LATER
MEDIEVAL EUROPE

◆

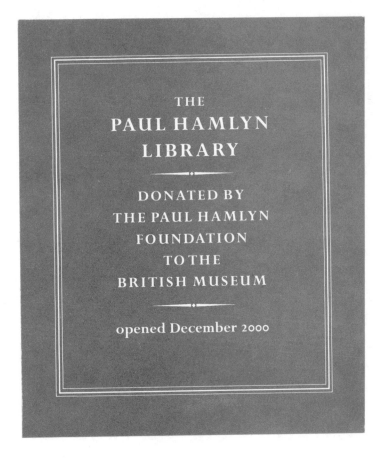

LATER MEDIEVAL EUROPE

◆

1250–1520

Daniel Waley

Third Edition revised
by Peter Denley

Longman

An imprint of **Pearson Education**

Harlow, England · London · New York · Reading, Massachusetts · San Francisco
Toronto · Don Mills, Ontario · Sydney · Tokyo · Singapore · Hong Kong · Seoul
Taipei · Cape Town · Madrid · Mexico City · Amsterdam · Munich · Paris · Milan

PEARSON EDUCATION LIMITED

Head Office:
Edinburgh Gate
Harlow CM20 2JE
Tel: +44 (0)1279 623623
Fax: +44 (0)1279 431059

London Office:
128 Long Acre
London WC2E 9AN
Tel: +44 (0)20 7447 2000
Fax: +44 (0)20 7240 5771
Website: www.history-minds.com

First published in Great Britain in 1964
Second edition 1985
Third edition 2001

© Longman Group Limited 1964, 1985
© Pearson Education Limited 2001

The right of Daniel Waley and Peter Denley to be identified as Authors
of this Work has been asserted by them in accordance
with the Copyright, Designs and Patents Act 1988.

ISBN 0 582 25831 6

British Library Cataloguing in Publication Data
A CIP catalogue record for this book can be obtained from the British Library

Library of Congress Cataloging in Publication Data
A CIP catalog record for this book can be obtained from the Library of Congress

10 9 8 7 6 5 4 3 2 1

Typeset by Graphicraft Limited in 10.5/12 pt Garamond MT
Printed and bound in Great Britain by Henry Ling Limited, Dorchester

The Publishers' policy is to use paper manufactured from sustainable forests.

CONTENTS

———◆———

PART III. THE FIFTEENTH CENTURY: NEW DYNAMICS

Contents

LIST OF MAPS

◆

FIGURE

◆

TABLE

◆

PREFACE TO THE THIRD EDITION

———— ◆ ————

*L*ater *Medieval Europe* now appears in a considerably longer version and with much augmented reading lists. Two of the chapters (15 and 16) are entirely new. The book is the work of two authors, the original one (Dr Waley) and the editor of the third edition (Dr Denley). The new edition has been undertaken in the shared belief that, whatever changes in historiographical fashion and focus there have been, an understanding of, and access to, the political history of the period continue to be important for aspiring medievalists of all kinds. The revisions and additions reflect this view, bringing the text up to date in the light of recent research, and expanding it further beyond the confines of 'western' Europe in particular, but not attempting to cover new areas and sub-disciplines of history. The text has been rearranged and sub-divided for the convenience of the reader. A particular feature of the book, its frequent recourse to the voices of contemporaries, has been further documented wherever possible, and references to published English translations of sources have also been added (except in the case of works such as Dante's *Comedy* and Machiavelli's *The Prince*, which appear in too many editions for page references to be helpful). A major change has been the inclusion at the end of each chapter of substantial bibliographical notes, both to reflect the developments in the subjects covered since the first edition of the book, and to provide detailed guidance for students and teachers alike on what is available in English. An explanation of the thinking behind this, and suggestions on how these sections can be used, appear in the 'Bibliographical note'.

Each of us would wish to thank his wife for their great support and helpful suggestions.

D. P. W.
P. R. D.
December 2000

PREFACE TO THE FIRST EDITION

◆

The aim of this book is to serve as an introduction to the history of Europe between the middle of the thirteenth century and the early part of the sixteenth. I hope to persuade my readers that this is an interesting period, and I have quoted a good deal from contemporary writings, because men's *ipsissima verba* are surely bound to be more striking and more convincing than the 'secondary' conclusions drawn from them. I have also assumed in my readers diverse intellectual temperaments. Those who are not attracted by past politics may find more interest in past economics, or in religion or art or the history of ideas, and quite substantial sections of the book are devoted to each of these topics. Yet politics remain the staple diet of the historian, and I have taken as my principal subject the growth of the power of the State and the manner in which this is reflected in ideas concerning politics. In treating a series of diverse themes I have tried to keep this main thesis in view. Thus, while the book begins and ends with contrasting chapters on the State and men's notions about it in the thirteenth century and the early sixteenth century, the chapter on the early Renaissance touches on the intensification of civic spirit, while, of the two chapters primarily concerned with religion, the former emphasises the patriotic element in the Hussite movement and the latter the decisive religious consequences of Germany's uncharacteristic political disintegration.

My thanks are due above all to my wife and to my friend Dr E. B. Fryde, who read the work in typescript: both of them have helped me with many suggestions. I have also benefited gratefully from the advice of Dr A. R. Bridbury (on Chapter V) and of Dr Nicolai Rubinstein and Dr A. T. Hankey (on Chapter VIII).

D. P. W.

PREFACE TO THE SECOND EDITION

◆

The first edition of this book appeared in 1964. Written twenty years ago, it bears the imprint of its generation, not least in the opinion, recorded in the Preface, that 'politics remain the staple diet of the historian'. The saying that 'everything has a history' would never have met with disagreement, but History as an educational subject, with syllabuses and examinations, and even as a field for study and publication, has been confined by convention within quite narrow boundaries. To recover the entirety of past situations and events does not make sense as an objective. Limits and definitions, dictated by the nature of surviving evidence from the past as well as by the practical realities of research and education, are a necessity for the historian.

Tastes in history, as in everything else, are bound to fluctuate. Recently the ebbing of interest in power, institutions and high-level thought has been accompanied by the rise of concern with demography, the family and household, popular religion and intellectual history in the broadest sense (*mentalités*). These changes, seen from the viewpoint of 1984, appear to be considerable; yet it is too early to say whether they are symptomatic of a long-term and far-reaching shift in the subject-matter of History.

The growth of an interest in aspects of the past once thought of as lying outside the historian's territory can be seen in the publication of new periodicals. To give only a few examples, the *Journal of Marriage and the Family* dates back to 1939 and *Population Studies* to 1947, but the *Journal of Family History* began publication as recently as 1976 and other new titles include the *History of Childhood Quarterly* and the *Journal of Psychohistory*. Practitioners of such branches of history see themselves as introducing their interests into the subject-matter of 'accepted' history and thus as enriching it. The process can be a painful one, but the words which concluded the colloquium held in Paris in 1974 on 'Family and Kinship in the medieval West' are realistic. 'What is important', said Professor Werner, 'is the simple fact of having introduced the subject into the domain of the "proper historian", so that those who play a part in history are no longer, for such historians, mere points in the passage of "events".'[1]

Whether those who accept these new traditions in historiography can be truthfully described as writing 'total history' is another matter, but a greater breadth of theme is apparent in many of the more ambitious books of the last two decades, particularly in France. The programme of Professor Le Roy Ladurie, set out in his *Peasants of Languedoc*, is characteristic. 'In this book', he says, 'I have tried to observe at different levels the long-term movements of an economy and the society enveloping it: base and superstructure, material life and cultural life, sociological development and collective psychology, all this within a rural world which remained very largely traditional in nature.'[2]

Such history, which is social history in the most serious sense, provides at its best a more profound treatment of what it felt like to live in the past, as well as being a necessary base for studies in government and politics. It can include domestic realities and the mental attitudes which accompanied them. It can take the student deeper than that social history of 'manners', such as dress and the life of royal courts, which has often been thought colourful and particularly appealing to children. Going more profoundly into the life of a more statistically respectable sample of people, there seems no reason why the subject matter should not be suitable for schoolchildren, and it can include the 'older' social history rather than supersede it. What people ate, how much they ate and when, deserves to be a major historical theme, and courtly feasting does not merit exclusion from this but a minor place within it.

There is room to mention here only a few of the fresh themes broached by historians, with varying degrees of success, in the last two or three decades. A typical pioneering work, concerned with attitudes to childhood and the treatment of children, was Philippe Ariès's *L'enfant et la vie familiale sous l'ancien régime* (1960). Much has also been written on the history of education with the emphasis less strongly on institutions and syllabuses than was the case in such classics as Rashdall's *Universities of Europe in the Middle Ages*. Instead the reader now encounters (for example) university students in early sixteenth-century Germany living by begging and in the summer 'sleeping rough'—in the cemetery. It is a natural feature of this movement (observable in historical research generally) away from the study of institutions that it has been accompanied by greater dependence on unofficial sources, at the expense of the archives which the institutions themselves created.

Other books have confronted the history of attitudes towards nature and the external world, the history of humour, the realities of sex and marriage and related attitudes. Even if many of the questions raised by such enquiries are unanswerable, to refuse to ask them is a symptom of being incurious about the past. The same author who put childhood on the historical map (if not the syllabus) has written on attitudes to old age and death. Though that book does not reach the standard of his earlier work it appears to have tapped an even richer vein. Often the *obiter dicta* and detail of such works do more to 'bring the past to life', as the cliché goes, than the authors' principal findings. Nothing is more convincing, for example, in Ariès's book on childhood than his remark that 'one was never alone' and 'life was passed in public'. Such fundamental and unspoken features of life, taken for granted by contemporaries, have often been missed by historians.

There is another advantage, from the educational viewpoint, of the move away from History as 'past politics'. The broader the subject-matter, the greater and clearer should be the differentiation between past and present. Hence it should be easier for the teacher to convey that History is not a continuous drama performed by variously attired representatives of an unchanging 'human nature', but that in the past it felt different to be alive. The superficial notion that 'the more it changes, the more it's the same' is the antithesis of a historical outlook. Analogies in the past and between the present and the past can be fruitful and interesting, but no more than that; as the Greek philosopher put it, one 'never bathes twice in the same stream'.

The patristic definition of the traditional Christian faith as 'that on which all have always been agreed' (*quod ab omnibus, quod ubique, quod semper*) exemplifies well the contrary outlook which sees and emphasises resemblances between past and present. If there had been topics on which all men had always been agreed the landscape of the past would be a monotonous one and maps drawn accordingly would be boring as well as misleading.

Recent developments in historiography have not been all gain, as teachers could testify who have been confronted by pupils acquainted with the past of witchcraft and astrology who have no grounding in 'facts' and chronology and are unable to ascribe to the right century the Hundred Years War, Thirty Years War or Seven Years War. Yet the insight into the past to be gained through these recent historiographical developments ought to bring about a greater and more serious contact with reality. There should be less danger of history as an educational subject implying merely a vicarious and perhaps snobbish acquaintanceship with the courts and cabinets of princes.

The purpose of the new chapter [Chapter 17] in this edition of *Later Medieval Europe*, concerned with the demographic history of the period and the structure of the family and household, is to introduce the theme of reconstructing the realities of past society, one which is perhaps little reflected as yet in general introductory works of history. Hence a considerable proportion of the chapter deals with a particular, well-documented example: the society of part of central Italy in the 1420s.

The inclusion of an additional chapter is the principal innovation in the present edition of *Later Medieval Europe*. The suggestions for further reading, last revised for the paperback edition of 1975, have again undergone considerable alterations and the opportunity has been taken to make changes in the text of several chapters.

My thanks are again due to my wife, this time for much help with the new index.

D. P. W.
November 1983

NOTES

1. *Famille et Parenté dans l'Occident Médiéval* (École Française, Rome, 1977), p. 444.
2. E. Le Roy Ladurie, *Les Paysans de Languedoc* (Paris, 1966), I, p. 633.

ACKNOWLEDGEMENTS

◆

We are grateful to the following for permission to quote copyright material:

De Agostini Rights Limited for an extract from *The Hussite Movement in Bohemia* (2nd edition) translated by J. Macek, published by Orbis publishing; Cambridge University Press for an extract from *Selections from the Works of Conrad Celtis 1459–1508* translated by Leonard Foster, published by Cambridge University Press 1948; Oxford University Press for an extract from *Selections from the Notebooks of Leonardo da Vinci* edited by I. A. Richter, published by Oxford University Press: World Classics 530; and Penguin Putnam Inc. for an extract from 'Letter to Loelius' in *Rerum Familiarum Libri* published in *Petrarch: The First Scholar and Man of Letters* by J. H. Robinson, published by Penguin Putnam Inc.

Map 7 adapted from map on p. xvi in *Lithuania Ascending: A Pagan Empire within East-Central Europe, 1295–1345*, published and reprinted by permission of Cambridge University Press (Rowell, S. C. 1994).

BIBLIOGRAPHICAL NOTE

———— ◆ ————

T he bibliographical sections throughout this book aim to introduce the reader to the main works on late medieval Europe published recently in English. This restriction has been made for practical reasons. Thirty years ago it was not possible to study the period without a reading knowledge of at least some other European languages. German, Spanish or Slavic history were virtually closed books to the monoglot, while Italian history was just beginning to be more accessible. This situation has changed dramatically over a generation, both through research by native English speakers and (to a much lesser extent) through the translation of the works of eminent scholars. However, while this is of benefit to students, it also brings with it an increased danger of narrowness and ethnocentricity. The fact that the present list is confined to works in English should not be taken to imply that English-language publications have been the most important in these international topics.

Regard has been given to works which are in print or widely available in libraries of higher education in the English-speaking world. Articles in periodicals have been included where particularly important. As many of the topics are inter-connected, readers should be prepared for the need to cross-refer throughout the bibliography.

GENERAL HISTORIES OF THE PERIOD

The most authoritative compendium is now *The New Cambridge Medieval History* (hereafter *NCMH*) which replaces *The Cambridge Medieval History* of the early twentieth century. The volumes covering this period are *Volume V: c.1198–c.1300*, ed. David Abulafia (Cambridge, 1999), *Volume VI: c.1300–c.1415*, ed. Michael Jones (Cambridge, 2000) and *Volume VII: c.1415–c.1500*, ed. Christopher Allmand (Cambridge, 1998). Other general volumes covering or including the period include: Robert Fossier, ed., *The Cambridge Illustrated History of the Middle Ages III. 1250–1520* (Cambridge, 1986); Malcolm Barber, *The Two Cities. Medieval Europe 1050–1320* (London and New York, 1992); John H. Mundy, *Europe in the High Middle Ages, 1150–1309* (2nd edition, London, 1991); Denys Hay, *Europe in the Fourteenth and Fifteenth Centuries* (2nd edition, London, 1989); George Holmes, *Europe: Hierarchy and Revolt, 1320–1450* (London, 1975; 2nd edition, Oxford, 1999); David Nicholas, *The Transformation of Europe 1300–1600* (London, 1999); Eugene F. Rice, Jr. with Anthony Grafton, *The Foundations of Early Modern Europe, 1460–1559* (2nd edition, New York, 1994); Thomas A. Brady Jr., Heiko A. Oberman and James D. Tracy, eds, *Handbook of European History 1400–1600*, 2 vols (Leiden, 1994–5, paperback Grand Rapids, Mich., 1996); De Lamar Jensen, *Renaissance Europe: Age of Recovery and Reconciliation* (Lexington, Mass., and Toronto, 1981); Margaret Aston, *The Fifteenth Century. The Prospect of Europe* (London, 1971).

GENERAL MEDIEVAL HISTORIES

George Holmes, ed., *The Oxford Illustrated History of Medieval Europe* (Oxford, 1988, 2nd edition 1990); also published without illustrations as *The Oxford History of Medieval Europe* (Oxford, 1992); Jacques Le Goff, *Medieval Civilisation 400–1500* (Oxford, 1988); Jacques Le Goff, ed., *The Medieval World* (London, 1990); David Nicholas, *The Evolution of the Medieval World. Society, Government and Thought in Europe, 312–1500* (London, 1992).

REFERENCE WORKS

The fullest in English is Scribner's *Dictionary of the Middle Ages* (New York, 1982–9), in 13 volumes; more accessible is H. R. Loyn, *The Middle Ages. A Concise Encyclopaedia* (London, 1989). S. Fletcher, *The Longman Companion to Renaissance Europe 1390–1530* (London, 2000) is a useful manual.

ATLASES

A. Mackay and D. Ditchburn, eds, *Atlas of Medieval Europe* (London, 1996); D. Matthew, *Atlas of Medieval Europe* (Oxford, 1983); C. McEvedy, *The New Penguin Atlas of Medieval History* (London, 1992); R. I. Moore, ed., *The Hamlyn Historical Atlas* (London, 1981). For atlases covering central and eastern Europe *see also* under Chapter 15.

COLLECTIONS OF DOCUMENTS IN TRANSLATION

Alfred J. Andrea, ed., *The Medieval Record* (New York, 1997); Patrick J. Geary, ed., *Readings in Medieval History* (Ontario, 1991); David Englander, Diana Norman, Rosemary O'Day and W. R. Owens, eds, *Culture and Belief in Europe 1450–1600. An Anthology of Sources* (Oxford, 1990); D. Herlihy, ed., *Medieval Culture and Society* (London, 1968); C. Warren Hollister, Joe W. Leedom, Marc A. Meyer and David S. Spear, eds, *Medieval Europe. A Short Sourcebook* (3rd edition, New York, 1997); J. B. Ross and M. M. McLaughlin, eds, *The Portable Medieval Reader* (Harmondsworth, reprinted 1977), and *The Portable Renaissance Reader* (Harmondsworth, reprinted 1978); D. Weinstein, ed., *The Renaissance and the Reformation 1300–1600* (New York, 1965); Brian Tierney, ed., *The Middle Ages, I. Sources of Medieval History* (6th edition, New York, 1999). Other collections on specific topics are given below.

INTERNET SOURCES

Although historians by and large do not publish directly on to the Internet, a number of websites have been established for the purposes of exchanging information, sources, teaching materials, etc. Many of these are presented in an exciting and accessible way. A note of caution is necessary; the Net is a medium in which anyone can publish, so the quality is variable and indeed so is the level for which the material is intended. Moreover, although an extensive number of sources in translation are available on the Net, most of these are old translations which can be put there because they are no longer in copyright. The Net should be regarded as a liberating resource, but one of variable quality.

The following current sites are of particular interest for students of later medieval Europe. They are also for the most part refereed by recognised medievalists.

The Labyrinth—http://labyrinth.georgetown.edu—the standard starting point for Medieval Studies on the Internet.

ORB Online Reference Book for Medieval Studies—http://orb.rhodes.edu/— an online textbook, with both primary and secondary resources.

Internet Medieval Sourcebook—http://www.fordham.edu/halsall/sbook.html

NetSERF: The Internet Connection for Medieval Resources—http://www.netserf.org

ARGOS—Limited Area Search of the Ancient and Medieval Internet—http://argos.evansville.edu

World Wide Web Virtual Library/Medieval—http://www.msu.edu/~georgem1/history/medieval.htm

Medieval Sources*online*—www.medievalsources.co.uk—a web-based learning resource published by Manchester University Press.

Specific sites are referred to in the appropriate place.

MAPS

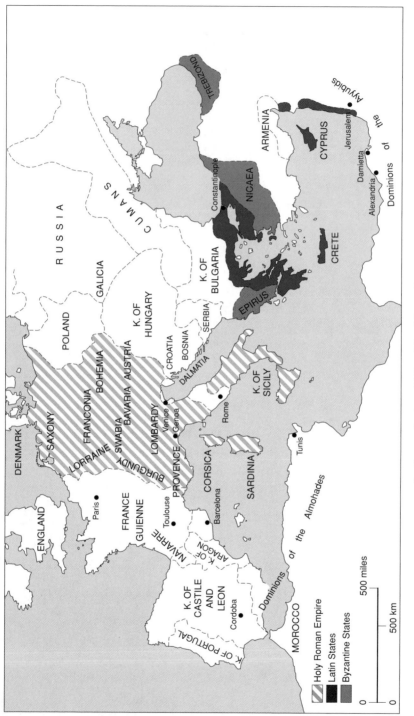

1. Europe in the middle of the thirteenth century

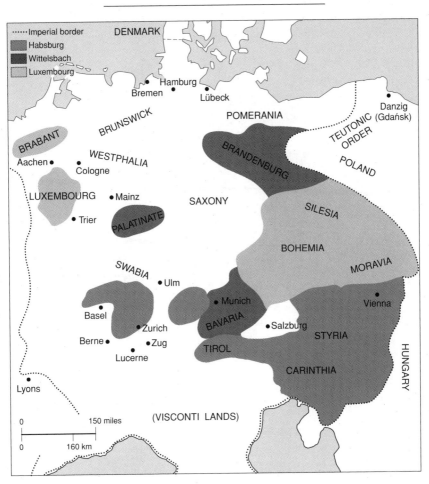

Legend:
- ······ Imperial border
- Habsburg
- Wittelsbach
- Luxembourg

DENMARK

Hamburg
Bremen
Lübeck

BRUNSWICK

POMERANIA

Danzig (Gdańsk)

TEUTONIC ORDER

BRABANT

WESTPHALIA

Aachen
Cologne

BRANDENBURG

POLAND

LUXEMBOURG
Mainz

Trier

PALATINATE

SAXONY

SILESIA

BOHEMIA

MORAVIA

SWABIA
Ulm

Basel

Zurich

Berne
Zug

Lucerne

Munich

BAVARIA

Salzburg

Vienna

STYRIA

TIROL

HUNGARY

CARINTHIA

Lyons

0   150 miles

0   160 km

(VISCONTI LANDS)

2. The territorial base of the late medieval emperors

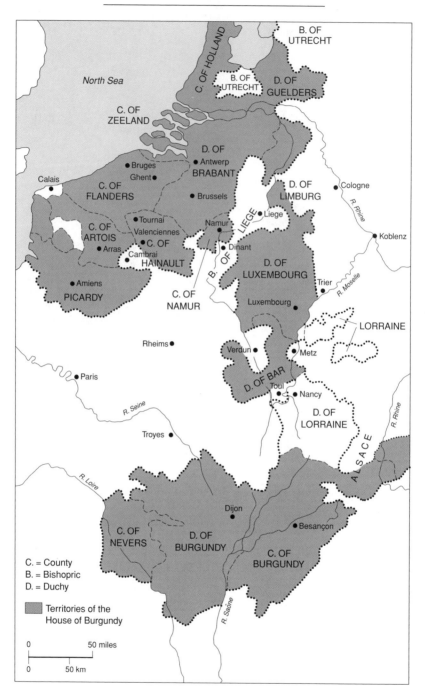

3. The duchy of Burgundy in the fifteenth century

4. The Italian states in 1494

5. The eastern Mediterranean, *c.*1340

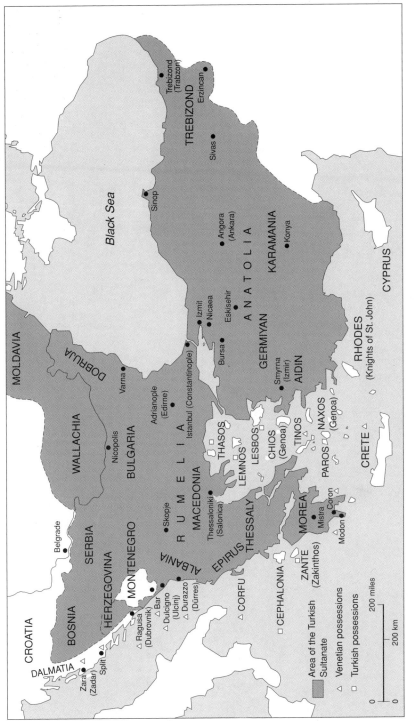

6. South-eastern Europe, 1481

Area of the Turkish Sultanate

△ Venetian possessions

□ Turkish possessions

CROATIA
DALMATIA
Zara (Zadar) △
Split △
BOSNIA
HERZEGOVINA
Ragusa (Dubrovnik) △
MONTENEGRO
Bar △
Dulcigno (Ulcinj) △
Durazzo (Dürres) △
ALBANIA
EPIRUS
CORFU △
CEPHALONIA □
ZANTE (Zakinthos)
Belgrade
SERBIA
Skopje
MACEDONIA
RUMELIA
Thessaloniki (Salonica)
THESSALY
MOREA
Mistra
Coron
Modon △
Black Sea
MOLDAVIA
WALLACHIA
Nicopolis
BULGARIA
DOBRUJA
Varna
Adrianople (Edirne)
Istanbul (Constantinople)
THASOS □
LEMNOS □
LESBOS
CHIOS (Genoa)
TINOS △
NAXOS (Genoa)
PAROS □
CRETE △
Sinop
Trebizond (Trabzon)
Erzincan
TREBIZOND
Sivas
Angora (Ankara)
ANATOLIA
KARAMANIA
Konya
Izmit
Nicaea
Eskisehir
Bursa
GERMIYAN
Smyrna (Izmir)
AIDIN
RHODES (Knights of St. John)
CYPRUS

0   200 miles
0   200 km

7. East central Europe in the late Middle Ages. The borders of Lithuania are as in *c*.1340.
   After G. C. Rowell, *Lithuania Ascending: A Pagan Empire within East-Central Europe,*
   1295–1345 (Cambridge, 1994), p. xvi

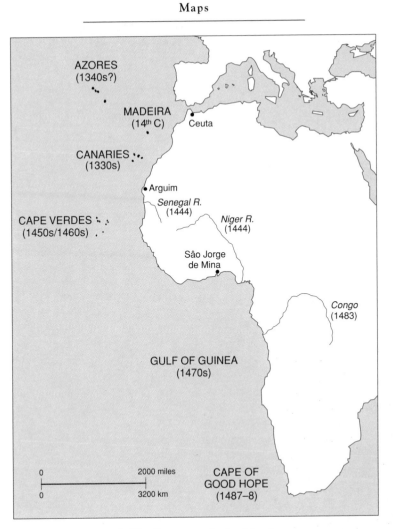

AZORES
(1340s?)

MADEIRA
(14th C)   Ceuta

CANARIES
(1330s)

Arguim
Senegal R.
(1444)   Niger R.
(1444)

CAPE VERDES
(1450s/1460s)

Sâo Jorge
de Mina

Congo
(1483)

GULF OF GUINEA
(1470s)

| 0 | 2000 miles |
| 0 | 3200 km |

CAPE OF
GOOD HOPE
(1487–8)

8. The Portuguese in the Atlantic

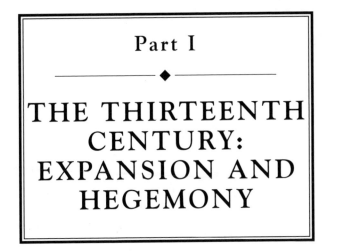

Part I

THE THIRTEENTH
CENTURY:
EXPANSION AND
HEGEMONY

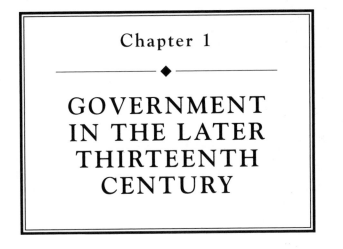

Chapter 1

◆

GOVERNMENT IN THE LATER THIRTEENTH CENTURY

THE POLITICAL CONTOURS OF THIRTEENTH-CENTURY EUROPE

One of the main themes of this book is the development of government during two centuries and a half, foreshadowing and culminating in the 'modern' nation-state of later periods. We may begin, therefore, by describing some of the ways in which political power was exercised at the start of our period.

The most centralised forms of government are evidenced in western and northern Europe. In France, where St Louis IX (1226–70) had added immeasurable prestige to the territorial and administrative gains of Philip (II) Augustus (1180–1223), the monarchy already displays the powerful basis of its later achievements.[1] Similar trends can be seen in Christian Spain and in England. In their relationship with the great men whose attitude would do most to determine their success as rulers, these kings were feudal overlords. The magnates, lay and ecclesiastical, owed the king fealty as vassals and in particular had the obligations of attending his court when summoned to give counsel and of rendering him military service—the amount of which was normally defined in some detail. In that he had been crowned a king and anointed as a sign of his semi-sacred calling—everything possible was done to exploit the mystical aspects of kingship on his behalf—the monarch was more than first among equals, and in thirteenth-century France the doctrine was becoming accepted that in no circumstances could he be himself a vassal of an uncrowned lord.

The picture is less consistent elsewhere. The western emperors, heirs to Charlemagne, had uncertain claims to suzerainty over these kings, but in practice the lands of Germany and northern Italy had no ruler between the death in 1250 of Frederick II and the election in 1273 of Rudolf of Habsburg, a princeling from south-western Germany who enjoyed papal support but had no resources to compare with those of the kings. Germany was a feudal body without a head. In Italy, this long-standing situation had given rise to a multiplicity of independent or quasi-independent territories in which government took a variety of forms, from monarchy in the south (beyond the confines of the Empire) to city-state in the north.

Beyond the territories that formed the core of western Europe, there were even fewer signs of stability. The eastern emperor, restored to Constantinople from the time of Michael Palaeologus (1261), ruled over 'the shade of that which once was great'; most of what had been Byzantine territory was now parcelled out among the Turks, Bulgars, Italian maritime republics and Frankish lords. Poland and Bohemia were Slav kingdoms in part populated by Germans and often unsettled by pressure from the rulers of Germany. Russia was overshadowed by Mongol domination and Hungary by the power of both Mongols and Germans. The Scandinavian kingdoms had not yet achieved even the relatively civilized techniques of government in western Europe and have left less written testimony to their activities.

MONARCHS AND SUBJECTS

It is with France and Spain that I shall be principally concerned, then, in describing the characteristic structure of the feudal kingdom, with its 'empire within an empire' or, more accurately, its series of 'Chinese boxes' intervening between the all-inclusive monarchy and the humble individual in his own locality (in 'the last place on earth', as I once heard a French peasant describe his village). 'Every baron is sovereign in his own barony', says Beaumanoir, the thirteenth-century French lawyer,[2] and indeed each was entitled to wage his own wars, so long as these were not incompatible with his fealty to the king. Linguistic differences accentuated this social and political localism. In France the great dividing line ran between the Provençal south, whose tongue (the 'langue d'oc') had received a smaller element of Teutonic influence from the barbarians, and the northerners whose 'yes' was 'oui' (the 'langue d'oïl') and who have shaped the French language of today. Brittany, of course, spoke an entirely different, Celtic, tongue. The great French fiefs were Aquitaine (whose duke was the king of England), the duchy of Burgundy, and the counties of Flanders, Brittany and Champagne. At St Louis' death (1270) the other powerful counties were in the hands of the king or his immediate family; his brother Charles held Anjou and Provence and a nephew Artois.

Each of these lordships was a state in itself, with its own machinery of central and local government, exercising legislative and judicial powers, taxing and coining money, exacting military service and counsel. Even excluding Aquitaine, which was altogether exceptional through its connection with the English Crown, these fiefs rivalled and in some cases surpassed the king's own administration in the degree to which they had developed an intricate structure of government. Both Champagne and Flanders had local *baillis* at least as early as the Crown—in the late twelfth century—and indeed the Flemish counts, who had a precocious chancery in the eleventh century, tapped the wealth of their industrial cities through a highly organised office for receipts by the middle of the thirteenth. For the majority of French nobles, their lord was one of these great magnates. Before St Louis set out on crusade he had called his barons to Paris to swear that they would 'keep faith and loyalty to his children if anything happened to him on his journey'. Joinville, the king's future biographer, refused to take this oath, 'since I was not then his vassal'.[3] He was a vassal of the count of Champagne only and his refusal was entirely justified. Nearly 200 years later the royal official at Vaucouleurs in the county of Bar—between Champagne, which had now come to the Crown, and Lorraine—was Robert de Baudricourt. When a shepherdess came to him with a strange tale of supernatural visions, it was to the duke of Lorraine that she was sent. Only later did Baudricourt reluctantly despatch the persistent Joan of Arc to Charles VII at Chinon.

But it would be misleading to give an impression of France as a neat pattern of clearly demarcated territorial lordships. The situation was much more intricate than this. The count of Champagne, for example, held lands of the emperor, the duke of Burgundy, the archbishops of Reims and Sens and of several bishops, as well as of the king of France. The title of count was not an indication of tenancy-in-chief (i.e. of the king) and many counts were numbered among the count of Champagne's own vassals. The powerful subjects of later medieval England were still less regional in the basis of their strength. Edward III's sons, the Black Prince and John of Gaunt, were little less than kings, and the latter (who was, indeed, titular king of Castile) on occasions raised about half the nation's armed forces from his own men. The Black Prince was prince of Wales and Aquitaine, duke of Cornwall and earl of Chester; Gaunt was duke of Lancaster, but geographical titles gave little indication of their power and Gaunt's 'palatinate' was more independent and stronger.

The Spanish monarchies present a different picture in some respects, for they were themselves composite structures. Alfonso X was king of 'Castile, Toledo, León, Galicia, Seville, Cordova, Murcia, Jaen and Algarve' and the Aragonese ruled not merely Aragon but also Catalonia, Valencia, the Balearics and the county of Barcelona. These titles to some extent corresponded to divisions in the work of government: the component parts of the Aragonese kingdom had their own royal households and councils, their own stewards and chancellors, courts and parliaments. The absence here of a small class of great lay feudatories did not imply that the king exercised greater power, indeed it could not, for all kings faced the same situation and lacked the financial means to secure direct obedience over wide areas. Hence all were compelled to divide the work of government with local powers such as feudal magnates or municipalities. The degree of independence achieved by urban institutions serves as a sort of barometer of the king's strength, for where he is most powerful— in southern Italy and in England—the town receives a strictly limited right to order its own internal affairs, and where he is weakest—in the imperial territory of northern Italy—republics arise paying, at the most, occasional lip-service to their overlord.

Since the Carolingian period, in circumstances that had been unpropitious to central control, western Europe's most characteristic institution had been the zone of private jurisdiction, the 'liberty' or 'immunity'. The king's efforts had to be directed to seeing that 'self-government at the king's command' was performed satisfactorily and on terms which were clearly defined and as much as possible in accordance with his own interests. His vassals owed him aid in war and peace and he would also attempt to reserve the right to hear judicial appeals. He would normally reserve the right to intervene if his vassal failed to render justice, and might even reserve for his court all major criminal suits. A grant made by Alfonso IX of Castile to the Order of St James (1229) will serve as an illustration.[4] The Order received from the king gave jurisdictional rights in certain places in return for normal feudal services. 'Moreover I [the king] am to exercise justice in these *villae* should either you or the representative [*vicarius*] deputed by you for this purpose be negligent in doing justice.' Should this circumstance arise, however, the Order was nevertheless to receive the property of the criminal. The king also reserved to himself the power to hear appeals from the Order's court.[5]

Arrangements of this nature prevailed all over Europe (and others bearing some resemblance to them over a good deal of Asia). The Spanish kingdoms were not exceptional in the ubiquity of ecclesiastical lords. In imperial territory north of the Alps (that is, an area centred on modern Germany) the pious donations of lay magnates had combined with the policy of emperors intent on securing a literate and celibate governing class to place a very high proportion of the land in the hands of the Church, a situation which had been fateful for German history in the eleventh century, when the emperors fought the new claims of the papacy to control the whole Church, and was to be so again in Luther's time.[6] In the Slav lands, Germany east of the Elbe and Scandinavia, bishops and monasteries occupied a dominant position in society as the heirs of recently triumphant missionaries. Some churchmen, too, benefited by the general rule that in the 'marches' or border territories the local potentates were entrusted with special powers to strengthen their hand in the military emergencies of frontier existence. Thus the bishop of Durham, the king of England's bulwark against the Scots, ruled a palatinate which was unvisited by the king's sheriffs and normally paid the king no taxes.

The energetic ruler kept himself constantly informed concerning his rights and struggled to increase them or at least preserve them intact. In particular he sought to extend his judicial activity, for this gave him greater control in his kingdom and also, by bringing in money, made possible further gains. Often a vital contest was waged over appellate jurisdiction.[7] The popes of the later thirteenth century fought a long struggle to prevent the communes of the Papal State from hearing appeal suits, but their attempt to secure a monopoly of these cases were not successful. At the same time (1278) Philip III of France legislated to forbid the setting up of appeal benches by any of his vassals not then in possession of such courts.

The bureaucratic apparatus of the western monarchies will be described later. The king was, in orthodox but somewhat archaic theory, expected to 'live of his own', content with what he received as a lord exploiting his own feudal revenues or domain. To an enormous extent he was dependent on the productiveness of this domain. With some exaggeration, the success of the thirteenth-century French kings may be ascribed to their acquisition of Normandy in 1204, and the failure of the emperors to their inability to acquire the confiscated duchy of Saxony some years earlier. But in the last analysis the king was dependent on the loyalty of his vassals, a virtue doubtless fostered by the knowledge that they in turn needed their own vassals to be loyal.

To these vassals the king was a feudal overlord, but he could be seen in other ways: to legists he was the source of law, to theologians the means through which

God worked his purposes on earth. Before going further into the realities of thirteenth-century government it may be well to look at some of the theories expressed concerning rule and rulers and, first of all, to see what kings themselves and popes thought about kingship.

KINGSHIP AND LAW

St Louis, handing on to his son Philip III the lessons of a righteous and successful career, explained that a king must love God and strive after justice. He must avoid favouring the rich and powerful and must show complete impartiality in cases in which the Crown's own rights are involved: 'If you should discover that you are in wrongful possession of anything, even if possession of it was acquired by your ancestors, surrender it forthwith.'[8]

A few years before this, St Louis' brother, Charles of Anjou, had been the recipient of similar advice from Clement IV on acquiring the throne of Sicily and Naples.[9] The pope too had emphasised justice. Royal judges should sit daily and should be salaried and incorruptible. Any complaints against officials should be investigated rapidly and there should be a special post (held by a monk or some *miles affabilis*, a good-natured knight) concerned with petitions, to ensure that these were heard expeditiously. The king should never take innocent parties as hostages or make them pay for the guilty. When enquiries were held concerning royal rights the burden of proof should only be placed on his subjects when circumstances made this reasonable.[10] The pope had also some advice to offer on administration and the king's relations with his baronage; he should be careful not to abuse his feudal right to intervene concerning marriages (of his tenants' daughters) and above all he should remedy the serious trouble about this present year's taxes by reaching agreement with his barons, prelates and men of the towns about the circumstances in which he may impose taxation.

Both Philip and Charles may well have thought that their duties were being emphasised at the expense of their rights, but this was in keeping with medieval views of kingship. The king was, by general consent, bound by the law—and whatever doubts there might be as to what constituted 'the law', the essential point was that the monarch had responsibilities and did not wield absolute power. In England the king took an oath at his coronation to keep peace with the Church, exercise justice in his judgments, preserve good customs and extirpate bad ones,[11] and Magna Carta—reissued several times in the thirteenth century—was testimony to circumstances in which a king's powerful subjects might force him into less imprecise promises. It was not the attitude of theorists, but the relative strength of king and subjects and their interdependence in practice which effectively determined the king's position. Coronation oaths reveal this clearly enough, though the often-cited oath of the Aragonese nobles to their king ('We who are each worth as much as you, and, united, more than you, offer you our obedience if you keep our liberties, and if not, not') is a later forgery.[12] It was orthodox doctrine in thirteenth-century France that a vassal denied justice might declare war on the king, hence St Louis was doing more for his son than enumerating personal virtues. In the crusading kingdom of

Jerusalem, where a monarchy had been installed ready-made rather than growing up by evolutionary processes, the mutual duties of ruler and ruled were yet more clearly defined. The 'assizes' declared it the duty of the people to prevent their lord from breaking his oath and refusing to administer law and justice, and the court of all the king's vassals, the 'Court of Burgesses of Jerusalem', could declare any vassal absolved from his obligations.

The constitution of the crusading state established in the Holy Land demonstrates the limitations of feudal monarchy, emphasising the weak position of a king chosen as the ostensible apex of a pyramid whose sturdier blocks were the lords who had carved for themselves slices of formerly Islamic and Byzantine territory in the Levant. In western Europe there were many who claimed for their anointed kings a much less circumscribed and purely utilitarian position. Such men were to be found particularly among the Roman lawyers, for whom law was not a statement of custom (as it was to the men of the early Middle Ages) but a corpus of positive enactments, handed down from the classical period. Inevitably such an outlook implied emphasis on the supreme position of the ruler responsible for enunciating and enforcing the law; indeed a famous Roman maxim had it that 'whatever has pleased the ruler has the force of law'. The study of Justinian's legal code had revived in the west during the eleventh century, and by the thirteenth those who attempted to define the position of the king produced a strangely compounded portrait of two incompatibles, a classical emperor superimposed on a feudal overlord.

Such a picture is found in the great legal work of the court of Alfonso X of Castile (1252–84), the *Siete Partidas*, a curious combination of codification with treatises on the law, the constitution and the duties of different ranks in society. The *Siete Partidas* ('Seven Parts') pronounce that 'no one can make law except the emperor or king or another on their orders', but elsewhere the need to take counsel with subjects is admitted. Statements of custom need 'the counsel of good men . . . the wish of the lord and the consent of those who are to be bound', the king can only rescind laws in a 'great council of all the "good men" of the land, that is the best and most honoured and learned ones', and to amend them he must take counsel with 'the "good men" and those who understand and are learned in law: he must do this with as many good men as he can gather from as many parts as possible, so that they are as much as possible in agreement, *for it is a noble and good thing to make law, and the more it is agreed on and understood the better and firmer it is*'.[13] Even the Romanist lawyers of the Castilian court emphasise that the king has responsibilities, that he must fear God, love justice and truth, and must himself set an example by obeying the law.

Something of the same atmosphere prevails in the political ideas of the best known and most representative of thirteenth-century thinkers, St Thomas Aquinas (*c.*1226–74). Aquinas's birth, upbringing and education help to explain his broadly based outlook, for he was descended from a line of Lombard nobles in southern Italy, and received his earliest schooling at Monte Cassino, the Benedictine mother-house, and at the emperor Frederick II's university at Naples, before embarking on the conventional scholastic training of a Dominican at Paris and Cologne. In his writings is to be found the same characteristically medieval blend of classical influences with those of contemporary society: his views on politics comprise in essence an attempt to apply a Christianised version of Aristotle's thought to the feudal monarchies of his own day. Thus he takes from Aristotle the view that the State is a 'natural' expression of man's nature, thereby departing from St Augustine's pessimistic view of it as a necessary evil, 'the remedy of sinfulness'. From the same source—Aristotle's *Politics* only became widely known in the west in the thirteenth century, through translations into Latin—he adopted the idea of the 'common good' as the touchstone of political action and organisation. This was the test of everything, of the justification for levying a tax, for example, and of different types of constitution. A law had to be *ad bonum commune* and 'if rule is ordered not for the common good of the multitude but for the private good of the ruler this is unjust and perverse rule' and 'such a ruler is called a tyrant.'[14] The concept of the common good—which is as much his key to politics as the 'general will' is Rousseau's—also helps Aquinas to define the role of the individual in the community. 'The good of a single man is not the ultimate end: it should be ordered to the general good',[15] and 'since each man is part of the city [society], no man can be good except in so far as he is well proportioned to the common good'.[16]

When he approaches the question of legislation and the ideal constitution Aquinas reveals more clearly that he is aware of the monarchies of his own day. Custom, he says, is the main source of law, and he gives this statement of Teutonic practice theological and philosophical justification by explaining that men's actions, like their words, are an expression of reason. He does not come down firmly for either prince or people as the source of law, but states that the ruler may change the law if this is expedient. At this point he again calls in the 'common good'—never long absent from the stage—and explains that it is right to change the law only 'in so far as the common utility is served by such a change'. Moreover there must be 'evident utility'—this concept comes from Ulpian, a Roman lawyer—for custom and law should coincide as far as possible and 'the constrictive force of law is diminished in so far as custom is taken away'.[17] When Aquinas comes to the problem of the best form of government he once again follows Aristotle who, like many writers in antiquity, advocated a 'mixed constitution'. In the *Summa Theologica* he explains that this means 'a well combined constitution' (*politia bene commixta*), consisting of elements from monarchy, aristocracy and democracy. Again he is able to clothe his Greek wisdom in Hebrew garments, for he supports his case with the example of Moses and his successors, who ruled with the assistance of chiefs and wise men (Deuteronomy 1:15, in the Vulgate these are *sapientes et nobiles*) and of 'able men from all the people' (Exodus 18: 21: *de omni plebe viros potentes* in the Vulgate).[18] The conciliar role of the magnates in the feudal kingdoms of his day was doubtless in Aquinas's mind when he advocated an aristocratic element in the government of the ideal state, but it is difficult to see what institutions he had in mind when he spoke of a democratic one. Either its inclusion represents the acceptance of Aristotle without any contemporary reference, or possibly he recalled the burgher representatives of the towns present in the parliamentary assemblies of southern Italy (under Frederick II) and the Papal State and in German *Reichstage*.[19]

Aquinas's views on the state have been discussed here because they illustrate the supreme exponent of the scholastic outlook face to face with the monarchies of his day. After this preliminary consultation with lawyers and theorists it is time to return to the realities of government, but we cannot leave the quintessential product of thirteenth-century education without a word concerning his general approach and reasoning. St Thomas's political, like his other opinions, and like those of the many 'scholastic' writers he epitomises, are the result of the *deductive* method, that is to say he reasons from the general to the particular. There is no question of considering the workings of particular states, for instance (as Aristotle had done), and of *inducing* from this study general laws applicable to the science of politics as a whole. Instead, scholastic writers begin with universal principles, using their knowledge to illustrate their working. A characteristic passage on the advantages of 'government by one' (kingship) may be cited as an instance:

That is best which most nearly approaches a natural process, since nature always works in the best way. But in nature, government is always by one. Among members of the body there is one which moves all the rest, namely, the heart: in the soul there is one faculty which is pre-eminent, namely reason. The bees have one king,[20] and in the whole universe there is one God, Creator and Lord of all. And this is quite according to reason: for all plurality derives from unity. So, since the product of art is but an imitation of the work of nature, and since a work of art is the better for being a faithful representation of its natural pattern, it follows of necessity that the best form of government in human society is that which is exercised by one person.[21]

CONSENT AND CONSULTATION: MEDIEVAL PARLIAMENTS

The right of an overlord to obtain 'counsel', emphasised by the *Siete Partidas* and implicitly mentioned by Aquinas, was no abstract doctrine but a recognition of the obvious fact that orders could only become effective if they had the support of the powerful men of the lordship. Moreover their advice would help to decide whether a proposed innovation was practicable. The barbarian kings had held such gatherings of leading warriors and churchmen—witness the Anglo-Saxon *witan*—at which attendance had been less a right than a duty. In the thirteenth century assemblies of great council—formal meetings of the king and his permanent leading officers reinforced by the presence of powerful men and sometimes by representatives of towns and localities—were becoming characteristic of the monarchies of England, Castile and Aragon. In France, as we shall see, they appear later and their development is stunted. In the south Italian kingdom representatives of the towns had been called by Frederick II to Foggia as early as 1232, and Aragonese influence was later to give Sicily a famous parliament. Pope Innocent III called an assembly of the lands of the Church in 1207 and during the second half of the century several provinces of the Papal State were holding frequent gatherings of this nature. The condition of the empire was not conducive to the growth of centralized institutions, but Frederick II held spasmodic meetings of town representatives in imperial Italy, and around the middle of the century William of Holland (king of the Romans, 1247–56) gathered several *Reichstage* or *colloquia generalia* of lords and cities in the Rhineland. In 1274, after the long interregnum, Rudolf of Habsburg summoned a 'general court' 'for the reformation of the collapsed state of the empire and the common tranquillity of the faithful', but more characteristic of Germany were the *Landstage* of the princes. Rudolf's summons quoted in support of the king's action the maxim of Justinian's *Codex* that 'what concerns all must be approved by all' ('*quod omnes tangit ab omnibus comprobari debet*'). In 1295 Edward I of England was to cite the same passage in calling the clergy to parliament, and again one is reminded of how the Roman lawyers could confer classical respectability on rude medieval institutions.

'Institution' is indeed perhaps too exact a term for parliaments in the period of their informal development when they were organs of royal government but occasions rather than institutions. The word *parlamentum* (*parlement* in French and Anglo-Norman) merely meant 'speaking'. Another Latin word, *colloquium* (colloquy = speaking together) was more or less a synonym for *parlamentum* in the thirteenth century and the Spanish equivalents were termed *cortes* (courts: in Catalan, *corts*). That they were not yet technical terms shows clearly enough in the remark of the English *Fleta* that 'the king has his court in his council in his parliaments'. At this stage there was no 'parliament' capable of enjoying independent power to check the actions of the king. Yet the gatherings were witnesses to the existence of a *de facto* limitation of the royal power and hence of the possibilities of formal, constitutional, circumscription. In Aragon this situation was exploited by the subjects of Peter II as early as 1283. At the *cort* of Catalonia held at Barcelona that year a petition made 'in the name of the whole *universitas* [corporation] of Catalonia' was granted, providing that a general *cort* was to be held at least once a year and that representatives of the towns, as well as lay barons and prelates, were always to be present. Statutes were only to be promulgated 'with the approbation and consent of the prelates, barons, knights and citizens of Catalonia, or (providing they have been called) of the greater and wiser part of the same'.[22] Such agreements were not reached without often tense negotiations, as may be seen in the Appendix to this chapter.

Everything that has already been said on the subject should make it evident that attempts to define and delimit the activities of parliamentary sessions are bound to fail or to end in the vague assertion that they dealt with 'important matters of public concern'. Such a formula at least testifies to a correct reluctance to make anachronistic distinctions. It must include not only consideration of state affairs and all matters requiring publicity,[23] but also the presentation and consideration of petitions, the hearing of judicial suits, the promulgation of laws and consent to taxation. It was natural that consultation on executive action should normally take place only after initial decisions had been made. Thus James I of Aragon was determined on his expedition to the Balearics (1228) and conquest of Valencia (1232) before he summoned his *corts*, though in each case he consulted with them to secure their co-operation. As early as 1188 Alfonso of León had recorded a promise that 'I shall not make war or peace or any judgment [*placitum*: a better translation might be "treaty"] except with the counsel of the bishops, nobles and "good men", by whose counsel I ought to be ruled'.[24] But in practice the questions 'Shall I wage war?', and so on, were liable to be of the type known to the Romans as 'questions expecting the answer *Yes*'.

I have already quoted the opinion of the Castilian *Siete Partidas* that the king must take counsel when he makes or changes the law and the same view was expressed by the legal writers of other kingdoms. 'Thus it is,' says Beaumanoir, writing on the customs of the region of Beauvais in the 1280s, 'the king can make new orders [*établissements*], but he must take great care that he does so for a reasonable cause and for the common good and after taking "great counsel" [*par grant conseil*].'[25] When a king issued legislation he was careful to precede it with formulae such as 'by common assent and counsel of my court and barons', 'by common deliberation', or 'I, Alfonso, have made this law after much discussion, with the consent of all'.

Whatever the king's attitude to his assemblies, there remained the fact that 'counsel' and 'assent' implied the possibility of 'unwelcome advice' and 'refusal'. The most obvious circumstances in which these might arise was a demand for taxation. In England and the Spanish kingdoms it was understood that the ruler could raise 'extraordinary' (i.e. non-feudal) subsidies only with parliamentary consent. The fourteenth century was to see the constitutional exploitation of this notion and in particular the appointment of committees to watch over the administration of grants and other agreed measures. As early as 1301 such committees, to act between parliamentary sessions, were appointed in Catalonia; each represented a locality and its members—a knight, a burgess, a lawyer and a notary—were named by the king.[26] More than a decade before this the pope's rector had met with some outright refusals to grant taxes in the provincial assemblies of Romagna, a region in which papal authority fought in vain against the strength of such tyrants as the Polenta of Ravenna and the Malatesta of Rimini. The denial of scutage (*tallia militum*) by these two cities in 1287 is a reminder that in the last analysis the nature of parliaments depended on the relative strength of ruler and ruled.

The presence of representatives of towns—unthinkable in the Teutonic Europe of the early Middle Ages—was testimony to an 'urban revolution' and to the need to recognise their weight in the nation. In León the towns were ordered to send men to the *cortes* as early as 1188, and in Catalonia by 1214, but it was only in the second half of the century that they began to play a prominent part in the Castilian assembly; they were then summoned ten times during the reign of Alfonso X (1252–84), four times by Sancho IV (1284–95), and no less than 15 times by Ferdinand IV (1295–1312). We have already seen that in 1283 the Catalan towns secured a promise from their ruler that they would be consulted annually. The fiction whereby representatives spoke for a community and made promises on its behalf created certain difficulties, for the novel idea that men not present could be bound by the word of others who were present was not easy to grasp—especially the unpleasant financial implications of a blank cheque. Again the Roman lawyers could be of assistance. Justinian's *Code* defined the method whereby a corporation could give its agents full powers (*plena potestas*) to represent its interests and hence to consent to the jurisdiction of judges and to their decisions. By the same means towns could give a mandate to 'proctors' and promise to 'hold firm' whatever these representatives had agreed to in the assembly. Soon kings were insisting that all representatives must have the necessary full powers to bind the corporation or community on whose behalf they were present. Attempts were made by the cautious to confer limited powers or to add powers to defend the town's privileges and liberties, hence Philip IV's instructions that representatives must have full powers 'without the excuse of giving an account'—*plena potestas absque excusatione relationis facienda*—in other words they must not be able to plead the necessity of referring back for further instructions.

GOVERNMENT AND ADMINISTRATION

The monarchies have been treated hitherto in terms of 'pure' feudalism, but every king had available a certain bureaucratic machinery to assist him in enforcing his will. Inevitably the extent and efficiency of this machine depended largely upon the wealth of the crown, the availability of educated men, and the existence of a tradition of literate and loyal administration. In the later thirteenth century governmental officialdom was probably to be seen at its most powerful in the Sicilian kingdom of Charles of Anjou, though the Palaeologan relic of the Eastern Empire was heir to an even longer and greater tradition. The compact kingdom of England also made an impressive showing, but France on the whole less so—we have already seen that in this respect it as yet barely ranked ahead of some of its own great fiefs. The Iberian kingdoms lacked well-developed systems of administration, while the Empire tended to lag behind all the rest, partly through the tragic adversities of its recent history, but more fundamentally because the elective principle effectively hindered the development of any continuity in personnel, traditions and archives.

The king governed through his 'court' and departmentalisation within this court developed very slowly. There was no clear differentiation between the ruler's own finances and the national treasury, and officials did not normally specialise in particular aspects of administration. The seneschal (or steward) and marshal, once the principal men in the king's household, had retained little power, but other officials of the household continued to play a leading part in government, particularly in England. The personnel of central administration consisted of a body of 'familiars' or royal officials, most of whom were normally 'clerks' at least in minor orders, though there was a growing lay element, mainly of men trained in the law. This central civil service was expected to display versatile competence in financial, judicial and military administration. The clerics did not normally receive salaries from the crown but lived mainly on the revenues of their ecclesiastical benefices; naturally they were absentees and pluralists, though this was less serious when they held canonries and prebends without 'cure of souls'. Promotion to the episcopate was the equivalent of promotion today into the higher reaches of the civil service and royal administration was one of the principal routes to ecclesiastical preferment. To govern a diocese conscientiously while remaining in the king's service was beyond the capacity of any normal man, and there were some who expressed dissatisfaction with an arrangement which was taken for granted by most—indeed any other system of paying officials would have placed an intolerably heavy burden on the king's finances and would have led to very heavy taxation or the virtual disappearance of the class of officials.

One occupation of the king's clerks was naturally the drafting of correspondence, a task undertaken by clerics of the royal chapel; as institutions became more formalised the principal of these became known as the chancellor and his office as the chancery. Later these were reinforced by lay notaries, particularly in the Latin countries possessing schools of Roman law and hence a larger class of literate laymen.

Not only did the chancery tend to become something of a separate department within the court, but its head at times assumed an independent status which menaced the king's own supremacy. It was for this reason that the chancellorship was left vacant for long periods in France, England and Castile. The French kings entrusted the headship of the writing-office from 1227 till 1314 to a 'keeper of the seal' who was either a clerk of comparatively low rank (he was never a bishop) or a layman. In Castile the archbishop of Toledo and the archbishop of Santiago became ex officio nominal chancellors of Castile and León respectively, while the work was done by a chief notary. We may be justified in applying one general test to these chanceries in an attempt to secure an impression of what degree of bureaucratic efficiency prevailed within them: did they regularly preserve copies of outgoing letters? To do so was a heavy burden on the small staffs of clerks, for dozens of letters, many of them concerning trivial or routine matters, must often have been despatched in a single day—yet how could government be carried on effectively if the king had no record of the orders that he himself had sent? The answer to our question is surprisingly unfavourable to thirteenth-century administration. The popes had regularly kept registers of important out-letters since the eleventh century, and perhaps earlier. The Angevin rulers of southern Italy also made registers of their letters: the full series of 378 volumes survived intact until 30 September 1943, when they were intentionally burnt by German troops, with the other documents of the Naples State Archive. The English chancery enrolments open on an impressive scale from the reign of John (1199–1216) and the Castilian kingdom had registers (which have disappeared) from the time of Alfonso X. The French court was slow to embark on a policy of regular registration, which was begun only in 1307. In France, as in England, the recipient of a letter had to make a payment to secure its registration.[27]

Inevitably the financial aspects of administration, as the essential basis of all the rest, bulked largest, and this is reflected in the emergence of exchequers as separate departments in England and Sicily. Again France was slow to follow suit. At the time of St Louis' death there was no equivalent to the exchequer, the supervision of revenue being entrusted largely to the *chambre aux deniers* in the household and to the occasional sessions of special commissions of the court charged with overseeing the accounts of the officials of the royal domain. The treasury, situated at the Paris house of the Order of the Templars, was also much involved with both revenue and expenditure. The consolidation of a separate accounting department (*chambre des comptes*) was again a fourteenth-century development. The Iberian monarchs also lagged behind in financial organisation, Castile perhaps inevitably since the king had virtually no domain lands to exploit, while in Aragon finance was the concern of the households of its various parts.

Equally crucial was the field of local administration, and it was here that the French king outstripped the English from whom he had learnt so much. Local government in the Middle Ages could mean anything from the mere recognition of regional magnates (granted office as royal officials and perhaps misleadingly viewed as such from the royal court) to the appointment of men strictly appointed and paid by the crown, responsible and loyal to it, independent of all local ties. Indeed, from the barons of the post-Conquest decades to the royal officials 'raised from the dust', the English sheriffs occupy every position in this spectrum between the eleventh century and the thirteenth. For the king to maintain real control over an official who was truly his servant it was desirable that the man should be imposed from above and without—not recruited locally. He was also more likely to give satisfactory service if he was the recipient of a fixed salary and not a 'farmer' who had secured office in return for a promise of paying a certain sum, and was thus obliged to raise from his zone of activity sufficient money to recoup his farm and achieve a margin of profit for his own pocket. The local representative of French royal power, whose wide functions defy definition, was the bailiff (*bailli*—or, in the south, 'seneschal'). This official met almost all the requirements stated above. He was not a local man and he tended to be moved fairly frequently (on an average every two or three years). Furthermore, if he was a native of the north, he was probably posted to southern France, and vice versa. He was not permitted to acquire property or even to find a wife or husband for his children within his zone of office, except with the king's permission. He was paid a salary and was required to remain in his bailiwick for 40 days after his resignation (or transfer), during which time his finances were subject to a special enquiry. He was also liable to periodical inspection by officials appointed by the king to oversee local administration, the *enquêteurs*. The Aragonese local officers also, unlike the English sheriffs, were salaried, but feudal and municipal powers greatly restricted their activities. The position of the Castilian regional *adelantado* implied recognition of a similar situation and came close to that of the English 'baronial sheriff'; there was virtually no true royal local administration in Castile, for the provinces were ruled by nobles and towns.

COMMUNES: THE MEDIEVAL CITY-STATE

Hitherto in this chapter municipal government has been mentioned only as detracting from royal control. In a general picture of the exercise of political power this is inadequate, for by the thirteenth century there were two considerable areas in Europe within which the towns were autonomous republics rather than self-governing units within the monarchical structure of rule. These parts were Flanders and northern and central Italy.

Before discussing the institutions of these 'communes' we must consider why more independence was gained in the two areas named and to what extent they may be considered as democracies introducing a broader element of the population to the responsibilities of power. In the first place it is evident that the city-republics were part of an equation in which the other factor was the power of the king or lord; other things being equal, they were most likely to succeed in asserting their autonomy where external pressure was weakest. In Lombardy, Tuscany and the Veneto they benefited by the rarity of effective imperial intervention. In the Low Countries the French king and the emperor made only intermittent appearances on the scene, while the count of Flanders, by tradition and necessity, was an ally who drew money from the towns rather than sought to rule them. Where the claims of a lord were most effective in limiting municipal independence, as at Liège, Cambrai and Utrecht, the lord was a bishop.

In essence, however, it was the towns' own strength that made of them something more than a 'collective feudatory', and this strength was derived from a sizeable population possessing formidable financial and military resources. Such urban nuclei had each some thousands of inhabitants; both Italy and Flanders ran to many towns of around 10,000, but probably only the exceptional places—Bruges and Ghent in the north, Milan, Venice, Florence and perhaps a few others in the south—exceeded 30,000 at the end of the thirteenth century. Their growth was of course connected with the expansion of trade and industry. Many Flemish towns were centres of cloth manufacture, dependent largely on wool shipped from England and exporting their products by North Sea routes (particularly eastwards to northern Germany and the Baltic) and overland to the Mediterranean. Of the larger Italian towns Venice, Genoa and Pisa were most dependent on maritime trade, but these, like the other great towns of Lombardy, the Veneto, Tuscany and Emilia, had a mixed economy embracing textile industries and other crafts, long-distance and local trade, banking and finance, shop-keeping and agriculture. The inhabitants of these centres, and still more of the smaller towns, should not be envisaged as a 'new class', urban, mercantile, divorced from and antagonistic to the feudal outlook. In the Mediterranean town-life had a long tradition behind it, and both malaria and the dangers of war and raiding drove men to gather in those hill-top settlements of agriculturalists—often tilling land many miles distant—which still characterise some parts of southern Europe. Land-owning knights had been an important element in the formative stage of the Italian commune in the eleventh and twelfth centuries, furnishing its cavalry and often half the consuls (the governing officials). Italy and the Languedoc had also a large and powerful class of lawyers and notaries.[28] Even in Flanders there was no clear-cut division between archaic rustic nobles and slick urban businessmen; money made from the soil was often invested in trade and industry, and in turn the profits of these activities could be converted into nothing safer than land. Such a cycle was still more natural in Italy where the climate encouraged the purchase of a villa for the summer *villeggiatura*. Southern France is one obvious exception which disproves the fallacious 'rule' that only communities of merchants could set up independent institutions. Here Toulouse virtually won self-rule in the 1230s as an ally of its count in the struggle against the military power of northern France, and even smaller places, such as Avignon and Beaucaire, possessed such 'Italian' institutions as consuls and *podestà* and won the vassalage of the surrounding countryside. Inevitably, self-government was not government 'by the people' or even 'for the people'. 'The rich men possess rule in the towns', says Beaumanoir, and this French generalisation holds true elsewhere. The wealthier people had more time at their disposal and more education behind them, to strengthen their speeches and recommend their administrative services. There was much in the government of the town—particularly fiscal policy—that directly and obviously affected their well-being; in such matters to lack interest in politics might be to condemn oneself to poverty. Above all, they possessed the means of bringing pressure to bear upon the rest of the population, dependent on them for employment and patronage and liable to be overawed, at a pinch, by a show of strength from armed retainers. In a sense the inevitable presence of powerful and interested citizens makes an oligarchy the 'natural' form of government of any autonomous city. In ready recognition of this tendency, contemporaries spoke of *maiores, boni homines, potentiores* and *divites* or *ditiores*—in the Italian vernacular, of *grandi, magnati and ottimati*.[29] Rather later the Florentine Francesco Guicciardini thought that a senate of 150 would contain 'all the qualified men of the city'; a larger one would be bound to include the 'ignorant and ill-born'.[30] This oligarchical conformation was typical also of cities enjoying merely municipal status. Beaumanoir explains well the reasons for this and its effects:

We have seen many disputes in the towns, the poor against the rich, and the rich against each other—when for example, they cannot agree on the nomination of a mayor, or proctors, or lawyers; or when one party accuses another of not dealing properly with the town's revenue and of having spent excessively; or when the administration is in a bad condition on account of the quarrels and hatreds that turn one family against another . . . There are some towns in which the poor burgesses and even those of middle rank take no part in the administration of the town, this being entirely in the hands of the rich because the common people fear them on account of their wealth and connections. Men become mayor or *jurés* or *receveurs* and then the next year they pass on the office to their brothers or nephews or close relatives—so that in ten or twelve years the rich hold all the offices in the towns.[31]

In London, where a similar situation prevailed, the courageous John of Northampton (in the late fourteenth century) led an unsuccessful assault by the lesser crafts and minor members of the greater ones against a well-entrenched regime which, characteristically, followed a monopolistic policy injurious to both small traders and consumers. *De jure* might lag behind *de facto*, but sooner or later the town's constitution was likely to reflect the oligarchical trend. At Ghent this had happened as early as 1228, with the introduction of a sort of rota system whereby the 13 *échevins* for the year shared power with the 13 holders of the office for the two previous years. Every three years the same men reappeared as the 'new' *échevins* and in practice office for life was held by 'the Thirty-nine'. Venice, the best Italian instance of formalised oligarchy, 'closed' its great council in 1297. Thereafter only those whose ancestors had sat in this council were eligible for membership.[32]

A rigid, fossilised system of political oligarchy, however, is doomed to defeat through its very rigidity, for it defies the essential mutability of men's fortune—or, as the sociologists would have it, 'social mobility'. In an age when a single fortunate trading venture or loan might produce a colossal profit and when taxes (by modern European standards) were low, ability and good luck could rapidly make a poor man rich—the reverse, of course, also held. At times a general increase in wealth might apply to considerable area—we are perhaps in the realm here of the 'take-off' dear to writers on the economy of developing countries—and often many men in a single town were making fortunes contemporaneously. We may see this occurring in Florence in the two or three decades after the city's bankers had financed Charles of Anjou's conquest of southern Italy—which became something of an economic colony—in 1265–6. Florence's walls, which had been expanded in 1172–6, had to be extended again after 1284 to take in a vastly increased population. Assisted by the fact that 'conspicuous consumption' is most conspicuous in climates which encourage people to live in the open air, the population was itself aware of such changes. The great Florentine poet and intellectual, Dante, thought that his city's period of true greatness was to be found in the past, before it had become corrupted by wealth. 'New people and rapid wealth', he said, had led to pride and *dismisura* (a lack of proportion), and Florence was already suffering from the effects of this.[33] In a moving passage in the *Paradiso* (written *c*.1315) he puts into the mouth of his great-grandfather, Cacciaguida, a description of this Golden Age of the twelfth century. 'Within the old walls Florence was at peace, sober and pure.' Women did not wear necklaces and tiaras, skirts and belts covered with ornaments. Fathers were not then appalled at the birth of a daughter, for they married less early and their dowries were smaller. Family homes were smaller and did not seem half-empty, and they too were not over-decorated. Women did not use cosmetics and were not left lonely by husbands going to France on business. They tended their babies in the cradle, chanting the traditional lullabies, or worked at their spinning and told the old tales of Troy, Fiesole and Rome.[34]

Dante's contemporary Giovanni Villani, though writing of a less archaic period, recounted the same contrast, with the same underlying 'primitivist' belief—strengthened perhaps by the Franciscan ideal—in the moral superiority of the simple life:

And note, that at the time of the said Popolo [1250−60] and before and afterwards for a long time, the citizens of Florence lived soberly, and on coarse food, and with little spending, and in manners and graces were in many respects coarse and rude: . . . but they were true and trustworthy to one another and to their commune and with their simple life and poverty they did greater and more virtuous things than are done in our times with more luxury and more riches.[35]

This knowledge of and admiration for the austerity of the past was not confined to Florence, and the same feeling is to be found in Riccobaldo of Ferrara's *Universal History*, written at the end of the thirteenth century:

Manners and ways of living were rough in Italy in the times of this emperor [Frederick II, 1220−50]. The men wore a head-dress of iron mail. Man and wife would eat from one dish and the use of wooden trenchers at table was not yet known. A family would have only one or perhaps two goblets. When people ate at night they lit their tables by oil-lamps or by faggots held by a boy or servant, for tallow and wax candles were not then in use. Men wore leather or cloth cloaks, without a lining, and a light cloth hood. The women wore tunics of the same cloth, both at their marriage and after. For both sexes it was a plain way of life, little if any gold or silver was displayed on their clothing and they were frugal in their meals. The common people ate fresh meat three times a week. They would eat vegetables cooked with meat and keep some of the meat to eat cold in the evening. Not everyone drank wine in summer, and people thought themselves rich if they had just a little money. Wine-cellars were small then and granaries were not large, for people were satisfied with what was distributed. Girls married with a small dowry because they were frugal in their ways and before marriage they were content to wear a light cloth tunic and over this a flaxen cloak. Neither maidens nor married women decorated their heads with expensive ornaments. The wives wore a band round their temples and cheeks which tied under the chin. Among men it was thought glorious to be proficient in arms and on horseback, and among the wealthy nobles to possess towers; some of the Italian cities were renowned for the towers which abounded in their midst.[36]

In so far as oligarchy was a formal political structure it had to possess the means of assimilating 'new men', and at times this needed to be a rapid process for many were pressing for admission. There were certainly diehards who objected to the *nouveaux riches*, but their exclusion was a danger and might prevent a town from exerting its full potential strength, as well as weaken it through internal divisions. In the armies of the Italian republics the 'nobles' fought as cavalrymen and it was wasteful not to use in this role a man capable of maintaining a horse and fighting on it. The towns themselves ennobled their own citizens—the ceremony of dubbing had to be performed by one who was himself a noble—but some republics compromised by compelling wealthy non-nobles to serve on horseback as *milites pro communi*. The dangers of failing to assimilate at a sufficient rate are illustrated by the 'popular' anti-magnate movements which flourished in many Italian towns in the later thirteenth century.[37] Such movements were essentially an attempt by the leading 'outsiders' to weaken the hold of the 'top people' and in particular to neutralise by legislation their formidable social strength. The nature both of this strength and of the measures used to oppose it are well illustrated by some laws for its members promulgated in 1260 by Perugia's 'Popolo':

1. No man is to become the vassal of any other, or swear fealty to him; any one doing so is to be decapitated, as is the man receiving such an oath and the notary recording such a transaction.
2. No member of the *popolo* may have recourse to any 'magnate' concerning any business he had in the commune's court before the *podestà* or captain or any other official . . .
3. No member of the *popolo* is to dare to hold conversation with any magnate or to be in his company when going to or returning from the court or palace of the commune, or in any other part of the city at a time when this magnate is involved in a fight or quarrel.[38]

In Florence similar moves against the 'magnates' began in 1281 with the decision to draw up a list of these, each of whom should be compelled to make a payment of 2,000 *lire* as security for his future good conduct. Twelve years later a more powerful popular movement formulated the 'Ordinances of Justice', whereby an official, the *Gonfaloniere di Giustizia* (standard-bearer of justice), was added to the six priors, with the special responsibility of punishing magnates; any magnate killing a member of the *popolo* was to be automatically sentenced to death, his property confiscated and his house promptly destroyed by the popular militia under the command of the *Gonfaloniere*. If the guilty man could not be traced, his next of kin was liable to punishment; in this way the magnates' family solidarity was exploited and used against them. Magnates were excluded from membership of the guilds and hence from the priorate. Any family of which a member during the last 20 years had been a knight was to rank in the black list with 'those whom the general opinion calls *potentes*, *nobiles* or *magnates*'. This list included about 150 families, 72 of which resided mainly in the city.

Opposition to an oligarchy inevitably looked for external allies, and the sort of situation that might arise from this is well illustrated by events in Flanders during the reign of Philip IV of France (1285–1314). At this period the count, Guy of Dampierre, was co-operating with anti-oligarchic elements in the towns in an attempt to weaken the hold of such cliques as the Thirty-nine of Ghent; the count's main purpose was of course to gain control himself. The result was the formation in 1287 of a rival coalition between the patriciate (henceforth the *Leliaerts* or 'men of the lilies') and the French king. The long and inconclusive struggle that ensued combined the bitterness of class hatred with the patriotic hatred of Fleming and Frenchman.

INSTITUTIONS OF URBAN GOVERNMENT

We can now turn from this necessarily rather long description of the setting to the institutions of urban government. In origin the communes had taken shape as corporations of individuals undertaking joint political action. Normally the citizens had been united by an oath of mutual co-operation, and there is much truth in the view that contrasts this 'horizontal' oath between equals with the 'vertical' feudal oath linking vassal and lord. The double origin of many Italian communes, however, comprising distinct noble and non-noble organisations, is a reminder that even here the democratic element in the towns may easily be exaggerated. In Italy the characteristic institutions of the early communes had been the *arenga* (the parliament of all the citizens) and the consuls, who were administrative officials. By the early years of the thirteenth century divisions within the consular class had led to the replacement of the consuls by a single official called in from another town, a sort of 'town manager'. This man, the *podestà*, was normally in turn dispossessed of the *de facto* headship of the commune by the guild organization, the *popolo*. We have already seen how pressure was constantly exerted on the powers that be by a class of 'new men', and the *popolo* was essentially an organisation headed by such men, expressing their interests through the guilds and often forming a military force subdivided according to the different 'regions' of the town. The *popolo* was usually at first headed by an external 'captain'—in this respect its organisation was based on that of the commune itself—but the reverse now occurred to what had happened in the change from consuls to *podestà*, for the captain of the *popolo* often lost his importance to local officials. In Florence the captain, who had come to power in 1250, was virtually superseded in 1282 by guild representatives, the six priors.[39] But there was no secure resting place for the institutions of these towns. No individual was permitted to retain an important office for a long period lest he attempted to set up a tyranny: Florence's priors, for example, held office for two months at a time, after which they were ineligible for the next two years. In this paralysed condition the city-states sought not merely to organise their domestic affairs and to conduct diplomacy and (almost ceaseless) warfare; they also ruled most of the countryside. The *contado*, or zone of subjection, had been acquired in opposition to neighbouring towns for its strategic value, as a source of taxes and soldiers, above all as an insurance against starvation:[40] it was made to provide the town with food. The internal history of most of the towns is a hectic tale of internal class disputes, complicated by feuds inside the nobility, with 'new men' putting forward claims, while the strongest among the 'old' are never dispossessed of power. This explains the numberless constitutional changes, the incurable tendency to experiment with new types of council, new ways of voting, new combinations of the contrasting principles of voting and choice by lot. The constitutional solution to the town's problems was always felt to be just round the corner, and Dante's criticism of Florence was entirely justified:

> Athens and Lacedaemon, still well known
> for ancient laws and civil discipline
> showed but the faintest signs of order then
> compared to you, who plan so cleverly
> that by the time November is half done
> the laws spun in October are in shreds.
> How often within memory have you changed
> coinage and customs, laws and offices,
> and members of your body politic!
> Think back, and if you see the truth, you'll see
> that you are like a woman, very sick,
> who finds no rest on her soft, sumptuous bed,
> but turns and tosses to escape her pain.[41]

The conclusion of this tale was almost invariably the same: the *signoria*, government by a single tyrant.

In Flanders and north-western France the characteristic feature of republican institutions was the *échevinage*. The *échevins* (in Latin, *scabini*) were in origin the men chosen by the lord to perform judicial offices in the town, and were appointed to this position for life. As the towns achieved independence the *échevins* were gradually transformed; they ceased to be the lord's men and became the city's governing body or council, no longer holding office for life but now normally for one year only at a time. This at least was the theory, and at first the practice: but at Ghent the annual rotation of 13 *échevins* was so manipulated that the city was ruled by a closed council of 39.[42] In all the city-states the lesson is evident that any constitutional structure was vulnerable to pressure and would be modified and reshaped by the powerful, whether these were Flemish oligarchs crystallising their control through the Thirty-nine or Italian anti-oligarchs installing their 'popular' institutions to check or supersede those of the magnates. In the towns where a powerful overlord, the bishop of Liège, was able to retain control of the *échevinage* and prevent its development as a town's own council, an analogous process took place: there also two rival governmental structures existed side by side, for the townsmen set up against the bishop's *échevins* their own 'sworn men' or *jurés*.

CONCLUSION

Monarchical and municipal governments as they existed in the thirteenth century both illustrate that weakness of central control which is the most striking contrast with the modern state. 'Feudalism', even where its institutions are imposed by the monarchy (as in England and southern Italy), is essentially the formalisation of this situation. In their lack of salaried officials and full-time soldiers, above all in their implicit compromise with the powerful subject, these monarchies are feeble creatures beside the Leviathans of the sixteenth and seventeenth centuries. Within their limitations, however, great gains could be made. Much depended on the fortunes of family descent, on avoiding minorities and disputed successions. The Capetians of France produced an undisputed male heir in 11 successive generations, from the tenth century to the fourteenth, and it was in part due to this genetic triumph[43] that when they gained new territories—Normandy, Poitou and Toulouse in the thirteenth century, Champagne and part of Flanders early in the fourteenth—they were sufficiently strong for these to prove a source of strength and not an impossible burden. With them one may contrast the unfortunate house of Castile, hopelessly debilitated in the fourteenth century by disputed successions and resultant civil warfare. The collapse of imperial power in Germany must be imputed largely to the failure of earlier rulers to install hereditary succession in place of the archaic elective principle—but that failure is in turn evidence of the feeble resources of these kings and of the dispersion of political power within the Empire.

APPENDIX

King James I negotiates with the Catalan Estates, 1264

(From *The Chronicle of James I, King of Aragon*, chs ccclxxxiii–ccclxxxvii. Based on the translation by J. Forster (London, 1883), vol. II, pp. 503–7.)

We[44] departed thence, went to Catalonia, and called together the Court[45] at Barcelona. When they were assembled, 'rich men',[46] citizens and clergy, we asked them, since they and theirs had always helped us in such undertakings as that of Majorca and others, that they would now help us in this one, as was much needed. Their answer was that they would deliberate thereupon, and as the lord Ramon de Cardona and some of his house claimed redress for some wrongs they had suffered of us, they would first speak with us thereupon, and then make such answer as would satisfy us. We replied that anyone in our land who had any complaint to make should come forward at once, and right would be done to him; that ought not to be a reason for refusing us the aid we asked for. It was not good sense, we said, that whilst we asked them for one thing, they should reply by talking of another quite unconnected with it. Wherefore we prayed and commanded them to think better of it, for certainly the answer they gave did not become such good men as they were. They deliberated again and then gave us answer as bad as, or worse than, the first.

When we saw how badly they behaved to us, we told them that they had not sufficiently considered what might happen thereafter. If the King of Castile ultimately lost what was his own, we and they would find it harder to keep our property than we had done till then. We then addressed the clergy in these words: 'What will you gain by the churches where our Lord and His Mother are now worshipped being lost, and the name of Mahomet worshipped therein? And if what belongs to kings be lost, how can you expect to keep what you yourselves own? Why answer us so ill and so basely! We never thought that we should assemble the Court in Catalonia without obtaining from them what was reasonable; for surely had we asked from you urgently what was unreasonable, we really think we should have prevailed with you to grant it to us. But since such is your answer, we will depart from you, as much displeased as any lord ever was with his people.'

Saying which we arose, and would hear nothing more from them and went to our house; they prayed us earnestly not to be angry, for they would again deliberate and give us an answer. But for all that we would not wait; some of them followed us to our house, others remained behind; but ultimately those who had come with us went back to the others.

And we were in this state, and would not eat, when they sent us the lord Berenguer Arnau, the lord Pedro de Berga, and two other 'rich men', whose names we do not recollect, who begged to speak to us. We took them aside and heard what they had to say. They told us that it had never been, and never should be, the mind of the Court on any account that we should seek counsel or aid of the prelates and 'rich men' of Catalonia without finding it at once. And that as we intended to leave the town, and had said so to some, they begged us to remain, saying that, if we did, they would behave in such wise that we should be satisfied with them. And this they prayed so much and so earnestly of us, that we had to grant it.

At vespers they came to us again, saying that on no account would they (that we ought to believe) let us leave in anger with them. We ought to hear what they had to say, for their words in the first instance were not intended in bad sense. They therefore begged us, before they granted what we asked of them, to do what Ramon de Cardona had begged us. It was, they said, their intention to grant us after that the service known by the name of *bovatge*,[47] although they maintained we had no right to it, having already had it twice since the beginning of our reign; once when we came to the throne, and again when we went to Majorca. They would, however, grant it again, since we wished it, and would serve us in that business so that we should have reason to thank them. We were content with their answer, and called together the Court in Aragon, to be present at Zaragoza within three weeks.

FURTHER READING

The political contours of thirteenth-century Europe

Good overall surveys of government in the thirteenth century are Malcolm Barber, *The Two Cities. Medieval Europe 1050–1320* (London and New York, 1992), Part III, and John H. Mundy, *Europe in the High Middle Ages, 1150–1309* (2nd edition, London, 1991), Part IV. The classic work is H. Mitteis, *The State in the Middle Ages. A Comparative Constitutional History of Feudal Europe* (tr. Amsterdam, Oxford, New York, 1975); Part IV relates to the period covered in this book. Further references can be found under reading suggestions for Chapter 18 below. For the histories of individual countries, *see* the respective sections below.

Monarchs and subjects

Of the sources cited in the text, Joinville's *Life of St Louis* has been translated by M. R. B. Shaw in Joinville and Villehardouin, *Chronicles of the Crusades* (London, 1963). Beaumanoir's work has been translated by F. R. P. Akehurst, *The Coutumes de Beauvaisis of Philippe de Beaumanoir* (Philadelphia, Pa., 1995). Other French sources of interest are in Theodore Evergates, tr., ed., *Feudal Society in Medieval Europe. Documents from the County of Champagne* (Philadelphia, Pa., 1993), and Theodore Evergates, tr., ed., *The Etablissements de St Louis. Thirteenth-Century Law Texts from Tours, Orléans and Paris* (Philadelphia, Pa., 1996). Selections of cases heard by

Louis IX's *enquêteurs* in Normandy in 1247 have been translated in Patrick J. Geary, ed., *Readings in Medieval History* (repr. Peterborough, Ont. and Lewiston, N.Y., 1992), vol. 2, pp. 353–63.

On the relationship of monarchs and subjects, *see* Susan Reynolds, *Kingdoms and Communities in Western Europe, 900–1300* (Oxford, 1984); Susan Reynolds, *Fiefs and Vassals. The Medieval Evidence Reinterpreted* (Oxford, 1994), especially ch. 7 (a provocative reassessment of the traditional view of feudalism). On France and Spain generally, *see under* Chapters 3 and 12 respectively.

Kingship and law

The essential political passages of St Thomas Aquinas's *Summa Theologica* and other works were translated in Aquinas, *Selected Political Writings*, ed. A. P. D'Entrèves, tr. J. G. Dawson (Oxford, 1959, repr. 1981 without Latin text—the edition quoted here), in Dino Bigongiari, ed., *The Political Ideas of St Thomas Aquinas* (New York and London, 1953, repr. New York, 1997), and in P. E. Sigmund, ed., *Thomas Aquinas on Politics and Ethics* (New York, 1988). On Aquinas generally *see* the short biography by Anthony Kenny, *Aquinas* (Past Masters Series, Oxford, 1979); on the contemporary, as opposed to the scholastic, influences on his views *see* J. Catto, 'Ideas and experience in the political thought of Aquinas', *Past and Present*, 71 (1976), pp. 3–21. On theories of the common good, *see* M. Kempshall, *The Common Good in Late Medieval Political Thought* (Oxford, 1999). The *De Regimine Principum* has now been translated in its entirety by James M. Blythe, *On the Government of Rulers. De Regimine Principum. Ptolemy of Lucca with Portions Attributed to Thomas Aquinas* (Philadelphia, Pa., 1997). A selection of other related texts can be found in Cary J. Nederman and Kate Langdon Forman, *Medieval Political Theory—A Reader. The Quest for the Body Politic, 1100–1400* (London and New York, 1993).

The classic study on medieval kingship is Ernst H. Kantorowicz, *The King's Two Bodies. A Study in Medieval Political Theology* (Princeton, N.J., 1957, repr. 1981). On the development of Roman law in the Middle Ages, M. Bellomo, *The Common Legal Past of Europe, 1000–1800* (Washington, D.C., 1995), and on its influence on ideas of sovereignty, K. Pennington, *The Prince and the Law, 1200–1600: Sovereignty and Rights in the Western Legal Tradition* (Berkeley, Cal., 1993). General works on medieval political ideas include J. Canning, *A History of Medieval Political Thought, 300–1500* (London, 1996); A. Black, *Political Thought in Europe, 1250–1450* (Cambridge, 1992); J. H. Burns, ed., *The Cambridge History of Medieval Political Thought c.350–c.1450* (Cambridge, 1988); W. Ullmann, *Medieval Political Thought* (3rd edition, London, 1975); W. Ullmann, *Principles of Government and Politics in the Middle Ages* (3rd edition, London, 1974). *See also* J. M. Blythe, *Ideal Government and the Mixed Constitution in the Middle Ages* (Princeton, N.J., 1992). More generally *see* M. Colish, *Medieval Foundations of the Western Intellectual Tradition* (New Haven, Conn., 1997).

Consent and consultation: medieval parliaments

The most recent overview of the literature is Wim Blockmans, 'Representation (since the thirteenth century)', in *NCMH*, VII, ch. 2. A. Marongiu, *Medieval Parliaments. A Comparative Study* (tr. London, 1968), and A. R. Myers, *Parliaments and Estates in Europe* (London, 1975) are general works of synthesis; T. N. Bisson, ed., *Medieval Representative Institutions. Their Origins and Nature* (Hinsdale, Ill., 1973) reprints selected passages from the historiography. On methods of classifying parliaments, *see* W. P. Blockmans, 'A typology of representative institutions in late medieval Europe', *Journal of Medieval History*, 4 (1978), pp. 189–215. Monographs include E. Procter, *Curia and Cortes in Leon and Castile, 1072–1295* (Cambridge, 1980); J. F. O'Callaghan, *The Cortes of Castile–León 1188–1350* (Philadelphia, Pa., 1989); and T. N. Bisson,

Assemblies and Representation in Languedoc in the Thirteenth Century (Princeton, N.J., 1964), and his *Medieval France and its Pyrenean Neighbours. Studies in Early Institutional History* (London, 1989), Part I: Consultation and Representation.

Government and administration

The issues in this section are treated in a number of general works and monographs. For France, *see* E. M. Hallam, *Capetian France, 937–1328* (London and New York, 1980), ch. 5; J. W. Baldwin, *The Government of Philip Augustus. Foundations of French Royal Power in the Middle Ages* (Berkeley and Los Angeles, Cal., 1986); J. R. Strayer, *The Reign of Philip the Fair* (Princeton, N.J., 1980), chs 2 and 3; F. J. Pegues, *The Lawyers of the Last Capetians* (Princeton, N.J., 1962); and James Given, *State and Society in Medieval Europe. Gwynedd and Languedoc under Outside Rule* (Ithaca, N.Y. and London, 1990). For Spain, J. N. Hillgarth, *The Spanish Kingdoms 1260–1516*, 2 vols (Oxford, 1976–8), vol. 1, *1250–1516*, ch. 3; J. F. O'Callaghan, *History of Medieval Spain* (Ithaca, N.Y. and London, 1975), ch. 18; A. MacKay, *Spain in the Middle Ages. From Frontier to Empire, 1000–1500* (London, 1977), ch. 5; and J. F. Powers, *A Society Organized for War. The Iberian Municipal Militias in the Central Middle Ages, 1000–1284* (Berkeley, Cal., 1988). On administration and the keeping of records, *see* R. Britnell, ed., *Pragmatic Literacy, East and West, 1200–1330* (London 1997) and, for England, M. T. Clanchy, *From Memory to Written Record: England 1066–1307* (London, 1979, 2nd edition, Oxford, 1993).

Communes: the medieval city-state; Institutions of urban government

Excerpts of the Ordinances of Justice have been translated in B. C. Kohl and A. Andrews Smith, eds, *Major Problems in the History of the Italian Renaissance* (Lexington, Mass. and Toronto, 1995), pp. 139–42. There are many translations of Dante's *Divine Comedy*; the one cited here is by Mark Musa (Bloomington, In., 1971–84, and London, Harmondsworth, 1984–6); on Dante's relationship with Florence, John M. Najemy, 'Dante and Florence', in *The Cambridge Companion to Dante*, ed. Rachel Jacoff (Cambridge, 1993), pp. 80–99. A partial translation of Giovanni Villani's *Chronicle* is *Villani's Chronicle. Being Selections from the First Nine Books of the Croniche Fiorentine of Giovanni Villani*, tr./ed. R. E. Selfe and P. H. Wicksteed (2nd edition, London, 1906), esp. Books VIII and IX. A good introduction to Villani is Louis Green, *Chronicle into History. An Essay on the Interpretation of History in Florentine Fourteenth-Century Chronicles* (Cambridge, 1972), ch. 1. An even more contemporary view for Dante's period is *Dino Compagni's Chronicle of Florence*, tr. Daniel Bornstein (Philadelphia, Pa., 1986). On the themes discussed here, *see also* J. K. Hyde, 'Contemporary views on faction and civil strife in thirteenth- and fourteenth-century Italy', in his *Literacy and its Uses. Studies on Late Medieval Italy*, ed. D. P. Waley (Manchester, 1993), ch. 3.

On the Italian city-states, a great deal has now been published in English. For overviews, D. P. Waley, *The Italian City-Republics* (3rd edition, London, 1988); J. K. Hyde, *Society and Politics in Medieval Italy* (London, 1973); J. Larner, *Italy in the Age of Dante and Petrarch, 1216–1380* (London, 1980); Lauro Martines, *Power and Imagination. City-States in Renaissance Italy* (New York, 1979 and London, 1980), esp. chs 3–8; Giovanni Tabacco, *The Struggle for Power in Medieval Italy. Structures of Political Rule* (tr. Cambridge, 1989), esp. ch. 6; and the magisterial P. J. Jones, *The Italian City-State. From Commune to Signoria* (Oxford, 1997). A wide-ranging collection of essays is Anthony Molho, Kurt Raaflaub and Julia Emlen, ed., *City-States in Classical Antiquity and Medieval Italy* (Ann Arbor, Mich., 1991). Individual cities have received varying coverage. The most studied is Florence. A basic narrative acount is F. Schevill, *Medieval and Renaissance Florence* (2 vols, revised edition, New York, 1963). For the thirteenth century, *see especially* G. A. Holmes, *Florence, Rome and the Origins of the Renaissance* (Oxford, 1986), and Carol Lansing, *The Florentine Magnates. Lineage and Faction in a Medieval Commune* (Princeton, N.J., 1991). Siena has also been intensively studied: D. P. Waley, *Siena and the Sienese in the Thirteenth Century* (Cambridge, 1991); W. M. Bowsky, *A Medieval Italian Commune. Siena under the Nine* (Berkeley and Los Angeles, Cal., 1982); and more generally J. Hook, *Siena. A City and its History* (London, n.d.). Amid the profusion of works on Venice, introductions are Frederic C. Lane, *Venice. A Maritime Republic* (Baltimore, Md., 1973), and John Julius Norwich, *A History of Venice* (Harmondsworth, 1983). Monographs on other city-states (and towns with considerable independence) include: S. A. Epstein, *Genoa and the Genoese, 958– 1528* (Chapel Hill, N.C., 1996); D. P. Waley, *Medieval Orvieto: the Political History of an Italian City-State, 1157–1334* (Cambridge, 1952); J. K. Hyde, *Padua in the Age of Dante. A Social History of an Italian City State* (Manchester, 1966); and D. Herlihy, *Pisa in the Early Renaissance. A Study of Urban Growth* (New Haven, Conn., 1958, repr. Port Washington, N.Y., 1973), and his *Medieval and Renaissance Pistoia* (New Haven, Conn., 1967).

Much less is available in English for Flanders. D. Nicholas, *Medieval Flanders* (London, 1992) is an important work of synthesis; *see also* the older work of Henri Pirenne, *Early Democracies in the Low Countries: Urban Society and Political Conflict in the Middle Ages and the Renaissance* (New York, repr. 1963); and J. A. van Houtte, *An Economic History of the Low Countries 800–1800* (London, 1977), esp. Part 1.

The literature on medieval cities generally is extensive. For introductions, *see* David Nicholas, *The Growth of the Medieval City: From Late Antiquity to the Early Fourteenth Century* (London, 1997), esp. Part 3, and id., *The Later Medieval City, 1300–1500* (London, 1997); E. Ennen, *The Medieval Town* (tr. Amsterdam, 1979); and the older F. Rörig, *The Medieval Town* (tr. London, 1967). *See also* under Chapter 18 for works on the relationship of city and state.

NOTES

1. *See* Map 1.
2. Philippe de Beaumanoir, *Coutumes de Beauvaisis*, ch. 34, § 1043, ed. A. Salmon (1900, repr. Paris, 1970), II, pp. 23–4. The work has been translated by F. R. P. Akehurst, *The Coutumes de Beauvaisis of Philippe de Beaumanoir* (Philadelphia, Pa., 1995): for this excerpt see p. 368.
3. *Life of St Louis*, ch. XXVI, in Joinville and Villehardouin, *Chronicles of the Crusades*, tr. M. R. B. Shaw (London, 1963), p. 192.
4. *Bullarium Equestris Ordinis Sancti Jacobi* (Madrid, 1719), p. 150.
5. The chain of appellate jurisdiction was often a long one. Thus in Castile *c.*1274 appeal from the court of the town *alcalde* was to the local *adelantado* (governor), thence to the king's *alcalde*, thence to the royal court (*adelantados mayores de Castilla*) and finally to the king himself. In León and Andalusia the second court was one of 'three men learned in the law' and the fourth of these five stages was omitted.
6. It has been calculated that in the late eleventh century 53 German counties were in the possession of the episcopate alone.
7. 'Appeal' as such is not characteristic of Germanic law and did not exist in Flanders, for example, but analogous concepts enabled the party losing a suit to claim denial of justice or false judgment.
8. Joinville, *Life of St Louis*, as *above*, pp. 347–9. A number of different versions of these 'Instructions' have survived.
9. Martène (E.) and Durand (U.), *Thesaurus Novus Anecdotorum* (Paris, 1717), II, cols. 505–8.

10. The pope refers here to the 'enquiry' allegedly held by Charles's predecessor Manfred into the possession of horses and sheep. When the owner could not prove the animals were his they became the king's.

11. W. Stubbs, *Select Charters and Other Illustrations of English Constitutional History: from the Earliest Times to the Reign of Edward the First* (9th edition, Oxford, 1942), p. 244 (oath of Richard I, 1189: cf. the similar oath of Henry I, 1100, p. 116).

12. This was demonstrated by R. E. Giesey, *If Not, Not: the Oath of the Aragonese and the Legendary Laws of Sobrarbe* (Princeton, N.J., 1968).

13. *Siete Partidas* (Madrid, 1974 facsimile of Salamanca, 1555 edition), I, 2, II.

14. *De Regimine Principum*, ch. 1, in Aquinas, *Selected Political Writings*, ed. A. P. D'Entrèves, tr. J. G. Dawson (Oxford, 1981 edition), pp. 2–5. This is the only chapter of the *De Regimine Principum* that most scholars still agree might have been the work of Aquinas himself; the rest is considered to be the work of one or more of his pupils. On this issue (and for a more recent translation), *see* James M. Blythe, *On the Government of Rulers. De Regimine Principum. Ptolemy of Lucca with Portions Attributed to Thomas Aquinas* (Philadelphia, Pa., 1997).

15. *Summa Theologica*, Q. 90, Art. 3, ad 3um; in *Selected Political Writings*, cit., p. 57.

16. *Summa Theologica*, Q. 92, Art. 1, ad 3um; op. cit., p. 60.

17. *Summa Theologica*, Q. 97, Art. 2; op. cit., pp. 72–3.

18. *Summa Theologica*, Q. 105, Art. 1; op. cit., pp. 75–6.

19. It is less likely that St Thomas knew about burgher representatives in English and Spanish assemblies (for these *see below*, pp. 10–13).

20. This biological fallacy was inherited from the ancient world.

21. *De Regimine Principum*, ch. 2; op. cit., pp. 6–7. This part of the work was probably written by Ptolemy of Lucca.

22. *Cortes de los antiguos Reinos de Aragón y de Valencia y Principado de Cataluña* (Madrid, 1896–1922), I, p. 145.

23. It is characteristic that the *Siete Partidas* require public accusations of treason to be made in the king's court and in the presence of at least 12 nobles.

24. *Cortes de los antiguos Reinos de León y de Castilla* (Madrid, 1861–1903), I, pp. 39–42.

25. Beaumanoir, *Coutumes de Beauvaisis*, ch. 49, § 1515; ed. A. Salmon, cit., II, p. 264; in Akehurst's translation, cit., p. 542.

26. *Cortes de los antiguos Reinos de Aragón de Valencia y Principado de Cataluña*, cit., I, pp. 192–3.

27. The chancery of Rudolf of Habsburg seems not to have kept proper registers but many of the king's letters have survived in the 'formularies' compiled by his notaries.

28. Padua, not one of the largest of Italian cities, had over 500 notaries *c.*1300. J. K. Hyde, *Padua in the Age of Dante. A Social History of an Italian City-State* (Manchester, 1966), p. 162.

29. Recent writers have tended to prefer the anachronistic 'patricians' and 'patriciate'.

30. F. Guicciardini, *Dialogo e Discorsi del Reggimento di Firenze*, ed. R. Palmarocchi (Bari, 1932), p. 116; English translation *Dialogue on the Government of Florence*, tr. Alison Brown (Cambridge, 1994), pp. 112–13.

31. Beaumanoir, *Coutumes de Beauvaisis*, ch. 50, ed. A. Salmon, cit., II, pp. 267–9; in Akehurst's translation, cit., pp. 543–9.

32. Qualification was decided by membership of the council since 1172. Though the *serrata* applied in practice from 1297, the list of eligible families was only drawn up in 1315 and the 'closure' became formal in 1322.

33. *Inferno*, XVI, 73–5.

34. *Paradiso*, XV, 97–126.

35. G. Villani, *Cronica*, ed. F. Gherardi Dragomanni (Florence, 1845), Bk. VI, ch. 69; in new edition as *Nuova Cronica*, ed. Giuseppe Porta (Parma, 1990–1) as Book VII, ch. 69

(vol. 1, pp. 363–4). The translation is based on that of Rose E. Selfe, in *Villani's Chronicle. Being Selections from the first Nine Books of the Croniche Fiorentine of Giovanni Villani*, tr./ed. R. E. Selfe and P. H. Wicksteed (2nd edition, London, 1906), p. 167.

36. Riccobaldo of Ferrara, 'Historia Universalis', *Rerum Italicarurum Scriptores* (Milan, 1726), IX, col. 128 (also in the same author's 'Compilatio Chronologica', ibid., col. 2478). On this phenomenon, Charles T. Davis, 'Il Buon Tempo Antico', in *Florentine Studies*, ed. Nicolai Rubinstein (London, 1968), pp. 45–69, repr. in his *Dante's Italy and Other Essays* (Philadelphia, Pa., 1984), pp. 71–93.

37. These movements also show the inadequacy of the approach which would describe these towns as 'controlled by a patriciate'.

38. *Regestum Reformationum Comunis Perusii (1256–60)*, ed. V. Ansidei (Perugia, 1935), pp. 162–6.

39. A similar change occurred in many towns at this time, the Five taking over power at Perugia in 1270, the Nine at Siena in 1287 and the Seven at Orvieto in 1292.

40. The view that the *contado* was won primarily to open for trade the roads that had hitherto been dominated by marauding barons is a myth connected with the legend that the communes were essentially congregations of merchants.

41. *Purgatorio*, VI, 139–51, translated by Mark Musa (Harmondsworth, 1981), p. 61.

42. *See above*, pp. 19–20.

43. It is of course impossible to calculate the odds against the survival of the father by a legitimate male heir in 11 successive generations over this period, but they must have been enormous.

44. The king uses the royal 'we' in this passage. Occasionally he slips into the use of 'I' elsewhere in the *Chronicle*, a fact which has been used to support his personal authorship. It is unlikely that this error would be made by someone composing the work in the king's name.

45. The word *cort* here signifies 'estates' or 'parliament'.

46. Rics-hòmens': the nearest English equivalent is 'barons'.

47. This was a tax paid by clergy and towns, not merely on oxen as the name seems to imply.

Chapter 2

◆

ITALY AND THE MEDITERRANEAN IN THE SECOND HALF OF THE THIRTEENTH CENTURY

ITALY AFTER 1250

The death of the emperor Frederick II (December 1250) provides a convenient beginning point for viewing the framework of government in action. Frederick's career had galvanised European politics. The emergence of a German emperor who was also king of Sicily was perceived by the papacy as an unprecedented threat to its authority, and the dispute between the two powers had become one of the central ideological and geo-political themes of the first half of the thirteenth century. Although Frederick had for the most part abandoned the imperial lands north of the Alps to their lay lords and to the towns, his energetic attempt to dominate the Italian peninsula had achieved a sort of crystallisation, the dissolution of which marked a decisive change in the course of European history. There is also some convenience in starting in southern Europe because the Mediterranean zone, from the Pillars of Hercules to the Bosphorus, possessed a certain unity; it is conspicuously true of an age of difficult land transport that the sea served to join rather than to divide. In this period the political fates of Aragon, southern Italy and Byzantium were so interdependent that a classic work on the 'Sicilian Vespers' of 1282 justly bears the subtitle 'A history of the Mediterranean world in the later thirteenth century'.

Throughout Frederick's struggle to dominate Italy, the emperor had employed as a tolerably secure base his Sicilian kingdom, consisting of the island of Sicily and the southern mainland: this was organised along lines not dissimilar to the two great monarchies of northern Europe, France and England. Italy north of Rome, however, contrasted radically with this centralised kingdom, for it was a land of city-states: one might almost say that it was ancient Greece to Frederick's Persia. The central Italian zone claimed by the papacy provided no exception, since the pontiffs could not rule the communes who were their theoretical subjects. Further north still, in Tuscany, Emilia, Lombardy and the Veneto, the towns were yet more pre-eminent. In this alien world Frederick's achievement had been to polarise the rivalries between the cities, one system of alliances relying on his aid while the other defied his pretensions. Even to the former he was no more than an ally; he never came very close to being the ruler of northern Italy. To interpret the history of twelfth- and thirteenth-century Europe as 'the struggle of pope and emperor' is to impart a fictitious unity to a complicated theme and, above all, to neglect the feeble temporal resources of these two contestants. The unaided power of each was rarely greater than that of one of the more powerful communes, and in writing of Italy the numerous cities deserve much more attention than either pope or emperor. That eyes have often been diverted from the direct evidence of their actions has been in part the effect of the articulateness of these two shadow-boxers; the ingenious pronouncements of their publicists have been listened to with unmerited attention, and it has become conventional to discuss this phase of history in terms of allegorical swords at the expense of material ones.[1] It is in keeping with this lack of realism in official and semi-official pronouncements that Innocent IV should have declared Frederick deposed (Lyons, 1245) and that this deposition should in itself have been virtually without influence on the course of events in Italy. The titular successors found for the emperor achieved no hold south of the Alps.

After Frederick's death the Italian political scene lacked a pattern; the cities were like filings meaninglessly dispersed after the removal of a magnetic force. The situation resembled that of half a century before, when Henry VI had died prematurely, leaving Frederick as an infant heir; now Frederick in his turn had no adult legitimate heir in the peninsula. Events at once revealed the readiness of individuals and city-republics to take up the heritage of power in a thoroughly fragmented Italy. In Lombardy and the Veneto Ezzelino da Romano and Uberto Pallavicino, hitherto allies of Frederick, were able to construct precocious tyrannies, the former controlling for a time Verona and Padua, the latter Cremona and Pavia. Although neither could hold together a lasting *signoria*, it was already clear that in the north republican institutions were losing ground and would soon normally be replaced by the rule of a single lord. The Este family dominated Ferrara and the Della Torre and Visconti alternated as rulers of Milan. In Tuscany the time of the dissolution of imperial power was the first great era of Florentine expansion in southern Tuscany and on the Tyrrhenian coast. Further south still, the republic of Rome demonstrated clearly enough by its successful imperialism under a popular leader, the Bolognese Brancaleone degli Andalò (1252–5 and 1257–8), that even in papal territory the towns rather than the pope could benefit by the absence of imperial pressure.

SICILY: THE STRUGGLE FOR SUCCESSION

In the Sicilian kingdom, where the towns had long before submitted to the powerful rule of the Normans, the situation evolved in an entirely different manner. Here a struggle for the succession ensued which was decisive for Italy's political geography and for the future of the papacy. The southern kingdom was held, at least in theory, as a papal fief. Thus constitutional right as well as the pressing need to emerge from the century-long nightmare of Hohenstaufen 'encirclement' justified Innocent IV (1243–54) in seeking a new ruler for Sicily. The absence of a legitimate claimant *in situ* (Conrad, Frederick's surviving legitimate son, was in Germany) strengthened Innocent's hopes, but he hesitated between the alternatives of placing the kingdom under direct papal rule and calling in a temporal conqueror to assume the crown. He had not yet made a decision when Conrad (IV) appeared in Italy (January 1252) and began the conquest of his father's kingdom. This setback drove Innocent to negotiate with potential aspirants to the Sicilian monarchy, such as Charles of Anjou (brother of Louis IX of France) and two members of the English royal family, Henry III's brother, Richard of Cornwall, and the king's younger son Edmund.[2] Innocent was still engaged in these negotiations when he received the news of Conrad's premature death (May 1254).

This renewed incidence, in alternate generations, of early death (Henry VI, like his grandson, had survived his father by less than a decade) was not extraordinary ill-luck by medieval standards. It might have settled the problem of the south decisively in the pope's favour, but there was another contender in the person of Frederick's illegitimate son Manfred, Prince of Taranto. Innocent at first attempted to reach terms with Manfred while himself assuming rule in the Sicilian *Regno*, but this paradoxical alliance was short-lived. Manfred went into revolt and the papal army which entered Apulia was routed. The news of this defeat reached Innocent IV at Naples just before his death in December 1254. His successor Alexander IV encountered a still more decisive defeat in Apulia in the summer of 1255. Manfred was now in a position to assert his succession to his father's standing throughout the peninsula. Beginning with a Genoese alliance (1257) he set about the construction of a system which would serve as a screen against claimants entering Italy from the north. In August 1258 he had himself crowned at Palermo. The same autumn he invaded the March of Ancona, the Adriatic province of the Papal State. He found friends in the north of Italy in Pallavicino and the Este family and in Tuscany formed links with the Sienese, leaders of the anti-Florentine cause. As well as continuity with the Hohenstaufen tradition—or Ghibellinism, as it was now generally styled—Manfred was able to offer the more tangible asset of a force of German soldiers, well trained and dependent for their livelihood on successful warfare. These men were the heroes of the great victory of Montaperti (September 1260), a crushing defeat for the Florentines which established Ghibelline authority throughout Tuscany. If any further event was needed to bring home to Alexander IV the revolutionary change in the balance of power to Manfred's advantage, it was the latter's election in 1261 by a pro-Hohenstaufen faction as senator of the city of Rome. Further afield Manfred made a powerful ally and at the same time greatly enhanced the prestige of his line by the marriage of his daughter Constance to Peter, elder surviving son of James I of Aragon (June 1262).

THE PAPACY, THE ANGEVIN ALLIANCE AND THE DEFEAT OF THE HOHENSTAUFEN

The story of Manfred's overthrow and supersession begins with the death of Alexander IV and the election of a Frenchman, Urban IV (August 1261), as his successor. This was one of the most fateful of all papal conclaves, for Urban's decision that unfavourable terms with a French prince were preferable to a continuance of Hohenstaufen domination inaugurated an era of French predominance in southern and central Italy. Urban promptly relinquished the lengthy and fruitless negotiations carried on by his predecessor with the foolish Henry III of England, to whom Bismarck's comment 'such a large appetite, such poor teeth' would have been well suited.[3] To renew the approaches already made to Charles of Anjou was not altogether easy, for Charles would require the consent of his brother Louis and, as a king, Louis was bound to consider more seriously than did the pope the claim to the Sicilian kingdom of Conrad, the young son of Conrad IV. The scruples of the future saint were overcome and in June 1263 Urban was able to announce that he had chosen Charles as king. The terms of the agreement then reached provided that Charles should pay the pope the handsome sum of 50,000 marks immediately after the conquest of his kingdom and thereafter an annual feudal rent of 10,000 gold ounces. He was to leave Provence within a year with an army of at least a thousand knights and 300 crossbowmen.

In contrast with Henry III, Charles of Anjou possessed ability to match his ambition. He had achieved a firm hold in Provence, and Marseilles provided him with a port and a fleet, though the enmity of the Genoese and others deterred him from the attempt to bring the bulk of his forces to Italy by the sea route. An energetic cardinal, Richard Annibaldi, helped to bring about Charles's election in 1263 as senator of Rome, but Urban naturally feared an arrangement whereby the city might have remained permanently under Charles's control and persuaded him to give a secret undertaking to relinquish the senatorship after conquering his kingdom. Alliances in northern Italy were essential for the passage of his army, and with great skill Charles secured a league in Piedmont with the Marquis of Montferrat and in Lombardy with Milan and a number of other cities. The critical year for the papacy was 1264, when Manfred, aware of the approaching invasion, launched a three-pronged attack on Orvieto, Urban's Umbrian retreat; this came so near to success that the pope in haste turned everywhere for local crusaders to repel the threat. The leader of one of Manfred's columns was drowned fording a river and his troops somehow failed to press home their attack. When Urban died in October 1264 Charles's preparations were almost complete.

Urban's death greatly strengthened the position of Charles who was already much the stronger partner in the alliance. As well as interrupting the continuity of papal government, it replaced one Frenchman by another who was both less forceful and more French in his loyalties; Clement IV had served as a counsellor of Louis IX. Charles reached Rome by sea in May 1265 and was crowned as king the following month. To raise his army he had had to make a supreme financial effort. About 200,000 *lire* had been loaned to him by Florentine bankers, Guelfs whom

Montaperti had driven into exile. These men had every reason to desire the victory of his cause, and his success was to turn southern Italy, from the economic viewpoint, into something of a Florentine colony. From the Roman bankers Charles was able to borrow about 50,000 *lire*, but this still left him desperately short of money, and Clement IV had to raise more by pawning the plate from his own chapel. In January 1266 the pope learnt with relief of the arrival at Rome of Charles's main forces, which had crossed the Alps late in 1265.

Complete success was not long delayed, for on 26 February Charles shattered Manfred's forces near Benevento. Manfred himself was killed in the battle and after it Charles met little resistance in the Sicilian kingdom. His task of organising government was simplified by Manfred's thorough control: as heir to a highly efficient machine, Charles was content to preserve the bureaucratic traditions of his German and Norman predecessors. Only one break in continuity was essential, the installation as feudatories of Charles's chief French and Provençal supporters. The confiscated fiefs of Manfred's men provided many of these, but the king also found it necessary to part with a good deal of royal domain; he had to content more than 700 land-hungry followers.

As has been mentioned already, Conrad IV had an heir in Germany. 'Conradin', king of the Romans, was now 15 and his advisers persuaded him that Charles of Anjou's conquest had given him a great opportunity of gaining the kingdom that was rightly his. In 1267 he invaded Italy and won a good deal of support among the imperialist towns of the north. Rome, under the senatorship of a Castilian prince, also welcomed him. Clement IV, who had fled to Viterbo, is said to have expressed his pity for the young man whom he saw leading his army, a lamb going to the slaughter, but this pity was very nearly misplaced, for the battle of Tagliacozzo (August 1268) was a 'near-run thing'. A well-hidden corps in reserve ultimately won the day for Charles, after fortunes had fluctuated. This victory, too, was complete and was followed by the capture of the fugitive king. A few weeks later Conradin was executed at Naples.

One important consequence of Conradin's venture was that a frightened papacy granted new powers to its protector. The untrustworthy citizens of Rome were now placed for 10 years under Charles's senatorship; in this matter Clement entirely abandoned the position of his predecessor. At the same time, at the invitation of the Tuscan Guelfs and without consulting the pope, Charles assumed the title of imperial vicar in Tuscany; in the following years his representatives exercised much power in that zone, while a host of allies in Lombardy and Piedmont enabled him to play the role throughout the peninsula which Manfred had sought in the 1260s. This northern screen was a 'pattern of alliances', municipal and feudal, rather than overlordship based on direct local power, but it gave to Charles a standing similar to that enjoyed by the man whom he had come to displace, Frederick II.

Frederick had been matched and fought by Innocent IV, Manfred by Urban and Clement, but in the years of his greatest influence Charles had no counterpoise, since the papal see was vacant for more than three years after Clement's death (November 1268–December 1271). During this time the Papal State became virtually a northern extension of the Sicilian kingdom and Charles's long occupation of the Roman senatorship was the clear sign of his dominance; for 10 years after Benevento no pope resided permanently in his own see. The problem for the popes was now the choice between full co-operation as an Angevin ally and the alternative policy of relying on family territorial position as a counterweight and source of independence. The first pope in this situation to choose the latter alternative was Nicholas III (1277–1280), who before his election had served a long apprenticeship as leader of the anti-French element among the cardinals. The Angevin supremacy and Clement IV's creation of many French cardinals had split the papal court into French and Italian factions.[4] Nicholas, an Orsini, came of a family that had long been associated with the papal see and was well entrenched in the feudal territory to the south of Rome. He exploited his local connections by securing for himself the senatorship of Rome on the expiration of Charles's 10-year period of office, having previously issued a constitution forbidding lay rulers and nobles to hold rule in the city in future. He appointed one of his nephews rector of the papal province north of Rome, the Patrimony in Tuscany, and sent two others (one of them a cardinal) to gain control in Romagna, the fertile but warlike zone in the south-eastern part of the Po valley which had been ceded to the papacy by the recently elected king of the Romans, Rudolf of Habsburg. Ruling in Rome through a series of vicars (the first was his brother), Nicholas took up residence in the city itself, thereby emphasising his intention of putting an end to the era of Angevin domination. But rule in papal territory through nephews had its disadvantages. The cardinal, alleging ill-health, had an understandable tendency to be at Florence when he was supposed to be at Bologna, and the pope was driven to tell him that it would ill befit the dignity of the family that Bertold, the other nephew, should be forced to serve under a legate who was not an Orsini. Both were reminded by their uncle that the assumption of power in Romagna, a land of powerful barons, was no easy matter: 'in matters of this sort you must make much use of dissimulation, keep many things hushed up, and feel your way cautiously.'[5]

The greatest danger of a family policy of this sort was that it evoked the jealous enmity of the other feudal dynasties of the Roman Campagna. No sooner was Nicholas in his grave than the Annibaldi organised a coup in Rome and a rising at Viterbo which dispossessed Orso Orsini of his rectorate and overawed the papal conclave; two Orsini cardinals were seized in an attempt to extort promises from them concerning their votes in the election. After six months this situation was ended by the choice of a pope thoroughly acceptable to Charles of Anjou. Martin IV (1281–5), a Frenchman, had, like Clement IV, been a counsellor of Louis IX. Urban IV had raised him to the cardinalate and made him legate in France during the negotiations which preceded the Angevin conquest. 'He disturbed the Church of God through his love of his own people and wanted to rule the whole world in the French manner', says the German chronicler Alexander of Roes.[6] As rectors for the major provinces of the papal state he took councillors of Charles of Anjou. A 'crusading' tenth levied in France produced 100,000 *lire* towards the expenses of the burdensome campaign against his unwilling subjects in Romagna. Having been voted the Roman senatorship, Martin proceeded to pass on this office to Charles, in defiance of his predecessor's decree, for the duration of his pontificate. Reverting to the traditions of Urban and Clement, Martin settled in Umbria, under the protection of an Angevin garrison. He could thus leave a free hand in the city to the Angevins, while he himself was closer to Romagna—in which region his armies were composed largely of Angevin and French troops. The conqueror of southern Italy had by this time extended his domination throughout the peninsula.

Jean de Meun, who in the late 1270s added a second part to the *Roman de la Rose*, took as an instance of that great medieval commonplace, the mutability of human fortunes, the fate of Manfred who

> by force
> And guile long peacefully held all the isle
> Until at last the good Charles of Anjou,
> Count of Provence, made war on him and won.[7]

A few years later any Frenchman would have tactfully avoided this example, for Manfred's conqueror, whose Italian triumph has been the theme of the first section of this chapter, was in turn to suffer a fall. To account for this turn of Fortune's wheel it is necessary to outline developments in the eastern and western Mediterranean, in Byzantium and Aragon.

VENICE AND THE LURE OF BYZANTIUM

Byzantium was the traditional goal of ambitious Sicilian rulers; in the late twelfth century Henry VI had planned an invasion, only to have his fleet wrecked in port by a storm. After this the Eastern Empire, already weakened by territorial losses in Asia and by constant dynastic disputes, underwent the tragic and decisive experience of the Fourth Crusade (1204), which left its shattered frame divided among many masters. The legitimate heir fled to Nicaea in Asia Minor, while the largest share of the dismembered empire went to count Baldwin of Flanders, who became ruler of an upstart 'Latin Empire', within which one-quarter of the land was retained by the emperor, the rest being shared equally between Venice and the knights who had participated in the crusade. Many others disputed the body of this prototype 'Sick Man of Europe'. A Greek empire in Trebizond (Trabzon) was set up as a rival to Nicaea. Another Byzantine, an Angelus, founded a 'despotate' based on Epirus. The Bulgarians soon greatly extended their hold in Thrace, at the expense of the Latins. Among many westerners to pose their own local solutions to this 'Eastern Question' were Boniface of Montferrat, who became king of Thessalonica, and the Villehardouin princes of Achaia.

Those who gained most of all were the experienced economic imperialists, the Italian maritime cities, and in particular Venice, which had organised the 'crusade' and played the chief part in it. Already dominant along the eastern littoral of the Adriatic, the Venetians were anxious to extend their empire into the eastern Mediterranean. Their share of the spoils, which consisted almost entirely of harbours and islands, extended from the Adriatic into Ionian Greece (including Crete) and to the Hellespont and the Sea of Marmora. The principal commodities imported from and through this area by Venice (and thence distributed over western Europe) were 'spices', a comprehensive term for exotic goods which included sugar, dyes, glue, perfumes, pepper, cloves and nutmeg. Other considerable imports were gold, silver and jewellery, cotton and raw silk, and slaves, particularly from the Black Sea. Italian merchants, never specialists, were also sufficiently versatile to turn their hands to banking. Venetian commerce in the Mediterranean was closely regulated by the republic; by the fourteenth century most of it was conducted through a minutely organised annual convoy of some 10 to 20 huge armed galleys. Non-Venetians were excluded from trading through Venice and the balance of trade was safeguarded by forbidding the export of currency and limiting that of goods.

Venice, which thus became the insular centre of a great oriental mercantile empire, is in many ways reminiscent of eighteenth-century England. The *chiarissimi* —the equivalent of the 'nabobs'—returned in middle age to take up the political burden of their closely guarded oligarchy, after having spent much of their lives abroad as holders of territorial fiefs or as merchants. The wealthier firms had permanent representatives in Greece and the Levant, though much commerce was also conducted by agents who sailed as representatives of the owners of shares ('carats') in the cargo. Altogether Venetian wealth was securely based, for the richer Venetians spread their risks not only by thus dividing the cargo, but by having interests in the local coasting trade, in the republic's funds, and in town property, as well as in the rural properties which provided food for their households and villas for their summer holidays.

Although Venetians secured the leading position in east Mediterranean trade after 1204, their advantage was diminished by Genoa's gains later in the century. The Treaty of Nymphaeum (1261) with the Byzantine ruler Michael Palaeologus gave the Genoese the right to trade free of duty throughout the Eastern Empire. They received absolute possession of Smyrna and very full extraterritorial rights in Constantinople itself and nine other commercial centres. Finally the Greeks promised to close the Black Sea to other traders, except the Pisans who, however, were no longer serious competitors in this area, their interests being limited mainly to the western Mediterranean. In return for all this the Genoese had only to offer the emperor the aid of 50 vessels whenever he requested it—and the crews were to be paid by the Greeks. Thus the Genoese were able to build up a rival empire in the Levant, which was the scene of the exploits of such men as Benedetto Zaccaria (c.1240–1307) who held the island of Chios, yielding a crop of mastic worth 16,000 Genoese *lire* a year, and Phocaea, with its yet more valuable alum.[8] At one time Zaccaria was chartered by the French to serve as an admiral against England, but here his Midas touch failed him, for Philip IV's projected invasion never materialised. A reminder of the nature of these settlements of homesick Italians is a Genoese dialect poem which runs:

> So many are the Genoese,
> And so spread over the earth,
> That where they go and settle
> They make another Genoa.[9]

Michael Palaeologus, the emperor who restored Greek rule to Constantinople in these circumstances of economic dependence, was a usurper. Though descended from three imperial dynasties, Michael came to power only through 'by-paths and indirect crook'd ways'. He dispossessed John IV Lascaris in 1258 and later imprisoned him and, on Christmas Day 1261, had him blinded. Michael's victory against the weak Latin empire was the tardy result of a series of wars which involved the Bulgars and the other successor states. His decisive defeat in 1259 of the allied forces of Michael of Epirus, William of Achaia and Manfred, opened the way to Constantinople. In 1261 the Latins were finally driven from the city.

Michael, however, as the terms of Nymphaeum suggest, had come into a shrunken and enfeebled heritage.[10] Of what is now Greece, he regained only part of Thessalonica and the Morea; the Franks retained Achaia and the duchy of Athens. His military strength was inadequate—in part, perhaps, because he was afraid to maintain a really powerful army, which might have restored the rightful Lascarid line. Yet the dominant element in his policy was the threat of Charles of Anjou, the heir not only to Manfred's Sicilian kingdom but to his (and Henry VI's) visions of a 'push towards the East'. Well placed for an assault in the Balkans (for Albania lies within sight of the heel of Italy), Charles set about uniting the anti-Palaeologan forces. His aim was nothing less than the imperial crown. Since Charles would be able to present his campaign as a crusade on behalf of Roman Christianity against the heterodox and schismatic Greeks, it was important for Michael to detach the popes from schemes for religious conquest in the east. This he was able to accomplish in 1274 by the titular submission of the Greek Church to papal obedience. Such a policy had immense dangers, and this desperate step testifies to the emperor's overpowering fear of Charles: it caused great discontent and unrest in Michael's territories, arousing so much opposition that its application was found impracticable. This policy of religious appeasement became yet more difficult to justify after 1281, when the new pope, Martin IV, placed his alliance with Charles[11] before any hopes of peaceful religious reunification with Byzantium.

ARAGONESE EXPANSION

Charles of Anjou was faced, however, with the prospect of a war on two fronts. As well as the not very formidable enemy in the east, whose emergence has been described in the preceding pages, he had to reckon with a more intimidating power in the west, the Aragonese monarchy. There was no danger that the claims of Constance, Manfred's daughter, to the Sicilian throne might be forgotten at the Aragonese court: she had assumed the title of 'Queen of Sicily' immediately after receiving the news of her father's death, and three years later (1269) her husband, the future Peter the Great, made a treaty with a number of Gascon and Aragonese nobles and knights which bound these men to uphold her rights in the kingdom. The Sicilian exiles at James I's court included Constance's relative Conrad Lancia. Moreover Peter himself had old grievances against Charles concerning Provence and Sardinia and Charles's support of Aragonese rebels. In 1276 this very able man succeeded to the throne on the death of his father.

Aragon's emergence as a great sea-power in the Mediterranean, heralded by the conquest of the Balearics in 1229–35, can have been no surprise to Charles. It was made possible by the growth of the naval and mercantile strength of Barcelona, carefully nurtured by the monarchy. In 1227 James I gave the Barcelonese traders, then already sailing to Ceuta, Alexandria and Syria, a monopoly of the commerce of their home port. These merchants and sailors urged the conquest of the Balearics, which would shorten their routes and make them safer. The planning of the ensuing expedition—which was of little benefit or interest to the other citizens of Aragon, who would have preferred an assault on Valencia—was entrusted to a Barcelonese, Raymond de Plegamans. One hundred and fifty ships took part and the men of Barcelona benefited greatly by its success, securing rights of free trade throughout the Balearics. Thereafter James continued to smile on his fruitful *protégé*. In 1267 he again denied foreign merchants the right to freight any ships at Barcelona except their own. The following year he accorded the city the privilege—which it already enjoyed *de facto*—of appointing consular representatives in foreign ports. Finally, in 1274, a royal grant gave Barcelona something of the independence of an Italian republic. The city's five counsellors were to be its real rulers, the royal vicar and bailiff having to swear to follow their counsel. The king renounced his criminal jurisdiction within the city and excused it payment of the heavy *bovatge* tax. Besides all this, Barcelona gained very considerable weight in the parliamentary assemblies of Catalonia.[12]

The rapid expansion of Barcelona's trade can be traced in the city's consular representation and in the diplomatic negotiations which marked her peaceful economic penetration of North Africa. She had a consul at Tunis before 1258, one at Alexandria a few years later, one at Pisa by 1275. Pisan predominance in western Mediterranean commerce was seriously shaken by Barcelona around this time and more so still after the disastrous defeat by Genoa at Meloria (1284). Though her trade with Syria continued, the great area of Barcelona's activity was the Maghreb, the western part of the Mediterranean littoral of Moslem Africa. Envoys from the king of Tlemcen came to the city in 1250 to reach a trading agreement, and in 1263 it was found necessary to mint a special currency imitating Moslem coinage. Barcelona's friendly relations with the North African powers naturally led her to oppose St Louis' crusade against Tunis in 1270. The following year a new commercial treaty was made with the Tunisian ruler al-Mustansir and a later agreement with this sultan also provided for his payment of a tribute and regulated the status of Christian mercenaries in his service. Meanwhile, in 1274, James I promised the king of Morocco the assistance of 50 ships for a proposed attack on Ceuta.

The main justification for Barcelona's privileged status within the Aragonese kingdom was, of course, the city's provision of a fleet, there being then no distinction between trading and naval vessels. The activity of the shipyards is constantly mentioned in James I's time (1213–76), when the harbour had frequently to be enlarged. By the 1280s, 10 galleys could be built at one time. In 1282 the Aragonese put 140 ships to sea, of which 64 were large vessels (galleys, tarids and 'arrows'). Valencia, by then won from the Moslems, and Tortosa helped to provide this great fleet, but the leadership of Barcelona was emphasised by an order to the Valencians that their ships should be 'painted with the arms of Barcelona as well as those of the King'.

There was no danger that the Barcelonese should fail the Aragonese crown, for their interests coincided admirably. The conquest of Sicily by Peter III would assist them to dislodge the Pisans and Genoese from their hold on the island's valuable trade. When this was accomplished, much direct commerce developed between Barcelona and Sicily, which provided food—in particular grain, wine, cheese, oil, fish and vegetables—for the Aragonese. Before the middle of the fourteenth century the Catalans had 'consuls'—and thus trading colonies—in 18 Sicilian towns. Besides, they naturally took over the Sicilians' own interests in north Africa. The failure of the Aragonese to make gains on the Italian mainland can in part be attributed to the satisfaction of the Barcelonese with their trading bases in the island, which from an economic viewpoint was a much greater attraction. Their hold there had much to do with their triumphant expansion in the fourteenth century, the golden era of Barcelona's commerce.

THE SICILIAN REVOLT

Though Charles of Anjou looked ambitiously to the east and nervously to the west, the conclusive phase in the story belongs to his own subjects, whose discontent was brought to the boil by the energetic labours of bitter Manfredian exiles. The Sicilian islanders were heavily taxed by the Angevin government, particularly when naval preparations began for the campaign against Byzantium. Charles's officials were perhaps too little supervised by a king who preferred to reside on the mainland. More influential than any precise grievances over methods of rule were Sicily's immemorial opposition to government from the European 'continent' and the natives' xenophobic hatred of the French. There was still a strong Greek element in the Sicilian population, a potential source of disaffection in view of Charles's well-known schemes for a Byzantine conquest. Many, too, must have remembered Manfred's younger children held by Charles in perpetual imprisonment, and the situation was exacerbated by several years of disastrously poor harvests.

By the spring of 1282 Charles's plans for the conquest of Constantinople were far advanced. He had the Venetians (dissatisfied with their standing in the Palaeologan empire) as powerful allies, and 200 ships were ready in the harbour at Messina. Michael Palaeologus, who was in deadly danger, had not failed to make diplomatic contact with Peter of Aragon, and was greatly assisted in these moves by the Manfredian exiles. An Aragonese official, Taberner, was probably at Constantinople in 1278 and again in 1279, while Michael's envoy to Catalonia was the Genoese Zaccaria who stood to lose much of his fortune if driven from Phocaea and Chios by the Angevins and Venetians.[13] It is not possible to reconstruct the full story of the conspiracy of these years, over which Sicilian and Italian patriotism has cumulated a great accretion of myth: in these legends the hero's role is allotted to the Salernitan doctor John of Procida, once Manfred's chancellor and subsequently chancellor of Aragon. Undoubtedly Michael sent money contributions to assist Peter III's naval preparations and he probably sent money to Sicily also. He was able to record in his brief autobiography that 'the Sicilians, who had only scorn for the forces remaining to the barbarian king [Charles], dared to take arms and deliver themselves from servitude, and if I dared to claim that I was God's instrument in bringing them liberty, I would be telling only the truth'.[14]

History, like a Shakespearian play, often proceeds on two planes, the lively characters of the sub-plots appearing unaware of the more deliberate proceedings of the dignified actors of the high diplomatic drama. Thus it was in the 'Sicilian Vespers'. On Easter Monday of 1282 (30 March) a French sergeant arrogantly pressed his attentions on a young married woman in the *piazza* of the Church of the Holy Ghost at Palermo. He had little time to realise the unwisdom of his behaviour, for the affronted husband stabbed him to death. Soon his companions had been despatched in the same manner. As the church bells rang for Vespers the streets echoed to the cry of 'Death to the French!' and the massacre of the occupying forces became general. The news of the revolt spread rapidly. Within a few days Corleone had followed the example of Palermo and about a month later Charles suffered a supreme blow through the insurrection of Messina, his main naval base. The first action of each of the rebel towns was to declare a commune; undoubtedly their citizens envied the privileged towns of northern Italy and hoped to attain the same independent status. In their innocence they sent emissaries to the papal court to ask for protection, but the reply of Charles's ally Martin IV was excommunication.

In this spring of 1282, though the Latin Christian state in Syria languished unnoticed and near to extinction, the talk was all of crusades. Charles of Anjou's proposed expedition against Constantinople had been duly recognised by Martin IV as a crusade, but the pope was more doubtful about the request of Peter of Aragon that he should be granted a crusading subsidy for the fleet with which he was preparing to go to the assistance of the governor of Constantine, a potential Christian convert, against the king of Tunisia. Peter's real purpose was of course the invasion and conquest of Sicily, though he may have hoped to combine this with a reassertion of his overlordship in Tunis, or even have regarded the African scheme as a second best if the Sicilian venture fell through. Like Charles, he was taken unawares by the Sicilian rising. He appears to have had no contact with the rebels at first. Only in June did his impressive fleet sail for the Algerian coast, where Peter learnt of the death of the governor whose protection was the ostensible purpose of his expedition. In August he was still encamped at this site, and it was there that he received a visit from a delegation despatched by Palermo and Messina to ask him for aid and to offer the throne to his wife Constance, rightful queen of Sicily. This was the signal for the transference of the Aragonese armada to southern Sicily and on 30 August Peter disembarked at Trapani.

There is no call to recount the endless fluctuations of the ensuing war. Peter was proclaimed king at Palermo on 4 September and soon Charles had to evacuate his forces to the mainland. The naval and military campaigns for the control of mainland Sicily put an end to Charles's oriental ambitions and long outlasted the lifetime of all the principal participants in the opening scenes, for Michael Palaeologus died in 1282 and Charles, Peter and Martin IV in 1285. With the support of the papacy the Angevins continued the struggle, and Peter's son James, his heir in Sicily, was even persuaded to go over to their cause. The war was thus brought back to the island, now defended by James's younger brother, Frederick. The effect of the Peace of Caltabellotta (1302), which put an end to the struggle, was to perpetuate the military situation of 20 years before: the Aragonese Frederick retained the island of Sicily as 'king of Trinacria', while the Angevins were to rule the southern mainland.

THE LATE THIRTEENTH-CENTURY PAPACY

The Sicilian war that humbled Charles of Anjou was also a heavy burden to the papacy, which was committed by the policy of the preceding decades to support of the Angevin cause. Boniface VIII, who was pope from 1294 to 1303, expended something like a quarter of a million florins each year: much less than half of this was spent on the papal court and the government of the western Church, and the war ranked very high among the other, political items. With this financial expense should be reckoned the imponderable loss of spiritual impetus entailed by the attention devoted by popes and many of the ablest churchmen to the papacy's temporal business.

Throughout the war the two rival traditions of 'local' popes seeking support from baronial dynasties and 'French' popes dependent on a wholehearted alliance with the Angevins continued to alternate. Martin IV's pontificate revealed so clearly the disadvantages of the second of these that it was natural that a Roman should be chosen as his successor. This was Honorius IV (1285–7) whose family, the Savelli, were prominent baronial landowners and had already provided one pope. Honorius received the senatorship of Rome for life and, like Nicholas III, was able to depute rule there and in the surrounding papal patrimony to relatives; in comparison with the situation in Martin IV's time, this was a considerable territorial gain at the expense of the Angevin ruler of the Sicilian kingdom.

The Savelli stood with the Annibaldi and Caetani in the second rank of the nobility of the Campagna: none of these could attain the uncontroverted, time-honoured status of the Colonna and Orsini. The originality of Honorius's successor Nicholas IV (1288–92) lay in his decision to base his temporal policy on the support of the Colonna, although he was not himself a member of that family. Nicholas was a friar, the first mendicant to become pope. His own descent was neither Roman nor baronial, but his connection with the Colonna dated back to the period when he had been bishop of Palestrina (this town being the centre of the Colonna estates in the Campagna) and Colonna support probably assisted his elevation to the papacy. Like Honorius, he received the Roman senatorship for life and was able to reside in the city; this office and the provincial rectorships of the Papal State were of course held by members of the Colonna family. Contemporaries were not slow to remark the humiliating element in Nicholas's position, and one cartoonist depicted him as a scarcely visible figure between two substantial columns.

A long vacancy followed Nicholas's death and was only ended by recourse to an eccentric variant of the Angevin tradition. This was the choice of Peter of Morrone (Celestine V), a hermit who had won a great reputation as a saint and reformer. Utterly unskilled in politics and administration, Celestine could be seen by the spiritual as the protagonist of a radical departure from the temporal preoccupations of his predecessors and by the Angevins (for he was a native of Abruzzi and subject of

Charles II) as a harmless and convenient tool. The latter proved the better prophets. During the five months of his pontificate Celestine never moved from the kingdom. Eight Frenchmen were raised to the cardinalate and Angevin officials took over the Roman senatorship and most of the papal provinces. The choice of the hermit of Monte Morrone was perhaps too extreme a swing of the pendulum. His office made demands that the pathetic Celestine was quite unable to fulfil and in December 1294 he resigned.

Celestine's eager successor represented the furthest possible swing in the direction of worldly ability and interests and dependence on family territorial support. Benedict Caetani, who now became Pope Boniface VIII, had served a long apprenticeship in the papal court and had been a cardinal since 1281. He was capable and, as a chronicler puts it, 'prudent and wise in the affairs of this world'. This is a euphemism: Boniface was not merely prudent, he was cynical. In recording this it must be remembered that he was no strange sport amid a body of uniformly dedicated men of God. It was normal in the baronial milieu for the clever younger sons to receive an education which prepared them for the Church, and those who were able and had a powerful family behind them would reach the top, however little their temperament inclined them to spirituality. It was long indeed before this dilemma disappeared: Stendhal's *Le Rouge et le Noir* is concerned with the perpetuation in the nineteenth century of an analogous situation. The members of the college of cardinals had only to attach a little too much importance to administrative talent or to underestimate a little too charitably a candidate's lack of holiness for them to find themselves saddled with a Nicholas III or a Boniface VIII.

Fearing that his predecessor—whose resignation was unique and controversial—might become the centre of opposition, Boniface arrested Celestine and placed him in confinement, where he died. Within a few years there was certainly no lack of criticism. Dante, exiled from Florence through Boniface's Tuscan policy, proclaims in the *Inferno* that Nicholas III will have to move lower down among the simoniacs to make way for Boniface.[15] Jacopone da Todi, spokesman for a party among the Franciscans, addressed a number of poems to him, one of which begins:

> Pope Boniface, you have led a joyous life in this world,
> But I do not think that you will leave it joyfully.[16]

One of the remarks attributed to Boniface is that 'unless there is discord between the great families of Rome the pope cannot be a true pope or dominate the city and the lands of the Church'.[17] His own policy was certainly to lead to this type of discord, but this was due less to a calculation that he could divide and rule than to the impossibility of following a policy of family aggrandisement in the Campagna without arousing bitter hostilities. Boniface's principal difficulty was that, as has been remarked above, he lacked a really imposing territorial base. To some extent he compensated this by his precocity in embarking on a dynastic policy. During his cardinalate his brother and nephews had strengthened their holdings between Rome and the Neapolitan kingdom (in which they held the county of Caserta), securing a chain of places along the Via Appia and Via Latina, the two main routes of this zone, with outliers on a lateral road to the east. There can be no doubt that these moves were based on hopes of the cardinal's promotion; even before becoming pope he made an agreement with a town, promising the cession of some papal land (in the event of his election) in return for a fief which he coveted for a nephew. This deal in due time became effective and enabled Boniface to extend his family's domain to the north of Rome, but his greatest efforts were reserved for the Campagna, the traditional stronghold of the 'local' popes and the region where his rivals were strongest. Linked with and assisting these territorial acquisitions was the control of the Caetani in the papal provinces, which were normally ruled by members of the family. At the same time Boniface strove, with considerable success, to gain the friendship of the numerous towns of his State by granting them, for money, *de jure* enjoyment of rights which they already exercised *de facto*, and by issuing a series of reforming ordinances to check the abuses of his provincial officials and judges.

Boniface took care not to antagonise all the other baronial families, and in particular ingratiated himself with the Orsini. But his megalomania could only be satisfied by the dispossession of those who were already entrenched. The crisis came when his schemes along the Tyrrhenian coast demanded the purchase of Ninfa, which was the property of cardinal Peter Colonna. Stephen, the man of action among the Colonna, now set an ambush just outside Rome on the Via Appia and was able to capture most of the money intended for the purchase of Sermoneta, a fortress recently bought from the Annibaldi. There followed an extraordinary war. This typical feudal dispute was pronounced a crusade, and the Colonna were excommunicated, deprived of their cardinalates and other ecclesiastical offices and driven into exile. The lands of which they were dispossessed were either retained by the Caetani or used to ensure the neutrality of the Orsini and Annibaldi.

It is possible that Boniface's landed power might have gone on from strength to strength after his defeat of the Colonna had he not also become involved in a desperate quarrel with the French king, Philip the Fair. Philip's younger brother, Charles of Valois, whom Martin IV had ineffectively named king of Aragon at the time of the Vespers, was in 1302 Boniface's chief temporal ally in the Sicilian war. Philip himself, however, was unwilling to accept Boniface's claim to tax and control the clergy of his kingdom. This dispute, which will be discussed in the next chapter, came to a head when, in 1303, Philip despatched his minister Nogaret to Italy with instructions to capture the pope and bring him before a general council of the Church. Nogaret enlisted the aid of the Colonna and of three other families of the Campagna which had suffered at the hands of the Caetani. Thus was gathered the strangely assorted force which stormed the papal residence of Anagni on 7 September 1303, the day when, in Dante's phrase, 'Christ was made captive in the person of his vicar'.[18]

CONCLUSION

The sequence of events related in this chapter, which covers half a century, brought about major changes in the situation in southern Europe. The story began with the creation of a power vacuum in the Italian peninsula after the death of Frederick II, and the most conspicuous of all the changes was the elimination of the emperor as a great power in Italy. Later emperors were to make an occasional reappearance on the Italian stage and in the fourteenth century Dante could believe in an imperial solution to the political problems of the peninsula, but this was the anachronistic dream of a poet. The principal beneficiaries of the new state of affairs were the city-republics. The cultural achievements of the town milieu, conventionally described as the 'Renaissance', will be discussed in a later chapter. The commercial hold of the maritime republics in the Levant, mentioned above, contributed greatly to the wealth of these towns and is evidence of their strength. The theme treated here at length, the involvement of the papacy in the political fate of central and southern Italy, was not a new development: Gregory IX and Innocent IV had been as fully involved in the territorial struggle against Frederick II as their successors were in the wars over the Sicilian kingdom. But the support given to Charles of Anjou and the foundation of a new tradition of French pontificates did bring an entirely new element to the Church's political preoccupations. This involvement with the French dynasty and the growth of a strong French party in the Roman court are the essential preliminaries to the fourteenth-century papal developments which are also the subject of a later chapter. Equally striking as a break with the past is the appearance of Aragon as a great Mediterranean power, with Barcelona, virtually an independent ally of the monarchy, now rivalling Pisa in its pre-eminence in western Mediterranean commerce. The role of maritime trade in all the transformations described in this chapter is noteworthy. Byzantium's weakness shows in its lack of active participation in this no less clearly than in its loss of territory. A Greek empire was brought back into being, and was enabled by Michael Palaeologus to escape extinction, but this institution, far older in origin than the others discussed here, was now only 'the shade of that which once was great'. Apart from the city-states and the Aragonese (it would perhaps be more accurate to say the Catalans), the power that had improved its position most notably was the French monarchy, with its related Angevin ally. There was more than a little truth in the cleric's arrogant assertion that both *sacerdotium* and *regnum* were now transferred to the French. We must now turn to an investigation of this claim.

FURTHER READING

General

Few works treat the Mediterranean as a whole, Steven Runciman, *The Sicilian Vespers. A History of the Mediterranean World in the Later Thirteenth Century* (Cambridge, 1958, paperback 1982), remains the most wide-ranging narrative study. David Abulafia, *The Western Mediterranean Kingdoms, 1200–1500. The Struggle for Dominion* (London, 1997) also has a broad scope. In their different ways, both take Sicily as their main focus and demonstrate its pivotal role in Mediterranean politics.

On Frederick II, three scholarly biographies have been published in English (along with a large number of less scholarly ones): the classic but eccentric E. Kantorowicz, *Frederick II* (tr. London, 1931), the detailed Thomas Curtis Van Cleve, *The Emperor Frederick II of Hohenstaufen: Immutator Mundi* (Oxford, 1972), and the lively David Abulafia, *Frederick II: A Medieval Emperor* (London, 1988), which focuses especially on Italy. The immense amount of recent research in this area by Italian, German and other scholars has not yet percolated through to literature in English.

Italy after 1250

J. Larner, *Italy in the Age of Dante and Petrarch, 1216–1380* (London, 1980), ch. 3 covers the political events, as does, from a Florentine perspective, G. A. Holmes, *Florence, Rome and the Origins of the Renaissance* (Oxford, 1986), chs 1 and 2. *See also* D. P. Waley, *The Papal State in the Thirteenth Century* (London, 1961); P. Partner, *The Lands of St Peter* (London, 1972), chs 7 and 8; John Larner, *The Lords of Romagna. Romagnol Society and the Origins of the Signorie* (Ithaca, N.Y., 1965); P. J. Jones, *The Malatesta of Rimini and the Papal State. A Political History* (Cambridge, 1974), chs 1 and 2; and the monographs given above under Chapter 1.

Sicily: the struggle for succession

Steven Runciman, *The Sicilian Vespers. A History of the Mediterranean World in the Later Thirteenth Century* (Cambridge, 1958, paperback 1982) remains the best narrative account. On Sicily's internal history from this point, *see also* S. R. Epstein, *An Island for Itself. Economic Development and Social Change in Late Medieval Sicily* (Cambridge, 1992); C. R. Backman, *The Decline and Fall of Medieval Sicily. Politics, Religion, and Economy in the Reign of Frederick III, 1296–1337* (Cambridge, 1995); and D. Mack Smith, *Medieval Sicily* (London, 1969), Part 2.

The papacy, the Angevin alliance and the defeat of the Hohenstaufen

The most detailed account is Norman Housley, *The Italian Crusades. The Papal-Angevin Alliance and the Crusades against Christian Lay Powers, 1254–1343* (Oxford, 1982). Jean Dunbabin, *Charles I of Anjou. Power, Kingship and State-Making in Thirteenth-Century Europe* (London, 1998) is a rounded and thoughtful biography of a critical figure.

Venice and the lure of Byzantium

On the western European interests in the east, a general overview is P. Lock, *The Franks in the Aegean, 1204–1500* (London, 1995, paperback 1998); *see also* references under Chapter 14. On Venice's relationship with Byzantium over the centuries, *see* Donald M. Nicol, *Byzantium and Venice: A Study in Diplomatic and Cultural Relations* (Cambridge, 1988); also on Venice and its trading empire, Frederic C. Lane, *Venice. A Maritime Republic* (Baltimore, Md., 1973), chs 5–7. On the specific years covered here, *see especially* D. J. Geanakoplos, *Emperor Michael VIII Palaeologus and the West, 1258–1282: A Study in Byzantine-Latin Relations* (Cambridge, Mass., 1959); Nicol, *Byzantium and Venice*, cit., ch. 11; Donald M. Nicol, *The Last Centuries of Byzantium, 1261–1453* (London, 1972), Part 1; Donald M. Nicol, *The Despotate of Epiros, 1267–1479. A Contribution to the History of Greece in the Middle Ages* (Cambridge, 1984), ch. 1; J. Gill, *Byzantium and the Papacy, 1198–1400* (New Brunswick, N.J., 1979).

Aragonese expansion

T. N. Bisson, *The Medieval Crown of Aragon. A Short History* (Oxford, 1986, paperback 1991), ch. 4 is a brief introduction; *see also* J. N. Hillgarth, 'The Problem of a Catalan Mediterranean Empire, 1229–1324', *English Historical Review, Supplement 8* (London, 1975); and David Abulafia, *A Mediterranean Emporium: The Catalan Kingdom of Majorca* (Cambridge, 1994). On Barcelona, *see* S. Bensch, *Barcelona and its Rulers, 1096–1291* (Cambridge, 1995), especially ch. 7; Felipe Fernández-Armesto, *Barcelona. A Thousand Years of the City's Past* (Oxford, 1992), ch. 2.

The Sicilian revolt

For the details of the revolt and its aftermath, Runciman, *Sicilian Vespers*, cit., ch. 13 onwards; for an analysis of its significance and an overview of the historiography, Abulafia, *The Western Mediterranean Kingdoms*, cit., ch. 2. On the role of crusading interest and ideals at the time, Norman Housley, *The Later Crusades. From Lyons to Alcazar, 1274–1580* (Oxford, 1992), chs 1 and 2.

The late thirteenth-century papacy

For general histories of the papacy, *see under* Chapter 6. The late thirteenth-century popes have been rather neglected by historians, and even the critical figure of Boniface VIII has lacked a biographer for over 60 years. T. S. R. Boase, *Boniface VIII* (London, 1933).

NOTES

1. A modern analogy may illustrate the dangers of relying on propagandists for the reconstruction of history. Ribbentrop's Introduction to the German White Book (1940) refers to 'the magnanimous and infinitely patient statesmanlike endeavours of the Führer to place German-Polish relations on a basis which does justice to the interests of both sides'. *100 Dokumente zur Vorgeschichte des Krieges. Auswahl aus dem amtlichen deutschen Weissbuch* (Berlin, 1940), p. 10. This passage is not normally quoted by historians as evidence concerning Hitler's policy during the years before the 1939–45 war.
2. The negotiations concerning Edmund, who was a child (b. 1245), were conducted with his father Henry III.
3. Alan Palmer, *Bismarck* (London, 1976), p. 218.
4. These factions are well illustrated by a letter written in 1270 by a French cleric at the conclave to elect a new pope. This derides the south Italians for their 'rustic, clownish ways' and the barrenness of their soil: the author is confident that both lay and ecclesiastical power (*regnum* and *sacerdotium*) have been transferred permanently from Rome to France. See G. de Luca, 'Un formulario della cancelleria francescana e altri formulari tra il XIII e XIV secolo', *Archivio Italiano per la Storia della Pietà*, I (1951), pp. 219–393 (this passage is published on pp. 347–8).
5. F. Kaltenbrunner, *Aktenstücke zur Geschichte des deutschen Reiches* (Vienna, 1889), pp. 218–25.
6. 'Notitia saeculi' in Alexander of Roes, *Schriften*, ed. H. Grundmann and H. Heimpel (Stuttgart, 1958), pp. 162–3. A dictum of Martin IV current in Vienna was: 'I wish I were a stork and the Germans were frogs in the marshes, so I could devour them all; or else a pike in a lake and they fish, so I could eat them this way' ('Continuatio Vindoboniensis', in *Monumenta Germaniae Historica, Scriptorum*, IX (Hanover, 1861, repr. Leipzig, 1925), pp. 712–13. On Alexander of Roes, *see below*, p. 63, n. 11.
7. Guillaume de Lorris and Jean de Meun, *The Romance of the Rose*, translation by H. W. Robbins (New York, 1962), p. 203. More recent translations include those by Charles Dahlberg (3rd edition, Princeton, N.J., 1995: *see* p. 129) and Frances Horgan (Oxford, 1994: *see* p. 101).
8. On alum, *see below*, p. 92.

9. 'E tanti sun li Zenoexi/ e per lo mondo sì dextesi,/ che und'eli van o stan/ un' atra Zenoa ge fan.' *Anonimo genovese: Poesie*, ed. Luciana Cocito (Rome, 1970), 138: 195–8, p. 566.

10. *See* Map 1.

11. *See above*, p. 34.

12. *See above*, pp. 11–12.

13. For Zaccaria, *see above*, p. 36.

14. Quoted in D. J. Geanakoplos, *Emperor Michael Palaeologus and the West, 1258–1282: a Study in Byzantine-Latin Relations* (Cambridge, Mass., 1959), p. 367.

15. *Inferno*, XIX, 76–8.

16. 'O papa Bonifazio, molt'ài iocato al mondo:/ pensome che iocondo non te'n porrai partire!' *Laude*, ed. F. Mancini (Rome, 1974), no. 83, pp. 248–50.

17. P. Dupuy, *Histoire du différend d'entre le pape Boniface VIII et Philippes le Bel* (Paris, 1655), p. 344.

18. *Purgatorio*, XX, 87.

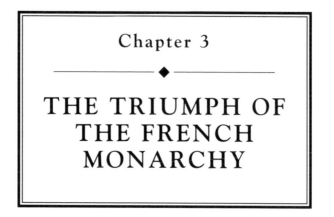

Chapter 3

◆

THE TRIUMPH OF
THE FRENCH
MONARCHY

THE LATE THIRTEENTH-CENTURY CAPETIANS

The last chapter was largely concerned with a French outlier, the Angevin kingdom in southern Italy. The combination there of a powerful bureaucratic tradition—having successive Byzantine, Arabic, Norman and German strata— and a conquering French baronage made up a formidable state whose ruler not only threatened to control the Mediterranean but also exercised so great an influence over French policy that successive kings of France died invading Tunis and Aragon on his behalf. Yet the kingdom of France itself demonstrates still more clearly what strength monarchy could generate at the turn of the thirteenth and fourteenth centuries whenever the mighty official was not counterbalanced by that rival, feudal, figure stigmatised by generations of loyal historians as the 'over-mighty subject'.

Louis IX of France (1226–70) added to the practical achievements of his grandfather Philip 'Augustus' his own inestimably precious contribution of prestige. The French monarchy was fortunate that these two great representatives should have made their appearance in this order, since Louis' role was essentially a complementary one: France could only afford a king with a burning zeal for justice and the crusade after she had made territorial gains, particularly at the expense of the kings of England. The reputation of St Louis was reflected in the many requests for his arbitration. He settled the tangled problem of the inheritance of the county of Flanders and a few years later pronounced in favour of Henry III of England in the matter of that king's dispute with his barons (the Mise of Amiens, 1264). His prestige as a crusader and saint (he was canonised in 1297) made men look back on his reign as a golden age: the feudal malcontents of 1314–15 demanded a return to his laws, and Edward III and the later English kings who claimed the throne of France described themselves as 'descendants of St Louis'. Yet Louis had contributed also to his house's tangible assets, in particular by appointing *enquêteurs* to check local officials and protect royal interests, by insisting that the royal currency should be valid throughout the kingdom, and by strengthening his predecessors' alliance with the towns, especially in the frontier zones.

Under St Louis' son and successor, Philip III 'the Bold' (1270–85), there was no strong indication of a move in the direction of bureaucratic centralisation. A conventional, pious, mediocre man and an exemplar of the ideals of thirteenth-century chivalry, Philip set himself the aim of imitating his father. As a young man he had been so submissive to parental authority that he had taken an oath to accept his mother's wardship, in the event of his father's death, until he attained the age of 30: fortunately his father came to hear of this rash promise and persuaded pope Urban IV to free him from it. He nevertheless remained deeply conservative by instinct. What had been good enough for his father was good enough for him, and owing to the brevity of his reign he was not faced with the problem of seeking a new set of servants to replace those of St Louis. Mathieu de Vendôme, abbot of St Denis (who acted as regent during the Tunisian and Aragonese campaigns) was retained as a virtual prime minister by Philip, together with most of his father's other councillors and officials.

Whatever the temperament of the king, deeper and stronger currents were already bearing the French monarchy in the direction of change. The chief of these was an increasingly pressing need for money. Philip III's invasion of Aragon in 1285 cost more than 1,200,000 *livres tournois*, a tremendous sum by the standards of the time. Moreover it was the expensive culmination, inspired by Charles of Anjou and Martin IV, of a series of French interventions beyond the Pyrenees: disputed successions in Navarre and Castile had already involved Philip in a Navarrese war on behalf of an infant heiress who was betrothed to his elder son, and in an abortive invasion of Castile. The Angevin link was a heavy financial burden in other ways, drawing French forces into the war for Sicily (in which Philip's younger brother Peter of Alençon was killed) and the campaigns fought to gain for the papacy the province of Romagna.[1] Philip III had also to pay the remaining expenses of his father's Tunisian campaign and to send much aid to the Latin state in the Holy Land, now in its dying throes. The constant danger of war with Edward I of England over Edward's fief of Aquitaine was another expensive matter, although open hostilities began only in the following reign.

By Philip IV's time (1285–1314) war with Edward had become the main burden, in combination with a series of campaigns in Flanders. The Flemish war was closely connected with the struggle for Aquitaine, since Edward made an alliance with the county of Flanders to threaten the French on two fronts. But in 1297, after four years of warfare, Edward withdrew: it now seemed to Philip that the wealthiest of the great fiefs lay open to royal control. He was soon to learn that industrialisation and urbanisation made the Flemings formidable and difficult subjects. Following the policy that had succeeded well in the towns of central and northern France, Philip formed an alliance with the dominant oligarchy, only to find that in these textile-manufacturing cities the patricians were confronted by powerful popular forces. The first rising against French government and oligarchic control was the 'Matins of Bruges' (18 May 1302), culminating in a decisive victory for the Flemish infantrymen over 10,000 French knights (Courtrai, 11 July 1302). This shattering blow, which drove the French from Flanders, was followed by two years of indecisive campaigning. The battle of Mons-en-Pévèle (18 August 1304) set the seal on French recovery and the following summer peace was made at Athès-sur-Orge. But the terms of Athès were so humiliating to the Flemings that they failed to achieve a settlement. Besides providing a large money indemnity, the Flemings were to send the French king 500 troops, to be at his disposal for a year. Thereafter they were to owe him military service even against their own count. Ghent, Bruges, Ypres, Lille and Douai were to undergo the razing of their walls, and Bruges was to expiate the revolt of 1302 by sending 3,000 of its men on pilgrimage, 1,000 of them to the Holy Land. The terms also provided that all Flemings aged over 14 should swear to observe the treaty; this oath was to be renewed every five years, besides which officials were always to take it on entering office. If the terms were broken the county was to be placed under interdict. The main consequence of this exigent peace was the prolongation of the period of heavy military expenditure by the French. With victory apparently achieved, the French were still compelled to call out large armies in an attempt to threaten Flanders into obedience, and naturally the expense of these peacetime armies of 1312–15 and 1318–19 was much resented.

The decisive feature in the development of all the western European states in the later Middle Ages is their adaptation to the financial demands of war, but this is particularly true of the French and English monarchies. In their long struggle the sides competed to wage war more continuously and on a larger scale. To fall behind would be to risk defeat, and hence in both countries new demands had to be made on subjects and new ways found of tapping their wealth. Thus the wars were reflected in another, internal, struggle, in which officialdom strove to increase fiscal pressure without yielding constitutional ground. In the early decades of the fourteenth century this situation was making or breaking the power of monarchical governments. The French bureaucracy was gaining as clearly as the English—driven back by baronial discontents and by nascent parliamentary institutions—were losing; there was as yet no sign that Edward III's victories would come to the rescue of the English monarchy. Naturally, heavy taxation could not by itself bring into being a stronger state: that would require also, on the positive side, jurisdictional gains for the crown and the growth of national feeling, on the negative side a weak and divided opposition to the king's expansion. In addition it would require an efficient and devoted corps of royal servants.

A noteworthy development of Philip IV's time was the employment as ministers and officials of a number of men trained in the law. Educated in a discipline which made an ideal preparation for administrative duties, these lawyers were an immense asset to the Crown, and worked hard on its behalf, especially to extract money from the Templars and other clerics, from Lombards and Jews, from ministers who had forfeited the king's favour, and indeed any subject whom it was worth while to harass. Some historians have seen in them a 'new class', raised from the dust by the king to serve his interests, and owing allegiance to no other power. There are, however, various difficulties about this view. In the first place, there was no clearly defined group of 'royal' lawyers, for those who served the Crown normally acted also for members of the nobility and ecclesiastical bodies. Moreover the 'stereotype' of these men has been based too exclusively on the personality of Guillaume Nogaret, keeper of the seal from 1307 to 1313. Nogaret was a native of the Languedoc who taught law at Montpellier before entering the service of the Crown and being entrusted with the management of Philip's relations with the papacy. He was of non-noble birth and remained a layman—though he was described as *clericus* during the years of his legal studies. Nogaret was not the only royal legist of this type; another was Raoul de Presles, a lawyer of Laon, who had been born a serf and gained great territorial wealth, perhaps in part through his evidence against the Templars. Others of Philip's officials, however, were of noble origin, among them Pierre Flote, keeper of the seal from 1298 till his death (in battle at Courtrai) in 1302. Moreover, many were clerics, and some of the most important figures among the lawyer-officials were both nobles by origin and clerics by status. Aicelin was an Auvergnat noble who became archbishop of Narbonne (and later of Rouen), and Pierre de Belleperche, another keeper of the seal, who died as bishop of Auxerre, also probably came of a noble family. Certainly there was no decision to have recourse to a new breed of godless and unprincipled Machiavellians, nor was the royal council dominated by legists. Nogaret himself was a man of at least conventionally religious views, perhaps even a pious man: to oppose the pope was not necessarily to be an unbeliever or neo-Albigensian. When on his way to Italy to summon Boniface VIII before a general Council, Nogaret wrote to a bishop, who was a friend:

May the Lord through His Grace direct your footsteps ... pray to the Lord that if my way is pleasing to God He may direct me in it and that if it is not He may prevent me from it by death or as He pleases

and later, after his 'Outrage of Anagni'[2] he sought (and obtained) papal permission to have a portable altar.

We must now return to the Crown's territorial gains, an element of enormous importance in its general advance in authority. The groundwork in this respect had been accomplished during the reign of Philip Augustus. The greatest acquisition of this time was the appanage formerly held by St Louis' brother Alphonse of Poitiers, which came to the Crown when Alphonse and his wife died within a few days of each other in August 1271. Philip III thus added to his domain the counties of Poitiers and Toulouse together with much of Auvergne and some rights in the neighbouring lordships of Albigeois, Rouergue and Quercy. Philip acted at once on receiving news of the death of Alphonse and his wife, for the Aragonese and English kings also had claims in these areas: he himself visited Poitou and then entered Toulouse at the head of an army. The takeover of the county of Toulouse, though mainly peaceful, was a long-drawn-out affair of investigating rights, confirming privileges and receiving oaths; the last judicial enquiry concerning baronial rights in the county on the occasion of its being placed directly under the Crown was not heard until 1285. Even more gradual was the acquisition by Philip IV of the kingdom of Navarre and the counties of Champagne and Brie, through his marriage to the heiress Joan: these areas came under effective royal control in 1285, but the counties were not formally absorbed into the domain until the second half of the following century, by which time the Navarrese kingdom—a source of expenditure rather than profit—had been divided from them.

In total, Philip III's achievement in the territorial extension of royal power almost deserves to rank with that of Philip Augustus. In Aquitaine his officials fought a ceaseless judicial battle on behalf of his rights, and his gains in the south-west coincided with a greatly enhanced degree of overlordship in Flanders, due to a disputed succession and the consequent separation of Hainault from Flanders.

Successes in Aquitaine were double gains, for they were won at the expense of the English king, but they were hardly more important in the long run than the slow, ubiquitous coralline accretion of lands and rights. Philip III bought the county of Guines from its heavily indebted count, the barony of Nemours, the viscounty of Pierrefonds, the town of Harfleur, and many other lordships. Philip the Fair's main purchases were the counties of Chartres, of La Marche and Angoulême, and of Burgundy (Franche-Comté). The monarchy usually made such purchases by paying the vendor both a lump sum and an annual pension for his lifetime. In two wealthy and important towns the Crown gained control by a process of attrition which eroded the jurisdiction of the previous lords; these towns were Lyons and Montpellier, the evicted lords of which were respectively the archbishop and cathedral chapter and the king of Aragon. The acquisition of Lyons was one of many gains made in the east, often at the expense of imperial rights, but this was certainly not part of a general preconceived plan for a systematic advance eastward; the Capetians took whatever chances came their way and they came from no single direction. The total effect of the additions now made to the royal domain was so overwhelming that by 1328 the domain covered a total area about three times that of the great appanages and fiefs.

At the same time the monarchy was coming to enjoy a thorough control over the internal affairs of the municipalities. This was in part at the wish of the communes themselves, for they frequently had recourse in their disputes to royal arbitration, while indebted towns sought the advice and aid of royal officials concerning fiscal measures and other financial matters. From this it was a small step to unsought royal intervention, since the Crown could demand to inspect a commune's accounts in order to have a check on its taxes and its financial position. The towns' charters were also open to revision by the king. So thorough was this process of monarchical permeation in the government of the towns that municipal officials came to find themselves entrusted with tasks that should more properly have been those of the king's own agents: after 1284, for example, the officers of the guilds took over from the royal serjeants the administration of ordinances concerning currency. Such administrative innovations were the exception. For the most part the king's government was acquiring more work to do and doing it in the old ways. It was the king's business to investigate his rights and to ensure that these were not usurped by other lords, hence innumerable enquiries were held into the exercise of feudal jurisdiction, comparable with Edward I's *Quo Warranto* proceedings in England. The doctrine that all suits touching the king's sovereignty could be called to the king's court lay behind the great development of royal justice at this time, for every 'breaking of the peace' could be interpreted as such a case. The power of hearing appeals was the Crown's other great judicial asset, and from St Louis' reign onwards the appellate business of the royal court grew steadily and rapidly. This was also the principal way in which the French kings were able to assert their overlordship in Aquitaine. All these gains are reflected in Beaumanoir's statement that 'all lay jurisdiction is held as a fief of the king'[3] and in the increasingly accepted doctrine that the king could in no circumstances hold land as a vassal, a principle stated in the time of Philip Augustus, but only formally proclaimed under Philip the Fair, in 1303.

CROWN AND CHURCH: PHILIP THE FAIR AND BONIFACE VIII

If the French kings were to secure sufficient money for their military enterprises it was vital that they should gain a share in the revenues of the Church. They would have suffered an immense disadvantage—and the laity would have had to bear a far heavier burden—if the possessors of a very large proportion of the nation's wealth had enjoyed exemption from direct taxation. In Philip the Fair's time a levy on the Church of a tenth of its estimated annual income yielded about a quarter of a million pounds, which was one-fifth of the total cost of his father's Aragonese war. Such a tax required, by time-honoured custom, the consent of the pope. In certain circumstances there was no difficulty in gaining this consent. There was no inevitable clash of interests and it was often possible for king and pope to arrange a mutually satisfactory accommodation whereby each took a slice from the wealth of the French Church. Such a situation prevailed in Martin IV's time, when the pope awarded the French the Aragonese crown, proclaimed their campaign a crusade and aided it with the grant of a clerical tenth for four years, while his royal ally reciprocated by assisting Martin in Sicily and the Papal State.[4] On that occasion papal legates were involved in the supervision of the levy and the atmosphere of co-operation in a joint enterprise was rounded off by an arrangement whereby part of the proceeds—no less than 100,000 *livres tournois* in 1284—was allotted to the pope.

This type of profit-sharing, however, called for good relations between the two sharers and an absence of dogmatic principle and exaggerated rapacity in either party. Philip IV, who had inherited a crown impoverished by the disastrous campaign in Aragon, was probably anxious to eschew the pro-papal alignment of his father. The election of Boniface VIII (1294) brought about a crisis because the new pope did not relish the diminution of authority implicit in his predecessors' compromises with the French monarchy and he himself coveted the wealth of the French Church for his own Italian policy and the Sicilian war. In 1296 the pope took the initiative by issuing the bull *Clericis laicos* forbidding lay taxation of the clergy except with papal consent, on pain of automatic excommunication: the kings of France and England were warned by Boniface of this measure. Philip IV's retort was to issue a decree forbidding the export of money from his kingdom, thereby depriving the pope also of the possibility of taxing the French Church effectively. His dependence on French support in Italy made Boniface's position a weak one and he soon failed to give the French clergy the backing they required if they were to achieve exemption from royal taxation. Under pressure from Flote and Philip's other administrators the French archbishops and bishops petitioned the pope to be allowed to pay the tenth refused by Boniface. Early in 1297 the pope gave way, a double tenth was granted and the bull *Etsi de statu* proclaimed the king the judge of the expediency of clerical taxation. Thus the French clergy were routed in this first engagement through the defection of their ally. At this juncture Boniface canonised Louis IX, Philip's grandfather: it appeared that the alliance of Martin IV's time had been re-established.

The alliance was a brief one, however, for a second clash occurred, in 1301, this time concerning the general question of jurisdiction over the French clergy. The occasion was Philip's arrest and trial of the bishop of Pamiers, Bernard Saisset. Boniface now revoked Philip's privileges and summoned the leading French prelates to Rome. His letter *Ausculta fili* stated his grievances and claimed for the papacy a position superior to the French Crown; Philip's officials had a copy of this bull burnt in Paris and issued a disrespectful parody. The king also summoned clerical representatives to a gathering and secured their support, but almost half the French bishops obeyed Boniface's summons to Rome. Ineffective negotiations both preceded and followed the issue in 1302 of *Unam Sanctam*, the general statement of papal supremacy in which Boniface declared it 'necessary to the salvation of all human creatures' to be subject to the Roman pontiff. By the spring of 1303, despite his defeat in Flanders, Philip made the decision to press his assault on the pope, accusing him of having secured election unjustly, and denouncing him in a conciliar assembly. That summer Nogaret was despatched to Italy to bring Boniface to trial before a general ecclesiastical council. These were the events which led to the pope's humiliation at Anagni[5] the day before that on which he had intended to declare Philip excommunicated.

TAXATION: POLITICS, PERSECUTION AND CONSENT

The comparative rapidity with which even the bitter dispute of 1301–3 was healed confirms that the logic of the situation—or perhaps one should say the wealth of the French Church—made the pope and king natural allies. In 1296 and the following years heavy loans and taxation were accompanied by the manipulation of the coinage in the interests of the Crown. When Philip again asked for a tenth (1303), the Church retorted by demanding in return a promise that permanent judicial sessions should be held at Paris and that the currency should be reformed and no monetary changes be made in future except with the consent of the barons and clergy. Rather than make these concessions, Philip abandoned negotiations, but the succession in 1305 of the weak and French-born Clement V reintroduced the situation that had prevailed under Martin IV. Tenths were granted with papal consent in 1307, 1308, 1310, 1312 and 1313–15, with no compensating constitutional concessions. Thus the principal victim was the Church in France.

The circumstances of the Avignonese papacy (1305–78) will be described in a later chapter, but some reference may be appropriately made at this point to the 'Affair of the Templars', since the suppression of this order admirably illustrates the power of the French monarchy in the early fourteenth century. The Order of the Temple had been founded to assist the defence of the crusading state and the disappearance of that state in 1291 removed its principal *raison d'être* and provided the Order's enemies with a convenient prima facie case for their actions. Philip IV's motives in the matter are not entirely clear, but it is highly probable that his principal purpose in seeking the downfall of the Templars was financial gain, although the results achieved in this respect were disappointing. To describe money as the main motive is not to deny that Philip was genuinely convinced that the Templars were guilty of the crimes of which they were accused, nor to impugn the sincerity of his schemes for the fusion of the two military orders in the interests of the crusade. The king's part in this grim story has been described as 'an act of faith', but his constant pressure on the pope, who was persistently threatened with a posthumous trial of Boniface VIII, suggests a more secular outlook. Here we are concerned with the king's methods rather than his psychology. In the years 1305–7 Nogaret was employed in collecting evidence against the Templars, and on 13 October 1307 all members of the Order were arrested throughout the French kingdom: this simultaneous action is in itself a reminder of the power of the monarchy. The pope had not been notified in advance of the intention to make these arrests.

The charges brought against the Templars included idolatry, sacrilege (on admission to the Order, it was claimed, a knight was compelled to spit three times on a crucifix) and compulsory sodomy. The wholesale confessions obtained, normally under torture, have puzzled many western European historians, but they should present no difficulty at all to those who have read confessions made under duress in totalitarian states in the twentieth century. They cannot be taken as evidence of guilt, but the vulnerability of the Templars to such pressure reflects unfavourably on their mutual loyalty and the profundity of their religious convictions. Throughout the affair Philip exerted influence on the pope to hasten individual trials and the general suppression of the Order. In 1308, having recourse to a technique already employed against Boniface VIII, he called a general assembly of nobles, prelates and towns, which gave its approval to the royal request that a petition should be forwarded to the pope demanding the judgment and condemnation of the Templars. The matter dragged on, much to Philip's indignation, and it was only in 1312, at the council of Vienne, that his pressure persuaded Clement to take the ultimate step of suppressing the Order. Many of its members had already died under torture or been burnt as relapsed heretics, and in 1314 this fate overcame the Grand Master, Jacques de Molay. Throughout France and in the territories that were under French domination—such as the kingdom of Naples and the Papal State—the Templars confessed and were found guilty. That they did not confess elsewhere is the surest evidence of the efficacy of Philip IV's intervention, whether we are to attribute this situation to the Templars' innocence or (less plausibly) to the inability of other rulers to persuade their subjects to assist in the Order's destruction. Philip gained for himself the money deposited at the Paris Temple and the possessions of this house, as well as a handsome gift of 200,000 *livres tournois* from the frightened sister order, the Hospitallers. Allegedly these payments were to compensate the French Crown for money owed it by the Temple and to pay for the expenses of the trial. A further 50,000 *livres tournois* were paid in 1317. This was certainly not a negligible contribution to his hard-pressed finances, but it may be a tribute to papal resistance that the principal beneficiary from the downfall of the Templars was the Order of the Hospital.

The triumphant tale of Philip IV's relations with the French clergy—whom he taxed heavily in 24 of the 30 years of his reign—was in part made possible by his success in securing the backing of his subjects. His method was to make use of parliamentary institutions to demonstrate the degree of support that he enjoyed, and though popes must have known that it was not easy for Frenchmen to express disapproval of a carefully prepared royal statement, it was difficult for them to express scepticism in the face of these manifestations of public consent. As early as 1277 Philip III employed this technique and called a baronial assembly which asked Nicholas III's approval for special taxation in support of a projected crusade. We have seen how his son used similar gatherings to demonstrate the nation's solidarity in opposing Boniface VIII's claims to jurisdiction over the Church in 1302–3 and in the matter of the Templars in 1308. The 'publicising' nature of parliament was also useful to Philip V, who summoned an assembly to recognise his title to the throne on the occasion of his controversial succession (1316) to his brother Louis X.

By far the most important role of these gatherings was their function in assisting the taxation of the laity. Up to the time of Philip the Fair the main source of revenue had been the royal domain, supplemented by clerical taxation and by the levying of money fines on the laity in lieu of military service. Philip found these arrangements quite inadequate to meet his expenditure, but it would be misleading to dignify his experimental struggles for cash with the title of 'fiscal policy'. His methods were above all pragmatic and improvisatory. It was normally his custom to 'consult' and obtain consent from some sort of gathering before embarking on taxation, but there was no attempt to give formality to the occasion or to the approval gained. More-over the composition of the assemblies was quite flexible. In 1295, for example, some nobles from southern France met in various assemblies to approve a tax of $1\frac{1}{2}$ per cent on real estate in that area. The following year a small but rather more general gathering agreed to a 2 per cent property tax. In 1303 some nobles and a few others gave consent to an income tax, and in 1304 a slightly reinforced conciliar meeting approved a demand for military service. In 1308 some prelates and towns sent representatives to the court to agree to taxation. Even the greater gathering of 1314, designed to assist the raising of an army to fight in Flanders, contained representatives of the cathedral cities only, and it was characteristic that their main task was to hear and disseminate the propagandistic speech against the Flemings of the principal minister, Enguerrand de Marigny.

The same informality prevailed four years later when Philip V needed an army to threaten the Flemings. Forty-six towns of northern France were ordered to send representatives to Paris and 56 of the south to Toulouse; the towns were selected more or less arbitrarily, and all communes were later asked for a contribution whether or not they had been summoned and whether or not they had offered assistance. Normally these assemblies were merely the preliminaries to local bargaining between the king's officials and towns or feudal lords: indeed one of their purposes was probably to enable the central government to become better informed about the resources of the localities. 'Compounding' or paying a fine for exemption was the usual way of settling a tax demand; each town made some sort of offer and after prolonged haggling agreement was commonly reached over the payment of a lump sum. Occasionally these negotiations had to be eased by small concessions and by (ill-kept) promises of reform, of exemption from other taxes or of the 'once for all' nature of the levy. Noble support had sometimes to be won by permitting feudatories to keep a proportion of the proceeds of their own lands. The concessions granted in 1304 will serve as an instance of this process. On that occasion currency reform was promised, together with payment for military provisions and the right to deduct from the amount due debts outstanding from the Crown; finally, the towns' own estimates of their population were to be accepted instead of being subject to official inspection. The nobles of Auvergne further gained two charters confirming their judicial rights. Throughout this experimental double process of 'consultation' and local bargaining there was no notion that consent had to be given: the purpose of the assemblies was merely to find out public opinion, to influence it and to commit it. Their role was 'collaboration not discussion'.

The informal nature of the French parliamentary gatherings of this time is the main explanation of the fact that, in contrast with contemporary developments in England, they did not lead to constitutional concessions by the Crown. Since no cut-and-dried assent was required, there was no need to win it by granting concessions. Owing to the technique of local bargaining by royal officials, the only renunciations made were local ones, and these tended to take the form of temporary contracts or even meaningless formulae. The multiplicity of assemblies also meant that there was no possibility of a demand for money being rejected unanimously. It is clear, nevertheless, that the French barons had some opportunity of making use of the king's financial needs to check his power, and that they failed to take it. This may have been due in part to a failure to realise that direct taxation was to become a permanent feature of government, but its main explanation lies in the strength of provincial separatism and in the baron's predominant concern with his own lordship. The feudatories were content to seek independence of the Crown, rather than trying (as in England) to gain control of the government. The king's strength did not appear a menace and, paradoxically, the disunity of the French kingdom assisted the monarchy. Thus the nobles made no attempt to co-operate with other classes, seeing no community of interests with them. The prelates alone seem to have relished their role in central conciliar gatherings, for the towns were quite content with the less costly local assemblies.

Thus it came about that the French kings had only to modify their policies in comparatively unimportant ways. The most significant changes made were currency reforms, the decisions after 1297 to drop forced loans and the unpopular sales tax and, at the end of Philip IV's reign, the return to a form of direct taxation based on the military liability. In any case, Philip's financial stringencies were greatly eased after 1305 by the renewed alliance with the papacy. When a movement of discontented barons was organised early in Louis X's reign (1314–15), the major lords played little part, and the provincial charters issued by the king contained no important concessions. For the most part these charters confirmed feudal rights and embodied vague promises of fiscal moderation: they put no effective limitation on the Crown's power to tax and they positively aided the growth of royal jurisdiction. The assemblies of Philip V (1316–22) were entirely local and no attempt was made to use them to check the power of the Crown: this king, too, was exceptionally successful in threatening to turn clerics and townsmen against the nobles and thus deterring any moves for co-operation between the three estates.

CONCEPTS AND IMAGES OF MONARCHY AND NATION

Regional and local feeling was still intensely strong, far stronger than the nascent stirrings of national patriotism. It is extremely difficult to know what the 'average' Frenchman thought, yet there are some signs among the more articulate that the monarchy's increasing strength was reflected in a growing awareness of nationality and a new sense of being bound by French loyalties. It has already been suggested, in connection with pro-French and anti-French sentiments in the papal court in the 1260s,[6] that such feelings were essentially negative in origin, the product, especially in circumstances of antagonism, of meeting strangers speaking a different tongue and reared in an alien environment. That the Curia continued to breed these prejudices is shown clearly enough by the alleged dictum of Boniface VIII that 'he would rather be a dog or an ass than a Frenchman'.

The principal basis for the consequent sentiment of solidarity was certainly linguistic. Though Italy was long to remain a 'geographical expression', Dante had no doubts at the beginning of the fourteenth century of who were the Italians; they were those who spoke Italian, the inhabitants of the area between Pola in Istria and the northern border of Genoese Liguria.[7] Edward I of England brought the accusation against the French king that he planned 'to delete the English language throughout the land'. There were difficulties about a linguistic basis for patriotism, since Edward and most of his leading subjects spoke French as their first language (as did many of his Flemish allies), while Philip's own subjects in southern France spoke a language differing profoundly from French.

Despite the illogicalities of the situation, national feeling was now a powerful force, as may be seen from the attitude of the French clergy during Philip the Fair's dispute with the papacy. The contest for the loyalty of the clergy was crucial, both because these men were the educated class and because they had a rival allegiance to the supranational Church. In general they sided with the king, and it is notable that the religious houses which did not do so were those the majority of whose members were not French. The Franciscan house at Paris stood by the pope, but it is known that at the most 17 of its 87 friars were French, so that this is a true instance of the exception 'proving' the rule. The French clerics could have claimed with justification that Boniface was unworthy to be the representative of a spiritual cause but, whatever their outlook, their conduct contrasts strongly with the fidelity a century earlier to Innocent III of both the French and English clergy, in the time of the disputes with Philip Augustus and John. For some of them national loyalty was a more positive sentiment. When Philip IV attacked Flanders, a French priest preached a sermon in which he proclaimed that 'those who die for the justice of the king and the realm shall be crowned by God as martyrs', and a contemporary scholar at Paris, Henry of Ghent, even contended that to die for the community might be compared to Christ's supreme sacrifice for mankind.

If some of the French clergy were thus prepared to declare that 'God is on our side', this was in part the consequence of the high theoretical claims now put forward on behalf of the lay state by its propagandists. Philip IV was careful to justify his taxation in 1302 with the classical plea that it was required for the defence of the native land 'and the venerable antiquity of our ancestors ordained warfare on behalf of the Fatherland, putting its care before the love of descendants'. In the realm of unofficial propaganda, Philip's writers made use of Aristotle's doctrine concerning the moral purpose of society to claim self-sufficiency and independence for secular authority: they demanded for the state spiritual powers and absolute control over justice, legislation and the persons and property of the king's subjects. Such writings moved in a world of legal theory that had no influence on the ideas of the average man. But if the propagandists were to justify their employment they had to change the outlook of influential men. Hence they did not merely elaborate logically contrived abstractions; they were forced to come down to earth. One sees this in the ironical descriptions of the clerics who scandalously failed in their role as Frenchmen, 'lying in the shade eating luxuriously, drinking joyfully, resting on their ornate beds, sleeping quietly and basking comfortably amid sensuous furnishings'.[8] In the same vein, the anonymous author of the *Antequam essent clerici* wrote that 'Just as any part refusing to give help to the body is a wicked part, and as it were useless or paralysed; so all those men, be they clerics or lay, nobles or villeins, who refuse to perform their required duties towards the head or the body of society, the king or the kingdom, show by their refusal that they are like useless or paralysed members'.[9] Another French pamphleteer implicitly emphasised Philip IV's claim to ecclesiastical supremacy. Not only the pope, he explained, had delayed in acting against the Templars, but his nepotism was such that he had given relatives 'more benefices than the forty popes before him'.[10]

The forces forging a strong central government in France were men and money, officials working to levy taxes which both paid for armies and in turn made possible the employment of more officials. This practical fiscal, administrative and judicial pressure on subjects was the primary and essential process of which a broader national consciousness, diminishing regional patriotism, was a secondary product. But it was also powerfully reinforced by the remarkable extent to which, in the thirteenth century, the Capetians were able to draw together the many strands of political development to forge an image of strength, unity of purpose and European pre-eminence. The continuity of the dynasty, and the sustained pattern of expansion that is evident in the hundred years from the late twelfth century, made possible a continued accretion of the ideology and paraphernalia associated with the monarchy. As usual, images and symbols reinforced texts. From coronation to burial, from the 'sacred touch' whereby the Capetians were believed to heal scrofula to the bearing of banners in battle, rituals were continued, developed and embellished; the association of the monarchy with pious works, the building and patronage of religious institutions and the preservation of holy relics was unbroken, and kept in prominence. The royal entourage played a full part in all this. Like Abbot Suger in the twelfth century, Joinville wrote a laudatory biography of the monarch he had served, directing its precepts at a descendant. The mythologising of Louis' life added to the stock of images of royalty that had been growing for over two centuries—and what more potent and symbolic image could there be than the austere and saintly king directly dispensing justice under an oak tree? The administration of that justice was all the more effective with the settlement of royal administration in Paris which, rather ahead of other monarchies, gave it a geographical focus; not yet a 'capital' in any modern meaning of the word, but in a sense co-resident with one in the shape of the University of Paris, the theological and perhaps even intellectual capital of Christendom.[11] The presence of the university had both direct and indirect advantages for the monarch. To the prestige value of playing host to the seat of knowledge and doctrine were added the practical advantages of being able to draw on its personnel for advice, expertise and support; much of the ideological weaponry used in the conflict with Boniface VIII, including the treatise of John Quidort 'of Paris' *On Royal and Papal Power*, came from this quarter.

The thrust of Capetian ideology was towards unity of territory and of purpose under a quasi-sacred ruler; a unity which gave both ruler and kingdom a special role in Christendom. It has justly been encapsulated in the title of a publication on the subject as 'France: The Holy Land, the Chosen People, and the Most Christian King'.[12] A great practical boost to this image was the growing role that the Capetians played on the international scene. The arbitration of Louis IX between pope and emperor, his leadership of two crusades, the connections with the Angevin presence in the Mediterranean, and most dramatically the conflict with Boniface VIII are only the most obvious examples. If the first three demonstrated the Capetians' role as champions of the Church, it required little modification to present the fourth, albeit directed against the incumbent of the papal throne, as of similar moral value. France's dominant role in European politics can be gauged in 1308, when Philip IV went as far as to put up a candidate for the imperial vacancy. Although this can hardly have been more than a gesture, it played a critical role in the electors' decision to choose the candidate deemed likely to be the most sensitive and resistant to French ambitions on the western border of the empire.[13]

The external and internal roles of the monarchs reinforced each other. We have outlined Philip IV's success in meeting the financial exigencies of his international policies by attaining an unprecedented level of internal consent and support. The cohesion that made this possible owed much to the ideological foundations and programme of the monarchy. The durability of such weapons is another matter. The military and political crisis with which this apparently robust state was confronted in the middle decades of the fourteenth century, a crisis which came close to nullifying all the labours of Nogaret and Philip the Fair, will be the subject of a later chapter.

FURTHER READING
The late thirteenth-century Capetians

The best general introduction to the Capetians in English is Elizabeth M. Hallam, *Capetian France, 937–1328* (London, 1981). Older works are R. Fawtier, *The Capetian Kings of France. Monarchy and Nation* (tr. London, 1960), and C. Petit-Dutaillis, *The Feudal Monarchy in France and England from the Tenth to the Thirteenth Century* (tr. London, 1936). A general and very readable history of medieval France is Georges Duby, *France in the Middle Ages, 987–1460* (tr. Oxford, 1991). A major reference work is W. W. Kibler, G. A. Zinn *et al.*, eds, *Medieval France* (New York, 1995).

Much has been written on the almost legendary figure of Louis IX. For English readers, J. Richard, *Saint Louis: Crusader King of France* (tr. Cambridge, 1992: an abridged version of the original work of 1983) can now replace M. W. Labarge, *Saint Louis. The Life of Louis IX of France* (London, 1968). *See also* W. C. Jordan, *Louis IX and the Challenge of the Crusade* (Princeton, N.J., 1979). On specific aspects of his reign, *see*: L. Little, 'Louis IX's involvement with the friars', *Church History*, 33 (1964), pp. 125–48; R. Bartlett, 'The impact of royal government in the French Ardennes: the evidence of the 1247 *enquête*', *Journal of Medieval History*, 7 (1981), pp. 83–96.

On Philip IV, the fundamental work in English is Joseph R. Strayer, *The Reign of Philip the Fair* (Princeton, N.J., 1980). Despite his importance and the work done on him, the personality of Philip has remained elusive. He can be seen as the arch-manipulator, boxing Boniface VIII into a corner and then relentlessly continuing his campaign after Boniface's death—or, as the dissident Bernard Saisset described him, an owl, looking decorative but saying nothing, hiding behind his advisers and discarding them in turn as their policies failed. On the debate about the degree of Philip's own involvement in government, *see* Joseph R. Strayer, 'Philip the Fair—a "constitutional" king', *American Historical Review*, 62 (1956), pp. 18–32, repr. in his *Medieval Statecraft and the Perspectives of History* (Princeton, N.J., 1971), pp. 195–212 (the volume also contains other essays on Philip). *See also*: Malcolm Barber, 'The world picture of Philip the Fair', *Journal of Medieval History*, 8 (1982), pp. 13–27; and E. A. R. Brown, 'The prince is the father of the king: the character and childhood of Philip the Fair of France', *Medieval Studies*, 49 (1987), pp. 282–334, repr. in her *The Monarchy of Capetian France and Royal Ceremonial* (London, 1991), ch. 2.

Many works in English now treat aspects of the Capetians in power and government. A. W. Lewis, *Royal Succession in Capetian France: Studies on Familial Order and the State* (Cambridge, Mass., 1981) deals with the complexities of dynastic policy; *see also* his 'The Capetian apanages and the nature of the French kingdom', *Journal of Medieval History*, 2 (1976), pp. 119–34; and C. T. Wood, *The French Apanages and the Capetian Monarchy 1204–1328* (Cambridge, Mass., 1966). On the impact of royal expansion on regions, James Given, *State and Society in Medieval Europe. Gwynedd and Languedoc under Outside Rule* (Ithaca, N.Y., and London, 1990); and T. Evergates, *Feudal Society in the Bailliage of Troyes, 1152–1284* (Baltimore, Md., 1975). On the relationship of the monarchy to the towns, C. Petit-Dutaillis, *The French Communes in the Middle Ages* (tr. Amsterdam, 1978), Book II chs 1 and 2; on aspects of royal justice, S. H. Cuttler, *The Law of Treason and Treason Trials in Later Medieval France* (Cambridge, 1981). On royal advisers, bureaucracy and administration, F. J. Pegues, *The Lawyers of the Last Capetians* (Princeton, N.J., 1962), and J. H. Shennan, *The Parlement of Paris* (2nd edition, Stroud, 1998), ch. 5; Joseph R. Strayer, 'Viscounts and viguiers under Philip the Fair', *Speculum*, 38 (1963), pp. 242–55, revised version in his *Medieval Statecraft and the Perspectives of History*, cit., pp. 213–31; H. Takayama, 'The local administrative system of France under Philip IX (1285–1314)', *Journal of Medieval History*, 21 (1995), pp. 167–93 on the differences between *baillis* and seneschals. On the political struggle over Flanders, David Nicholas, *Medieval Flanders* (London, 1992), ch. 8.

Crown and Church: Philip the Fair and Boniface VIII

The standard introduction, with documents in translation, is B. Tierney, *The Crisis of Church and State, 1030–1300* (Englewood Cliffs, N.J., 1966), Part 4, chs 3 and 4. On the ideological issues at stake, an effective introduction is J. A. Watt, 'Spiritual and temporal powers', in *The Cambridge History of Medieval Political Thought, c.350–c.1450*, ed. J. H. Burns (Cambridge, 1988, paperback 1991), ch. 14, esp. pp. 397–410; *see also* Antony Black, *Political Thought in Europe, 1250–1450* (Cambridge, 1992), pp. 48–55. A selection of readings on the episode is Charles T. Wood, ed., *Philip the Fair and Boniface VIII. State vs. Papacy* (Huntington, N.Y., 1976). On Boniface, *see above* under Chapter 2.

Taxation: politics, persecution and consent

The trial of the Templars has attracted a great deal of popular attention; not all works on the subject are scholarly. The definitive work is Malcolm Barber, *The Trial of the Templars* (Cambridge, 1978); *see also* the readable account of E. Burman, '*Supremely Abominable Crimes*'. *The Trial of the Knights Templar* (1994, 2nd edition, London, 1996). On the way in which posterity has overlaid the story with fantasy, Peter Partner, *The Murdered Magicians. The Templars and their Myth* (Oxford, 1982). On the Templars generally, Malcolm Barber, *The New Knighthood. A History of the Order of the Temple* (Cambridge, 1994), and his 'The Knights Templars', *The Historian*, 60 (Winter 1998), pp. 4–9; Edward Burman, *The Templars, Knights of God* (London, 1986); H. Nicholson, *Templars, Hospitallers and Teutonic Knights* (Leicester, 1995); Alan Forey, *The Military Orders: from the Twelfth to the Early Fourteenth Centuries* (London, 1992).

On taxation, *see* Joseph R. Strayer, 'Consent to taxation under Philip the Fair', in Joseph R. Strayer and Charles H. Taylor, *Studies in Early French Taxation* (Westport, Conn., 1939). On the role of assemblies, Thomas N. Bisson, *Assemblies and Representation in Languedoc in the Thirteenth Century* (Princeton, N.J., 1964).

Concepts and images of monarchy and nation

The most important tract, on the French side, to come out of the conflict between Philip and Boniface was John of Paris, *On Royal and Papal Power*, tr. J. A. Watt (Toronto, 1971), also translated by Arthur P. Monahan (New York and London, 1974).

The public face of the Capetians and the ideology and rhetoric deployed on their account has been the subject of intense investigation in recent years. Articles by J. R. Baldwin, W. C. Jordan and E. A. R. Brown on Philip II, Louis IX and Philip IV, respectively were published under the title '*Persona et Gesta*: The Image and Deeds of the Thirteenth-Century Capetians', in *Viator*, 19 (1988), pp. 198–246. *See also* Joseph R. Strayer, 'France: The Holy Land, the Chosen People, and the Most Christian King', in *Action and Conviction in Early Modern Europe*, eds T. K. Rabb and J. E. Seigel (Princeton, N.J., 1969), pp. 3–16, repr. in his *Medieval Statecraft and the Perspectives of History*, cit., pp. 300–14; Elizabeth M. Hallam, 'Philip the Fair and the cult of Saint Louis', *Studies in Church History*, 18 (1982), pp. 201–14; and G. M. Spiegel, 'The cult of Saint Denis and Capetian kingship', *Journal of Medieval History*, 1 (1975), pp. 43–69. C. Beaune, *The Birth of an Ideology: Myths and Symbols of Nation in Late-Medieval France* (Berkeley, Cal., 1991) focuses primarily on the period after 1300 but has plenty of information on the whole Capetian period as well.

NOTES

1. *See above*, pp. 34 and 40–1.
2. *See above*, p. 43.
3. Beaumanoir, *Coutumes de Beauvaisis*, ch. 11, § 322, ed. A. Salmon, cit. (*above*, p. 26, n. 2), I, p. 158; in Akehurst's translation, cit., pp. 121–2.
4. *See above*, p. 34.
5. *See above*, p. 43.
6. *Above*, pp. 34 and 46, n. 4.
7. *Inferno*, IX, 115: *De vulgari eloquentia*, I, viii, x; *see* the translation by Marianne Shapiro, *De Vulgari Eloquentia. Dante's Book of Exile* (Lincoln, Neb., 1990), p. 55.
8. 'Disputatio super potestate praelatis ecclesiae' in M. Goldast, *Monarchia S. Romani Imperii* (Hanover, 1611), I, p. 16.
9. P. Dupuy, *Histoire du différend d'entre le pape Boniface VIII el Philippes le Bel* (Paris, 1655), pp. 21–2.
10. S. Menache, *Clement V* (Cambridge, 1998), p. 223n.
11. The German canon Alexander of Roes, writing around 1285, proposed the replacement of the traditional binary division between the spiritual and temporal powers by a three-fold division between priesthood, empire and university, with responsibility for them allocated respectively to Rome, Germany and France. H. Grundmann, 'Sacerdotium, Regnum, Studium', *Archiv für Kulturgeschichte*, 34 (1952), pp. 5–21; *see also* L. Scales, 'France and the Empire: the viewpoint of Alexander of Roes', *French History*, 9 (1995), pp. 344–416.
12. By Joseph R. Strayer, in *Action and Conviction in Early Modern Europe*, eds T. K. Rabb and J. E. Seigel (Princeton, N.J., 1969), pp. 3–16, repr. in his *Medieval Statecraft and the Perspectives of History* (Princeton, N.J., 1971), pp. 300–14.
13. *See below*, pp. 72 and 75–6.

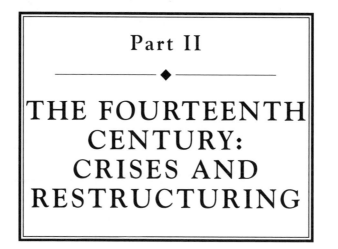

Part II

◆

THE FOURTEENTH CENTURY: CRISES AND RESTRUCTURING

Chapter 4

◆

FRAGMENTATION
IN GERMANY

THE MEDIEVAL EMPIRE

France in the early fourteenth century shows the potential strength of a medieval monarchical state in favourable circumstances, the Crown flourishing on the snowball principle that nothing succeeds like success. The German territories at the same time illustrate no less clearly the contrary process of fragmentation, lack of central control fostering the institutions of local political independence and traditions of regionalism. Much of this was due to the peculiar position of the German Crown. From the high Middle Ages the notional ruler of the Germanic lands was burdened with the additional status of 'emperor'—the successor to Charlemagne, whose coronation as emperor in 800 had signalled a self-conscious revival of the title of ancient Rome, as well as a reassertion of western European interests in such a title as counterweight to that of the emperors of Byzantium. The legacy of this episode was complex. During the disputes between the German ruler and the papacy, imperial propagandists had elevated their patron to the status of chief secular power, even God's secular representative on earth, with a unique relationship to the chief spiritual power and to the other secular rulers of Christendom. The territory of the emperor also extended well beyond Germany and covered an area which no medieval ruler could realistically hope to control; yet a belief in the rights and therefore duties that came with the imperial office—and perhaps also the difficulties in asserting their authority in their humbler capacity as rulers of Germany—impelled successive emperors into the international ideological and geo-political arena. Our concern here will be less with the universalist aspirations and obligations of the emperor than with the dramatically different story of their fortunes in Germany itself, and the very different question of how Germany developed in consequence.

The most obvious disadvantage suffered by the emperor was the elective nature of his throne. A strict rule of inheritance had not applied in the early period of the 'Germanic' kingdoms, when the leader had to be a strong man, and the people could not be exposed to the danger of rule by a child or an obviously incompetent weakling. The new king had to secure the acceptance of the leading men before he could enjoy power, and this situation was formalised in his 'election' or the recognition ('acclamation') of his succession (subtle distinction between these two concepts would be out of place in discussing early medieval society). Normally the new king would be the eldest or most prominent son of his predecessor, but it was only slowly that more settled political conditions tended to make this common practice a constitutional rule, and even then agreement on such refinements as primogeniture was extremely slow: hence, for example, the dispute on the death of Richard I of England in 1199 as to whether the true heir was the youngest brother of the late king (John) or the son of an elder brother (Arthur). While the monarchies in France and England became in practice hereditary, the Empire remained elective—at times, under the Saxons and Ottonians, in theory only, but when there was no direct heir in practice also. At the end of the twelfth century Henry VI had striven energetically to persuade the German princes to make the imperial succession hereditary, so that his son Frederick might follow him automatically in the imperial lands as he would in the Sicilian kingdom, but his efforts had met with no success. This was a decisive moment; the possibility of setting the Empire on a hereditary basis was not to recur for several centuries.

Elective kingship meant, above all, lack of continuity. This was a tremendous disadvantage in administration. Each time a new feudal family assumed the coveted burden of imperial rule, new officials took over and a new archive was set up; whatever resources this family enjoyed in the way of a bureaucracy embarked without the benefit of their predecessors' experience and records on the Sisyphean task of government. Whichever noble or royal house gained the Empire was dependent also on its own domain: by the late thirteenth century there was virtually no crown land and exceedingly little royal revenue from fiscal sources. The French monarchy had, it is true, advanced from a situation that in some respects was similar: until the mid-twelfth century the royal domain had been very small, and regional divisions in France remained extremely strong. But the Capetians had drawn prestige from the long duration of their house and the central position of their domain was an inestimable asset. Their initial weakness may have saved them from the attacks of other feudal houses, but in Germany the monarchy could not benefit even from this paradoxical advantage: its feebleness was such that nobles and towns were forced to make their own political arrangements, and there seemed no prospect of the monarchy acquiring the strength that would enable it to inherit these states in miniature, as the French had incorporated Normandy, Toulouse, Champagne and so much else.

In writing of Germany, however, there is a strong danger of interpreting that country's development in the light of anachronistic hindsight. We know that German unification was only achieved in the nineteenth century and hence tend to assume that in some way its medieval rulers failed to prepare the way for the 'unity' achieved by France, Spain and England in the early sixteenth century. Hence the whole of medieval German history is often looked on as the history of a political failure and each of its ages is interpreted by different writers as the era in which things went irreparably wrong. Yet Germany might well have been united in the sixteenth century if only Charles V had had to face slightly fewer problems outside Germany: the reasons for the failure to unify Germany at that time were not solely

German reasons, and had they not existed there would be much less temptation to see the history of medieval Germany as a tragic tale of frustration. The tragedy, if there was one,[1] should perhaps be ascribed to the sixteenth century, and in any case the history of the Italian peninsula should have made historians—even liberal nationalist historians—more sceptical concerning the blessings of unity and the evils of regionalism.

Some writers have regarded the late eleventh century as the decisive stage in Germany's development and have blamed the reforming papacy for supporting the German Church and lay nobility in their opposition to the Salian emperors. Others have emphasised the role of the empire's expansion eastward and have attributed the strength of the princely houses to their ability to build up their power in these zones of new settlement untrammelled by the counterbalancing influence of a feudal baronage. Some also have seen the long tradition of 'the Italian adventure', bringing about lengthy royal absences from the homeland, as well as heavy expenditure, as the all-important factor. But these views surely put the decisive phases in Germany's political development too early: if there was a period when the German ruler's power shrank seriously in contrast with that of the other monarchies of the west it must be placed in the thirteenth century. Frederick II had disliked Germany, with its 'long winters, muddy towns, dark forests and rugged castles' and he regarded his Sicilian kingdom as both wealthier and easier to govern. He himself spent comparatively little time north of the Alps and was content for the most part to enjoy the title that Germany provided for him, while entrusting power there to the princes. These princes, both lay and ecclesiastical, were the beneficiaries of the two great privileges of 1220 and 1232, of which the latter (the 'Constitution in favour of the princes') gave them full control over justice and currency. Individual magnates also received valuable privileges—the Welf Otto, a former enemy of the Hohenstaufen, was bribed by the creation for him of the duchy of Brunswick—and domain territory was alienated on a considerable scale. Most paradoxical of all the features of Frederick's policy was his support of the feudal magnates against the towns, the obvious and traditional allies of the monarchy. This alignment was a cause of the revolt of his son Henry, for Henry was more familiar with German conditions and hence less prone to his father's notion, based on Italian experience, that towns were harder to manage than feudatories. When Henry turned traitor and was deposed and imprisoned, Frederick set up another son, Conrad, in his place, but this time with the intention of keeping him under close control. At this juncture, however, the emperor's Italian policy and his consequent bitter struggle with the papacy were responsible for a new and yet more serious deterioration in his position in Germany. Innocent IV, after deposing him, sought with considerable success to deprive him of the vital support of the Church, and Frederick found himself engaged in a competition to outbid the pope's offers to the lay nobility. Another feature of the papal offensive was the election of two successive anti-kings, Henry Raspe, landgrave of Thuringia, a pious 'clerics' king' who was prepared to surrender all control over the German Church to Innocent's legates, and count William of Holland, chosen because there was little danger of his acquiring much political power beyond the border territories of the Low Countries and Rhineland.

After Frederick II's deposition (1245), fate itself seemed determined that no one man should be granted time to face the problems of governing the Empire. Raspe, chosen to succeed Frederick, died in 1247, only a year after his election. Frederick himself died in 1250 and his son Conrad in 1254. William of Holland was killed in battle in 1256. In the following year imperial prestige declined to its nadir through the 'double election' of Richard of Cornwall and Alfonso X of Castile. Richard earl of Cornwall was the younger brother of Henry III of England and his appearance on the German scene was part of the unsure and over-ambitious structure of scheming evolved by Henry, which included the plan of gaining the Sicilian kingdom for Edmund 'Crouchback'.[2] He also had the support of a party in Flanders, whence he first received the proposal that he should become a candidate for the throne. Well-directed bribes then won Richard a following among the German nobility and some of his backers crossed to England to persuade the justly suspicious barons that Richard had already been elected. He in fact secured—on conditions—the votes of the archbishops of Cologne and Mainz and of the duke of Bavaria. A little later king Ottokar of Bohemia was persuaded to add his support. The election of Alfonso of Castile, which took place some two months after Richard's (on 1 April 1257) came about in a very different fashion, but was in its essentials a similar product of 'vaulting ambition which o'er-leaps itself'. Alfonso had high schemes for extending his influence outside the Iberian peninsula (in Sicily as well as Germany) and he enjoyed the advantage of Hohenstaufen descent, his mother being a first cousin of Frederick II. The initiative which led to his election, however, came from Italy, where the Ghibelline city of Pisa turned to him as protector and announced its recognition of Alfonso as king of the Romans. A series of bribes in Germany procured for Alfonso the votes of the archbishop of Trier, the duke of Saxony, the margrave of Brandenburg and the king of Bohemia. Ottokar of Bohemia had thus cast a vote for both candidates, and Alfonso's case was not assisted by the fact that the archbishop alone had voted in person, the other electors having appointed him as their proctor. Subsequent events in Castile were to reduce Alfonso's claim to an empty formality; he was never able to put in an appearance on imperial soil. Richard of Cornwall's performance was scarcely more substantial: he visited the Rhineland in 1257–9, 1260 and 1268, but was unable to institute any firm control even in that area. This period of *de facto* interregnum was probably the time of the greatest loss of imperial lands, much of the domain being usurped or pledged by powerless rulers who were seeking backers.

The failure of both Richard and Alfonso to establish themselves in the empire meant that for two decades Germany learnt to do without a ruler. It also led to a more formal recognition of the existence of a fixed electoral college of seven princes, since each claimed during the subsequent proceedings in the papal court that the four votes that he had secured constituted a majority. In earlier periods the 'election' had been the concern of the greater lay nobles (as representatives of Germany's tribal divisions) and of the most powerful prelates: at times (as mentioned above) hereditary succession had made election a formality, but after the death of Henry VI and particularly during the subsequent struggle between the Hohenstaufen and the papacy it had been very much a reality. The limitation of the electoral college to seven assisted the worst of the abuses which had accompanied the events of 1257, for the number of principal recipients of bribes from those seeking election was now firmly fixed—at first the number only, not the names, since for a time the dukes of Lower Bavaria challenged the Bohemian kings for the seventh vote. Thus the choice of the emperor[3] became, by fixed constitutional practice, the affair of seven magnates, and the man elected would be he whose choice was most compatible with the selfish interests of these seven princes.

IMPERIAL POLITICS FROM 1273

The election in 1273 of Rudolf of Habsburg well exemplifies this generalisation. In Rudolf the princes chose with care the representative of a house whose power could not compare with their own. The Habsburgs held land in Alsace, the upper Rhine and what is now Switzerland; there was as yet no indication of the family's future greatness. Rudolf was so much the dependent of the electors that they were able to make him promise to alienate none of his domain except with their consent. His election was to a considerable extent the product of Gregory X's desire to raise up a northern counterweight to the overwhelming strength of Charles of Anjou, yet the man whom the electors chose was not powerful enough for the role. He was naturally forced to concentrate his attention on his own domain and the advancement of his family; his policy could not be an imperial one in the wider sense, but within its limits it was successful, for Rudolf gained Austria and Styria for his sons. Thus the family's territorial basis shifted further east:[4] some of Rudolf's successors, indeed, were to be rulers of southern or south-eastern Germany only, though their control was not so strictly limited as that of William of Holland and Richard of Cornwall in the north-west.

This concentration on the south-east made possible friendly relations with the French monarchy, the interests of which had tended to clash with those of the empire along the border, in the Carolingian 'Middle Kingdom'.[5] But the long struggle between France and England served to exacerbate disunity within the empire, because each side attempted to recruit military support there. The Low Countries and Rhineland provided the most promising base for an English assault on the Île de France, while the French in turn exploited local disputes in the same region to build up a party favourable to them. Meanwhile growing national sentiment in France and England made Germany's disunity still more pronounced in comparison, and the French Crown was able to nibble away at imperial land in the no-man's-land of Franche-Comté, Lorraine and the Lyonnais.

Rudolf of Habsburg so frightened the princes by his territorial gains that on his death (1291) the electors rejected his son and instead turned again to a weak candidate, Adolf of Nassau. Adolf was soon deeply involved on the English side in the struggle for power in the Netherlands, was then challenged by Albert of Habsburg and fell in battle (1298). Albert in turn was drawn into war, against the Bohemian dynasty; the weakness of his standing is well illustrated by Boniface VIII's attempt to persuade him to cede Tuscany and to recognise formally that any imperial election might be quashed by a pope.

Henry of Luxembourg, Albert's successor (1308), was a compromise candidate, chosen because he was neither a Capetian (French aspirations to the empire now reappeared) nor a Habsburg, and because the comparative obscurity of his house made it likely that he would remain dependent on the princes who had elected him. By abandoning imperial claims in Thuringia and confirming Habsburg rights in Austria and Styria Henry conformed to the expectation that in his time Germany would remain without a strong ruler. Like his predecessors, however, he set out to strengthen the position of his own family and he secured the succession to Bohemia and Moravia through the marriage of his son John (1311). The main shift in imperial policy under Henry was his return to an ambitious policy in Italy. Initially the result of a natural wish to revive imperial claims south of the Alps, this policy benefited from the encouragement of the pope (Clement V) who saw it as a means of restoring some order to the peninsula and of counterbalancing the formidable power of France. Henry's intention was to stand above the Italian maelstrom as a neutral, but he had gone no further than Milan when he abandoned this attempt and was drawn into the struggle by the appeals of the Ghibellines. The high hopes that these men placed in Henry's role may be seen at their most extreme in Dante's letter saluting 'the successor of Caesar and Augustus' and begging him to fulfil his task throughout northern and central Italy,[6] and in the same writer's fervently anachronistic *De Monarchia* (*On Monarchy*), which founds the empire's position on that of the ancient Romans, who ruled the world through God's will. Henry also discovered that Aragonese support compelled him to take sides against the Angevins, the other contenders for the south. Finally, after much hesitation, the pope himself declared against Henry, who thus came to dedicate the last three years of his short life to fruitless campaigning in Italy. Whatever Dante's hopes, Henry cannot be regarded as reviving the tradition of the Hohenstaufen, for he had the worst of both worlds and achieved dominance neither north nor south of the Alps.

Henry's death (August 1313) was followed by a disputed election, the rival candidates being the Habsburg Frederick and Lewis of Bavaria. The latter was the heir to the votes cast in 1308 for the house of Luxembourg; Henry's son John was young and, besides, papal pressure told against him. In the main Lewis was stronger than his rival, but he held only half of the old Bavarian duchy and the territorial basis of his power was inconsiderable. A bitter war between Frederick and Lewis caused great devastation and even Lewis's decisive victory at Mühldorf (1322) did not bring the struggle to an end, for the pope, John XXII, took advantage of the disputed succession to claim the imperial vicariate in Italy and, later, administration of the 'vacant' empire. When the pope, after excommunicating Lewis, sought out a pro-French emperor among the Habsburgs and considered also reviving the candidacy of John of Bohemia, Lewis retorted by declaring himself joint emperor with his former rival Frederick: this arrangement lasted from 1325 till Frederick's death in 1330. Lewis salvaged some degree of prestige for the empire by his intervention in Italy: he was never able to lay his hands on more than 4,000 horsemen, but in the fragmented peninsula even this force counted for much. In any event Lewis, a practical man and an opportunist, was not aiming at an imperial restoration in thirteenth-century style. He saw Italy as a source of money and knew that if he could assert himself there even a little, the many tyrants who sought a constitutional basis for their *signorie* would pay him handsomely for the title of 'imperial vicar'. During his six years in Italy he was able to install an imperialist anti-pope, but the main effect of his Italian policy was to keep alive memories of the empire's former greatness. Lewis never visited northern Germany, but his dynastic policy gained for him the Tyrol and the Brandenburg March and (by his marriage) Hainault, Zeeland, Holland and Friesland.

Lewis' successes were meagre. He was able to play off Habsburg against Luxembourg, and his conflict with the papacy was given a further edge by the fact that, although he could by no stretch of the imagination be called cultured, his court at Munich became a focus for papal dissidents. Marsilius of Padua fled there after he was exposed as the author of the controversial *Defender of the Peace*, and he was later joined by the Franciscan philosopher William of Ockham. But despite the stridently anti-papal tone of the most famous of their political works, neither of these writers contributed much to the imperial cause itself; they were refugees rather than spin-doctors at court. The fact is that Lewis never came close to achieving an imperial revival. Indeed such a revival had never been practical politics during the century which had passed since Frederick II's deposition. The strength drained from the ruler had flowed continuously to the princes, and the princes had affirmed their constitutional position by declaring (at Rhens, in 1338) that the king elected by them had no need of papal confirmation. It was also the princes who took the lead at Frankfurt in 1346, when they chose Charles of Bohemia (the son of John of Bohemia and grandson of Henry VII), to supplant Lewis. Charles (born 'Wenceslas') was the candidate brought forward by the strongly pro-French pope Clement VI: he had been educated at the French court, and had met Clement there. In the history of the empire the importance of Charles's reign lies in his promulgation of the Golden Bull (1356) which gave official recognition to the triumph in Germany of the particularist principle. This edict reaffirmed that the only necessary stage in the choice of an emperor was election by the seven princes. The electoral college was thus more formally constituted, and its members were singled out by another clause which forbade them to partition their territory. A number of special powers granted to the princes ratified their position as virtually independent rulers. Offences against them were to rank as *lèse-majesté* (treason). No appeal was to lie from their law courts to the emperor's. They were to have control over the currency of their lands. The bull also prohibited the formation of leagues between towns and among the nobles. In appearance a constitutional abdication of a ruler in favour of seven powerful subjects—and a sensible recognition of political realities—the Golden Bull was also an invitation to the other great feudatories, secular and lay, to assume similar authority, for it would be difficult to confine this virtual independence to the electoral princes.

Much of Charles's negative reputation derives from fifteenth-century writers whose denigration of him was cumulative and programmatic.[7] Aeneas Silvius Piccolomini accused him of pawning the empire; epithets he acquired posthumously included 'augmenter of Bohemia, diminisher of the Empire', and 'father of Bohemia, arch-stepfather of the Empire'. There is some limited truth in these accusations; recent estimates have shown that the greatest reduction of imperial territory in the late Middle Ages (through pawning, pledging or selling off) took place under Charles.[8] Yet there was a rationale for it, and Charles's two roles of emperor and king of Bohemia, far from being mutually antagonistic, can perhaps more usefully be seen as complementary and even in harmony. His dynastic policy (*Hausmachtpolitik*) was certainly effective; four astute marriages, and a sustained programme of economic and cultural development in Bohemia itself (to which we will return in Chapter 6) make Charles's achievements as ruler of Bohemia impressive. The Luxembourg possessions as left by Charles have been assessed as the largest territorial block hitherto amassed by one German princely family.[9] Undeniably he bought this opportunity, literally and figuratively, from rival dynasties and through pacts with the other chief internal powers that are reminiscent of Frederick II; but Charles was much more active and present than Frederick, both as ruler of Germany and as emperor. He travelled almost constantly throughout the territory, cultivated good diplomatic relations with France and the papacy, and established one of the most impressive courts of the time in Prague. He even expanded the imperial borders, welding in the peripheral acquisitions of Lusatia and Silesia, and thus ensuring that at his death the extent of the empire was larger than ever before. The justification of his dynastic policy, at the time and in retrospect, was that an effective emperor had to have a real power-base. His achievement perhaps was to establish one that did not threaten the other dominant princely families. Indeed, his relations with them are characterised by careful and balanced behaviour, generosity and pressure being applied in roughly equal measure. Being first among equals at home allowed him to function unhindered as emperor on the international scene. The nickname of *Pfaffenkaiser*, or 'priests' emperor'—acquired because of and during his negotiations for support for the imperial title in 1346—is only partly appropriate; more than anything he was the princes' man.

Despite Charles's achievements, the tenuous position of the emperor meant that there was absolutely no guarantee of continuity. It says much about him that the imperial electors chose two of his sons for the title, but the first of these soon squandered his heritage and the second found himself up against formidable problems. The rulers that followed Charles call for no more than a brief mention, since their melancholy history is not the history of Germany; after the issue of the Golden Bull 'the history of German internal development passes from the whole to the parts, and each separate principality requires individual treatment'.[10] Charles's drunken son Wenceslas (1378–1400) was tied to Bohemia by the struggle against Hussitism.[11] This most disastrous of reigns proved that 'elective' kingship was no protection against the succession of the totally incompetent. Rupert of the Rhine replaced Wenceslas on his deposition, but achieved no hold outside his own lands during his rather brief reign (1400–10). On Rupert's death the electors turned to Sigismund, Charles IV's younger son, who had already acquired the crown of Hungary. Sigismund (1410–37) enjoyed some popularity in his lifetime and his knightly personality and his initiative in forwarding the council of Constance perhaps did a little to revive royal prestige. Such power as he possessed, however, was based entirely on Bohemia and Hungary, and most of his reign was devoted to a series of unsuccessful crusades against the Hussite risings. In the north he sold Neumark, conferred the duchy of Saxony on Frederick of Meissen and granted Brandenburg to Frederick of Nuremberg, thus assisting the foundation of Hohenzollern power. The Swiss Confederation also gained considerably in autonomy during his time. Sigismund's political ability was limited to a certain skill in exploiting the internal divisions of the towns. An instance may be given to illustrate this technique in action. In 1414 he promised a popular regime newly installed in Lübeck that for 25,000 florins he would give the city a 'privilege' whereby the former oligarchs were to remain in perpetual exile and the city's consuls to be recruited only from the lesser guilds; this handsome bribe was disguised as a loan, the privilege being valid only if repayment had not been made by a fixed date. Sigismund was of course powerless to prevent the return of Lübeck's exiles in 1416, by which time he was haggling for another gift of 16,000 florins. Even shamelessly cunning methods of this sort could come nowhere near to solving the problem of Sigismund's notorious insolvency. At times the king was reduced to wearing tattered clothes. In 1416, on his return journey from England, he had to pawn part of the insignia of the Order of the Garter, which he had recently received, and after the Council of Constance he was forced to leave some of his linen with the municipality: this proved unsaleable because it was stamped with the imperial arms. Sigismund's son-in-law and successor, Albert of Austria, reigned for a single year only (1438–9), but his cousin Frederick III was king till 1493. Under Frederick III, while the king struggled to retain control of his own Austrian duchy, much of Prussia was lost to Poland and Silesia and Moravia to Hungary; for a time, too, much imperial territory was in the hands of Charles of Burgundy.

Underlying the tortuous story of imperial succession outlined above is a far from obvious trend, namely a gradual shift of the political weight of the empire towards the east. From 1273 to 1346, the calculations at each imperial election included a number of factors; a wish to deny any individual family the opportunity for continuity that could lead to the establishment of the hereditary principle; a wish to counteract some of the policies of the previous emperor; and, most frequently, a wish to provide an effective counterweight to French aspirations on the western border of the Empire. The fact that four of the seven electors had their power-bases in western Germany close to the French border ensured that this issue had priority. The consequences of this cocktail were unpredictable but profound. Each of the dominant dynastic houses to occupy the imperial throne used the opportunity of power for dynastic aggrandisement, but in an unforeseen way; in each case there was territorial expansion in the less populated and geo-politically less sensitive areas of the east.[12] The Habsburg family, as has been seen, began as relatively small landowners in southern Germany, and within the span of the career of its first emperor had established a far larger territorial power-base in the then Austria, Styria and Carinthia, subsequently extending through Carniola down to the Adriatic. Lewis, again beginning from the Wittelsbach holdings in Bavaria and the Palatinate, soon added Brandenburg to the family's holdings. The most spectacular example of this phenomenon was perhaps the house of Luxembourg. Henry was chosen, as has been seen, as an unprepossessing candidate who nonetheless was expected to stand up to the French. What none of the electors could have calculated was that marriage would so rapidly propel the lineage to the throne of Bohemia. Although this was initially little more than titular—John, like his father Henry, disliked Bohemia and made little effort to govern it—by the time of Charles IV the situation was very different, as has been seen. Charles's ambitious intention to put Bohemia on the map translated into economic policy, for example in the creation of a trade network from Frankfurt via Nuremberg through to Prague. The extent of commitment to the eastern part of the empire can be seen in his grandiose plans to re-route Venetian trade by opening up a new eastern route from the Adriatic through the Moldau and Elbe rivers to Hamburg.[13]

This eastern emphasis was of great significance. First, it had consequences for Germany's relations with its eastern neighbours. There is a sense in which the *Drang nach Osten*, the 'push towards the east', which played such a prominent part in high medieval German history, was continued into the fourteenth century, a period by which elsewhere in Europe (except in the Iberian peninsula) colonisation and territorial expansion had largely ceased. This will be discussed later. Second, it took the focus of imperial politics out of the western heartlands in which it had become so conflictual. The imperial succession was a much less controversial matter after the election of Charles. Conventionally this is ascribed to the Golden Bull, which regulated the process; others have seen the decline in controversy as a signal that the job of emperor was hardly worth competing for. Another factor, though, must be the increased stability of the power-balance among the major dynasties between which the title oscillated. Henceforth the role of emperor was left to families in the eastern part of the empire which could use it to their advantage provided they did not encroach on the development of other power-bases and constitutional arrangements in the west—or indeed on the interests of their neighbours, be they French or Italian. The eastward power shift freed up the west for different avenues of government and different forms of experimentation. The rise of the Swiss Confederation, the development of principalities and leagues, all took place in a context of the absence of imperial opposition. That does not necessarily imply weakness or ineffectiveness, or even opposition. Diversity is the most striking aspect of late medieval German government, and it is not necessarily helpful to see the Crown and the other forms of political life in conflict with each other. It is these forms of government that we must now address.

FRAGMENTATION AND CONFEDERATION

In 1457 an Italian cardinal received a letter from his friend Martin Meyr, the chancellor of the archbishop of Mainz, lamenting the condition of Germany, which was being bled white by papal taxation. This cardinal, Aeneas Silvius Piccolomini, had travelled much in Germany during the previous quarter of a century and had indeed lived there for several years, some of which were spent in the service of Frederick III. He replied in a spirited work in which he described the wealth of many German cities and diagnosed the true sources of the woes of the Church in Germany as 'luxury and ambition'. The main trouble, however, was the political situation:

You acknowledge the emperor as your king and lord, but he seems only to rule on sufferance, and his power amounts to nothing. You obey him only so far as you wish, and this is very little indeed ['*tantum ei paretis quantum vultis, vultis autem minimum*']. Liberty is pleasing to everyone and neither cities nor princes render to the Emperor what is due to him: he has no revenue and no treasury. Everyone wishes to be the manager and arbiter of his own affairs, hence the constant quarrels and perpetual wars which rage in your midst, from whence there arise pillage, slaughter, conflagration and a thousand other kinds of evil. How essential it is to intervene in such a situation, where there is not one ruler but many.[14]

The 'many rulers' were not merely princes, but also towns and those leagues of towns that had been condemned by the Golden Bull. Of the latter the most celebrated was the Hanseatic League, a loose association of German cities trading in the area between Russia and Scandinavia in the north and Flanders in the west. This Hanse was formed principally to protect the mercantile interests of the towns concerned and in particular to concert their relations with Scandinavian rulers and the other powers with whom they had dealings. Their co-operation achieved its greatest success in the Peace of Stralsund (1369) which gave them complete free-dom of trade in Denmark. The *raison d'être* of the league was the absence of any ruler capable of protecting the towns' own interests, but it was an ad hoc political entity and never evolved a firm constitution of its own. Lübeck was always the leader among the Hanse towns and the assemblies of the league were frequently held there, but attendance at the *Hansetage* was slack and meetings were irregular. Many towns drifted into and out of the league, so that it is impossible to define its scope: at the greatest recorded gathering (1447) 38 towns were represented. It was difficult for this amorphous body to bring pressure to bear on recalcitrant members, but at times it made use of the most obvious weapon available, 'unhansing', or deprivation of membership.

In its commercial motivation, its loose structure and its long duration, the Hanseatic League was untypical; the nature of a more characteristic league in the Rhineland is well described in some passages in a chronicle from Mainz:

Around the year 1381 some powerful cities, to wit Ratisbon and Nuremberg and thirty-six Swabian towns in the Rhineland (Basle, Coblenz, Strasburg, Speier, Worms, Mainz and Cologne) and Frankfurt, Freiburg, Wetzlar and Gelnhausen in Wetterau and some other royal towns and cities, together with various barons, nobles, knights and squires (in particular Counts John and Rupert of Nassau) formed a league called *der stede bundt*.[15] They hired many lancers, paying them heavy wages. The purpose of the troops was to oppose vagrant robbers in those parts, for the barons there so encouraged these wicked bandits and it was unsafe for anyone to move between one town and another.

But the chronicler soon lost his enthusiasm for the league:

At the same period [1382] the evil league called *der bund*, after capturing this town [Scholten], had become so arrogant that it entirely despised the princes, barons and knights of those parts and turned to the extirpation of the clergy. At Mainz it infringed ecclesiastical liberties in every way, and forbade its members under heavy penalties to work for the clergy as pur-veyors of salt or wine or in many other trades. The result of this was that for many years no services were said at Mainz,[16] which worried the citizens not at all, in fact they were happy about it, for heresy flourished.

In 1386 the citizens of Worms were cited a number of times by the clergy to the court of Wenceslas king of the Romans, on account of their violent actions against them [the clergy]. But the citizens persisted in their disobedience, refusing to appear in the court to defend their case because they were confident of the power of their confederation, *der stede bundt*. In consequence they were sentenced by the king to a fine of several gold marks.

Finally he was able to report with satisfaction that

the cities in the confederation had spent tremendous sums of money on the payment of their army, for they had in their pay two hundred lancers, not to mention a vast throng of armed townsmen, artisans and peasants. These had done an enormous amount of harm and had served no useful purpose at all; also they were meeting defeat on all sides. Consequently Adolf archbishop of Mainz, the bishop of Babenburg and John of Venningen, the Master of the Teutonic Order, intervened and made peace after Whitsun [1389]: some of the cities had to pay large sums of money to lords as compensation for the harm done to the peasantry. They also had to endure the considerable shame and disgrace of these heavy payments. And so the whole conspiracy of the confederation of cities was annihilated and dissolved, and quiet restored in place of strife.[17]

This chronicler's grievances against the Rhenish League of 1381–9 were principally those of a churchman, but his account of the activities of the league's armies shows clearly enough that when this type of response to central weakness occurred the cure closely resembled the disease. Every German annalist of the fourteenth and fifteenth centuries has his own local version of this tale of brigandage and of warfare between towns and barons—often 'robber' barons whose castles were notorious as nests of thieves—as well as of violence and bitter class cleavages within the towns. Private warfare had become 'an accepted instrument of politics and war'. At times princes granted jurisdictional and other powers to towns and town leagues. Thus in 1322, after Anklam, Demmin, Greifswald and Treptow had destroyed the castle of Bugewitz, the duke of Pomerania gave these cities the authority to destroy any other castle within the duchy. These tactics could never provide a satisfactory solution to the problems of government, and in any case they were increasingly hindered in the fifteenth century by the general economic and political decline of the towns. Some places were rising in this period, particularly in southern Germany—Augsburg is an instance—and in the Lower Rhineland the cities continued to hold their own against the nobles, but this was exceptional. In the north-east the Hanse lost much of its Baltic trade to the Dutch and English. Many cities of this zone, enfeebled also by agrarian depression, forfeited their independence to the dukes of Pomerania and the Hohenzollern margraves of Brandenburg.

THE SWISS CONFEDERATION

Contrasting with the general tale of the failure of the local leagues is the great success story of the rise of the Swiss Confederation. The emergence of a new state from the debris of imperial decentralisation not only is of interest in its own right but serves also to illustrate the particular conditions under which local political institutions could consolidate and flourish.

Of the three different elements that made possible the growth of Switzerland, the most fundamental was perhaps the prior existence of the social and political institutions out of which the confederation developed. Local *Landfrieden* could only become effective as means of joint action and judicial arbitration and co-operation if they involved communities already enjoying a certain degree of self-government. The communities of Uri, Schwyz and Unterwalden, forest valleys around Lake Lucerne, were already 'corporations' and the free peasantry, which comprised perhaps as much as two-thirds of the population, probably chose the 'judges' exercising rights of lower justice. Geographical factors were hardly less important. The lake united the three cantons, facilitating communications between them. Their command of the northern approaches to the St Gotthard pass, which by the thirteenth century was the most important of the alpine routes, gave them strategic importance, and its tolls yielded them considerable revenue. They thus had both lake and pass in common, and the aim of a good deal of their subsequent expansion was control over the southern approach to the St Gotthard. Another source of unity was the preponderance of the pastoral way of life, and the people also had in common their poverty: hence their willingness to take the career of a mercenary soldier as a means of escape. The medieval Swiss had a common language, for the area that came into the confederation early was entirely German speaking.

These positive factors would not have brought about the crystallisation of Switzerland without the decisive negative pressure of the Habsburgs. Imperial weakness made the threat of local noble control a real one when the ruler was not a Habsburg, and did nothing to remove it under the Habsburg kings. The first defensive league of the three Forest Cantons probably dates from the time when count Rudolf IV, after his election as king of the Romans, sought to build up a really strong territorial state in south-western Germany. When this alliance was confirmed at the time of Rudolf s death (1291) it was described optimistically as a 'permanent league' and its constitutional basis was strengthened by a decree that judges within the cantons must be locally born men. By the early fourteenth century the cantons were appointing their own 'headmen' and soon these *Landammänner* came to exercise higher justice.

Lewis of Bavaria's disputed election (1314) gave the Swiss the opportunity to assert their direct allegiance to this emperor against his Habsburg rival Frederick. When the Habsburgs launched their first war against the Swiss (1315), the troops of Frederick's brother Leopold were routed at Morgarten.[18] This victory was followed by a new union (9 December 1315) proclaiming the open intention of mutual co-operation against the Habsburgs. One clause prescribed that the members

should be as one person, like man and wife, and should be obedient in rendering reasonable services to their rightful lords, when their lord or lords use no violence against them and do not try to impose illegal demands by force. But they should perform no services so long as their lords act unjustly towards them.

Other clauses were directed towards giving the confederation greater cohesion. Hence:

We also agree that none of the members of the confederation should take an oath or make an agreement with any outside power except after consulting the other members, and

None of the members should have any negotiations with outside powers except after consulting the other members and securing their consent, so long as the members are lordless.[19]

The pact of 1315 was, however, only the beginning of the confederation's struggles. The emperor could never be a reliable ally against the Habsburgs, and the original territories had to expand if they were to achieve economic self-sufficiency. In the course of the fourteenth century they secured the adherence of the neighbouring rural zones of Glarus and Zug and of three towns, Lucerne, Zürich and Berne. The urban communities were valuable allies, but their interests, as municipalities and textile-producing centres, contrasted with those of the original rural cantons, and there could be no confidence that they had come to stay. Lucerne joined as a fellow rebel against Habsburg lordship, but the circumstances that brought in the other towns were more or less ephemeral: Zürich turned to the Swiss when its tyrant, Brun, found that the exiles opposed to his regime had gone to the Habsburgs for support, while Berne was in need of allies to assist in the conquest of the surrounding rural area. The great asset of the Swiss during this period was the Habsburgs' concentration on their Austrian territories and the spasmodic nature of their attempts to assert overlordship further west. When the Habsburgs did at last wage determined war over Lucerne's adherence to the confederation (1385–9), the Swiss won another resounding victory, at Sempach (1386), in which Leopold of Austria, nephew of the Leopold defeated at Morgarten, met his death. Other successes in this war made it of decisive importance in the development of Swiss expansion and unity, but the 'confederation' was not yet a single organisation, some of its members being linked with some but not all of the others. Antecedents of the firmer constitutional structure of later times are to be found by 1370 in a joint agreement concerning clerical privilege, and this trend is still more marked in the *Sempacherbrief* (Charter of Sempach) of July 1393.[20] The most important clause of this statute laid down that:

It is our unanimous opinion that henceforth no town or territory among us should enter upon a war . . . without giving notice in accordance with the sworn agreement linking all the towns and territories.

This was an important principle, though it was sometimes defied. Since the Swiss were entirely dependent for their position on the strength and prestige of their arms it was essential that some code should regulate the conduct of the confederation's forces. The *Sempacherbrief* not only forbade attacks on Church property and on women 'unless they are helping the enemy', but incorporated a clause concerning looting which is worth quoting for the light that it throws on the warfare of the age:

Let it be known also that in this battle many of the enemy escaped . . . who would not have done so had our men pursued them instead of plundering before the battle was entirely won and finished, . . . so that those who were fleeing gathered together and won back command of the field and the bodies and possessions of the dead. We consider unanimously that, whenever the occasion arises, everyone should do his best as an honourable man to harm the enemy and hold the field, without plundering whether in fortresses, towns or the open countryside, up to the time when the battle has ended and been won, and the commanders permit plunder. Then all present may plunder whether they are armed or not and the loot is to be handed over to the commanders and it is to belong to them, and they shall divide it fairly among those of their men who are present, according to their number. And when they have divided the plunder among the men everyone should be content with his proper share.

A torrent of new accessions was inaugurated by the acquisition of the Valais as an ally in the early fifteenth century. Among these the Aargau was of particular importance for the constitution and for the growth of mutual interests among its members, since this formerly Habsburg territory was held in common between the confederates and taxed and governed by them jointly. By 1461, when the Thurgau, west of Lake Constance, was gained, the Habsburgs retained almost nothing of their former lands south of the Rhine, and in the last two decades of the century there began another series of important accessions, Fribourg and Solothurn joining the confederation in the 1480s and Basle and Schaffhausen around 1500. Between the late 1460s and 1476 the Swiss were threatened by the rise of the Burgundian duchy,[21] and for a time they received money from both Sigismund of Habsburg and Louis XI of France to stimulate their opposition to the duke. When Charles of Burgundy invaded Switzerland in 1476 he was decisively defeated by the Swiss pikemen in the battles of Grandson and Morat. The Swiss could not always resist the temptation to indulge in military expeditions which were little more than large-scale looting forays into the Savoy and Franche-Comté, Vaud and the duchy of Milan. But a firmer agreement was reached concerning co-operation in foreign policy and military engagements (Compact of Stans, 1481) and further unity was conferred on the confederation by the ill-judged decision to neglect it in the constitutional reforms of the *Reichstag* of Worms of 1495.[22] Four years later the Swiss beat off the forces of Maximilian and the Swabian league and the emperor was compelled to recognise the confederation as virtually independent.

The success of the Swiss is clearly attributable to their military strength and to the fact that the Habsburgs so rarely put this to the test in a prolonged war. The cavalry, conventionally the master of medieval battlefields, could make little headway in the mountains,[23] and the Swiss were hardy infantrymen, well armed with halberds and pikes. They were carefully trained to maintain an unbroken formation even in difficult terrain and this made them formidable both when standing firm on the defensive against a ragged charge and when themselves advancing in slow-moving but implacable attack. Mercenary service helped to keep the Swiss in training and to gain them experience. By the end of the fifteenth century the prestige of their pikemen was unchallenged in western Europe. Machiavelli thought the Swiss the sole surviving heirs of Rome's military greatness. His *Art of War* is full of praise for their methods,[24] and when he was charged with the organisation of the newly formed Florentine militia in 1506 he recommended that it should be drilled in the Swiss manner. Yet the military power of the Swiss would not have been sufficient to win them independence had not the confederation evolved a constitution which bound the members sufficiently firmly in the face of opposition and which was yet sufficiently loose to allow for the inevitable strains of diverging interests. Around 1500 there were 13 confederate 'cantons' which voted in the diets of the 'Great League of Upper Germany'; the cantons sent representatives with instructions to the meetings of the diet, the powers of which were undefined although it was the league's only federal authority. Membership was not yet a fixed and permanent affair, and in the mid-fifteenth century Zürich had deserted the league for a time and even fought some of its members. Outside the confederation stood a number of 'allies', two of which were groups of communities (Valais and Grisons), while others were country districts, towns and abbeys; many of the allies were still linked by treaty to some, but not all, of the cantons, and some of the cantons had their own subject territories, both singly and jointly. This complicated but flexible machinery worked successfully, and in the sixteenth century Switzerland was to show itself a power to be reckoned with in war and diplomacy, as well as in religion.

THE DIFFUSION OF POWER

Confederations, whether successful or not, have been presented as a response to the power vacuum at the centre of the empire. A similar diagnosis is possible of the principalities, many of which grew in strength in the fifteenth century in particular. (They will be discussed in Chapter 13.) But these developments are only symptoms of what was wrong at the top. Below this level is another important form of power whose roots are controversial but whose extent and significance is now appreciated by historians. Communities in late medieval Germany, both urban and rural, evolved a level of self-government that is striking in its extent, diversity and vigour. In village communities this took the form of 'communes', associations of landholders on a basis of equality, with a legal 'personality' (in other words the right to maintain peace and order, and to sue at law), an elected headman or leader, assemblies of its members, collective responsibility for the maintenance and defence of shared land and resources, and extensive powers of self-regulation (particularly of economic affairs). The relationship of these 'communes' to the local and territorial lords was complex and often strained, but it was mostly a working one in which both parties co-operated. Urban communities were similar in some respects, different in others. The term covers a wide spectrum, from small townships, whose differentiation from villages was not always clear-cut, to large cities, many with considerable practical autonomy, some effective republics. There was, unsurprisingly, greater sophistication of political and administrative institutions in the towns, and internal hierarchies and tensions are also more evident, socially, economically and politically. Guilds played a prominent part, but so did tensions between the town government and their overlords and neighbours.

The significance of these communes has been much debated. There is a temptation to see them as the antecedents of democratic institutions, but this view should be treated with care. The extent of democracy was in practice very small. Rural communes consisted only of male landholding heads of household in village communes, and urban ones of male married citizens (a category which is tightly defined and jealously guarded). Despite the constitutions of these towns, they demonstrated the same strong tendency towards oligarchy that is evident in the Italian city-states. Yet communes and 'communalism' were a ubiquitous feature of late medieval German society. They clearly played an important role in the formation of some of the confederations discussed above, especially the Swiss Confederation, but also in the neighbouring areas of southern Germany where the institution was particularly strong and where one of the possible avenues of development was 'to turn Swiss'. Their proliferation could undoubtedly be seen as a force that could work in favour of a mentality of independence and indeed of beliefs in the right of resistance, and attempts have been made to establish the impact of this on the Reformation, as will be seen later.

The virtual absence of central government, the weakness of the emperor, the mixed record of a variety of confederations, the history of regional territorial consolidation, the long parade of local and regional conflicts and the success of the Swiss in moving towards independence from the empire give a negative impression of German history in the late Middle Ages. Yet this is only so if we begin with the teleological assumption that a society's performance can be gauged in terms of its 'progress' in building up to the form of government that is considered to be its 'destiny'—or at least the form currently preferred. This problem of perspective was mentioned above.[25] Judged purely by its success in creating a nation-state, German history has to be deemed a failure until the nineteenth century. Judged by other criteria, including for example the evolution of self-government—though this is only another teleology—the record is much more positive. Without plumping for any of these single approaches, one can point to the late medieval period as one in which Germany saw the development of a wide variety of forms of power. Evaluation of the varying durability and political success of these forms is only one aspect of their history. During their period of influence they underpinned economic and cultural activity, spheres in which any picture of Germany's 'backwardness' is soon dispelled. They deserve study and appreciation in their own right.

APPENDIX

The Battle of Morgarten, 1315

(Translated from the Chronicle of John of Winterthur, ed. F. Baethgen, *Monumenta Germaniae historica, Scriptores rerum Germanicarum*, n.s., 3 (Berlin, 1924, repr. 1955), pp. 77–81.)

In the year of our Lord 1315 a certain rustic people living in the valleys called 'Swiz' which are almost surrounded by high mountains, denied Duke Leopold the obedience and payments and customary services that they owed him: they prepared to resist him, trusting in the well-fortified strength of their mountains. Duke Leopold was enraged at this and made no secret of the fact that he was assembling an army which was to be ready by St Martin's Day [11 November]. He is said to have mustered no less than twenty thousand men from the places subject to him and from friendly-disposed neighbours: this army was raised to defeat, despoil and subjugate the rebellious mountain folk. The force collected by the Duke was a strong, determined body of specially chosen well-trained troops, met together as one man to subdue and humiliate these rustics gathered within their wall of mountains. To make certain of utterly defeating, capturing, destroying and despoiling the region, the Duke's soldiers were provided with cord and ropes to assist them in carrying off sheep and cattle. When the news of these preparations was known the inhabitants of the weaker places were very frightened and they strengthened their defences with walls and ditches and in every other possible way, and commended themselves to God by prayer, fasting and litanies. They 'possessed themselves beforehand of all the tops of the high mountains'[26] and the men in those parts where the army was likely to pass were ordered 'to keep watch where the way was narrow between the mountains'. They did as was 'commanded them' and 'every man cried to God with great fervency and with great vehemency did they humble their souls' in fasting 'both they and their wives' and they 'cried to God all with one consent earnestly that he would not give their flocks for a prey and their wives for a spoil, and their villages to destruction and their honour and virtue to profanation'. They 'cried unto the Lord with all their power, that he would look upon their people graciously', saying 'O Lord God of heaven and earth, behold their pride, and pity the low estate of our nation and show that thou forsakest not them that trust on thee, and that thou humblest them that presume of themselves, and glory in their own strength'. They also did penance and begged with all their might for peace and forgiveness for their disobedience: this they did through the offices of a certain Count of Toggenburg, a man noble both in body and mind, who acted as arbiter and tried to make peace between the two parties and to put an end to the quarrel. This Count worked hard and faithfully in the interest of both sides, but he could make no headway with Duke Leopold, who was 'very wroth' with the Swiss 'and his anger burned in him': he was unwilling to accept the humble terms that they offered him through the Count of Toggenburg, as it was his intention to destroy them and to scatter them with his forces. When the Swiss heard this 'they were struck with great fear and trembling'. And so the Swiss 'took up their weapons of war' and they remained 'in those places where the passage was strait and they took mountainous paths, and watched all day and night'.

On St Othmar's Day Duke Leopold tried to advance with his army into the area between a certain mountain and a lake called the *Egeri See*, but was hindered by the height and steepness of the mountain. Almost all the knights had thrust themselves eagerly to the fore in the hope of gaining loot but, however daring their advance, it was completely impossible for them to climb the mountain on horseback; indeed it was impossible even for the infantry to find a footing there. The Swiss knew beforehand, through the Count, that this was the direction from which the attack was coming and they realized that this part was particularly difficult of access. They were much heartened, and they now came down from their hiding-places, surrounded their enemies till they were like fish caught in a net, and put them to slaughter without meeting any resistance. They had no difficulty in finding a footing on even the steepest slopes, where neither the enemy nor his horses could stand at all, with the aid of certain iron contrivances with chains[27] which they attached to their feet, as was their custom. Also the Swiss were armed with a lethal kind of battleaxe which is called 'halberd' in the vernacular: with this terrifying weapon they could cut up even well-armoured opponents as though with a razor, slicing them in pieces. This was not a battle but rather, for the reasons that have been given, it was a massacre of

Duke Leopold's men who came 'like sheep for the slaughter' to fall at the hands of the mountain folk. These spared nobody and took no prisoners but 'smote them all until they were dead'. Those who were not killed were drowned in the lake into which they had plunged in the hope of swimming to the other side. When the infantry heard their valiant knights being struck down in such terrifying fashion by the Swiss some were so frightened and driven out of their wits by fear of this horrifying death that they too threw themselves into the lake, preferring to fling themselves into the deep waters rather than fall into the hands of so dreadful an enemy. It is said that fifteen hundred men fell 'by the sword' in this battle, apart from those who were drowned in the lake. So many knights from the territories around were killed that for some time afterwards there was a lack of knights: almost all those who were killed were knights and nobles who had been trained to arms from childhood. The troops who were going into the attack by other approach routes avoided the blood-stained hands of their enemy, because they 'fled for their lives' when they heard of the ferocious slaughter that had taken place. A number of men from the surrounding cities, towns and villages were killed, and everywhere 'the voice of mirth and gladness' was silent and the only sound to be heard was 'lamentation and weeping'. From the town of Winterthur one man only was killed and he was one who had become separated from his fellows and had the misfortune to be with the cavalry: all the others returned home unharmed. Duke Leopold on his retreat was to be seen among these, looking half dead in his great distress. I saw this with my own eyes, for I was then a schoolboy away from home and I and the other schoolboys ran happily to watch from the town-gate. And indeed Duke Leopold had cause to look melancholy and afflicted, for he had lost the flower and strength of his army. All this happened on 15 November 1315 on St Othmar's day while the Duke's brother Frederick was in Austria. After the battle the Swiss took the weapons of the men who had been killed and drowned and whatever booty they could recover, so that they were greatly enriched in money and arms. They also proclaimed that the day was to be celebrated annually as a feast and holiday in perpetuity, on account of the victory granted them by God.

FURTHER READING
General

English-language histories of medieval Germany tend to take shorter rather than longer periods. Alfred Haverkamp, *Medieval Germany, 1056–1273* (tr. Oxford, 1988), and Benjamin Arnold, *Medieval Germany, 500–1300. A Political Interpretation* (London, 1997) cover the early part of the period discussed in this chapter; *see also* Benjamin Arnold, *German Knighthood 1050–1300* (Oxford, 1985), and A. Haverkamp and H. Vollrath, eds, *England and Germany in the High Middle Ages. Challenge and Change* (Oxford, 1996). Joachim Leuschner, *Germany in the Late Middle Ages* (tr. Amsterdam, New York and Oxford, 1980) and F. R. H. Du Boulay, *Germany in the Later Middle Ages* (London, 1983) cover the period from 1200 to 1500, the former with an emphasis on the first part of the period, the latter concentrating on the fourteenth and fifteenth centuries. G. Barraclough, *The Origins of Modern Germany* (Oxford, 1946, repr. 1966) covers German history from 800 to 1939; its medieval chapters still have relevance. H. S. Offler, 'Aspects of government in the late medieval Empire', in *Europe in the Late Middle*

Ages, eds J. R. Hale, J. R. L. Highfield and B. Smalley (London, 1965), pp. 217–47 is a fine, sharp introduction to the history of late medieval Germany. Hermann Heimpel, 'Characteristics of the late middle ages in Germany', in *Pre-Reformation Germany*, ed. Gerald Strauss (London, 1972), pp. 43–72 is more discursive. Finally Bob Scribner, ed., *Germany. A New Social and Economic History*, vol. 1: *1450–1630* (London, New York, etc., 1996) is an excellent introduction to many aspects of late medieval Germany; despite its title, many chapters go back to 1300.

The medieval empire

On the empire and its significance, D. J. A. Matthew, 'Reflections on the medieval Roman Empire', *History*, 77 (1992), pp. 363–90 is a broad review of the whole issue. A number of older works are of interest; G. Barraclough, *The Medieval Empire: Idea and Reality* (London, 1950); W. Ullmann, 'Reflections on the medieval empire', *Transactions of the Royal Historical Society*, 5th series, 14 (1964), pp. 89–108; R. Folz, *The Concept of Empire in Western Europe from the Fifth to the Fourteenth Century* (tr. London, 1969); F. Heer, *The Holy Roman Empire* (tr. London, 1968). *See also* K. Hampe, *Germany under the Salian and Hohenstaufen Emperors* (tr. Oxford, 1973). On the electoral system, C. Bayley, *The Formation of the German College of Electors* (Toronto, 1949), on which *see also* K. Leyser, 'A recent view of the German College of Electors', *Medium Aevum*, 23 (1954), pp. 76–87.

Imperial politics from 1273

Dante's *De Monarchia*, referred to in this section, has recently been translated by Prue Shaw: Dante, *Monarchy* (Cambridge, 1996), and Richard Kay: *Dante's Monarchia* (Toronto, 1998). It is discussed in George Holmes, *Dante* (Oxford, 1980), ch. 4. His *Letters* are published in *Dantis Alagherii Epistolae. The Letters of Dante*, ed. & tr. P. Toynbee (2nd edition, Oxford, 1966); letter VII, translated on pp. 100–5, is to Henry VII. For Dante's political ideas see also U. Limentani, 'Dante's political thought', in *The Mind of Dante*, ed. U. Limentani (Cambridge, 1965), pp. 113–37; C. T. Davis, *Dante and the Idea of Rome* (Oxford, 1957); A. P. d'Entreves, *Dante as Political Thinker* (Oxford, 1952); J. M. Ferrante, *The Political Vision of the Divine Comedy* (Princeton, N.J., 1984); and John A. Scott, *Dante's Political Purgatory* (Philadelphia, Pa., 1996). The Golden Bull was translated in E. F. Henderson, *Select Historical Documents* (London, 1894), pp. 220–61; repr. in Patrick J. Geary, ed., *Readings in Medieval History* (repr. Peterborough, Ont. and Lewiston, N.Y., 1992), vol. 2, pp. 312–333.

Little has been written in English about the individual emperors of this period. The political developments are most fully covered by the old *Cambridge Medieval History*, vol. VII (Cambridge, 1932), chs 3–9 (to the mid-fourteenth century), and thereafter by Du Boulay, *Germany in the Later Middle Ages*, ch. 2. J. Bérenger, *A History of the Habsburg Empire, 1273–1700* (tr. London and New York, 1994), chs 1–4 has a little to say on Rudolf and Albert. W. M. Bowsky, *Henry VII in Italy. The Conflict of Empire and City-State, 1310–1313* (Lincoln, Neb., 1960) focuses on the critical episode of Henry's Italian venture. On Lewis's court as a centre for scholarship (and dissent), Dick E. H. de Boer, 'Ludwig the Bavarian and the scholars', in *Centres of Learning: Learning and Location in Pre-Modern Europe and the Near East*, eds J. W. Drijvers and A. A. MacDonald (Leiden, 1995), pp. 229–44; and C. K. Brampton, 'Ockham, Bonagratia and the Emperor Lewis IV', *Medium Aevum*, 31 (1962), pp. 81–7. Despite much German interest in the figure of Charles IV, motivated particularly by the sixth centenary of his death in 1978, there has been no recent biography in English; see B. Jarrett, *The Emperor Charles IV* (London, 1935), which includes an abridged translation of his autobiography, pp. 33–68, repr. in Patrick J. Geary, ed., *Readings in Medieval History* (repr.

Peterborough, Ont. and Lewiston, N.Y., 1992), vol. 2, pp. 296–311; for the full text and translation see B. Nagy (ed.) and P. W. Knoll (tr.), *Autobiography of Charles IV of Luxembourg, Holy Roman Emperor and King of Bohemia* (Budapest, 2000). František Kavka, 'Politics and culture under Charles IV', in *Bohemia in History*, ed. M. Teich (Cambridge, 1998), pp. 59–78 is a good introduction, broader than its title indicates; *see also* S. Harrison Thomson, 'Learning at the court of Charles IV', *Speculum*, 25 (1950), pp. 1–20.

Fragmentation and confederation

On the history of German leagues and confederations, F. R. H. Du Boulay, *Germany in the Later Middle Ages* (London, 1983), chs 2 and 5(c); on some of the background to them, *see also* his 'Law enforcement in medieval Germany', *History*, 63 (1978), pp. 345–55. On the Hanse, the classic work is P. Dollinger, *The German Hanse* (4th tr. edition, London, 1989). Johannes Schildhauer, *The Hansa. History and Culture* (2nd tr. edition, Dorset Press, 1988) is a rounded and accessible work. For specific aspects of Hanseatic history, *see* J. A. Gade, *The Hanseatic Control of Norwegian Commerce during the Late Middle Ages* (Leiden, 1951); T. Lloyd, *England and the German Hanse 1157–1611. A Study of their Trade and Commercial Diplomacy* (Cambridge, 1991); J. Fudge, *Cargoes, Embargoes and Emissaries. The Commercial and Political Interaction of England and the German Hanse 1450–1510* (Toronto, 1995); and the bibliography on late medieval trade, under Chapter 5.

The Swiss Confederation

E. Bonjour, H. S. Offler and G. R. Potter, *A Short History of Switzerland* (Oxford, 1952) is still the basic work in English though it is now outdated. For a more recent summary, *see* Roger Sablonier, 'The Swiss Confederation', in *NCMH*, 7, pp. 645–70. An effective general introduction is J. Steinberg, *Why Switzerland?* (Cambridge, 1976). On the later period, some important work is represented by T. A. Brady, *Turning Swiss: Cities and Empire, 1450–1550* (Cambridge, 1986). Randolph C. Head, *Early Democracy in the Grisons: Social Order and Political Language in a Swiss Mountain Canton, 1470–1620* (Cambridge, 1995) investigates one of the last regions to join the confederation.

The diffusion of power

The best introduction in English is F. R. H. Du Boulay, *Germany in the Later Middle Ages* (London, 1983). German historians have for a long time been focusing on localised power, on regional developments, on the formation of territorial states and particularly on communities, be they rural or urban, as sources of explanations for the peculiar course of German history. Two of the most influential older works in German historiography have lately been translated: O. von Gierke, *Community in Historical Perspective*, ed. Antony Black (Cambridge, 1990), and O. Brunner, *'Land' and Lordship: Structures of Governance in Medieval Austria*, tr. H. Kaminsky and J. van Horn Melton (Philadelphia, Pa., 1992). Both are accompanied by excellent introductions placing the works in historiographical perspective. Prominent in this enterprise has been Peter Blickle, who has placed great emphasis on the community and its independent development, using these features to counter the traditional optic whereby German history was always judged in the perspective of the formation of a strong state. His views are most accessibly translated in Peter Blickle, *Obedient Germans? A Rebuttal. A New View of German History* (tr. Charlottesville, Va., 1997); see also his 'Communalism as an organisational principle between medieval and modern times', tr. in his *From the Communal Reformation to the Revolution of the Common Man* (Leiden, 1998), pp. 1–15. The Blickle thesis is assessed in R. W. Scribner, 'Communalism: universal category or ideological construct? A debate on the historiography of early modern Germany and Switzerland', in *Historical Journal*, 37 (1994), pp. 199–207. Finally an excellent historiographical overview is offered by Bob Scribner, 'Communities and the nature of power', in *Germany. A New Social and Economic History*, vol. 1: *1450–1630*, ed. Bob Scribner (London, New York, etc., 1996), pp. 291–325.

A few more specialised works on these themes have been written in or translated into English. A good description of communalism, with Swiss examples, is in Head, *Early Democracy in the Grisons*, ch. 1. On towns, Peter Moraw, 'Cities and citizenry as factors of state formation in the Roman-German Empire of the late middle ages', *Theory and Society*, 18 (1989), pp. 631–62, repr. in *Cities and the Rise of States in Europe, AD 1000 to 1800*, eds C. Tilly and W. P. Blockmans (Boulder, Colo., 1994), pp. 100–27 provides a broad analysis of the political dynamics with special reference to the role of German towns, while H.-C. Rublack, 'Political and social norms in urban communities in the Holy Roman Empire', in *Religion, Politics, and Social Protest*, ed. K. von Greyertz (London, 1984), pp. 24–60 discusses urban structures and political ideas. Benjamin Arnold, *Princes and Territories in Medieval Germany* (Cambridge, 1991) traces the development of the German principalities from the twelfth century to, roughly, the early fourteenth. For works on the principalities after that, see below under Chapter 13.

NOTES

1. For further discussion of this topic and the way recent historians have reassessed it, *see below*, p. 83.
2. *See above*, p. 31.
3. The emperor-elect was known as king of the Romans until he had been crowned by the pope.
4. *See* Map 2.
5. *Above*, p. 52.
6. *Dantis Alagherii Epistolae/The Letters of Dante*, ed. P. Toynbee (2nd edition, Oxford, 1966), Letter 7, pp. 87–100, tr. pp. 100–5.
7. Beat Frey, *Pater Bohemias—Vitricus Imperii. Böhmens Vater, Stiefvater des Reichs. Kaiser Karl IV. in der Geschichtschreibung* (Berne, 1978).
8. Ernst Schubert, *König und Reich. Studien zur spätmittelalterlichen deutschen Verfassungsgeschichte* (Göttingen, 1979), summarised in F. R. H. Du Boulay, *Germany in the Later Middle Ages* (London, 1983), pp. 24–7.
9. Ferdinand Seibt, 'Karl IV. und seiner Welt', in *Kaiser Karl IV. Staatsmann und Mäzen*, ed. F. Seibt (2nd edition, Munich, 1978), p. 13.
10. G. Barraclough, *The Origins of Modern Germany* (repr. Oxford, 1966), p. 321 n. 2.
11. *See* Chapter 6.
12. *See* Map 2.
13. W. von Stromer, 'Der kaiserliche Kaufmann—Wirtschaftspolitik unter Karl IV.', in *Kaiser Karl IV. Staatsmann und Mäzen*, ed. F. Seibt (2nd edition, Munich, 1978), pp. 63–73 (pp. 66–9); and *see* F. Kavka, 'Politics and culture under Charles IV', in *Bohemia. A History*, ed. M. Teich (Cambridge, 1998), pp. 59–70 (p. 67).
14. Aeneas Silvius Piccolomini (Pius II), 'De ritu, situ, moribus et conditione Germaniae descriptio', *Opera Omnia* (Basle, 1571), pp. 1060–1.
15. This phrase ('the league of cities') is in German in the chronicle, which is written in Latin.
16. This is probably a hyperbolical statement, not to be taken literally.
17. *Chronici Moguntini Miscelli Fragmenta Collecta* in J. F. Böhmer, *Fontes Rerum Germanicarum*, IV (repr. Aalen, 1969), pp. 376–83.

18. For a contemporary account of the battle *see below*, pp. 83–5.
19. *Amtliche Sammlung der ältern Eidgenössischen Abschiede*, 1 (Lucerne, 1839), doc. 2.
20. Ibid., 1, doc. 30.
21. *See* Chapter 9.
22. *See below*, p. 234.
23. *See* the account of the battle of Morgarten *below*, particularly pp. 83–5.
24. N. Machiavelli, *The Art of War*, tr. E. Farneworth (1775; revised edition New York, 1965, repr. 1990), esp. pp. 86–7, 97–8, 209.
25. *See* pp. 68–9.
26. Many phrases in this passage are biblical quotations or reminiscences, particularly from the book of *Judith*: these phrases are indicated by inverted commas.
27. Crampons.

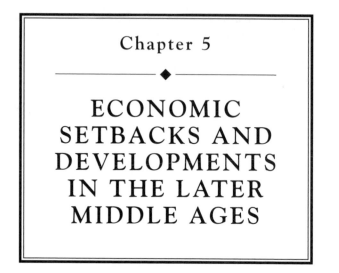

Chapter 5

♦

ECONOMIC SETBACKS AND DEVELOPMENTS IN THE LATER MIDDLE AGES

INTRODUCTION

E conomics is the science of wealth and economic historians like to pose the all-important question of 'how much wealth?' Unfortunately this question, when asked of a medieval archive, will receive at the very best a murmured and ambiguous reply. This is in part the explanation of the fact that historians who have despaired of a reliable answer to this query have preferred instead to ask 'how?' and have come away with answers about such economic institutions as the manor and the guild.

The sources available for quantitative research into economic movements in the medieval period can only provide a discontinuous picture, a little clearer for some areas and periods than for others, but never really distinct. Occasionally statistics can be gained from Customs accounts—many of these are extant for English and Hanse ports for part of the fourteenth and fifteenth centuries—and some of the contemporary estimates of industrial production and of exports were probably based on official sources. Even the official evidence is difficult to interpret, particularly since it normally refers only to overseas trade in certain commodities. As the evidence for medieval prices and population is no less spasmodic than that for production and trade, the economist has none of his essential preliminary data in a secure form. This is not to imply that full statistics would eliminate controversy or that economic aspects are a particularly tenebrous and frustrating region of medieval history; on the contrary, the need to work from inadequate sources is the very essence of the study of these centuries, the only possible justification for the conventional division between 'medieval' and 'modern' history.

The specific difficulty, to come to the fourteenth century, is to decide whether the impression, gained by many who have investigated this period, that Europe's economy went through a time of serious, widespread and prolonged depression, is based on particular information that is indeed characteristic of a general situation. 'The Fourteenth Century: Was There A Recession?' was a dominant theme of historiography for much of the mid- and late twentieth century. It will be our starting point, but as will soon be seen, other questions have come to the forefront. Above all—and with this the long catalogue of preliminary cautions is at an end—one must emphasise the extreme rashness of generalising about the economy of 'Europe', particularly at a time when the typical activity was the production of food for a local market. Regional conditions were all-important and, on the whole, difficulties, particularly of transport, caused different regions to be less interdependent than they were to become later.

THE EUROPEAN ECONOMY TO THE END OF THE THIRTEENTH CENTURY

The central period of the Middle Ages presents so clear-cut a picture of economic expansion that the warnings given above can easily be forgotten. It is evident that between the eleventh century and the thirteenth the population of Europe grew very considerably. New land was colonised and brought under cultivation on a very large scale, most notably in the 'frontier' territories of Germany east of the Elbe, but also on soil hitherto spurned as too densely wooded, too marshy or liable to flood, or in some other way too poor in quality to justify the expense of initial labour and capital. In the west the greatest areas were gained in low-lying Flanders, in the valley of the Po where a tremendous work of dyking and embanking was initiated, on the Atlantic coast of Gascony, and perhaps in the parts of Spain reconquered by the Christian kings. While these *villes neuves* and colonised lands provided one outlet for the increasing population, many of the older towns were also growing rapidly. There are plentiful indications of the widespread extension of the practice of producing food and textiles for sale, rather than for local or seignorial consumption, expanding population having contributed to a considerable rise in the price of grain and other food. The boom did not, however, necessarily imply a rise in individual standards of living. More people survived, but they did so for the most part in extreme discomfort and poverty, on a diet that was little above subsistence level. Many of the peasants produced wheat that went to make bread for their lord—or for him to profit by its sale for consumption in a town—while they themselves ate coarser bread made from rye, barley or oats. In a bad year even this might be a luxury and acorns, normally valued as food for pigs, were not unaccustomed diet for humans in some parts of western Europe.

In the age of expansion long-distance maritime trade came to flourish on a considerable scale in both south and north. In the Mediterranean, Venice, Genoa and Pisa dominated western Europe's commercial link with Byzantium, Syria, Egypt and the lands beyond. In the North Sea the most active route lay between Bruges, London and the other English and Flemish ports of the 'narrows' in the south, while at the farther end of this axis were the Hanse towns of the Baltic and North Sea, exporting mainly the fish, furs, timber, wax and honey of the north, and east

German grain, and receiving cloth from the west. The principal link between these two zones of maritime trade was by land, over the Brenner Pass from Venice or (for a larger proportion of goods) across the Alps and through eastern France, where lay the normal meeting point for the merchants and financiers of the two regions, at the fairs of the Champagne. By the end of the thirteenth century this connection by land was coming to be superseded by the sea-route through the Strait of Gibraltar, which was regularly employed by Genoese galleys from the year 1298. The main industry feeding long-distance commerce was cloth manufacture, situated principally in the Low Countries and Tuscany, and dyes concerned with this industry, as well as alum (a sulphate of potassium and aluminium used as mordant to cleanse fabric and help the dye to bond), were other commodities of major importance. Other textiles (silk and cotton) and metals (in particular iron) were wares of note, and the foodstuff that ranked second only to grain was wine, much of which was shipped along a route lying outside those mentioned above, the export area being Gascony (with Bordeaux as its principal port) and the main recipient England, which was French in tastes but too northerly to have many vineyards of its own.[1]

These major trade-routes are those most easily investigated and they have tended to monopolise the attention of historians. It by no means follows that they occupied the energies of more men at the time or even that more money was made from them. There was a great deal of local trade by land, centred on fairs and markets dealing mainly in agrarian produce and craftsmen's wares, and trade by sea also was not confined to the great convoys of the Levant and Baltic. Local 'coasters' plied down and across the Adriatic, based on Venice and elsewhere, and the Tyrrhenian ports—less conveniently placed for oriental commerce—did much of their trade between Provence in the north (with an occasional extension into Catalonia) and Sicily in the south. Thus Portovenere, a small place between Genoa and Pisa, traded entirely within the Tyrrhenian, principally with Sardinia, sometimes with Corsica, Pisa, or the small grain-ports north-west of Rome, more rarely farther south to Naples and Sicily. Sicily, an exporter of grain and other food,[2] was a considerable importer of textiles, and around the middle of the thirteenth century an enterprising Pisan, Lazarius Talliapanis, made a fortune largely through the export of hats to Sicily. Lazarius was farmer, industrialist and merchant; the hats were manufactured by him from the wool of his own sheep. Men such as he were famous for their business acumen and the speed with which they became rich, and the *Novellino*, a thirteenth-century collection of stories, preserves one far-fetched tale from the many that must have been told about the methods of these parvenu millionaires:

A merchant was voyaging with hats. They got wet and he laid them out to dry. A lot of monkeys appeared and each one put a hat on its head and ran up into the trees. This seemed a grievous matter to the merchant. He went back and bought breeches and thus he regained the caps[3] and made a good profit on them.[4]

A man like Lazarius Talliapanis, however, would not normally have travelled with his own wares. It is characteristic of a great change in commercial and financial methods that by the thirteenth century the 'merchant' himself was normally no longer peripatetic; he left the conduct of his affairs in distant markets to representatives. These might be factors employed solely by him, like the men paid by the Tuscan and other bankers to staff their various branches; the Bardi of Florence alone had 25 branches in the early fourteenth century, and such employment was a common way to start on a business career. On the other hand it was also habitual for a merchant to make use on a commission basis of the services of an agent residing abroad who was also acting for a number of other men or firms. The introduction of bills of exchange facilitated the technique of the 'sedentary' financier by obviating the need to move currency in specie. This development, as well as the increasing use of the sea-route through the Strait of Gibraltar, played a part in the rapid decline of the Champagne fairs after about 1320. Earlier, these fairs had been primarily occasions for dealing in commodities; now that their business was mainly financial and that the Italian bankers had branches established at Bruges it was no longer necessary to have a meeting place halfway between Europe's two zones of maritime trade.

THE PROBLEMS OF THE FOURTEENTH CENTURY

During the first half of the fourteenth century economic expansion was checked in many parts of Europe. The process of extending the area of land under cultivation may have come to an end in France and southern England as early as the middle of the previous century, but clear signs that a depression had set in in some sectors of the European economy date from about a quarter of the way through the fourteenth. In accordance with the theories of Malthus, the population of certain parts of Europe had so outstripped food supplies that a series of poor harvests brought about appalling famines. These were followed by epidemics of bubonic plague (of which the most serious was the 'Black Death' of 1348–9, of which more below), and recovery was further hampered by widespread warfare associated with the dislocation of economic life and with heavy taxation. Evidence, particularly concerning the movements of Swiss glaciers, suggests that there may also have been climatic deterioration, with colder weather.

The story should perhaps begin with the famines of 1315–17, which affected all northern and eastern Europe and parts of the Mediterranean region. Three successive bad harvests (1314–16) led to a disastrous shortage of grain in Scandinavia, the Slav countries, Germany, Flanders, France, Britain and northern Italy. The price of grain in England rose from five shillings a quarter in 1313 to 26s. 8d. in 1315 and at Antwerp the price tripled in a period of seven months. Animals became scarce and sober chroniclers record appalling stories of cannibalism. The situation was most acute in the Low Countries, where the numerous towns were normally dependent on grain imports from northern France and eastern Germany. During the summer of 1316 more than 3,000 people—about one-tenth of the population—died in Ypres alone.

All the chronicles of the time record the same story, and two may serve as exemplars:

In the year of Our Lord 1316 famine, hunger and great mortality prevailed. A *modius* of spelt was then worth 4 of the large, old shillings (*solidi*) or more.[5]

So great was the universal pestilence that many corpses of poor people who had died of hunger or plague were to be found lying in the roadways, and a number of towns had general pits dug in the cemeteries and fixed the dues to be paid for burial of such corpses in these.[6]

Plague and famine were allies, for fields and flocks were neglected in time of epidemic,[7] while undernourishment may have weakened resistance to disease.[8] Both were in turn assisted by war, which is the hardest to assess of all these factors. There seems to be a consensus of opinion that warfare was more continuous in Europe during the fourteenth century and the first half of the fifteenth than during the preceding two centuries, and that the wars of this period were more ruinous in their economic consequences. But these things cannot be measured and such an impression is not susceptible of demonstration; the evidence is so piecemeal that it must be presented merely as an impression. Campaigns were normally brief and confined to the summer months, but companies of unemployed mercenaries lived off the land even in peace. The most usual way to harm an enemy was to damage his crops—no misconception about the past is so fatuous as the belief that military action against civilians is an invention of the twentieth century—so that even a short campaign might mean a year of starvation. The Hundred Years War certainly involved larger bodies of troops and wrought enormous destruction in parts of France between the early fourteenth century and the mid-fifteenth, and the belief that the quantity or volume of warfare increased at this time is based mainly on that prolonged struggle and on the Hussite and other wars in eastern Europe. The appalling condition of France during the Hundred Years War and the despair to which it gave rise can be seen in this extract from the diary of a Frenchman for 1422:

Item, the King of England was at this time before Meaux and he spent the New Year and Epiphany there. His men were all over the region of Brie and were pillaging everywhere, so that on account of them and the others [Burgundians] it was impossible to till the soil or sow anywhere. Many were the complaints to these lords [the English], but they only mocked and laughed, and their men behaved worse even than before. Most of the peasants abandoned work in the fields and were in despair. They left their wives and children and said to one another: 'What shall we do? let us give everything over into the hands of the devil, for it cannot matter what becomes of us. To do our worst will profit us as much as doing our best. The Saracens would treat us better than the Christians do, and we may as well do our worst, they cannot do more than kill us or make us prisoners. Thanks to the false government of traitors we have had to leave our wives and children and flee to the woods like lost animals. This has not lasted one year or two; the tragic dance began as long as fourteen or fifteen years ago'.[9]

Moving from the north-east of France to the south-west, to consider the effects of the hostilities in the area around Bordeaux, one finds that much land was abandoned at times, particularly in the zone of the French-Gascon frontier, whence many peasants fled to the towns. There were severe epidemics in Gascony in 1348, 1362, 1410–11 and 1414. The first of these was preceded by campaigning and famine, and by 1349–50 wine exports from Bordeaux had diminished to a quarter of the average figures for the first third of the century. A recovery followed in the 1350s and 1360s, but 1373 was another year of famine and 1374–9 a period of intensive fighting, during which much land was deserted. When the war ended in the mid-fifteenth century the frontier zone of the Entre-deux-Mers (the wine-growing region between the Garonne and the Dordogne) had declined greatly, and here in particular many houses and fields were abandoned. Most of the seignorial families of the area had suffered through the loss of land by confiscation (even a general willingness to change sides did not make it possible to be always on the side that was winning), and through the need to alienate land to supporters and to diminish the services of the hard-pressed peasantry. Confiscations meant frequent changes of ownership, and a general loss of confidence must also have served to discourage enterprising cultivation. Even after the end of the war recovery was slow, and Gascony was treated by the French monarchs as a defeated colony rather than as a recovered province. In that region the greatest change wrought by the war was the decline of the nobility, but this was probably untypical of France as a whole. There may have been some truth in the view of the Englishman Sir John Fortescue (expressed in 1465) that the French peasants lived in misery 'in the most fertile kingdom in the world'.

The case of Gascony shows clearly how a single wave of devastation was not by itself the cause of serious economic decline: permanent setback followed only when a prolonged series of campaigns and military occupations deprived an area of the means or even the will to restore ravaged fields and to rebuild. Probably the loss of a year's harvest, appalling though its effects may have been, was less lasting in its consequences than loss of livestock. Medieval soldiers, living admittedly off the land, were likely to take every opportunity of supplementing their 'rations' off the hoof. It would have been difficult to keep armies adequately fed by any other means, and a meal could be made off local livestock far more quickly and easily than off local stores of grain. Enormous damage must have been done in this way, and the soldiery, it may be supposed, gave no thought to the problem of the priority of chicken or egg, but made away with the chickens at the expense of their own future consumption of eggs. The countryside had to bear the burden not only of soldiers employed in campaigns against the forces of an enemy, but also of temporarily unemployed bands of 'adventurers' organised to exploit the possibilities of a parasitic way of life. The consequences of such a situation may be studied in Froissart's account of the activities of Aymerigot Marcel in the Rouergue in south-western France in 1391, during the period midway between Edward III's and Henry V's French campaigns:

Aymerigot Marcel was much displeased with himself for having sold and delivered the strong castle of Aloise [Alleuse] . . . for he found his former authority much decreased thereby, and perceived well that he was the less feared. For all the time that he kept it he was doubted and feared, and honoured by all men of war of his party, and had kept a great establishment always in the castle of Aloise: the contributions of countries that he held in subjection was well worth twenty thousand florins yearly. When he remembered all this he was sorrowful; he thought he would not diminish his treasure; he was wont daily to search for new pillages, whereby he increased his profit, and then he saw that all was closed from him. Then he said and imagined that to pillage and to rob, all things considered, was a good life, and so repented him of his good doing. On a time he said to his old companions: Sirs, there is no sport nor glory in this world among men of war, but in such a life as we have formerly passed; what a joy was it to us when we rode forth at adventure and sometimes found by the way a rich prior or merchant, or a troop of muleteers of Montpellier, Narbonne, Limoges, Fougans [Fanjeaux], Béziers, Carcassonne, or Toulouse, laden with cloth . . . of Brussels . . . or leather-ware, coming from the fairs . . . or laden with spicery from Bruges, Damascus, or Alexandria; whatsoever we met was all ours, or else ransomed at our pleasures; we daily got new money, and the villeins of Auvergne and Limousin constantly provided and brought to our castle wheat-meal, ready-baked bread, oats for our horses, and litter, good wines, beef and fat sheep, poultry and wild fowl: we were always supplied like kings; when we rode forth all the country trembled with fear; all was ours, going or coming . . .

Then Aymerigot viewed the place, to see if it were worth fortifying: and on an accurate survey of the situation, and the defence that might be made there, it pleased him much. Then they took it and fortified it by degrees, before they committed any depredations on the country: and when they had made the place strong enough to withstand a siege or assault, and that they were well horsed, and provided with everything necessary for their defence, then they began to ride abroad in the country, and took prisoners and ransomed them, and pro-vided their stronghold with flesh, meal, wax, wine, salt, iron, steel and every other requisite; there came nothing amiss to them, without it having been too heavy or too hot. The country all about, and the people, expecting to have been at peace by reason of the truce between the two kings and their realms, they began then to be alarmed; for these robbers and pillagers took them in their houses, and wherever they found them, even labouring in the fields: and they called themselves adventurers.[10]

Heavy taxation was another consequence of war, but this would not necessarily fall on the areas in which fighting was taking place—indeed the sufferings of these regions and the need of governments to retain their loyalty meant that the burden was likely to be heavier elsewhere. Nor is it easy to judge who was ultimately the poorer through heavier taxation. England's expenditure on the Hundred Years War was met to a considerable extent by heavy customs duties on the export of wool. In the early phases of the war the burden of these seems to have fallen mainly on the English graziers, but after the middle of the fourteenth century the price of English wool on the Continent rose considerably, and it appears that Flanders was by then paying much of the cost of England's war.

Another factor, depopulation, is more complex. Whatever the sequence of causes may have been, it is clear that the period of demographic growth had come to an end in many parts of Europe before the Black Death of 1348–9 and that this disaster merely accentuated an existing trend. Conservative estimates suggest that in the worst-hit areas the population was diminished by more than a quarter by this epidemic, and that later outbreaks prevented the achievement of a significant recovery during the next twenty years.[11] Gascony's deserted villages had their counterparts in many other places at this time. It is never possible to be certain to what extent this phenomenon represents migration to other places—in particular to towns—for we have extremely few figures for population at this time, but it is surely significant that in the fourteenth century, for the first time since the later Carolingian period, there is much evidence of rural depopulation, coming from widely separated areas in Scandinavia, Germany, France, England and Italy.[12] The figures in Table 1,[13] relating to some of the few towns for which we possess estimates, suggest that depopulation in the countryside cannot be explained in terms of migration into the cities.

Table 1. Population figures for some late medieval towns

	1335	1350	1367	1379	1385	1385–6	1398	1405	1468	1500
Freiburg im Breisgau	—	—	—	—	9,000	—	—	—	—	6,000
Zürich	—	12,000	—	—	—	—	—	—	5,000	—
Montpellier	—	—	22,500	5,000	—	—	—	—	—	—
Toulouse	30,000	—	—	—	—	26,000	24,000	22,500	—	—

	1326	1338	1351	1359	1380	1462	1477	1482	1497	1526
Perpignan	—	—	—	18,000	—	—	—	—	15,500	—
Modena	22,000	—	—	—	—	—	—	8,000–9,000	—	—
Florence	—	110,000	45,000–50,000	—	70,000	—	—	—	—	70,000
Barcelona	—	—	—	38,500	—	38,000	20,000	—	29,000	—
Lerida	—	—	—	6,000	—	—	—	—	3,500	—
Tarragona	—	—	—	5,500	—	—	—	—	4,500	—

Sources: R. Lopez, 'The Trade of Medieval Europe: the South', in *Cambridge Economic History of Europe*, vol. II (2nd edition, Cambridge, 1987), p. 386; P. Wolff, *Commerces et Marchands de Toulouse: vers 1350–vers 1550* (Paris, 1954), pp. 68–86. For Barcelona *see* J. Vicens Vives, ed., *Historia Social y Economica de España y America*, vol. II (2nd edition, Barcelona, 1972), pp. 51–2: these figures are affected by the revolution of 1477 and by the growth of Valencia from a city of *c.*40,000 in 1418 to *c.*75,000 in 1483.

In some well-documented sectors the nature of Europe's economic setbacks is at least clearer than their causes, though even here the evidence is often ambiguous. After the famines of 1314–16 the price of grain fell in France and England to a level considerably lower than that prevailing in the early years of the century. The fall in prices was in turn reflected in manorial profits, and the value of land naturally fell in sympathy.[14] Such a decline is recorded in various parts of England and France and Scandinavia and was probably widespread, as grain farming for the market was increasingly abandoned. Again it must be emphasised that collective contraction did not necessarily imply individual impoverishment. Men who might otherwise have worked for wages took up farms, and the consequent relative shortage of wage labour caused a marked rise in wages. In agriculture, as in industry, there is no evidence of a fall in output per head, and it was on this that standards of living depended.

Cloth production in Flanders is another instance of fourteenth-century decline. This major industry was largely dependent on exports of raw wool from England, which fell fairly steeply in the second half of the century, as may be seen from the following:

1350–60:	(average in sacks per annum) over 30,000
1380–90:	c.20,000 sacks p.a.
after 1393:	never above 20,000 sacks p.a.[15]

Exports of English cloth rose considerably during the same period (the average for the 1390s being roughly treble that for the years 1360–80) and it seems clear that the main explanation of the decline of the Flemish industry lies in the growth of cloth-making in England. It is not, however, possible to tell whether there was an overall decline in English wool production, as there are no reliable figures for the amount of English cloth consumed in the home market during the fifteenth century. The Flemish had to compete with the Italians for English wool, and suffered from English fiscal policy, which alternated embargoes on export to north-western Europe with high export duties. English exploitation during the French wars of Flemish dependence on English wool involved rapid fluctuations for the textile industry and, in particular, periods of disastrous unemployment. The Flemish craftsmen reacted to this by attempting to wrest political and industrial control from their employers —the anti-French revolution of 1302 has been mentioned above[16] and there were further serious risings in 1324–8 and 1379–82—and this unrest must in turn have affected unfavourably Flemish ability to compete with Italy and England. The textile industry of the Low Countries is typical, however, in that it presents no simple picture of all-round regression: the decline of the Walloon towns, such as Arras, Lille and Douai, coincided with the rise in Brabant of Brussels, Louvain and Malines, and increased exports from Bruges to both north-eastern Europe and the Mediterranean may have offset the decline of the French market.

Italy also experienced some marked industrial and commercial setbacks during the fourteenth century. Florence suffered severely in the 1340s through the bankruptcy of the Bardi and Peruzzi, involving the fall of almost all the other important Florentine banking companies, and in the ensuing period the Italians were to lose the near-monopoly in European finance that had been gained by their commercial advantages and precocious techniques. Local bankers appeared and sapped the position of the Italians in many parts of Europe, particularly in economically advanced areas such as Flanders, England and France. Textile manufacture had been of importance in thirteenth-century Florence, but it was not till the 1320s that the city gained a lead among the Italian producers of high-quality cloth.[17] They also made use of new techniques of mixing wool with other textiles, learnt from the more advanced industry of Flanders. From the same period the Florentines were assisted, both as purchasers of wool in England and elsewhere, and as cloth exporters throughout the Mediterranean world, by the serious decline of the Flemish draperies. Though the first half of the fifteenth century saw a decline in the output of Florentine cloth, a considerable recovery was achieved later in that century and maintained into the sixteenth.

PLAGUE AND POPULAR MOVEMENTS

Our survey of the period would not be complete without a further word about the plague which first reached Italy from the east in the winter of 1347/8 and in the next two years continued its devastating path northwards across western Europe. In a famous passage in his *Decameron*, the contemporary Florentine writer Giovanni Boccaccio described its impact as follows:

Now, because I would wander no further in every particularity concerning the miseries happening in our city, I tell you that, extremities running on in such manner as you have heard, little less spare was made in the villages round about; wherein (setting aside enclosed castles which were like cities in little) poor labourers and husbandmen, with their whole families, died most miserably in out-houses, yea in the open fields also; without any assistance of physic or help of servants; and likewise in the highways, or their ploughed lands, by day or night indifferently, yet not as men, but like brute beasts. By means whereof they became lazy and slothful in their daily endeavours, even like to our citizens; not minding or meddling with their wonted affairs, but as a waiting for death every hour, employed all their pains, not in caring any way for themselves, their cattle, or gathering the fruit of the earth, or any of their accustomed labours; but rather wasted and consumed even such as were for their instant sustenance. Whereupon it so fell out that their oxen, asses, sheep and goats, the swine, poultry, yea their very dogs, the truest and faithfullest servant to men, being beaten and banished from their houses, went wildly wandering abroad the fields, where the corn still grew on the ground without gathering or being so much as reaped or cut. Many of the foresaid beasts (as endued with reason) after they had pastured themselves in the day time would return full fed at night home to their houses, without any government of herdsmen or any other.

To leave the country now and return to the city, what more can I say? Such was the cruelty of heaven, and perhaps in part that of men too, that between March and July, owing to the illness itself and the abandonment or neglect of many of the sick by those who were afraid to approach them, it is thought that certainly more than a hundred thousand people died within the walls of Florence. Before the plague many might not have known that the population of the city amounted to so many.

How many fair palaces! How many goodly houses! How many noble habitations, filled before with families or lords and ladies, were then to be seen empty, without any one there dwelling, without even a silly servant? How many kindreds worthy of memory! How many great inheritances! And what plenty of riches; were left without any true successors? How many good men! How many worthy women! How many valiant and comely young men, whom not even Galen, Hippocrates, and Aesculapius (if they were living) could have reputed any way unhealthful; were seen to dine at morning with their parents, friends and familiar confederates, and went to sup in another world with their predecessors?[18]

The Black Death, as it became known only much later, has had a recurrent fascination for historians of many persuasions and specialisms. For many, this dramatic and highly visible human catastrophe in the middle of the 'century of transition' epitomised the many other ill winds of the period, and perhaps even brought them to a head in what can retrospectively be seen as a sort of 'defining moment'. This currently fashionable but imprecise phrase has much to recommend it here, as it avoids the implications of causation that have bedevilled the historiography. In many respects historians are less clear about the Black Death than they thought they were thirty years ago. For example, even the nature of the disease itself has been called into question.[19] What is striking, however, is the persistence of the belief that, because it was such a dramatic event, it must have had a profound effect.[20] This has become an *idée fixe*, perhaps a consequence of the profession's vested interest in identifying clear causes of change. Historians have found in the Black Death seductively simple explanations for developments as diverse (and contradictory) as the economic crisis under discussion here, the explosion of popular unrest, the undermining of authority and the birth of a lay spirit, the transformation of religious devotion, the revival of higher education, the acceleration of technological innovation, the 'modernisation' of medicine and the birth of scientific thought, the increase of state intervention and control and the growth of national sentiment, the formation of the nuclear family and even the rise of the individual. When most of these theories are examined, they tend to collapse under their own crudity; yet, seemingly undeterred, historians have moved rapidly from the discrediting of one theory to set up the next. It is one thing to identify immediate consequences of the demographic impact of plague.[21] It is another matter to evaluate the impact this had on economic balance, as opposed to volume, even in the short term. The immediate impact on prices, wages, labour shortages and perhaps land tenure can be traced, though many of these changes appear to have been superficial and transient, and were far from homogeneous across Europe. It is more problematic still to assess the role of plague in subsequent and long-term developments. 'From the matrix of forces shaping the late medieval world, it is impossible to factor out those attributable to plague alone.'[22] Economic historians have by and large retreated from the proposition that the Black Death had a profound identifiable effect.[23] Indeed, it might be more profitable to start, not from the assumption that the plague must have had a profound impact on so many aspects of human behaviour, but from the fundamental resilience of the species, demographically, economically and culturally.

To the extent that long-term effects can be ascertained, they are more credible in areas that are less capable of being measured. It seems perfectly sensible to posit a link between the plague and the changes in attitudes to death that many have observed in the late fourteenth and particularly in the fifteenth century. Again, though, this is qualitatively very different from the immediate, dramatic and traumatic reactions of Boccaccio and many others in 1348. Most of all, such attitudes are formed through the realisation, that dawned with the second wave of plague (1361–3) and grew after subsequent epidemics, that this was not an isolated 'bolt from the blue' but something that could occur again and again.[24] Analogous observations could be made about the economic and social aspects of the plague. Its arrival was sensational but also in many respects superficial. The most lasting economic impact of plague was perhaps its addition to an already long list of problems that generated an enduring sensation of insecurity.

This age of economic setback and change was also an age of popular unrest, of revolts by the 'blue-nails' in Flanders and the *Ciompi* at Florence, of *Jacqueries* in France and the English Peasants' Revolt. There is clearly a connection between the developments described above and these democratic movements. The weakening of manorialism and consequent demands for the end of villeinage lie behind the English revolt of 1381, while the French risings were directly connected with that country's sufferings during the Hundred Years War. As for the movements of the clothmakers, these had led to violence in Flanders and some parts of Italy well before the close of the thirteenth century. Serious troubles at Siena (in 1329 and 1342) preceded the first momentous impact of democratic feeling on Florentine politics, the achievement of a temporary tyranny with popular backing by the Frenchman Walter of Brienne (1342–3). Brienne gave the textile workers, or *sottoposti*, some share in the city's government, but after his fall they lost this position. The Black Death led to an improvement in their pay, thanks to the drastic decline in Florence's population, but an expensive war against the papacy in the mid-1370s aggravated fiscal grievances and discontent with the narrow oligarchic regime of the Albizzi. This was a time of popular movements in a number of central Italian towns: the *popolo minuto* came to power at Lucca in 1369, at Siena in 1371, at Perugia in 1372. The programme of the Florentine *Ciompi* in 1378 shows clearly enough what the *sottoposti* wanted. These men included owners of small workshops, petty entrepreneurs as well as wage labourers. Though 'disenfranchised' in the sense that guild membership was denied them, it would not be correct to think of them as proletarian workers in the factories of a highly capitalised industry. The Florentine rising of 1378 involved 'patricians' who were aiming at a widening of the ruling group, as well as small entrepreneurs and workers in the textile industry, and their programme was certainly not an extreme one framed to forward the interests of the proletariat. For a time the *Ciompi* gained control in Florence and new guilds were formed of dyers, shirtmakers and the undifferentiated *popolo minuto*, but the regime faced very serious financial problems, and its fiscal measures, which included unpopular forced loans, helped to bring about its disintegration and fall. In the ensuing period the position of the Florentine clothworkers worsened considerably.

Florence was not exceptional in refusing guild status within the textile industry. There were indeed a very few Italian towns, such as Venice and Verona, which permitted the formation by *sottoposti* of *scholae* or confraternities. Normally, however, any institution of this sort was regarded with fear and horror by the authorities. There is a parallel between the struggle of these workers for the right to organise against town merchant oligarchies and the conflict of the English trade unionists with a national trading oligarchy between the First and Third Reform Acts.

NEW DEVELOPMENTS

The greatest difficulty in attempting to decide whether or not to accept the thesis of a century-long slump is that a story of success can be set beside almost every story of decline, and that there is inadequate information to measure the two against each other. Just as Brabant gained at the expense of southern Flanders, so Antwerp came forward to take the place of Bruges, now affected by silting as well as by the decline of its industrial hinterland. When the German Hanse lost its near-monopoly of Baltic and Scandinavian trade the beneficiaries from the later fourteenth century were the English, and in the mid-fifteenth the Dutch, both of whom exploited skilfully the conflicting interests of the Hanseatic ports. New towns were also coming to the fore in south Germany and Switzerland as industrial and commercial centres, notably Augsburg and Nuremberg, and Pisa's sharp decline was connected with the rise of Marseilles and of Barcelona, which in turn lost ground to Valencia. In England Lincoln and some other wool-marketing towns fell on hard times, but Hull advanced as a cloth port, and new industrial areas emerged in East Anglia, in Gloucestershire, Wiltshire and Somerset, and at Coventry.

In Italy Lucca and the south lost their quasi-monopoly of silk manufacture at the same time as the Florentines were yielding their unrivalled primacy in cloth: Milan, Venice, Genoa, Bologna and Florence all had considerable silk industries by the end of the fourteenth century. In Florence itself new banking houses came to the fore after the collapse of the Bardi and Peruzzi, among them that of the city's future rulers. In 1373 Foligno de' Medici wrote pessimistically of his family's decline from its former greatness: 'so great were we once', he records, 'that there used to be a saying "You are like one of the Medici"; every man feared us'. In Foligno's day the many branches of the family were concerned principally with agriculture, but Vieri di Cambio (who retired in 1392) was a wealthy financier. He it was who trained Giovanni di Bicci, who founded the fortunes of the Medici Bank in Rome in the 1390s. Early in the following century the bank had its headquarters at Florence, with branches at Rome and Venice, and by the time of Giovanni's death (1429), thanks originally to their friendship with John XXIII, the Medici were the papacy's principal financiers. Until the mid-1470s they normally retained this position, which brought them immense prestige and gained for them the task of organising the housing and financing of the many ecclesiastical councils of the period. Under Cosimo, Giovanni's son, there were also permanent branches at Pisa, Milan, Geneva, Avignon, Bruges and London. This international structure was of immense assistance to the Medici when they became, after 1434, *de facto* rulers of Florence; they were able, for example, to obtain rapid news from all parts of Europe through the firm's own channels. Nor were Cosimo's commercial activities confined to banking; he was involved in the textile industry and he dealt in commodities, particularly alum. In the diversity of his interests Cosimo was a characteristic figure. Specialisation in economic activity dates from a much later period, and at this time it was normal throughout Europe for such men with predominantly urban backgrounds and interests to enjoy at the same time considerable agrarian incomes. Only in Italy, however, were these sources of revenue supplemented by interest derived from holdings in government stock.

The history of the Medici is an important part of Europe's political and cultural history, and we therefore return to it in a later chapter.[25] A glance at the careers of two fifteenth-century Venetian businessmen may illustrate better how enterprising people could flourish in an age when the total volume of Mediterranean commerce may well have been contracting. Andrea Barbarigo (1399–1449) came of a family which had connections and estates in Crete, but his recorded dealings relate mainly to trade in other parts. At one stage he is to be found buying cotton through an agent at Acre, but he quarrelled with this agent and then suffered through a dispute with the sultan which interrupted trade with Syria. After this affair Andrea turned to Valencia, whence he shipped Spanish wool and olive oil to Venice. Shortly after this he was doing business in England, where he sold gold thread and pepper and bought cloth. At the same time as he suffered by the sultan's embargo he experienced similar difficulties in southern Germany, where political troubles led to the closing of the main land-route between Venice and the north of Europe. These problems and Andrea's readiness to switch his interests rapidly from one foreign market to another illustrate both the advantages of Venice's position as a centrally placed 'universal middleman' and the knowledge and judgement required to make correct decisions involving distant countries in times of great economic and political fluctuations. It was the very essence of the methods of such men that they were not specialists and that they could shift their interests constantly while retaining the support of the system of galley convoys organised and controlled by the Venetian state.

Barbarigo's descendants withdrew from mercantile affairs and lived mainly on the proceeds of the estates bought by Andrea on the Italian mainland near Treviso and Verona. It was a time of constant warfare between Venice and Milan, and they suffered heavily when these lands underwent enemy occupation. Nor was the later fifteenth century a good period for holders of government bonds, and this was another source of worry to the Barbarigo, though some of the family benefited from salaries earned as state officials in Venetian territories overseas and in the expanding empire on the *Terraferma*.

The activities of Barbarigo's contemporary Guglielmo Querini (*c.*1400–68) show a close resemblance to those of Andrea. Like Barbarigo, he himself played a sedentary role in Venice, at least from his adult years. He, too, did much business in Italy, some of it almost locally. When he ranged farther afield, it was sometimes to Spain, sometimes to England and Flanders, sometimes to Greece and the Levant. The pattern is not entirely the same, however: Querini traded at Geneva and in southern France, and his most original line was the sale of Sicilian grain at Tunis and on the island of Djerba. These men benefited immensely from their city's Mediterranean empire[26] and a policy which insisted that all export from that empire must be to Venice and on Venetian vessels. The city probably drew about one-fifth of its own grain supplies from its dominions, as well as wine, honey, cheese and oil, cotton, alum, iron, wax and timber. Most of its imported grain came from non-Venetian territory such as southern Russia and Thrace, and through the Levant came silk, spices, dyes and slaves. Thus the main role of the ports of Venice's empire, even of Candia, was to serve as entrepôts, and bases and points of call for the galleys. They constituted a defensive system for the maritime routes thanks to which these versatile Venetian patricians were able to retain their prosperity.

In the final analysis the problem of Europe's wealth in the later Middle Ages should be judged in relation to agriculture, for this was the pursuit of by far the biggest element in the population. Yet here we return to the difficulty that changes in organisation are far more certain than changes in wealth. It is clear that in most parts of Europe there was a decline in seignorial authority, that lords tended increasingly to become *rentiers*, particularly when labour shortage, after the Black Death, made domain farming dearer. In western Germany this change was accentuated by unsettled political conditions, for lords frequently alienated their lands to pay for soldiers or else lost them to bailiffs. However the *rentier* solution characteristic of England, France and western Germany was not universal, and in the corn-exporting areas of east Germany and Prussia the knightly class was building up its domains and turning to farming in earnest, while many of the peasantry suffered eviction. Here heavier dues and services were imposed on men who lacked the alternative of flight to the towns. If the period was marked by an increased proportion of payments in money, there was certainly no abandonment of payments in kind, indeed one form of this, share-cropping (French *métayage*, Italian *mezzadria*), was becoming more common. When payments were made in money, much depended on the frequency with which dues could be increased in times of rising prices; the impoverished nobles were those who could not change rents often enough. Their decline must have been made more conspicuous by the ascent of the most assiduous and fortunate among the peasantry.

CONCLUSION

Some historians have seen the fourteenth century as a time of economic tragedy, the fifteenth as one of recovery. For instance the cultivation of rice and of mulberries was first undertaken at that time on a large scale in the Po valley, where a great deal of land was reclaimed. Between 1439 and 1475 55 miles of canals, with 25 locks, were constructed in the plain south of Milan, and this is but one of many striking instances of fifteenth-century technological progress, to be found in both southern and northern Europe, in shipbuilding, in the use of water power and in the mining and processing of metals. Nor were the successful financiers of fifteenth-century Italy all Florentines: apart from the Genoese, one may mention the Sienese Chigi and the Borromeo, Tuscans turned Milanese. Yet the peninsula had owed its economic primacy above all to its position in the Mediterranean, and it is unlikely that in the fifteenth century the total volume of sea trade in the Mediterranean increased. That this was the situation is strongly suggested by the failure of the Pisan galleys. Florence acquired this long-coveted port in 1406 and soon attempted to organise convoys of galleys there after the Venetian model. The scheme took twenty years to get under way, it was immensely subsidised, and yet by 1480 it had been virtually abandoned.

It seems unlikely that the fifteenth century marked a general recovery in the north. The misery of Prussia in this period has already been noted, as has the general decline of the German Hanse in the face of the challenge of the English and Dutch. In England land values continued to fall and the enclosure of land for sheep farming brought a new form of unrest. One northern area to achieve a very marked advance in maritime trade during the last quarter of the century was Normandy, and this development is significant both because it signals France's recovery after the Hundred Years War and because Normandy soon began to look to the west, to Spain and the New World, rather than to the north. Another area of economic advance is the network of south German towns.

Are we, then, to accept the view that the economy of Europe in the later Middle Ages underwent a century of crisis? The evidence discussed above suggests that it should rather be considered as passing through a series of setbacks and change—troubles that may indeed also have marked the ill-documented earlier centuries of expansion. For all the calamities of famine and disease, there was never a breakdown in the fabric of commercial interdependence. That local specialisation could make new advances in this age is shown by the gains of the salt trade of the Bay of Bourgneuf, on the Atlantic coast of France, which now achieved the leading position in the English market, at the expense of native English salt. Historical research has illuminated great changes in Europe's economy in the first half of the fourteenth century. Further investigation may make it possible to decide whether or not this was followed by a long period of general economic contraction.

FURTHER READING

Introduction

From its development as a sub-discipline early in the twentieth century, economic history was a much more international enterprise than other branches of history. Consequently much more has been published in English, the lingua franca. The bibliography below gives an introductory selection only; in many of the areas covered, much more is available.

The most useful single-volume introduction is N. J. G. Pounds, *An Economic History of Medieval Europe* (2nd edition, London, 1994); *see also The Fontana Economic History of Europe*, vol. 1, *The Middle Ages*, ed. Carlo M. Cipolla (London, 1972), and the trio of textbooks published by Cambridge University Press in the 1970s: R. S. Lopez, *The Commercial Revolution of the Middle Ages, 950–1350* (Cambridge, 1976); Harry A. Miskimin, *The Economy of Early Renaissance Europe, 1300–1460* (Cambridge, 1975); Harry A. Miskimin, *The Economy of Later Renaissance Europe, 1460–1600* (Cambridge, 1977). The most authoritative reference work is the *Cambridge Economic History*, vol. 1, *The Agrarian Life of the Middle Ages*, ed. M. M. Postan (2nd edition, Cambridge, 1971), vol. 2, *Trade and Industry in the Middle Ages*, eds M. M. Postan and Edward Miller (2nd edition, Cambridge, 1987), and vol. 3, *Economic Organization and Policies in the Middle Ages*, eds M. M. Postan, E. E. Rich and Edward Miller (Cambridge, 1963). Broad surveys which cover the late medieval period include Carlo M. Cipolla, *Before the Industrial Revolution. European Society and Economy, 1000–1700* (London, 1976); Douglass C. North and Robert Paul Thomas, *The Rise of the Western World. A New Economic History* (Cambridge, 1973). For histories of individual regions or countries, *see* G. Luzzatto, *An Economic History of Italy* (tr. London, 1961); Stephan R. Epstein, *An Island for Itself. Economic Development and Social*

Change in Late Medieval Sicily (Cambridge, 1992); R. E. Cameron, ed., *Essays in French Economic History* (Homewood, Ill., 1970), Part 1; J. A. van Houtte, *An Economic History of the Low Countries 800–1800* (London, 1977); Bob Scribner, ed., *Germany. A New Social and Economic History*, vol. 1: *1450–1630* (London, New York, etc., 1996).

The European economy to the end of the thirteenth century

On the 'internal' expansion of Europe *see especially Cambridge Economic History*, vol. I, ch. VII; on land reclamation, some of the essays in Salvatore Ciriacono, ed., *Land Drainage and Reclamation* (Aldershot, 1998), and T. F. Glick, *Irrigation and Society in Medieval Valencia* (Cambridge, Mass., 1970); on the growth of towns, David Nicholas, *The Growth of the Medieval City. From Late Antiquity to the Early Fourteenth Century* (London and New York, 1997), especially Parts 2 and 3; on the phenomenon of new towns, M. Beresford, *New Towns of the Middle Ages. Town Plantation in England, Wales and Gascony* (London, 1967). Finally a thorough survey of Europe at the opening of the fourteenth century is Norman J. G. Pounds, *An Historical Geography of Europe, 450BC–AD1330* (Cambridge, 1973), ch. 6, pp. 313–433.

Trade has been extensively covered. E. S. Hunt and James Murray, *A History of Business in Medieval Europe, 1200–1550* (Cambridge, 1999) is an admirable synthesis; *see also* R. S. Lopez, *The Commercial Revolution of the Middle Ages, 950–1350* (Cambridge, 1976), chs 3–5. A lively overview is J. Favier, *Gold and Spices. The Rise of Commerce in the Middle Ages* (New York and London, 1998). On northern European trade and traders in particular, M. M. Postan, *Medieval Trade and Finance* (Cambridge, 1973), E. M. Carus-Wilson, *Medieval Merchant Venturers* (2nd edition, London, 1967) and J. Day, *The Medieval Market Economy* (Oxford, 1987) are useful collections of essays; *see also* J. A. Van Houtte, 'The rise and decline of the market of Bruges', *Economic History Review*, 19 (1966), pp. 29–47. On Italian trade, The *Journal of Medieval History*, 20 (1994) is a special issue on 'The Genoese and their rivals in medieval Mediterranean commerce'; on merchants and bankers, R. De Roover, *Money, Banking and Credit in Medieval Bruges. Italian Merchant-Bankers, Lombards, and Money-Changers. A Study in the Origins of Banking* (Cambridge, Mass., 1948) and some of the essays in R. De Roover, *Business, Banking and Economic Thought in Late Medieval and Early Modern Europe* (Chicago, Ill., 1974); J. R. Strayer, 'Italian bankers and Philip the Fair', in *Economy, Society, and Government in Medieval Italy: Essays in Honor of Robert L. Reynolds*, eds D. Herlihy, R. S. Lopez and V. Slessarev (Kent, Oh., 1969), pp. 113–21, repr. in J. R. Strayer, *Medieval Statecraft and the Perspectives of History* (Princeton, N.J., 1971), pp. 239–47; R. W. Kaeuper, *Bankers to the Crown: The Riccardi of Lucca and Edward I* (Princeton, N.J., 1973), and R. W. Kaeuper, 'The Frescobaldi and the English crown', *Studies in Medieval and Renaissance History*, 10 (1973), pp. 41–95; E. S. Hunt, *The Medieval Super-Companies. A Study of the Peruzzi Company of Florence* (Cambridge, 1994); and E. S. Hunt, 'A new look at the dealings of the Bardi and Peruzzi with Edward III', *Journal of Economic History*, 50 (1990), pp. 149–62. English trade with the Continent has attracted a lot of attention: T. H. Lloyd, *The English Wool Trade in the Middle Ages* (Cambridge, 1977); J. H. A. Munro, *Wool, Cloth and Gold. The Struggle for Bullion in Anglo-Burgundian Trade, 1340–1478* (Toronto, 1972), and J. H. A. Munro, *Textiles, Towns and Trade. Essays in the Economic History of Late Medieval England and the Low Countries* (Aldershot, 1994); W. R. Childs, *Anglo-Castilian Trade in the Later Middle Ages* (Manchester, 1978), and W. R. Childs, 'Anglo-Portuguese trade in the fifteenth century', *Transactions of the Royal Historical Society*, 6th series, 2 (1992), pp. 195–219. A useful collection of sources in translation is Robert S. Lopez and Irving W. Raymond, *Medieval Trade in the Mediterranean World. Illustrative Documents* (repr. Columbia, N.Y., 1990).

The problems of the fourteenth century

The issue of climatic change has been debated in works such as E. Le Roy Ladurie, *Times of Feast, Times of Famine: a History of Climate Since the Year 1000* (tr. London, 1972). On the famines, a recent overview is W. C. Jordan, *The Great Famine. Northern Europe in the Early Fourteenth Century* (Princeton, N.J., 1996); *see also* H. S. Lucas, 'The Great European Famine of 1315, 1316 & 1317', *Speculum*, 5 (1930), pp. 341–77, repr. in *Essays in Economic History*, vol. II, ed. E. M. Carus-Wilson (London, 1962), pp. 49–72; I. Kershaw, 'The Great Famine and Agrarian Crisis in England, 1315–1322', *Past & Present*, 59 (1973), pp. 3–50. B. M. S. Campbell, ed., *Before the Black Death: Studies in the 'Crisis' of the Early Fourteenth Century* (Manchester, 1991) is a collection of essays; *see in particular* J. H. Munro, 'Industrial transformation in the north-west European textile trades, *c.*1290–*c.*1340: economic progress or economic crisis?', pp. 110–48.

On the economic problems in France, Guy Bois, *The Crisis of Feudalism. Economy and Society in Eastern Normandy, c.1300–1550* (tr. Cambridge and Paris, 1984); but *see also* the survey of James L. Goldsmith, 'The crisis of the late middle ages; the case of France', *French History*, 9 (1995), pp. 417–450, which argues against the view that there was a downturn before the Black Death. On the effects of taxation in France, *see under* Chapter 7 below. On the vicissitudes of the textile industry, David Nicholas, *Medieval Flanders* (London, 1992), ch. 10, and David Nicholas, *The Metamorphosis of a Medieval City: Ghent in the Age of the Arteveldes, 1302–1390* (Lincoln, Neb., 1987), ch. 6; A. R. Bridbury, *Medieval English Clothmaking. An Economic Survey* (London, 1982); and N. B. Harte and K. G. Ponting, eds, *Cloth and Clothing in Medieval Europe. Essays in Memory of Professor E. M. Carus-Wilson* (London, 1983). On Italian industrial and commercial problems, *see* some of the works on banking cited above; and Maureen Fennell Mazzaoui, *The Italian Cotton Industry in the Later Middle Ages, 1100–1600* (Cambridge, 1981).

Plague and popular movements

The most accessible and approachable introduction to the Black Death is a volume not by a medieval specialist: Philip Ziegler, *The Black Death* (2nd edition, London, 1998, with an additional essay by Colin Platt, 'The Black Death in recent historiography', pp. 322–9; the original text is also available in an illustrated edition, Stroud, 1997). Good collections of sources are Rosemary Horrox, tr. and ed., *The Black Death* (Manchester, 1994)—now accessible on the internet at Medieval Sources*online* (www.medievalsources.co.uk)—and Johannes Nohl, *The Black Death. A Chronicle of the Plague Compiled from Contemporary Sources* (repr. London, 1971); the latter is written in narrative form, unfortunately presented as anecdotal information without bibliographical references. David Herlihy, *The Black Death and the Transformation of the West* (Cambridge, Mass., 1997) is a posthumous publication of three lectures, not revised by the author. The best feature of this work is Samuel Cohn's introduction and excellent references which are a good way into the literature. W. M. Bowsky, *The Black Death: a Turning Point in History?* (Huntington, N.Y., 1979) contains a selection of readings from many historians; D. Williman, ed., *The Black Death. The Impact of the Fourteenth-Century Plague* (Binghamton, N.Y., 1982) contains several original essays including J. M. W. Bean, 'The Black Death. The crisis and its social and economic consequences' (pp. 23–33). R. S. Gottfried, *The Black Death. Nature and Human Disaster in Medieval Europe* (New York and London, 1983) has been discredited. Various documents on the Black Death are available on the internet site 'Plague and Public Health in Renaissance Europe', at http://jefferson.village.virginia.edu/osheim/intro.html.

On the Black Death in comparison with other epidemics: J. F. D. Shrewsbury, *The History of Bubonic Plague in the British Isles* (London, 1970); W. H. McNeill, *Plagues and Peoples* (repr. London, 1977); Sheldon Watts, *Epidemics and History. Disease, Power and Imperialism* (New

Haven, Conn., 1997), ch. 1. G. Twigg, *The Black Death. A Biological Appraisal* (London, 1984) questioned whether the epidemic was in fact plague; his work is finally beginning to get the attention it deserves. Analyses of the effects of the Black Death in specific countries or regions include A. R. Bridbury, 'The Black Death', *Economic History Review*, 26 (1973), pp. 557–92; his view that the Black Death did little damage to the English economy is amplified in his *Economic Growth. England in the Later Middle Ages* (2nd edition, Brighton, 1973); R. Emery, 'The Black Death in Perpignan', *Speculum*, 42 (1967), pp. 611–23; J. Henneman, 'The Black Death and Royal Taxation in France', *Speculum*, 43 (1968), pp. 405–28; W. P. Blockmans, 'The social and economic effects of the plague in the Low Countries', *Revue belge de philologie et d'histoire*, 58 (1980), pp. 833–63; Michael W. Dols, *The Black Death in the Middle East* (Princeton, N.J., 1977). Finally Samuel K. Cohn, Jr., *The Cult of Remembrance and the Black Death. Six Renaissance Cities in Central Italy* (Baltimore, Md., 1992) analyses changes in attitudes to death.

The history of popular unrest in the late Middle Ages, and in the fourteenth century in particular, has attracted much fragmented interest. Attempts at synthesis are rarer, not least because of the scale of the subject. Two overviews are M. Mollat and P. Wolff, *Popular Revolutions of the Later Middle Ages* (London, 1973), and G. Fourquin, *Anatomy of Popular Rebellion in the Middle Ages* (Amsterdam, 1978). On unrest in individual countries or regions, *see*: R. H. Hilton, *Bond Men Made Free: Medieval Peasant Movements and the English Rising of 1381* (London, 1973); R. B. Dobson, ed., *The Peasants' Revolt of 1381* (2nd edition London, 1983), a collection of documents in translation; D. M. Bessen, 'The Jacquerie: class war or co-opted rebellion?', *Journal of Medieval History*, 11 (1985), pp. 43–59; W. TeBrake, *A Plague of Insurrection: Popular Politics and Peasant Revolts in Flanders, 1323–1328* (Philadelphia, Pa., 1994), a reminder that such disturbances were by no means an invention of post-Black Death society; on Italy, G. A. Brucker, 'The Ciompi revolution', in *Florentine Studies. Politics and Society in Renaissance Florence*, ed. N. Rubinstein (London, 1968), pp. 314–56, and Samuel K. Cohn, Jr., *The Laboring Classes in Renaissance Florence* (New York and London, 1980) (controversial); on Spain, P. Wolff, 'The 1391 pogrom in Spain: social crisis or not?', *Past and Present*, 50 (1971), pp. 4–18, and A. Mackay, 'Popular movements and pogroms in fifteenth-century Castile', *Past and Present*, 55 (1972), pp. 33–67, and 'Faction and civil strife in late medieval Castilian towns', *Bulletin of the John Rylands Library*, 70 (1990), pp. 119–31; on Germany, P. Blickle, 'Peasant revolts in the German Empire in the late Middle Ages', *Social History*, 4 (1979), pp. 223–39; Rhiman A. Rotz, 'Urban uprisings in Germany: revolutionary or reformist? The case of Brunswick, 1374', *Viator*, 4 (1973), pp. 207–23, and Rhiman A. Rotz, 'Investigating urban uprisings with examples from Hanseatic towns', in *Order and Innovation in the Middle Ages*, eds W. C. Jordan, B. McNab and T. F. Ruiz (Princeton, N.J., 1976), pp. 215–33. On the social context of unrest, Michel Mollat, *The Poor in the Middle Ages. An Essay in Social History* (tr. New Haven, Conn., 1986).

New developments

On the changes in trading patterns and the fortunes of towns and industries generally, see *Cambridge Economic History*, vol. 3, the textbooks by Miskimin mentioned at the beginning of this section, and works on trade listed above. *See also*: S. R. Epstein, 'Regional fairs, institutional innovation and economic growth in late medieval Europe', *Economic History Review*, 47 (1994), pp. 459–82; D. Nicholas, 'Economic reorientation and social change in fourteenth-century Flanders', *Past and Present*, 70 (1976), pp. 3–29; H. Van der Wee, *The Growth of the Antwerp Market and the European Economy in the Fourteenth to the Sixteenth Centuries*, 3 vols (The Hague, 1963); R. Davis, 'The rise of Antwerp and its English connection 1406–1510', in

Trade, Government and Economy in Pre-Industrial England: Essays Presented to F. J. Fisher, eds D. C. Coleman and A. H. John (London, 1976), pp. 2–20. On Italian bankers and merchants, R. De Roover, *The Rise and Decline of the Medici Bank, 1397–1494* (New York, 1966); F. C. Lane, *Andrea Barbarigo, Merchant of Venice 1418–1449* (repr. New York, 1967); and the well-known and readable I. Origo, *The Merchant of Prato* (London, 1957, many reprints). Finally J. E. Dotson, tr. and ed., *Merchant Culture in Fourteenth-Century Venice: the Zibaldone da Canal* (Binghamton, N.Y., 1994) is a merchant's miscellany rich in information on business and culture.

Late medieval agriculture has been the subject of equally intense study. The best compendium is *Cambridge Economic History*, vol. I. General studies include, most recently, Werner Rösener, *Peasants in the Middle Ages* (tr. Oxford, 1992); also B. H. Slicher van Bath, *The Agrarian History of Western Europe* (tr. London, 1963); W. Abel, *Agricultural Fluctuations in Europe from the Thirteenth to the Twentieth Centuries* (tr. London, 1980), Part I; G. Duby, *Rural Economy and Country Life in the Medieval West* (tr. London and Columbia, S.C., 1968); and R. Fossier, *Peasant Life in the Medieval West* (tr. Oxford, 1988). Collections of essays include Del Sweeney, ed., *Agriculture in the Middle Ages. Technology, Practice, and Representation* (Philadelphia, Pa., 1995); M. M. Postan, *Essays on Medieval Agriculture and General Problems of the Medieval Economy* (Cambridge, 1973); and M. Bloch, *Land and Work in Medieval Europe* (collected essays, tr. London, 1967). A recent comparative survey is Tom Scott, ed., *The Peasantries of Europe: from the Fourteenth to the Eighteenth Centuries* (London, 1998). On the social significance of developments in agriculture, a survey of a key debate is T. Aston and C. H. E. Phillips, eds, *The Brenner Debate. Agrarian Class Structure and Economic Development in Pre-industrial Europe* (Cambridge, 1985). On individual areas, M. Bloch, *French Rural History: an Essay on its Basic Characteristics* (published posthumously 1952; tr. London, 1966, paperback 1978) is a classic work. German agriculture is surveyed by Werner Rösener, 'The agrarian economy, 1300–1600', in *Germany. A New Social and Economic History*, vol. 1: *1450–1630*, ed. Bob Scribner (London, New York, etc., 1996), pp. 63–83; *see also* a stimulating series of articles by M. Toch: 'Lords and peasants: a reappraisal of medieval economic relationships', *Journal of European Economic History*, 15 (1986), pp. 163–82; 'Ethics, emotion and self-interest: rural Bavaria in the later Middle Ages', *Journal of Medieval History*, 17 (1991), pp. 135–47; and 'Agricultural progress and agricultural technology in medieval Germany: an alternative model', in *Technology and Resource Use in Medieval Europe. Cathedrals, Mills and Mines*, eds E. B. Smith and M. Wolfe (Aldershot, 1997), pp. 158–69. Finally R. C. Hoffman, *Land, Liberties and Lordship in a Later Medieval Countryside. Agrarian Structures and Change in the Duchy of Wrocław* (Philadelphia, Pa., 1989) illustrates the rather different development of a part of central eastern Europe.

NOTES

1. The chronicler Froissart reports the men of Bordeaux as saying: 'We have more commerce with the English than French, in wool, wines, and cloth, and they are more naturally inclined to us'. *Chronicle*, Book IV, ch. 117; trans. T. Johnes (London, 1939 edition), vol. II, p. 703.

2. *See above*, p. 39.

3. Presumably the monkeys put on the breeches, which made them less agile.

4. *Il Novellino*, n. XCVIII; adapted from the translation of E. Storer (London and New York, 1925), pp. 206–7. On Talliapanis, *see* David Herlihy, *Pisa in the Early Renaissance. A Study of Urban Growth* (New Haven, Conn., 1958, repr. Port Washington, N.Y., 1973), pp. 177–9.

5. *Die Chronik der Grafen von der Mark, von Levold von Northof*, ed. F. Zschaeck, *Monumenta Germaniae Historica, Scriptores rerum germanicarum*, n.s., 6 (Berlin, 1929), p. 67.

6. *Gesta Trevirorum*, eds J. H. Wyttenbach and M. F. J. Müller, 2 vols (Trier, 1836–9), II, p. 235. A *modius* as a measure of capacity was equivalent to about 8.6 litres.

7. *See below*, pp. 99–100.

8. The link between plague and famine has been questioned by M. Livi-Bacci, *Population and Nutrition: an Essay in European Demographic History* (Cambridge, 1991).

9. *Journal d'un Bourgeois de Paris sous Charles VI et Charles VII*, ed., A. Mary (Paris 1929), pp. 154–5. This work has been translated by Janet Shirley, *A Parisian Journal, 1405–1449* (Oxford, 1961): the passage *above* is on p. 167.

10. From Froissart's *Chronicle*, Book IV, ch. 35: based on Lord Berners' translation (London, 1814–16 edition), vol. IV, pp. 129–31.

11. For the Black Death *see also* pp. 99–101 and 297–8 *below*.

12. One example from central Italy will serve as an instance. A tax register of 1426 concerning the 'district' (the area within 100 miles radius of the city) of Rome records 105 villages as 'destroyed and uninhabited'. Giuseppe Pardi, 'La popolazione del distretto di Roma sui primordi del Quattrocento', *Archivio della Società Romana di Storia Patria*, 49 (1926), pp. 331–54.

13. *Below*, p. 97.

14. For English corn prices *see Cambridge Economic History of Europe*, vol. II (2nd edition, Cambridge, 1987), p. 255. For English examples of declining manorial profits and land values, E. Miller, *The Abbey and Bishopric of Ely: the Social History of an Ecclesiastical Estate from the Tenth Century to the Early Fourteenth Century* (Cambridge, 1951), p. 105, and F. G. Davenport, *The Development of a Norfolk Manor, 1086–1565* (Cambridge, 1906), pp. 55 and 78–9.

15. *Cambridge Economic History of Europe*, vol. II (2nd edition, cit.), p. 241: cf. E. M. Carus-Wilson, *Medieval Merchant Venturers: Collected Studies* (repr. London, 1967), p. xviii and graph.

16. *See* pp. 49–50.

17. The statistics concerning cloth production given by the chronicler Giovanni Villani (Bk. XI, ch. 94) probably greatly exaggerate total production (and also tend to over-emphasise the degree of Florence's dependence on English wool). G. Villani, *Cronica*, ed. F. Gherardi Dragomanni (Florence, 1845), p. 325: in new edition as *Nova cronica*, ed. Giuseppe Porta (Parma, 1990–1) as Book XII, ch. 94 (vol. 3, p. 199). For careful criticism of them *see* H. Hoshino, *L'arte della lana in Firenze nel basso medio evo. Il commercio della lana e il mercato dei panni fiorentini nei sec. XIII–XV* (Florence, 1980), esp. pp. 194–203.

18. G. Boccaccio, *Decameron*, Introduction to the First Day; partly taken from an anonymous translation of 1620. Modern translations include that of G. H. McWilliam (Harmondsworth, 1972).

19. G. Twigg, *The Black Death. A Biological Appraisal* (London, 1984), and David Herlihy, *The Black Death and the Transformation of the West* (Cambridge, Mass., 1997), ch. 1.

20. Beside the title under which Herlihy's lectures were published, see also the title of George Huppert's *After the Black Death. A Social History of Early Modern Europe* (2nd edition, Bloomington and Indianapolis, In., 1998).

21. Touched on *above*, p. 96 and *below*, pp. 297–8.

22. Herlihy, *The Black Death and the Transformation of the West*, cit., p. 19.

23. In a conference representing a major survey of historical thinking on this subject in the early 1980s, a number of the contributors came to the conclusion that there was no 'general crisis' in the later Middle Ages; and there was general agreement that the impact of the Black Death has been greatly exaggerated. F. Seibt and W. Eberhard, eds, *Europa 1400: die Krise des Spätmittelalters* (Stuttgart, 1984).

24. The argument of—amongst others—Samuel K. Cohn, Jr., *The Cult of Remembrance and the Black Death. Six Renaissance Cities in Central Italy* (Baltimore, Md., 1992), who demonstrates that the change in attitudes observable in wills is much more marked after 1363.
25. Chapter 10, esp. pp. 192–6.
26. *See above*, Chapter 2, esp. pp. 35–7.

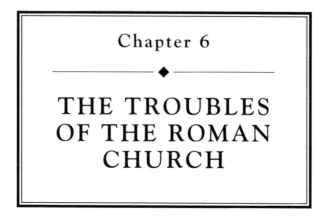

Chapter 6

◆

THE TROUBLES OF THE ROMAN CHURCH

THE AVIGNON PAPACY

The aftermath of the conflict between Philip IV and Boniface VIII, and the latter's death a few weeks after the attack on him at Anagni, took the papacy into uncharted waters, yet there was nothing inevitable about the subsequent turn of events. The domicile of the papacy beyond the Alps between 1305 and 1377 marks no sudden break. Since the 1240s residence in Rome had been exceptional and the sojourns at Lyons of Innocent IV (1244–51) and Gregory X (1273–5) had shown that the pope could continue his functions outside Italy. The Avignon papacy does, however, mark with topographical incontrovertibility the triumph in the Curia of the French element which had become so powerful since the election of Urban IV and the triumph of Charles of Anjou.[1]

On 5 June 1305 the conclave gathered at Perugia elected as pope Bertrand de Got, a Gascon who was archbishop of Bordeaux. Four days later the cardinals wrote to Bertrand in terms which reveal their realisation that Clement V might wish to reside outside Italy.

There can be no doubt [they argued] that the see of Peter will be a stronger residence for you and that you will shine there more resplendently, and will be able to live more tranquilly in his territory. If you are farther from kings, princes and their subjects, they will think more highly of you and you will gain greater devotion and obedience from them, for everyone is stronger in his own house than elsewhere and finds sweeter repose in his own church. The part of the sword that cuts deepest is that which is furthest from the hilt: what is seen often is despised and what is easily reached and attained is little esteemed. Come, then, and we pray you again that your benignity should yield on this point to our prayers.

Clement was reminded that Clement IV and Gregory X, the last two popes to be elected when outside Italy, had rapidly made their way to the peninsula, and yet again asked 'to prepare yourself for the journey to the apostolic see'.[2]

The terms of the cardinals' letter show their implicit acceptance of the fact that relations with Philip IV of France would take precedence on the new pope's agenda.

The main reason for this was the unresolved conflict which had reached its climax at Anagni in 1303; the cardinals of 1305 were sharply divided between protagonists of Boniface and Philip, and the latter still awaited a reply to his request for the calling of a general council which should pronounce on Boniface's deeds and his doctrines. But there were also important secondary considerations. The French Crown, by far the greatest power in the west since the decline of imperial strength, was involved in an endless dispute with the English monarchy over the English king's tenure of Gascony. The quarrel implicated Flanders and Scotland as well, and as long as it lasted there could be no hope of mounting a successful crusade, although the urgent need for such an expedition had been recognised ever since the fall in 1291 of Acre, the last Christian stronghold in Palestine. Moreover Clement V, as a Gascon subject of Edward I of England, was in a promising position to effect a pacification between the English and French kingdoms. There were also negative reasons, as the cardinals well realised, which might persuade Clement to remain for the time being north of the Alps. South of Rome a war raged between the dispossessed Colonna and the Caetani, the family of Boniface VIII, for domination in the Campagna. In the rest of the Papal State central authority since the 'Outrage of Anagni' had been even weaker than usual. Thus Rome seemed out of the question as a base and Umbria, where the conclave had met, scarcely more inviting.

Finally it was pressure from the French king that prompted in Clement the fateful decision to postpone his journey to Italy. Threatening a posthumous trial of Pope Boniface, Philip insisted on the transfer of the coronation from Vienne (in imperial territory) to Lyons. The king's further intention, of inducing Clement to settle in France, was frustrated, but Clement remained beyond the Alps, postponing his departure till he should have made a thorough recovery from his chronic state of ill health. After four years of peregrinations he settled at Avignon, which was an Angevin enclave in the papal territory of the Comtat-Venaissin; the halt was intended to be a temporary one and much of the machinery of administration, such as the archive, still remained in Italy. In 1310, however, Clement took the step of appointing a vicar to represent him at Rome. The city on the Rhône was never thought of as a permanent base, and schemes for a move to Italy were more or less constantly under discussion. In 1332 detailed plans were worked out for a move to Bologna, though it is very doubtful whether this independent and turbulent city, adjoining the still more turbulent Romagna, was really a practicable compromise between Avignon and Rome. The decision of Benedict XII (1334–42) to build a palace at Avignon marks a belated acceptance of the fact that the 'captivity' was something more than a passing visit. Not until 1367 was a return made to Rome, by Urban V, and this proved abortive, for three years later Urban deserted the city once more. It was left to his successor, Gregory XI, to make an Italian journey, in 1377, from which there was no return. As well as the predilections of the preponderant French element in the Curia, inertia, the old age and illness of successive popes, and the tempting strength of Avignon (which in 1348 was purchased from the Angevins) all played a part in this prolonged sojourn of seven decades.

Urban V met so much opposition from the cardinals when he began preparations for his move to Rome that he is said to have had to overcome it by threatening to 'swamp' the objectors by a wholesale creation of new cardinals. This episode, if true, is characteristic of the strife within the college between French and Italians, which led to a curious war of pamphlets regarding the respective merits of Avignon and Rome. While Frenchmen depicted the horrors of a malarial Eternal City, decayed and desolate, and vaunted the delectable vintages of the Languedoc, Italians deplored the abandonment of the Church's time-honoured home. Periodically embassies came from the widowed city to implore the popes to return and rescue it from obscurity and economic collapse. As early as 1308 Italians wrote of the papal *captivatio*, and a succession of patriotic writers, of whom Dante was one of the first and Petrarch the most fervent, denounced 'carnal' Avignon as the new Babylon. In a conversation with Clement VI Petrarch told the pope that it was unfortunate that he did not know Italy as well as he knew France and England, and later he addressed two long and eloquent hortatory letters on the subject to Urban V.

Your see is wherever you wish [says the poet], but the only one that is your own true see of old, for the benefit of the faithful and the advantage of all, is Rome, that place grateful to God, venerable to men, the desire of the pious, the terror (when you are there) of rebels. That is the see fitted to reform the world, to rule over monarchs, the see that till now has known no equal and, unless I am misled by the wishes of my heart, will know none in future . . . All other cities have their spouses, subject to you but ruling over their own churches; Rome alone has none but you. Though you are the superior in all others, in the city of Rome you are the only Pontiff, the only spouse.[3]

In Italy all the Avignon popes were regarded with extreme suspicion as patriotic Frenchmen. It was even rumoured that when the cardinals elected Clement V they thought him already dead, while a story was current in Germany that a papal official had accepted a bribe of 16,000 florins to hand over the whole of Benedict XII's treasury to Philip VI.[4] This view would not have been that of the French kings. Clement V, as we have seen, was a Gascon, and none of his Avignonese successors was born north of the Loire: John XXII was from Quercy, Benedict XII from Foix, Clement VI, Innocent VI and Gregory XI from the Limousin, Urban V from the southern part of the Massif Central. No fewer than 113 of the 134 cardinals created by these popes came from greater France, but their court was Languedocian, rather than 'French'. Their native tongue differed from the Languedoïl as much as it did from Italian and, with the partial exception of Clement V, they were certainly not puppets of the French kings. Clement V was terrified by the threats of a posthumous trial for Pope Boniface into a humiliating participation in the shameful Affair of the Templars. Clement VI, once keeper of the seal to Philip VI, made enormous loans to his former master; between November 1345 and February 1350 these totalled no less than 592,000 florins and 5,000 crowns. Apart from this, there is no reason to accept the contemporary Italian view of the Avignon popes. The belief of most of them that they could hope, as true neutrals, to end the Hundred Years War, was genuine, and—unlike the Italians—they rightly saw in this war the greatest political problem of western Europe. Moreover their principal preoccupation—war for their Italian lands, relations with the Empire, the crusade, ecclesiastical taxation, theological controversies—were their own, not those imposed by an external authority.

In a way their very independence of the French was a source of weakness to these popes in their Italian policy, which was the most pressing of their temporal concerns. The Neapolitan kingdom was neutralised, first by war with Aragonese Sicily, then by economic decline and political collapse. The empire was weak and was in any case still inconceivable as an ally. Finally, France became so involved in the war with England that the popes found themselves facing alone the intolerable double burden of anarchy in the Papal State combined with the enmity of the immensely powerful Visconti of Milan. When these men are blamed for their failure to return to Italy, it must be remembered that a series of crises faced them in the peninsula with a relentless recurrence just when circumstances might seem to have made the transfer possible. In 1310–13 it was Henry VII's Italian expedition, then the growth of Ghibellinism in Tuscany and the challenge of the Visconti, followed by Lewis of Bavaria's invasion of 1327–30, which in turn gave way to the quasi-imperialist schemes of John of Bohemia. After a brief interlude, the Visconti war was renewed in 1341, coalescing later with the long-standing revolt in Romagna. Only in the 1350s did it become possible for the popes to think in terms of a positive Italian policy and, later, Albornoz' achievements were immediately followed (in 1370) by renewed opposition from the Visconti, with support from within the Papal State, and by the Florentine 'War of the Eight Saints' (1375).

Throughout this time the papacy had lost almost all authority in central Italy, which was in a condition of endemic lawlessness. Revenues from papal territory fluctuated enormously in these circumstances, but they can rarely have attained half of the sum nominally due, and expenditure—particularly on mercenary armies, now predominantly German—was enormous. Warfare in Italy was the financial haemorrhage that necessitated the notorious fiscality of these popes, whose total revenues were often insufficient to meet this source of expenditure alone. The most interesting of a number of governmental experiments tried at this time in papal Italy was the vicariate, an institution taken over from imperial practice and first employed by the papacy in 1329. The essence of the vicariate was a bargain with local rulers, who now gained official recognition of their jurisdiction in exchange for certain obligations —mainly financial—which they by no means always fulfilled. There was much to be said for this realistic semi-abdication of rule, less for appointments to offices in the Papal State which alternated between French relatives or protégés and local men who were often feudal magnates. Nepotism did enormous harm, particularly in Clement V's time, when central Italy became a rich pasture for the d'Albret and other Gascon relatives, but it was not always an improvement when such a man was succeeded by an Orsini or a Farnese, while Italians who lacked any local standing might secure no obedience at all. The common belief was that prelates were less likely to be rapacious than laymen, but Tavernini, an ecclesiastic who was treasurer of the Tuscan Patrimony for many years, was so unpopular as to provoke riots and left a fortune of over 35,000 *lire*.

The first papal envoy to attempt a general appeasement in Italy was Cardinal Bertrand du Poujet, legate from 1320 to 1334, who conducted a strenuous struggle against the Visconti, but failed to gain reliable allies and was finally overcome by the strength of local tyrants. Cardinal Gil Albornoz, a Spanish archbishop who was appointed legate in Italy in 1353, accomplished with weak resources and little backing the immense task of pacifying the papal lands. In achieving this Albornoz made cunning use of the disunity of his antagonists. His method was to work his way up gradually from the south, tackling first his opponents in the neighbourhood of Rome and eventually reaching Romagna, where in 1356–9 he fought a successful war against the Ordelaffi thanks to the alliance of the Malatesta. After this he was able to fight the Visconti, first at Bologna and then farther north. Albornoz was a statesman who knew when to compromise with his adversaries and a legist who never failed to make very precise terms when he compromised. He was in command of considerable mercenary armies at times, but neither Innocent VI nor Urban V gave him wholehearted support; he was removed from his legation in 1357 and, though he returned the following year, he was finally superseded in 1364 by a legate who was prepared to come to terms with the Visconti. Albornoz has been regarded as 'the founder of the Papal State', mainly on account of the impressive code of laws which he promulgated in 1357, but his achievement was bound to disintegrate. By 1375 Florence was at war with the papacy and stimulated revolts in many major towns of the Papal State by calling them to arms against the French 'whose ambition has left no honour to the Italians and whose insatiable avarice has left nothing unravaged'. The papacy was only able to return after a new series of notable concessions to its subjects, and whatever remained of Albornoz' work was undone in the anarchy of the next thirty years.

Although the Avignon popes were compelled to keep Italy in the forefront of their minds, they were not condemned to purely negative political and military activity. All were active in seeking to put an end to the Anglo-French conflict, and attempted to forward the crusade. All but John XXII were notable theologians, and Benedict XII, Urban V and Gregory XI were men of outstanding piety. Even John XXII, who quarrelled with the Franciscans and drove the extreme 'Spirituals' into the imperialist camp, entered the realm of theology and condemned the doctrine of the absolute poverty of the disciples, a move welcomed by the Dominicans, some of whom are said to have repainted their crucifixes to depict Christ taking money with one hand. Assisted by the conveniently central position of Avignon, which was admirably situated to facilitate communications with France, Flanders and England to the north and the empire and Spain to the east and west, as well as with Italy, the popes greatly strengthened the financial and general administration of the papacy. The chancery was reorganised in seven offices and the judicature in four tribunals. Under the pressure of Italian requirements, the fiscal organisation was also systematised, special regional collectors being regularly used, while a new source of revenue, the annates, was exploited with great success. The Church throughout western Europe was brought more strictly under central control than hitherto, not only in financial matters, but in appointments to benefices: the number of cases in which 'provision' was automatically made by the papacy was now greatly increased.

The greatest organisational change of the time, however, probably lay in the increasingly independent status of the college of cardinals. The role played by these dignitaries and their households in the Curia's notorious luxury was visible enough:

Clement VI spent 8,000 florins a year on clothes for his household, and the cardinals, one of whom entertained Clement at a banquet of 27 courses, were not to be outdone in conspicuous consumption. One cardinal required 10 stables for his horses, another 51 houses for his entourage, and a characteristic expression of their outlook is perhaps to be found in the will of Cardinal Pierre Bertrand (d. 1361), who bequeathed 100 florins to the papal see, the same amount to his cook and only a little less to his falconer, baker and butler respectively.[5] Many of these prelates were papal relatives, a fact which in part explains their determination not to be outshone by their fortunate and benevolent patron; John XXII appointed nine new cardinals from Quercy, of whom five were related to him, while 12 of Clement VI's 15 appointments were Limousins. But the new element in the situation, growing invisibly but inexorably, was the tendency of each cardinal to conduct his own policy and intrigues as a semi-independent magnate and—more important still—for the college to regard itself as a separate institution, having its own interests, which were not necessarily those of the pope. This development was encouraged by the independent financial organisation of the college, which had its own chamber and after 1289 was supposed to receive half of various forms of papal revenue. In the conclave following the death of Clement VI the cardinals' oligarchic proclivities came into the open for the first time. Almost all the cardinals present then swore an agreement to bind the future pope: no major decisions concerning papal territory or papal taxation should be taken without the consent of at least two-thirds of the cardinals, and the same majority would be required for the appointment of a cardinal, while the members of the college were never to number more than 20. Innocent VI, who was elected in this conclave, was among those who had added a 'saving clause' when consenting to this 'compromise', and he proceeded to annul it on the grounds that it contravened canon law, though some of its terms in fact constituted no radical departure from existing law. The events of 1352, though they had no immediate effect, reveal the cardinals very clearly in their baronial role. The wider results of this development in church government were to appear a quarter of a century later, on the death of Clement's nephew, Gregory XI.

Gregory, the man who brought the 'exile' to an end, disembarked from his galley opposite S. Paolo, outside the gate of Rome, on 17 January 1377. He lived in the city for a year, though even this residence was broken by more than five months of residence at Anagni. On 27 March 1378 he died. Ten days later the conclave gathered in the Vatican, while, in the *piazza* outside, the throng vociferously expressed its wishes: 'Romano lo volemo, o al manco italiano' ('We want him to be a Roman, or at least an Italian'). The 16 cardinals present, of whom seven were Limousins and another four Frenchmen, proceeded to an election on the very first morning of the conclave. The man on whom their choice fell was a Neapolitan, Bartholomew Prignano, a pious and learned legist who had served as papal vice-chancellor under Gregory XI and was now archbishop of Bari. The noisy behaviour of the crowd was later used to justify the claim that undue pressure prejudiced this election and made it invalid, but it seems certain that Urban VI was elected 'in fear, but not through fear'. The original choice was rapidly confirmed, to banish any possible doubts, by 13 of the electors, the six cardinals who had remained at Avignon hastened to convey their homage and in the early days of the pontificate no cardinal refused Urban his recognition.

The new pope's position, however, was not an easy one. A man of violent and tactless temperament suddenly found himself raised above the cardinals whom he had long served in a subordinate capacity. To make matters more embarrassing, Urban was a man of relatively humble birth who lacked the social polish of the prelates whose gracious living he saw as an insult to his schemes for radical reform. St Catherine of Sweden (daughter of St Bridget) was later to explain the sequence of events by attributing them to 'the rigorous justice of the pope, who was not gentle to the cardinals when they made requests, but attempted to reform them'.[6] One of these cardinals put it in similar terms: 'if the archbishop of Bari had been a prudent man and had had *savoir-faire* he could have been a pope ... but he was in no way fitted to govern the Church', and the future Benedict XIII complained that 'he turned everything upside-down through his violence'.[7] Urban's forthrightness and refusal to compromise showed from the very start. He ordered the cardinals to have only one course at each meal and to abandon the time-honoured custom of accepting retaining 'pensions' from lay rulers. He had flaming rows with the Cardinal of Limoges, whom he once attempted to strike in a consistorial assembly.[8] In another consistory he launched a tirade against the Cardinal of Amiens, whom he accused of accepting bribes from both the French and English when engaged in peace negotiations with these two nations.[9] He rejected angrily suggestions that the Curia should return to Avignon, and when a 'whispering campaign' began to hint at the possibility of his resignation he said to the bishop of Todi: 'They don't know me well: if they pointed a thousand swords at my neck, I still wouldn't give up.'[10] All this serves as a reminder that the 'constitutional' issue between pope and cardinals was no mere paper dispute over legal principles; it was the outcome of a series of bitterly felt grievances against autocratic monarchs.

THE GREAT SCHISM AND THE CONCILIAR MOVEMENT

Intrigues against Urban had started soon after his election. The messenger despatched to announce the election to Charles V of France cast some doubt on his legal position, and a second embassy to Charles mysteriously failed to arrive. An ambassador to Castile and Portugal played an equally ambiguous role. The bishop of Amiens, Jean de la Grange, who was a former councillor of Charles V, had not been present at the conclave. It was he who set out to organise Urban's downfall. By June (1378) he had gathered at Anagni a number of cardinals who proceeded to declare Urban's election invalid and to demand his deposition. These cardinals then moved to Fondi, south of the Neapolitan frontier, where they received a letter from Charles of France encouraging them to go ahead with their plans. Two days later, on 20 September, they met in conclave and 13 cardinals gave their vote to Robert of Geneva, bishop of Cambrai. Robert, who was the brother of the count of Geneva and whose mother was a cousin of Charles V, took the title of Clement VII, thereby expressing his allegiance to the Avignonese tradition.

Since France was already committed to the cardinals' party, it was natural that Charles (with the support of the University of Paris) should proceed to recognise Clement. The summer after his election (1379) Clement was forced by rioting to leave Naples, and in June he took up residence at Avignon. Thus, less than three years after Gregory XI's departure, Avignon was again opposed to Rome, but this time with a rival pontiff, not merely as a rival tendency within the Curia. Each side created its own cardinals—Urban 29 in September 1378, Clement nine that December—and soon the schism was reflected throughout western Christendom. There was a general topographical pattern in this division, with most of France, the Iberian kingdoms, and Scotland declaring for Clement, while the other areas were predominantly Urbanist, yet each pope had his supporters in 'enemy' territory, and the rift came to bisect even the smaller subdivisions of the Church. Religious orders sometimes had two rival masters, sees two bishops and chapters, monastic houses two abbots. Adversity made Urban no more tractable, and the cardinals adhering to him were driven to consult a lawyer about what action could be taken against a pope who showed himself incapable of governing the Church. Learning of this, he had the five prelates involved imprisoned and tortured, and only one of them survived.

When Urban died in 1389 he was at once succeeded by a less unpopular Italian, Boniface IX. Clement lived on till 1394, and it is possible that his death failed only by a few hours to put an end to the schism: the slowness of medieval communications may for once have played a decisive part in events, since Charles VI of France wrote to the cardinals on hearing of Clement's death, ordering them not to proceed to an election—but the conclave had opened just before the king's letter arrived, and the cardinals agreed that it should be read only after an election had been made. Clement's successor, the Aragonese Peter de Luna (Benedict XIII), was an elderly cardinal who had played the leading part in winning over the Iberian kingdoms to the Clementist cause. Like his fellow participants in the conclave Benedict had agreed to renounce the papacy if this was necessary to end the schism, but he proved to be a character of extraordinary tenacity. France was the power most likely to be able to bring the contest to an end by exerting pressure on both popes, but French action was at the mercy of ducal intrigues for Charles VI was frequently insane. Only in 1398 did the French Church withdraw its obedience from Benedict XIII, and this action proved indecisive and was abandoned after five years. Boniface IX was succeeded by two more Italian popes, Innocent VII (in 1404) and Gregory XII (in 1406). The participants in the conclave which elected Gregory XII made an agreement that, if elected, they would resign on condition that Benedict XIII did the same. After almost thirty years some progress was at last made towards healing the schism, but it was a slow and painful business. A meeting between the two sides was planned, but Gregory failed to appear. The French again withdrew their obedience from Benedict, and a number of other states, including the Empire, now declared their neutrality. In 1409 a council at Pisa was attended by cardinals previously in either camp, but both popes boycotted its proceedings and held councils of their own. Anxious to retain the initiative, the Council of Pisa perhaps acted precipitately in failing to secure the representation of all the major lay powers and in accusing both popes of heresy. Its only immediate effect was to secure the election of a third pope, Alexander V, who survived less than a year and was then succeeded by the Neapolitan John XXIII, a 'great man in temporal matters' and a worthy antagonist of Benedict XIII.

The new council which met at Constance in 1414 was at last able to bring the schism to an end. John XXIII was deposed, Gregory XII resigned, and Benedict XIII was eventually condemned as a heretic and schismatic. A decree (*Frequens*) was promulgated ordaining that a general council of the Church should be held at intervals of not more than 10 years. Any future papal schism was to be settled by a council within a year of its occurrence. In November 1417 a new pope was elected by a special body of 23 cardinals and 30 prelates, representing the six 'nations' into which the council was divided: the man on whom their choice fell was Cardinal Oddo Colonna, who became Pope Martin V.

Inevitably the schism had given rise to much discussion in ecclesiastical circles about the constitutional method to be used in bringing it to an end, and a voluminous literature was compiled on the subject. Even before Clement VII was elected some Italian cardinals had mooted the idea of a new council to decide whether Urban's election was valid, and a little later opinion in the University of Paris came to favour a council as the most practicable solution to the schism, in preference to the appointment of arbitrators ('compromise') or a mutual agreement to abdicate ('cession'). The common-sense argument in favour of the conciliar method (as framed by Henry of Langenstein), was this:

New and dangerous emergencies which arise in any diocese are dealt with in a council of that particular diocese or a provincial synod, and therefore it follows that new and arduous problems which concern the whole world ought to be discussed by a General Council. For what concerns all ought to be discussed by all, or by the representatives of all.[11]

From such a view there was a natural progress to the extreme claims put forward by theorists of conciliar authority, that the pope was subject to a general council in matters of faith; if the only infallible body on earth was the universal Church, it followed that a council should have the power to judge and condemn a pope's doctrines and to depose him if he proved obstinate. Such theories found support by analogy from two secular classical concepts, of the lawfulness of resistance to an unjust ruler, and of mixed government (advocating a judicious combination of monarchy, aristocracy and democracy). These ideas lie behind the famous decree of the Council of Constance which has been called 'the most revolutionary official document in the history of the world'. This decree proclaimed that:

This holy synod of Constance ... declares, being legitimately met in the Holy Spirit and a General Council which represents the Catholic Church, that it holds its powers directly from Christ, and that everyone, of whatever status or dignity he may be, even if he is the pope, is bound to obey it in matters pertaining to faith, to the extirpation of this schism and to the reform of the Church in its head and members.[12]

After the ending of the schism the tide of conciliarism rapidly receded from this high water mark. Martin V certainly feared the institution that had elevated him, but the events of the following thirty years were to show the difficulties in normal circumstances of holding together a composite institution against an individual and the manifold advantages enjoyed by an ecclesiastical autocrat. Martin had to convoke a council, which met in 1423 at Siena, and his forebodings seemed justified by the radical nature of the measures proposed by the French reforming party, but such was the dissension within the council that it accomplished nothing and concluded ignominiously in dissolution by the papal legates. The next council met at Basle in 1431, again with the pope's reluctant consent, though Martin died before the opening session was held. His successor, Eugenius IV (1431–47), soon quarrelled with the council, mainly over its willingness to open negotiations with the Bohemian Hussites. For a time the council seemed to have triumphed over the pope, but the reforms proposed in 1435 (which included the abolition of annates) were radical and probably unrealistic, and later Eugenius contrived to take into his own hands the negotiations for reunion with the Byzantine Church (1438–9). This was, of course, *par excellence* the sort of field in which a great assembly was handicapped by the difficulty of formulating an agreed policy and conducting prolonged bargaining. In 1439 the council, with some support from France and the emperor, took action against Eugenius and formally deposed him. The conciliar anti-pope was Amadeus, the pious duke of Savoy, who took the name of Felix V, but a conciliarist pope proved—as might have been foreseen—a paradox more unfeasible than a Ghibelline pope. Felix resented his treatment by the Council, achieved little recognition, and at last (in 1449) abdicated. One of the last acts of the venerable council was to 'elect' as pope Nicholas V, who two years earlier had succeeded to Eugenius.

The background to the immediate occasion of the schism had been the constitutional issue between pope and cardinals, but the main cause of its prolongation arose from political developments in western Europe. The long-standing dispute between French and Italian in the Curia, going back to the period of the papacy's struggle with the Hohenstaufen, was both protracted and remoulded by the increasing power of the nation-state. Political alignments crystallised the schism, and the council, the institution which brought the schism to an end, could only be effective if it was organised in a manner that recognised national identities—while at the same time this recognition served in turn to harden nationalist feeling.

The situation that shaped the alignment of the two sides during the schism was the long French struggle to resist domination by England. Thus French leadership of the Clementist cause involved the participation on Urban's side of Flanders and Gascony, the two French fiefs that fought with England in the war. With the same inevitability France's ally Scotland was drawn to Clement's party—with the by no means negligible consequence that Scots no longer went to study at Oxford or Cambridge and hence universities had to be founded in Scotland at St Andrews, Glasgow and Aberdeen. When local ecclesiastical councils were held in the Iberian kingdoms, the German parts of the empire, Bohemia and Hungary, each made its choice by virtue of its diplomatic relations *vis-à-vis* France rather than by a consideration of the legal merits of the cases presented by the rival popes. Portugal was at first hesitant, but in 1385, thanks to the intervention of John of Gaunt, it came within the English sphere of influence and thus henceforth Portugal was Urbanist. The kingdom of Aragon was also slow to decide its allegiance, but in 1387 it declared for Clement and the election in 1394 of an Aragonese successor brought this kingdom to the fore as a zealous supporter of Benedict XIII. Eventually it became clear that the schism could only be ended by efforts to cut across diplomatic loyalties; hence the French secured the support of England, Castile and the emperor before the 'withdrawal of obedience' of 1398. The same spirit shows in the willingness of most states to accept the pope named by the Council of Pisa; after this council only Castile, Aragon and Scotland still held out for Benedict XIII, while the kingdom of Naples, Poland and a few parts of the Empire persevered in their allegiance to Gregory XII.

The councils had to recognise the nature of the Schism and to assume the only form of organisation that was adapted to healing it: *de facto* they were gatherings of discordant nations, and if agreement was to be effective their structure had to reflect this. At Pisa most of the major lay powers—France, England, the Empire, Poland and Portugal—were represented, though the king of Aragon confined his intervention to an embassy asking that Benedict XIII's representatives should be heard. This was the first council to be divided into four 'nations' (France, England, Germany and Italy); the institution was based on one already existing in that forcing-house of xenophobia, the medieval university. At Constance the voting for the first time took place by nations, the Spaniards being added as a fifth nation after 1416. Each nation met separately in the initial phases of discussion, having its own president; laymen were permitted a vote. Measures agreed on by the 'nation' were then proposed, *nationaliter*, in a general congregation of the nations, and if they secured acceptance at this stage were further considered, *concilialiter*, in a general session wherein each nation remained a voting unit. At Siena again, in 1423–4, voting was by nations, and each nation was instructed to draw up its own programme of reform—an unlikely recipe for securing agreement on reform. The Council of Basle was not organised by 'nations', but national feeling was prominent in its deliberations and had to be recognised by an arrangement whereby each of the nations was represented on the four 'deputations'—concerned respectively with heresy, pacification, reform and ecclesiastical organisation—through which the council transacted its business. It was impossible to ignore the tendencies that were turning the ecumenical assembly into an international conference.

THE HUSSITE REVOLUTION

The medieval Church rightly saw heresy as a serious threat only when it had the support of lay authorities, as in the county of Toulouse in the early thirteenth century. The history of the Schism illustrates clearly the strength in the later Middle Ages of those secular loyalties which might cut across loyalty to the universal Church, and subsequent events were to show how they could give new force to theological heresy. This occurred on a large scale for the first time in Bohemia.

In the kingdom of Bohemia there existed all the necessary ingredients for a precocious growth of national consciousness. This Slav territory, bounded to the west by the 'Bohemian Forest' and to the north by two mountain ranges, the Erzgebirge and Riesengebirge, had considerable geographical unity, and German proximity and German settlement in the towns had made of it a frontier zone highly conscious of its ethnic personality. As early as the twelfth century a Czech chronicler had written bitterly of 'the innate arrogance of the Germans, who in their puffed-up pride always hold in contempt the Slavs and their language'. Czech sentiments were particularly strong in the towns, where German merchants and craftsmen monopolised most of the wealth, and strongest of all in the capital, Prague.

Under the long regency and rule of Charles IV (1334–78) Prague had acquired a 'new town'—populated entirely by Czechs, many of them peasants who had moved in from the surrounding countryside—as well as an archbishopric and a university. Feeling ran high in the university between German and Slav, the latter elements gaining ground as new *studia generalia* were founded in Germany. Prague's first archbishop was Charles's chancellor, Ernest of Pardubice, a scholar, lawyer, ascetic and patron of learning and the arts. He was the leading figure in Charles's attempts to make the Prague court a prominent centre of culture. One of Charles's main interests was the promotion of historical writing tending to enhance the prestige of his family and to foster loyalty to it, and a consequence of these activities was the growth of a school of patriotic Czech erudition. Beneš of Weitmil, the author of the *Cronica ecclesie pragensis*, was virtually Charles's official historiographer, and the king himself assisted Beneš in collecting material. He also commissioned Přibik Pulkava's Bohemian chronicle as well as the *History of Bohemia* of the Italian Giovanni da Marignola, and himself finished a life of the royal saint, king Wenceslas. Charles also encouraged writing in the vernaculars, both Czech and German; chronicles and lives of saints, as well as the Bible, were translated into Czech, and a Czech encyclopedia and Czech–Latin dictionary were compiled.

When Charles IV persuaded his friend Clement VI to free Prague from its ecclesiastical subordination to Mainz he was insisting on the independence of his own country. He and his archbishop rebuilt the cathedral and Prague became a centre of religious reform as well as cultural activity. The leaders of reform in Charles's day were Conrad Waldhauser and John Milič. Hymns sung in the vernacular, the denunciation of ecclesiastical corruption and of excessive reverence for images and relics and the advocacy of daily communion were a central part of this movement, which gained strength through the grievances felt during the papal Schism. Such grievances were increased by the territorial wealth of the Church, which held no less than half of the land in Bohemia. The Crown held approximately one-third of the remainder, but the estates gained considerably in power in Charles's time, and under his son and successor Wenceslas aristocratic opposition was even more effective. The king's authority was circumscribed by a permanent council, and for a time Wenceslas was imprisoned. These movements gave the Bohemian baronage increased cohesion at a time when a nationalist element was entering into Czech religious fervour. The contrast drawn between 'native' religious feeling and the luxurious and rapacious Church of Rome naturally tended to become intertwined with anti-German feeling. To contemporaries the two were inseparable, as may be seen from the words of a chronicler who wrote that 'in Prague the people got very infuriated against some priests and monks and against the Germans, and they drove them out of the town, and others fled on their own account. For at that time it was common for Germans to be on the council and in the town offices'.[13] The later 'crusades' against Bohemia by predominantly German armies merely served to strengthen a tendency in Hussitism which was strong from the very start.

John Hus began his studies in the university at Prague as a young man around 1390 and had a distinguished career there as a student of theology. In 1401 he became the dean of the faculty of arts, and the following year he began to preach (in Czech) in the new Bethlehem chapel, a centre of the reforming religious movement which could house a congregation of 4,000. Hus was a student of the English scholastic theologians and his affinity to Wyclif was to prove a matter of some embarrassment to him, for in 1403 the university condemned a number of Wyclif's opinions. Still more dangerous to his position was Hus's constant criticism of the clergy, concerning which serious complaints were first raised in 1408. During the Schism in the Church it was always likely that disputes over doctrine would lead to differences in papal affiliations and this now occurred at Prague, where the archbishop remained loyal to Gregory XII at a time when Hus had already accepted the decisions of the Council of Pisa. The quarrel was intensified after 1409 when Hus became the rector of the university: the archbishop now ordered him to cease preaching and placed him under excommunication. In 1412 the circumstances of the Schism were again decisive in driving Hus and his supporters towards the defiance of authority which was to lead to a struggle lasting a quarter of a century.

In that year John XXIII declared a 'crusade' against his enemy king Ladislas of Naples and indulgences were sold in Bohemia to raise funds for the campaign. Some of Hus's supporters were executed for their protests, Prague was placed under interdict and Hus himself was excommunicated by the pope and summoned to his Curia. For two years Hus abandoned the capital, but in 1414 he agreed to the suggestion of Sigismund, king of the Romans, that he should accept a safe-conduct and attend the Council at Constance. Soon after his arrival there he was imprisoned, despite the terms of the safe-conduct, and accused of holding heretical, Wycliffite opinions. Hus refused to recant his doctrines unless they could be proved erroneous by evidence from the Scriptures, and on 6 July 1415 he was condemned and burned.

A fifteenth-century Bohemian writer tells us that Hus

began to preach, and to castigate the people for their sinful life ... But then he began to preach also against the sinfulness of the clergy, sparing neither the Pope on his throne nor the lowliest priest, and he preached against their haughtiness and their greed, against simony and concubinage, and he said that priests should not wield worldly power nor have worldly estates, and he preached also that in the Holy Communion the Body of Christ and also the Blood of Christ should be given to the common people.[14]

The main burden of Hus's preaching, in fact, as with the earlier Prague reformers, was clerical corruption. Ecclesiastical morals occupied much more time than theology, and even the theology was by no means whole-heartedly Wycliffite. It was a case of affinity rather than influence, for Wyclif was a fellow scholastic with the same preoccupations: both men were opponents of nominalism and, what is more important, both felt doubts about the authority of a worldly papacy and the claims of a Church which had great possessions. Hus rejected Wyclif's doctrine concerning transubstantiation, he even felt doubt about the Englishman's view that priests who sinned forfeited their priestly status; although he sympathised with this position, he considered it too absolute and preferred to regard such priests as unworthy rather than illegal. He agreed, however, on the fundamental point that 'the Church' consisted of Christ and all the elect, not of the pope and cardinals. It was this democratic ecclesiology which led logically to the view that the laity should receive the Communion in the same form as the clergy, that is in the 'two kinds', the wine as well as the bread. This symbolic levelling of priest and people, which was to give the Hussites their most cherished liturgical idiosyncrasy, was first practised in Prague about 1414, after Hus's departure, by two of his followers, Jauoubek of Stříbro and Nicholas of Dresden. The chronicler quoted above erred in ascribing 'utraquism' to Hus himself, but Hus was informed of this development and expressed his approval. In rejecting erring priestly authority he had no intention of installing in its place religious anarchy: there was still a supreme authority, and this was the Bible. All disputes could be settled by reference to the Bible, and obedience was due to the Church, as Hus insisted at his trial, only when this was in conformity with the Bible.

When Hus was put to death the story of Hussitism as a social and political force was only at its beginning. In the face of great 'crusading' invasions by foreign forces the Hussites were to perform extraordinary military feats—all the more extraordinary because of the constant tension within the movement between extremists and moderates. The men who had rejected the Church's authority were free also to reject traditional religious practice, and soon after Hus's death there were important developments in this direction: Hussite priests married, auricular confession and the Latin liturgy were abandoned, 'images' fell into complete disfavour. In the fortress of Tabor, which was founded in 1420, Hussitism became a popular movement. Leaders were elected and property was held in common. The Taborites held the millenarian belief, characteristic at various times of the religion of the poor, that 'the end of the world is approaching, resplendent castles shall fall into ruins, proud cities shall perish, magnificent monasteries crumble into dust, all existing society is to be destroyed'. Soon Christ would descend, 'place supreme power in the hands of the people' and 'faith will blossom forth and justice flourish'.

Some extracts from the 'Articles' of Tabor will make clear the nature of the religious and social ideals of the extremist party:

First, that in our time there shall be an end of all things, that is, all evil shall be uprooted on this earth.

That this is the time of vengeance and retribution on wicked men by fire and sword so that all adversaries of God's Law shall be slain by fire and sword or otherwise done to death.

So that in this time whoever will hear the Word of Christ, then let them that be Jews [*sic*][15] flee to the mountains, and those that will not leave the towns, villages and hamlets for the mountains or for Tabor shall all be guilty of mortal sin.

Everyone that will not go to the mountains shall perish amidst the towns, villages and hamlets by the blows of God.

In this time nobody can be shielded from God's blows but on the mountains.

The Taborite brethren are in this time of vengeance the messengers of God sent to purge away all offences and evil from Christ's kingdom, all wickedness from good people and from the Holy Church.

The Taborite brethren shall take revenge by fire and sword on God's enemies and on all towns, villages and hamlets.

Every church, chapel or altar built to the honour of the Lord God or of any saint shall be destroyed and burnt as a place of idolatry.

Every house of a priest, canon, chaplain or other cleric shall he destroyed and burnt.

In this time of vengeance only five towns shall remain and those who flee to them shall be saved . . .

As in Hradiště or in Tabor nothing is mine and nothing thine, but all is common, so everything shall be common to all forever and no one shall have anything of his own; because whoever owns anything himself commits a mortal sin.

Debtors who flee to the mountains or the aforesaid five towns shall be acquitted of paying their debts.

Even now, at the end of the ages, all shall see Christ bodily descend from Heaven to accept His kingdom here on earth . . .

In this time no king shall reign nor any lord rule on earth, there shall be no serfdom, all dues and taxes shall cease, nor shall any man force another to do anything, because all shall be equal, brothers and sisters.

Holy Mass shall not be sung or read in the Latin tongue, but only in the language of the people.

Missals sung in Latin, prayer books and other books, priestly vestments, surplices, silver or golden monstrances and chalices, silver or golden belts, ornamented or richly embroidered garments, finely made or costly robes: all these things shall not exist and must therefore be spoilt and destroyed.

Priests shall have no payments nor hamlets nor cattle nor estates nor houses in which to dwell nor anything of the like, even if they were given such things as alms, even if they held them by secular law and governance.[16]

It may seem strange that the Bohemian baronage ever co-operated with the men who proclaimed such a revolutionary political and social programme. That they did so at times can only be attributed to the increasingly strong patriotic element in the movement. In 1419 the 'Taborites' acquired a great military leader in the person of John Žižka, a squire who had previously served as a mercenary captain in his own country and in Poland. The spirit of the ensuing struggle between the Hussites and the forces of king Sigismund is typified by the terms in which Žižka called for support from the inhabitants of Domažlice: 'Defend yourselves bravely against the misdeeds which the Germans commit against you and follow the example of the Czechs of old who, having made ready for the march, defended not only God's cause but their own also.' Žižka, who was an original military thinker, based his tactics on the use of mobile fortress-camps; the perimeter was held by wagons, the crews of which were organised like modern tank-crews, and the fortress was normally sited on a hilltop. Žižka's infantrymen were often armed with flails, but his force was no mere mob of peasants. He possessed quite powerful artillery and learnt to use his guns tactically in the offensive; he was the first European commander to make effective use of artillery other than in siege warfare. This unorthodox general also knew the advantage of surprise and employed it ingeniously: he was to have a profound influence on later warfare in Germany and Hungary. Nor did he fail to understand the importance of morale, and he neatly expressed the religious bellicosity of his army by adopting the chalice, the symbol of utraquism, as his emblem.

Sigismund raised an invading army and in 1420 the religious struggle became a national war.

The Germans [says Žižka's early biographer] sought the lives of the Czechs and the Czechs of the Germans . . . when the Germans got hold of a Czech, even if he was of their own party in his creed, they did not even ask him about that, but as soon as they laid eyes on him they took him and burned him. And this went on until even those Czechs who were of the king's own party grew indignant against him.[17]

In 1420 Žižka achieved the extraordinary feat of holding Prague against the invaders. The following year he became completely blind, but the greatest of his campaigns, which brought about the defeat of Sigismund's new crusading armies, was fought in 1421–2.

The German electors invaded the land [says 'The Very Pretty Chronicle of John Žižka'] with a very strong army, and with them there were many princes, counts, bishops, and also the Margrave of Meissen. And they committed many cruelties, and whenever they got hold of a Czech they killed or burned him . . .

Then the Hungarian King came with a vast army to Bohemia, having with him Turks and Wallachians, Croatians and Hungarians, Cumans and Yassyans, Germans and other people from many different countries.[18]

Whether or not the atrocities of this heterogeneous army are exaggerated by the chronicler, his account confirms that the Czechs were now involved in a national struggle against an external foe. The invaders were routed and driven from Bohemia, but inevitably the passing of the crisis led to renewed discord between the moderate Hussites and the chiliastic extremists. Žižka's last opponents before his death in 1424 were the Catholic nobility, but by then he had already been involved in warfare against the radical Taborites.

After Žižka's death the Hussites found a new commander in Prokop the Bald, under whose generalship the struggle continued until 1433, defence against the crusading forces of Cardinals Beaufort and Cesarini alternating with raids into Austria, Silesia, Slovakia and Hungary. By this time Hussitism had permeated into neighbouring territories, particularly to Brandenburg and to south-western Germany, where there was a hierarchy of four Hussite bishops. Meanwhile the social and military consequences of Hussite warfare also spread wider afield, thanks to the formation and extension of more bands of soldiers. The last acts of the drama saw Hussites negotiating with the Council at Basle and with its representatives at Prague at the same time as Prokop was fighting on behalf of the Taborites and the 'Orphans' of Žižka against a league of Bohemian barons. After the league's capture of Prague and Prokop's death the less extreme party among the Hussites agreed to the 'Compactata' of 1436, a compromise which permitted the continuation of utraquism. In the same year Sigismund was at last accepted as king of Bohemia and soon Hussite resistance was at an end. In one sense the compromise of 1436–7 marks the beginning of the Reformation, but a group among the Hussites refused to accept it and exists today as the Moravian Church, the survivor, with the

Waldensians, of the medieval protestant movements. The most profound consequences of this great upheaval, however, were social and political. The entire structure of the Bohemian feudal Church was dismantled, the principal beneficiaries being the nobles and gentry. Once the Church lost its estates the gains, in the absence of a powerful monarchy, were bound to go to the local magnates. A typical story concerns the estates of the monastery of Zlata Koruna in southern Bohemia, which were confiscated in 1419–20 by the Hussite supporter Oldřich (Ulrich) of Rožmberk. A few years later this baron went over to the crusaders, but he contrived to retain the monastery's lands by becoming its 'Catholic protector'. While the lords gained, the peasantry suffered: the famines and epidemics that accompanied the wars bore particularly heavily on them, and in general the status of the villein was depressed. Lastly, the long struggle had sharpened Bohemian nationalism and given it a 'myth'. Consciousness of being Czech was stronger than before, particularly in the towns, and thus religious war had served to strengthen the rival loyalty that challenged the Church, in Prague as in the councils and in the papal Curia itself.

FURTHER READING

General

Excellent brief general histories of the medieval church are John A. Thomson, *The Western Church in the Middle Ages* (London, 1998), and Bernhard Schimmelpfennig, *The Papacy* (New York, 1992). Geoffrey Barraclough, *The Medieval Papacy* (repr. London, 1975), W. Ullmann, *A Short History of the Papacy in the Middle Ages* (London, 1972), R. W. Southern, *Western Society and the Church in the Middle Ages* (Harmondsworth, 1970) and more recently Joseph H. Lynch, *The Medieval Church. A Brief History* (London, 1992) give less space to the later medieval church. S. Ozment, *The Age of Reform 1250–1550. An Intellectual and Religious History of Late Medieval and Reformation Europe* (New York and London, 1980) is fuller, and takes the account through the Reformation. Finally Jacques Verger, 'Different values and authorities', in *The Cambridge Illustrated History of the Middle Ages*, vol. III, *1250–1520*, ed. Robert Fossier (Cambridge, 1986), pp. 119–91 is an excellent, wide-ranging survey.

The Avignon papacy

There are two general surveys: Y. Renouard, *The Avignon Papacy, 1305–1403* (tr. London, 1970), and more extensively G. Mollat, *The Popes at Avignon* (tr. Edinburgh, 1963). B. Smalley, 'Church and state, 1300–77: theory and fact', in *Europe in the Late Middle Ages*, eds J. R. Hale, J. R. L. Highfield and B. Smalley (London, 1965), pp. 15–43 is a brilliant essay. In recent years French, German and Italian scholars in particular have been working extensively on the administrative records of the Avignonese, though relatively little of their work has percolated through to English. (An outstanding example is B. Guillemain, *Le cour pontificale d'Avignon, 1300–1376: étude d'une société* (Paris, 1966).) Only two of the Avignon popes have had biographies in English: S. Menache, *Clement V* (Cambridge, 1998), and D. Wood, *Clement VI. The Pontificate and Ideas of an Avignon Pope* (Cambridge, 1989). Geoffrey Barraclough, *Papal Provisions* (repr. Westport, Conn., 1971) is a useful account of the process by which papal administrative control was extended. H. S. Offler, 'Empire and papacy: the last struggle', *Transactions of the Royal Historical Society*, 5th series, 5 (1956), pp. 21–47 describes the conflict with Lewis the Bavarian. N. Housley, *The Italian Crusades. The Papal-Angevin Alliance and the*

Crusades against Christian Lay Powers, 1254–1343 (Oxford, 1982) deals with some aspects of the papacy's Italian policy. The Ordinances of Cardinal Albornoz are translated in E. Emerton, *Humanism and Tyranny. Studies in the Italian Trecento* (Gloucester, Mass., 1925), pp. 197–251. On the crusading policy of the popes, *see* N. Housley, *The Avignon Papacy and the Crusades, 1305–1378* (Oxford, 1986). One aspect of the papal court is discussed in Bernhard Schimmelpfennig, 'Papal coronations in Avignon', in *Coronations: Medieval and Early Modern Monarchic Ritual*, ed. J. M. Bak (Berkeley, Cal., and Oxford, 1990), pp. 179–96.

The Great Schism and the conciliar movement

W. Ullmann, *The Origins of the Great Schism. A Study in Fourteenth-Century Ecclesiastical History* (1938, repr. Hamden, Conn., 1972) is an extensive narrative account of events of 1378. Richard C. Trexler, 'Rome on the eve of the Great Schism', *Speculum*, 42 (1967), pp. 489–509 adds useful background.

The most accessible introduction to the conciliar movement is C. M. D. Crowder, *Unity, Heresy and Reform 1378–1460. The Conciliar Response to the Great Schism* (London, 1977), a translation of selected documents with an excellent introduction and commentary. Antony Black, 'Popes and councils', *NCMH*, vol. V, pp. 65–86 is a crisp, up-to-date account. L. R. Loomis, *The Council of Constance. The Unification of the Church*, eds J. H. Mundy and K. M. Woody (New York, 1961) is a translation of the main chronicle sources for the Council of Constance. P. Stump, *The Reforms of the Council of Constance (1414–1418)* (Leiden, 1994) rehabilitates the reforming achievements of the council. R. N. Swanson, *Universities, Academics and the Great Schism* (Cambridge, 1979) is a thorough account of the growth of the movement seen especially through academic eyes, and demonstrates the critical role played—for once—by academics in a vital political process. On the role of the cardinals, R. N. Swanson, 'The problem of the cardinalate in the Great Schism', in *Authority and Power. Studies on Medieval Law and Government Presented to Walter Ullmann on his Seventieth Birthday*, eds B. Tierney and P. Linehan (Cambridge, 1980), pp. 225–35. On the sense and meanings of 'nationality', L. R. Loomis, 'Nationality at the Council of Constance. An Anglo-French dispute', *American Historical Review*, 44 (1939), pp. 508–27, repr. in *Change in Medieval Society. Europe North of the Alps, 1050–1500*, ed. Sylvia L. Thrupp (repr. Toronto, 1988), pp. 279–96; L. R. Loomis, 'The organization by nations at Constance', *Church History*, 1 (1932), pp. 191–210.

Conciliar theory produced an immense contemporary literature, and has been much studied for its position in the development of late medieval political ideas. A thoughtful review of the historiography is A. Black, 'What was conciliarism? Conciliar theory in historical perspective', in *Authority and Power. Studies on Medieval Law and Government Presented to Walter Ullmann on his Seventieth Birthday*, cit.; *see also* Antony Black, *Political Thought in Europe, 1250–1450* (Cambridge, 1992), ch. 6, and Antony Black, 'The conciliar movement', in *The Cambridge History of Medieval Political Thought, c.350–c.1450*, ed. J. H. Burns (Cambridge, 1988), pp. 573–87. B. Tierney, *Foundations of Conciliar Theory. The Contribution of the Medieval Canonists from Gratian to the Great Schism* (Cambridge, 1955) outlines the intellectual background to the movement; see also E. F. Jacob, *Essays in the Conciliar Epoch* (2nd edition, Manchester, 1953), and J. B. Morrall, *Gerson and the Great Schism* (Manchester, 1960).

Recent attention has focused particularly on the movement after Constance. See J. A. F. Thomson, *Popes and Princes, 1417–1517. Politics and Polity in the Late Medieval Church* (London, 1980), especially ch. 1; A. J. Black, 'The political ideas of conciliarism and papalism, 1430–1450', *Journal of Ecclesiastical History*, 20 (1969), pp. 45–65; A. J. Black, *Monarchy and Community. Political Ideas in the Late Conciliar Controversy, 1430–1450* (Cambridge, 1970). On specific councils and figures, A. Black, *Council and Commune. The Conciliar Movement and the Fifteenth-Century*

Heritage (London, 1979); Joachim W. Stieber, *Pope Eugenius IV, the Council of Basel, and the Secular and Ecclesiastical Authorities in the Empire: The Conflict over Supreme Authority and Power in the Church* (Leiden, 1978); J. Gill, *Eugenius IV, Pope of the Christian Union* (Westminster, Md., 1961); J. Gill, *The Council of Florence* (Cambridge, 1959); J. Gill, *Personalities of the Council of Florence and Other Essays* (Oxford, 1964); G. Alberigo, ed., *Christian Unity: the Council of Ferrara-Florence, 1438/9–1989* (Louvain, 1991); Paul E. Sigmund, *Nicholas of Cusa and Medieval Political Thought* (Cambridge, Mass., 1963). One of the chief commentaries on the Council of Basle is Aeneas Sylvius Piccolominus, *De Gestis Concilii Basiliensis Commentariorum Libri II*, tr. and eds Denys Hay and W. K. Smith (Oxford, 1967).

The Hussite revolution

Good brief introductions are M. D. Lambert, *Medieval Heresy. Popular Movements from Bogomil to Hus* (2nd edition, Oxford, 1992), especially chs 15–18; G. Leff, *Heresy in the Late Middle Ages. The Relation of Heterodoxy to Dissent c.1250–c.1450* (Manchester, 1967), ch. 9. The fullest account in English is H. Kaminsky, *A History of the Hussite Revolution* (Berkeley and Los Angeles, Cal., 1967); J. Maček, *The Hussite Movement in Bohemia* (2nd edition, Prague, 1958; repr. London and Prague, 1965 and New York, 1980) is a briefer introduction which includes a number of texts in translation. The most recent monograph in English is Thomas A. Fudge, *The Magnificent Ride: the First Reformation in Hussite Bohemia* (Aldershot, 1998). František Šmahel, 'The Hussite movement: an anomaly of European history?', in *Bohemia in History*, ed. M. Teich (Cambridge, 1998), pp. 79–97 is an excellent summary and evaluation; František Graus, 'The crisis of the middle ages and the Hussites', in *The Reformation in Medieval Perspective*, ed. S. E. Ozment (Chicago, Ill., 1971), pp. 76–103 also attempts to sum up the significance of the revolution. R. R. Betts, *Essays in Czech History* (London, 1969) remains a useful collection of essays.

On the background to the revolt, František Kavka, 'Politics and culture under Charles IV', in *Bohemia in History*, ed. M. Teich (Cambridge, 1998), pp. 59–78. On the religious background, M. Wilks, '"Reformatio Regni": Wyclif and Hus as leaders of religious protest movements', in *Schism, Heresy and Religious Protest*, ed. Derek Baker. Studies in Church History, 9 (Cambridge, 1972), pp. 109–30; W. R. Cook, 'John Wyclif and Hussite theology 1415–1436', *Church History*, 42 (1973), pp. 335–49; F. Šmahel, 'Wyclif's fortune in Hussite Bohemia', *Bulletin of the Institute of Historical Research*, 43 (1970), pp. 16–34. On Wyclif, A. Kenny, *Wyclif* (Oxford Past Masters, Oxford, 1985), and A. Kenny, ed., *Wyclif in his Times* (Oxford, 1986). On Hus himself, M. Spinka, *John Hus: a Biography* (Princeton, N.J., 1968; repr. Westport, Conn., 1979); M. Spinka, *John Hus' Concept of the Church* (Princeton, N.J., 1966); M. Spinka, *John Hus and the Czech Reform* (repr. Hamden, Conn., 1941); M. Spinka, *John Hus at the Council of Constance* (New York, 1965). On the role of the university in the revolution, H. Kaminsky, 'The University of Prague in the Hussite revolution: the role of the masters', in *Universities in Politics*, eds J. W. Baldwin and R. A. Goldthwaite (Baltimore, Md., 1972), pp. 79–106; on social factors, J. M. Klassen, *The Nobility and the Making of the Hussite Revolution* (New York, 1978).

Thomas A. Fudge, 'The "crown" and the "red gown": Hussite popular religion', in *Popular Religion in Germany and Central Europe, 1400–1800*, eds Bob Scribner and T. Johnson (Basingstoke, 1996), pp. 38–57 is a good description of the religious aspects of the conflict; *see also* Ernst Werner, 'Popular ideologies in late medieval Europe: Taborite Chiliasm and its antecedents', *Comparative Studies in Society and History*, 2 (1960), pp. 344–63; and Howard Kaminsky, 'Chiliasm and the Hussite Revolution', *Church History*, 26 (1957), pp. 43–71. On the later political history of the revolution, F. G. Heymann, *John Žižka and the Hussite*

Revolution (Princeton, N.J., 1955, repr. New York, 1969); F. M. Bartoš, *The Hussite Revolution, 1424–1437* (tr. New York, 1986); O. Odložilík, *The Hussite King. Bohemia in European Affairs, 1440–1471* (New Brunswick, N.J., 1965); F. G. Heymann, *George of Bohemia King of Heretics* (Princeton, N.J., 1965). Finally on the political history of Bohemia after the revolution, Josef Maček, 'The monarchy of the estates', in *Bohemia in History*, ed. M. Teich (Cambridge, 1998), pp. 98–116.

NOTES

1. *See above*, pp. 32–4.
2. Mansi, *Sacrorum conciliorum, nova et amplissima collectio* (repr. Graz, 1960–1), XXV, cols 125–8.
3. *Senilia*, VII, I; *see* English translation in Francis Petrarch, *Letters of Old Age. Rerum senilium libri*, tr. A. S. Bernardo, S. Levin and R. A. Bernardo, 2 vols (Baltimore, Md., and London, 1992), I, pp. 227–62 (these passages are on pp. 245 and 235 respectively). *See also* Letter IX, I (pp. 304–27).
4. Heinricus Dapifer de Diessenhoven, in *Fontes Rerum Germanicarum*, ed. J. F. Böhmer (repr. Aalen, 1969), IV, p. 34 (*ad* 1340).
5. F. Du Chesne, *Histoire de tous les Cardinaux francois de naissance*, vol. II (Paris, 1660), pp. 359–68 (the text of Cardinal Bertrand's will).
6. W. Ullmann, *The Origins of the Great Schism* (1938, repr. Hamden, Conn., 1972), p. 43.
7. Ullmann, op. cit., pp. 173–4.
8. Ullmann, op. cit., p. 45.
9. Ullmann, op. cit., pp. 46–8.
10. E. Baluze, *Vitae Paparum Avinonensium*, ed. G. Mollat, vol. II (Paris, 1927), p. 758.
11. Henry of Langenstein, 'Consilium Pacis', in *Magnum Oecumenicum Constantiense Concilium*, ed. H. v. D. Hardt (Frankfurt and Leipzig, 1697), vol. 2, cols 2–61 (this passage in col. 28). There is an abridged translation in *Advocates of Reform: From Wyclif to Erasmus*, ed. M. Spinka (London, 1953), pp. 106–39 (this passage on p. 117).
12. C. Mirbt, *Quellen zur Geschichte des Papsttums und des Römischen Katholizismus* (3rd edition, Tübingen, 1911), p. 169. Excerpts are translated in C. M. D. Crowder, *Unity, Heresy and Reform 1378–1460. The Conciliar Response to the Great Schism* (London, 1977), pp. 82–3.
13. Trans. from 'The Very Pretty Chronicle of John Žižka', in F. G. Heymann, *John Žižka and the Hussite Revolution* (Princeton, N.J., 1955), p. 4.
14. Quoted from 'The Very Pretty Chronicle', tr. Heymann, cit., p. 3.
15. Evidently the intention was to quote Mark 13:14: 'let them that be in Judaea . . .'.
16. Slightly adapted from the translation in J. Maček, *The Hussite Movement in Bohemia* (2nd edition, London and Prague, 1965), pp. 130–3.
17. From 'The Very Pretty Chronicle', tr. Heymann, cit., pp. 5–6.
18. Op. cit., pp. 7–8.

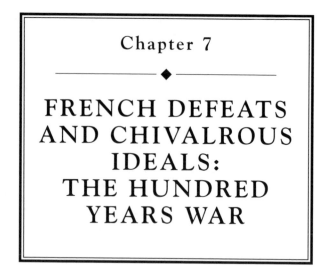

Chapter 7

◆

FRENCH DEFEATS AND CHIVALROUS IDEALS: THE HUNDRED YEARS WAR

THE BACKGROUND TO THE WAR

A previous chapter described the strength of the French monarchy at the beginning of the fourteenth century, and some mention has already been made of the economic effects of the prolonged struggle with England which dictated the course of French history from that time till the end of the following century. The main cause of war was the old and insoluble dispute concerning Aquitaine, the remaining fief of the English kings in the French kingdom. As the power of the French monarchs increased it became both more intolerable to them that much of southwestern France should be held by another sovereign and more conceivable that firm administrative and military action might dispossess the English Crown of Aquitaine.

The question remained dormant during the brief reigns of Louis X and Philip V (1314–22), but Charles IV (1322–8) was confronted by less baronial opposition than they and was encouraged by the contrast with the deteriorating internal situation of Edward II of England. Moreover the worsening relations between Edward and his queen, who was Charles's sister, removed one of the brakes on French action. The conventional methods of the French in Aquitaine had been to exploit to the full the inextricably complicated legal status of the duchy by transferring lawsuits from its courts to Paris and instigating intervention by French officials on the ground that the duke's failures to secure justice justified intervention by the overlord. Disputes over action of this sort combined with commercial rivalry in the Channel, French support of the Scots and English involvement with Flanders to keep Anglo-French relations in a state of perpetual hostility. Despite the appointment of numerous commissions of reform and constant changes in official personnel, English administration in Gascony was unsuccessful and expensive. A seneschal was appointed to rule the whole duchy in 1323, but he was handicapped by the lack of an appellate court in the duchy (itself an encouragement to the French in their tactics of citing cases to the royal court), and Gascony, which needed financial aid from England, was expected to run at a profit.

In 1324 war broke out over an incident at the disputed village of St Sardos. Charles IV declared the duchy confiscated to the French Crown on account of Edward II's failure to perform homage for it, and French forces advanced, meeting little effective resistance. By 1326 only a small coastal strip remained in English hands. Edward II was too occupied with the unsuccessful attempt to retain his own crown to organise a systematic defence of Gascony or of Ponthieu, the area round the mouth of the Somme which he had inherited from his mother and which now also fell to the French. In 1327 an agreement gave the French a solid return for their victories by assigning them most of the disputed frontier territory.

When Charles IV, Philip the Fair's youngest son, died in 1328 there was no direct male heir: after three and a half centuries the Capetians had at last come to the end of their genealogical luck. The line was not extinct, however, and there was a fairly obvious successor in the person of Philip of Valois, the son of Philip the Fair's brother Charles. A case could be made for the claim of the new king of England, since Edward III was the son of Charles IV's elder sister, but there was almost every conceivable practical objection to this candidate; he was the king of England, he was only 15 years old, and he was under the control of his disreputable mother Isabella and her lover Mortimer. It was natural that the assembly of peers and prelates should declare for Philip, who had a firm base in France's feudal structure as count of Valois, Anjou, Maine, Chartres and Alençon.

Although Philip was a man of 35 he had not yet had much experience of political affairs. He had not been educated in the expectation that he would become king of France, but his father, Charles of Valois, had once been claimant to the throne of Aragon[1] and was to be the son, brother and father of kings. Charles was sufficiently optimistic to have a special history text-book compiled for his son, designed to instil in him the wish to emulate the virtues and deeds of the Jews, Greeks, Trojans and Romans. Philip VI was a pious man, able and willing to take on the pope in an argument about the Beatific Vision, and an enthusiast—too much of an enthusiast from the viewpoint of French interests—for the crusading ideal. The papacy was favourably disposed towards him[2] and granted him valuable powers in appointing to benefices and taxing the French clergy. He also had a close ally in king John of Bohemia, whose daughter was later to marry his son. Philip shared the conventional chivalrous outlook of his day, but he was not a popular character. He had the good fortune to begin his reign with an overwhelming victory at Cassel over Flemish insurgents, but the ferocity of his reprisals against these clothworkers and peasants is sufficient to explain his unpopularity in that region.

The change of dynasty of 1328, even though it took place in circumstances which gave the English king a claim to the throne, disturbed France far less profoundly than England was unsettled by the revolution of 1326–7 and the subsequent super-session of his mother and Mortimer by Edward III (1330). Philip VI can hardly be blamed for failing to foresee the extraordinary tenacity and success of the English onslaught on France in the following decades. As the ruler of a monarchy enjoying unrivalled political and cultural prestige in Europe and possessing perhaps three times as many subjects as those of Edward III, he had no strong reasons for fearing a house which had recently seemed much more likely to lose all of Aquitaine than to gain new territory in France.

Anglo-French relations came to a crisis in 1337 when Philip VI retorted to Edward's claim to the French throne by declaring Gascony confiscated. By this time both sides were recruiting allies in the Low Countries. An English mission, well supplied with money, purchased the support of Brabant, Hainault, Berg, Juliers, Limburg, Cleves and Marck; finally they triumphantly bought the alliance of Lewis IV, and Edward became the emperor's vicar-general in imperial Flanders. The French king's feudatory, the Count of Flanders, and his allies, Luxembourg, Liège and Cambrai, made a less impressive showing. The stage was set for what would clearly be a crucial trial of strength.

THE FIRST PHASE OF THE WAR

A mere chronological account of the campaigns which have gained the rather misleading name of the 'Hundred Years War' would do the reader no favours. The military successes won by the apparently weaker power require explanation, and some suggestions may be offered concerning advantages enjoyed by the English. In the first place, the strategic initiative lay with them, in that they could select the direction from which assaults were launched against the Île de France and could synchronise or co-ordinate assaults from more than one base. Aquitaine and the Low Countries provided the original bases, but after 1341 the English gained a third foothold by supporting Jean de Montfort, one of two rival claimants to the duchy of Brittany. Moreover, French provincialism made it possible for the English cause to gain some sympathy in other regions, notably in Normandy. The war was fought almost entirely on French soil, its characteristic strategic feature being the *chevauchée* (cavalry raid) launched from friendly territory by the English across France. In the intervals between the regular campaigns France was plagued by marauding companies of unemployed mercenaries;[3] for the civil population a truce rarely signified peace. So long as she could launch her armies from secure bases against the heartland of France, England was a formidable adversary, and the vigour with which her commercial wealth was mobilised to keep her armies in the field meant that the French were challenged powerfully and frequently. Finally it was a disadvantage to the French that they had no zone which acted as a permanent training ground. The English were able to employ the well-tried manoeuvres which had won successes in the frequent hostilities in Wales and Scotland, where the lessons of the longbow had been learnt. These theatres of war to some extent occupied the position that centuries later was to be held by the Indian north-west frontier.

The phase of the war which opened in 1337 and concluded in 1361 with the Treaty of Brétigny was marked by two disastrous French defeats, Crécy (1346) and Poitiers (1356). A brief account of these two battles will make it clear that weaknesses in the French methods of conducting war were no less critical than French strategic disadvantages. Edward III's campaign of 1346 was based on Normandy, an exiled feudal lord of the Cotentin having persuaded him of the advantages of this approach. Edward struck south as far as the walls of Paris, then turned north-east. Near Abbeville he was caught by the French pursuit, and each side felt strong enough to risk an engagement in the open field, though the English numbered only some 2,500 heavy cavalry and the same number of horse-archers. Horse-archers had been used to bring the Scots to battle as long as 50 years before, and these tactics had been employed with success at Falkirk (1298), Dupplin Moor (1332) and Halidon Hill (1333). The English victory at Crécy was due to the rashness of the French in assaulting a very strong position. The tactics of the English were to extend their wings forward, so that the advancing cavalry met fire from three sides. The assault of the French, launched through their own crossbowmen, who suffered heavily, was ill disciplined and appallingly costly, as attack always is when directed against a well-armed and well-positioned enemy. The English archers and horsemen had been trained to fight together and the longbow, the principal English weapon, had a rate of fire at least three times as great as that of the French crossbow: it was almost as though machine-gunners were fighting riflemen. Despite the tremendous casualties, this French defeat was not decisive: the English were too weak to exploit their victory, and for the next 12 months they were occupied with achieving the submission of Calais.

For several years after 1347 there was little fighting in France. During this time Philip VI died (1350) and again fortune favoured the English, for Jean le Bon, though an amiable man, was an incompetent ruler, whereas the English king was a capable and experienced general backed by a son whose military ability was no less than his own. In 1356 one English force attacked Normandy from Brittany, while another, under Edward's son the Black Prince, broke out of Aquitaine in a northerly direction. The prince had no more than 2,600 horsemen and the ensuing battle near Poitiers was a much more close-run thing than Crécy. The French commanders made the mistakes that had been made 10 years before. In a preliminary council of war Marshal Clermont, who recommended caution, was accused of cowardice, whereupon he walked out and launched a rash assault. Eventually the French were defeated when attacked from the rear by the Gascon Captal de Buch. This time the inability of the English to attempt a territorial exploitation of their victory was of little importance, for they already held the trump card: the French king had been taken prisoner. Jean's captivity was all the more disastrous in that the young dauphin was faced by risings in Paris and elsewhere and by a formidable enemy in the person of his cousin Charles of Navarre. The subsequent Treaty of Brétigny, which was never fully effective, granted the English three million crowns as a ransom for the French king, together with a greatly enlarged Aquitaine (now including all the disputed borderlands on its eastern frontier) as well as Ponthieu and Calais. The French were to be compelled to pay heavily indeed for the military ineptitude which had twice led them into the trap laid by their experienced adversary.

The financial burden of war fell heavily on the English too, but success, which reconciles men to military expenditure, in this case also helped to diminish it, since large ransoms were paid for the captive French nobles. Meanwhile the fiscal problems of the French were increased by the dislocation of their trade: customs receipts were down by one-third in 1344 as compared with 1332. Apart from clerical taxation and debasement of the currency, the French king had to rely mainly on loans. For these he turned everywhere, to the pope and the French clergy, to towns, feudatories, royal officials and the communities of Italian and Jewish merchants.

INTERNAL PROBLEMS OF THE FRENCH MONARCHY

It might be supposed that the great defeats of 1346 and 1356 should have cost the French Crown heavily in prestige and constitutional standing as well as in money, but this was not the case. Even during the early critical years of king Jean's captivity the French estates failed to strengthen their position. The assemblies called to give consent to taxation were normally local ones, and although they did not fail to demand reforms and to seek control over the distribution of the subsidies and even over the troops themselves, they made no solid gains in this sense. The very fact of the king's captivity may have hindered those seeking effective concessions from the Crown. Certainly it strengthened sentiment concerning the monarchy; there was a feeling of national mourning after Poitiers, as is witnessed by the decision that no minstrels or *jongleurs* should perform in the Languedoc. Demands for radical constitutional 'reform' were indeed put forward at this juncture. It was proposed that 28 counsellors, from all three estates, should temporarily take control in France, that in future some counsellors should always be nominated by the estates, and that the estates themselves should decide when meetings should be held: the local assemblies were to be discontinued. In 1357 nine 'reformers' were actually appointed. Yet all schemes for reform foundered because the different discontented elements failed to collaborate. Étienne Marcel's movement of 1357–8 in Paris was entirely local and the rural *Jacquerie* was also independent.

Jean le Bon returned from his captivity in 1360, but soon afterwards the duke of Anjou, who was hostage for the payment of the remainder of the king's ransom, broke his oath and fled to France. Rather than allow the honour of his house to be tarnished, Jean returned voluntarily to his English prison and died as a captive.

His son and successor Charles V (1364–80) was an able man whose comparatively early death was to cost his country very dear. Charles, who had a considerable library, took an interest in the theory as well as the practice of kingship; experiencing difficulty in reading Aristotle in Latin, he had a French translation of the *Politics* made for his own use. He realised that fiscal embarrassment might restrict the constitutional powers of the French monarchy, and hence was careful to evade consultation with the estates; moreover he was singularly successful in levying taxes which had hitherto required consent. He approached warfare in a much more business-like spirit than his grandfather and father, appointing as his principal commander Bertrand du Guesclin, an unpolished Breton knight who defied the traditions of chivalry in that he cherished his men and attempted to avoid engagements in the open field.

By 1380 there seemed every reason to suppose that France had weathered the storms of the English onslaught. Edward III, the initiator of the war and the hero of its early phase, was dead and England was under the rule of a mere boy, Edward's grandson Richard. That France underwent a second and far more dreadful crisis was the consequence of a series of misfortunes, beginning with the early death of Charles 'the Wise' and the succession of his incompetent son Charles (VI) at the age of 11. The tragic tale of Charles VI's relations with his uncles and of the family quarrel which drove the powerful Burgundian duchy into alliance with the English cannot be related here, though in part it will form the theme of a later chapter.[4] After 1392 Charles underwent recurrent periods of mental illness, and later he became incapable of carrying on the business of government. The length of his life (he died in 1422) was as unlucky for his country as was the brevity of his father's.

Even this combination of calamities might have been ineffective had it not coincided with the succession to the English throne in 1413 of a king resolved to be the reincarnation of Edward III. Henry V's first attempt to win glory in France began unpromisingly with a lengthy siege of Harfleur, and looked like ending disastrously when the 6,000 English archers making for Calais were intercepted by a much stronger French force. But at Agincourt (25 October 1415) the story of Crécy and Poitiers was repeated. The French cavalry was handicapped by the wet conditions and a narrow front did not permit the horsemen to deploy and thus benefit from their superior numbers. Again the stationary archers were victorious. Some 7,000 Frenchmen were killed. Agincourt had no decisive strategic consequences, but its effect on English opinion helped Henry to renew the war in 1417 with ambitious plans for the capture of Paris. At first progress was not rapid, but the murder of Jean sans Peur, duke of Burgundy, carried out at the instigation of the French dauphin, drove Burgundy into alliance with the English (December 1419). After this Charles VI and his advisers saw no hope of further resistance and the following spring they agreed to the humiliating terms proposed by the English. By the Treaty of Troyes the dauphin was disinherited, the French king recognised Henry as his regent and heir, and Henry agreed to marry Charles's daughter, Shakespeare's 'plus belle Catherine du monde'. Henry still had to reduce to terms the very considerable area of France (approximately from Paris southward) which now supported the dauphin, but this did not appear to be an impossible task. The French estates duly ratified the Treaty of Troyes, Paris itself fell to the English before the end of 1420, and the dauphin lacked a formidable governmental machine to control the zones which acknowledged him. Disastrous though 1356 was, 1420 marks the very nadir of French fortunes.

THE IDEALS OF CHIVALRY

In 80 years the apparently powerful French kingdom had been brought to its knees. There seemed every likelihood that within the next decade the king of England would also in fact be king of France, though there was as yet no intention of merging the two monarchies. How had this extraordinary situation come about?

In order to attempt an answer to this question it is necessary to return to the military methods of the two sides, and this in turn involves a discussion of attitudes towards the conduct of war in the later Middle Ages. We must consider, in fact, the outlook and institutions comprised by the abstraction 'chivalry'. 'Chivalry' means, literally, 'horsiness'; it was the code of the men who fought on horseback, the knightly class. It owed its existence to the pride of this class in what differentiated it from its social inferiors, and to the deep-seated human desire to formulate and define distinctions within society. Manners softened in this age of late feudalism, but they also crystallised and became more formal. Pride of 'birth' was felt and displayed by the medieval nobility with a confident directness denied to later aristocrats. What these men had in common was a certainty of superiority over the socially ineligible, and particularly over those whose ways of life brought them closest to what birth denied them, the wealthy bourgeois and the non-noble cavalry sergeant.

This certainty of pertaining to a privileged and higher category of humanity emerges clearly in three episodes recounted by Joinville in his *Life of St Louis*. The first concerns a discussion between Joinville himself and Robert de Sorbon, the king's confessor and founder of the college which later gave its name to the university of Paris. Sorbon had rebuked Joinville for being more nobly dressed than the king. The retort that he drew on himself was as follows:

Master Robert, with your permission, there is nothing to blame in me if I wear fur and green cloth; for this is the clothing that my father and mother left me. On the contrary, it is you who are doing something blameworthy, for you are the son of villeins and you have given up the clothing of your father and mother and are wearing richer cameline cloth than the king is.[5]

The next story is of an episode which occurred in Palestine, during St Louis' first crusade:

One of the king's sergeants, a man named Goulu, laid his hand on one of the knights of my *corps de bataille*. I went and complained to the king. The king told me that he thought I might well let the matter drop, as the sergeant had only given the knight a push. I told him that I would not allow it to drop, and that if he did not grant me justice I would leave his service, since his sergeants pushed knights about. He granted me justice and the justice [verdict] was thus, in keeping with the usage of the country: the sergeant came to my tent, barefoot and wearing only his underpants, carrying his drawn sword, and he kneeled down before the knight, took hold of the sword by the point and held out the pummel to the knight, saying 'Sire, I make amends to you for having laid my hand on you, and I have brought this sword so that you may cut off my hand if you wish.' And I asked the knight to pardon the sergeant's offence; and he did so.[6]

Joinville's other tale concerns Henry 'the Generous', Count of Champagne:

Artaud of Nogent was the burgher in whom the Count trusted most of all the burghers in the world, and he was so rich that he built with his own money the castle of Nogent l'Artaud. Now it happened one Whitsun that Count Henry was going out of his rooms at Troyes to hear mass at St Stephen's. At the foot of the staircase there was kneeling a poor knight, who said to the Count: 'Sire, I beg you for the love of God to give me money, so that I may marry these two daughters of mine whom you see here.' Artaud, who was walking behind the Count, said to the poor knight: 'Sire knight, it is not courtly to ask of our lord, for he has given away so much that he has no more to give.' The generous Count turned to Artaud and said: 'Sire villein, you are not telling the truth when you say that I have no more to give; I have something, for I have you. Take him, sire knight, for I give him you, indeed I will guarantee him to you.' The knight was not taken aback but got hold of Artaud by his cloak and told him that he would not let go until they had come to terms. And by the time Artaud got away they had come to terms to the tune of five hundred pounds.[7]

All three of these stories illustrate the essentially exclusive nature of chivalry; the pleasure in being a member of an élite comes solely from the contrast between one's position and that of the non-elect. Above all, this class mystique was nourished by the contrast between the code or conduct of the nobles and those of the rich but 'low-born' merchants, the Artauds of the world. This shows clearly in the verses addressed by a fifteenth-century poet, Jean Molinet, to the bourgeoisie, lines obviously intended to be acceptable to a noble reader:

> You lead a comfortable life, peaceful, secure,
> While they endure mortal suffering in the fray.
> You sleep warm in the city, restfully,
> And they out in the fields, still armed.
> You dream of adding to your rank,
> And they are dying for you and your inheritance.[8]

Bertrand de Born, the Provençal freebooter of an earlier century, emphasised the same contrast in a poem celebrating the delights of war:

And it will be a happy time, for the usurers will be robbed of their property and pack-animals will no longer be able to journey in peace on the roads, nor will the townsmen and the merchants on the road from France travel in safety. He who takes willingly will become wealthy.[9]

This bellicose ideology was the prerogative of those who had been inducted or 'dubbed' as knights by being struck a blow with a sword by one who was already a knight. The symbolism involved in this magical transmission of special powers is a reminder that the occasion was essentially a quite primitive initiation ceremony, though the Church worked strenuously to 'infiltrate' chivalric ideas by adding religious and social obligations to the list of the knight's duties, and dubbing became a sacrament whereby the knight and his arms were consecrated. When he was admitted to the chivalrous class the warrior was expected to train seriously as a cavalryman: the tournament was the peace-time form of exercise in which he learnt and practised the skilled art of fighting on horseback in close formation. So profound was the division between the man who waged war on a horse and he who fought on foot that it was felt by some nobles to be unfitting that a knight should be killed by an infantryman; indeed the duke of Julliers hanged one of his foot soldiers who was so rash as to claim responsibility for the death in battle of the duke's enemy the count of St Pol.

The virtues most prized by the chivalrous were military prowess, loyalty to a feudal overlord, and 'courtesy'—considerate manners, that is, towards the other members of the chivalrous class. The 'romance' literature of the Middle Ages elaborated on these qualities as they had been displayed by the knights of king Arthur's court and by Charlemagne's paladins, and to the men who set the tone of the chivalrous society of the later Middle Ages these were very real heroes. 'We had great need to-day of the good knights of the Round Table', said John I of Portugal at the siege of Coria, 'for surely, if they had been here, we should have taken this place'.[10] Charles the Rash of Burgundy, later in the fifteenth century, was a great reader of Arthurian literature, and used to speak of his desire to emulate the knights of chivalrous romance and the heroes of antiquity; 'he was great of heart', says Chastellain, 'in his desire to be known and highly regarded for his outstanding deeds'.[11] Imitation of the great men of the past was the way to glory, it was believed, and Charles had his court at Dijon decorated by tapestries depicting the siege of Troy, the labours of Hercules and the voyage of the Argonauts, Trajan and Caesar, Alexander the Great and Charlemagne, king Arthur, Godfrey of Bouillon and the rest of the Nine Worthies. Similar collections of noble exemplars were to be found depicted at any court, and may still be seen, for instance, at the ducal palace of Urbino. But the modest opinion, characteristic of the earlier Middle Ages, that the men of latter, degenerate days could never rival the heroes of antiquity, was lacking. Instead, attempts were made to inaugurate a sort of cult of those contemporaries who showed to perfection the virtues of chivalry. Such an attitude is strongly marked in a number of laudatory biographies, particularly those of Du Guesclin, of marshal Boucicaut and of Jacques de Lalaing, the Burgundian *bon chevalier* whose knight errantry is described in the *Livre des faits*, and who was fair as Paris, pious as Aeneas, wise as Ulysses and passionate as Hector—and yet *courtois, débonnaire* and even *humble* towards his opponents. As for Boucicaut, the eulogistic biography published in his lifetime tells us that beside accomplishing imperishable feats of arms, he was so devout that he daily prayed for three hours and heard two masses, and never failed to wear black each Friday.

CHIVALRY AND WARFARE

So much for the ideals of chivalry. It is now time to come to the difficult question of their influence on the conduct of the war. Exponents of chivalric theory saw warfare as a series of equal engagements conducted in such a manner as to test and show the prowess of the individual knightly participants. As late as the sixteenth century it was normal to propose the settlement of wars by individual combat. Such schemes were never effective, although the elaborate plan to resolve the Sicilian dispute by a personal combat at Bordeaux between Charles of Anjou and Peter III of Aragon (1283) was not entirely insincere and came somewhere near to fruition. Similar proposals were sometimes made for contests between small teams representative of the two sides; thus marshal Boucicaut suggested during the siege of al-Mahdiya (1390) a combat of one, or 10, or 20, or 40 representatives of the king of Tunis and of the crusaders, who were to advance on each other from the two sides of a closed field. This view of warfare also entailed the elimination of any form of unjust advantage which might vitiate the verdict of battle as a test of military prowess. It was by some considered unfair to set ambushes or even to make use of side-roads in campaigning. A head-on clash was the most impartial trial, and during the English siege of Calais (1346–7) William of Hainault suggested that a truce should take effect for three days while a bridge was built which would conveniently enable the English and French armies to meet in battle.

The chivalric virtue of 'courtesy' implied kind treatment of knightly prisoners of war, and the well-known passage in which Froissart describes the Black Prince's generosity towards the French nobles after Poitiers shows that this could be effective in practice:

That evening the prince of Wales gave a supper in his lodging to the French king, his son Philip, and the most part of the counts and barons that were prisoners. The prince seated king John, the lord James of Bourbon, the lord John d'Artois, the count of Tancarville, the count of Étampes, the count of Dammartin, the count of Joinville and the lord of Parthenay, at one high table . . . and other lords, knights, and squires, at other tables; and the prince always served the king . . . very humbly, and would not sit at the king's table, although he requested him: he said he was not qualified to sit at the table with so great a prince as the king was. Then he said to the king: 'Sir, for God's sake, make no bad cheer, though your will was not accomplished this day; for, Sir, the king my father will certainly bestow on you as much honour and friendship as he can, and will agree with you so reasonably, that you shall ever after be friends. And, Sir, I think you ought to rejoice, though the battle be not as you wish, for you have this day gained the high renown of prowess, and have surpassed all others on your side, in valour. Sir, I say this not to mock you, for all our party, who saw every man's deeds, agree in this, and give you the palm and chaplet.'

Therewith the Frenchmen whispered among themselves, that the prince had spoken nobly, and that most probably he would prove a noble man, if God preserved his life, to persevere in such good fortune.[12]

The Black Prince's courtesy was of course assisted by his fluency in French, which remained the first language of the English court, and was in a sense the international language of chivalry. Moreover, this generous treatment of fellow aristocrats in the hour of victory should not be taken as a typical occasion. The Black Prince and the English nobles would naturally have felt generous after gaining a decisive victory which put the French kingdom at their mercy and promised to win fortunes for many of them in ransom money; yet the very fact that many went to war to seek financial gain rather than glory was incompatible with chivalric ideals. Treatment of the non-noble classes was quite another matter. The Black Prince himself was responsible for the sack of Limoges in 1370, when the city was burnt and more than 3,000 of its people put to death. Infantry taken in battle were entitled to none of the consideration granted to the nobility and no ransom could be expected for them; they were often slaughtered rather than being suffered to become a burden on the victor's food resources.

In so far as it affected warfare, then, the chivalrous outlook detracted from the efficient conduct of war; its emphasis was on the manner of accomplishment rather than the thing accomplished, on glory rather than 'results'. To be chivalrous was to be unbusiness-like in the matter of achieving victory, and thus to be handicapped. We have seen that the French met defeat in the three great actions of Crécy, Poitiers and Agincourt at least in part because they employed the conventional chivalric mode of attack, the cavalry charge, against armies whose strength lay in a non-noble weapon, the longbow. Does it follow from this that the English won their victories because they were more sceptical of the noble mirage of chivalry and, specifically, were less inhibited by chivalric notions of warfare?

Certainly the English were unashamed to proclaim the unaristocratic longbow as their characteristic weapon. By Edward I's Statute of Winchester (1285) it became an obligatory weapon for English foot-soldiers and Edward III made compulsory the holding of archery contests on holidays. The great folk hero of later medieval England, Robin Hood, was a renowned archer with the longbow, a man who could 'slice the wand' again and again from a range of many hundred yards:

> I was com[p]ted the best archere
> That was in mery Englonde.[13]

If the English archery and tactical combination of archers with other arms suggest a professional approach to war which contrasts with French dilettantism, the explanation of this must be sought in the constant wars of the English with their Celtic neighbours, from whom, indeed, the use of the longbow had been learnt. Frequent campaigning in difficult terrain against the Welsh and Scots compelled the English to give much thought to strategy, tactics, weapons and the other problems of war; the consequences of military conservatism for them would have been expensive and humiliating and there was constant need for inventiveness. Throughout the 80 years of war the English had their eyes on the serious proposition of gaining the French kingdom rather than the pageantry of chivalric pomp: it is symbolic of this that Henry V, when he married Princess Catherine in June 1420,[14] refused to hold any tournament but instead hurried off his knights to besiege Sens.

The French had indeed had opportunities to learn the dangers involved in launching knights against well-disciplined infantry—as witness their defeat by the Flemish in 1302 at Courtrai—but the lesson had not been learnt. In all the three major engagements the French cavalry was unleashed in a courageous but rash charge, and such tactics were not confined to their wars with the English. It was the French and Burgundian element which insisted on a headlong assault against the Turks at Nicopolis in 1396, despite the warnings of the king of Hungary who was accustomed to warfare against the Ottomans and refused to commit his own troops to mass suicide. Du Guesclin was able to show that successes could be won if only battle was not made the occasion of an undisciplined display of valour, but in opposition to him was a strong and respected tradition which reasserted itself at Agincourt. Such a tradition is exemplified by the reported refusal of the French to accept the services at Agincourt of 6,000 archers offered by the city of Paris: 'what need have we of these shop-keepers?' they proudly enquired, and it was suggested that the principles of knightly honour would be contravened if the French army thus came to outnumber the English. It is not altogether just to adopt Froissart, who was a native of Valenciennes in Hainault and spent several years at the English court, as the characteristic representative of the French chivalric attitude to war, yet nowhere outside his pages are these campaigns depicted in such chivalrous colours as a series of knightly deeds in which the nobles of the contending sides were joined by a common devotion to valorous and 'courteous' enterprise. For Froissart, who set out to describe feats of arms and wondrous deeds as an encouragement to valour, the bowmen who actually won the decisive battles were an insignificant rabble of boors. Yet Froissart's stupid snobbery must not blind one to the nobler side of chivalry, the side that is seen in king Jean's decision to return voluntarily to imprisonment in England when his hostage absconded.

A difficult question remains to be answered. Should the French reliance on cavalry and preference for bravery over tactics be ascribed to mere military conservatism, or is this anachronistic emphasis on the aristocratic arm symptomatic of a more profound difference between the two countries? Did the French suffer merely from bad generalship or was their exaggerated respect for the horse-soldier and contempt for the infantryman indicative of a more hierarchical society? Certainly the English governing class was more content to recruit assistance in war from the lower ranks, and co-operation in war would in turn tend to foster a stronger feeling of community. It may well be that for England, like Switzerland, an unusual reliance on infantry had consequences for social and political structure (more developed representative institutions, greater potential for revolt) that were not present in France.[15] But if the question of differences in social structure is answerable, it is certainly not through sources such as those that have been under discussion. Froissart, and others mentioned here, give the chivalric, aristocratic viewpoint, mostly in literary form. The social realities cannot be measured in this way. Even military realities are more complex. The persistent myth that the three famous English victories demonstrated the superiority of longbow infantry over cavalry may be congenial to a particular brand of English national sentiment, but it is an oversimplification. For one thing, as has been seen, position and timing played even more determinant roles in the battles than weaponry. For another, the English archers, too, 'remained firmly grounded in a military context that was dominated by horseback-riding aristocrats'.[16] Chivalric accounts, with their natural interest in glamourising the role of cavalry, do not tell us much about the close co-operation between mounted and foot soldiery that is in evidence on both sides and over a long period. Finally the subsequent history of warfare should make us wary of exaggerating the significance of these battles. The appearance of the longbow was quickly met by better protective armour and more flexible tactics, and the role of the cavalry as shock troops capable of breaking formations persisted long into the era of gunpowder. The French military revival of the mid-fifteenth century, which will be discussed in Chapter 11, is a reminder of how rapidly the balance of fortunes could change.

A case could be made for the statement that the war was embarked on in a spirit of chivalry on both sides and that this view of warfare prevailed for a whole generation—until the Peace of Brétigny or perhaps the death of Edward III (1377) —to perish thereafter except in its disastrous revival by the French at Agincourt. King Edward, the founder of the Order of the Garter, was the very soul of chivalry and would have been puzzled at the argument that the English waged war less chivalrously because they relied to a greater extent on archery. For Froissart the great days of knightly feats of arms ended with this phase of the war, and when he returned to England in 1395 he found that there were Englishmen who shared his point of view and asked:

What has become of the great ventures [*entreprises*], the valiant men, the fine battles and the fine conquests? Where are the knights of England now, to accomplish such things? In those days the English were feared, and spoken of everywhere. Since good King Edward's death things have gone from bad to worse . . . and now King Richard of Bordeaux only seeks rest and pleasures.[17]

It must be remembered, of course, that the sentimental Froissart was then an elderly man who would easily fall prey to nostalgia.

By the time that Richard II ruled England (1377–99) the French had begun to reflect on the causes of their defeats. Honoré Bouvet's *Arbre des Batailles* (issued in 1387) is a practical handbook on war, not a treatise on chivalry and honour; it advocates defensive tactics in battle and suggests that the French should make more use of their peasantry, who are accustomed to a rigorous life. By the middle of the following century such views were commonplace, and similar warnings against indisciplined impetuosity and advice in favour of reliance on infantry and defensive warfare are to be found in Jean Juvénal des Ursins' 'Remonstrances' (1453) and Jean de Bueil's *Le Jouvencel*. The latter work (*c.*1466) went directly against chivalric doctrine by forbidding any form of fraternisation with the enemy: the author makes his hero reject a suggestion from the enemy commander that 12 knights from each side should pick out a convenient and impartial site for battle, on the ground that 'there is a common saying, and it is thought to be a very old one, that one should never do anything on the enemy's initiative'.[18]

In the 1370s an anonymous author presented to Charles V of France a weighty book of advice in the form of a dialogue entitled *Somnium Viridarii* or *Dream in the Pleasure-garden* (better known under its French title as *Le songe du vergier, qui parle de la disputacion du clerc et du chevalier*). The cleric who is a participant in this dialogue remarks sarcastically that 'The knights of our day have foot-battles and cavalry engagements painted on the walls of their rooms, so that through their eyes they may take delight in imaginary battles, which they would not dare to witness as members of an army, or even to be present at in person'.[19] This suggestion that there was now a strong vicarious element in chivalry, that its reality was a thing of the past, contains much truth. Every such ideal must look back to a golden past that can never have existed in reality, but it is particularly true of chivalry that the less of it there was the more it was talked about and the more strenuous were the attempts to revive it. Characteristic of this late, formalised, self-conscious chivalry is the highly organised and pedantic pageantry of heraldry, with its learned glorification of noble descent, and such chivalric foundations as Edward III's Order of the Garter (*c.*1348) and Philip the Good of Burgundy's Order of the Golden Fleece (1430). The Golden Fleece was inaugurated by Duke Philip

from the great love we bear to the noble order of chivalry, whose honour and prosperity are our only concern, to the end that the true Catholic Faith, the Faith of Holy Church, our Mother, as well as the peace and welfare of the realm may be defended, preserved and maintained to the glory and praise of Almighty God our Creator and Saviour, in honour of His glorious Mother, the Virgin Mary, and of our Lord, St Andrew, Apostle and Martyr, and for the furtherance of virtue and good manners.[20]

Membership of this order was restricted to 24 (later 30) noble knights. Four officers and a chancellor, secretary and treasurer served under the master and sovereign, who was always the reigning duke. Naturally France was most prolific of these orders. Among the French foundations may be mentioned King Jean's Order of the Star (1352), whose 300 members took an oath never to flee in battle (and which ceased to exist after only one year when more than a quarter of the knights were killed in a single engagement), and Boucicaut's Order of the White Lady, founded in 1398 for the defence of ladies and maidens in distress.

William Caxton, in the epilogue to his translation of Lull's *Order of Chivalry*, expressed his conviction that chivalry was decadent in his day:

O ye Knights of England, where is the custom and usage of noble chivalry that was used in those days? What do ye now but go to the baths and play at dice? And some not well advised, use not honest and good rule, against all order of knighthood. Leave this, leave it! and read the noble volumes of Saint Graal, of Launcelot, of Galahad, of Tristram, of Perseforest, of Perceval, of Gawain, and many more. There shall ye see manhood, courtesy, and gentleness. And look in latter days at the noble acts since the Conquest, as in King Richard's days Coeur de Lion, Edward the First and Third and his noble sons, Sir Robert Knolles, Sir John Hawkwood, Sir John Chandos and Sir Walter Manny; read Froissart, and also behold that victorious and noble King Harry the Fifth and the captains under him, his noble brethren, the Earls of Salisbury, Montagu, and many others whose names shine gloriously by their virtuous noblesse and acts that they did in the honour of the order of chivalry. Alas! What do ye but sleep and take ease, and are all disordered from chivalry?[21]

Not all Caxton's heroes, it will be noted, came from the distant past. It has already been suggested that attempts were made in their own lifetime to raise on to a chivalric pedestal such figures as marshal Boucicaut (1366–1421) and Jacques de Lalaing (1421–53), the latter of whom was denied a knightly end in that he was killed by a cannon ball. In the following century the same treatment was accorded to Bayard, the *chevalier sans peur et sans reproche* who met his death from arquebus fire in Lombardy in 1524. In Bayard's day the emperor Maximilian strove hard to revive chivalry, writing a verse autobiography (1517) in which his adventures in the tourney and chase were recounted in the tradition of chivalrous literature, and assisting in the preparation of *Der Weiszkönig*, a similar work on his father Frederick III and himself. Throughout the sixteenth century, jousting, though it had lost much of its utility as a form of military training, remained the aristocratic sport *par excellence*. King Henry II of France was killed jousting in 1559 and in the half-century after this the English court fêted its queen in the annual accession-day tilts.

The brief account given here of the splendours and miseries of chivalric warfare has no claim to constitute a description of the phenomenon 'Chivalry'. Almost nothing has been said of chivalry and 'courtoisie' as literary *genres*—or one should perhaps say as a literary *Zeitgeist* witnessing to a *Zeitgeist* general among the classes of society who read or were read to. *The Adventures of Don Quixote*, that 'light and mirror of all knightly chivalry' (1604–14), bears witness to the fact that the valour of knights and their 'courtesy' to ladies remained the favourite topic of Europe's fiction readers long after the armoured knight had ceased to be the characteristic figure of the battle-field. Don Quixote, it will be remembered, 'filled his mind with all that he read in his books, with enchantments, quarrels, battles, challenges, wounds, wooings, loves, torments and other impossible nonsense; and so deeply did he steep his imagination in the belief that all the fanciful stuff he read was true, that to his mind no history in the world was more authentic'. And so it came about that Don Quixote repaired his ancestor's rusty armour and fitted it with a pasteboard visor because 'he thought it fit and proper, both in order to increase his renown and to serve the state, to turn knight errant and travel through the world with horse and armour in search of adventures, following in every way the practice of the knights errant he had read of, redressing all manner of wrongs and exposing himself to changes and dangers, by the overcoming of which he might win eternal honour and renown'.[22]

Don Quixote is not merely a satire on chivalry but also the great prose poem of the sunset of chivalry. In Elizabeth I's England, Cervantes' contemporary Edmund Spenser was writing in his *Faerie Queen* of another 'gentle knight', 'for knightly giusts and fierce encounters fitt'. As in architecture there was no clear break between the last of 'true' Gothic and the beginning of the Gothic revival, so in literature there was no interruption between this prolongation of medieval romance and the Romantic revival of medieval taste as witnessed in the ballad collections of Bishop Percy and J. G. Herder and the European popularity of Macpherson's *Ossian* and Scott's *Ivanhoe*.

Even today international law enshrines the chivalric notion of warfare in the clauses of the Geneva Convention which govern the treatment of prisoners of war. The terms of these provide that 'other ranks' who are captured may be forced to work for the imprisoning power, but it is illegal to compel officers to work; they are the heirs of the nobles who dined with the Black Prince after Poitiers.

FURTHER READING
The background to the war

The best introduction to the war is now C. Allmand, *The Hundred Years War. England and France at War, c.1300–c.1450* (Cambridge, 1988), which also has a good thematic bibliography. The classic work is E. Perroy, *The Hundred Years War* (tr. London, 1951), which is still irreplaceable as narrative. Anne Curry, *The Hundred Years War* (Basingstoke, 1993) is written explicitly from the English point of view: J. Sumption, *The Hundred Years War*, vol. 1, *Trial by Battle* (London, 1990) and vol. 2, *Trial by Fire* (London, 1999) is a full and readable account. K. Fowler, ed., *The Hundred Years War* (London, 1971) includes a variety of essays; H. S. Lucas, *The Low Countries and the Hundred Years War* (repr. Philadelphia, Pa., 1976) is a substantial monograph. On the build-up to the war, M. Vale, *The Origins of the Hundred Years War. The Angevin Legacy, 1250–1340* (Oxford, 1996; revised version of *The Angevin Legacy and the Hundred Years War, 1250–1340*, Oxford, 1989); and P. Chaplais, 'English arguments concerning the feudal status of Aquitaine', *Bulletin of the Institute of Historical Research*, 21 (1948), pp. 203–13. R. W. Kaeuper, *War, Justice and Public Order. England and France in the Later Middle Ages* (Oxford, 1988) is an important study of power in both countries.

The best-known chronicle source for the fourteenth century is Froissart, *The Chronicles* (tr. G. Brereton, Harmondsworth, 1968) (excerpts); one older translation, by Lord Berners (several editions, including the modernised and abridged one by G. I. Macaulay, London, 1908), is available on the internet from the University of Virginia Library, Electronic Text Center (http://etext.lib.virginia.edu/). *See also* J. J. N. Palmer, ed., *Froissart: Historian* (Woodbridge and Totowa, N.J., 1981); and, with a wider literary perspective, P. F. Ainsworth, *Jean Froissart and the Fabric of History: Truth, Myth and Fiction in the* Chroniques (Oxford, 1990).

The first phase of the war

Most of the focus in English has been from the English viewpoint. C. J. Rogers, 'Edward III and the dialectics of strategy', *Transactions of the Royal Historical Society*, 6th series, 4 (1994), pp. 83–102; H. J. Hewitt, *The Organization of War Under Edward III, 1338–62* (Manchester, 1966); J. Campbell, 'England, Scotland and the Hundred Years War in the fourteenth century', in *Europe in the Late Middle Ages*, eds J. R. Hale, J. R. L. Highfield and B. Smalley (London, 1965), pp. 184–216. From the French side, *see* J. B. Henneman, *Royal Taxation in Fourteenth Century France. The Development of War Financing, 1322–56* (Princeton, N.J., 1971). J. J. N. Palmer, *England, France and Christendom, 1377–99* (London, 1972) is a chronological narrative account, very much from the English point of view.

Internal problems of the French monarchy

On internal dissent, A. L. Funk, 'Robert Le Coq and Étienne Marcel', *Speculum*, 19 (1944), pp. 470–87; D. M. Bessen, 'The Jacquerie: class war or co-opted rebellion?', *Journal of Medieval History*, 11 (1985), pp. 43–59. The theory that over-mighty subjects came to pose the biggest threat to the monarchy and to the cohesion of France was put by J. Le Patourel, 'The king and the princes in fourteenth-century France', in *Europe in the Late Middle Ages*, eds J. R. Hale, J. R. L. Highfield and B. Smalley (London, 1965), pp. 155–83. A case in point is Brittany: *see* M. Jones, *Ducal Brittany 1364–99. Relations with England and France during the Reign of Duke John IV* (Oxford, 1970); Michael Jones, *The Creation of Brittany A Late Medieval State* (London, 1988) (essays). *See also* J. B. Henneman, 'The military class and the French monarchy in the Late Middle Ages', *American Historical Review*, 83 (1978), pp. 946–65; C. T. Allmand, *Society at War. The Experience of England and France during the Hundred Years War* (Edinburgh, 1973); and C. T. Allmand, ed., *Power, Culture and Religion in France, c.1350–c.1550* (Woodbridge, 1989), a collection of essays.

The ideals of chivalry

M. Keen, *Chivalry* (New Haven, Conn., and London, 1984) is the best introduction in English. A broad view of medieval society taking chivalry as its focus is taken in the essays published in G. Duby, *The Chivalrous Society* (tr. London, 1977). *See also* J. Bumke, *The Concept of Knighthood in the Middle Ages* (New York, 1982) (on German literature of the 12th and 13th centuries); A. Borst, 'Knighthood in the high middle ages: ideal and reality', in *Lordship and Community in Medieval Europe: Selected Readings*, ed. F. Cheyette (repr. Huntington, N.Y., 1975), pp. 180–91; Benjamin Arnold, *German Knighthood, 1050–1300* (Oxford, 1985); and R. H. Lucas, 'Ennoblement in late medieval France', *Medieval Studies*, 39 (1977), pp. 239–60. A broad survey of the literary context is A. Scaglione, *Knights at Court: Courtliness, Chivalry and Courtesy from Ottonian Germany to the Italian Renaissance* (Berkeley, Cal., 1991). Recent studies include R. Barber, *The Knight and Chivalry* (repr. Woodbridge, 1995); J. Vale, *Edward III and Chivalry. Chivalric Society and its Context, 1270–1350* (Woodbridge, 1982); R. Kaeuper, *Chivalry and Violence in Medieval Europe* (Oxford, 1999), and the series of conference proceedings edited by Christopher Harper-Bill and Ruth Harvey: *The Ideals and Practice of Medieval Knighthood*, vol. I (Woodbridge, 1986), vol. II (1988) and vol. III (1990), and *Medieval Knighthood*, vol. IV (1992) and vol. V (1995). On the commentators of the time cited here, *see* Paul D. Solon, 'Popular response to standing military forces in fifteenth-century France', *Studies in the Renaissance*, 19 (1972), pp. 78–111.

Chivalry and warfare

For the general context of medieval warfare, see P. Contamine, *War in the Middle Ages* (tr. Oxford, 1984) (with a systematic methodology and extensive bibliography); M. Keen, ed., *Medieval Warfare. A History* (Oxford, 1999); J. F. Verbruggen, *The Art of Warfare in Western Europe during the Middle Ages* (2nd edition, Woodbridge, 1997); H. Delbrück, *History of the Art of War*, vol. III. *Medieval Warfare* (repr. Lincoln, Neb., 1990). The excellent overview of Bernard S. Bachrach, 'Medieval military historiography', in *Companion to Historiography*, ed. M. Bentley (London, 1997), pp. 203–20, is among other things a sharp antidote to much of the myth making about medieval military history. On late medieval and renaissance warfare, Michael Mallett, 'The art of war', in *Handbook of European History 1400–1600*, eds Thomas A. Brady jr., Heiko A. Oberman and James D. Tracy (Leiden, 1994–5), vol. 1, pp. 535–62 is a good introduction, as is Christopher Allmand, 'War', in *NCMH*, vol. 7, ch. 8. K. Devries, *Infantry Warfare in the Early Fourteenth Century* (Woodbridge, 1996) discusses the most significant battles of the period. *See also* the excellent Bert S. Hall, *Weapons and Warfare in Renaissance Europe: Gunpowder, Technology, and Tactics* (Baltimore, Md., 1997), which begins with the late Middle Ages; and, with a slightly later focus, J. R. Hale, *War and Society in Renaissance Europe, 1450–1620* (London, 1985).

Works dealing with the Hundred Years War in particular include A. Curry and M. Hughes, eds, *Arms, Armies and Fortifications in the Hundred Years War* (Woodbridge, 1994), and M. Prestwich, *Armies and Warfare in the Middle Ages. The English Experience* (New Haven, Conn., 1996).

On the specific issues of the impact of chivalric ideas on the conduct of warfare, *see* M. Vale, *War and Chivalry: Warfare and Aristocratic Culture in England, France, and Burgundy at the End of the Middle Ages* (Athens, Ga., 1981). On the role of the longbow and its social implications, Clifford J. Rogers, 'The military revolutions of the Hundred Years' War', *Journal of Military History*, 57 (1993), pp. 241–78 (esp. pp. 249–57). On Robin Hood, *see* J. G. Bellamy, *Robin Hood: an Historical Inquiry* (Bloomington, In., 1985); R. B. Dobson and J. Taylor, *Rymes of Robin Hood: an Introduction to the English Outlaw* (revised edition, Stroud, 1997); J. C. Holt, *Robin Hood* (London, 1989); and M. Keen, *The Outlaws of Medieval Legend* (London, 1961; revised edition, 1979). Honoré Bonet or Bouvet's *The Tree of Battles* is translated with an introduction by G. W. Coopland (Liverpool, 1949). Finally on the chivalric orders, D'A. J. D. Boulton, *The Knights of the Crown. The Monarchical Orders of Knighthood in Later Medieval Europe, 1325–1520* (Woodbridge, 1987).

NOTES

1. *See above*, p. 43.
2. *Above*, p. 114.
3. *Above*, pp. 94–6.
4. Chapter 9.
5. Joinville, *Life of St Louis*, ch. VI; in Joinville and Villehardouin, *Chronicles of the Crusades*, tr. M. R. B. Shaw (London, 1963); this passage is on p. 171.
6. Joinville, op. cit., ch. XCIX; in Shaw's translation, p. 293.
7. Joinville, op. cit., ch. XX; in Shaw's translation, p. 186.
8. Jean Molinet, *Chroniques*, eds G. Doutrepont and O. Jodogne, 3 vols (Paris, 1935–7), vol. I, p. 69.
9. M. de Riquer, ed., *La Lírica de los Trovadores* (Barcelona, 1948), vol. I, p. 427.

10. Fernão Lopes, *Crónica de D. Joâo I*, Pt. II, ch. LXXV, ed. Almeida and Basto (Porto, 1949), vol. II, p. 187. Excerpts of this source have been translated in Fernão Lopes, *The English in Portugal, 1383–1387* (Warminster, 1988).

11. *See below*, p. 180.

12. Froissart, *Chronicle*, Book I, ch. 168; adapted from Lord Berners' translation (London, 1814–16), vol. I, p. 126; in G. Brereton's translation (Harmondsworth, 1968) this passage is on pp. 143–4.

13. 'A Gest of Robyn Hode', in *The Oxford Book of Ballads*, selected and ed. James Kinsley (Oxford, 1969, pb. edition 1982), pp. 420–90 (p. 487).

14. *See above*, p. 137.

15. An argument recently restated by Clifford J. Rogers, 'The military revolutions of the Hundred Years' War', *Journal of Military History*, 57 (1993), pp. 241–78 (esp. pp. 252–5).

16. Bert S. Hall, *Weapons and Warfare in Renaissance Europe: Gunpowder, Technology, and Tactics* (Baltimore, Md., 1997), p. 39.

17. Quoted by Baron Kervyn de Lettenhove, *Oeuvres de Froissart, Chroniques*, vol. I. (Introduction) (Brussels, 1870), pt. I, pp. 418–19.

18. Jean de Bueil, *Le Jouvencel*, ed. L. Lecestre with introduction by C. Favre, 2 vols (Paris, 1887–9), vol. I, p. 210.

19. *Le songe du vergier*, Book 1, ch. 3, § 8, ed. M. Schnerb-Lièvre, 2 vols (Paris, 1982), vol. I, p. 15.

20. O. Cartellieri, *The Court of Burgundy* (tr. 1929, repr. London, 1972), p. 57.

21. Caxton, *The Book of the Ordre of Chyvalry*, ed. A. T. P. Byles (Early English Texts Society, 1926: modernised here), pp. 122–4. Caxton continues: 'How many knights be there now in England that have the use and the exercise of a knight, that is to wit that he knoweth his horse and his horse him?'

22. *Don Quixote*, ch. I; translation by J. M. Cohen (Harmondsworth, 1950, repr. 1987), pp. 32–3.

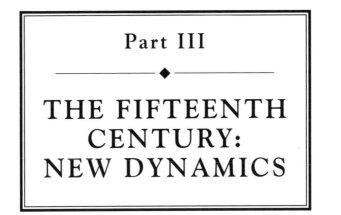

Part III

◆

THE FIFTEENTH
CENTURY:
NEW DYNAMICS

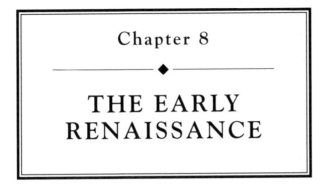

Chapter 8

◆

THE EARLY RENAISSANCE

THE URBAN AND SECULAR CULTURE OF ITALY

Consideration of military events in fourteenth-century France in the previous chapter led on to a discussion of the role of 'chivalry' in the social and literary culture of later medieval Europe. This discussion was almost entirely confined to Europe north of the Alps, and we must now turn to the culture of the wealthiest and most advanced region in western Europe, the Italian peninsula. Although this chapter is prefaced by the time-honoured abstract noun, 'Renaissance', its subject is perhaps better defined as the intellectual and cultural history of Italy in the fourteenth and the earlier part of the fifteenth centuries.

This culture differed from that of contemporary northern Europe in that its tone was set as much by town-dwelling merchants and lawyers as by feudatories from courts and castles, and more by all these than by clerics. The chief element in the contrast between Italian civilisation and that of Europe north of the Alps was secular education. The lay schoolmaster had never disappeared from medieval Italy. By the thirteenth century he was to be found even in the smaller towns, and in the great cities he was ubiquitous. The mercantile classes sent their children to receive an education that was at least in part professional—there was a strong emphasis on mathematics—and in the towns of northern Italy the literacy rate must have been high. Giovanni Villani reports that at Florence in the 1320s some 8,000 to 10,000 children were in attendance at elementary schools at any one time. Villani estimates that the total population of the city at the time was in the region of 90,000. Owing to the high death rate, the age structure of the population was very different then from now, but if 10 per cent of the population was indeed attending elementary school it is likely that a majority of the male citizens received some schooling. The proportion of Florentines that went on to receive further education was less considerable. According to Villani more than 1,000 boys attended the six abacus schools (which provided training for business) and the four grammar schools had a total of 600 pupils, but probably a good many boys and girls were taught at home by a tutor at this stage.[1]

The tone of the Italian culture of this period is markedly urban in the most direct sense. Collections of amusing stories, like the *Novellino*—from which one tale has already been quoted[2]—were immensely popular, and a theme that ranked in favour with the quick-witted merchant and his prompt retorts was his rustic counterpart, slow of understanding and easily imposed upon. The satirists made no attempt to spare the feelings of the peasant, for he was not part of their public; and without the stock figure of the credulous, gullible yokel, Boccaccio and Sacchetti would be deprived of much of their subject matter. But, if the countryman was a mere figure of fun, the countryside itself was the object of a new admiration. This revolution in the history of sensibility is directly connected with the urban quality of the culture of the time. The man who appreciates the beauty of the rural land-scape is the man who visits it for his summer holiday (the fourteenth-century Florentine merchant usually spent four months a year at his villa) or to picnic and to hunt, not he who struggles to wrest a living from it. No doubt it was partly their reading of the Latin poets which made them see beauty in rural scenery, but its effect went deep, and men now not only read pastorals but again wrote pastoral poetry with sincerity of feeling. Shepherds and shepherdesses had come back to decorate the literary scene for many a century. In no one is this feeling for the country stronger than in Petrarch (1304–74), whose joy in scenery even shines through his self-conscious literariness. It was typical of his time that Petrarch should contrast the 'convenience of the city' with the 'leisure of the country'. His letters contain many descriptions of scenery and in one he declares that 'I always have felt, from my earliest childhood, a hatred of cities, implanted in me by nature, and a love of sylvan life'.[3]

If the countryside was an escape from town and business, there was another world of escape into the imagination provided by that very literary tradition, native to France, which was described in the preceding chapter. For the merchant nothing was more delightful than to sit comfortably in his chair and to read of the perilous, valiant and exhausting deeds of chivalrous knights. Thus he took his risks and his exercise vicariously, and as his modem counterpart travels to the polar regions or climbs Everest so he in his mind's eye fought with Hector and king Arthur and Charlemagne, or mingled with such chivalrous heroes of a more recent age as the 'Young King' (the son of Henry II of England) and Saladin. Dante himself confessed attachment to memories of such reading of:

> the ladies and the knights, the toils and ease
> which roused in us both love and courtesy
> where now so evil have all hearts become.[4]

And when Folgore of San Gimignano, also writing in the early fourteenth century, composed a series of sonnets on the months, his April was 'the gentle country-side all flowering with fresh grass' and his May pure chivalric nostalgia, a picture of horses, banners, trappings, shields, jousting-spears, lances and garlands.[5]

These men were also patriotic citizens of precarious city-republics and normally they played an energetic part in the political life of their state. Coluccio Salutati, who served Florence as chancellor from 1375 to 1405, was one of a number of literary men who defended the 'active life' which was contrasted in time-honoured controversy with the religious and philosophical 'contemplative life'. Again and again it was urged that a 'complete man' should play an active part in public affairs (Cicero was often quoted to this effect) and that he should have a family. Before the middle of the fifteenth century such a view was a commonplace. Giannozzo Manetti (1396–1459) attacked Pope Innocent III's ascetic work on *Contempt of Worldly Things*, and elsewhere quoted with approbation the tag from Terence 'I am a man and I think nothing human alien to me'. Matteo Palmieri's *Della vita civile* (*On Civil Life*, finished in 1439) attacks 'idle men who live in solitude away from all public affairs, contributing nothing to the common good of other mortals and concerned only with their own health . . . Mere sanctity does no good to anything but itself'.[6] L. B. Alberti's *Della famiglia* (*On the Family*), written in the same years, teaches the same doctrine:

the true citizen will love tranquillity, but his own less than that of other good men; he will delight in his own leisure, but not less in that of the other citizens; he will wish for unity, quiet, peace and tranquillity in his own household, but still more for these in the affairs of his city . . . Wise men say that good citizens should undertake the affairs of the republic and bear the burdens of their *patria* . . . to maintain the general well-being of the citizens.[7]

In these phrases concerning the 'common good', we return, it will be noted, to Aristotle, the fountain-head of political writers.[8]

The civic patriotism that received this theoretical justification was a powerful force which had no need of literary backing. *Campanilismo*—the narrow preference for one's native town—is still a strong sentiment in Italy, and was far more potent in an age when towns were independent republics having their own political traditions and a long history of warfare against their neighbours. The *palazzo comunale* or communal palace, the outward sign of the commune's personality, had to be worthy of the town's prestige, as did its other ecclesiastical and municipal monuments. The patronage of the republics was thus an important influence in 'Renaissance' artistic achievement. A city would pay well a man who could enhance its beauty, but the worker in the visual arts was still an 'artist' only in the sense that he was a member of an *arte* (guild); he had no great pretensions and as yet he was vexed by no problems concerning his 'role in society'. Versatility was expected of him as a conscientious craftsman—not as an 'all-round personality'—and he had to be able to turn his hand to the design of fortifications and aqueducts and fountains, as well as being ecclesiastical architect, sculptor and painter. By the early fourteenth century, however, the successful Florentine artist could already hope to enjoy a certain prestige. In 1300 the council called Arnolfo di Cambio, the master of works at the cathedral and the campanile, 'the most famous master and greatest expert in church building known in these parts',[9] and in 1334 they were proud to appoint Giotto to 'the honourable and worthy mastership and governorship of the work at the church of S. Reparata and of the construction and perfection of the walls of the city of Florence . . . and the other connected works of the said city'.[10]

A CULTURAL 'REBIRTH'?

At the beginning of this chapter it was stated that its theme would be Italian culture in the fourteenth and early fifteenth centuries, yet the phrase 'Renaissance' has already been brought into use. How has it come about that the civilisation of the period has received this highly adhesive label, and can the use of this abstraction be justified? The answer to the first of these questions is comparatively straightforward: it is, in brief, that influential writers in Florence, from the fourteenth century to the sixteenth, believed themselves to be living in an age of cultural 'rebirth'. Soon after the middle of the fourteenth century Boccaccio proclaimed that the muses had long been banished from Italy, but Dante had opened the way for their return and Petrarch restored them. He praised Giotto in similar terms as 'one of the lights of Florence's glory', who 'brought painting back into the light after it had been hidden for many centuries under the errors of those who aimed to please the eyes of the ignorant rather than the understanding of the wise'.[11] In his own day, he thought, individuals not unlike the men of antiquity were seeking immortality, and the tiny spark of their efforts raised a hope that the lost light of antiquity might be restored. Giotto had already figured in Giovanni Villani's *Chronicle* as 'the most sovereign master in painting of his day and the one who could best depict people and their movements in a lifelike way',[12] but only rather later, in the writings of the chancellor Salutati and Villani's nephew Filippo, can this view be seen to have crystallised as an agreed (but highly Florence-centred) version of cultural history. Salutati says that the study of 'letters' declined from late classical times, but emerged again with the Paduan Mussato and with Dante, Petrarch and Boccaccio. Filippo Villani in his *Lives of Famous Florentines* (*c.*1400) echoes his uncle's view of Giotto but names Cimabue as the first restorer of artistic standards. The first post-classical poet whom he notes is Dante and he mentions six more recent 'moderns'.

In the 1430s the same interpretation is to be found in Matteo Palmieri who proclaims that:

before Giotto painting was dead and pictures of people risible; he raised it up and his followers have maintained this. Carving and architecture for an extremely long period produced only stupid marvels, but in our time they have risen again and come back into the light after being polished and perfected by many masters. As for letters and liberal studies, it would be better to be silent than to say little. The principal leaders and true masters of men in every good attainment were so forgotten for more than eight hundred years that there was no one who had any true knowledge of them.

But 'Latin elegance' and 'the sweetness of the Latin tongue' were restored by Leonardo Bruni (1370–1444), and now men should thank God that they have had the good fortune to be born in an age when 'the excellent arts of skill are flourishing more than they have for a thousand years'.[13] The same tremendous confidence appears in Leon Battista Alberti's dedication—addressed to Brunelleschi, the designer of the dome of Florence cathedral—to his work *On Painting*:

I believed that it was as many people told me, that nature, the mistress of things, had now indeed grown old and weary, and, just as she no longer brought forth giants, so with talents, which in her younger and more glorious times, so to speak, she brought forth plentifully and wonderfully.

But after I was brought back here to this city of ours [Florence], adorned above all others, from the long exile in which we Alberti have grown old, I realized that in many, but especially in you, Filippo, and in our dear friend Donato [Donatello] the sculptor, and in those others, Nencio [Ghiberti], Luca [della Robbia], and Masaccio, there was talent for every noble thing not to be ranked below any who was ancient and famous in these arts.[14]

This was the sort of optimism that in 1464 caused Giovanni Rucellai to thank God in all sincerity for having made him a Christian born in Italy, 'the most worthy and noble part of Christendom', in Tuscany 'esteemed one of Italy's most worthy provinces' and, above all, at Florence, 'the most beautiful city not only in Christendom, but in the whole world'—and for the fact that his lot had fallen 'in the present age, which all who understand aright know full well transcends in splendour every age that has passed since Florence was first built'.[15] This Florentine certainty of existing in a great time of rebirth was finally incorporated and crystallised in Giorgio Vasari's immensely influential *Lives of the most excellent Painters, Sculptors and Architects* (1550), and it secured acceptance by Michelet, John Addington Symonds and Burckhardt, who in the nineteenth century popularised the idea of the Renaissance in French, English and German. The concept of an age of the Renaissance, then, was the product of the age itself—indeed it states the period's estimate of itself.

To decide whether the concept of a 'Renaissance' is justified by the culture of fourteenth- and fifteenth-century Italy is much more difficult. There is certainly no clear break in the continuity of Italian culture. The classical studies of the fourteenth-century 'humanists' (the word implied a contrast with 'divine', or theological, learning) were in the tradition of a rhetorical education which had never been abandoned. Lawyers had long studied the art of writing and speaking eloquently in accordance with classical models. The Paduan lawyer Mussato (1261–1329), mentioned by Salutati, and his contemporary Lovato, may have seen Roman civilisation as a living thing because their studies of Roman law gave it reality, but their taste for reading Latin authors was nothing new. They were exceptional only in their extension of the principle of classical imitation: Mussato composed a drama, *Eccerinis*, on the model of the classical tragedies, concerning the thirteenth-century Ghibelline tyrant, Ezzelino da Romano. The corpus of classical literature known to Mussato differed little from that available to thirteenth-century scholars, but he was acquainted with some books of Livy's *History* which had long been unread. The circle of humanists at Padua was not unique: others existed at the same time at Verona—where the Chapter library housed many little-known classical works— at Naples and in the papal court at Avignon.

One resident of Avignon was Petrarch (1304–74), the most important figure in the literary culture of fourteenth-century Italy. Petrarch, a Florentine by descent, had been sent to study law at Montpellier and Bologna, but neglected his studies and conceived a fanatical admiration for the works of Cicero. He even addressed ardent letters, couched in his best Ciceronian Latin, to the long-dead author, and behaved in so unbalanced a manner that his enraged father burnt some of his books, though he eventually spared Cicero's *Rhetoric*. Abandoning the legal career, Petrarch took

minor orders and, thanks to the patronage of the Colonna, received several prebends and a priorate. He visited Paris, the Netherlands and the Rhineland, and once
undertook a mission to Naples on behalf of the pope, but for many years resided
mainly at the papal court, living on his unearned ecclesiastical income as a self-
consciously literary figure, a sort of fourteenth-century Jean-Jacques Rousseau, an
author in several genres and a scholar. In middle age he returned to Italy, living at
Parma, Padua, Milan and finally in and near Venice.

Petrarch's writings serve admirably as a reminder of the high degree of continuity
in fourteenth-century Italian culture. There was little change in legal or medical education, and philosophy and theology continued to be studied in the scholastic tradition, based on Aristotelian logic. The theme of Petrarch's *Secretum*, which is perhaps
his most deeply felt work, is the preference which should be given to virtue over
glory.[16] In form the book is a dialogue, in which Petrarch holds a discussion with
St Augustine, the greatest of the fathers of the Church, and there is nothing in his
conclusions which would have shocked the readers of the intervening medieval
centuries. 'Some people in their pride', he says elsewhere, 'have sought to secure by
force the secrets of nature and the high mysteries of God, which we receive with
humble faith.' He goes on to quote with approval (from Romans 11: 34): 'For who
hath known the mind of the Lord?' and 'But what is commanded thee, think thereupon with reverence; for it is not needful for thee to see the things that are secret. Be
not curious in unnecessary matters: for more things are showed unto thee than men
understand' (Ecclesiasticus 3: 22–3).[17] It would scarcely be possible to be more
'medieval' than this and more antagonistic to that spirit of enquiry which is often
considered the very essence of the 'Renaissance'. Moreover, another of Petrarch's
works, *De vita solitaria* (*The Life of Solitude*), is an essay in one of the most popular of
all medieval genres: far from being a protagonist of the civic and family virtues, he
wrote a defence of the monastic life.[18] In one of his letters Petrarch describes an
ascent of Mont Ventoux (near Avignon), and both this gratuitous undertaking and
his account of the climb and of the view from the top—which is perhaps fictitious
—have been held to mark an epoch in the evolution of human sensibility.[19] But the
significant point is Petrarch's reflection after the climb that St Augustine is right, and
that 'men admire mountains and sea, river, oceans and stars' but 'nothing is truly
wonderful except the soul'.[20] Nor is Petrarch exceptional among the early humanists
in the closeness of his adherence to traditional ways of thought. His friend Giovanni
Boccaccio (1313–75), also a scholar and a versatile author, in many respects followed the footsteps of the writers of medieval romances and *fabliaux* in both style
and content, while such works as his *De viris illustribus* (*On Famous Men*)[21] had French
analogues in writings of the same century which advocated imitation of the virtues
of the ancient Romans.[22]

So much for the element of continuity. But the 'Renaissance' is not a mere delu-
sion; there were new cultural threads interwoven with the old. Some of these are
connected with the re-discoveries of classical writings already mentioned. Petrarch
himself, who was a good textual scholar, found an unknown work by Cicero at Liège
and a better text of Livy at Chartres. A friend of Petrarch's made similar discoveries
in the monastic library at Monte Cassino, and Boccaccio was responsible for putting

back into circulation, as it were, the great historian Tacitus and some works of Cicero, Seneca and Ovid. In certain moods of Petrarch one may detect a new confidence in his attitude towards intellectual authority. He defiantly mocks those who accept every word of Aristotle as true: 'I think he was a great man,' he says, 'but he was a man . . . and I do not doubt that he was totally wrong about some things . . . even important ones.' Yet his deference towards Cicero and St Augustine perhaps tended to substitute a Roman for a Greek authority. 'Among the many subjects which interested me,' he says, 'I dwelt especially upon antiquity, for our own age has always repelled me, so that, had it not been for the love of those dear to me, I should have preferred to have been born in any other period than our own.'[23] The belief that imitation of Roman virtues could restore the great days of classical Italy shows clearly in Petrarch's account (not necessarily an entirely veracious one) of his meeting with the emperor Charles IV at Mantua in 1354. He promised to present the emperor with his still unfinished *Lives of Famous Men* when Charles had become distinguished not only by his title 'but also by your deeds: and when, by the greatness of your character, you shall have placed yourself upon a level with the illustrious men of the past. You must so live that posterity shall read of your great deeds as you read of those of the ancients'.

Following up the opportunity afforded by my words, I presented him with some gold and silver coins, which I held very dear. They bore the effigies of some of our rulers—one of them a most lifelike head of Caesar Augustus—and were inscribed with exceedingly minute ancient characters. 'Behold, Caesar, those whose successor you are,' I exclaimed, 'those whom you should admire and emulate, and with whose image you may well compare your own. To no one but you would I have given these coins, but your rank and authority induce me to part with them. I know the name, the character, and the history, of each of these who are there depicted, but you have not merely to know their history, you must follow in their footsteps; the coins should, therefore, belong to you.' Thereupon I gave him the briefest outline of the great events in the life of each of the persons represented, adding such words as might stimulate his courage and his desire to imitate their conduct.[24]

The influence of Greek antiquity on fourteenth-century Italian culture was small. Throughout the medieval period there had been many in the formerly Byzantine territory of southern Italy who knew Greek; both Petrarch and Boccaccio had sought assistance from natives of this region, but neither managed to acquire a good knowledge of the language. Before the end of the century a number of Greeks, such as Manuel Chrysoloras, left Byzantine soil and taught Greek in Italy, and at this time the direct influence of Plato's own works began to be felt. Earlier, his impact had come only through the *Timaeus*, an uncharacteristic book and, more strongly, through neo-Platonic writers. Far more influential than Greek writings, however, was the contribution of France, and in particular of French imaginative literature. This went back to the chivalresque epics and to romance poetry—the *Roman de la Rose* was much read in Italy—and above all to the Provençal troubadours, who were the delight of St Francis of Assisi and did much to form the *dolce stil nuovo* ('sweet new style') of Dante's predecessors in Tuscany. Dante himself pays tribute to the troubadours in the *Divine Comedy* when he breaks into eight lines of Provençal.[25] Nor was it uncommon for Italians to write works in French, though this became rarer in the course of the fourteenth century. Brunetto Latini—placed by Dante in his *Inferno*—compiled in the 1260s a sort of encyclopedia in French (the *Livre dou Tresor*) and Marco Polo's *Travels*, dictated by Marco during his Genoese captivity in 1298–9, also first appeared in the French of his fellow prisoner Rustichello of Pisa, the author of a number of French romance works. The strong French element in the writings of Boccaccio has already been mentioned.

WEALTH, FAMILY AND PATRONAGE

To complete this attempted answer to our second question—how valid is the concept 'Renaissance'?—we must return to the milieu. The civilisation of a period requires consideration in terms of its volume (to express it crudely) as well as its content, and these need to be seen in the light of contemporary patronage. The achievements of Italy in learning and the arts in the fourteenth and fifteenth centuries would have been impossible without the wealth of the traders and financiers of the time, and in an infinite number of ways they reflect the outlook of these men. Boccaccio's *Decameron* has been called a 'mercantile epic' and most of his tales derive their setting and action from the world of the cosmopolitan merchant of his day. Much of the contents of the *Decameron* could be defined as stories written about commercial travellers for commercial travellers, and more than two-thirds of the surviving early manuscripts are known to have belonged to merchant families. The importance to the visual arts of the patronage of these families is evident. One has only to recall the names of the chapels in which are to be found frescoes by Giotto (or attributed to him). These are the chapels of the Bardi and Peruzzi (both great banking houses, which together lent Edward III of England £125,000 in 1338–9) in Santa Croce (Florence) and at Padua the chapel of the Scrovegni founded by the wealthy Paduan merchant Enrico Scrovegni. Contemporaries of course realised that the wealth and the cultural achievements of their time were connected. Giovanni Rucellai—whose gratitude for being born a fifteenth-century Florentine has already been recorded—has another striking passage in his Notebook (*Zibaldone*), in which he lists the various aspects of Florence's greatness in his day (he is writing in about 1458). The Italians, he says, are now pre-eminent in arms; literary style has reached a level unapproached since Cicero; Florence has added greatly to its subject territory; the appearance of the city has been wonderfully improved by the skilful architects of churches, palaces and other buildings; there have been notable painters and workers in the other arts; people are now dressed and their houses decorated with greater luxury, and they have many more slaves than formerly;[26] the manufacture of new types of costly textiles has begun; the Florentines now trade (from Pisa) in heavy galleys; dowries have been increased, thanks to the ingenious invention of dowry funds as part of the city's public debt; and Florence has seen recently four 'notable citizens worthy to be remembered'. These are Palla Strozzi, happy, learned and wealthy; Cosimo de' Medici, 'perhaps the richest Italian there has ever been', an extremely able man who 'controlled the government of the city as though he had been its lord'; Leonardo Bruni, scholar and eloquent writer; and Filippo Brunelleschi, the greatest architect since Roman times. 'The revenues of the commune of Florence are greater than ever before', churches are wealthy and religious observance flourishing. There is a possibility that all citizens may be exempt from taxation for 10 years. Even the middle ranks of society now dress in the best quality cloth and 'the city is richer than ever in ready money, merchandise, property, and holdings in the public funds, and therefore tourneys, weddings and other feasts have become richer and more magnificent than they ever were in the past'. Rucellai ends, as a true merchant, with some statistics. Among these are his estimate of the wealth of Florence's citizens in specie and commodities alone at one and a half million florins: the same figure, he thinks, would have held good 30 years before, but in 1418–23, before the expensive campaigns against the Visconti, it might have reached two million florins.[27]

Rucellai, it will be observed, deals with economics and the arts together, but he does not imply a simple relationship between wealth and cultural achievement of cause and effect. It has been argued that this causation in a sense worked in reverse because merchants tended to spend more money on artistic patronage when the returns from mercantile ventures diminished.[28] This hypothesis supposes an extreme degree of rationality in the merchants and it receives little support from parallel circumstances, but it serves as a useful reminder of the truism that there is no simple equation whereby greater wealth creates greater artistic and intellectual achievement.

Although Rucellai dwelt on the wealth and flourishing condition of the Florentine church, the culture of his day had a secular tone which contrasted strongly with the characteristically medieval culture of European scholasticism. For the first time since the classical period the educated layman was not an exceptional figure. Italy, with its considerable class of lawyers and notaries, had increasingly constituted an exception, but by and large the educated men of western Europe for a millennium were clerics and therefore had no children—or were supposed to have no children.[29] The cultural effects of clerical celibacy, though quite impossible to measure, must be taken into account in discussing the social background to Renaissance culture. The fact that a high proportion of the most educated men did not reproduce had an important consequence; it limited the direct continuity of intellectual achievement within the family. The home was rarely an environment within which intellectual traditions could be handed down from generation to generation, although certain monastic houses came near to substituting for this the nurture of a religious 'family'. The growing interest that fathers who were merchants or lawyers took in the upbringing of their sons brought a new form of cultural transmission into being, and pride in family traditions ensured that this new force should be a powerful one. The same spirit of family pride and loyalty played a direct part in encouraging cultural patronage, since no distinguished family wished to be outshone in the fashion of expending its money on the 'right' artists and men of letters. No work illustrates the strength of these family traditions better than L. B. Alberti's dialogue *Della famiglia*, although (or because?) Alberti's father was an illegitimate descendant of this illustrious Florentine house. Again and again Alberti returns to the family's great past, its military deeds, its distinction in the law and in administration:

Our family, the Alberti, which has always been most honest in all its undertakings, has long conducted its commercial transactions in the West and in many other parts of the world, with such honesty and integrity that we have won universally no inconsiderable or undeserved fame. There was never a single man amongst us who permitted any dishonest practice in trading. All observed the terms of every transaction with entire, scrupulous probity, and thus we became known as great merchants in Italy and abroad in Spain, in the west [England and Flanders], in Syria, Greece and indeed in every port. Moreover the Alberti have been of no little assistance to the state. Of every thirty-two *danari* spent by the state [Florence] in those days, one at least had been provided by our family. A great sum indeed this, but our goodwill and affection towards our State and our furtherance of its interests have always been yet greater! And so we have won fame and reputation with all, but more good feelings and love from strangers than from our own fellow-citizens.[30]

The purpose of this harangue, addressed to two young members of the family by Lionardo Alberti, is to ensure 'that you should always continue as devoted as you are to our family, and equally desirous of increasing its dignity, authority, fame and glory in every way that is open to you; for it would be shameful should you fail to preserve the reputation won by our ancestors'. The Alberti have been considered among the wealthiest of Florentine families for more than two hundred years; no other family has had so long a history of prosperity, for the Cerchi, Peruzzi and many others have fallen into distress. The Alberti have always kept their word, and their continuing affluence must be a divine reward for this. 'I have tried to show you', Lionardo adds, 'that not a few occupations by which wealth may be gained are praised and are honest ones, and that one of these is the merchant's profession.'[31] Elsewhere Lionardo gives his views on education. 'I should wish to see a young noble with a book in his hand more frequently than a hawk on his fist; I never liked that common saying that it is sufficient to know how to write your own name and add up the money due to you. I prefer the old custom of our family. Almost all we Alberti have been considerable men of letters.' He then expatiates on the distinction of no fewer than seven Alberti in theology, mathematics and other fields. 'Any family, but particularly one like ours, should bring up its boys so that with age they increase in wisdom and knowledge, not merely to conform with this ancient and admirable custom of ours, but also on account of the other advantages that a family derives from its men of letters.'[32]

The same atavistic version of the Renaissance principle of *imitatio* figures promin-ently in another dialogue of the same period, Matteo Palmieri's *Della vita civile*, which is dedicated to Alessandro degli Alessandri, 'born of a noble line, begotten by an excellent father, and brought up to study the arts' in the hope that in him 'the glory of the perfect virtue of Ugo, your excellent father, and of your other most renowned and glorious ancestors, may achieve its climax'.[33] In Book I Palmieri deals with educa-tion, and throughout he assumes that a boy's father will be directly concerned with his upbringing. 'A father to whom a son has been born should above all have ideal hopes for him and should expect him to grow up a virtuous and worthy man . . . the father would not be willing to weary his mind on the education of one for whose future he cherished no hopes.'[34] When the child enters adolescence 'the father should start to observe his son closely, for this is the age when the boy first thinks that he already knows things, and when he begins to be free to make decisions and to live in his own way'.[35] 'It is unnecessary to say anything of grammar [Latin], for every father should know positively that without that foundation any learning that may be built up is bound to tumble into barren ruin.'[36] Beyond this, the father should hope that his son will acquire some special talent displaying 'a reverent readiness of the body or a worthy employment of the mind which is an adornment to life'.[37]

FLORENCE AND THE SPREAD OF NEW IDEAS

The greatest of Florentine mercantile families, the Medici, have not been discussed in this account of Renaissance culture and families—there will be some mention of them in a later chapter—but Rucellai, Alberti and Palmieri were all Florentines, and the emphasis on Florence in this chapter requires explanation. Florence is regularly referred to as the 'cradle' of the Renaissance, and if a relatively narrow time-span is taken—roughly the first four decades of the fifteenth century—it can be demonstrated that the label is merited. The concentration of innovative writers who self-consciously placed a premium on the value of classical studies, and who evolved a broadly coherent set of ideas (as described above), was matched by a similar grouping of significant artists and architects—Masaccio, Brunelleschi, Ghiberti, Donatello and others—whose achievements were patent for all visitors to see. The atmosphere of achievement was enhanced by skilful drawing on antecedents. Dante, Petrarch and Boccaccio were cast as Florentine heroes (even if the first of these had spent his last two, most productive, decades in exile and the second was associated with Florence only by the fact that the same fate had befallen his father), and a similar place was occupied by Giotto in terms of artistic innovation. The interaction and even cohesion of these groups is also significant. The relationship between humanists and artists is not easy to pinpoint but it was clearly a fertile one. In due course painting was a beneficiary of the humanistic exploration of classical themes, as exemplified in Boccaccio's encyclopedic *On the Genealogy of the Gods*, which came to be used as a reference work on classical mythology. More immediately, humanists were quick to point out the parallels between the principles underlying classical rhetoric and those of proportion and perspective being developed by the early Renaissance artists. They proclaimed a common aesthetic and a unity of purpose between the disciplines or 'arts'. Though the emphasis on these parallels was itself to a degree celebratory rhetoric, it proved to be one of the most influential and enduring aspects of the movement.

The factors that proved conducive to such a flowering, and the mechanisms that prompted it, are less easy to establish. Florence was in many respects a relatively young city that shot to economic prominence in the thirteenth century and thereafter to political influence, with its pivotal position in the papal-Angevin alliance. From the late thirteenth century to the early fifteenth its territory expanded until it controlled two-thirds of Tuscany; and it did so during a period of comparative internal stability, albeit stability which entailed the steady encroachment of oligarchy.[38] One suggestion, that Florentine humanists found their ideological focus very suddenly during the crisis of a war with Milan at the turn of the century, has rightly concentrated attention on the civic ideology that was so prominent in subsequent decades, though ultimately historians have not accepted this as an explanation for the 'movement' as a whole.[39] Another view is more tempting. Thirteenth-century Florence's economic and political precocity was not immediately matched by academic prominence; in comparison to Paris or Bologna, the largest university centres in Europe, Florence was, if not exactly an intellectual backwater, certainly in a second league. It only had a university from 1349, which has been deemed less than central to the humanist movement. It has been suggested that this peripheral status of Florence partly accounts for the eclectic and highly original nature of Dante's thought; and, moreover, that the absence of the formal and constraining educational framework of the university world also goes some way towards explaining the originality of the humanists.[40] Certainly freedom from rigid curricula and academic hierarchy may have helped the humanists, and the stated opposition of some of them to scholastic culture would seem to support this view. However, it would be unwise to make much of these declared antagonisms, which form part of the humanists' rhetorical output, and the role of universities as educators of humanists and subsequently as centres for their own teaching has been seriously underestimated. A more satisfactory evaluation would be that a combination of political, economic and cultural factors permitted, encouraged and helped finance a dramatic increase in cultural activity in a highly educated, articulate, secular, civically minded community with recent but lively intellectual and artistic traditions. Finally it is worth stressing the importance of the 'internal' and technical history of those traditions. As has been seen, writers could build on the work of their predecessors, and the cumulative effect of such knowledge paid off. For example, it has often been remarked that the great manuscript discoveries of Poggio Bracciolini and others came about not fortuitously, but because the discoverers were already sufficiently deeply immersed in, and advanced in their approach to, classical scholarship to know what they were looking for. Much beyond that it would not be wise to go; if 'originality' could ever be fully explained, that would be the moment of its evaporation.

Florence in the early Renaissance is only the first and perhaps most dramatic instance in our period of a cluster of individuals, working in different 'disciplines', whose contribution we can group together and talk about as a 'movement'. Its relationship to other centres of learning and culture is complicated. It would be tempting to view this in terms of 'transmission' or 'reception', and in some measure this is useful. The relationship is exemplified by Coluccio Salutati, the long-serving chancellor of Florence, who has already been mentioned. Salutati became one of the most influential humanists, not so much because of his set-piece writings (in which interest was belatedly revived in the twentieth century) but because of his position as fulcrum, and eventually doyen, of the growing community of men of letters, a community that knew few geographical boundaries. His voluminous correspondence over three decades includes exchanges with almost all the major classicising scholars of Italy, many of whom came to rely on the chancellor for news of discoveries and writings. Florence's alleged centrality owes much to this highly productive yet sedentary figure. His life is in complete contrast to that of Petrarch, for whom, as has been seen, peripatetic scholarship was both a way of life and an ideal. The next generation of humanists by and large demonstrated the qualities of the latter model more than the former. Like other humanists, many Florentine scholars—Poggio Bracciolini is a prime example—spent substantial parts of their careers in other cities, and almost all had contacts across the peninsula and beyond. Different towns absorbed the new ideas of the humanists—it is too narrow to speak of them as even predominantly Florentine—in different ways. One thing almost all had in common was that they adopted the humanistic educational programme, perhaps the single most effective method by which humanism took root, both in Italy and, some decades later, across the whole of Europe. In this, incidentally, Florence played only a minor role. Beyond the field of education, the degree to which humanist concepts were adopted could vary considerably. Only thirty miles down the road from Florence, Siena continued to spend lavishly on a full programme of patronage—buildings, art, its university— but showed comparatively little interest in what strike us as the most obvious characteristics of humanism. Genoa did not acquire a tradition of patronage, though it is noteworthy that some Genoese showed a stronger enthusiasm for contemporary Flemish painting than was normally found elsewhere in Italy. This taste was certainly acquired through Genoa's trading links with the Flemish textile cities and with Bruges.

'Transmission', with its implications of an active participant and a passive one, is ultimately not an adequate model of what occurred. The processes whereby such ideas were exchanged were reciprocal and multifarious. The major centres—Rome, Milan, Naples and Venice—made the new culture decisively their own, in the process focusing on different ideas and genres and taking scholarship and creativity in new directions, but also influencing other centres, including of course Florence, in turn. A similar observation could be made about the spread of humanism and artistic fashions beyond the Alps. Much of this is the history of the culture of courts, which will be discussed further in Chapter 10. Here just two further remarks are necessary. First, such courts did not simply adopt Florentine trends second-hand. Early *signori* such as the Della Scala of Verona and the Carrara of Padua were patrons respectively of Dante and Boccaccio, and courts had been important centres of culture and patronage throughout the period. Second, it would be easy but misleading to contrast the 'courtly', princely or aristocratic culture of some other city-states with the 'republican' tones of what has been described in early fifteenth-century Florence, and even more misleading to contrast this aristocratic culture with the merchant-dominated world of the Florentines. The emphasis that has been placed in this chapter on the bourgeois nature of the Renaissance milieu would have been indignantly denied by many of the most characteristic figures of the time. Dante thought of himself as a town-dweller of noble, rural descent, and many Florentine thinkers and writers of the fourteenth and fifteenth centuries (those for instance who were members of the intermarried Strozzi and Acciaiuoli families) considered themselves in the same light. This was in part the consequence of the general permeation of chivalrous, aristocratic ideas, while the snobbery of merchants who made good naturally took the form of hankering after noble status. Yet there was much justification for this attitude, since such families drew much of their income from landed property. The merchants of Florence and Venice retained their connection with the countryside and invested their profits by purchasing more land, hence they cannot be contrasted with rural property-owners.[41]

We must now return to our central problem: is the culture of this time aptly described by the epithet 'Renaissance'? Questions concerning the applicability of generic terms are not, of course, answerable in terms of straight positives and negatives. Historians accept or reject such concepts by subjective pragmatic criteria; they arrive at a judgement on the utility to them in considering and describing cultural developments in fourteenth- and fifteenth-century Italy of employing the concept 'Renaissance'. In practice the term is so generally used that its complete rejection in either thinking or writing seems unattainable. The idea of a Renaissance cannot now be abolished, but there remains the danger that, through illogical thinking, it may be accepted as something more than a label or generalisation. The 'Renaissance' was not a 'thing' or 'force', to which consequences may be attributed. Nothing caused 'the Renaissance', nothing resulted from it, nothing was part of it and nothing lay outside it. Some aspects of the cultural development of the time are characteristic of humanism (in the restricted sense of classical learning), but to describe any of them as characteristic of 'the Renaissance' is another dangerous abuse of language. The term must be applied to that development in all its manifestations, not confined to supposedly new trends within an indivisible cultural complex.

FURTHER READING

General

An immense amount of literature is available. Good short introductions to the Renaissance are Alison Brown, *The Renaissance* (London, 1988; 2nd edition 1999); Peter Burke, *The Renaissance* (2nd edition, London, 1997), and George Holmes, *The Renaissance* (London, 1996). D. Hay, *The Italian Renaissance in its Historical Background* (Cambridge, 1961) is a stimulating survey. Fuller accounts are Peter Burke, *The Italian Renaissance. Culture and Society in Italy* (2nd edition, Cambridge, 1987); J. Stephens, *The Italian Renaissance. The Origins of Intellectual and Artistic Change Before the Reformation* (London, 1990), an impassioned plea for the originality of the Renaissance. Albert Rabil, Jr., ed., *Renaissance Humanism. Foundations, Forms, and Legacy*, 3 vols (Philadelphia, Pa., 1988) is an authoritative multi-authored assessment of the subject. The classic work is J. Burckhardt, *The Civilisation of the Renaissance in Italy* (first published 1860; many editions), which effectively marked the rebirth of Renaissance studies; its thesis is still discussed. (A survey of past historiography is Wallace K. Ferguson, *The Renaissance in Historical Thought. Five Centuries of Interpretation* (Cambridge, Mass., 1948).) K. R. Bartlett, *The Civilization of the Italian Renaissance. A Sourcebook* (Lexington, Mass., 1992) is a collection of documents in translation, while Benjamin C. Kohl and Alison Andrews Smith, eds, *Major Problems in the History of the Italian Renaissance* (Lexington, Mass., 1995) is a 'reader' of essays and documents. J. R. Hale, *A Concise Encyclopaedia of the Italian Renaissance* (London, 1981) is a useful small reference work. Finally 'The Italian Renaissance' at http://history.hanover.edu/early/italren.htm is a helpful website.

The urban and secular culture of Italy

Histories of Italy which provide the background include Denys Hay and John Law, *Italy in the Age of the Renaissance 1380–1530* (London, 1989); J. Larner, *Culture and Society in Italy, 1290–1420* (London, 1971); and L. Martines, *Power and Imagination. City-States in Renaissance Italy* (New York, 1979 and London, 1980), a more controversial work. On Florence an excellent introduction is G. A. Holmes, *The Florentine Enlightenment 1400–1450* (London, 1969, rev. Oxford, 1992); *see also* his 'The emergence of an urban ideology at Florence, *c*.1250–1450', *Transactions of the Royal Historical Society*, 5th series, 23 (1973), pp. 111–34.

On secular education in Italy, *see* P. Grendler, *Schooling in Renaissance Italy: Literacy and Learning, 1300–1600* (Baltimore, Md., 1988); P. F. Gehl, *A Moral Art. Grammar, Society, and Culture in Trecento Florence* (Ithaca, N.Y., 1993); and Charles T. Davis, 'Education in Dante's Florence', *Speculum*, 40 (1965), pp. 415–35, repr. in his *Dante's Italy and Other Essays* (Philadelphia, Pa., 1984), pp. 137–65. A stimulating approach to the *novelle* of the period is L. Martines, *An Italian Renaissance Sextet: Six Tales in Historical Context* (New York, 1994). On urban perceptions of the countryside, E. Sereni, *History of the Italian Agricultural Landscape* (tr. Princeton, N.J., 1997), Parts 4 and 5; on chivalric literature in Italy *see* A. Scaglione, *Knights at Court: Courtliness, Chivalry and Courtesy from Ottonian Germany to the Italian Renaissance* (Berkeley, Cal., 1991), especially Part 4. The exaltation of the active life over the contemplative is well summarised in E. Garin, *Italian Humanism* (tr. Oxford, 1965), ch. 2, and discussed more broadly in P. O. Kristeller, 'The active and the contemplative life in Renaissance humanism', in *Arbeit, Musse, Meditation. Betrachtungen zur 'Vita activa' und 'Vita contemplativa'*, ed. Brian Vickers (Zurich, 1985), pp. 133–52, repr. in his *Studies in Renaissance Thought and Letters*, vol. IV (Rome, 1996), ch. 12, pp. 197–213. For the expression of civic pride in communal building, *see*, among many works, L. Benevolo, *The European City* (Oxford, 1993), esp. chs 2 and 3; the relevant chapters in John White, *Art and Architecture in Italy 1250–1400* (3rd edition, New Haven, Conn., and London, 1993), in John T. Paoletti and Gary M. Radke, *Art in Renaissance Italy* (London, 1997) and in Diana Norman, ed., *Siena, Florence and Padua. Art, Society and Religion 1280–1400* (New Haven, Conn., and London, 1995); and, for detailed case studies, N. Rubinstein, *The Palazzo Vecchio, 1298–1532. Government, Architecture, and Imagery in the Civic Palace of the Florentine Republic* (Oxford, 1995), and Diana Norman, *Siena and the Virgin. Art and Politics in a Late Medieval City-State* (New Haven, Conn., and London, 1999).

A cultural 'rebirth'?

Good orientations in the immense subject of renaissance humanism are Robert Black, 'Humanism', *CMH*, vol. VII, ch. 12, pp. 243–77; C. Trinkaus, 'Humanism', in *Encyclopaedia of World Art*, vol. 7 (New York, 1963), pp. 702–34, repr. as 'Renaissance humanism, its foundation and development' in his *The Scope of Renaissance Humanism* (Ann Arbor, Mich., 1983), pp. 3–51; and Jill Kraye, ed., *The Cambridge Companion to Renaissance Humanism* (Cambridge, 1996). E. Garin, *Italian Humanism* (tr. Oxford, 1965), and P. O. Kristeller, *Renaissance Thought and Its Sources* (New York, 1979) are accessible introductions to the works of these highly influential scholars.

On Petrarch, N. Mann, *Petrarch* (Oxford, 1984) is a concise introduction; *see also* M. Bishop, *Petrarch and his World* (London, 1964); Giuseppe Mazzotta, *The Worlds of Petrarch* (Durham, N.C., 1993); and K. Foster, *Petrarch: Poet and Humanist* (Edinburgh, 1984). Many of his works have been translated; those referred to in the text include *Letters from Petrarch*, tr. M. Bishop (Bloomington, Ind., 1966); Petrarch, *Letters on Familiar Matters, I–VIII*, tr. A. S. Bernardo (Albany, N.Y., 1975), and *IX–XVI* (Baltimore, Md., 1982); *Letters to Classical Authors*, tr. M. Cosenza (Chicago, Ill., 1910); *The Life of Solitude* (tr. J. Zeitlin, Urbana, Ill., 1924); and *Secret*, tr. W. H. Draper (London, 1911) and D. A. Carozza and H. J. Shey (New York, 1989). Boccaccio is best introduced by V. Branca, *Boccaccio. The Man and His Works* (tr. New York, 1976); translated works include *The Decameron*, tr. G. H. McWilliam (Harmondsworth, 1972) and *On Poetry: Being the Preface and the Fourteenth and Fifteenth Books of Boccaccio's 'Genealogia deorum gentilium'*, tr. C. G. Osgood (Indianapolis, Ind., 1956). Coluccio Salutati, one of the most influential of the early humanists after Petrarch because of his extensive network of scholarly contacts, has been portrayed in Ronald G. Witt, *Hercules at the Crossroads. The Life, Works, and Thought of Coluccio Salutati* (Durham, N.C., 1983). For Bruni, *see* Gordon Griffiths, James Hankins and David Thompson, *The Humanism of Leonardo Bruni. Selected Texts* (Binghamton, N.Y., 1987) (including a biographical introduction). Many of the Florentine humanist treatises mentioned in the text have been at least partially translated; there is a growing body of 'readers' through which their work is accessible. *See:* Benjamin G. Kohl and Ronald G. Witt, eds, *The Earthly Republic. Italian Humanists on Government and Society* (Manchester, 1978); R. N. Watkins, tr. and ed., *Humanism and Liberty. Writings on Freedom from Fifteenth-Century Florence* (Columbia, S.C., 1978); Albert Rabil, ed. and tr., *Knowledge, Goodness, and Power: the Debate over Nobility among Quattrocento Italian Humanists* (Binghamton, N.Y., 1991); David Thompson and Alan F. Nagel, eds, *The Three Crowns of Florence. Humanist Assessments of Dante, Petrarca, and Boccaccio* (New York, 1972); Jill Kraye, ed., *Cambridge Translations of Renaissance Philosophical Texts* (Cambridge, 1997), vol. 1: *Moral Philosophy*, vol. 2: *Political Philosophy*; W. Gundersheimer, *The Italian Renaissance* (1965, repr. Toronto, 1993); and E. Cassirer, P. O. Kristeller and J. H. Randall, Jr., eds, *The Renaissance Philosophy of Man* (Chicago, Ill., 1948). Giannozzo Manetti's *On the Dignity of Man* is translated in B. Murchland, ed. and tr., *Two Views of Man: Pope Innocent III and Giannozzo Manetti* (New York, 1966), pp. 63–103.

Interesting aspects of the discoveries of classical writings are brought out in P. W. Goodhart Gordan, ed., *Two Renaissance Book-Hunters: the Letters of Poggius Bracciolini to Niccolaus de Niccolis* (New York, 1974, repr. 1991); *see also* R. Weiss, *The Renaissance Discovery of Classical Antiquity* (2nd edition, Oxford, 1969). On the influence of Greek and Greek culture, D. J. Geanakoplos, *Constantinople and the West. Essays on Late Byzantine (Palaeologan) and Italian Renaissances and the Byzantine and Roman Churches* (Madison, Wis., 1989). Brunetto Latini is treated in Charles T. Davis, 'Brunetto Latini and Dante', *Studi medievali*, 3rd series, 8 (1967), pp. 421–50, repr. in his *Dante's Italy and Other Essays* (Philadelphia, Pa., 1984), pp. 166–97; his *Livre dou Tresor* is translated by Paul Barrette and Spurgeon Baldwin (New York, 1993). Marco Polo's *Travels* are translated by R. E. Latham (Harmondsworth, 1958) among others; *see also* J. Critchley, *Marco Polo's Book* (Aldershot, 1992), and John Larner, *Marco Polo and the Discovery of the World* (New Haven, Conn., and London, 1999).

Wealth, family and patronage

Alberti's *Della famiglia* has been translated as *The Family in Renaissance Florence*, tr. R. N. Watkins (Columbia, S.C., 1969); on him, *see also* J. Gadol, *Leon Battista Alberti, Universal Man of the Early Renaissance* (Chicago, Ill., 1969). Much work has been done recently on Florentine patrician families; notable are R. A. Goldthwaite, *Private Wealth in Renaissance Florence. A Study of Four Families* (Princeton, N.J., 1968); F. W. Kent, *Household and Lineage in Renaissance Florence. The Family Life of the Capponi, Ginori, and Rucellai* (Princeton, N.J., 1977); and A. Molho, *Marriage Alliance in Late Medieval Florence* (Cambridge, Mass., 1994). The subject of their patronage can be traced through a variety of works, including Richard A. Goldthwaite, *The Building of Renaissance Florence. An Economic and Social History* (Baltimore, Md., 1980), and F. W. Kent, *A Florentine Patrician and His Palace*, vol. 2 of *Giovanni Rucellai ed il suo Zibaldone* (London, 1981); and from the abundant general literature on patronage in the period: Mary Hollingsworth, *Patronage in Renaissance Italy from 1400 to the Early Sixteenth Century* (London, 1994); F. W. Kent and P. Simons, eds, *Patronage, Art and Society in Renaissance Italy* (Oxford, 1987); G. F. Lytle and S. Orgel, eds, *Patronage in the Renaissance* (Princeton, N.J., 1981); and D. S. Chambers, ed., *Patrons and Artists in the Italian Renaissance* (London, 1970) (documents in translation). *See also* Brian Kempers, *Painting, Power and Patronage: the Rise of the Professional Artist in*

Renaissance Italy (London, 1992), and A. Martindale, *The Rise of the Artist in the Middle Ages and Early Renaissance* (London, 1972); Richard A. Goldthwaite, *Wealth and the Demand for Art in Italy 1300–1600* (Baltimore, Md., 1993); and Lisa Jardine, *Worldly Goods. A New History of the Renaissance* (London, 1996), an introduction to Renaissance culture from the perspective of what might be called consumerism. Finally many of E. H. Gombrich's essays on the art of the Renaissance are collected in his *Norm and Form* (London, 2nd edition 1971), *Symbolic Images* (London, 1972), *The Heritage of Apelles* (London, 1976), and *New Light on Old Masters* (London, 1986); repr. as *Gombrich on the Renaissance*, vols 1–4 (London, 1985–98). These supplement his *The Story of Art* (London, 16th edition, 1995), of which *see* esp. chs 12–16.

Florence and the spread of new ideas

On the relationship of humanists and artists, an overview of the problems is Charles Hope and Elizabeth McGrath, 'Artists and humanists', in *The Cambridge Companion to Renaissance Humanism*, ed. Jill Kraye (Cambridge, 1996), pp. 161–88. Michael Baxandall, *Giotto and the Orators: Humanist Observers of Painting in Italy and the Discovery of Pictorial Composition 1350–1450* (2nd edition, Oxford, 1986) is a highly original enquiry into humanist writings about art; *see also* Francis Ames-Lewis, *The Intellectual Life of the Early Renaissance Artist* (New Haven, Conn., and London, 2000).

Hans Baron, *The Crisis of the Early Italian Renaissance* (rev. edition, Princeton, N.J., 1966), and *In Search of Florentine Civic Humanism. Essays on the Transition from Medieval to Modern Thought*, 2 vols (Princeton, N.J., 1988) are the key works in his thesis that profound changes in what he defined as 'civic humanism' originated in the Florentine political crisis of the years around 1400. Recent assessments of this view are J. Hankins, ed., *Renaissance Civic Humanism: Reappraisals and Reflections* (Cambridge, 2000); J. Hankins, 'The "Baron thesis" after forty years and some recent studies of Leonardo Bruni', *Journal of the History of Ideas*, 56 (1995), pp. 309–38, and a 'forum' of articles on Baron's influence by Ronald Witt, John M. Najemy, Craig Kallendorf and Werner Gundersheimer in *American Historical Review*, 101 (1996), pp. 107–44.

On humanist ideas on education, W. H. Woodward, ed., *Vittorino da Feltre and Other Humanist Educators* (Cambridge, 1897, repr. New York, 1963) is an excellent introduction which includes translations of the key texts. *See also* his *Studies in Education during the Age of the Renaissance 1400–1600* (Cambridge, 1896, repr. New York, 1967); and P. Grendler, *Schooling in Renaissance Italy: Literacy and Learning, 1300–1600* (Baltimore, Md., 1988).

On the relationship of Florence to other centres, and the question of the spread of humanism and the Renaissance generally, *see*: Anthony Goodman and Angus Mackay, eds, *The Impact of Humanism on Western Europe* (London, 1990); Charles G. Nauert, Jr., *Humanism and the Culture of Renaissance Europe* (Cambridge, 1995); R. Weiss, *The Spread of Italian Humanism* (London, 1964); and Peter Burke, *The European Renaissance: Centres and Peripheries* (Oxford, 1998). Roy Porter and Mikuláš Teich, eds, *The Renaissance in National Context* (Cambridge, 1992) questions the customary Italo-centric assumptions about the Renaissance; Robert Black's contribution ('Florence', pp. 21–41) is a balanced summary.

NOTES

1. G. Villani, *Cronica*, ed. F. Gherardi Dragomanni (Florence, 1845), Book XI, ch. 94, p. 324; in new edition as *Nuova Cronica*, ed. Giuseppe Porta (Parma, 1990–1) as Book XII, ch. 94 (vol. 3, p. 198). The reliability of Villani's figures has been much debated; a formidable, though excessively mechanistic, attack is P. Grendler, *Schooling in Renaissance Italy: Literacy and Learning, 1300–1600* (Baltimore, Md., 1988), pp. 71–4.

2. *Above*, p. 92.

3. Petrarch, letter on the nature of poetry, *Rerum familiarum libri*, X. 4; translation in James Harvey Robinson, *Petrarch, the First Modern Scholar and Man of Letters. A Selection from his Correspondence* (New York and London, 1914), pp. 261–75 (pp. 268–9). The *Rerum familiarum libri* is also translated by A. Bernardo as *Letters on Familiar Matters*, 3 vols (New York and Baltimore, Md., 1975–85); this letter is in vol. 2, pp. 69–75.

4. *Purgatorio*, XIV, lines 109–11; translated by A. L. Money (London, 1910).

5. *Sonetti burleschi e realistici dei primi due secoli*, ed. A. F. Massèra (Bari, 1940 edition), pp. 159–60.

6. M. Palmieri, *Vita civile*, ed. G. Belloni (Florence, 1982), Bk. I, p. 53.

7. L. B. Alberti, *Della famiglia*, Bk. 3; translated by R. N. Watkins as *The Family in Renaissance Florence* (Columbia, S.C., 1969). The relevant passage is on p. 178.

8. *See above*, p. 9.

9. W. Braunfels, *Mittelalterliche Stadtbaukunst in der Toskana* (1952, 3rd edition Berlin, 1966), doc. 24, p. 260.

10. Braunfels, op. cit., doc. 27, pp. 262–3.

11. *Decameron*, Day VI, story 5.

12. *Cronica*, Book XI, ch. 12 (Gherardi Dragomanni edition, p. 232; in Porta edition, Book XII, ch. 12, vol. 3, pp. 52–3).

13. Palmieri, *Vita civile*, cit., Bk. I, pp. 43–4.

14. L. B. Alberti, *De Pictura*, Dedications; translation from E. G. Holt. *A Documentary History of Art*, vol. I (New York, 1957), pp. 205–6.

15. Giovanni Rucellai, *Zibaldone*, ed. A. Perosa (London, 1960), pp. 117–18.

16. It is translated as *Secret*, by W. H. Draper (London, 1911), and more recently by D. A. Carozza and H. J. Shey, *Petrarch's 'Secretum' with Introduction, Notes and Critical Anthology* (New York, 1989).

17. *De sui ipsius et multorum ignorantia* (*On His Own Ignorance and That of Many Others*), in *Opere latine di Francesco Petrarca*, ed. A. Buffano, 2 vols (Turin, 1975), vol. II, pp. 1025–1151 (p. 1066). There is an English translation by H. Nachod, in *The Renaissance Philosophy of Man*, eds E. Cassirer, P. O. Kristeller and J. H. Randall, Jr. (Chicago, Ill., and London, 1948), pp. 47–133 (this passage is on p. 76).

18. Translated as *The Life of Solitude*, by J. Zeitlin (Urbana, Ill., 1924).

19. The letter is translated in M. Bishop, *Letters from Petrarch* (Bloomington, In., 1966), pp. 45–51.

20. M. Bishop, *Letters from Petrarch*, cit., p. 49.

21. Petrarch, *De viris illustribus*, ed. G. Martellotti, 2 vols (Florence, 1962–4).

22. *Above*, p. 133.

23. 'Letter to posterity', tr. in Robinson, *Petrarch*, cit., p. 64; also in M. Bishop, *Letters from Petrarch*, cit., pp. 5–12.

24. 'Letter to Lœlius', *Rerum familiarum libri*, XIX.3, tr. in Robinson, *Petrarch*, cit., pp. 370–6 (pp. 371–2); cf. M. Bishop, *Letters from Petrarch*, cit., pp. 156–60, and Bernardo's translation, cit., vol. 3, pp. 77–82.

25. *Purgatorio*, XXVI, lines 140–7.

26. These were mostly oriental and Circassian slaves shipped to Italy from the Levant. On this trade, *see* K. Fleet, *European and Islamic Trade in the Early Ottoman State. The Merchants of Genoa and Turkey* (Cambridge, 1999), ch. 4, and on its impact on Tuscany, I. Origo, 'The Domestic Enemy: the Eastern Slaves in Tuscany in the Fourteenth and Fifteenth Centuries', *Speculum*, 30 (1953), pp. 321–66.

27. *Zibaldone*, cit., pp. 60–2.

28. Robert S. Lopez, 'Hard times and investment in culture', in *The Renaissance: A Symposium* (New York, 1953), repr. in *The Renaissance: Six Essays* (New York, 1962), pp. 29–54. For an assessment *see* J. Brown, 'Prosperity or hard times in Renaissance Italy', *Renaissance Quarterly*, 42 (1989), pp. 761–80.

29. In practice there was little attempt to enforce celibacy among the lower clergy until the eleventh century.

30. *Della famiglia*, Bk. 2 (in Watkins' translation, cit., p. 143).

31. Op. cit. (Watkins, cit., pp. 143–4).

32. Op. cit., Bk. 1 (Watkins, cit., pp. 80–1).

33. M. Palmieri, *Vita civile*, cit., pp. 9–10.

34. Op. cit., p. 17.

35. Op. cit., p. 34.

36. Op. cit., p. 29.

37. Op. cit., p. 28.

38. On Florentine politics *see* Chapter 10.

39. The views of Hans Baron; *see* Further reading at the end of this chapter. One of the responses to this view has been the rediscovery of a strong civicist and sometimes republican tradition of political ideas from at least the thirteenth century. *See*, for example, Nicolai Rubinstein, 'Political theories in the Renaissance', in *The Renaissance: Essays in Interpretation*, ed. A. Chastel (tr. London, 1982), pp. 153–200; J. H. Mundy, 'In praise of Italy: the Italian republics', *Speculum*, 64 (1989), pp. 815–34; and Quentin Skinner, 'The vocabulary of Renaissance republicanism: a cultural *longue-durée*?', in *Language and Images of Renaissance Italy*, ed. Alison Brown (Oxford, 1995), pp. 87–110.

40. G. A. Holmes, 'The emergence of an urban ideology at Florence, *c.*1250–1450', *Transactions of the Royal Historical Society*, 5th series, 23 (1973), pp. 111–34; *see also* G. Brucker, 'Renaissance Florence: who needs a university?', in *The University and the City: from Medieval Origins to the Present*, ed. Thomas Bender (New York, 1988), pp. 47–58, repr. in his *Renaissance Florence: Society, Culture and Religion* (Goldbach, 1994), pp. 225*–36*.

41. This generalisation, however, does not hold true for Genoa, whose merchants had little taste for buying land, while the aristocratic landowners of Liguria played scarcely any part in the city's business life.

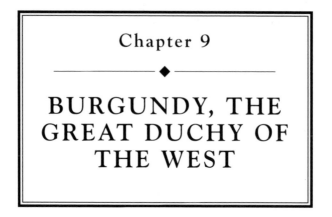

Chapter 9

◆

BURGUNDY, THE GREAT DUCHY OF THE WEST

FRANCE'S INTERNAL CRISIS AND THE RISE AND FALL OF BURGUNDY

The crisis of the French monarchy in the early fifteenth century has been mentioned above (Chapter 7), and reference has been made to France's disunity during the reign of the mad Charles VI and the emergence of a powerful and quasi-independent duchy of Burgundy.[1] Between the first onset of the king's insanity (1392) and the death in battle of duke Charles the Rash (1477), the course of French history was largely dictated by the policy of successive dukes of Burgundy. Burgundian abandonment of the English cause (1435) was the turning point in the Hundred Years War, and 40 years later the downfall of the duchy was equally decisive in the revival of the French Crown between the close of the war and the French campaigns in Italy. This long and vital role in the history of France justifies the allocation of a chapter to the great period of Burgundy's history.

Burgundy emerged as a duchy, from a combination of counties, during the time of Carolingian decay. It fell to the Capetian house in the eleventh century, was granted by Robert the Pious to a younger son, and descended in this cadet line of the royal house for over 300 years. The power of the dynasty, which often intermarried with the direct royal line, increased greatly during this long period. The advance of the duchy in cohesion and wealth was a gradual achievement, dependent on purchasing land and vassals, gaining from escheats (the reversion of a fief to the lord), increasing revenue from judicial, monetary and ecclesiastical rights, and benefiting from the towns of the duchy, with their tolls, fairs and markets, their desire for privileges and willingness to provide loans. The greatest territorial gain, the acquisition of the imperial county of Burgundy (Franche-Comté) was made by duke Eudes IV (1315–49) who was brother-in-law of Louis X and Philip VI and son-in-law of Philip V.

In 1361 the direct ducal line came to an end on the premature death of Philip de Rouvres, grandson of Eudes IV. The duke's cousin, king Jean le Bon, hastened to Dijon and took over the duchy, claiming it as next of kin. He made no attempt to

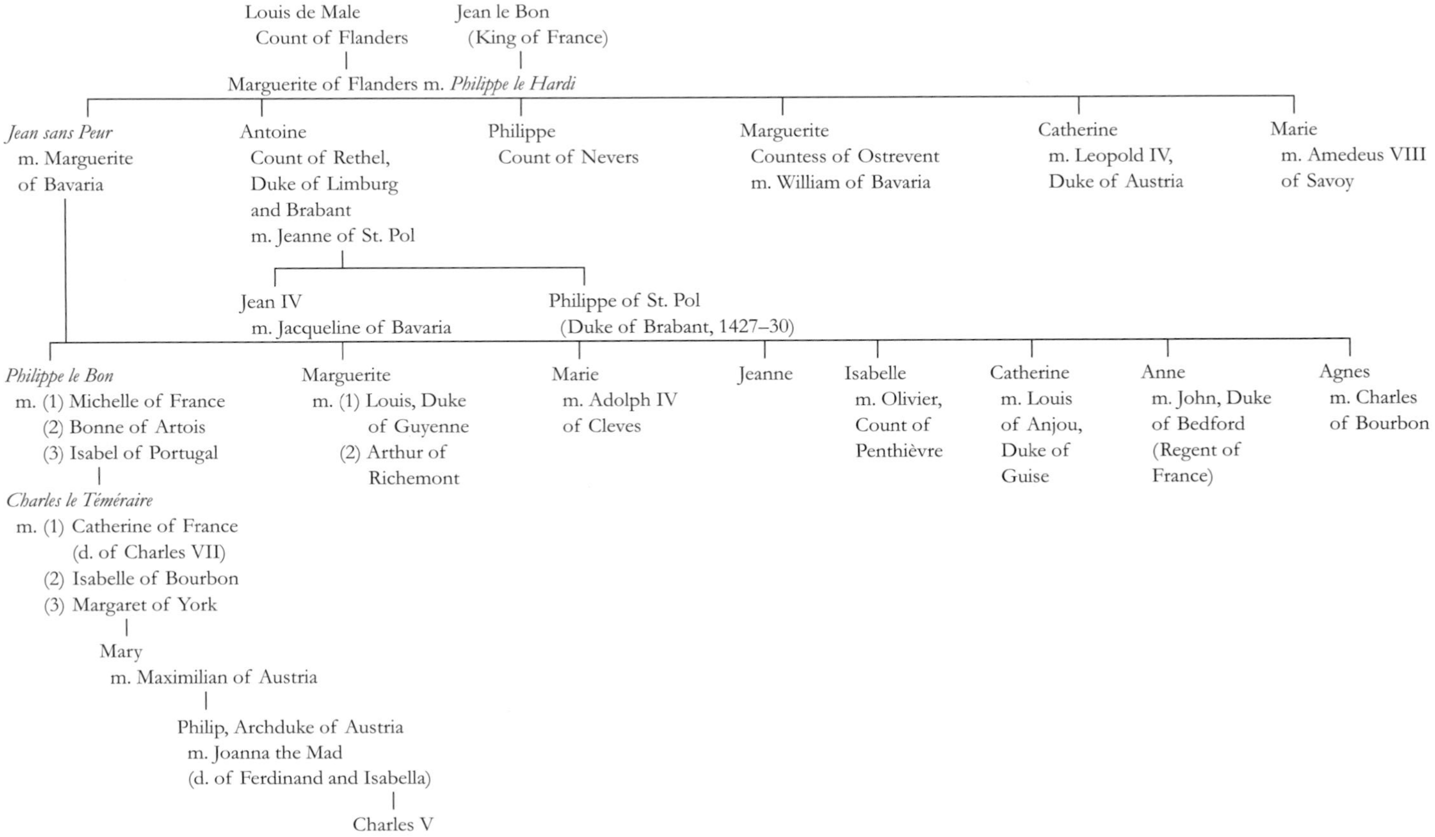
Louis de Male
Count of Flanders
Jean le Bon
(King of France)
Marguerite of Flanders m. *Philippe le Hardi*
Jean sans Peur
m. Marguerite
of Bavaria
Antoine
Count of Rethel,
Duke of Limburg
and Brabant
m. Jeanne of St. Pol
Philippe
Count of Nevers
Marguerite
Countess of Ostrevent
m. William of Bavaria
Catherine
m. Leopold IV,
Duke of Austria
Marie
m. Amedeus VIII
of Savoy
Jean IV
m. Jacqueline of Bavaria
Philippe of St. Pol
(Duke of Brabant, 1427–30)
Philippe le Bon
m. (1) Michelle of France
(2) Bonne of Artois
(3) Isabel of Portugal
Marguerite
m. (1) Louis, Duke
of Guyenne
(2) Arthur of
Richemont
Marie
m. Adolph IV
of Cleves
Jeanne
Isabelle
m. Olivier,
Count of
Penthièvre
Catherine
m. Louis
of Anjou,
Duke of
Guise
Anne
m. John, Duke
of Bedford
(Regent of
France)
Agnes
m. Charles
of Bourbon
Charles le Téméraire
m. (1) Catherine of France
(d. of Charles VII)
(2) Isabelle of Bourbon
(3) Margaret of York
Mary
m. Maximilian of Austria
Philip, Archduke of Austria
m. Joanna the Mad
(d. of Ferdinand and Isabella)
Charles V

Figure 1. Genealogical table of the house of Burgundy

gain the Franche-Comté, which went, with Artois and Champagne, to Margaret, the widowed countess of Flanders, while some of Philip's other lands were allotted to the house of Boulogne. Thus a number of possible claimants were satisfied. The king's decision to grant the duchy in appanage to his youngest son Philip, duke of Touraine, rather than annexing it to the Crown, perhaps requires explanation. The later consequences of this action were so unfortunate that it seems obvious to condemn it; but it must be remembered that Jean, after Brétigny and his first period of imprisonment, was beset with potential enemies—of whom the chief was Charles of Navarre—and felt unable to add to his own immediate responsibilities. The award to Philip, attributed by popular report to the youth's courageous bearing at Poitiers, was only made public on his father's death in 1364.

During the reign of Charles V, Philip the Bold of Burgundy ranked, with his other brothers Louis, duke of Anjou and John, duke of Berry, as one of the three great royal feudatories. His principal preoccupations were the pursuit of the war against the English and the giving of counsel to his royal brother. When Charles VI acceded in 1380 at the age of only 11, Philip's duty of counselling his nephew became a yet more pressing obligation. Although the first moves in the process that was to build up the duchy to greatness took place in Philip the Bold's time, there was as yet no hint that these gains could be disadvantageous to the French Crown. Indeed the intention of Philip's marriage to Margaret, daughter and only surviving child of Louis de Male, count of Flanders, was to bar English pretensions in the Low Countries. Margaret had been betrothed to Edmund of Langley, a son of Edward III, but pope Urban V had given aid to the French cause—and perhaps to that of peace—by refusing a dispensation for this marriage within the prohibited degrees. Her marriage to Philip took place in 1369, her father having finally given his consent in return for a considerable money payment and the return to Flanders of the territories lost to France in 1305. When the count died in 1384 Philip succeeded him in Flanders, Artois, Franche-Comté and the smaller counties of Nevers and Rethel.

The great acquisitions of 1384 were the beginning of the fortunes of the Burgundian house (see Map 3). These gains could certainly be reckoned an extension of French power. Hence Charles VI's readiness to assist Louis de Male and then Philip in subjugating Ghent, and to arrange marriages for Philip's children, which spread his sphere of influence still further to the east: a son and a daughter married into the Bavarian ducal house (which was also heir to Hainault, Holland and Zeeland), the other two daughters into the houses of Austria and Savoy. Nevertheless Philip was clearly exploiting his hold over his nephew, and doing so to such effect that between 1382 and 1403 he received one and a third million *livres* from Charles in 'gifts' alone. Towards the end of his life nearly half of Philip's revenues were drawn from the French Crown in the form of pensions, gifts and grants of royal taxation.

Philip quarrelled with his brothers the dukes of Anjou and Berry, and for a time lost much of his dominance through Charles VI's decision, in 1388, to take over the government of the kingdom. Four years later the king's madness brought to a head the struggle for control between Philip and Louis, duke of Orléans, Charles's younger brother. The pathetic king was at times so hopelessly insane that it was necessary to disguise as black-faced devils the strong men who had the task of changing his clothes. Meanwhile the bitter division which prevailed at the French court prevented France from exploiting the English civil disputes of the last part of Richard II's reign and the dynastic change of 1399.

Philip the Bold died in 1404, and was succeeded both in his duchy and in his dissensions by his son John 'the Fearless'. John made skilful use of demagogy to win over the people of Paris to his side. When an armed gang murdered the duke of Orléans in November 1407, John was almost at once forced to confess his responsibility for the deed, but the king took no action against him. John was even permitted to present a justification through the theologian Petit, who defended the murder as a case of 'tyrannicide', the killing of an infamous tyrant or traitor in accordance with morality and with natural and divine law. Three years passed between the murder and the outbreak of civil war, during which time the leadership of the Orleanist cause came to be shared between the duke's son and successor Charles and the latter's father-in-law, the count of Armagnac. When the fighting began the two sides inevitably competed for English support. The English hesitated between Burgundian and Armagnac; it was clear that either side could do much to re-establish English power in France, but Henry IV could wait to see which would offer the more handsome terms. The disastrous civil wars and disturbances of this period, which culminated in the Agincourt campaign of 1415, need not detain us here. Henry V, long a supporter of the Burgundian alliance, secured the duke's neutrality and so John, now virtually an independent power, stood aloof while France suffered overwhelming defeat. Later he was to regret his absence from Agincourt, in which battle both his younger brothers were killed, but for the time being John's feelings against the Armagnacs were too bitter. Meanwhile Agincourt greatly strengthened John's situation as well as Henry V's. In 1417 he came to an agreement with queen Isabel, Charles VI's discarded wife, and the two of them governed much of northern France from Troyes; he also reached a secret understanding with the English king whereby he accepted Henry's claim as heir to the French throne. The following year duke John's party gained Paris, and from this immensely strong position he embarked on negotiations for an agreement with the dauphin. On 10 September 1419, when the two leaders met on the bridge at Montereau, where the Yonne flows into the Seine, John the Fearless was assassinated.

Whether or not the dauphin was personally responsible for this murder, the crime would inevitably serve to drive the duke's heir into a new alliance with the English. This heir, duke Philip the Good (1419–67), was married to the dauphin's sister. He was entirely French by education, and he could feel his cause to represent French patriotism better than that headed by a king who was mad and a prince whom he thought a murderer. He hesitated before reaching a rather humiliating *entente* with Henry V, but his urgent wish for revenge and Henry's already dominant position in northern France sufficiently explain his decision—and do something to justify the alleged words of a monk who a century later showed John's skull to Francis I, saying, 'This is the hole through which the English made their way into France'. Philip the Good's acceptance of Henry as regent in France and heir to Charles immediately preceded the peak of Henry's achievement, the Treaty of Troyes of May 1420.[2]

Not till 15 years after Troyes did Philip abandon the English, but the story of the relations between these two powers, whose interests differed radically, is one of increasing coldness. This was due both to the general decline of the English cause and to direct diplomatic conflict in the Low Countries. Philip soon found that he had no say in the government of France, that his own subjects were reluctant to accept Henry as the French heir, and that Henry's promises of a marriage alliance and more land meant little. As it turned out, Henry V was to die shortly before Charles VI, in August 1422. John, duke of Bedford, who then ruled in northern France on behalf of his infant nephew Henry VI, had to make considerable concessions to retain Philip's friendship: Philip had indeed been offered the regency, but refused it as a doubtful blessing. Bedford married Philip's sister (1423) and offered him more territory—on condition, however, that he conquered it for himself, from the dauphin. When Philip lost influence in France his eyes turned further east, and it was there that he and the English clashed, thanks to the foolish policy of Bedford's younger brother, Humphrey, duke of Gloucester. The Burgundian house had long had an interest in Brabant and Limburg, which had passed through marriage to Anthony, son of Philip the Bold, and thereafter to his son, John IV. This duke John was married to Jacqueline, countess of Hainault, Holland, Zeeland and Frisia, but the match, a great success for John the Fearless on the diplomatic plane, was a failure on the human level. Jacqueline left her husband and gained the protection of Gloucester, who married her (although duke John was still alive), and by his ambitions in the Low Countries wrecked his brother Bedford's hopes of a continuing Burgundian alliance. For several years Philip of Burgundy campaigned intermittently against Gloucester, till the latter at last withdrew, and Jacqueline finally resigned to Philip the counties of Hainault, Holland and Zeeland and the lordship of Frisia (1433). Philip had already gained Brabant through the death without heirs of duke John's younger brother, the count of St Pol.

Throughout these years, when the war in France was beginning to swing in favour of the dauphin, Philip had given little assistance to the English, with the notorious exception of the handing over of the captive Joan of Arc (1430). By the beginning of 1435 the strength of Charles VII (the former dauphin) was such that Philip prepared to abandon neutrality and move over to the French side. A preliminary peace was concluded in February 1435 and formal terms promulgated at Arras in September of the same year. The French were compelled to pay heavily—or so it appeared on paper—to secure Burgundian withdrawal from the struggle. Charles sought Philip's forgiveness for the murder at Montereau, offered to establish many pious foundations for the repose of the soul of Philip's father and promised to search out and punish the murderers. Philip was exempted from the obligation of doing homage to Charles as king of France, and even received the right to appoint 12 counsellors at the Paris *parlement*. His more substantial gains included the towns and counties of Macon, Auxerre and Boulogne, and the domains of the French Crown on either bank of the Somme and between that river and Flanders. These 'towns of the Somme', however, were liable to compulsory repurchase by the French king if he could produce a sum of 400,000 gold crowns. Other clauses promised Philip an enormous revenue from fiscal rights in these territories and the county of Artois.

In practice Philip was to receive a good deal less from Charles VII than he had been offered by the terms of Arras. His perpetual hope that he might be accepted by Charles as a leading counsellor, the greatest of France's feudatories, was frustrated: the murders of 1407 and 1419 and the bitter opposition of the following years had inevitably made the relationship a deeply suspicious one. On the other side the murderers were never punished, the pious foundations were never forthcoming, and Charles did much to impede Philip's enjoyment of the fiscal and judicial rights ceded to him by the agreement of 1435. During the last five years of Charles's reign (1456–61) his relations with Philip were further poisoned by his quarrel with his son, the future Louis XI, and the latter's flight to Philip's territory.

For all these disappointments, Philip remained a great figure in Europe. Again failure in the west was counterbalanced by acquisitions in the east. Philip acquired the governorship of the duchy of Luxembourg from his aunt, Elizabeth of Görlitz, and he was able to extend his influence into the bishoprics of Utrecht and Liège by securing the election to these sees of a bastard son and a nephew. But, like his old enemy, Philip was saddened during his last years by serious disputes with his heir. One of the points at issue was the desire of Louis XI, Charles VII's successor, to buy back the 'Somme towns' under the terms of 1435. It was primarily in order to pay for a crusade that Philip accepted this repurchase, to which his son Charles was firmly opposed. Philip, whose father had fought in the heroic and disastrous crusade of Nicopolis (1396), was not least a Frenchman in his devout and anachronistic attachment to crusading schemes.

Under Philip's son and successor, duke Charles the Rash (1467–77), Burgundy came to play a different role in French history, both on account of the duke's own ambitious temperament, and because England's withdrawal from France and involvement in her own civil war gave Burgundy the position of an independent challenger rather than the weight in the Anglo-French scales. This is not the place to recount the involved story of Charles's relations with Louis XI of France. While still count of Charolais he joined in alliance with various feudatories and challenged Louis in the ill-named War of the Common Weal (1465).[3] Then in 1468 he married Margaret, sister of Edward IV of England, and his support played a big part in the Yorkist restoration of 1471, achieved at the expense of the French-aided Lancastrians.

Charles's greatest efforts, however, were reserved for his attempt to gain Lorraine, Alsace and Champagne, the wide corridor which divided the Burgundian Low Countries from Burgundy proper (see Map 3). In 1469 he achieved his first success in this endeavour when he received Alsace from the archduke Sigismund as a pledge for repayment of a loan of 50,000 florins, needed by the archduke to raise an army against the Swiss Confederation. Sigismund's lordship over Alsace was little more than nominal, but the title was worth acquiring, and it must have seemed unlikely that the debt would be repaid (as stipulated) in a lump sum. Despite difficulties in securing control in Alsace and Guelders (which he annexed in 1473), Charles now turned against the French in a frenzied attempt to destroy the structure of Louis XI's kingdom. Already his debts to towns, bankers and his own officials amounted to an enormous sum, so that by 1473 of the Italian bankers in Flanders only the Medici were willing to lend him money; the others had recently been charging him rates of interest rising to 48 per cent and even 55 per cent. Portinari, the Medici's manager at Bruges, became a councillor of Charles, and his unauthorised commitment to the duke was responsible for heavy losses leading to the belated withdrawal of the Medici from the branch in 1480–1. The armies raised with this money were of very considerable size and De la Marche, who was present as commander of the ducal guard, tells us that in 1474 at the siege of Neuss Charles had 18,000 cavalry (including the archers brigaded with the horsemen), 300 cannons, and an unspecified number of infantry companies of 300 men each.[4] But Charles was now detested by his overtaxed subjects, that year the Flemish estates refused him an *aide* (tax), and several of his officials had already deserted to the service of Louis XI. The League of Constance (March–April 1474) was a grand alliance, of which the backbone was the town forces of Strasbourg, Basle and Berne, that was to bring about Charles's defeat.

Meanwhile an astonishing agreement with Edward IV (Treaty of London, 1474) provided for what was virtually a division of France. Edward was to be king, but would have little territory in eastern France—though Charles graciously allotted him Rheims, for the day of the coronation ceremony only! By now Charles's pigeons were coming home to roost in inconveniently large numbers. Alsace was in revolt and Louis XI giving aid to the rebels, new enmities were being stirred up by Charles's expansion into Germany and Sigismund unexpectedly produced (thanks again to Louis) the money which gave him the right to resume his lordship in Alsace. From the end of 1474 Charles's downfall was rapid. Louis XI, 'the universal spider', was already an ally of the Swiss and in close touch with Sigismund of Austria. In December 1474 he signed the Treaty of Andernach with Frederick III. Soon the duke of Lorraine was brought into the alliance. Louis at last attacked Burgundy directly in the spring of 1475, by which time Charles had no money to pay his troops except those serving on the French frontier. When Edward IV's invading army landed, toward midsummer, it received so little of the support promised by Charles that Edward permitted himself to be bought over by the French. This treacherous abandonment was achieved at a cost to France of 75,000 crowns down, a pension of 50,000 crowns a year and a dowry for the dauphin's marriage to Edward's daughter Elizabeth (who was in fact destined to become the queen of Henry VII). After this treaty (Picquigny, August 1475), Louis was able to follow the slightly less expensive policy of signing a truce with Charles and fighting him through parsimonious subsidies to the Swiss and the duke of Lorraine. Unwisely attempting a winter campaign against the Swiss, Charles was defeated by their pikemen at Grandson on Lake Neuchâtel (March 1476). Three months later he lost still more decisively at Morat, on the route to Berne. Finally, now without money or allies, and with a much smaller army, he challenged duke René's reconquest of Lorraine, but was overwhelmed and killed at the battle of Nancy (5 January 1477).

THE BURGUNDIAN STATE

This renascent middle kingdom of Lotharingia was made possible above all by Anglo-French rivalry, which allowed the dukes to play off the two sides against each other, but also by the particular circumstances of Charles VI's insanity and his son's lack of spirit. The English required the goodwill of Burgundian Flanders if they were to conquer northern France, and this area derived much of its economic importance from its proximity to England. Skilfully though they used their initial strength to achieve territorial expansion to the north and east—and their marriage policy was greatly favoured by fortune—the Burgundian dukes never entirely transcended the status of 'overmighty subjects'. The sumptuousness of their court and the intricate formalities of its etiquette were famous throughout the west. No chivalric order surpassed in prestige Philip the Good's foundation of the Golden Fleece. From the time of John the Fearless's leadership at Nicopolis the Burgundian house was recognised as the natural director in every scheme for a crusade. Philip the Good's protection of the dauphin Louis emphasised still further Burgundy's position as a sort of Third Force. Yet the dukes fatally lacked 'the sweet fruition of an earthly crown'.

There was talk of a royal title for Philip the Good in 1447, during his negotiations with Frederick III, but Philip was thinking in terms of something more grandiose than the kingdom of Brabant that Frederick was willing to consider. In 1473 Frederick III approached Charles the Rash with a new scheme for the erection of the duchy into a kingdom, which again came to nothing, presumably because the duke asked for too much—perhaps for a new Middle Kingdom that would include Provence. The dukes liked to recall the barbarian Burgundian kingdom 'usurped by the Franks', but contemporaries seeking complimentary names for Philip or Charles were constrained to call them 'the great Dukes of the West'. One fundamental difficulty about their position, and about schemes for their recognition as kings, was that, although their heterogeneous subjects spoke a variety of tongues approximating to French and Dutch, the dukes thought of themselves primarily as Frenchmen. They liked to be described by court writers as *bon et entier Franchois* ('good and complete Frenchmen'), and Philip the Good, even after the murder of 1419, was accustomed to bemoan his own absence from Agincourt. Only Charles the Rash departed from this tradition and expressed anti-French feelings, a sign of the way in which a Burgundian national tradition might have been forged had not Burgundy undergone disaster through Charles's ambition, and later absorption into the imperial state of Charles V. Charles the Rash, it should be remembered, was one-eighth English by descent (his mother, Isabella of Portugal, was a grand-daughter of John of Gaunt and Blanche of Lancaster) and his third wife was English. He spoke Flemish, and also English, as appears from Commynes' account of his agonised discussion with his brother-in-law Edward IV after the latter had deserted him at Picquigny: 'the Duke talked in English and spoke of some of the great deeds performed by kings of England who had crossed to France, and of the suffering they had undergone in order to gain honour there; he complained strongly of the truce . . . but the King of England took his words very ill'.[5]

When the Anglo-French war ended at last—and this momentous discussion on the road between Peronne and Picquigny perhaps marks its true conclusion—Burgundy could no longer be parasitic on the flank of a mutilated France. Charles's fall was sudden and complete owing to his folly in antagonising too many of his neighbours at the same time, but the doubt remains whether his state could otherwise have survived as a considerable power. Its role in European diplomatic affairs had been great, far transcending its relations with France and England. The dukes were a factor in Iberian affairs, as allies of Aragon and Portugal, and in Italy as allies of the king of Naples and would-be rulers of Genoa. Further afield still Burgundy exerted influence through its constant preparations for the crusade and, less notably, through the feeble and ineffective campaigning which ensued from them. Yet the loose bundle of territories gathered together by the four dukes—primarily through their marriage policy—lacked all unity, and no time was granted for consolidation. The duke's subjects, wrote Georges Chastellain, the official historiographer of Philip and Charles, are 'of various countries and various conditions, and their temperaments [*natures*] also are various as are their ancient loyalties [*affections*]'.[6] North was divided from south by a wide corridor, and for long Luxembourg constituted an isolated enclave to the east (*see* Map 3). There was no true capital, though much the same was true of the nascent states elsewhere—particularly perhaps of Castile. The dukes, who were constantly on the move, tended increasingly to become involved in the urgent affairs of their northern territories: Philip the Good never visited Dijon, the capital of the old duchy, after 1455, and Charles the Rash never resided as duke in either French or imperial Burgundy.

There was not much progress in the direction of administrative centralisation, but it must be remembered that provincial institutions had the advantage of guaranteeing contact with local potentates. From the time of Philip the Bold there were two *chambres de conseil et des comptes* (council and accounts office) for the transaction of judicial and financial business, one at Dijon for Burgundy and the Franche-Comté, the other at Lille for Flanders and Artois. John the Fearless then subdivided the latter of these, taking the judicial part first to Audenarde and later to Ghent. After 1447 another financial chamber at Brussels covered a very wide area, taking in Holland, Zeeland and Frisia as well as Brabant and Limburg, while the *chambre* at Lille dealt with the Somme towns and the other lands of the western Low Countries as far as Hainault, as well as with Flanders and Artois. The dukes naturally possessed a chancery and counsellors of their own, drawn from the different parts of their lands; their 'civil service' was probably the best in Europe. Fundamental departure from the principle of ruling each territory through its own existing institutions is only to be found under Charles the Rash, who levied a general tax on all his lands in the Low Countries in 1465 and later (1473) set up a single court for the same region. Apart from this, taxes were demanded of the various provincial estates, and the areas retained their own *bailliages* and other units of local administration, their own councils and sometimes chanceries. Representatives or relatives of the duke might gain experience in the provinces, as Charles did in Holland before his accession, and Corneille—one of Philip the Good's 15 acknowledged bastards—in Luxembourg.

The territories in the Low Countries inevitably preoccupied the dukes most because they provided most of their revenues. In the time of the last two dukes (1419–77), *aides* accounted for one-third of the extraordinary revenues, and 75 per cent of the ducal income from *aides* was derived from the Low Countries. 'Ordinary' revenue was a small and diminishing proportion of the total, but it is notable that under Charles the Rash only 5 per cent of this was yielded by the 'two Burgundies' (the duchy and Franche-Comté). Receipts from domain and customs, as well as from direct taxation, increased enormously as the dukes acquired new lands. The table of revenue of expenditure compares annual averages of certain receipts and of expenditure under Philip the Bold and Charles the Rash, and illustrates the great expansion achieved in less than a century.[7]

	Ave. ann. revenue (livres)	Ave. ann. expenditure (livres)
Philip the Bold (1364–1404)	340,000	324,000
Charles the Rash (1467–77)	773,000	761,000

The main financial asset of the dukes was the prosperity, and in particular the commerce, of the Low Countries. The countryside was scarcely less valuable than the sea coast, which included the mouths of the Scheldt and Rhine, and its industrial hinterland. When Philip the Bold took possession of Flanders in 1390 he found it wretched and depopulated after six years of wars and floods; the ports had been damaged (the Hanseatics had abandoned Bruges) and Ghent and Ypres had suffered equally. During the next half-century an enormous improvement in conditions came about, thanks largely to peace and good administration. Monetary unification facilitated commerce and regulations carefully fostered the gold currency, though a deflationary policy may have had adverse effects on banking and industry. Communications improved, and in general there was greater security. The rural areas profited most because they benefited also from the declining political power of the towns and the increased willingness of burghers to sink their capital in schemes for reclaiming flooded land. Bladelin of Bruges, Philip the Good's last financial adviser, reclaimed a vast area of marshland on which the new town of Middelbourg was built. Farming methods improved, and the population increased, certainly up to about 1464—when Philip the Good probably had some two million subjects in the Low Countries—after which period there began a slow decline.

The wealth of Holland, Zeeland, Hainault and Brabant was predominantly agrarian, but Flanders was severely affected by industrial decline. Competition from the English industry and the increasing tendency for Italians to import their wool in galleys direct from England brought the Flemish cloth manufacture to its knees.[8] Ghent at least had its grain market, but Ypres, which had no other source of wealth, dwindled to a skeleton. Cloth production for local consumption continued in the countryside and a linen industry began to grow up, but the overall loss was severe. Commerce, a more important source of revenue, underwent great changes but no general decline. In the fourteenth century Bruges was the greatest financial and trading town of Europe north of the Alps. Until late in the following century it lost none of its importance as a banking centre and still presented the appearance of a flourishing city. Louis of Bruges, lord of Gruuthuse, built a superb *hôtel* (now the Musée Archéologique) between 1420 and 1470, and the visits of the dukes were celebrated with undiminished splendour. But Bruges was no longer a great entrepôt for trade between the Netherlands and England. Its commercial importance was coming to lie mainly in its relations with the Iberian countries: of 75 vessels known to have called at the port in 1486–7, 33 were from Spain and six from Portugal. By then the Zwin was already badly silted up, and early in the following century carts were able to cross the river at low tide. A survey of 1494 mentions between 4,000 and 5,000 ruined houses at Bruges.

The sharp decline of Bruges provides an instance of circumstances in which the dukes' economic policy could not benefit all their subjects. When Charles the Rash aided Bruges—in return for a grant of taxation—mainly with assistance in dredging works, he did so in the face of appeals from Ghent and Ypres, and the direct opposition of Antwerp. It was a case of directly contrasting interests, and the duke was compelled to take sides, though he could play a double game by turning a blind eye to Antwerp's flouting of the regulations against importing English cloth. In such circumstances no general policy was possible; Flanders and Brabant had to be allowed to make their own, independent commercial treaties. Antwerp was growing as Bruges declined, and largely at Bruges's expense. It was already a centre of some importance for the transit trade of Germans from the Rhineland and Italians in the early fourteenth century, and was assisted by the prominent role of alien traders. The Hanse merchants turned to Antwerp from Bruges in the fifteenth century, as did the English from the 1440s, and the visits of the Venetian galleys began in 1459. The Antwerpers themselves also owned ships, and the population figures in the table (number of 'hearths') bear witness to the rapid advance of their town as a centre of commerce.[9]

Number of 'hearths'

1435	3,440
1480	5,689
1496	6,801
1526	8,785

In comparison with the Low Countries, Burgundy was of small economic importance, yet Dijon grew with the power of its dukes—its population doubled between 1436 and 1460—and the area already had a significant export trade in wines.

The wealth of their lands enabled the Valois dukes of Burgundy to display a courtly luxury which was perhaps a compensation for their unattained kingship. Every form of patronage which could enhance their prestige was considered to be worth lavish expenditure. Guests were entertained at banquets of unparalleled splendour,[10] and a series of official historiographers recorded the deeds of the dukes, who took their last rest in the superb tombs of the Charterhouse at Champmol near Dijon. Claus Sluter, the great sculptor of Champmol, was a Dutchman who was Philip the Bold's 'ymagier et varlet de chambre'. The 'peintre et varlet de chambre' of Philip the Good was Jan van Eyck, who was taken into the duke's employment in 1425 at a retainer of 100 *livres* per annum, and rendered him service as both a painter and a diplomat. Van Eyck travelled to Portugal for the duke to paint for him a portrait of the princess Isabel, during the negotiations for their betrothal, and the duke stood as godfather to one of the painter's children. Many aspects of the life of the duchy's greatest days survive in Van Eyck's pictures, such as the portraits of Philip's greatest minister, the chancellor Rolin, of Cardinal Albergati, who helped to negotiate the peace with France, and of Giovanni and Giovanna Arnolfini, the Tuscan merchant family trading at Bruges. One regrets the more the loss of all the paintings he executed for the duke himself, including the portrait of Isabel, the portraits that he must surely have executed of the duke, and a spherical map of the world. Duke Philip's patronage was not the mere outcome of his determination to be outshone by no king, but reflects his miscellaneous personal tastes: a typical page from his account-books records payments to an illuminator, a bookbinder, three jesters, several minstrels, heralds and trumpeters and the keeper of his dromedary.[11] Much money was spent on tapestries—one famous scene depicted the deeds of Jason, the model of the Order of the Golden Fleece—and on illuminated manuscripts, another characteristic taste of the time. The ducal library included at least 900 works at the time of Philip the Good's death, and was added to by Charles, who had a passion for reading about the heroes of antiquity and commissioned translations of Caesar and Xenophon.

CONCLUSION

Charles's irremediable lack of wisdom brought him to destruction. It is easy now to see his history as a model tragedy of overwhelming pride punished by fate. So it fell out, not merely because Charles was monstrously ambitious but also because it was unrealistic, in the face of French opposition, to attempt to enlarge dominions that had not had time to acquire cohesion. What the dynastic matchmakers had joined together other men could very easily put asunder.

After the collapse of Charles the Rash's power, Louis XI gained for France the old French duchy of Burgundy, Picardy and Artois, and later Franche-Comté. But this was outweighed by the losses, as north-eastern territories long in dispute finally and definitively passed out of French control. Flanders and the Low Countries, the richest share of the Burgundian legacy, were transferred to Mary, Charles's only child, and she became the wife of the emperor Maximilian and grandmother of Charles V. Moreover, Artois and Franche-Comté receded to Maximilian in 1493. To a sixteenth-century historian the role of the dukes was that of 'founders of the Belgian empire', for their marriage policy had brought together the lands which composed Charles V's greatly valued 'Circle of Burgundy'. Burgundian rule in the Low Countries left its mark in England, where the anachronism of referring to those lands as 'Burgundy' long continued: in *Richard III* Shakespeare makes Clarence recount his fearful dream:

> Methought that I had broken from the Tower,
> And was embark'd to cross to Burgundy . . .

England, through its war, had done much to bring Burgundy to greatness. The fateful failure of France, and the success of the house of Habsburg in the struggle to become its principal legatee, will be discussed in a later chapter.[12]

APPENDIX

Philip the Good's Banquet at Lille, 1454

(Translated from Olivier de la Marche, *Mémoires*, eds H. Beaune and J. d'Arbaumont (Paris, 1883–8), Bk. I, ch. 29; vol. 2, pp. 351–4.)

The second table (which was the longest) had a pie in which were twenty-eight live people who, when it came to their turn, played musical instruments. The second set-piece at this table was a castle, representing Lusignan; at the top of its highest tower was Melusine, in the form of a serpent, and from two of the lower towers orange-water flowed into the moat. The third was a windmill on a mound, and on the highest sail of the mill was perched a magpie; around were people of all ranks, with bows and crossbows, all aiming at the magpie, to show that shooting magpies is an occupation common to all sorts of men. The fourth was a barrel in a vineyard containing two different wines, of which one was sweet and good, the other bitter and nasty; on the barrel was a finely dressed figure holding in his hand a notice saying: 'Help yourself'. The fifth represented a desert in which a wonderfully lifelike tiger was engaged in a struggle with a large serpent. The sixth was a wild man mounted on a camel which appeared to be wandering through the countryside. The seventh included a man on a perch beating a bush full of little birds, while nearby, in a charming orchard hedged by climbing roses, a knight and his lady sat at table eating the little birds from the bush; the lady pointed with her finger to the man beating the bush, to indicate that he was working in vain and wasting his time. The eighth was a madman on the back of a bear, amid strange mountains and rocks from which there dangled fine mirrors. The ninth scene was a lake on the shores of which stood towns and castles; on the lake sailed a handsome vessel, fully equipped and in constant movement.

The third table (which was the smallest) had a marvellous forest, like an Indian forest, within which were strange beasts, moving as though they were alive. The second set-piece at this table portrayed a lion tied to a tree in the middle of a meadow, and nearby a man beating a dog. The third and last was a merchant passing through a village, carrying a basket full of all sorts of haberdasher's wares . . .

Half-way down the hall, near the partition and facing the long table, was a high pillar on which was carved a naked woman. Her hair was so long that it covered her back to below her waist, and she wore a very fine hat. She was wrapped in a loose cloth on which there was Greek writing, and throughout the meal hippocras wine flowed from her right breast. Nearby a live lion was tied to another large pillar by an iron chain; the lion was the guard over the woman, and this pillar bore a buckler on which was written in letters of gold: 'Do not touch my lady.'

FURTHER READING

France's internal crisis and the rise and fall of Burgundy

On the crisis of the reign of Charles VI, *see especially* R. C. Famiglietti, *Royal Intrigue. Crisis at the Court of Charles VI, 1392–1420* (New York, 1986); and works cited above for Chapter 7.

The standard works on the duchy of Burgundy are the biographies of the four dukes by Richard Vaughan: *Philip the Bold. The Formation of the Burgundian State* (London, 1962), *John the*

Fearless. The Growth of Burgundian Power (London, 1966), *Philip the Good. The Apogee of Burgundy* (London, 1970) and *Charles the Bold. The Last Valois Duke of Burgundy* (London, 1973); a summarised version in a single volume is his *Valois Burgundy* (London, 1975). The older work of Joseph Calmette, *The Golden Age of Burgundy* (tr. London, 1962 and New York, 1963) is still useful. A crisp survey is Bertrand Schnerb, 'Burgundy', in *NCMH*, vol. 7, pp. 431–56. An interesting attempt to put the history of Burgundy in a longer context is Christopher Cope, *Phoenix Frustrated. The Lost Kingdom of Burgundy* (London, 1986). *See also* C. A. J. Armstrong's collected essays, *England, France and Burgundy in the Fifteenth Century* (London, 1983).

The Burgundian state

The splendidly produced W. Prevenier and W. Blockmans, *The Burgundian Netherlands (1380–1530)* (Cambridge, 1985) is an excellent survey of the northern part of the Burgundian territories from social, economic, cultural and political viewpoints; a substantially revised version, without the illustrations, is W. Blockmans and W. Prevenier, *The Promised Lands. The Low Countries under Burgundian Rule, 1369–1530* (Philadelphia, Pa., 1999). David Nicholas, *Medieval Flanders* (London, 1992) devotes the final three chapters to the Burgundian period, and gives an excellent example of the impact of Burgundian government on one region. P. Spufford, *Monetary Problems and Policies in the Burgundian Netherlands, 1433–1496* (Leiden, 1970) traces aspects of financial policy. For economic history *see* references under Chapter 5.

The court of the Burgundian dukes and Burgundian culture have been studied by many. An old synthesis is Otto Cartellieri, *The Court of Burgundy* (tr. 1929, repr. London, 1972 and New York, 1979). An important recent survey, which reassessed the widely assumed significance and originality of the Burgundian court, is Werner Paravicini, 'The court of the Dukes of Burgundy: a model for Europe?', in *Princes, Patronage, and the Nobility: the Court at the Beginning of the Modern Age, c.1450–1650*, eds R. G. Asch and A. M. Birke (Oxford and London, 1991), pp. 69–102. Graeme Small, *George Chastelain and the Shaping of Valois Burgundy. Political and Historical Culture at Court in the Fifteenth Century* (Woodbridge, 1997) is a study of the most eminent official Burgundian historian. P. Arnade, *Realms of Ritual. Burgundian Ceremony and Civic Life in Late Medieval Ghent* (Ithaca, N.Y., 1996) is a recent example of the many studies of the use of ritual in Burgundian politics; *see also* contributions to Barbara A. Hanawalt and Kathryn L. Reyerson, eds, *City and Spectacle in Medieval Europe* (Minneapolis, Minn., and London, 1994).

On Burgundian culture generally, Johan Huizinga, *The Waning of the Middle Ages. A Study of the Forms of Life, Thought, and Art in France and the Netherlands in the Fourteenth and Fifteenth Centuries* (tr. 1924; repr. Harmondsworth, 1968) is a deeply influential broad study; the new translation, as *The Autumn of the Middle Ages*, by R. J. Payton and U. Mammitzsch (Chicago, Ill., 1996, pb. 1997) is preferable. Craig Harbison, *The Art of the Northern Renaissance* (London, 1995) is a useful broad introduction; *see also* Erwin Panofsky, *Early Netherlandish Painting, Its Origins and Character*, 2 vols (Cambridge, Mass., 1953); and James Snyder, *Northern Renaissance Art: Painting, Sculpture and the Graphic Arts from 1350 to 1575* (New York, 1985). *See also* Frits Pieter Van Oostrom, *Court and Culture: Dutch Literature, 1350–1450* (tr. Berkeley, Cal., 1992); and Reinhard Strohm, *Music in Late Medieval Bruges* (rev. edition Oxford, 1990).

NOTES

1. *See* Map 3 and Figure 1, Genealogical table of the house of Burgundy (p. 173).
2. *See above*, p. 137.
3. *See below*, pp. 209–10.

4. O. de la Marche, *Mémoires*, eds H. Beaune and J. d'Arbaumont (Paris, 1883–8), vol. IV, pp. 82–94.

5. Philippe de Commynes, *Mémoires*, Bk. IV, 8. *See* the translation by Michael Jones (Harmondsworth, 1972), p. 251.

6. G. Chastellain, 'Exposition sur Vérité mal Prise', *Oeuvres*, 18 vols, ed. Baron Kervyn de Lettenhove (Brussels, 1863–6), vol. VI, p. 369.

7. *See* M. Mollat, 'Recherches sur les finances des Ducs Valois de Bourgogne', *Revue Historique*, 229 (1958), pp. 285–321. These figures relate to the finances handled by the 'receipt-general of the finances'. They omit surpluses from individual territories and some revenue from *aides*.

8. *See above*, p. 98.

9. H. Pirenne, *Histoire de Belgique* (2nd edition, Brussels, 1908), vol. II, p. 435.

10. *See* the appendix to this chapter, *above*, p. 184.

11. Marquis de Laborde, *Les Ducs de Bourgogne*, Part ii, *Preuves* (Paris, 1849), vol. 1, p. 249.

12. *Below*, pp. 211–12.

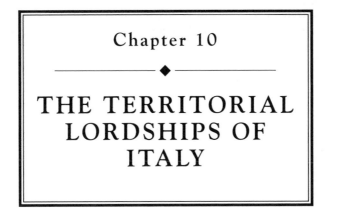

THE DECLINE OF THE REPUBLICS

The institutions of the Italian city-republics[1] were constantly reshaped and at last effaced by the interplay of the forces of social and aristocratic faction, combined with frequent external crises and the pressure of individual ambition. Before the end of the thirteenth century a number of towns had fallen to the rule of a despotic dynasty, and by the middle of the fifteenth Venice alone among the greater cities had maintained its independence and preserved a fully republican system of government.

The triumph of tyranny constitutes the pragmatic criticism of Italy's free communes. These republics had existed in an atmosphere of continual instability, and the normal outcome of endemic political disequilibrium is of course dictatorship. The communes suffered not only the normal constitutional handicaps of democracy —slow decisions, lack of secrecy and hamstrung diplomacy—but also the disadvantages of a discontinuity in personnel and policy which was in part imposed by the shadow of the fate which ultimately befell them. The executive officials of the republics held power for periods which rarely exceeded six months and were often as brief as two; longer periods in office would have failed to ensure a proper rotation among those regarded as eligible, and would have facilitated the schemes of any man set on suppressing the commune to his own advantage. Constant changes in the executive can be palliated by the existence of a permanent civil service—as was the case under the French Third and Fourth Republics—but the Italian cities had few permanent officials and none of high rank, until in the later fourteenth century the chancellor in some cities began to provide a certain element of diplomatic continuity.

By that time, however, in most cases it was too late. The perpetual struggle of the states within the state, 'popular', Guelf and Ghibelline,[2] encouraged these factions to entrust leadership to an individual, and what began as a measure of defence usually resulted in the overthrow both of republicanism and of the faction itself. The leader of the successful party became lord of the city, and thereafter those most likely to be 'purged'—as Machiavelli noted[3]—were the very men who had helped him to power. The occasion for the grant of special, unconstitutional powers to an individual was frequently an external crisis. Warfare between the towns, particularly between neighbours, was almost continuous, and was exacerbated by the periodic intervention of external powers, in particular the empire. Military crisis was of course normally accompanied by fiscal crisis, and failure in war was the most propitious of all circumstances for a potential tyrant.

A well-known case of such a transfer of power was the overlordship offered by Florence to Walter of Brienne, titular duke of Athens, in 1342 after the city's humiliating defeat at the hands of the Lucchese.[4] This was untypical only in that the initiative came mainly from the citizens. More commonly the tyrant accomplished his own ascent to power through a carefully planned *coup d'état*. However recognisable such a coup may be to the eyes of historians, it was usually possible at the time to disguise and minimise it. The city commonly in the first instance granted special powers to an individual for a fixed period only—alleging the need in a time of crisis to suspend for a while the normal workings of the constitution—but both the duration of the grant and the width of the powers were often extended later. Even when full powers had been made over, it was usual for the commune to maintain its own legal existence, its former institutions surviving though in practice they came under the control of the tyrant. Many *signori* (lords) regularised their position by securing a grant of special powers from a 'parliament' held to represent all the citizens, this anachronistic assembly having never formally lost its position as the commune's sovereign body. Commonly such an election continued to be made in each successive generation, the heir sometimes even taking an oath to protect the well-being of the commune. Normally *signori* came to acquire the power of appointing their successor—usually a son or nephew—and sometimes they associated him in office when they became elderly. A formal agreement on hereditary succession was likely to be a quite late development; it is only found at Verona, for example, after 1359, when the Scaligeri (Della Scala) had been lords of that city for almost a century.

In seeking recognition of his status the despot had a double task, however. A constitutional agreement with his nominal superior was desirable, as well as with those whom he ruled. The title of 'vicar' had long been held by local representatives of imperial power and the vicariate proved a convenient method for conferring respectability on tyrannical rule. Thus in 1311 Henry VII recognised Matteo Visconti as imperial vicar of Milan, Cangrande della Scala as vicar of Verona and Rizzardo de Camino as vicar of Treviso. The vicariate, a useful juridical arrangement, was soon adopted widely. It granted to lords powers that they already normally enjoyed in practice, giving them a recognition for which they were willing to pay. In consequence the institution flourished most under those emperors (from Charles IV onwards) who enjoyed least authority in the peninsula, and who were content to part with paper rights in exchange for much-needed revenue. As lords extended their dominions, new grants extended the areas of their vicariates. In theory vicariates were granted usually for the lifetime of the grantor only, but the successor was often willing to extend the arrangement, and clauses making these grants revocable in case of rebellion were ineffective in practice, as emperors discovered when they attempted to enforce them against the Visconti. Naturally the vicariate was of equal utility to the empire's frail twin-brother, the papacy, always ready 'to make a bad bargain, sooner than no bargain at all, with powerful subjects'.[5] The Este became papal vicars of Ferrara in 1329, the Malatesta were granted the same status at Rimini in 1355, and by the end of the Great Schism (1417) the Montefeltro of Urbino and the tyrants of many other towns in Romagna, the March of Ancona and Umbria held vicariates of the papacy.

One imperial title was more impressive than that of vicar, and the lords of Milan gained a unique position in 1395 when, for 100,000 florins, king Wenceslas conferred on Giangaleazzo Visconti the proud style of duke. This rank was transmitted both to Giangaleazzo's hereditary successors and to the Sforzas who ruled the city after 1450. A good deal later there were to be dukes of Urbino, Ferrara and Florence.

The general defeat of republican institutions in Italy was a very long process, extending over some two hundred years. For the most part it occurred sooner in the plain of Lombardy and the Veneto than in the hilly landscape of Tuscany and the Papal State. The earliest firm tyrannies in important towns were achieved by feudatories who owed their position in part to alliances with Frederick II. Of these Ezzelino da Romano held Verona from 1232 and added Padua in 1237, while by the time of the emperor's death (1250) Uberto Pallavicino was lord of Cremona and Pavia. With the dissolution of Frederick's authority all northern Italy went into the melting-pot, and soon after the mid-century a number of new *signori* emerged. From 1258 mastery at Milan alternated between two rival families, the Della Torre (Guelf) and the Visconti (Ghibelline). At the same period a 'popular' family, the Della Scala, was gaining a control in Verona which received formal recognition in 1277 when Alberto della Scala was elected captain general of the city for life. In the first half of the following century the Scaligeri built up a considerable empire, acquiring Vicenza, Padua, Treviso and even, for a time, Parma, Reggio and Lucca. By then tyranny was already the norm in Lombardy, the Veneto and Romagna and was becoming common in Tuscany, Umbria and the March of Ancona.

The first Tuscan *signorie* were the work of mercenary commanders, Uguccione della Faggiuola (lord of Pisa and Lucca from 1314 to 1316) and Castruccio Castracane (lord of Lucca, 1320–8). In the particularly unsettled era which followed the death of Henry VII (1313) Tuscany was a prey to constant warfare between Ghibelline and Guelf powers: the lordships of Uguccione and Castruccio arose from this situation, as did the more circumspect grants of special powers in Florence to the Angevins—Robert of Naples (1313–22) and Charles, duke of Calabria (1325–8). These abortive Florentine *signorie*, which were followed by a brief taste of sterner Angevin rule (under Walter, duke of Athens in 1342–3), illustrate well both how often the origins of tyranny lay in an external crisis and how difficult it was for a despot to retain control when he lacked local roots.

In some cases a great feudal family almost overshadowed the commune from its very origin. At Ferrara, for instance, the house of Este disputed control over the town with a rival dynasty, the Salinguerra, from the very early thirteenth century, if not before, and many smaller towns never fully escaped the mastery of a feudal castellan. The force which usually proved too strong for republican institutions was the old-established family having a deeply rooted territorial position, a powerful military retinue and allies linked by marriage and interest: these provided the financial and social means which could break its enemies and make its friends. Often the commune was heavily in debt to such great men before they became its lords, and above all they could overawe opposition by a show of armed force and by the wealth which could 'corrupt' the *popolo*.

To discuss the scores of tyrannies which developed throughout northern and central Italy is inevitably to generalise and thus to be misleading, for the regimes of different lords and cities differed greatly from each other. Characteristic instances have already had to be selected in the foregoing treatment of tyrannical origins, and in dealing with fully grown despotism it will also be necessary to select examples, and to confine the discussion primarily to Milan and Florence.

THE RISE OF THE *SIGNORI*: THE CASE OF MILAN

The history of tyranny at Milan involves two celebrated names, those of Visconti and Sforza. The Visconti—whose name bears witness to their feudal origin—ruled Milan for nearly two centuries and much of northern Italy for a considerable time, but their acquisition of power was not rapidly or easily accomplished. The Guelf Della Torre controlled the city from 1258 to 1278, and the subsequent regime of archbishop Ottone Visconti and his nephew Matteo was ended by a Della Torre reconquest in 1302. In 1311, however, with the support of the emperor Henry VII, Matteo Visconti regained power, and this time Visconti rule lasted until 1447. Their recognition as imperial vicars and dukes has already been mentioned. The story of their immensely successful expansionist policy is too involved to be recounted here at length. Matteo Visconti, inheriting earlier Milanese ambitions, embarked on the conquest of Lombardy and forced several neighbouring cities into submission. This first Visconti empire crumbled, but was reconstructed and enlarged by Azzo and Luchino Visconti in the 1330s and 1340s. In 1350 Giovanni Visconti secured a foothold in papal territory by acquiring Bologna, and for a time (1353–6) the Visconti held the vastly more valuable prize of Genoa. The greatest age of Visconti imperialism came under Giangaleazzo, who between 1385 and 1402 was perhaps within reach of setting up a north Italian state. Within a few years he overthrew the Della Scala to gain Verona and Vicenza and the Carrara to win Padua, and was thus in a position to thrust further south. From 1399 his pressure on Tuscany was very strong: Pisa and Siena fell to him, he became protector of the lord of Lucca and to the south-east he won Perugia and other places in Umbria. But Florence remained as an immensely energetic leader of the opposition to Giangaleazzo and the duke died in 1402 with his conquests incomplete. The Visconti then lost their more southerly territories and the Venetians combined with the Florentines to keep Milan in check.

The triumphs of the Visconti were made possible by an efficient and strictly controlled internal administration. Two small councils and two committees concerned with finance were the main institutions of government. The old 'great council' of 900 lost all real power and after 1396 its members were nominated instead of being elected. Milanese municipal affairs were directed by a 'vicar', with the assistance of the Twelve of the 'Office of Provisions'. Subject communes kept their local institutions; but, naturally, political and financial policy were under Viscontean control. Despite their centralising ambitions, the Visconti were obliged to reach compromises with the strong traditions of particularism: Giangaleazzo's special council at Verona for the territories east of the Mincio represents the only serious attempt to make inroads into local multiformity.

When the Visconti descent in the male line came to an end in 1447 the Milanese proclaimed a republic, but municipal revolts and war with Venice persuaded the republic's leaders to turn for salvation to a *condottiere* (mercenary leader), Francesco Sforza. Francesco, himself the illegitimate son of a mercenary commander, had served Filippo Maria Visconti and after a long and chequered engagement married his illegitimate daughter Bianca Maria. At one time he had carved out a state for himself in papal territory, but later had been dispossessed of this. Francesco won victories for the republic, but after Pavia made him its lord he was regarded with much suspicion, and ultimately he justified this by going over to the Venetians. The Milanese decision to make peace with Venice failed to save the republic from having to capitulate to Sforza, who became duke of Milan in 1450. Marriage to the late duke's illegitimate daughter gave Francesco no strong claim to the duchy, but he was extremely successful in his diplomatic policy. Medicean Florence and the kingdom of Naples became loyal allies to Francesco, enabling him to survive Venetian hostility and the difficult years of the Sforza regime's infancy. Within the duchy he attained a stronger position of autocracy than that won by any of the Visconti. He kept a characteristically tight hold over the Church, retaining the revenues of all vacant benefices and winning from the papacy effective control over nominations to bishoprics and abbacies; indeed, under Pius II (1458–64) all ecclesiastical appointments within the duchy were the concern of a special office which was under Sforza influence. From 1454 Francesco's brother was Milan's archbishop. Immunities and private jurisdiction were whittled away, and foreign affairs conducted by the duke with the assistance of his secretary Cecco Simonetta.

An unsettled period for the Sforza followed Francesco's death in 1466, and the family had difficulty in retaining the duchy. His son Galeazzo Maria was assassinated in 1476. Giangaleazzo Sforza was aged only seven on his accession that year, and after a long factional struggle between his uncles, he fell under the control of one of these, Ludovico 'il Moro', who kept him a virtual prisoner and executed Simonetta. Ludovico came to be haunted by his lack of a rightful claim and by the opposition of the Neapolitan royal house, the king's grand-daughter having married the lawful duke. His fear of the Neapolitans persuaded him to encourage Charles VIII of France to invade that kingdom in 1494, and his formal accession to the duchy after his nephew's death in the same year did nothing to increase his popularity. Contemporaries believed—probably wrongly—that Ludovico was guilty of this death, and when a new French invasion, directed against the duchy, occurred in 1499, he had very little support from his subjects. The following year he lost his state and he died a prisoner in France. His sons Massimiliano (in the years 1512–15) and Francesco II (in the years 1522–35) returned as nominal dukes under imperialist protection, but Ludovico was the last true *signore* of Milan.

FLORENCE AND THE MEDICI

The Medicean tyranny at Florence presents many contrasts with that of the Visconti and Sforza, notably in the long coexistence of republican forms of government with the practice of *signoria*. Moreover, Cosimo de' Medici's initial power was based upon money as undeniably as Francesco Sforza's upon arms, and this great banker won his lordship not as a single victor over a republic but as the leader of a successful party among competing factions.

After the defeat of the popular rising of 1378, power in Florence became the preserve of a fairly narrow oligarchy. The dominant clique was for long headed by Maso degli Albizzi, but after his death (1417) control was shared between Maso's extremely autocratic son Rinaldo and Niccolò da Uzzano. Though Florentine publicists contrasted their city's *libertas* with the tyranny of Milan, this was a 'liberty' that had nothing to do with democracy. In the time of Rinaldo degli Albizzi and Uzzano there were many dissatisfied elements in Florence, and the story of Medicean rule begins with the alliance formed between these malcontents and the nouveau riche banker Giovanni di Bicci de' Medici.[6]

Giovanni (who died in 1429) was recognised as head of the opposition to the prevailing oligarchs, and in this position—as well as in control of the Medici Bank—he was succeeded by his son Cosimo. Cosimo was then aged 40. He was not perhaps entirely a politician by temperament, but it was accepted that men of rank in the city should play an appropriate role in politics, and to withdraw from this was to accept serious social and financial disadvantages. 'It is not a good life in Florence for the rich unless they rule there', said Cosimo's grandson Lorenzo, referring to the heavy taxes levied on those who could afford to pay and had failed to win a say in the city's fiscal arrangements. When the moderate Uzzano died in 1433, Rinaldo degli Albizzi's fear of Cosimo led to the latter's arrest and banishment for one year, a sentence later increased to 10 years' exile. The accusation brought against Cosimo —that he was planning a *coup d'état*—was probably intended to provoke a death sentence, and may have failed to do so only because Cosimo was careful to keep pace with Albizzi in his bribes to the officials. Meanwhile Albizzi, by his increasingly tyrannical methods, was alienating some of his leading supporters, and in the autumn of 1434 Cosimo was recalled by an unexpectedly recalcitrant set of priors. There was not room in the city for both Albizzi and Medici, and the banishment of the former was decreed at the same time as the recall of the latter.

Cosimo had achieved no easy position of complete control: 'conspiracies' against him were foiled in 1444, 1457 and 1458. His great advantages were the reputation of the Medici as a 'popular' family and the wealth of his bank, then the most famous house of all Europe. The bank gave Cosimo a voice in the affairs of external powers as well as rapid news of foreign events and a valuable link with the papacy. Together with his many commercial and industrial interests, it provided him with an immense fortune.

Cosimo's system of rule—he rarely held office in person—involved dependence on a body of supporters, some of whom were powerful men in their own right. Constitutional methods of distributing office, which included the use of the 'lot', had to be manipulated to secure the choice of safe Mediceans. It would have been too blatant to abolish the 'lot', but Cosimo could not risk being overthrown, like Albizzi, by a single unfavourable priorate. The choice of priors, however, was often admittedly made deliberately ('by hand') rather than being entrusted to chance. From 1458 the system of choice 'by hand' became permanent, and a surviving petition to Cosimo's son asking for the leading position in the next priorate illustrates the reality of Medicean control. Moreover, taxation bore far more heavily on Cosimo's opponents than on his supporters. Cosimo's friendship with Francesco Sforza was responsible for a great diplomatic revolution which aligned Florence with its traditional enemy, Milan, in opposition to its old ally, Venice. This daring defiance of Florentine republican convictions led to an unpopular war, but the ensuing Peace of Lodi (1454) gave Florence a decade without hostilities.

Cosimo's description of a man as having 'a ready money sort of mind' (*'il cervello in danari contanti'*) might well be applied to himself. Remembering the origins of his family's popularity, he was careful to avoid ostentation in dress and to be noted for his friendliness towards the peasants. He was businesslike even in his patronage of learning and the arts, and his assistance in reorganising Florence's university certainly had the object of bringing students and money to the city as well as of forwarding education.

Cosimo died in 1464 and for five years the reins of power were held by a far less formidable figure, his semi-invalid son Piero. The next quarter-century (1469–92) was the age of the greatest of all the Medici, Lorenzo the Magnificent. At the time of Piero's death his son Lorenzo was a young man of 21. In practice the city's *signore*, in law he remained an ordinary private citizen. The paradox was of course remarked by contemporaries, including Lorenzo, who regarded his republican mask as an advantageous disguise and warned his own son that on diplomatic missions he should not take precedence over his elders, for 'you are but a citizen of Florence, as they are'. 'Lorenzo made himself master of the *essence* of government while he left the *appearance* of it entirely to the officials', said a writer of the time,[7] and this duality had a curious effect on the conduct of external relations. Florentine ambassadors might be compelled to seek pardon 'both on behalf of the city and of Lorenzo', and they had to conduct correspondence with Lorenzo himself as well as through 'official channels'. Lorenzo normally appointed ambassadors and they were in reality dependent on him and tended increasingly to write to him only, though he sometimes passed on their letters to the officials of the republic. Foreign powers also found themselves compelled to conduct a double correspondence, and at times were puzzled to find some contradiction between the 'line' taken by Lorenzo and that of the officials. They must have realised that the former was the one that really mattered, for they could see that even ambassadors were accompanied and watched by 'chancellors' appointed by Lorenzo.

Lorenzo could afford to leave no aspect of Florentine life unsupervised. Since there was always a potential opposition among the powerful families and alliances between these could be forwarded by marriage unions, marriages within this class came to require Lorenzo's consent. In the law courts, particularly those of the dependent towns, Medicean supporters had preferential treatment. Fiscal favouritism was less glaring than under Cosimo now that the Medici were more firmly in the saddle, but men who wrote to petition for a less heavy assessment took care to mention that they were faithful Mediceans. Moreover, Lorenzo occasionally secured special exemptions from taxation for himself and it was generally believed that he laid hands on a great deal of public money. The bank was now much less flourishing than in his grandfather's time, and a vast source of expenditure was the purchase of a cardinalate for his son Giovanni, later Leo X. Yet a lot of Lorenzo's own money was spent on diplomacy, entertaining and a 'secret service', and it was not iniquitous that this should be recouped from the public purse.

If there was a check on Lorenzo's power, it was provided by the need to retain the support of his own men. Decisions were often made in small gatherings of trusted Medicean partisans, the resolutions of this caucus being passed later in formal committee meetings. The names of steadfast Medicean families, many of them linked by marriage, commercial partnership or employment, recur constantly in the lists of council members, and such supporters could be sure of advancement to well-paid office, particularly to governorships in the towns of the Florentine *dominio* (territory). Behind these were arrayed the devoted officials made by the Medici and dependent on them, the 'low-born men' whose position was resented by the patricians, particularly in the case of those whose origins lay not in the city but in its subject-territory. Normally the machinery of control by secretaries and supporters worked smoothly enough, but any institution which acted without Medicean consent felt at once the grip of the iron hand. In 1491 one Cambi, then Gonfalonier (flag-bearer) of Justice or titular head of state, acted on his own initiative in depriving certain councillors of office for absenteeism: he paid for his rashness by himself suffering permanent deprival of office, while the men he had deposed were immediately restored.

Although content with his own position as a 'private citizen', Lorenzo found it convenient to adjust the institutions of the republic to facilitate his autocratic rule. In 1471 he deprived the Council of the Commune and the Council of the Popolo of much of their competence, and thenceforth governed through a single council, the 'Hundred'. Seven years later he had to face the one severe crisis of his regime, the Pazzi conspiracy. The principal parties in this plot were the wealthy anti-Medicean Pazzi, pope Sixtus IV with his family, the Riarii, and the king of Naples. Their plan was to kill Lorenzo and his brother Giuliano in the cathedral of Florence during the celebration of High Mass (26 April 1478). At the agreed moment, that of the elevation of the host, two assassins set on Giuliano and killed him, but the men to whom Lorenzo had been allotted bungled their assignment, and he was able to make his escape. The intended *coup d'état* was abortive, and Lorenzo, the survivor, was accorded a great demonstration of popular support—as well as being freed, as the cynical remarked, from the possible rivalry of his brother. Lorenzo's enemies attempted to press home their attack by two military campaigns which drove Florence to the verge of defeat, and from which Lorenzo was only able to emerge thanks to the skill with which he persuaded the king of Naples to withdraw from the hostile alliance. After he had brought back 'peace with honour' from Naples, Lorenzo put through a more radical constitutional reform (April 1480) which geared Florence's conciliar and executive machine yet more closely to the Medicean regime.

A new body, 'the Seventy', now became the principal council, and the chief executive committees were to be chosen from its members or by them.

To the Italians of his day Lorenzo the Magnificent was pre-eminently the skilful diplomatist who maintained contact between the rulers of the peninsula and did much to keep the peace in a time of threatened catastrophe.[8] Of the other Italian powers, Venice and the papacy were always on the alert for possibilities of expansion at the expense of their neighbours, while the two 'satiated' states, Naples and Milan, were threatened both by internal dissensions and by fear of French claims.[9] By appealing for co-operation against the Ottoman and French menaces, particularly to the unreliable Ferrante of Naples and Ludovico of Milan, Lorenzo did much to preserve the peninsula in a condition of comparative peace, and it became a common-place to refer to him as 'the balance' that preserved Italy from upset and disaster. Luca Landucci, who kept a chemist's shop, spoke for all the Florentines when he noted in his diary on Lorenzo's death that 'he was a wise head, and everything he attempted turned out well . . . He ennobled not only his family but the whole city'.[10] Another writer thought that 'We have lost the splendour not only of Tuscany but of all Italy. Every day we shall learn more what we have lost . . .',[11] and Ferrante of Naples wrote prophetically that 'this man has lived long enough for his own immortal fame, but not for Italy'.[12]

In later times Lorenzo the Magnificent has been celebrated less as a ruler and statesman than as a delightful poet and a highly intelligent patron of learning and the arts. Something will be said of him as a patron below, but we may note, before turning briefly to the later period of Medicean rule, that posterity may have pardoned too readily this many-sided man's failure to supervise adequately the bank which had gained the Medici their authority in Florence. In this respect there is a clearly marked distinction between Lorenzo's personality and that of his grandfather Cosimo. A fictional parallel may be found in the theme of *Buddenbrooks*, Thomas Mann's novel of burgher life in nineteenth-century Lübeck, for the Buddenbrooks too turned towards the arts, their money-making urge diluted after several generations of fiercely energetic success.

Lorenzo the Magnificent's death in 1492 marks the beginning of a 40-year crisis for the Medici. His son and successor Piero fled from Florence in 1494 when a coalition of anti-Medicean magnates proved more adept than he in coming to terms with the French invaders. For 18 years the city reverted to genuine republicanism—the first three years under the spell of the Dominican firebrand Girolamo Savonarola—and the new regime was overturned only when disaster befell the French cause in Italy (1512) and the republic's own malcontents allied with Medicean exiles and sympathisers. From 1512 till 1527 Florence again came under the Medici, but the family was restored in circumstances that brought about a complete change in the nature of its rule. Lorenzo's son Giovanni and later his illegitimate nephew Giulio became popes (as Leo X, 1513–21, and Clement VII, 1523–34), and hence Florence was almost an 'annexe' of the papacy. Control there was entrusted to a series of Medici relatives, lay and ecclesiastical, and ultimately to a cardinal, Passerini, in whose time the Medici name was represented by two young bastards, one of them the son of an oriental slave.

Clement VII's disasters in 1527, when an imperialist army sacked Rome, were the occasion of a new republican revival, and for three years Florence defied empire and papacy. After his defeat of the French at Pavia (1525), however, the emperor Charles V was the real master of Italy, and when he was able to turn his attention to Florence the republic came to realise that for all its commercial wealth it was an anachronism in a new world of great powers. Clement wanted Florence back for the Medici, and in Charles's eyes the papacy was a more weighty ally than the Florentine republic. When a papalist-imperialist army besieged the city in 1529 the 'last republic' was doomed. It capitulated in 1530 and the Medici returned once more. In 1532 the old constitution was abolished and Alessandro, the illegitimate son of a grandson of Lorenzo the Magnificent, became the first of the line of Medici dukes which lasted into the eighteenth century.

THE ITALIAN POLITICAL SYSTEM

The history of Milan and of Florence illustrates quite well the development of the *signoria* in the peninsula as a whole. There are no significant general differences between the tyrants of the papal lands and those of imperial Italy, and indeed the chronology of the *signoria* of Bologna, the greatest city of the Papal State, resembles closely that of Florence, After an abortive fourteenth-century tyranny (that of the Pepoli in the years 1337–50), Bologna fell to the control of a single dynasty, the Bentivoglio, who ruled the city, with some interruptions, from 1401 until 1512. Like the Medici, the Bentivoglio never formalised their status as tyrants. Like the Visconti they gained recognition as vicars—of the pope. Bologna, however, was a less power-ful piece on the Italian chessboard, and hence its lords were more dependent on external favour than those of Milan and Florence. Thus Giovanni Bentivoglio ruled in 1401–2 with the support of the Visconti, Sante from 1446 to 1463 with that of Cosimo de' Medici and, for a time, of Francesco Sforza. In the sixteenth century the *signori* of the Papal State became victims of papal centralisation, and the extinction of Bentivoglio rule by Julius II (1512) was a salient episode in the downfall of tyranny in the state.

Bologna was of particular strategic significance, then as now at one of the main crossroads for the Apennines and a key town for traffic through, and control of, the Papal State. This ensured, as with Genoa, that the predatory attentions of powerful neighbours were never far away, and the threat of external pressure is often cited as one of the most common reasons why a despot could gain power. The trend towards lordship throughout northern and central Italy is ubiquitous. Even the exceptions are revealing. Florence, as has been seen, survived as a republic in name only, first undergoing sustained evolution towards explicit oligarchy, and then mov-ing to a hybrid system of a largely cosmetic constitution with an unofficial *signore* who could more than hold his own on Florence's behalf in the Italian political arena. Siena, one of the few remaining examples of republican government, was equally oligarchic and equally dependent on mechanisms for circumventing the more 'democratic' aspects of its constitution; it too succumbed to despotism for a while in 1500. Perhaps the most genuine exception is Venice, whose constitution had long been admired as a work of art. Its lack of a hereditary ruler was compensated by a range of mechanisms: a head of state, the *doge*, appointed for life, a tight and stable set of committees, a closed political elite and a highly sophisticated code of secrecy and presentation of its public face. It must of course be added that in this case the geo-political explanation is also relevant. For centuries Venice's main preoccupation had been with its international trading empire, and the late-fourteenth century decision to expand on the Italian mainland (*terraferma*) brought it into the mainstream of Italian politics much later, and at a much later stage of its own development, than was the case with any of its rivals.

The emphasis in this chapter on changing forms of government is not intended to obscure other developments. It has been argued that at least as important as the shift to despotism—which, as has been seen, was far from being a black-and-white transition from 'freedom' to 'tyranny'—was the change in size and power of several of these states. To an extent it is fair to speak of a transformation from 'city-state' to 'territorial state'. Not, of course, that the latter term would have been inappropriate at the beginning of our period; no 'city-state' could achieve anything without sufficient hinterland, or *contado*, for food, taxation and defence. However, many of these states remained precarious, and if one symptom of that was the move towards despotism, another was the Darwinian process whereby the weaker states fell under the control of the stronger ones. Between the late thirteenth century and the early fifteenth, Florence, Venice and Milan grew to new dimensions and became transformed in the process, developing the administrative sophistication of substantial powers with extensive regional control. What is more, together with the papacy and the kingdom of Naples they became the key players in the politics of the peninsula; the other surviving states increasingly took their cue from their more powerful neighbours, in some respects becoming little more than satellites. The political map of Italy became considerably simplified. The wars of the first half of the fifteenth century were more sustained than those of the fourteenth; they were also 'pan-Italian' in that they involved all parties either actually or potentially. The very scale of involvement, and the interconnectedness of all the protagonists, paradoxically ensured that, when the end eventually came in the form of the Peace of Lodi and the Italic League, all the major powers became signatories. The years 1454–5 can be seen, in current parlance, as a 'defining moment'. Henceforth the official agenda was the expectation and maintenance of peace and the preservation of existing territorial integrity rather than further aggrandisement.

Various factors have been adduced to explain this unexpected window of comparative peace in Italy's hitherto turbulent history: war weariness and financial exhaustion; a balance, or at least an impasse, of power; the development of techniques of diplomacy; the threat of invasion by external forces, be they French or Ottoman. Historians are still debating the relative weight of these factors, but on one point they are agreed—its ultimate failure. The relative stability only postponed by 40 years the greater crisis that was to engulf the peninsula when larger states found in Italy a suitable theatre in which to conduct an altogether larger war, in a sense the first pan-European war. This will be discussed in a later chapter. A number of historians have also speculated on how Italy's inability to resist the invading forces might have been connected with another feature thrown into prominence particularly after the peace, often referred to by the shorthand but elusive label 'the culture of the courts'. The territorial rulers had increasingly common interests, perhaps even to the extent, like twentieth-century royal families, of having more in common with each other than with the majority of their subjects.[13] These interests of course extended to their entourage—clients, dependants and courtiers—though rarely lower down the social scale. They found expression in a variety of ways. Diplomatic activity and ceremonial, feasting, drama and tournament, the celebration of learning and the patronage of the arts (of which more below) are obvious examples; so is the growing body of values that exalted the prince and courtly conduct itself. In this sense the dominant and fashionable cultural values and practices could be integrative for the elite. They were common to large states as well as small, and in large measure to republics as well as *signorie* (even though the existence of a 'court' distinguished official and unofficial *signorie* from republics such as Siena and Venice, the cultural environment was very similar). They were, however, not politically inclusive, and were anything but socially integrative, and some historians suggested that the elitism of Italian renaissance culture was a contributory factor in the crisis of the Italian wars. Crudely put, the view is that the protagonists of Italian public life were too engaged in the self-indulgence of patronage and court life to 'mind the shop', either economically or politically. The consequent neglect of the pattern of alliances between powers, of the cultivation of internal political stability and consensus and of investment in the productive sectors of the economy, are all alleged to have contributed to the crisis that began in 1494.[14]

RULERS AS PATRONS

Much has already been said about patronage in Chapter 8, but the Italian tyrants are so closely linked with this topic that we must return briefly to their share in fostering art and learning. For them it was a matter of prestige to be surrounded by handsome buildings and works of art and to be known as the patrons of distinguished artists, writers and thinkers. It came to be believed that this was a race in which no tyrant, whatever his temperament, could afford to lag behind; to do so would have been a confession of avarice, of petty-mindedness, perhaps even of poverty. For the same reasons it was important to keep pace with changes in taste; patronage of a genre which was no longer fashionable was almost as bad as no patronage at all. Inevitably such patronage grew snowball-wise, like the acquisition of Old Master paintings by American millionaires in the days of Duveen and Berenson, and of Impressionists and post-Impressionists in the second half of the twentieth century. Artists and humanist writers dictated swings in fashionable taste and enjoyed their own new-found prestige. No longer mere 'artists' (craftsmen), they revelled in the sellers' market which brought to men like Michelangelo and Raphael grovelling letters from rulers beseeching them to accept their patronage.

There is not room here to discuss all the leading centres of Renaissance court patronage. It will perhaps be convenient, since their rulers have already been mentioned, to deal with Milan, Florence and the papacy, omitting such important patrons as the Montefeltro of Urbino and the Este of Ferrara. A letter from Leonardo da Vinci to Ludovico 'il Moro' of *c*.1482 illustrates well the nature of Sforza patronage. In it Leonardo urges on Ludovico his skill as a military and naval engineer, offering to construct tanks ('covered cars') and other ingenious weapons: apart from this, he is skilful as an architect, in designing both houses and systems for conveying water, he is a painter and a sculptor in marble, clay and bronze, who longs to take in hand the proposed equestrian statue in bronze of Francesco Sforza.[15] Unfortunately no evidence has survived to reveal whether Leonardo's employment produced the practical military advantages that he promised.

The two greatest Medici rulers were both distinguished as patrons. Cosimo gave encouragement to Marsilio Ficino, the teacher of Lorenzo, and to other Neo-Platonic philosophers, besides subsidising Niccolò Niccoli in the collection of classical manuscripts which later came to his own library and to the public library he founded, the Marciana. Cosimo showed comparatively little interest in the visual arts, but his son Giovanni ordered the famous Gozzoli frescoes in the chapel of the Medici palace and his other son Piero, an invalid, spent many hours with his collections of gems and illuminated manuscripts. Lorenzo was another connoisseur who probably spent more money on antiques—medals, precious stones and jewellery were his speciality—than on contemporary art. He certainly devoted much time to the plans for his new villa at Poggio a Caiano, but painting does not seem to have been among his principal enthusiasms. He was often consulted by other rulers about Florentine artists and the effect of his advice was to disperse rather than to employ them, for Leonardo, as we have seen, moved to Milan, and Verrocchio to Venice and then to Rome, where he worked, like many other Florentines, for Pope Sixtus IV. As a fine poet himself, as the close friend of the philosopher Ficino and of the classical scholar and poet Poliziano, Lorenzo stands apart from other Renaissance patrons. He could well afford to emulate Maecenas in the munificent patronage that reflected his individual tastes.

The greatest of fifteenth-century Italian patrons in terms of money was the papacy. The proud tradition was firmly founded by Nicholas V (1447–55), himself a classical scholar and virtually the originator of the Vatican library. In Nicholas's chancery were such humanists as Poggio Bracciolini, Leon Battista Alberti and Lorenzo Valla, and he encouraged Valla and the Greek cardinal Bessarion to undertake translations of the works of Plato and Thucydides. He employed as painters Fra Angelico, Piero della Francesca and Andrea Castagno, and he formulated ambitious schemes for rebuilding. His fulsome biographer, Giannozzo Manetti, likens his buildings to those of Athens, to Solomon's Temple, the Colossus of Rhodes and the Pyramids, but his greatest contribution was the decision to build a new St Peter's. Nicholas's successor, Pius II, though himself a humanist—or perhaps *because* he had been a humanist—was no enthusiastic patron of letters, nor was his successor Paul II. The tradition, however, was resumed with enthusiasm by the Franciscan Sixtus IV (1471–84), who began the alterations at St Peter's, built the famous chapel which bears his name (the 'Sistine'), employed Botticelli, Ghirlandaio, Perugino, Signorelli and other noted artists, chose as his librarian the papal biographer Platina and encouraged the employment of humanists at the *Studium Urbis*, the city's university. His successors, Innocent VIII and Alexander VI, gave work to Mantegna and Pinturicchio, but the greatest products of papal patronage, the building of a new St Peter's, the addition of many suites of rooms to the Vatican palace, and the replanning of much of Rome, were to be the work of the sixteenth century.

To emphasise their rank, which placed them above the merely temporal rulers of Italy, the popes determined to outshine all others as patrons. Their activities came to a peak when princely and pontifical pride joined together in the Medici popes Leo X and Clement VII. But there was no slackening under Clement's Farnese successor (Paul III) nor under the popes of the Counter-Reformation. The building of the new St Peter's proceeded throughout the sixteenth century, and only in that century did Rome become—what Florence had been since the time of Brunelleschi—a 'Renaissance' city, bearing the marks of the classical theories of proportion and harmony which were restated by Leon Battista Alberti. By the later sixteenth century Rome was the only court in Italy that remained a centre of artistic patronage, but 'Renaissance' traditions had been taken up in the courts of the monarchies. Tastes were inherited as well as traditions, and the Queen of the greatest of English royal collectors, Charles I, was by descent a Medici.

APPENDIX

Leonardo da Vinci writes to offer his services to Ludovico 'il Moro' of Milan, c.1483

(From *Selections from the Notebooks of Leonardo da Vinci*, ed. I. A. Richter (The World's Classics, London, 1952), pp. 294–6.)

Most illustrious Lord. Having now sufficiently seen and considered the proofs of all those who count themselves masters and inventors of instruments of war, and finding that the invention and working of the said instruments do not differ in any respect from those in common use, I shall endeavour without prejudice to anyone else to explain myself to your Excellency, showing your Lordship my secrets, and then offering at your pleasure to work with effect at convenient times on all those things which are in part briefly recorded below.

1. I have plans of bridges, very light and strong and suitable for carrying very easily, and with them you may pursue, and at times flee from, the enemy; and others secure and indestructible by fire and battle, easy and convenient to lift and place in position; and plans for burning and destroying those of the enemy.

2. When a place is besieged, I know how to remove the water from the trenches, and how to construct an infinite number of bridges, covered ways and ladders and other instruments having to do with such expeditions.

3. Also if a place cannot be reduced by the method of bombardment either owing to the height of its banks or to its strength of position, I have plans for destroying every fortress or other stronghold even if it were founded on rock.

4. I have also plans of mortars most convenient and easy to carry with which to hurl small stones in the manner almost of a storm; and with the smoke of this cause great terror to the enemy and great loss and confusion.

And if it should happen that the fight was at sea I have plans for many engines most efficient for both attack and defence, and vessels which will resist the fire of the largest cannon, and powder and smoke.

5. Also I have means of arriving at a fixed spot by caves and secret and winding passages, made without any noise even though it may be necessary to pass underneath trenches or a river.

6. Also I will make covered cars, safe and unassailable, which will enter among the enemy with their artillery, and there is no company of men at arms so great that they will not break it. And behind these infantry will be able to follow quite unharmed and without any hindrance.

7. Also, if need shall arise, I can make cannon, mortars, and light ordnance of very useful and beautiful shapes, different from those in common use.

8. Where the operation of bombardment fails, I shall contrive catapults, mangonels, *trabocchi*, and other engines of wonderful efficacy and in general use. In short, to meet the variety of circumstances, I shall contrive various and endless means of attack and defence.

9. In time of peace I believe I can give perfect satisfaction, equal to that of any other, in architecture and the construction of buildings both private and public, and in conducting water from one place to another.

Also I can carry out sculpture in marble, bronze or clay, and also I can do in painting whatever can be done, as well as any other, whoever he be.

Moreover, the bronze horse may be taken in hand, which shall endue with immortal glory and eternal honour the happy memory of the prince your father and of the illustrious house of Sforza.

And if any of the aforesaid things should seem impossible or impracticable to anyone I offer myself as most ready to make trial of them in your park, or in whatever place may please your Excellency, to whom I commend myself with all possible humility.

FURTHER READING

General

Denys Hay and John Law, *Italy in the Age of the Renaissance 1380–1530* (London, 1989) is a thorough synthesis; Michael Mallett, 'The northern Italian states', in *NCMH*, 7, pp. 546–70, and Alan Ryder, 'The Papal States and the kingdom of Naples', op. cit., pp. 571–87 are crisp syntheses of the political history in particular. Trevor Dean, ed., *The Towns of Italy in the Later Middle Ages* (Manchester, 2000) is a wide-ranging collection of documents in translation. *See also* Lauro Martines, *Power and Imagination. City-States in Renaissance Italy* (New York, 1979 and London, 1980). Two collections of essays cover a range of political issues raised in this chapter: Anthony Molho, Kurt Raaflaub and Julia Emlen, eds, *City-States in Classical Antiquity and Medieval Italy* (Ann Arbor, Mich., 1991), and Julius Kirshner, ed., *The Origins of the State in Italy, 1300–1600* (Chicago, Ill., 1996).

The decline of the republics

P. J. Jones, 'Communes and despots: the city-state in late medieval Italy', *Transactions of the Royal Historical Society*, 5th series, 15 (1965), pp. 71–96, and D. M. Bueno de Mesquita, 'The place of despotism in Italian politics', in *Europe in the Late Middle Ages,* eds John Hale, Roger Highfield and Beryl Smalley (London, 1965), pp. 301–31 are two fundamental articles for this topic; C. Chittolini, 'Cities, "city-states", and regional states in north and central Italy', in *Cities and the Rise of States in Europe, AD 1000 to 1800,* eds C. Tilly and W. P. Blockmans (Oxford, 1994), pp. 28–43 pursues some of the issues raised in these articles. *See also* the useful Historical Association booklet by J. Law, *The Lords of Renaissance Italy* (London, 1981). L. Green, *Castruccio Castracani. A Study on the Origins and Character of a Fourteenth-Century Italian Despotism* (Oxford, 1986) is a valuable case study of one of the earlier *signori.* Examples of the vicariate system are discussed in P. J. Jones, 'The vicariate of the Malatesta of Rimini', *English Historical Review,* 67 (1952), pp. 321–51, and in his *The Malatesta of Rimini and the Papal State* (Cambridge, 1974); and in John Larner, *The Lords of Romagna. Romagnol Society and the Origins of the Signorie* (Ithaca, N.Y., 1965). The history of the *condottieri* can be traced through M. Mallett, *Mercenaries and their Masters. Warfare in Renaissance Italy* (London, 1974), his 'The condottiere', in *Renaissance Characters,* ed. Eugenio Garin (tr. Chicago, 1997), pp. 22–45, and M. E. Mallett and J. R. Hale, *The Military Organization of a Renaissance State: Venice c.1400 to 1617* (Cambridge, 1984), Part 1.

The rise of the *signori*: the case of Milan

Relatively little has been published in English on Milanese history. *See* D. M. Bueno de Mesquita, *Giangaleazzo Visconti, Duke of Milan 1351–1402. A Study in the Political Career of an Italian Despot* (Cambridge, 1941), and C. M. Ady, *Milan under the Sforza* (London, 1907) for the basic political history.

Florence and the Medici

Florence is the most intensively studied city of the Renaissance. General introductions to the period before and including the Medici include F. Schevill, *A History of Florence* (New York, 1961 edition) and G. Brucker, *Renaissance Florence* (New York, 1969). N. Rubinstein, ed., *Florentine Studies* (London, 1968) is a valuable collection of essays. The political history of fourteenth- and fifteenth-century Florence can be followed closely through a series of studies: G. Brucker, *Florentine Politics and Society, 1343–78* (Princeton, N.J., 1962); G. Brucker, *The Civic World of Early Renaissance Florence* (Princeton, N.J., 1977); J. M. Najemy, *Corporatism and Consensus in Florentine Electoral Politics, 1280–1400* (Chapel Hill, N.C., 1982); A. Molho, *Florentine Public Finances in the Early Renaissance, 1400–1433* (Cambridge, Mass., 1971); D. Kent, *The Rise of the Medici Faction in Florence 1426–34* (Oxford, 1978). Selected documents in translation are in G. Brucker, ed., *The Society of Renaissance Florence. A Documentary Study* (1971, repr. Toronto, 1998).

On the Medici period, a general introduction (going well beyond this period) is J. R. Hale, *Florence and the Medici: the Pattern of Control* (London, 1977). On Medicean government the definitive work is N. Rubinstein, *The Government of Florence under the Medici, 1434–1494* (2nd edition, Oxford, 1997); *see also* A. Brown, *The Medici in Florence. The Exercise and Language of Power* (Florence and Perth, 1992). Cosimo de' Medici has received less attention in English than his grandson. F. Ames-Lewis, ed., *Cosimo 'Il Vecchio' de' Medici 1389–1464. Essays in Commemoration of the 600th Anniversary of Cosimo de' Medici's Birth* (Oxford, 1992). There are many biographies of Lorenzo and several volumes of essays which appeared in the wake of the quincentenary of his death. C. M. Ady, *Lorenzo de' Medici and Renaissance Italy* (New York, 1955) is still consultable; *see also* J. Hook, *Lorenzo de' Medici* (London, 1984); M. M. Bullard, *Lorenzo il Magnifico: Image and Anxiety, Politics and Finance* (Florence, 1994); M. Mallett and N. Mann, eds, *Lorenzo the Magnificent: Culture and Politics* (London, 1996). On Florence after

Lorenzo, *see*: D. Weinstein, *Savonarola and Florence* (Princeton, N.J., 1970); Lorenzo Polizzotto, *The Elect Nation: the Savonarolan Movement in Florence, 1494–1545* (Oxford, 1994); H. C. Butters, *Governors and Government in Early Sixteenth-Century Florence, 1502–1519* (Oxford, 1985); J. Stephens, *The Fall of the Florentine Republic, 1512–1530* (Oxford, 1983).

Other states

The examples covered in this chapter are only selections. An immense amount has been published in English on Italian history, and it would be impossible to give a full bibliography here. A selection of introductory works is given for initial orientation only. For **Venice**, in addition to works cited under Chapters 1 and 2, *see* D. S. Chambers, *The Imperial Age of Venice, 1380–1580* (London, 1970); R. Finlay, *Politics in Renaissance Venice* (London, 1980); J. R. Hale, ed., *Renaissance Venice* (London, 1973); E. E. Kittell and T. F. Madden, eds, *Medieval and Renaissance Venice* (Urbana and Chicago, Ill., 1999) (essays); and D. S. Chambers and B. Pullan, eds, *Venice. A Documentary History 1450–1630* (Oxford, 1992). For **Naples**, the works of A. J. Ryder: 'The evolution of imperial government in Naples under Alfonso V', in *Europe in the Late Middle Ages,* eds John Hale, Roger Highfield and Beryl Smalley (London, 1965), pp. 332–57; *The Kingdom of Naples under Alfonso the Magnanimous. The Making of a Modern State* (Oxford, 1976); and *Alfonso the Magnanimous, King of Aragon, Naples, and Sicily 1396–1458* (Oxford, 1990); on the following period, David Abulafia, 'Introduction: from Ferrante I to Charles VIII', in *The French Descent into Italy, 1494–95. Antecedents and Effects,* ed. D. Abulafia (Aldershot, 1995), pp. 1–25, and David Abulafia, 'The crown and the economy under Ferrante I of Naples (1458–94)', in *City and Countryside in Late Medieval and Renaissance Italy. Essays presented to Philip Jones,* eds Trevor Dean and Chris Wickham (London, 1990), pp. 125–46. The **Papal State** is covered by P. Partner, in *The Papal State under Martin V* (London, 1958) and *The Lands of St Peter* (London, 1972); *see also* C. F. Black, 'The Baglioni as tyrants of Perugia, 1488–1540', *English Historical Review,* 85 (1970), pp. 245–81; C. M. Ady, *The Bentivoglio of Bologna. A Study in Despotism* (London, 1937); and under Chapter 13 for further references. Of the lesser states, **Ferrara** is well covered in English: W. L. Gundersheimer, *Ferrara. The Style of a Renaissance Despotism* (Princeton, N.J., 1973); T. Dean, *Land and Power in Late Medieval Ferrara. The Rule of the Este, 1350–1450* (Cambridge, 1988); and T. Tuohy, *Herculean Ferrara. Ercole d'Este (1471–1505) and the Invention of a Ducal Capital* (Cambridge, 1996). For **Padua** before its conquest by Venice *see* B. Kohl, *Padua under the Carrara, 1318–1405* (Baltimore, Md., 1998). Finally two studies of **Lucca**, one of the few states to survive as a republic in the period: C. Meek, *The Commune of Lucca under Pisan Rule, 1342–1369* (Cambridge, Mass., 1980), and her *Lucca 1369–1400. Politics and Society in an Early Renaissance City-State* (Oxford, 1978); and M. E. Bratchel, *Lucca, 1430–1494. The Reconstruction of an Italian City-Republic* (Oxford, 1995).

Rulers as patrons

Many aspects of Italian Renaissance courts have been studied by specialists. On **Milan**, G. Lubkin, *A Renaissance Court. Milan under Galeazzo Maria Sforza* (Berkeley and Los Angeles, Cal., 1994); and E. Welch, *Art and Authority in Renaissance Milan* (New Haven, Conn., 1995). On **Florence**, *see* the richly detailed D. Kent, *Cosimo de' Medici and the Florentine Renaissance* (New Haven, Conn., and London, 2000); E. H. Gombrich, 'The early Medici as patrons of art', in *Italian Renaissance Studies,* ed. E. F. Jacob (London, 1960), pp. 279–311, repr. in his *Norm and Form. Studies in the Art of the Renaissance* (London, 1966), pp. 35–57; A. D. Fraser Jenkins, 'Cosimo de' Medici's patronage of architecture and the theory of magnificence', *Journal of the Warburg and Courtauld Institutes,* 33 (1970), pp. 162–70; A. Beyer and B. Boucher, eds, *Piero de' Medici, 'il Gottoso' (1416–1469): Art in the Service of the Medici* (Berlin, 1993); and

M. Wackernagel, *The World of the Florentine Renaissance Artist: Projects and Patrons, Workshop and Art Market* (1938: tr. Princeton, N.J., 1981). Much is available on renaissance **Rome**; *see especially* Charles L. Stinger, *The Renaissance in Rome* (revised edition, Bloomington, In., 1998); John F. D'Amico, *Renaissance Humanism in Papal Rome. Humanists and Churchmen on the Eve of the Reformation* (Baltimore, Md., 1983, paperback 1991); Loren Partridge, *The Renaissance in Rome, 1400–1600* (London, 1996); C. W. Westfall, *In This Most Perfect Paradise. Alberti, Nicholas V and the Invention of Conscious Urban Planning in Rome, 1447–1455* (University Park, Pa., 1974); and P. A. Ramsey, ed., *Rome in the Renaissance: the City and the Myth* (Binghamton, N.Y., 1982). On **Naples**, *see* J. H. Bentley, *Politics and Culture in Renaissance Naples* (Princeton, N.J., 1987); and A. Atlas, *Music at the Aragonese Court of Naples* (Cambridge, 1985).

On the art of the courts *see also* general works: in addition to those cited under Chapter 8, Evelyn Welch, *Art and Society in Italy 1350–1500* (Oxford, 1997) is an excellent introduction; *see also* A. Cole, *Art of the Italian Renaissance Courts. Virtue and Magnificence* (London, 1995: also published as *Virtue and Magnificence. Art of the Italian Renaissance Courts*, New York, 1995). Other basic works are John White, *Art and Architecture in Italy 1250–1400* (3rd edition, New Haven, Conn., and London, 1993); James Beck, *Italian Renaissance Painting* (New York, 1981, repr. Cologne, 1999); John T. Paoletti and Gary M. Radke, *Art in Renaissance Italy* (London, 1997); F. Hartt, *History of Italian Renaissance Art: Painting, Sculpture, Architecture* (4th edition, revised by D. Wilkins, London, 1994); R. J. M. Olson, *Italian Renaissance Sculpture* (London, 1992); J. Pope-Hennessy, *An Introduction to Italian Sculpture*, vol. 2: *Renaissance Sculpture* (3rd edition, Oxford, 1986). *See also* B. Cole, *Italian Art, 1250–1550: the Relation of Renaissance Art to Life and Society* (New York, 1987); A. Thomas, *The Painter's Practice in Renaissance Tuscany* (Cambridge, 1995); and C. M. Rosenberg, ed., *Art and Politics in Late Medieval and Early Renaissance Italy, 1250–1500* (Notre Dame, In., 1990). On Leonardo, *see* Martin Kemp, *Leonardo da Vinci: the Marvelous Works of Nature and Man* (Cambridge, Mass., 1981); and Kenneth Clark, *Leonardo da Vinci* (revised by Martin Kemp, London, 1988).

NOTES

1. *See* Chapter 1.
2. *See above*, pp. 31 and 115.
3. *The Prince*, ch. 20.
4. *Below*, p. 189.
5. P. J. Jones, 'The vicariate of the Malatesta of Rimini', *The English Historical Review*, 67 (1952), pp. 321–51 (p. 321). For an earlier version of this policy, *see* pp. 42–3.
6. *See above*, p. 102.
7. J. Pitti, 'Istoria fiorentina', *Archivio storico italiano*, 1 (1842), pp. 25–107 (this passage is on p. 25).
8. *See* Map 4.
9. *See below*, p. 214.
10. L. Landucci, *Diario Fiorentino*, ed. I. Del Badia (Florence, 1883), p. 65; the work has been translated as *A Florentine Diary* by A. de Rosen Jervis (London, 1927); this passage is on p. 54.
11. Bartolommeo Dei, in a letter to his uncle Benedetto; translated in Janet Ross, *Lives of the Early Medici as told in their Correspondence* (London, 1910), p. 341.
12. Quoted in Ross, op. cit., p. 343.
13. The shocked reaction of fellow rulers to the assassination of Galeazzo Maria Sforza of Milan in 1476 is witness to this. Vincent Ilardi, 'The assassination of Galeazzo Maria

Sforza and the reaction of Italian diplomacy', in *Violence and Civil Disorder in Italian Cities, 1200–1500*, ed. Lauro Martines (Berkeley and Los Angeles, Cal., 1972), pp. 72–103.

14. These views characterise the closing chapters of Lauro Martines, *Power and Imagination. City-States in Renaissance Italy* (New York, 1979 and London, 1980). A more balanced assessment is Michael Mallett, 'The northern Italian states', in *NCMH*, 7, pp. 546–70, esp. pp. 564–70. For an assessment of the characteristics and role of courts, *see* T. Dean, 'The courts', in *The Origins of the State in Italy, 1300–1600*, ed. J. Kirshner (Chicago, Ill., 1996), pp. 136–51.

15. For a full translation *see* the Appendix *above*, pp. 200–1.

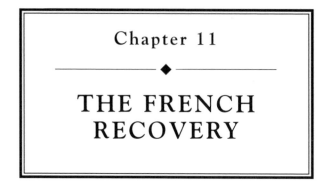

Chapter 11

THE FRENCH RECOVERY

ENGLISH TRIUMPHS AND REVERSALS: THE END OF THE WAR

The Treaty of Troyes of 1420[1] and its ratification by the French estates marked the lowest tide in the fortunes of France. The English, assisted by Burgundy, held most of northern France, and their king had been accepted as heir to the French throne. The finances of France were in a disastrous condition. The extravagance of the royal household was notorious; the 'Remonstrances' of Paris in 1413 claimed that the expenditure of the queen's household alone had recently risen from 36,000 to 154,000 *livres* a year. Even more serious were the financial consequences of the pressure exerted on the demented king by both Orléans and Burgundy during the years of their struggle for power; Louis of Orléans, besides an annual pension from the Crown of 12,000 *livres*, received 500,000 *livres* for renouncing his claims to Genoa, the same amount on the occasion of his son's marriage to the widow of Richard II of England and much else. The currency of the unoccupied zone was chaotic—and at Rouen groats were minted bearing the menacing legend 'Henricus rex Angliae heres Franciae' ('Henry, king of England and heir to France'). In Paris the population was for the most part more bitterly anti-Burgundian or anti-Armagnac (according to individual sympathies) than anti-English. Henry V of England was joyfully received in the city in 1420 and the following year the birth of his son was feted. This desertion of the French cause was not, of course, unanimous; when the Parisians took the oath of loyalty to the English in 1423 it was noted that 'some did so with a good heart, others most unwillingly'.[2] The effect of the treaty, in fact, was that the French were no longer clear where their allegiance lay.

After the treaty and the fall of Paris the disowned dauphin was able to carry on the war from Bourges, with other centres of support at Poitiers and Toulouse. The death of Henry V in 1422 brought some hope to the dauphin, and a few months later that of his father gave him a claim to the royal title, but France's dilemma was reflected in the very serious dissensions within his own party. These led to a series of campaigns between the chamberlain La Trémouille and the Angevin house, supported by the constable Richemont, amounting to a civil war within the framework of the greater struggle.

In 1429 the war at last took a favourable turn for the dauphin with the relief of Orléans, on the Loire. Not only was this fortress a key position for the defence of central and southern France, it was also the town of the captive duke Charles d'Orléans, and some held that in these circumstances the English were transgressing the rules of war in besieging it. French indignation at this action is mirrored in the decisive intervention of Joan of Arc, the symptom and at the same time the agent of French national sentiment. Joan's passionate patriotism was that of a frontier-territory; her village, Domrémy, lay on the boundary of the pro-Burgundian duchy of Bar, and it had once been destroyed by Burgundian troops. Her talk was as much of 'French blood' as of the saints, and the very words of her 'voices' are charac-teristic: 'Go to France, you will relieve Orléans'. Joan persuaded the dauphin of his legitimacy, then played a prominent part in the relief of Orléans. It is hard to assess her share in determining strategy and even to decide to what extent she ranked as a military commander, but her contribution for morale was great and vitally important in this turning point of the war. The English issued a proclamation against 'the cap-tains and soldiers who have abandoned their posts, influenced by the incantations of a maid', and the letter of Charles of France announced her successes as a miracle. After the relief, Joan took part in the further victory of Patay, then set the seal on her triumph by escorting the dauphin across France to Rheims, where he was crowned as Charles VII.

It was natural that Joan's achievements and her influence at court should make her enemies. La Trémouille in particular was jealous of her prestige and helped to rouse doubts concerning her when she met failure in an ill-prepared sally against Paris, in the course of which she was wounded for the third time. When she fell into the hands of the Burgundians at Compiègne (May 1430) the English paid 10,000 crowns for her to her captors. Her subsequent trial by the Inquisition was aimed, by implica-tion, at Charles also, for if she could be discredited, so was his coronation. Yet the French court now virtually disowned her and nothing was done to save Joan when she was sentenced to be burnt after being tricked into abjuring her errors. After her death (May 1431) she was remembered among the French people, but the monarchy did not obtain her official rehabilitation until a quarter of a century later. Recent writers, in reaction against the view which ascribes all historical developments to the deeds of outstanding individuals, have minimised the importance of Joan's inter-vention. Contemporary testimony leaves no doubt that her role was an enormously important one, and chroniclers as far afield as Lübeck[3] recorded her deeds and her death.

The momentous consequence of Charles VII's military revival was the gradual detachment of Burgundy from its English alliance. This was assisted by the dissolu-tion by death of the marriage alliance—Anne, duchess of Bedford, sister of the duke of Burgundy and wife of the English regent, died in 1432 and Bedford himself in 1435—but essentially it was the product of the shift in the balance of military suc-cess. At Arras in 1435 the Burgundians at last came to terms with the French Crown. The terms were humiliating for Charles, and in view of his circumstances they could not be otherwise: he had to yield the Somme towns, to excuse duke Philip homage, and to express contrition for the murder at Montereau. Nevertheless, the crisis in the struggle was now over. The following year Paris was reoccupied, and France entered the slow and painful process of recuperation. With England beset by internal dissension and France by bands of parasitic mercenaries, both sides were extremely weak. By 1439 Charles was able to begin a series of military reforms, asserting royal control of recruitment to the mercenary companies. After the truce of Tours (1444) there followed more effective military reorganisation, with the formation first of a regular cavalry force, the *compagnies d'ordonnance* consisting of 1,500 'lances' of six men each, then of a similar infantry force, the *francs-archers*, recruited by the provision of one archer from every 50 'hearths'. In time of peace the *francs-archers* were to be remunerated by exemption from tax. There was also some reform in financial organisation, four local receivers-general being appointed. Perhaps as influential in restoring order as these formal measures was Charles's success in the 1440s in loaning the baneful mercenary companies for employment by the emperor Frederick III and the duke of Lorraine.

In the mid-century the last decisive campaigns of the war were fought. Profiting by English political disunity and financial embarrassment, Charles recovered Normandy in 1449–50, and Guyenne between 1449 and 1453 after a temporary setback due to Gascon resentment of rule by Frenchmen. Charles lived on until 1461. His epithet, *le bien servi* ('the well-served') is perhaps a backhanded compliment. Despite his unimpressive personality, his achievements were immense. In some ways the most important of these was his success in bringing the monarchy out of the war with its hold over its noble subjects greatly strengthened. He checked the acquisition of new fiefs and the construction of new fortifications, limited seignorial taxation, and increased the scope of royal jurisdiction at the expense of the nobility. More nobles were taken into royal employment as officials and in office they enjoyed power in their capacity as officials rather than as nobles. Three times Charles had to face noble 'conspiracies', but only the *Praguerie* of 1440, which involved the dauphin as well as the dukes of Brittany, Alençon and Bourbon and the count of Anjou, was a serious threat: it was perhaps frustrated only by the refusal of the English to participate. The next reign was to show that the monarchy had by no means cowed the greater feudatories. The falling back of the lesser nobles and their tendency to become aligned with the Crown was an essential element in the extraordinarily rapid recovery of the French monarchy. Their recession is usually attributed to impoverishment by the war and inability to increase their incomes to meet the rising cost of fighting on their own account, but such explanations of general social changes are hard to establish, and this one cannot yet be regarded as proved.

LOUIS XI

Louis, son and heir of Charles, had long been in opposition to his father, and for the last five years of the reign had lived under the protection of the duke of Burgundy. The curious and interesting personality of Louis XI had much to do with France's continued recovery. He was a hard man and a hard worker, authoritarian, unscrupulous and expecting no scruples in others. Pious, jovial and in manner unassuming and unimpressive, he had no interest in ceremony, and at his coronation banquet he took off his crown, because he found it uncomfortable, and put it on the table. He had a passion for information and for diplomacy. Louis spoke Italian and admired the Italians, but in the opinion of Europe he had nothing to learn from them of diplomatic subtlety; certainly his comment on Francesco Sforza that 'he was never so great as when he was up to his neck in water' could be applied with equal truth to himself. The historians of his defeated rival, Burgundy, admiringly called him 'the universal spider', and Commynes, the servant and adviser whom he lured from the Burgundians, spoke from close acquaintance when he called him 'the cleverest man I have known at extricating himself from an adverse situation' and the one 'who worked hardest to win over a man who could serve him or do him harm'.

There is no room here to deal with Louis' diplomacy at length, and we must renounce, for example, the tale of his tangled negotiations in the Iberian peninsula, which occupied much of his time and energy. In his three principal aims, the overthrow of the virtually independent Burgundian duchy, the curbing of the other great French feudatories and the elimination of English intervention in France, he achieved success. These three themes are so interrelated that they cannot be treated in isolation. Philip the Good of Burgundy was the greatest of the feudatories, a fact he emphasised tactlessly at Louis' coronation by attending with a suite of 4,000 which greatly outnumbered the king's. Others were not far behind. The duke of Brittany almost ranked as an independent ruler, with his own administration and army, his own diplomacy and an agreement with the papacy which gave him very considerable authority over the dioceses of his duchy. Further south the Angevin descendants of Charles V's brother Louis held the middle Loire as well as Anjou and Maine and the isolated county of Provence; moreover, René of Anjou was claimant to the kingdom of Naples, his sister was the widow of Charles VII and his daughter the wife of Henry VI of England. In central France the duke of Bourbon dominated the upper Loire and Auvergne, thus completing a potentially hostile chain which terminated in the east with the duchy of Burgundy. Only a little after these greatest of nobles ranked the houses of Orléans and Alençon, and those of Armagnac and Foix in the south-west.

'On his accession he thought of nothing but revenge', says Commynes, and the dismissed officials of Louis' father played a leading part in the organisation of the great alliance of malcontents which was formed in 1464. The claim of this coalition to stand for the public weal (*le bien public*) bears witness only to the imagined persuasive strength of the tritest of all political commonplaces, and one to which the king himself subscribed when he advised his successor to rule *pour le bien commun* ('for the common good').[4] The Parisian writer who dated his poem from 'the year in which everyone put his own interest first' (*l'an que chacun à son profit tendait*) made the aptest comment on these pretensions. The chief characters in the conspiracy were Charles, count of Charolais (the heir of Philip of Burgundy), the duke of Brittany, René of Anjou's heir John of Calabria, the duke of Bourbon and the count of Armagnac; the king's brother Charles was its figurehead. Louis had the support of Normandy, Picardy and Champagne, of two of his uncles, the majority of the towns and a mercenary force provided by his ally Francesco Sforza, but his enemies were able to put well over 10,000 men into the field and his hopes of salvation lay mainly in their dissensions. In action the coalition proved a very piecemeal affair. The first attack was launched from Britanny in the spring of 1465 by the king's brother. Thereafter Louis was able to confront his opponents one by one, first defeating John of Bourbon, then checking Charolais at the indecisive battle of Montlhéry. By the autumn Charles of France had lost his enthusiasm for the war, but Louis was only able to extricate himself from the crisis by distributing sops to the principal plotters. By the Treaty of St Maur (October 1465) Burgundy received Boulogne, Guines and the recently ceded Somme towns, Bourbon the lieutenant-generalship of Languedoc and a gift of 100,000 crowns, Louis' brother Normandy, and the duke of Brittany and John of Calabria lesser rewards. A 'commission of reform' was appointed, but no reform followed. Soon afterwards Louis drove his brother from Normandy, which as a possible base for future English reconquests was a sensitive point; by then all Charles's former allies had forgotten the Public Weal, for none came to his defence.

Only once after the *bien public* did Louis have to face an acute crisis. This occurred after Charles of Charolais' accession to the Burgundian duchy (1467), when through over-confidence Louis enmeshed himself in the tortuous coils of his own diplomatic intrigue. In 1468 he pressed for a meeting with Charles the Rash, which took place at Péronne. But he had recently completed negotiations for a rising of Charles's subject city of Liège, and the news of this rebellion, together with Louis' evident complicity, reached the duke when the king, with almost no entourage (though he had troops nearby), was on his territory. For three days the angry duke held Louis virtually as a prisoner; the king was '*fort effrayé*' ('very frightened'), says Commynes, who goes on to recount how

that night, the third, the duke never took off his clothes. He only lay down on his bed two or three times, then started to pace up and down, as was his way when he was worried. I slept in his chamber that night and sometimes I walked up and down the room with him. In the morning he was in a greater rage than ever, he was making threats and was ready to carry out a great deed [*à exécuter grande chose*]. Nevertheless he decided to reduce his demands; he would be content if the king swore to keep peace [with him] and went with him to Liège to aid him in his revenge against the bishop of Lige, who was a close relative of the king's. And so he abruptly went off to the king's room to tell him this decision.[5]

The episode of Péronne and the subsequent campaign against his Liègois allies were a humiliation for Louis, but the duke had realised that international politics is not a game that ends with the capture of the king. In the event his gains were comparatively meagre. Louis yielded some jurisdictional rights and more territory. This time he granted his brother Champagne and Brie, which were dangerously adjacent to Burgundy, but later Charles was persuaded to accept instead Guyenne, tenure of which almost precluded friendship with England. Meanwhile an assembly of notables freed Louis from his engagements to the duke of Burgundy on the ground that these had been extorted under pressure.

As England early in the century had hesitated between support of Burgundian and Armagnac, so Louis now hesitated between Lancaster and York. During the 'public weal' he had been Yorkist and was fortunate in that Burgundy was then linked with the failing fortunes of Henry VI, whose brother-in-law John of Calabria was prominent in the League. Soon after this the Burgundians turned Yorkist, but the quarrel of Warwick 'the Kingmaker' with the Woodvilles and his flight to France gave Louis the opportunity to plan a Lancastrian restoration. He contrived to reconcile Henry's queen, Margaret of Anjou, with the man who had done so much to bring about her husband's deposition. In 1470 he assisted Warwick's invasion, and triumphed when Edward IV fled to the Low Countries and Henry VI was released from the Tower of London and restored to the throne. This success had its logical continuation when Louis sent an embassy to England to propose a joint attack on Burgundy; the duchy was to be carved up, England receiving the Low Countries.

But Louis had backed the wrong horse. Edward, with support from Burgundy, the Hanse and Brittany, invaded England and put an end to the Lancastrian restoration after less than a year. Now it was Burgundy's turn to prepare an attack on France, and the cycle of events became complete in 1474 when, by the Treaty of London, Charles of Burgundy came to terms with Edward IV for a partition of the kingdom of France.[6]

The following year Edward landed a large force at Calais, but he was disappointed to find that the promised aid from the dukes of Burgundy and Brittany did not materialise. Louis took his chance, arranged a personal meeting with Edward at Picquigny and bought him off for 75,000 crowns down, to be followed by an annual payment of 50,000. Charles of Burgundy was bitterly indignant at his ally's defection, but it was his own fault that he had committed himself to expansionist schemes in too many directions at the same time and was involved with his army in the Rhineland when he should have been assisting Edward: 'God had troubled his senses and his understanding', says Commynes. Picquigny marked the end of any serious English claim to the French throne and thus the liquidation of the Hundred Years War. It was characteristic of Louis that this should be achieved by money. As he explained in the *Rosier des guerres*: 'To fight is the most dangerous thing in the world . . . If one errs in anything else, one can amend it later, but when one has lost a battle there is no way of making amends.'[7] This preference for financial methods shows, too, in the handsome pensions later allotted by Louis to Edward's councillors, which were intended to secure English support for his Burgundian schemes after the death of Charles the Rash. Lord Hastings, the chamberlain, was the most favoured of these, at 2,000 crowns per annum—for which he was unwilling to furnish a receipt since he was also a pensioner of Louis' rival, Mary of Burgundy.

After Picquigny, Burgundy was by far the most important of Louis' preoccupations, but Charles, who 'would not have been satisfied with half Europe', did much to bring about his own destruction. The story of Louis' organisation of an alliance including the Swiss, Frederick III and the duke of Lorraine, and of Charles's frantic campaigns and downfall, has been recounted above. Louis' exploitation of Charles's death, however, cannot be ranked among his successes. The vital element in the situation was the future of Mary of Burgundy, Charles's only daughter, who was 19 when her father was killed at Nancy. Essentially Louis had to opt between supporting the heiress or opposing her: yet he fell victim to his characteristic fault of over-subtlety and, by attempting to reap the advantages of both courses, he gained little from either. He annexed Picardy, Artois, the towns of the Somme and—in the face of a good deal of opposition—the 'old' duchy (of Burgundy). These conquests by force were not easily reconcilable with Louis' plans for marrying Mary to his seven-year-old heir, and thus gaining the greater prize of the Low Countries. Mary was able to choose as her husband the obvious alternative, Maximilian, the son of Frederick III, and this marriage, possibly the most momentous in the entire history of Europe, took place in August 1477. The matter of the Burgundian lands was only settled, after some fighting, by the Peace of Arras of 1482. By the terms of Arras Louis gained Picardy and the Burgundian duchy. The intention was that Artois, the Franche-Comté and some other territories should also come to France, as the dowry of Mary's daughter Margaret, who was betrothed to the dauphin, but this marriage did not eventuate, and the lands proved untenable and had to be restored. All the rest of the great Burgundian inheritance was also gained by the hitherto weakly house of Austria. In the pragmatic test Louis' diplomatic expertise had not shown up well.

Nevertheless this was on the whole an era of continued monarchical recovery. We hear of Louis returning happy from a successful boar hunt 'singing a song written about the rout of the duke of Burgundy', and by the end of his reign there was a good deal else about which he could feel content. René of Anjou was survived by none of his male descendants, and after his death (1480) the Crown came into possession of the Angevin lands, including Maine, Provence and the county of Bar. One of Louis' daughters married the heir of John de Bourbon, another Louis of Orléans, and thus two of the great noble dynasties were more closely linked with the monarchy. More welcome still were the confiscated estates of Armagnac, St Pol and Nemours. Brittany was now the sole remaining quasi-independent fief, and even Brittany was not long to maintain this position.

If Louis preferred expenditure to war, he was fully aware that such a policy entailed a special care for his country's financial productivity. His attitude is reflected with striking clarity in his advice to his son, which breaks off strangely from the flow of political and military platitudes to culminate in some down-to-earth (if debatable) economics. The last words of this work are:

If all gilding was forbidden, this would be a good thing: for a lot of gold is lost in this way. Also no one should wear or use silk. And the old fairs of the kingdom should be revived. Thus all would be wealth.[8]

Louis' attempts to foster French fairs are seen at their most energetic in his support of Lyons, which he built up as a rival to Geneva—so overtly that its fairs were held on the same dates as Geneva's—with considerable success. Indeed, he experimented with almost every possible form of economic *étatisme* (state building). In the Mediterranean he backed a series of monopolistic ventures in state galleys, based first on Aigues-Mortes and other ports in the Languedoc, then, after its acquisition in 1482, on Marseilles. These however were unsuccessful, perhaps because the French were too accustomed to importing Levantine goods by land from other ports, such as Genoa. The small state arsenals set up originally at Tours, Rouen and Paris, and later at 18 other centres, were a rather less ambitious and more effective undertaking. Cannon foundries were also inaugurated at Tours, Rouen and Orléans. In the winter of 1480–1, requiring 5,500 pikes, 14,500 halberds and 18,500 daggers for the forth-coming campaign in Flanders, Louis was delighted to receive the total order within two months.

Typical of Louis' methods was his treatment of Arras when the burghers proved hostile to French rule after the occupation of Artois (1477). He had many of the inhabitants exiled, and in 1479 set out to repopulate the city by the compulsory settlement there of 3,000 families, drawn from every zone of France and each designated to follow a particular trade. For three years immense efforts were made to make the colonisation of Arras work. New families were drafted in, entailing tremendous administrative exertions at the recruiting end, economic privileges were lavished on Arras (now rechristened 'Franchise'!), royal officials organised the setting up of cloth firms and other towns were forced to purchase their produce at artificially high prices. Yet this impressive display of Colbertism before its time proved ineffective. The peace terms of 1482 permitted the return of the former inhabitants, and two years later such of the new colonisers as had remained were expelled.

Another enterprising but unsuccessful attempt at regulation was the plan to draw business from the great Burgundian fairs at Bruges and Antwerp. It was hoped to attract English trade away from them to newly founded fairs in Normandy —originally at Caen and later Rouen. In essence this scheme was one of Louis' many attempts at economic warfare, attempts which included military attacks on Burgundian crops and naval ones on the Flemish herring-fleet, and which are seen at their most ambitious in the great embargo on trade with Flanders in 1470. The latter was a serious measure of blockade which attempted to deny the Flemish towns the French grain on which they were dependent, in the hope that the starving population would rise against Charles the Rash in revolt. Louis' economic interven-tionism was significant rather for what it attempted than for what it achieved, but he had inherited a very formidable fiscal machine. There were already 'receiving' offices, each under a *receveur général* at Paris, Tours, Rouen and Montpellier, beside that for the Dauphiné, and to these Louis added offices for Burgundy and the Somme towns (1477) and for Provence (1484). Extraordinary taxation, which came under a central office of *généraux*, was organised by local units known as *élections*, and another net-work to ensure the collection of the salt tax (*gabelle*) covered most of the kingdom. The ultimate fiscal court, the *Chambre* or *Cour des aides*, had both judicial and adminis-trative functions. The extent of France's recovery shows in the fact that the average annual revenue from taxation of his country rose from about 1,800,000 *livres* at the start of Louis' reign to about 4,800,000 at the end,[9] though he may have inflicted hardship by excessive taxation, particularly in the countryside.

CHARLES VIII, LOUIS XII AND ITALY

Louis' heir, Charles VIII, was only 13 on his accession in 1483, and not a very intelligent 13 at that. He was under the guardianship of his elder sister Anne and her husband Pierre de Beaujeu, the heir to the duke of Bourbon, but the authority of this pair was challenged by the duke of Orléans, who was husband of the king's second sister Jeanne, and himself a cousin of the king. To maintain their control the Beaujeu made use of parliamentary institutions: the meeting of estates summoned to Tours, the first to be styled *États généraux* (estates general), was in substance merely a successful manoeuvre to confirm the regency. There was no strong demand for central estates in France, probably because regional feeling remained strong (and, indeed, some local estates continued to meet), and because the nobles, being exempt from taxation, took little interest.

The great political problem of the early years of the reign was that of Brittany, whose duke, Francis II, had no male heir. The duchy was the last great survival of feudal independence (its ruler no longer owed liege homage to the Crown), and there was always the danger that the English might again use it as the gateway to France, as they had done in the previous century. As with Burgundy a few years before, everything hinged on the marriage of the heiress, Anne. A prominent pretender to her hand was the duke of Orléans, who was seeking a divorce from his wife Jeanne. When Orléans rose in rebellion in 1484 (*La guerre folle*) he had some support from Brittany, as well as from king Maximilian and the king of Navarre. Duke Francis's death (1488) was followed by negotiations for a marriage between the heiress Anne and Maximilian, now a widower, and a proxy ceremony took place in 1490, but Maximilian lacked the means to intervene strongly in French affairs. The war in Brittany went in favour of the French Crown and in 1491 Anne was married to Charles VIII. Thus the last of the great fiefs lost its independence, and a new immense accession of domain was added to the recent gains of Anjou, Provence, Alençon and Armagnac. The very strong control over the French Church recognized by the Pragmatic Sanction of Bourges (1438) and the Concordat of Amboise (1472) rounded off for the monarchy a position of strength that would have been unimaginable during the long agony of Charles VI's reign.

Charles VIII had no difficulty in finding an arena within which to display this strength. The story of French interest and intervention in the Italian peninsula can be traced back without interruption to the conquest of Charles of Anjou in the 1260s. By the middle of the fifteenth century this tradition had been strengthened both by the claim of the new Angevin house—recognised by Queen Joanna II (d. 1435)—to the throne of Naples, and that of the Orléans line to the duchy of Milan, based on the marriage of Charles VI's brother Louis of Orléans to Valentina, daughter of Giangaleazzo Visconti. By Charles VIII's time the former of these claims had passed to the French Crown. The acquisition of Marseilles made Tyrrhenian Italy a tempting zone for nascent French naval power, while the city of Asti, Valentina Visconti's dowry, would serve as a convenient French base beyond the Alps. Long before 1494 Lorenzo de' Medici had realised the strong danger that the rivalry between the main Italian powers, and in particular the unstable regimes of Ludovico Sforza in Milan and of the feudalised Neapolitan kingdom—the two states to which the French monarchy possessed claims—might bring in the French and upset the precarious balance of the peninsula. Charles VIII was not the man to resist the temptation to win military renown. Diplomatic precautions came first, in the form of agreements to secure the neutrality of England (Étaples, 1492), Spain (Barcelona, 1493) and the empire (Senlis, 1493). There followed the military preparations which make it possible to explain the Dominican Savonarola's 'prophecy' of forthcoming invasion (December 1493) as no more than well-informed prediction.

In the years 1494–5, 30,000 Frenchmen conquered Italy, as it was said, 'with chalk' (the chalk with which they marked the billets for their troops), and the ensuing Italian wars continued, with interruptions, up to the Peace of Cateau-Cambrésis of 1559. The first French invasion ended in 1495 when Charles was frightened from Naples by an alliance including Spain and the empire, as well as most of the Italian powers. In 1499 Charles's cousin and successor, Louis XII, renewed the struggle, dispossessed the Sforza of Milan, and reached an agreement with the Spanish which promised him half the Neapolitan kingdom as well. Later, however, he too was driven out of southern Italy and at the end of his reign he lost Milan also, but this was regained by his successor Francis I (1515).

The experiences of Charles VIII and Louis XII showed that Spain and the empire were formidable opponents who were linked closely with the southern and northern parts of the peninsula respectively, and were unwilling to tolerate French supremacy in Italy. When a single ruler, in the person of Charles V, came to the throne of both Spain and the Empire (1519), the days of that supremacy were numbered. French power in Italy was shattered at the battle of Pavia (1525) and rarely reasserted. Direct rule in the south (Sicily and Naples) and the north-west (Milan) and predominance over the rest of the peninsula passed to Charles V and later to his son Philip II of Spain. This was the culmination of a series of campaigns which brought home to the Italians the strength of the great states who were their neighbours and whose battlefield they now supplied. The effect of this confrontation, which made some Italians see their own states as anachronistic survivors in a new world, will be discussed in the last chapter of this book.

FURTHER READING
General

Brief and useful profiles are Malcolm Vale, 'France at the end of the Hundred Years War (c.1420–1461)', in *NCMH*, 7, pp. 392–407, Bernard Chevalier, 'The recovery of France, 1450–1520', in *NCMH*, 7, pp. 408–30, and B. Chevalier, 'France from Charles VII to Henri IV', in *Handbook of European History, 1400–1600*, eds Thomas A. Brady jr., Heiko A. Oberman and James D. Tracy (Leiden, 1994–5, paperback Grand Rapids, Mich., 1996), vol. 1, pp. 370–401. For the political history of the period, see the early chapters of R. J. Knecht, *The Rise and Fall of Renaissance France* (London, 1996) (starts with Charles VIII). Emmanuel Le Roy Ladurie, *The French Royal State, 1460–1610* (tr. Oxford, 1994), takes up where Duby's first volume of *A History of France* (*see* under Chapter 3) leaves off. David Potter, *A History of France, 1460–1560. The Emergence of a Nation State* (Basingstoke, 1995) is a wide-ranging history from a less narrative perspective. *See also*: P. S. Lewis, *Later Medieval France: the Polity* (London and New York, 1968); and P. S. Lewis, *Essays in Later Medieval French History* (London, 1985). E. Perroy, 'Feudalism or principalities in fifteenth-century France', *Bulletin of the Institute of Historical Research*, 20 (1943–5), pp. 181–5, repr. in *Lordship and Community in Medieval Europe: Selected Readings*, ed. F. Cheyette (repr. Huntington, N.Y., 1975), pp. 217–21 raised some fundamental issues. Collections of essays include J. R. L. Highfield and Robin Jeffs, eds, *The Crown and Local Communities in England and France in the Fifteenth Century* (Gloucester, 1981), and P. S. Lewis, ed., *The Recovery of France in the Fifteenth Century* (New York and London, 1971), which includes translations of important work by French historians; *see especially* the articles by Lewis, Boutruche and Bossuat. H. A. Miskimin, *Money and Power in Fifteenth-Century France* (New Haven, Conn., and London, 1984) is a stimulating monograph.

Aspects of government in the fifteenth century are discussed in several works with a longer time-span. J. H. Shennan, *Government and Society in France, 1461–1661* (London, 1969) is a short and general work. J. H. Shennan, *The Parlement of Paris* (London, 1968) is a fundamental work; the revised edition (Stroud, 1998) includes an extensive new introduction. *See also* E. A. R. Brown and R. C. Famiglietti, *The Lit de Justice. Semantics, Ceremonial and the Parlement of Paris, 1300–1600* (Sigmaringen, 1994); J. R. Major, *Representative Institutions in Renaissance France, 1421–1559* (Madison, Wis., 1960); J. R. Major, *From Renaissance Monarchy to Absolute Monarchy: French Kings, Nobles and Estates* (Baltimore, Md., 1994), ch. 1; J. R. Major, 'The French Renaissance monarchy as seen through the Estates-General', *Studies in the Renaissance*, 9 (1962), pp. 113–25.

English triumphs and reversals: the end of the war

C. T. Allmand, 'The aftermath of war in fifteenth century France', *History*, 61 (1976), pp. 344–57 is a crisp introduction to many of the issues. M. G. A. Vale, *Charles VII* (London, 1974) remains the only modern biography of Charles in English. By contrast much more is available on the charismatic Joan. Marina Warner, *Joan of Arc: the Image of Female Heroism* (London, 1981) is a stimulating attempt to analyse her contemporary and subsequent significance; Frances Gies, *Joan of Arc. The Legend and the Reality* (New York, 1981) and the older Régine Pernoud, *Joan of Arc, by Herself and Her Witnesses* (tr. London, 1964) are more conventional biographies. Bonnie Wheeler and Charles T. Wood, eds, *Fresh Verdicts on Joan of Arc* (New York and London, 1996) includes essays on many aspects of the Joan 'phenomenon'. Roger G. Little, *The Parlement of Poitiers, 1418–1436: War, Government and Politics in France* (London, 1984) reassesses the role of the *Parlement* in the recovery of France; Martin Wolfe, *The Fiscal System of Renaissance France* (New Haven, Conn., 1972), ch. 2 casts light on the fiscal policies of Charles VII; Mark Spencer, *Thomas Basin (1412–1490), The History of Charles VII and Louis XI* (Nieuwkoop, 1997) is a study of one of Charles VII's officials and subsequent biographers.

Much attention has been devoted to English rule in France. G. L. Thompson, *Paris and its People under English Rule: The Anglo-Burgundian Regime, 1420–1436* (Oxford, 1991); C. T. Allmand, *Lancastrian Normandy 1415–1450. The History of a Medieval Occupation* (Oxford, 1983). Gascony has come under particular scrutiny: M. G. A. Vale, *English Gascony 1399–1453* (Oxford, 1970); M. G. A. Vale, 'The last years of English Gascony, 1451–3', *Transactions of the Royal Historical Society*, 5th series, 19 (1969), pp. 119–38; M. W. Labarge, *Gascony: England's First Colony 1204–1453* (London, 1980).

Louis XI

P. M. Kendall, *Louis XI* (London, 1971) is the standard work in English; the contemporary account of his reign by his servant Philippe de Commynes, *Memoirs*, tr. Michael Jones (Harmondsworth, 1972) is one of the richest of the period. Other works in English dealing with this reign are Robin Harris, *Valois Guyenne. A Study of Politics, Government, and Society in Late Medieval France* (Woodbridge, 1994) and D. Potter, *War and Government in the French Provinces: Picardy 1470–1560* (Cambridge, 1993), a case study.

Charles VIII, Louis XII and Italy

D. Abulafia, ed., *The French Descent into Renaissance Italy, 1494–95. Antecedents and Effects* (Aldershot, 1995) includes essays on many aspects of the war; for the military side, *see* F. L. Taylor, *The Art of War in Italy 1494–1529* (Cambridge, 1921, repr. London, 1993). J. A. Guy, 'The French king's council, 1483–1526', in *Kings and Nobles in the Later Middle Ages. A Tribute to Charles Ross*, eds Ralph A. Griffiths and James Sherborne (New York, 1986), pp. 274–94 discusses an aspect of politics. There is no recent English biography of Charles VIII, but *see now* F. J. Baumgartner, *Louis XII* (Stroud, 1994, paperback Basingstoke, 1996).

NOTES

1. *Above*, p. 137.
2. *Journal d'un Bourgeois de Paris*, ed. A. Mary (Paris, 1929), p. 171; the work is translated by Janet Shirley, *A Parisian Journal, 1405–1449* (Oxford, 1968) (this passage is on p. 185).
3. Hermann Korner, *Chronica Novella*, ed. J. Schwalm (Göttingen, 1895), pp. 509–10.
4. *Le rosier des guerres. Enseignements de Louis XI . . . pour le Dauphin son fils*, ed. M. Diamant-berger (Paris, 1925), ch. 3. The work may have been compiled by one of Louis' doctors, Pierre Choisnet, under royal direction: André Stegmann, 'Le rosier des guerres: testament politique de Louis XI', in *La France de la fin du XVe siècle—renouveau et apogée*, eds B. Chevalier and P. Contamine (Paris, 1985), pp. 313–23.
5. Philippe de Commynes, *Mémoires*, Bk. II, 9 (for the full passage see Michael Jones's translation, Harmondsworth, 1972, pp. 146–8). Louis was not as completely 'cornered' as Commynes implies.
6. *See above*, p. 178.
7. *Le rosier des guerres*, cit., ch. 6.
8. *Le rosier des guerres*, cit., ch. 7.
9. R. Gandilhon, *La politique économique de Louis XI* (Paris, 1941), p. 295. In the mid-seventeenth and late eighteenth centuries France was to demonstrate again how rapidly a nation can recover from financial and political disaster.

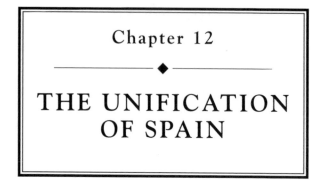

Chapter 12

THE UNIFICATION
OF SPAIN

INTRODUCTION

Iberian history holds invaluable keys to Europe's relations with its neighbours and eventually with the rest of the world. The peoples and political formations of the peninsula had much in common—the 'reconquest' of territory from Muslims, a 'frontier mentality', early practice in colonialism and eventually the impetus for exploration and discovery. The seeds of the consequent 'new world order' were sown in this period; but it would be dangerous to see the process from too teleological a point of view. Diversity and disunity are the dominant characteristics, which should not be brushed aside just because we can see the later consequences of the developments of the period. For example, the partial fusion of the crowns of Aragon and Castile under Ferdinand and Isabella in the late fifteenth century—and the fact that this proved to be a preliminary stage in a fuller state-building process so dramatically visible under Charles V—can leave the impression that it was the 'destiny' of 'Spain' to dominate the peninsula. Yet the area that in the event remained outside the growing Spanish hegemony, Portugal, played its own key role in Iberian and European development as well. Even within 'Spain', with its ethnic and cultural diversity, it is dangerous to assume homogeneity. The standard and enduring generalisations about the history and temperament of the Spaniards (their pride, their poverty, their faith, their reluctance to engage in commerce and industry) are misleading caricatures which have at most a partial and regional basis in fact. Indeed regional differences are still extremely striking in Spain. Even today a visitor may find the contrasts between Seville and Oviedo yet more marked than those between Marseilles and Lille or between Naples and Milan.

CASTILE AND ARAGON

Ferdinand and Isabella ruled not one kingdom but two. They differed from each other profoundly in their political and social traditions, and indeed had in turn been formed by earlier agglomerations of kingdoms—Castile and León on the one hand,

and Catalonia, Valencia and Aragon proper on the other. The history of Castile, eventually the senior of the two partners, was essentially that of the 'Reconquest' and the accompanying Christian settlement of lands previously held by the Muslims. The first great period of reconquest, during which Toledo and central Spain were recovered, occurred in the eleventh century. Another vast advance in the first half of the thirteenth won Seville and much of Andalusia, but Granada remained to the Muslims. When invited by Louis IX of France to join him on Crusade, Ferdinand III of Castile (1217–52) had retorted with complete truth: 'There is no lack of Moors in my own country.' Medieval Castile was in fact Christian frontier territory. The task of settlement was an immense one, for the defeated Muslims normally withdrew from the areas gained by the Castilians: in particular the towns were almost deserted. The size of the population clearly rose considerably over the late Middle Ages, though there is disagreement about the extent of its growth.

The most striking feature of medieval Castilian institutions is the weakness of the Crown, which was frequently enfeebled by minorities and disputed successions, and rarely benefited from tenure by really able and effective men. The kings struggled ahead on inadequate revenues, there was little wealth from trade or industry for them to exploit, and inevitably they lived off their capital by alienating the royal domain. Nor did they allow their ambitions to be held in check by their meagre resources, for they embarked on schemes for the conquest of Portugal and Aragon and even (in the case of Alfonso X) the empire. Anarchy was at its worst during the long war between two rival contenders, Peter the Cruel (1350–69) and his half-brother and successor Henry of Trastámara (1369–79), during which time Portugal, France and England were also drawn into the struggles of Castile. No period of recovery from this civil war was granted. Henry's son and successor, John I (1379–90), who sought to check the nobles by means of the peace guilds (*Hermandades*) and a regular army, died young. His son, Henry III (1390–1406), came to the throne after a long minority and died at the age of 27. Then Henry's infinitely less able son, John II (1406–54), succeeded, again after a minority, and Castile, like contemporary France, was haunted by the long survival of the unfittest. At times during this reign Castile was kept in some degree of order by the king's favourite, Alvaro de Luna, but, after several outbreaks of opposition to de Luna, and even civil war, he fell from power through the enmity of John's second queen, Isabella of Portugal, and was executed in 1453. The position of the monarchy was in no way strengthened by the accession of John II's feeble son, Henry IV 'the Impotent' (1454–1474), the troubles of whose reign will be mentioned below. Through a whole century of disputed successions and civil war Castile's rulers struggled for recognition and support by conferring land and offices on newly aggrandised magnates, into whose possession fell the pastures which were the country's principal source of wealth.

With the political and financial weakness of the Castilian monarchy went a correspondingly decentralised institutional structure. The nobles were powerful, not so much in formal feudal jurisdiction—which they could enjoy without requiring royal approbation—as in exemptions, and in the right to raise their own troops. Similar exemptions were enjoyed by the military orders and other religious corporations. The towns, too, inevitably had a high degree of formal independence, because during the Reconquest they could only be settled with adequate numbers of Christian inhabitants if their privileges were tempting. New frontiers had to be held, and hence the towns had to be granted considerable rights over the surrounding countryside, as well as much self-government. The standing of the towns in the kingdom shows in their early representation in the *Cortes*,[1] and in times of royal weakness—particularly in the late thirteenth and early fourteenth centuries—it was further strengthened by the formation of imposing leagues of towns.[2] In the fifteenth century, however, the towns tended to be drawn as dependencies into the struggles of the greater feudatories. Toledo, for example, which was virtually the capital, was frequently rebellious, but never in its own municipal interests. It is symptomatic of this situation that in the *Cortes* of 1442 the towns should have petitioned the Crown that men having more than 200 vassals should neither inhabit towns nor hold office in them.[3] So pronounced was the dominance of the nobles over the insignificant bourgeoisie that the *Hermandad general* of towns was prevailed upon to declare that civil war lay beyond its jurisdiction (1467).

The organs of central control, though withered through desuetude, were not lacking. The Crown still legislated, it exercised some influence over local jurisdiction through the institution of officials called *corregidores*,[4] and it possessed revenue from the trade tax (*alcabala*). There was no conciliar opposition, nor were the nobles—accustomed to sufficient independence in practice—in the habit of expressing opposition within the *Cortes*. The means were to hand, then, but the reality—during the two centuries before the accession of Ferdinand and Isabella—had normally been chaos.

The setting of Castilian history was the arid central plateau of the Iberian peninsula. Aragon differed fundamentally from Castile in that it possessed a window on to the Mediterranean, whence it drew most of its wealth and strength. The Aragonese kingdom had its own reconquest, culminating in the thirteenth century with the capture of the Balearic islands and Valencia, and since fewer of the Muslims had fled from these places their contribution to its population (which they increased by some 30 per cent) was much greater than that gained by the Castilians from their conquered territories. Much of Aragon lay inland and this was not fertile country, but it was the Catalans, with the assistance of the Valencians, who determined the nature of Aragonese achievements by their commercial and military expansion in the Mediterranean in the thirteenth and fourteenth centuries. Something has already been said about this expansion in connection with the Aragonese role in the 'Sicilian Vespers' of 1282.[5] The conquest of Sicily (1282–1302) was followed by that of the duchy of Athens (1311–88),[6] Sardinia became a dependency after 1326, and at times tribute was paid by the rulers of the Tunisian littoral. The trade that 'followed the flag' was mainly one in Sicilian grain and Sardinian silver, which were exchanged for Aragonese cloth. Further afield the Catalans had commercial links in the Adriatic (with Ancona and Ragusa), and above all in the eastern Mediterranean in Cyprus and Rhodes, at Alexandria, at Pera (the transpontine suburb of Constantinople) and in the Crimea. Barcelona's recession in the second half of the fifteenth century—in part offset by the continued expansion of Valencia—did not prevent the survival of its traditions of independence, as is evident from its leadership in the Catalan revolt of 1461–72. Aragon's eastward outlook shows most clearly in the policy of Alfonso V (1416–58), who undertook the conquest of the kingdom of Naples and when he had accomplished this task (1442) made Naples his normal residence. After his death Naples passed to a bastard son, and was again divided from Aragon and Sicily, but the link remained a close one. In this southern point of ingress and Aragonese connection there was already much that prefigured the eventual Spanish domination in Italy.

Aragonese political institutions in the later Middle Ages differed from those of Castile mainly in that prolonged constitutional opposition had gained more formal privileges for the nobility. The 'great' privileges of 1283 and 1287 promised 'due process of Law' and no forfeiture of fiefs except by decision of the council and *Justicia* (chief justice), no military obligations overseas for the upper nobility, annual meetings of the *Cortes* and the representation of all classes in the council. In 1287 the king was forced to offer 16 castles as security for his observance of these terms and to accept the right of the nobles to depose him if he failed in this. The struggle of the Aragonese feudatories against their king—the towns enjoyed less independence than those of Castile—is witnessed also by the terms of the famous but mythical coronation oath quoted in Chapter 1.[7] A particular point of dispute was the office of the *Justicia*, the supreme judge appointed to watch over the observance of the law and to settle suits between nobles and the Crown. It is significant that around the middle of the fourteenth century the long struggle for control of this office was resolved in favour of the king. At the same period the privileges of 1287, which were the outcome of the circumstances following Peter III's death and had never been fully effective, were formally annulled.

The history of the monarchy itself was rather less disturbed in Aragon than in Castile. The direct male line of the royal house came to an end in 1410 on the death of Martin I, but two years later the matter of the succession was satisfactorily settled by a commission which determined the so-called Compromise of Caspe, choosing Ferdinand of Antequera, who was Martin's nephew and a son of John I of Castile. The accession of a Castilian was of great importance for the future of the kingdom, yet it did nothing to alter Aragon's Mediterranean orientation; indeed, Ferdinand's son Alfonso V earned unpopularity with his Aragonese subjects by his desertion of them in favour of Naples. The continuance of profound differences between the two countries in the fifteenth century shows clearly in their contrasting literary traditions; that of Castile was strongly idealistic and religious, whereas Aragonese writing was more 'down to earth', practical and humorous, influenced less by French notions of courtly love and more by Boccaccio, Petrarch and the Italian schools.

THE MARRIAGE OF FERDINAND AND ISABELLA

The profoundly significant marriage of Isabella of Castile and Ferdinand of Aragon, the product of the policy of Ferdinand's father, John II, led to unification only because Henry IV of Castile had no undisputed heir. Henry himself, during a chaotic period of civil war, veered between accepting as his heir his queen's daughter Joanna (b. 1462), whose father was generally believed to be Beltran de la Cueva (she was known as *la Beltraneja*), and his own half-brother Alfonso; after the latter's death in 1468 he declared for Isabella, Alfonso's sister. The Castilian nobles foresaw the consequences for them of unification and strongly opposed the marriage project. Meanwhile John II, who was dogged by the threat of intervention by Louis XI and had to cede Roussillon and Cerdagne to the French, acquired the throne of Navarre, but was then compelled to face a full-scale revolt in Catalonia. His schemes came to fruition when the marriage ceremony was at last performed by the archbishop of Toledo on 19 October 1469, without the consent of Henry IV and with a forged papal dispensation: Ferdinand himself had reached Valladolid disguised as a muleteer. Henry now indignantly pronounced against Isabella as his successor, declaring again for Joanna *la Beltraneja*.

When Henry IV died in 1474, Isabella, who was convinced of Joanna's illegitimacy, had herself crowned at once. She faced a serious threat from the Portuguese king, Alfonso V, who invaded Castile in 1475, secured the support of some of the nobility, and became engaged to marry *la Beltraneja* (who was his niece). For a time they styled themselves king and queen of Castile and held court at Madrid. In 1476, however, Isabella's forces won a decisive engagement at Toro, and finally by the Treaty of Alcaçovas (September 1479) Alfonso abandoned his claims, as did Joanna, who became a nun. The end of the crisis in Castile coincided with the death of John II (January 1479) and the accession of Ferdinand in Aragon. It was fortunate for him that for four years he and Isabella had been able to concentrate on the menace of the Portuguese. As it was, he felt insufficiently strong to claim Navarre, which passed to his sister Eleanora, and he made no attempt to evict Louis XI from Roussillon and Cerdagne. For the time being the government of Castile and Aragon was a sufficiently heavy task for the dual rulers of the two kingdoms.

Ferdinand's Castilian descent did much to facilitate the unification. He seems to have thought of himself—and the revolt of the Catalans may well have emphasised this sentiment—as a Castilian rather than Aragonese. Indeed he went so far as to claim the throne of Castile in his own right on Henry IV's death, in competition with his wife, but there is no sign that he was dismayed when this claim was rejected. The arrangements for the dual monarchy set up a sort of loose confederation, within which Castile was the dominant partner. There was no 'kingdom of Spain' and each of the kingdoms retained its own political institutions, laws and law courts, fiscal and financial organisation and armed forces. Ferdinand had promised before his marriage that Castile would keep its own laws, and that he would not alienate the Castilian royal domain or make appointments in Castile; he also pledged himself to live there and to complete the reconquest by ending Muslim rule in Granada. Isabella, in fact, administered in Castile, but Ferdinand was more than a consort, and both of them signed letters and decrees. Any attempt to impose identical institutions in the two kingdoms would have been entirely impracticable, and presumably never occurred to Ferdinand or Isabella as a possibility.

Not least among the advantages of the *reyes catolicos* ('Catholic kings'—a title conferred on him by pope Alexander VI in 1494) were their complementary qualities, their conscientiousness and their mutual loyalty and co-operation. Isabella was hardworking, pious and a willing participant in the pomp and majesty of kingship, while

Ferdinand provided the cunning and parsimony so necessary to the success of their partnership. Each, too, had received a suitably stern political education. Ferdinand's childhood had been spent in the successive crises of the Catalan revolt—when still very young he had been besieged, with his mother, at Gerona by the rebellious forces—and Isabella's most impressionable years had been those of the struggle against *la Beltraneja*.

THE RULE OF FERDINAND AND ISABELLA

The elements of weakness in the royal situation were essentially those prevailing in Yorkist and Tudor England and in France after the Hundred Years War—powerful feudatories, fragmented jurisdiction and meagre financial means. In Spain, however, these were accentuated by two special difficulties, the contrasting nature of the two kingdoms and the presence of religious disunity owing to the existence of large communities of Muslims and Jews and doubtfully Christian 'converts'. The work of reorganisation undertaken by Ferdinand and Isabella in these unpromising circumstances met with an impressive degree of success. The anarchy in Castile was brought to an end mainly through the extension across the kingdom of the *Santa Hermandad*, a 'brotherhood' entrusted with the task of installing local law and order. The peace guilds could have achieved little but for the accompanying process of judicial and administrative repression of the greater feudatories, who lost ground to the Crown through a great Act of Resumption of royal domain (1480), the destruction of unauthorised castles and heavy punishment in the royal courts. The Crown also assumed the masterships of the military orders, which possessed enormous estates; in revenue alone these were worth about half a million *reals* a year, but the indirect gains in jurisdiction were immense.

Like other monarchs—and Italian *signori*—Ferdinand and Isabella naturally looked for ministers among the 'low-born' who had no territorial stake in the country and would be dependent on royal favour alone. The main instrument of rule in Castile was the Council, a continuous body with full powers, at whose meetings one at least of the monarchs was at first always present, though later a President was appointed. The reorganised Council had 12 or 13 members, of whom eight or nine were law graduates—hence trained administrators—while of the others three were nobles and one a prelate. In 1494 the Council of Aragon was reorganised on similar lines. The Council gained in power at the expense of the *Cortes*, though not before the latter had been employed to pass anti-baronial measures in 1476 and 1480. Thereafter the parliament—as in Yorkist England—was found to be of little use, and it was not called at all between 1483 and 1497. Later it was summoned occasionally to grant money, but in the main other sources of revenue were preferred to extraordinary taxation. Moreover, after 1480 only the representatives of towns were called, and these were now of exemplary subservience, thanks mainly to the institution of *corregidores*. These officials were supplemented by *veedores* (financial inspectors) and *pesquidores* (judicial commissioners). In Toledo the city's *alcade mayor* (chief official) was appointed by the Crown, though the municipality chose his two assistants. The town was pacified and brought thoroughly under royal control during

Gómez Manrique's long tenure of office as *corregidor* (1477–90). Elsewhere too the control in the towns of the aristocracy was superseded by that of the Crown. Financial recovery was due less to invention of new sources of revenue than to successes in checking the exemptions and corruption which had depleted the old ones, though exemption from taxation for the nobility remained a general rule. The *alcabala* tax on incomes which had rendered a mere 10 million *maravedís* a year under Henry IV realised nearly 25 million in 1478 and over 150 in 1482. The corresponding figures for total revenues have been estimated at under one million *reals* in 1479, 12 million in 1482 and over 26 million in 1504. In part this recovery was due to currency reform and to the increased yield of commerce and industry. Legislation played its part in stimulating the textile industry in Castile; after 1462 the importation of cloth was forbidden, and at least one-third of the Castilian wool crop had to be retained for home manufacture. Trading links, mainly through Bilbao, with Bruges and the Hanse ports had become important by the end of the fourteenth century and to the commerce in raw wool was now added that in Castilian cloth.

The greatest industry of Castile was pastoral farming and this implied transhumance, many of the flocks spending the winter in the southern plains and migrating during the summer to the central plateau. The organisation which controlled this vast biannual emigration of flocks, the *Mesta*, was the object of a royal privilege as early as 1273, but the financial possibilities of the *Mesta* were only fully exploited by the Crown from the time of Ferdinand and Isabella. Their manipulation of the *Mesta* provides an admirable instance of the new monarchy at work, and shows how initial intervention from above could be used to strengthen the sinews of the autocratic machine. The *Mesta* was now centralised in its judicial aspects and local taxation of migrant flocks was both systematised and restricted. Special judicial enquiries were held to investigate privileges bearing on the activities of the *Mesta*, which was encouraged to have recourse to the royal Council itself—as well as to the appellate court at Valladolid—as a court of first instance. The *Cortes* which met at Toledo in 1480 promulgated far-reaching reforms whereby royal towns had to furnish annual reports on local taxation affecting the *Mesta* and royal *veedores* were placed in charge of such taxation. Formerly royal tolls which had passed into private hands were now abolished, and in assuming the grand masterships of the military orders Ferdinand secured for the Crown their considerable revenue from sheep tolls. In 1500 royal control was formalised and again extended by the appointment of the senior member of the royal council as ex officio President of the *Mesta*. All this meant great acquisitions for the Castilian treasury—and the *Mesta* itself was often used as a sort of banking house for the Crown—but it also implied support, administrative and above all judicial, for pasturage in opposition to grain farming, and such a policy had grave economic dangers.

By the last decade of the century the monarchy had won great victories, though more notably in Castile than in Aragon. It had come to dominate the baronage and the Church, its council's administration was ubiquitous, its finances were vastly strengthened. These gains would only make Spain formidable if they were accompanied by military strength. As it was, the Spanish ranked with the Swiss as the great soldiers of western Europe. This was not due to changes in obligation and recruitment—though Ferdinand's assumption of the grand masterships virtually brought the military orders into the royal grand masterships virtually brought the military orders into the royal army—but to the reforms of a military genius, Gonzalo Fernández de Cordoba, the 'great captain'. Gonzalo organised the auxiliary arms, artillerymen and engineers, and 'brigaded' his troops so that he had at his disposition compact and self-sufficient formations accustomed to co-operate in action. His brigade included 300 heavy cavalry and the same number of light horsemen, but most feared of all was the square of heavily-armoured Spanish pikemen, moving forward and protecting a core of more lightly armed infantry. Gonzalo was also a highly successful military tactician, and as captain-general over both land and sea forces was well placed to ensure the efficient co-operation of the navy in the Granada campaign and the Italian ones that followed.

The final decisive war against the Moors to which Ferninand and Isabella were committed was made easier by the internal disputes of the Granada sultanate. They were able to use Boabdil, son of a previous sultan, against his uncle al-Zagal; to the Muslims, indeed, it must have appeared a civil war rather than a Christian conquest. But the campaigns naturally assumed a strongly religious tinge, and volunteers came from all parts of the peninsula and beyond. Malaga was captured in 1487 and the siege of Granada itself at last undertaken in 1491, Fendinand and Isabella being present to give solemnity to the last scene of the drama. The sultanate capitulated in November and the Ferdinand and Isabella made their entry into the city on the day of Epiphany (6 January) 1492.

This triumph was soon followed by an important acquisition for which no war had to be fought. In 1492 Charles VIII of France began to plan his Italian campaign. Certainty of Spanish non-intervention was essential for his plans, and this would not be easy to achieve, but the way to an *entente* might lie through the cession of Cerdagne and Roussillon, the provinces whence Ferdinand had not dared to dislodge Louis XI. Agreement was reached at Barcelona in January 1493 and, despite the disappointment of Charles's sister Anne over inadequate Spanish guarantees, Ferdinand and Isabella entered Perpignan in state that September. After Isabella's death (1504) Italian developments made possible yet another Pyrenean accession: the kingdom of Navarre, relinquished by Ferdinand's father, had come under the domination of the French, but in 1512 Ferdinand was able to dispossess Louis XII and secure confirmation of his hereditary title from his ally, pope Julius II.

These territorial successes on the Pyrenean frontier were but one aspect of a process, seen more clearly in Italy itself, whereby the French took the initiative but the Spaniards reaped the gains. In accordance with the agreement of Barcelona, Ferdinand stood aside while the French destroyed the Aragonese monarchy in Naples; yet the following year he was within his rights in responding to the appeals of Alexander VI when Charles VIII occupied papal territory and in helping to form the anti-French Holy League. After Charles's evacuation of Naples (1495), Ferdinand dropped hints to the French that a joint enterprise might carve up southern Italy to the mutual benefit of the two powers and in 1500 formal agreement on partition was reached at Granada. When the Aragonese house had been overthrown once more, Ferdinand was able to trump up a frontier dispute as *casus belli* and a series of brilliant campaigns under Gonzalo drove out the French by 1504. This was the beginning of the Spanish domination in Italy which was founded firmly in 1525 when Charles V, Ferdinand and Isabella's grandson and ruler of the empire as well as Spain, shattered the French at Pavia.

RELIGIOUS UNIFICATION

The peculiar problem presented by Spanish religious heterogeneity has already been mentioned—and of course the differences were profound social ones, not mere dissimilarities of faith. The situation was particularly inflammable in the towns, some of which housed large communities of *conversos*, former Jews, the genuineness of whose conversion was questioned and whose prosperity was regarded by the 'old Christians' with an envy inextricably mingled with religious disapprobation. Hatred of Jews and *conversos* played a very considerable part in the repeated riots and revolts of Toledo, where—in the face of papal disapproval—the old Christians obtained a royal privilege denying *conversos* the right to hold municipal office.

In any case no monarch could be strong without control of the fabric of religious institutions within the state. We have already noted how this was achieved by the Sforza in Milan and by the kings of France,[8] while other examples could be given from later medieval England. Sigismund had launched a crusade against his own Bohemian subjects rather than resign himself to rule a kingdom divorced from its church, and it was not conceivable that Ferdinand and Isabella's crusading state should act differently, however radical the policies involved. Characteristic agreements with the papacy—facilitated by the strong Spanish influence in the Curia— gave the Crown, from 1482, effective control over appointments to sees and the main abbacies. At the end of the century this satisfactory situation was further formalised by a new agreement with the Spanish pope Alexander VI. Meanwhile the authority of the monarchy in matters of belief had been secured by the quite abnormal institution of a national Inquisition, set up with the consent of Sixtus IV in 1478. Though the Supreme Council of the Inquisition represented both Crown and Church, all appointments as inquisitors were made by the kings, who also paid the inquisitors, supervised their instructions and received the property that they confiscated. In 1484 the work of the Supreme Council was extended to Aragon where, however, it was less appreciated than in Castile. The purpose of the inquisition was, as always, to investigate and stamp out heresy, but the specific heresy in its sights was the one regarded with most horror, apostasy or 'backsliding' by converts. The whole operation was directed almost exclusively against the *conversos*, and if this produced an unconventional form of anti-semitism it was no less virulent for that. The saving of Christian souls was an absolute priority, far greater than the obtention of fresh converts. Indeed, it has been suggested that the chief motivation for the eventual expulsion of the Jews was the belief that *conversos* were encouraged to revert to their former beliefs and practices by proximity to unconverted Jews. Separation of the two communities preceded the more drastic measures of 1492. The inquisition took time to build up to the central political role it attained in the sixteenth century

—those executed in the fifteenth century are probably numbered in hundreds rather than thousands—but the fears aroused by its institution galvanised the respective communities and set the stage for what followed.

The logic of religious unification under the Crown ultimately implied not only the conquest of Granada but also the extirpation from Ferdinand and Isabella's kingdoms of the religion of Islam and of Judaism. The monarchs went a long way down this eventual route, though how far this was in accordance with an overall plan is a matter of debate. The order to expel all Jews from Castile and Aragon was issued in March 1492. They were given four months, were not permitted to take valuables with them and found it hard to sell their possessions. Figures are difficult to establish, but recent estimates suggest that perhaps 40,000, or about half the Jews of Castile and Aragon, left, the rest opting for the decidedly mixed blessings of *converso* status.[9] Many went to Portugal or Navarre, only to be evicted in turn a few years later (1497 and 1498 respectively); in due course Spanish Jews migrated all over the Mediterranean, finding actual welcome only in parts of Italy and the Ottoman Empire. In the wake of the Jewish expulsions the authorities were encouraged to break the terms agreed when Granada capitulated in 1492, and attempted the mass conversion of the Muslims in 1499. The ensuing revolts strengthened the determination of the kings, and by 1502 the order was given for Muslims who refused to accept Christianity to be expelled from Granada and Castile. For those in Castile the terms were even harsher than those given to Jews; boys under 15 and girls under 13 had to be left behind. In practice the overwhelming majority remained and converted at least in name. At this point the programme halted; the decree was not extended to Aragon, with its substantial Muslim population (an estimated quarter of a million in Valencia alone), and only in 1525 was nominal mass conversion forced on them as well by Charles V.

The expulsions and forced conversions were religious and political acts, but there has been much debate about their social and economic implications. While in Aragon some Jewish property was seized by the Crown, and throughout Spain Jews were robbed with impunity, there is no evidence to support the assertion that material gain was one of the motives for the decision. It has been argued that the Jews were too small in number, and by 1492 of insufficient economic significance, to be enough of a temptation; their status had already been eroded by a century of persecution, and the emigration of many of the wealthier and more influential *conversos* in the preceding decade was much more lucrative for the authorities and more damaging to the economy.[10] The impact of the policy on the far more numerous Muslims is more complicated. In Granada, the entirely Muslim population of about 300,000 was subjugated within a decade by a sequence of developments: the emigration to North Africa of most of the nobility, the immigration of some 40,000 Christian colonists and administrators, the imposition of heavy taxes and eventually the forced conversions. The fact that the great majority of Muslims, both in Granada and elsewhere, converted rather than left, created a new problem, adding to the suspectedly crypto-Jewish *conversos* a much larger population of suspectedly crypto-Muslim *moriscos*, who became a dominant internal issue of the sixteenth century, finally in turn being expelled in 1609.

CONCLUSION

Spain is for the most part harsh and barren country, yielding a stern and meagre diet and an upbringing well calculated to prepare the Castilian infantrymen for the 'flinty and steel couch of war'. Francesco Guicciardini travelled a good deal in Aragon and Castile in 1512 as the ambassador of Florence, and his diary remarks repeatedly on the sterility of the land and the lack of inhabitants. In Catalonia 'the country is mountainous, wild and very barren; one finds a village with one big house, and some of the land around is cultivated, but after that for league after league there is no cultivation'. On his return home his official *Relazione* emphasised the poverty of the Spanish countryside and made the generalisation concerning the Spaniards, so often to be repeated by later observers: 'they do not engage in commerce, which they consider shameful'. Industry, he says, was a no less humiliating source of income.[11] Despite the predominance of agriculture and pastoral farming, the peninsula was not self-supporting in grain, which was imported from southern and western France, from Sardinia and Sicily and from parts of the eastern Mediterranean and Black Sea regions. Seville grew to a great city of some 75,000 inhabitants by the late fifteenth century, even before it became the centre of trade and communication with the Indies, but the previously flourishing economy of Catalonia (and in particular Barcelona) was in full decline by the same period. Catalan textiles had lost their place in the western Mediterranean to English cloth, and the merchants of Barcelona had been ousted, to some extent by Valencians and Castilians but much more by the Italians and English.

The policies of the Spanish rulers did nothing to resolve the paradox of strength combined with poverty. Attempts were made to foster a textile industry by limiting exports of raw wool, but in the long run protection of trade and industry would have been incompatible with the far more deeply rooted alliance with the *Mesta* and the large landowners; grain farming could only have been encouraged at the expense of the *Mesta*, an institution which became absorbed into the nation's financial structure. Connected with all this was the profound religious difficulty. A crusading state had been reluctant to back industry and trade wholeheartedly when so many of those concerned with these occupations were non-Christians. The religious element also aggravated the economic situation through the mass expulsions: in the words of the cynic's favourite cliché, they were worse than a crime, they were an error. The opening up of the New World, so often wrongly blamed for the decline of Spain because the importation of precious metals played a part in raising prices, perhaps came just in time to save Spain from economic disaster, but there was no escape from the country's fundamental poverty. Consideration of Spain's later decadence must also take into account the inquisition and the discouragement of the spirit of enquiry, but there is a great danger of making use of hindsight to over-emphasise these elements of weakness. On the death of Ferdinand in 1516 his Habsburg grandson Charles I succeeded to a well-administered state. Its 'Golden Age' lay still in the future, and after 1519, when under Charles its rule was joined with that of the empire, it became the dominant power in Europe west of the Ottoman lands.

FURTHER READING

Castile and Aragon

Angus MacKay, *Spain in the Middle Ages. From Frontier to Empire, 1000–1500* (London, 1977) is an excellent general history, as is Bernard F. Reilly, *The Medieval Spains* (Cambridge, 1993), which focuses more broadly on the Muslim world as well as the Christian. J. N. Hillgarth, *The Spanish Kingdoms 1260–1516*, 2 vols (Oxford, 1976–78) and Joseph F. O'Callaghan, *History of Medieval Spain* (Ithaca, N.Y., 1975) are detailed studies; Gabriel Jackson, *The Making of Medieval Spain* (London, 1972) is a lively cultural study. Glyn Redworth, *Government and Society in Late Medieval Spain. From the Accession of the House of Trastámara to Ferdinand and Isabella* (London, Historical Association, 1993) is a useful brief introduction to the century before the Catholic kings. R. Highfield, ed., *Spain in the Fifteenth Century, 1369–1516* (London, 1972) includes translations of essays by Spanish historians. For the economy, the standard work is J. Vicens Vives and J. N. Oller, *An Economic History of Spain* (3rd edition, tr. Princeton, N.J., 1969); *see also* Julius Klein, *The Mesta. A Study in Spanish Economic History, 1273–1836* (Cambridge, Mass., 1920).

Castile is surveyed in Angus MacKay, 'Castile and Navarre', in *NCMH*, 7, pp. 606–26, and is also served by a number of English-language monographs, including N. Round, *The Greatest Man Uncrowned: A Study in the Fall of Alvaro de Luna* (London, 1986), and W. D. Phillips, *Enrique IV and the Crisis of Fifteenth-Century Castile 1425–1480* (Cambridge, Mass., 1978); Angus MacKay, *Money, Prices and Politics in Fifteenth-Century Castile* (London, 1981); John Edwards, *Christian Cordoba: the City and its Region in the Late Middle Ages* (Cambridge, 1982); and T. Ruiz, *Crisis and Continuity: Land and Town in Late Medieval Castile* (Philadelphia, Pa., 1994). Angus MacKay, *Society, Economy and Religion in Late Medieval Castile* (London, 1987) is a collection of essays. **Aragon** is well introduced by T. N. Bisson, *The Medieval Crown of Aragon. A Short History* (Oxford, 1986; paperback 1991), and Mario Del Treppo, in *NCMH*, 7, pp. 588–605; *see also* A. J. Ryder, *Alfonso the Magnanimous, King of Aragon, Naples, and Sicily 1396–1458* (Oxford, 1990).

Ferdinand and Isabella

F. Fernandez-Armesto, *Ferdinand and Isabella* (London, 1975) is a wide-ranging biography; *see also* the colourful Peggy K. Liss, *Isabel the Queen. Life and Times* (New York, 1992). Two standard textbooks on early modern Spain which begin by placing the Catholic kings in a later perspective are J. H. Elliott, *Imperial Spain, 1469–1716* (Harmondsworth, 1963) and H. Kamen, *Spain, 1469–1714: a Society of Conflict* (2nd edition, London, 1991). Works on the political and administrative history of the reigns include M. Lunenfeld, *The Council of the Santa Hermandad: A Study of the Pacification Forces of Ferdinand and Isabella* (Coral Gables, Fla., 1970); M. Lunenfeld, *Keepers of the City. The Corregidores of Isabella I of Castile* (Cambridge, 1987); and R. Highfield, 'The Catholic Kings and the titled nobility of Castile', in John Hale, Roger Highfield and Beryl Smalley, eds, *Europe in the Late Middle Ages* (London, 1965), pp. 358–85.

Religious unification

D. Abulafia, *Spain and 1492* (Bangor, 1992) is a crisp introduction to the issues surrounding the events of 1492. Similar ground is covered in the lectures by B. Lewis, *Cultures in Conflict: Christians, Muslims and Jews in the Age of Discovery* (New York, 1995). Miguel Angel Ladero Quesada, 'Spain, circa 1492: social values and structures', in *Implicit Understandings. Observing, Reporting, and Reflecting on the Encounters Between Christians and Other Peoples in the Early Modern Era*, ed. Stuart B. Schwartz (Cambridge, 1994), pp. 96–133 is a deeper analysis of the same issues. John Edwards, *Religion and Society in Spain, c.1492* (Aldershot, 1996) is a useful collection of essays.

Interesting light is cast on relations between Castile and Granada in two articles in Roger Bartlett and Angus Mackay, eds, *Medieval Frontier Societies* (Oxford, revised paperback edition 1992): José Enrique López de Coca Castañer, 'Institutions on the Castilian-Granadan frontier 1369–1482' (pp. 127–50) and Angus MacKay, 'Religion, culture, and ideology on the late medieval Castilian-Granadan frontier' (pp. 217–43). Granada is the subject of the final chapter of Hugh Kennedy, *Muslim Spain and Portugal. A Political History of al-Andalus* (London, 1997). On the Muslims of Spain more generally, *see* L. P. Harvey, *Islamic Spain, 1250–1500* (Chicago, Ill., 1990); O. Rennie Constable, *Trade and Traders in Muslim Spain. The Commercial Realignment of the Iberian Peninsula, 900–1500* (Cambridge, 1994); and M. D. Meyerson, *The Muslims of Valencia in the Age of Fernando and Isabel: Between Coexistence and Crusade* (Berkeley and Los Angeles, Cal., 1991). Colin Smith, *Christians and Moors in Spain*, vol. 2 *(1195–1614)* (Warminster, 1989) is an anthology of documents in translation.

The literature on the Jews of Spain is immense. Y. Baer, *A History of the Jews in Christian Spain* (2nd edition, tr. Philadelphia, Pa., 1961–6) is the 'classic' work, still valuable; Jane S. Gerber, *The Jews of Spain. A History of the Sephardic Experience* (New York, 1992) is a popular account. John Edwards, *The Jews in Western Europe, 1400–1600* (Manchester, 1994) publishes a selection of documents in translation, the majority of them from fifteenth-century Spain. Space does not permit a full survey of earlier history, but Y. T. Assis, *The Golden Age of Aragonese Jewry. Community and Society in the Crown of Aragon 1213–1327* (London, 1997) is exceptionally rich and rounded. D. Nirenberg, *Communities of Violence. Persecution of Minorities in the Middle Ages* (Princeton, 1996) is a challenging study of the relationships between Christians, Jews and Muslims, mainly in Spain. The causes of the anti-semitic outbursts of 1391 are analysed in P. Wolff, 'The 1391 pogrom in Spain: social crisis or not?', *Past and Present*, 50 (1971), pp. 4–18, conveniently followed by Angus MacKay, 'Popular movements and pogroms in fifteenth-century Castile', *Past and Present*, 55 (1972), pp. 33–67, repr. in his *Society, Economy and Religion in Late Medieval Castile* (London, 1987). E. Kedourie, ed., *Spain and the Jews. The Sephardi Experience, 1492 and After* (London, 1992) offers a good introduction to the build-up to the expulsion; *see especially* Angus MacKay, 'The Jews in Spain during the middle ages', pp. 33–50, Eleazar Gutwirth, 'Towards expulsion: 1391–1492', pp. 51–73, and Henry Kamen, 'The expulsion: purpose and consequence', pp. 75–91 (but not the uncritical Haim Beinart, 'The conversos and their fate', pp. 92–122). Kamen also deals with the principal issues in his 'The Mediterranean and the expulsion of Spanish Jews in 1492', *Past and Present*, 119 (1988), pp. 30–55. B. R. Gampel, *The Last Jews on Iberian Soil: Navarrese Jewry, 1479–1498* (Berkeley and Los Angeles, Cal., 1989) is wider in scope than its title suggests. A recent contribution to the highly controversial issue of the beliefs of the *conversos* is N. Roth, *Conversos, Inquisition and the Expulsion of the Jews from Spain* (Madison, Wis., 1995). Much of the controversy relates to the traditional assumption that they were mostly crypto-Jews. The key scholar to challenge this view is Benzion Netanyahu; *see* most recently his *Toward the Inquisition. Essays on Jewish and Converso History in Late Medieval Spain* (Ithaca, N.Y., 1997).

NOTES

1. *Above*, pp. 11–12.
2. These leagues were known as *Hermandades* (brotherhoods), but were quite distinct from the peace guilds which went by the same name.
3. *Cortes de los antiguos Reinos de León y Castilla* (Madrid, 1861–1903), III, pp. 410–11.

4. M. Lunenfeld defines the *corregidor* as 'supervisor for municipality combining functions of mayor and judge, appointed either by a lord or the crown': *Keepers of the City: the Corregidores of Isabella I of Castile, 1474–1504* (Cambridge, 1987), p. x.

5. *Above*, pp. 37–41.

6. *See below*, pp. 252–3.

7. *Above*, p. 7.

8. *Above*, pp. 191 and 214.

9. Figures from Henry Kamen, 'The Mediterranean and the expulsion of Spanish Jews in 1492', *Past and Present*, 119 (1988), pp. 30–55, which debates the statistical controversy (p. 44). For further discussion *see* John Edwards, 'Jews and *conversos* in the region of Soria and Almazán: departures and returns', in his *Religion and Society in Spain, c.1492* (Aldershot, 1996).

10. Kamen, op. cit., and his 'The expulsion: purpose and consequence', in E. Kedourie, ed., *Spain and the Jews. The Sephardi Experience, 1492 and After* (London, 1992), pp. 75–91.

11. F. Guicciardini, *Scritti autobiografici e rari*, ed. R. Palmarocchi (Bari, 1936), pp. 120, 123, 12–30.

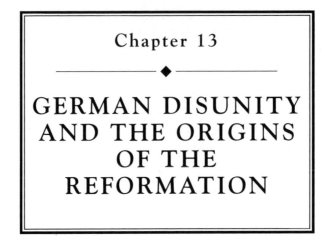

Chapter 13

◆

GERMAN DISUNITY AND THE ORIGINS OF THE REFORMATION

EMPEROR, PRINCES AND THE CHURCH

An earlier chapter has described the enfeeblement of central power in Germany during and after the thirteenth century and the gaining of *de facto* independence by the Swiss Confederation. In the fifteenth century imperial territory was also lost to Denmark, Poland and the Turks, while the emperor played an ever-diminishing role in Italy. For the future development of Germany, however, these losses were less important than the internal consequences of regionalism, which influenced and assisted the Lutheran Reformation, while the Reformation in turn was to do much to intensify political disunity.

The long reign of the Habsburg Frederick III (1440–93) was an uphill struggle for control. Until 1463 Frederick had to contest the control of his own Austrian and Tyrolean inheritance—his only territorial base—with his brother Albert. For 27 years (between 1444 and 1471) he never visited Germany west of these lands. He was threatened with supersession first by Philip the Good of Burgundy (1454), then by George of Poděbrady, king of Bohemia (1459–61) and finally by his own son Maximilian, and as late as 1485 he was driven from Vienna by Matthias Corvinus of Hungary. The constantly harassed circumstances of the reign made schemes for constitutional reform impracticable, although these were discussed and in 1455 a detailed plan was drawn up for an imperial council, an imperial court presided over by paid judges, and a general tax. Frederick's solitary triumph, which was of profound importance for the future of both the Habsburgs and the empire, was the marriage of his son Maximilian to the Burgundian heiress Mary, daughter of Charles the Rash (1477).[1] This marriage conveyed to the Habsburgs the wealth of the Low Countries on which had been founded the greatness of the Burgundian dukes, thereby strengthening enormously their territorial basis and perhaps virtually ensuring the continuation of their election as emperors. It also extended their interests so that the north-west of Germany now joined the south-east as the two potential strongholds of imperial power.

Frederick III's Concordat of Vienna with pope Nicholas V (1448) contrasts with the French king Charles VII's Pragmatic Sanction of Bourges (1438) in a way which illustrates clearly enough the difference between the authority of these two monarchs. The Pragmatic Sanction defined and checked papal authority over the Church in France to the advantage of the Crown. The Concordat, on the other hand, had to be acceptable to the imperial nobility as well as to the papacy; the German princes gained a very high price for their adherence to it and thereafter enjoyed an increased amount of ecclesiastical control. They won enlarged rights of presentation and a considerable share in the proceeds of ecclesiastical taxation. Church courts lost part of their jurisdiction to the princes, particularly in eastern Germany, and even to the municipalities. Moreover, the lay nobility even came to play a larger role in the organisation of religion, by issuing legislation concerned with matters of morality (such as gambling and false weights and measures), by intervening to reform or suppress ecclesiastical institutions and through its share in higher education. Of the 20 universities existing in Germany at the end of the Middle Ages, all but two (Würzburg and Mainz) had lay founders. One consequence of these developments was that religious reform came to be thought of as in many ways essentially the responsibility of the princes.

Ecclesiastical matters provide merely one instance of the general movement of the greater German feudatories into a position of complete dominance. Laymen or prelates, these men had a way of life in common, with their vast households (the margrave of Brandenburg had an entourage of 400 at the end of the fifteenth century) and their own traditions of expenditure on festivities and artistic and educational patronage. The princes had virtually carved up the kingdom. Naturally each sought to round off his territories and in the process quarrelled with his neighbour, particularly over disputed jurisdictional rights. Limits were set to their power, however, by lack of financial centralisation, by the existence of enclaves—particularly imperial cities and ecclesiastical lordships—within their dominions and most of all by the tendency to fission of lay property through division on succession. Thus there were two Saxonies (ducal and electoral) and several branches of the ruling house of Anhalt, Brunswick was divided from the early fifteenth century between three branches of the same family, and the Brandenburg lands were partitioned after the death of the Elector Albert Achilles (1486). The financial needs of the princes also subjected them to occasional pressure from meetings of estates, but in general the elements which might have kept them in check, the knights and the towns, were those which most conspicuously lost ground. As in France, the knightly class encountered great economic difficulties and began to play a much less significant part in the political scene. When ousted by professional soldiers of non-knightly origin, some of them sought an outlet from their poverty in the career of 'robber-knight'.

Though the knights complained bitterly of the social pretensions of the burghers and the enlarged jurisdictions of the municipalities, the towns, too, were losing authority. The decline of the Hanseatic ports has already been mentioned,[2] but the failure of the towns to 'balance' the nobility is as evident in other areas where there was no general recession, the only anomaly being the continued strength of the towns on the lower Rhine. The 'average' German town was of course primarily a centre for the marketing of grain, wine and other local agrarian produce. The major exceptions to this were Cologne and the other Rhineland towns, dealing in wine, coal, iron, cloth and silk, and closely connected with Antwerp and the towns of Flanders; Leipzig and Breslau (Wrocław) and other towns lying on the routes of the eastern and northern commerce in grain, fish, wax, honey and furs; and finally some rapidly developing cities in southern Germany. The chief among the latter were Nuremberg and Augsburg, both linked with Antwerp as well as with the commercial world of Italy, and benefiting from a spectacular advance of mining for silver and copper in the Tyrol and for gold and copper in Hungary. During the period 1460–1530 the annual output of silver and of copper in central Europe increased approximately fivefold, and in 1525 the emperor believed that 100,000 of his subjects were engaged in mining. Greatest of the Augsburg families were the Fuggers, the firm which financed Charles V's election to the empire: bankers to emperors and popes, they were also near-monopolists in their control of Tyrolean and Hungarian metals.

Whatever the achievements of the Fuggers, of other financiers such as the Hochstätters and Welsers, of lesser-known mining engineers and of the Swabian league of towns (which between 1488 and 1519 effectively opposed the Swiss and the dukes of Bavaria), the primary features of Germany's political landscape were the strength of the greater nobles and the impotence of the emperor. When Maximilian (1493–1519) succeeded his father Frederick III, there followed a still richer harvest of schemes for fundamental reform, all of them proposing a constitutional solution to the insoluble problem of governing an empire whose sovereign lacked the means to rule. The model for these was set at the prolonged *Reichstag* (parliament) at Worms in 1495, in which the estates put forward a detailed plan whereby the emperor was to have a Permanent Council (*Reichsrat*) of 17, the consent of which was to be required for all important royal acts: each of the six electors was to nominate one member of the council, the other spiritual and temporal princes were both to name four, the towns two and the remaining member, the president, was to be chosen by the king. This idea was naturally rejected by Maximilian, and the scheme for a quasi-federal tax (the 'Common Penny') was no more successful. Nevertheless the *Reichstag* of 1495 bore some fruit in the form of a supreme central court of justice, the *Reichskammergericht*. In 1500 the emperor himself advanced a scheme whereby many of his powers would pass to a central council (the *Reichsregiment*), but this proposal also was unsuccessful and provoked an open quarrel between Maximilian and the electors. The latter, led by the arch-chancellor, Berthold, archbishop of Mainz, would have been satisfied with nothing short of a quasi-federation within which the emperor would have lost control of both taxation and army. After these disputes Maximilian deprived Berthold of the arch-chancellorship, but compromise between imperial and electoral interests still proved impossible. New constitutional schemes were discussed ineffectively at Cologne in 1505, at Augsburg in 1510 and at Trier and Cologne in 1512; the last of these, perhaps the most radical, proposed the setting up of a permanent executive council of the *Reichstag* and an army organised by zones (*Kreise*).

These negotiations over constitutional change were brought about by the pressure of political events—by Maximilian's need for troops and money—but the same events made it impossible for the emperor to concentrate on the constitutional question. He had to work at the more practicable task of unification within his own Austrian lands (in which he achieved much success), to fight the palatinate over the succession to Bavaria (1504) and to oppose the Swiss and the Turks, as well as dealing with Germany's endemic anarchy. But the most onerous of all his preoccupations was the menace of French power in Italy. It would have been intolerable for any emperor, but it was particularly bitter for a man of Maximilian's chivalrous temperament, that his shortage of soldiers should cause the empire to cut such a wretched figure in Italy. Again and again imperial rights fell to the French by default, and meanwhile the insubordinate Swiss constantly counted for much more on the Italian scene. Enmity with Venice had originally caused Maximilian to welcome Charles VIII's invasion of 1494, but he soon recognised its dangers and joined the anti-French league of 1495, only to find that he could play no active part because the *Reichstag* wanted to talk about the constitution rather than provide him with an army. By 1496 he was ready to intervene in Italy, but did so feebly and achieved nothing. Maximilian wished for war against France on Charles's death in 1498, probably to add to his Burgundian acquisitions, but again the nobles would give him no support. When Charles's successor, Louis XII, captured the imperial duchy of Milan (1500) Maximilian could not even get an army into the field. Later he joined the league of Cambrai (1508) against his old enemy Venice, but once more his military contribution was negligible and so, therefore, were his territorial gains. Even in 1512 he played a diplomatic rather than a military role in defeating the French, and in any case Milan was in the hands of the French again by 1515. Revenge in Italy was only to come with the election to the empire in 1519 of Maximilian's grandson, the king of Spain.

GERMANY AND THE PAPACY

One consequence of imperial weakness and German disunity was to expose the Church within the empire to the authority, and in particular the fiscality, of the papacy. The constitutional discussions at Worms in 1495 included proposals for a 'German' Church, and Maximilian himself suggested the appointment of a permanent papal legate who should always be a German by birth, but these schemes were not put into effect and the empire failed to acquire the national ecclesiastical 'defences' of France, Spain and England. The feeling that Germany was paying more than its share to Rome in taxation, in expenses incurred over disputed episcopal elections, and so on, was a reasonable one. Indulgences to pay for German churches were one thing but, as Ulrich von Hutten put it, why should the Germans pay for Roman churches when Italy was wealthier than Germany?[3] Konrad Celtis the humanist had made a similar point: 'The Emperor rules in the German lands, but the Roman shepherd alone enjoys the pasture. When will Germany regain her old strength and shake off the foreign yoke?'[4] The logical conclusion of this attitude was to come with Luther's indignant opposition to papal fiscality and his invitation to the emperor and princes to forbid the payment of taxes to Rome.

This anti-papal sentiment was interwoven with the heightened national self-consciousness which was so evident also in the France of Joan of Arc and which had become more pronounced within the Church itself during the disputes of the conciliar era, while it was natural that religion should take on a more national tone in an age when the Scriptures were increasingly diffused in the vernacular.[5] During the fifteenth century there had developed a stronger interest in Germany's past, culminating in the appearance of the first history of Germany, Wimpfeling's *Epitome Rerum Germanicarum* (1505). The material for a nation's saga, both historical and mythical, existed in abundance. In the medieval past the imperial achievement of Frederick Barbarossa stood out, beyond that lay the epic deeds of Theodoric the Ostrogoth, and further back still there had shone the primitive virtues of the folk described and praised by Tacitus in his *Germania*. This work, first printed in Germany in 1473, appealed both to the classical interests and to the national pride of the German humanists—a pride often inflamed by much contact with patronising Italians. Konrad Celtis (1459–1508), a fierce German patriot, produced a new edition of the *Germania* and lectured on Tacitus, as well as planning a topographical *Germania Illustrata* and an epic poem on Theodoric.[6] Ulrich von Hutten (1488–1523), like Celtis, lived for some time in Italy, and shared his enthusiasm for the *Germania*, though he deplored the falling-away of the Germans from their pristine nobility. He it was who founded the 'myth' of Arminius, erecting into a national hero the chieftain who had defeated Varus's legions in AD 9. The strength of the patriotic currents which flowed beneath this classical surface may be gauged from the fantastic *Book of a Hundred Chapters* written in 1510 by an anonymous writer usually known picturesquely as 'the Revolutionary of the Upper Rhine'. This man believed that the Germans had once 'lived together like brothers', ruling all Europe in a Utopian communistic regime which had been destroyed by the Romans and the Church of Rome. The Latin peoples were the source of all wickedness and the eternal opponents of everything German. Yet 'the Germans once held the whole world in their hands and they will do so again, and with more power than ever'.[7]

National feeling and ecclesiastical grievances in Germany itself do not fully account for the widespread detestation of the papacy. While the humanists were confirmed in their indignation by Lorenzo Valla's exposure of the 'Donation of Constantine' as a forgery, of much greater general consequence were the effects of the prolonged, though gradual, descent of the papacy into an institution apparently concerned principally with the family policies characteristic of an Italian state. Nicholas V (1447–55) and Pius II (1458–64) had been well-meaning men who lacked the urgent reforming drive to halt these traditions. Their pontificates were separated by that of the first Borgia pope, Calixtus III (1455–8), who promoted to the cardinalate his nephew, the future Alexander VI. Paul II (1464–71), a Venetian and a nephew of Eugenius IV, was another pontiff who passively acquiesced in the traditions that he inherited, but his successor Sixtus IV (1471–84) was a scandalously secular character who promoted his criminal nephews and was an accomplice before the fact in the conspiracy to murder Lorenzo and Giuliano de' Medici. After the harmless but rather ineffective Genoese Innocent VIII (1484–92), there followed Alexander VI (Borgia) (1492–1503), who has often been made to bear the brunt of the moral blame levelled against the 'Renaissance' papacy. Like Sixtus, Alexander gave new impetus to the Curia's worldly outlook, and to the passionate advancement of his descendants he added more conspicuous defiance of the spiritual nature of his office. He it was who publicly kept a succession of mistresses and who attended that high-spirited party in the Vatican, hosted by his son Cesare, at which some most unusual games were played with the co-operation of 50 prostitutes.[8]

The prolonged political crisis in the peninsula ushered in by the French invasion of 1494 would in any case have made it difficult for the papacy to escape from the descending spiral of Italian politics and territorial rule, and in these circumstances expedience combined with bribery to ensure the election of men versed in the well-established ways of Sixtus and Alexander. Julius II della Rovere (1503–13) was a nephew of Sixtus IV and had been a very active and prominent member of the Curia during his uncle's pontificate: he no doubt found it natural that he should devote his energies primarily to the diplomatic situation in Italy and the reconquest of the Papal State. Leo X (1513–21) was no better equipped to break with the prevailing tendencies of the Curia; he was a son of Lorenzo the Magnificent, who had bought a cardinalate for him when he was 13, in 1489, and his preoccupation with French and Spanish power in the peninsula was complicated by the family connection which made him *de facto* ruler of Florence as well as of the Papal State.

Typical of many Germans who visited Rome at this time and reported unfavourably on it was the humanist Konrad Peutinger of Augsburg (1465–1547), who wrote of the city during Innocent VIII's pontificate:

Here I see everything for sale, from the highest to the lowest. Intrigues, hypocrisy and servility are praised, religion is falsified, base actions without number are perpetrated, and Justice sleeps. When I look at the ruined monuments of Antiquity I bewail the fact that the most honoured City is ruled by an alien [*peregrina*] people, who commit every sort of wickedness under the fair disguise of religion, and expect to receive praise instead of blame. When I criticize this, they tell me that it is ordained by Fate, and that if God wished otherwise people would act otherwise. The Patrimony of St Peter has to be governed thus, they say, because Fate wills it. I could write a long story, but do not wish to offend your ears further.[9]

In view of the reputation of Rome with the Germans, it is likely that the young Augustinian friar Martin Luther was prepared to find the worst when his house at Erfurt sent him to Rome in 1510, and anti-Italian feeling may surely be detected in his own comment that 'he went to Rome with onions and returned with garlic'. Whatever his expectations, he was shocked at the irreverent ways of the Roman clergy. Yet another German who came away with indignant impressions was 'Crotus Rubeanus' (part-author of the satirical *Letters of Obscure Men*), who reported of his visit to Rome in 1519: 'I saw the monuments of antiquity. I saw the chair of pestilence: what I saw both helps and disgusts me.'[10] One cause of this antagonism was presumably the contrast between northern and southern religious practices which persists to this day, for Catholics from northern Europe are still scandalised to find Italians walking about and talking during Mass. The same difference was noted by a visitor to Milan in the early sixteenth century who compared the 'irreligion' of that duchy with the crowded churches of Germany 'where they do not talk of merchandize nor amuse themselves as in Italy, but occupy themselves solely with hearing Mass and the divine offices and saying their prayers, all kneeling'.[11]

It would be quite misleading, however, to distinguish the pious North from the indifferent South. In both there were movements for reform: in Italy, for instance, those associated with the Franciscan St Bernardino of Siena (1380–1444) and the Puritan revivalism of Savonarola in late fifteenth-century Florence; in Germany and the Netherlands the less spectacular but more lasting and widely diffused movements associated with the Beguines and the Brethren of the Common Life. Moreover, the upper clergy in Germany produced examples of scandalous worldliness which ranked with the worst in Italy. Rupert von Simmern, bishop of Strasbourg from 1440 to 1478, was said never to have celebrated Mass, and Diether von Isenburg, archbishop of Mainz from 1460 to 1481, to have done so once only, on the occasion of his consecration. Such men became archbishops and bishops because these offices, involving immense political and territorial power, continued to be associated with the great feudal families who struggled to secure them for their members. The Church in Germany had remained largely the 'proprietary Church' of the early Middle Ages. It was as impossible for the archbishop of Cologne or Mainz to neglect his state and devote himself primarily to spirituality as it was for the pope to withdraw from the affairs of his State and of Italy. One consequence of this was a great rift between the prelates and the lower clergy, many of whom were to give their support to Lutheranism.

CRITICS AND REFORMERS

The principal currents in the reforming tendencies in the North, often described generically as the *Devotio Moderna*, were those associated with the Augustinian canons of Windesheim and the 'Brethren of the Common Life' whose movement centred on Deventer in the Netherlands. The second of these had originated in the fourteenth century with the work of Gerard Groote, the founder of a hostel where pious women lived as a community. In the fifteenth century many other 'colonies' were set up in the Low Countries and Rhineland, frugal households whose members took a vow of chastity, surrendered all their possessions to a common chest, and devoted much of their time to prayer. Hostels were also opened for the children of the poor, who thus received a religious education, but men like Groote were far from being 'humanists'. Groote himself advised against the vanity of 'books beautifully adorned' and the dangers of the useless learning of 'geometry, arithmetic, rhetoric, dialectic, grammar, songs, poetry, legal matters or astrology'.

I resolve [he wrote] never to take a degree in medicine, because I do not purpose to get any gain or preferment by such a degree; and the same resolve holds for Civil and Canon Law; for the purpose of a degree is either gain or preferment, or vain glorification and worldly honour, which latter things if they lead not to the former are simply useless, empty and most foolish, being contrary to godliness and all freedom and purity. I resolve not to study any art nor to write any book, not to undertake any journey nor any labour, nor to pursue any learning with the purpose of extending my own fame or repute for knowledge.[12]

The characteristic and most famous book of this *milieu* is the *Imitation of Christ*, probably written by Thomas à Kempis (1380–1471). The *Imitation*, too, dwells on the dangers of intellectual pride. Knowledge has little to do with piety, 'I would rather feel compunction than know how to define it', and 'What will it avail thee to dispute profoundly of the Trinity if by your lack of humility you are displeasing to the Trinity? Truly at the day of judgment we shall not be examined on what we have read, but on what we have done'.[13]

One who received some education in the schools of the Brethren of the Common Life at Deventer and s'Hertogenbosch in the 1470s and 1480s, but was unhappy there, was Erasmus of Rotterdam (?1469–1536). This illegitimate son of a priest of Gouda spent a period as an Augustinian canon, but left his monastery and became the most famous figure in the learned world of his day. We know much about Erasmus, thanks in particular to his letters, and there is insufficient room here to do justice to his many-sided importance or to discuss adequately the differences between his opinions and Luther's. First of all, Erasmus was a much-travelled cosmopolitan literary figure, moving between the Netherlands, France, England, Italy and Germany, and linking humanists in many lands. As a voluminous and much-read author (in Latin) he also exerted an enormous influence on the literature of sixteenth-century Europe, particularly through his collection of pithy Adages and the rather unoriginal but wise and well-phrased social commentary of the *Colloquies*. Erasmus's favourite targets were empty and superstitious observances and the other religious abuses of the age. Among the Spaniards the fervent commonsense of his moral criticism founded a school of thought the outlook of which is still evident in *Don Quixote*. Besides all this there was a great positive achievement in learning, of which the principal monument was Erasmus's New Testament. This was the first edition to be published in Greek (though it was made from extremely defective texts), and incorporated a new Latin translation, differing greatly in style from the Vulgate.

Among those who made use of Erasmus's New Testament was Martin Luther, who learned from it that the Vulgate's version of the Greek of St Matthew 4:17 rendered as 'Do penance' words which meant merely 'Be penitent'. From this Luther argued that the sacrament of penance lacked scriptural authority, a conclusion which strengthened him in his stand against the sale of indulgences. The indulgence was not in itself an innovation in Luther's day: for centuries crusaders, contributors to religious buildings and foundations and others had been promised certain defined benefits in the form of remission of sins. The idea had proved capable of considerable expansion, and indignation against its development is to be found already in the fourteenth century, when Chaucer depicted his crafty pardoner with a wallet 'brimful of pardon come from Rome all hot'.[14] Nor were the popes always successful in retaining control over this institution. For a time (particularly under Clement VI) some bishops who were resident not in their dioceses but at Avignon did a flourishing business in the issue of collective indulgences embellished with rather amateurish illumination. In the following century the benefit of indulgences was extended to souls in purgatory. Erasmus and other critics expressed doubts about these extensions and criticised the salesman's techniques of the pardoners, but this was essentially a grievance of the serious and educated; indulgences were not an important source of popular anti-clerical or anti-papal feeling.

The papal indulgence which aroused Luther's indignation was that preached in 1517 by the Dominican Tetzel. It was a dual affair in that half the money contributed to gain remission of sins for the donors and their dead friends and relations was to go to pope Leo X to assist in the rebuilding of St Peter's, the other half to the young Hohenzollern, Albert archbishop of Magdeburg and Halberstadt, to enable him to repay the loan of 10,000 ducats from the Fuggers which was to purchase the arch-bishopric of Mainz. Neither of these causes was a popular one in Germany, for the Hohenzollern had many enemies, and the long-planned rebuilding of St Peter's was felt to be a matter for the Romans. In any case it was a slow affair, the completed results of which were unlikely to be visible for a long time. The construction of a Renaissance St Peter's, though proposed in the middle of the fifteenth century by Nicholas V, had only been begun in earnest by Julius II in 1506. Though it was strenuously forwarded by Leo X, most of the work was carried out later still, with Michelangelo as the principal architect, and it was not completed until the seventeenth century.

Luther's protest against the indulgence of 1517 (the 'Ninety-five Theses') was important not in itself but because it became the first step towards a position of outright revolt. In the summer of 1518 Luther replied to a critic in a tract which appealed to the Scriptures and by implication elevated them as an authority above both pope and councils. When his case came before a papal legate at Augsburg that autumn he rejected the doctrine concerning the 'treasury of merit' which offered the orthodox justification and explanation of indulgences. In the argument that followed, Luther stated a new and revolutionary position when he claimed that the pope abused the Bible: 'I deny that he is above Scripture.' Luther then fled back to Wittenberg, confirmed his stand ('I damn and detest this decretal'), and appealed from the pope to a general Council. Luther went on to reject papal primacy, which he regarded as the product of the papal legislation of the last four centuries or so— the decretals—and as lacking the essential authority of the Scriptures. A bull of November 1518 ('Cum postquam') redefined doctrine on indulgences and made it clear that they did not in themselves remit guilt nor automatically diminish the penalties of purgatory, but by this time Luther had gone too far for reconciliation. Leo X's bull of June 1520 ('Exsurge Domine') condemned 41 Lutheran errors and ordered his works to be burnt. On 10 December Luther retorted by burning the bull.

If Luther's position was already far from that of Erasmus, who could not at any price condone a schism, that of his protector Frederick the Wise, elector of Saxony, was no less far from them both. At Wittenberg Frederick had not only his cherished university, in which Luther was lecturer on the Bible, but also a magnificent accumu-lation of holy relics, partly inherited but mainly acquired through his own energies. The catalogue of 1509 recorded 5,005 separate relics and by 1520 the holy bones alone numbered 19,013. Yet this pious collector of relics was greatly impressed by Luther, and Luther in turn accepted Frederick's protection, without which he could have achieved little. Practical reformers in Germany had long understood that religious institutions were so rooted in society that durable religious change could only be achieved with the support of lay power. Some years earlier Konrad Celtis and the satirical poet Sebastian Brant (the author of *The Ship of Fools*) had hoped that reform might come from Maximilian, but in Germany effective lay power could only mean the princes. It was primarily to these that Luther addressed himself in his *An den christlichen Adel deutscher Nation von des christlichen Standes Besserung* (*To the Christian nobility of the German Nation, concerning the Reform of the Christian Estate*) of 1520, an appeal to emperor, princes and nobles, ecclesiastical and secular, to assist in the reform of the Church. Recourse to the lay powers was accepted by Luther without reluctance, and he cannot have failed to realise that emancipation from the papacy implied for the nobility an immensely attractive prospect of increased wealth and authority from enlarged jurisdiction and the spoils of ecclesiastical property. He made clear his attitude in the statement that 'earthly government is a divine order and estate' and by his criticism of the proto-Anabaptist Müntzer and other sectaries who would not come to terms with the secular state. He was willing to consult with the elector, through the latter's chaplain Spalatin, and accepted the situation whereby the elector's court came to deal with suits involving ecclesiastical matters such as marriage, tithes and even church discipline. In 1527 Luther's *Instruction of Visitors to the Pastors* asserted that lay courts and officials should punish moral offences, false religious doctrines and non-attendance at church, and later the Lutherans established Consistorial Councils, whose members were named by lay lords, to deal with such matters. By then, with the formation of the League of Torgau (1526), there was an open Lutheran party among the princes, led by the Saxon elector and the landgrave of Hesse.

LUTHERANISM AND THE REFORMATION

Lutheranism drew strength from both German national feeling and German political disunity, but neither worked solely in its favour. Luther's defence of certain condemned articles of Hus (among them the statement that 'it is not necessary for salvation to believe the Roman Church superior to all others') earned him much unpopularity. He was hailed by his enemies as 'the Saxon Hus' in lands that had been fought over by the Bohemian Hussites, and must have lost some support through such accusations, though this label did not stick. Moreover, rivalry between electoral and ducal Saxony ensured antagonists for the Wittenberg professor in the ducal university of Leipzig, just as rivalry between religious institutions gained the Dominicans' support for Tetzel against the Augustinian. Nevertheless the strength of the elector of Saxony in relation to his imperial overlord was the essential element that enabled Lutheranism to become fully rooted in the critical decade after 1517.

The diffusion of Lutheranism would also have been a much slower and more difficult process but for the printing press. In the years before Luther's prominence Frankfurt had been the main centre for the printing of pamphlets concerning the Reuchlin controversy, a dispute (over the right of a scholar to pursue biblical investigations by studying Jewish literature) which had put the humanists at odds with papal authority. It was therefore natural that this city should become a sort of headquarters of Protestant printing. Erasmus was already a best-seller—75 editions of the *Adages* appeared between 1500 and 1525, and about 60 of the *Colloquies* in eight years after 1518—but the publication of Luther's writings was an even more profitable, as well as a pious, undertaking. Four thousand copies of the address *To the Christian Nobility* were sold within three weeks. The pamphlet war warmed up to such intensity that in the years 1518–25 no fewer than one-third of the German books sold were copies of works by Luther, while many of the rest were those of his supporters and antagonists.

Much of the remaining pamphlet literature was concerned with the question of peasant discontent. Since the early fifteenth century the German peasantry had suffered serious depression of its status at the hands both of hard-pressed knights and (particularly in the east) virtually independent lords. Sporadic risings culminated in *Bundschuh*[15] peasant revolts in Alsace in 1493, around Speyer, in 1502, in the Breisgau and many other parts of the west in 1513–14, in Austria in 1515, and in the Black Forest area again in 1517. In 1525 there followed the great and disastrous Peasants' War. Ultimately the principal effect of these revolts was to strengthen the already dominant position of the lords who played the leading role in their suppression, but they had religious consequences as well, in that nobles who might otherwise have devoted their energies to combating Lutheranism were distracted by the successive crises of agrarian discontent.

The principal responsibility for the extermination of heresy in Germany lay of course with the emperor Charles V, who had at the same time to conduct the struggle against Francis I in Italy and the critical defence of the empire against the Turks, as well as the multifarious internal negotiations of his vast domains. Charles's burdens were so manifold that his failure to bring sufficient force to bear in time against the rapidly rising Lutheran movement is readily understandable. In 1532 he was compelled to recognise the Protestant religion by the 'Common Peace' of Nuremberg, and in 1555 the Peace of Augsburg sealed the victory of territorialism in Germany by permitting the head of each state to decide the religion of his own lands.

In common with many accounts, this chapter has juxtaposed the topics of late medieval Germany and the origins of the Reformation. It is natural to consider them together as any other approach risks making of the Reformation something abstract and remote. However, attention must be drawn to the limitations of this approach. One is a specific instance of the general danger of looking for antecedents and causes of the Reformation—the ease with which one can come to see each protest against ecclesiastical shortcomings, or each doctrinal variant from the church's line, as a harbinger of what was inevitably to follow. This form of religious trainspotting neglects the broader picture. The unrest in Germany that preceded the Reformation and accompanied its early phase had many motives, political, social and economic as well as religious, and if all that is remembered is the anti-clericalism one is not much closer to an understanding of German history or indeed of the processes which brought about the Reformation. Anti-clericalism was widespread in other periods too, and by no means all directed against Italians or the papacy. It is certainly not acceptable to assume from these attacks that the spiritual vitality of Christendom was in decline.

The second danger is that of seeing the Reformation from a purely German viewpoint. German alienation from Rome is an extreme but not a unique case. This discussion has not tried to give a full account of the spiritual forces for change that fed into the Reformation; but the following observation holds good. The factor that allowed many different forces to come together—theological dissent, alienation and resentment of various kinds, but above all political expediency—was the ultimately insoluble managerial problem of trying to run a multinational enterprise that claimed such extensive authority in an age of increasing particularism and complexity. Lack of spiritual leadership in Rome was alleged at a time when the Church was wealthier and administratively more sophisticated than ever before, but also less able than before to enforce its wishes over equally 'modern' governments that had overtaken Rome in the degree of control they were able to exercise. The 150 years of challenges to the papacy's monolithic authority, through schism, the conciliar debates about church government and the open rebellion of the Hussites, had made the notion of full-scale detachment from the Church no longer unthinkable. The unfolding of the crisis as heralded by Luther had profound roots which were by no means confined to Germany and whose wider implications were not seen by anyone at the time.

APPENDIX

German National Sentiment in Celtis' Ingolstadt Address, 1492

(Translation by Leonard Forster, *Selections from the Works of Conrad Celtis, 1459–1508* (Cambridge, 1948), pp. 45–7.)

Let us be ashamed, I pray, that although we have waged and won many memorable wars in Hungary, France and Italy and against that cruel tyrant of Asia who wallows in Christian blood, not one of you should be found today to hand down to posterity the deeds performed by German courage. Yet many foreigners will be found who in their historical works, contrary to all historical truth, will hiss like vipers against our courage with all the pretentious cajolery of their style and seek with falsifications and lying inventions (with which that sort of men is most prodigal for the purpose of singing their own praises) to belittle our glorious achievements. And I am quite at a loss to say whether it is due to our wisdom or our carelessness that lately of our own accord we have surrendered the insignia of authors and their companion, the imperial laurel, to Rome—an unhappy omen, as it were, for our empire, this abdication to others of the right to confer the laurel, foreshadowing that in the end not a single privilege of empire will remain in our possession.

Assume, O men of Germany, that ancient spirit of yours, with which you so often confounded and terrified the Romans, and turn your eyes to the frontiers of Germany; collect together her torn and broken territories. Let us be ashamed, ashamed, I say, to have placed upon our nation the yoke of slavery and to be paying tributes and taxes to foreign and barbarian kings. O free and powerful people, O noble and valiant race plainly worthy of the Roman empire, our famous harbour is held by the Pole and the gateway of our ocean by the Dane! In the east also power-ful peoples live in slavery, the Bohemians, the Moravians, the Slovaks and the Silesians, who all live as it were separated from the body of our Germany. And I may add the Transylvanian Saxons who also use our racial culture and speak our native language. In the west is France, which is so friendly and bountiful towards us by reason of the immortal virtue and incredible wisdom of Philip, Palatine of the Rhine, who rules both banks of the famous river and will ever rule them with fair-omened sway,

> While the pole wheels the stars, while winds smite the shores.

But from the south we are oppressed by a sort of distinguished slavery, and under the impulse of greed, that old and accursed aid to the acquirement of comfort and luxury, new commercial ventures are continually established, by which our country is drained of its wonderful natural wealth while we pay to others what we need for ourselves. So persistent is fortune or destiny in persecuting and wiping out the Germans, the last survivors of the Roman Empire.

FURTHER READING

Emperor, princes and the Church

On fifteenth-century Germany generally *see* Tom Scott, 'Germany and the Empire', in *NCMH*, 7, pp. 337–66; F. R. H. Du Boulay, *Germany in the Later Middle Ages* (London, 1983); R. W. Scribner, ed., *Germany. A New Social and Economic History*, vol. 1, *1450–1650* (London, 1995); Michael Hughes, *Early Modern Germany, 1477–1806* (Basingstoke, 1992), ch. 2; and G. Strauss, ed., *Pre-Reformation Germany* (London, 1972), a collection of translated essays by German historians. On the empire and the emperors, Jean Bérenger, *A History of the Habsburg Empire, 1273–1700* (tr. London, 1994), chs 4–10; G. Benecke, *Maximilian I, 1459–1519. An Analytical Biography* (London, 1982); essays by F. Hartung and K. S. Bader, in Strauss, cit., *Pre-Reformation Germany*; S. W. Rowan, 'Imperial taxes and German politics in the fifteenth century', *Central European History*, 10 (1980), pp. 148–64.

The government and politics of several regions are covered in English: *see* F. L. Carsten, *Princes and Parliaments in Germany from the Fifteenth to the Eighteenth Century* (Oxford, 1959); H. J. Cohn, *The Government of the Rhine Palatinate in the Fifteenth Century* (Oxford, 1965, repr. Aldershot, 1991); H.-S. Brather on Saxony in Strauss, cit., *Pre-Reformation Germany*; T. A. Brady, Jr., *Turning Swiss. Cities and Empire, 1450–1550* (Cambridge, 1981); T. Scott, *Freiburg and the Breisgau* (Oxford, 1986); Hilary Zmora, *State and Nobility in Early Modern Germany. The Knightly Feud in Franconia, 1440–1567* (Cambridge, 1998); H. W. Koch, *A History of Prussia* (London, 1978), chs 1 and 2; and M. Burleigh, *Prussian Society and the German Order. An Aristocratic Corporation in Crisis, c.1410–1466* (Cambridge, 1984).

Germany and the papacy

G. Strauss, ed., *Manifestations of Discontent in Germany on the Eve of the Reformation* (Bloomington, In., 1971) is a collection of documents illustrating the range of causes of unrest, of which atti-tudes to the Church was one. D. A. Eltis, 'Tensions between clergy and laity in some western German cities in the later middle ages', *Journal of Ecclesiastical History*, 43 (1992), pp. 231–48 is a reminder that anti-ecclesiastical sentiment was by no means all targeted against Rome; *see also* M. Burleigh, 'Anticlericalism in fifteenth-century Prussia: the clerical contribution reconsidered', in *The Church in Pre-Reformation Society. Essays in Honour of F. R. H. Du Boulay* (Woodbridge, 1985), pp. 38–47. B. Moeller, 'Religious life in Germany on the eve of the Reformation', in Strauss, cit., *Pre-Reformation Germany*—another translation is 'Piety in Germany around 1500', in *The Reformation in Medieval Perspective*, ed. S. E. Ozment (Chicago, Ill., 1971), pp. 50–75—stresses how deeply acceptance of the Church's authority was ingrained. P. E. Tillinghast, 'An aborted reformation: Germany and the papacy in the mid-fifteenth century', *Journal of Medieval History*, 2 (1976), pp. 57–79 illustrates an earlier controversy which fizzled out.

On the papacy, J. A. F. Thomson, *Popes and Princes 1417–1517: Politics and Piety in the Late Medieval Church* (London, 1980) is an effective introduction. P. Partner, *The Pope's Men. The Papal Civil Service in the Renaissance* (Oxford, 1990) explores the administrative aspects (and their political implications); on papal finances *see also* P. Partner, 'Papal financial policy in the Renaissance', *Past and Present*, 88 (1980), pp. 17–62, and P. Partner, 'The "budget" of the Roman Church in the Renaissance period', in *Italian Renaissance Studies*, ed. E. F. Jacob (London, 1960), pp. 256–78. P. Prodi, *The Papal Prince. One Body and Two Souls: the Papal Monarchy in Early Modern Europe* (tr. Cambridge, 1987) discusses the power and problems of the papacy in a broader chronological context, while D. Hay, *The Church in Italy in the Fifteenth Century* (Cambridge, 1977) discusses the Italian ecclesiastical background. For individual popes, *see* C. M. Ady, *Pius II* (London, 1913), R. J. Mitchell, *Memoirs of a Renaissance Pope* (an abridged translation of the *Commentaries* of Pius II, ed. L. C. Gabel) (London, 1952); M. Mallett, *The Borgias* (London, 1969); and Christine Shaw, *Julius II. The Warrior Pope* (Oxford, 1993).

Critics and reformers

General introductions to late medieval religion include R. N. Swanson, *Religion and Devotion in Europe, c.1215–c.1515* (Cambridge, 1995); J. Bossy, *Christianity in the West 1400–1700* (Oxford, 1985); and F. Oakley, *The Western Church in the Later Middle Ages* (Ithaca, N.Y., and London, 1979). Selected texts of the **Devotio Moderna** are published in J. van Engen, ed., *Devotio moderna: Basic Writings* (New York, 1988); *see also* A. Hyma, *The Christian Renaissance. A History of the 'Devotio Moderna'* (2nd edition, Hamden, Conn., 1965); and R. R. Post, *The Modern Devotion: Confrontation with Reformation and Humanism* (Leiden, 1968). The controversy over the significance of this movement is assessed in H. A. Oberman, *Masters of the Reformation: The Emergence of a New Intellectual Climate in Europe* (Cambridge, 1981), ch. 4. **Thomas à Kempis**, *The Imitation of Christ* is available in several translations including that of Leo Shirley-Price (Harmondsworth, 1952). On **Erasmus** *see especially* James McConica, *Erasmus* (Oxford Past Masters, 1991); Lisa Jardine, *Erasmus, Man of Letters* (Princeton, N.J., 1993); R. H. Bainton, *Erasmus of Christendom* (New York, 1969 and London, 1970); and Margaret Mann Phillips, *Erasmus and the Northern Renaissance* (revised edition London, 1981).

Of the many biographies of **Luther** *see especially* R. H. Bainton, *Here I Stand: A Life of Martin Luther* (New York, 1950); M. Brecht, *Martin Luther: His Road to Reformation 1483–1521* (tr. Philadelphia, Pa., 1985); G. Ebeling, *Luther: An Introduction to his Thought* (tr. London, 1970); B. Lohse, *Martin Luther: An Introduction to his Life and Thought* (Edinburgh, 1987); James M. Kittelson, *Luther the Reformer: The Story of the Man and his Career* (Minneapolis, Minn., 1986) and Heiko A. Oberman, *Luther: Man between God and the Devil* (New Haven, Conn., 1989). Selected works of Luther are translated in Part I of Hans J. Hillerbrand, ed., *The Protestant Reformation. Selected Documents* (London, 1968).

Lutheranism and the Reformation

General works which take the Reformation as their main focus but also go back into its medieval roots include Andrew Johnston, *The Protestant Reformation in Europe* (London, 1991), a basic introduction; Euan Cameron, *The European Reformation* (Oxford, 1991)—with an excellent thematic bibliography—and Carter Lindberg, *The European Reformations* (Oxford, 1996); *see also* the essays in Andrew Pettegree, ed., *The Reformation World* (London and New York, 2000). Works with a focus on the intellectual roots of the Reformation include H. A. Oberman, *The Dawn of the Reformation* (Edinburgh, 1986); Steven Ozment, *The Age of Reform, 1250–1550. An Intellectual and Religious History of Late Medieval and Reformation Europe* (New Haven, Conn., 1980); Alister McGrath, *The Intellectual Origins of the European Reformation* (Oxford, 1987); and H. A. Oberman, *Masters of the Reformation: The Emergence of a New Intellectual Climate in Europe* (Cambridge, 1981). Works with a specifically German focus are A. G. Dickens, *The German Nation and Martin Luther* (London, 1974 and Glasgow, 1976); R. Po-Chia Hsia, ed., *The German People and the Reformation* (Ithaca, N.Y., 1988); and R. W. Scribner, *The German Reformation* (London, 1986) (a brief introductory book). R. W. Scribner, *Popular Culture and Popular Movements in Reformation Germany* (London, 1987) contains many insightful essays.

The impact of printing on the Reformation is best assessed through the standard works on the history of printing: S. H. Steinberg, *Five Hundred Years of Printing* (new edition revised by John Trevitt, London, 1996); L. Febvre and H. J. Martin, *The Coming of the Book: the Impact of Printing, 1450–1800* (tr. London, 1976); E. L. Eisenstein, *The Printing Press as an Agent of Social Change. Communications and Cultural Transformations in Early-Modern Europe* (Cambridge, 1979) —an abridged version was published as *The Printing Revolution in Early Modern Europe* (Cambridge, 1983, repr. 1993). R. W. Scribner, 'Oral culture and the diffusion of Reformation ideas', *History of European Ideas*, 5 (1984), pp. 237–56, repr. in his *Popular Culture and Popular Movements in Reformation Germany* (London, 1987), pp. 49–70 challenges the view that printing was primarily responsible for the transformation of popular sentiment.

NOTES

1. *See above*, p. 212.
2. *Above*, p. 102.
3. Cf. W. Andreas, *Deutschland vor der Reformation. Eine Zeitenwende* (1932; 6th edition Stuttgart, 1959), p. 70.
4. Op. cit., p. 71.
5. At least 16 German versions of the Bible were printed before Luther's.
6. *See* the Appendix to this chapter, pp. 243–4.
7. For 'the Revolutionary of the Upper Rhine' *see* N. Cohn, *The Pursuit of the Millennium* (1962, revised edition London, 1972), pp. 118–26.
8. J. Burchard, *Liber Notarum*, ed. E. Celani, in *Rerum Italicarum Scriptores*, new series, XXXII, I (Città di Castello, 1906), II, p. 303; translation by G. Parker, *At the Court of the Borgia, being an Account of the Reign of Alexander VI* (London, 1963); this passage is on p. 194.
9. Letter from Rome to Valentin Eber, 5 August 1491, in *Konrad Peutingers Briefwechsel*, ed. E. König (Munich, 1923), p. 9.
10. *'Fui nuper Rhomae cum Hesso nostro, vidi veterum monumenta, vidi cathedram pestilenciae: vidisse iuvat, vidisse piget'*, in Ulrich von Hutten, *Opera*, ed. E. Böcking, 5 vols (Leipzig, 1859–70), I, p. 311.

11. *Die Reise des Kardinals Luigi d'Aragona . . . v. A. de Beatis*, ed. L. Pastor (Freiburg in Breisgau, 1905), p. 107; translated as *The Travel Journal of Antonio de Beatis, Germany, Switzerland, the Low Countries, France and Italy, 1517–1518*, tr. J. R. Hale and J. M. A. Lindon, The Hakluyt Society, 2nd series, 150 (London, 1979). This passage is on p. 80.

12. Translation slightly adapted from Thomas à Kempis, *The Founders of the New Devotion: being the Lives of Gerard Groote, Florentius Redevin and Their Followers* (London, 1905), p. 57.

13. *Imitation of Christ*, Ch. I. A widely available translation is that of L. Sherley-Price (Harmondsworth, 1952, many reprints).

14. ('Bretful of pardoun comen from Rome al hoot'.) *The Canterbury Tales*, General Prologue, l. 687, in *The Riverside Chaucer* (3rd edition Boston, Mass., 1987), p. 34.

15. This was a type of shoe worn by peasants.

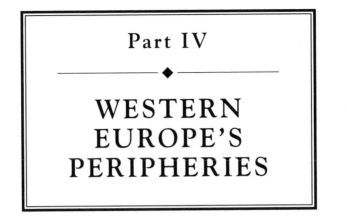

Part IV

◆

WESTERN EUROPE'S PERIPHERIES

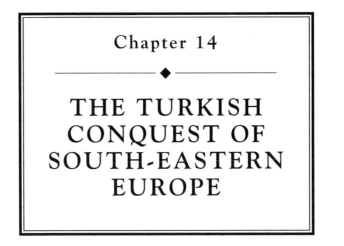

Chapter 14

◆

THE TURKISH CONQUEST OF SOUTH-EASTERN EUROPE

WESTERNERS IN THE EAST AND THE DECLINE OF BYZANTIUM

The role of the Burgundian dukes as the great protagonists of the crusading movement in their day—outlined in Chapter 9—can only be understood in the light of the events in south-eastern Europe which are the subject of the present chapter. The diminishing coastal strip of Palestine which remained in the hands of the western Christians in the thirteenth century finally disappeared with the fall of Acre (1291). Its history since the days of Saladin and Cœur de Lion had been so discouraging that one can sympathise with the disillusioned Knight Templar who wrote after the loss of Arsouf in 1265 that 'he is mad who seeks to fight the Turks since Jesus Christ does not deny them anything . . . God, who used to keep watch over us is now asleep, but Mahomet works with all his might'.[1] Meanwhile the restored Byzantine state of the Palaeologi was, as we have seen in Chapter 2, a mere skeleton, the relic of a body politic whose flesh had been consumed by Bulgars, Franks, Venetians and Genoese, not to mention such separatist Greeks as the Despots of Epirus. An account of military and political developments in Byzantine and formerly Byzantine Europe will make it clear why crusading triumphs filled the dreams and daydreams not only of the Avignon popes and the Burgundian dukes, but of Henry IV of England (1399–1413), who dreamt that he would die at Jerusalem, and of his son, Henry V, who liked to think of his French victories as mere preliminaries to greater exploits performed against the 'malignant and turban'd Turk'. Indeed, for all the great warrior-kings of the west the Turk came to figure as a sort of 'last enemy', the supremely formidable opponent who took his place at the end of a queue of more immediate minor foes: even Charles VIII's invasion of Italy in 1494 was presented as the prelude to a great Turkish campaign.

The weak condition of the Byzantine Empire at the beginning of the fourteenth century under Andronicus II (1282–1328) is well illustrated by the story of his employment of a body of Catalan mercenaries. The conclusion of the war of the Sicilian Vespers in 1302 meant that a great number of professional soldiers were out of work. Roger of Flor, a German mercenary commander who had served under Frederick II of Sicily, received permission to seek terms with Andronicus: it was known that a ruler who had lost 'more than thirty days of land' to the Turks would be grateful for the aid of Catalans and Aragonese, and particularly those who had been fighting against the hated Angevins. When Roger reached Constantinople he seems to have had no difficulty in gaining a contract. Pay was fixed for his followers at rates varying from four gold ounces a month for a fully armed cavalryman to 20 *tarins* for a crossbowman (the *tarin* was a small silver coin). Roger himself was to be the emperor's 'Megaduke' and to marry his niece. His men, numbering some 6,500, reached Constantinople in the autumn of 1302, and their deeds over the next eight years have been recorded by one of their number, Ramon Muntaner, in his *Chronicle*.

The Catalans began satisfactorily by crossing to Anatolia and fighting the Turks, but were bitterly resentful when (in 1304) they were asked to fight the Bulgars. Disputes arose over pay and other matters, and in 1305 the Greeks themselves attacked the Catalans and murdered their leader. During the next phase of its activity the company, hitherto based on Gallipoli, occupied most of Thrace and fought a number of campaigns against the Byzantines. Muntaner himself held Gallipoli against the Genoese in 1306, and the same year the Catalans accepted reinforcements from a new quarter:

And so the Turks came before Gallipoli, and one of their chiefs, Xemelic by name, came and asked to have speech, and said that if we agreed he would enter Gallipoli and talk with us. And I sent an armed ship and he came on it with two knights who were both relations of his. He announced to Rocafort and Ferran Xemenis and myself [Muntaner] that he was prepared to come over to us with all his company and their wives and children. They would take an oath and perform homage, promising to stand with us like brothers, he and all his company. They would stand against all the people in the world, would entrust their wives and children to our power, were willing to be under our command in all things and for all things as the lowest men of our company, and they would give up one-fifth of all their gains.

The Catalans were not the men to refuse an offer of this sort:

And so we ruled and rode up and down the Empire in our own way, and when the Turks and Turcopols went on cavalry campaigns those of our men who wished to go went too, and the Turks treated them most honourably and saw to it that they came away with twice as much gain as themselves. And so there was never any trouble between us and them.[2]

Later the Catalans fell out among themselves, pillaged Phocaea in Asia Minor with a ferocity that was exceptional even for them and, after fighting both with and against all the other variegated despoilers of Byzantium, turned at last to their old enemy and swore an oath of fealty to Charles of Anjou. After moving into Thessaly they took service with the Frenchman Walter of Brienne, duke of Athens (1310). At the end of six months, however, the Catalans had received only two months' pay. The duke made liberal promises in an attempt to retain a small body of 200 cavalry and

300 infantry, whom he hoped to detach from the rest of the company. But the Catalans refused to be divided and a bitter battle was fought when the duke attacked them on the river Cephisus in Boeotia (March 1311):

And the battle was very fierce [says Muntaner], but God, who always aids the just, gave our Company his aid, so that of all the seven hundred [Frankish] knights, only two escaped. The rest were all killed, the Count [Walter] and all the barons of the principality of Morea, who had all come to destroy the Company . . . And so all the cavalrymen of the whole country were killed there, as well as more than twenty thousand infantry. And thus the Company quitted the field, having won the battle and the whole Duchy of Athens.[3]

The Catalans offered their Turks several places in the duchy, but the Turks refused, saying that 'God had done well for them, and they were so rich that they wanted to go back to their friends in the kingdom of Anatolia'—an unfortunate decision, since the Genoese killed or captured most of them on the Hellespont, and the remainder were killed near Gallipoli by the Byzantines. As for the Catalans themselves, they ruled the duchy (Attica and Boeotia), and in 1318 extended it far to the north, into Thessaly.[4] They lost these northern lands to the Serb Dušan in 1349, but held the duchy itself till dispossessed by Neri Acciaioli, lord of Corinth, in 1388.

The tale of the Catalan company has been related only as an instance of the manner in which parasites, Frankish, Italian, Greek and Turkish, settled on hitherto Byzantine soil and brought about the political fragmentation of the southern parts of the Balkan peninsula. Dissension within the Palaeologan house itself was rarely lacking, nor was there any unity in the Slav regions farther north, which were divided between Bulgars, Serbs and Bosnians. The whole of south-east Europe was so segmented in race, religion and rule that warfare was constant, and warfare—as we have seen above—inevitably involved appeal to the powerful military support of the Turks.

THE OTTOMAN TURKS

It is now time to turn to the principal protagonists of the achievements described in this chapter, the Ottoman Turks. The Ottomans were a small emirate imbued with a strong spirit of religious militarism; they saw themselves as a community of *ghazis*, warriors of the Muslim faith. They first figure on the historical scene in the early fourteenth century when, with the assistance of warriors from other emirates, they began to make slow territorial progress against tenacious Byzantine resistance in western Asia Minor. They were sufficiently powerful to rank as attractive allies and to benefit by Greek disunity in 1345, when John VI Cantacuzenus called them in to aid him in Thrace against John V Palaeologus. The emir married John VI's daughter, while John recognised Ottoman control of Bithynia. The Ottomans then seized Gallipoli from another emirate, and by 1354 occupied the whole of this strategically important peninsula. At about the same time they gained Angora (Ankara) and other territory in Asia Minor. As the only intensely active *ghazi* state, they received much assistance from volunteers from the other emirates, and by 1360 they had begun to expand into the Balkans.

Ottoman advance in south-eastern Europe originally took the form of suzerainty, but gradually vassal dynasties were eliminated and direct Ottoman control replaced overlordship. During the 1370s the rulers of Bulgaria and Serbia and the Byzantine emperor himself became tributaries, to be joined soon by many lords in Greece and Albania, as well as in Anatolia. Under Bayezid I (1389–1403) direct rule was inaugurated, in Anatolia and Bulgaria, and this abandonment of the more cautious method of amassing overlordships may have been in part responsible for the disastrous defeat suffered at the hands of the great conqueror Timur ('Tamburlaine', 1339–1405). Timur's kingdom, a powerful amalgam of Turkish and Mongol (or Tatar/Tartar) elements, was transitory, while Ottoman direct rule survived and proved immensely effective. Newly conquered territories were the subject of elaborate statistical surveys (the *defters*), and these Domesday Books were both bases for fiscal exploitation and records establishing legal claims to land. Certain districts were specially appropriated to the military fisc, and the *defter* was used to assign revenue to the army as well as to regulate taxation. Thus Ottoman military, fiscal and legal arrangements came to supplant those of the conquered lands, but the transition was eased by the fact that there was no radical substitution of a new governing landed class. Christian seigneurs and *voyvods* (chiefs) often retained much of their estates by entering the Ottoman army as *askeri* (a military-administrative class) or securing feudal rank as holders of *timars*, feudal estates, owing cavalry service.

Ottoman government offered efficient rule, improved communications, tolerably light taxation and even a fair degree of religious toleration. Yet there could be no doubt that this was conquest. The subject population had to submit to the periodic levy of the *devshirme*, the tribute of children taken to serve as soldiers, administrators and pages. Equally characteristic of absolutist rule was the employment of mass deportation. Albanians, Serbs and Greeks were transferred in vast numbers to Anatolia and—after 1453—to Constantinople, while Anatolians (often nomads) were transplanted to Thrace, Bulgaria and the border zones of the Balkans. The purposes of compulsory migration were of course fiscal and military as well as political. The Ottomans' unsurpassed infantry of janissaries recruited from their Christian subjects and excellent system of cavalry service due from feudatories (timariots) presented a formidable picture of organisation and unity, which contrasted with the piecemeal resistance of their European victims.

Only at one moment did it seem possible that a powerful Christian kingdom in the Balkans might halt the progress of Ottoman conquest. This was during the reign of Stephen Dušan (1331–55), 'Emperor of the Greeks and Serbs'. Rascia, which later became Serbia, was one of the inland Balkan states owing vassalage to Byzantium which emerged from semi-independence in the time of Byzantine decline after the late twelfth century. Serbia's first king, Stephen, a Slav by birth but Byzantine by education, was crowned in 1217. The history of Serbia's brief hour of hegemony begins a century later with a decisive victory over the Bulgars at Kjustendil (Velbužd) in 1330. Stephen Uroš Dečanski III, the victor of Kjustendil, was deposed, and probably killed, in the following year by his son Dušan, who allied himself with a weakened Bulgaria, held the Hungarians at bay, kept the peace with Bosnia, and set as his aim the conquest of Constantinople, no less. Making use, as did the Ottomans, of the disputed Byzantine succession of 1341, Stephen gained Albania and Macedonia, and in 1346 ambitiously inaugurated a 'Serbo-Roman Empire'. As the self-styled successor to the Byzantines he was crowned *Imperator Rasciae et Romaniae* (Emperor of the Serbs and Romans) and his archbishop was made a patriarch. Turning his forces against northern Greece, he reached Volos on the Thessalian coast by 1348, and proposed to the Venetians a scheme for a joint conquest of Constantinople. Undeterred by Venice's refusal, he proceeded with plans for an unassisted assault on the city, but died in the year before that which he intended to mark the fruition of his career.

Dušan's empire disintegrated in the 20 years after his death in 1355. His Greek and Albanian lands soon went their separate ways, while internal disputes threatened Serbia and Macedonia. It is not easy to estimate whether Dušan's achievements would have lasted had he lived longer. He certainly envisaged consolidation, as his law code, promulgated in 1349 and amended shortly before his death, testifies. It was the first code of public law for Serbia, though it catered separately for the Serbian and Greek parts of his empire. In practice, however, his dominion was a makeshift affair, for with virtually no central administration or judicial system he had little control over his own nobility. Nor did he rule a wealthy country, though he derived a considerable revenue from the mining of gold, silver and iron, and there was a lively trade with the eastern Balkans in the mining towns and with Italy through Ragusa (now Dubrovnik) and other Dalmatian ports. These coastal cities rendered certain dues which no doubt facilitated the employment of a cosmopolitan mercenary force. Dušan had a personal guard of 300 Germans, and his paid troops played a considerable part in his military triumphs.

The aftermath of Dušan's career coincided with growing momentum in the Ottoman advance in Europe. Murad I (1360–89) soon conquered Thrace, making Adrianople (now Edirne) his main European base, and threatened Serbia. In 1371 his army inflicted a heavy defeat on Serbian forces at a critical battle on the river Marica, leaving what remained of Dušan's empire wide open to attack. The annexation of Macedonia and much of southern Serbia followed. The ruler of Bulgaria became his vassal, as did the emperor John Palaeologus (1373). Niš and Sofia were captured by 1386 and Salonika in the following year. A landmark came when an alliance between Bosnians and Serbs met Ottoman forces in June 1389 at Kosovo Polje. Much uncertainty hangs over this celebrated battle which, as is now notorious, subsequently came to occupy a central place in Serb nationalist ideology. Next to nothing can be said with assurance about the numbers and multi-ethnic composition of both armies, and conflicting legends have sprung up about the events of the day. The outcome of the battle itself was inconclusive; all that is certain is that both the emperor and the Serb prince Lazar Hrebeljanović were dead by the time it was over. At the end of the day the Christian troops withdrew, but the Ottomans also left rapidly as Murad's son Bajezid hastened to secure his succession. However, the consequences of the battle are clearer. The overall loss of troops had a much heavier impact on the Serbs than it did on the Ottomans, who were soon able to return and inflict further losses. With additional pressure on Serbia's northern and western borders with Hungary (which included Croatia), Lazar's widow Milica, as regent for her son, became an Ottoman vassal. By the end of 1392 almost all Serb territory was under Ottoman suzerainty, though direct Turkish rule only followed more gradually. By contrast the following year Bulgaria, already a Turkish vassal, was conquered, annexed and placed under direct Turkish rule.

LATE MEDIEVAL CRUSADING

The end of resistance to the Ottomans in Albania, northern Serbia and Bulgaria was to provoke energetic, though belated, action in the west. The Turks were in fact halted by Mongol armies from the east, not by the Christians from the west, but the 'Crusade of Nicopolis' of 1396 is an event of sufficient significance to justify a brief excursus on the history of crusading thought in the century after the disappearance of Christian rule in Syria. Throughout this period there was much discussion concerning the methods to be used to regain the territory now lost to Christianity. The ideas of the Catalan Ramon Llull (1232–1315/16) are of interest for their originality, though they had no practical effect. Llull had plans for military reconquest, but his most novel recommendation proposed the foundation of chairs of oriental languages in western universities. Muslims were to be converted by what might now be called 'brain-washing'. Special linguist-preachers should 'hold disputations with prisoners to convert them to the Holy Catholic faith', and they should read certain books which prove that Mahomet was not a true prophet.

Afterwards the ruler-commander [under whom the military religious orders were to be unified] should release these captives. He should pay them their travelling expenses with a fair and friendly expression on his face, and send them off to the Saracen kings and other rulers . . . so that they should make clear to them (the rulers) what we believe concerning the most holy Trinity . . . and this will be a way of converting the Infidels and of spreading our most holy faith.[5]

The most fundamental of the many disadvantages of this scheme was that the Christians very rarely succeeded in taking Muslim prisoners.

It was natural that the most active propagandists of the crusade should be those who were most closely threatened by the Moslem advance. Pierre de Thomas, a French Carmelite friar, went to the eastern Mediterranean around 1350 and spent the remaining 15 years of his life as papal legate in Crete and Cyprus. Among Thomas's disciples was Philippe de Mézières, who became chancellor of Peter I of Cyprus, planned to found a chivalrous order (to be called 'The New Order of the Passion of Jesus Christ') and wrote a number of works on the crusade after returning to France in 1369. King Peter (a Lusignan) was a close friend of both these men, and with their energetic encouragement and assistance he raised a fleet of 165 vessels and launched an expedition of which the anticlimactic outcome was the capture—for a single week—of the city of Alexandria.

The assault on Alexandria (1365) was the issue of three years' preparatory work, including a visit by king Peter to the west, where he held discussions with pope Urban V, John II of France, Edward III of England, the emperor Charles IV and the kings of Hungary and Poland. It took its place in a long and uninterrupted series of military failures, a list that includes Clement VI's league of 1343 (which did, however, capture Smyrna) and Peter's own earlier expedition against Asia Minor, which also captured a solitary port, Adalia (Antalya). It was followed by the 'Crusade' of Count Amadeus VI of Savoy, who took 15 galleys and several mercenary companies to the east in 1366, but was diverted into fighting against the Christian Bulgarians on behalf of the Byzantine emperor.

Almost a generation passed before the next ambitious scheme, the joint Franco-Genoese crusade of 1390 against the Tunisian port of al-Mahdiya. A hundred galleys sailed on this enterprise under the command of Louis II de Bourbon, uncle of Charles VII of France. The attack on al-Mahdiya, like all crusading ventures, was the product of mixed motives, motives which affected both the composition of the force involved and the outcome of the operations. The Genoese—who supplied 1,000 crossbowmen and 2,000 cavalrymen as well as the shipping—were principally concerned with al-Mahdiya as the home of corsairs who hindered their valuable north Africa trade. The French were sincere crusaders, benefiting from the respite afforded by the pacific policy of Richard II of England; they were indeed reinforced by English, Flemish and Aragonese elements. The siege proved a difficult undertaking, the Genoese were naturally the first to feel discouraged and negotiations soon resulted in their agreement to a 10-year truce which offered them all they really wanted. The reluctant French were compelled to follow suit and after three months the siege was abandoned.

The last of the major crusading ventures was the outcome of the great Ottoman victory of 1389.[6] Like the al-Mahdiya expedition, the Crusade of Nicopolis was made possible by the long lull in the Anglo-French war. In 1395 negotiations led to the formation of a league involving France, England, Hungary, Venice and Burgundy: Duke Philip the Bold was the principal promoter and his son John of Nevers (the future John the Fearless) commanded the Franco-Burgundian element. More than half of the very large Christian force involved were Hungarians. In the summer of 1396 this army advanced from Buda along the Danube and besieged Nicopolis. Sigismund of Hungary, experienced in warfare against the Ottomans, favoured cautious tactics, but the French could only think in terms of the headlong chivalric assault which had cost them so dear at Crécy and Poitiers. When Bayezid broke off the siege of Constantinople and came to the aid of Nicopolis the French at once launched an attack (25 September 1396). After winning ground in the early stages of the engagement, they were defeated with the loss of almost their entire force. The Ottomans then turned against the Hungarians, who had held aloof from the French battle, and they too were overcome. Most of the French prisoners were put to death, but Bayezid spared the nobles, who were later ransomed for a fee of 200,000 florins. Among these was John of Nevers, who reached home the following year.

The great military undertaking of 1396 had failed to halt the Turkish advance and Constantinople would almost certainly have fallen within a few years but for the defeat of Bayezid by Timur in 1402. Throughout the preceding century the western Christians had compared unfavourably with their opponents—whom they had consistently underrated—in every respect. Their tactics and discipline had been inferior and they had fought in unsuitable armour. Above all, their efforts had been spas-modic and had been frustrated by internal divisions and conflicting motives. As an old man, Philip of Mézières, the great crusading propagandist of the age, learned the news of the crushing defeat of his hopes at Nicopolis. In these last, sad years of his life he was accustomed to write of himself ruefully as a *vieil abortif* (an old failure).

Bayezid's defeat and capture near Ankara in 1402 postponed Ottoman domina-tion throughout south-eastern Europe for several decades. During this period both Venice and the kingdom of Hungary were sufficiently powerful to dispute what was left of the Eastern Empire with the Turks—though inevitably they were rivals and not allies. After the death of Sigismund (1437) Hungary lost much of its cohesion, and the eventual successor, Ladislas of Poland, had to struggle for control in Hungary as well as fighting the Turks in Serbia. The campaigns of 1442–4, which probably saved Constantinople from conquest by Murad II, were fought under the virtual leadership of John Hunyadi of Transylvania, a Wallachian noble who had come into prominence in the service of Hungary. Hunyadi was also involved in the attempt to exploit Murad's absence in Asia during 1444, which culminated in the disastrous defeat of Varna, in which king Ladislas was killed. Surviving this battle, Hunyadi became regent in Hungary for Ladislas Posthumus, the grandson of Sigismund and heir to Ladislas III. Hunyadi in his turn became preoccupied with internal factional strife, and in the following years the main role in opposing the Ottomans was assumed by the Albanian George Castriot, later known as Scanderbeg (born *c.*1405). Scanderbeg had been taken by the Turks in youth as a hostage and, as a Moslem, served them for many years before he fled to his native land and set up as the leader of resistance there in 1443.

MAHOMET II AND THE FALL OF CONSTANTINOPLE

As early as the 1420s western visitors to Constantinople were startled to find its population much under the influence of Turkish ways. The honour of suppressing the shrunken vestige of the empire founded by Augustus fell to Mahomet II 'the Conqueror' (1451–81). The man who achieved the success so long promised by God to the champions of the Islamic faith, and so long denied them, was in every respect worthy of his triumph. Mahomet was born in 1432, the son of Murad II by an unknown slave. An elder half-brother was murdered and Mahomet became heir presumptive as a young child; indeed, his father abdicated in his favour in 1445, but had second thoughts and resumed power in the following year. Mahomet's first campaign was probably the victorious one against Hunyadi which culminated in the second battle of Kosovo (1448). Murad died three years later, and Mahomet marked his succession by putting to death a young half-brother who was a potential centre of opposition. The same fate was later to befall a series of grand viziers, but Mahomet must be given credit for his punctilious observance of etiquette in such matters: when an important dignitary was executed his head was exposed on a silver plate, whereas that of a lesser official was only granted a plate of wood. The sultan's favourite method of execution was to order men to be sawn in half, and his whim-sical sense of humour permitted him to claim that he had been true to his word when he had 300 Italians killed in this way at Mytilene in 1462 after promising that 'they might keep their heads'. His methods did little to distinguish him from his Christian opponents, though in his reputation for brutality he was outdone by perhaps only one contemporary, the infamous Vlad 'the Impaler', ruler of Wallachia. At the height of his campaign against the Wallachians (also 1462), Mahomet's army apparently found itself in a 'forest' of 20,000 stakes on which Vlad's Turkish and Bulgarian victims had been impaled.

Mahomet was steeled by an unlimited faith in his own destiny. From childhood he had believed that Constantinople would be his, and later he was to dream of the conquest of Hungary and even of Rome. He had a great taste for Greek and Roman history, as well as for what we should now call medieval chronicles; these works were read to him presumably in Greek (for he knew this language, as well as 'Slav'), by Italians. A particular favourite was Alexander the Great, and there can be little doubt that Mahomet saw himself as the new Alexander, called by destiny to repeat in reverse the deeds of the old. 'The times have changed now', he is reported to have said, 'and I shall go from east to west as formerly the westerners penetrated the East.'

Mahomet's best-known military achievement, the conquest of Constantinople, was not his greatest feat of arms. This was merely the last symbolic act in the extinction of an empire which had long survived only by consent of the Turks. On the death of the emperor John VIII Palaeologus in 1448 the rival claimants, John's brothers Constantine and Demetrius, invited Murad to decide the succession. Not unnaturally Murad declared for Constantine, the despot of Mistra, who two years earlier had become his tributary. The city that Mahomet set out to subjugate in 1452–3 had long been encircled, but he took care to occupy the forces of the emperor's two brothers by launching a diversionary campaign in the Morea. The final siege began on 6 April 1453. Since the Byzantines were able to muster only some 9,000 men (of whom one-third were Genoese and Venetians) to hold four miles of wall, the outcome of the siege was a foregone conclusion once the sultan had turned his full might against the city. Nevertheless, tribute must be paid to the ingenuity which enabled the Ottomans to drag 70 ships across land from the Bosphorus to the waters of the Golden Horn, thus circumventing the chain which was supposed to protect the harbour against naval assault. The walls were at last breached on 29 May. The emperor Constantine died courageously among his men, and within hours the entire city was in Ottoman hands; inevitably there were appalling scenes of massacre and looting.

Mahomet fought an almost ceaseless series of campaigns in Europe and Asia. To chronicle them would be tedious, but without doing so it is difficult to give a sufficient impression of Ottoman military power at this period. In Asia the emperor of Trebizond, another beneficiary of Byzantine decay, was overthrown, as were a large number of Anatolian rebels and Persian challengers. To the north, naval and military campaigns made of the Black Sea a Turkish lake, with disastrous consequences for western European traders. Mahomet's onslaught on Europe was checked in 1456 by the heroic relief of Belgrade by Hunyadi and the crusaders of the friar Capistrano. Belgrade was to defy the Turks again, but by 1459 Mahomet had regained all Serbia and within three years of this he held Athens and the Morea. To his conquests in mainland Greece he soon added Mytilene (Lesbos) and various other islands, though the Venetians were able to retain Euboea, with its strategic trading post, Negroponte, till 1470. By that date Bosnia had fallen and resistance in Albania almost come to an end with the death of Scanderbeg (1468). From Bosnia marauding Ottoman irregulars launched annual raids as far to the north-west as Styria and Carinthia, and in 1477 a force pressed so far into Italy that the fires caused by its depredations could be seen from Venice. Three years later the Ottomans attacked southern Italy, captured Otranto, massacred every male in the city, and held it for over 12 months.

When Mahomet died in 1481, at the age of 49, Ottoman strength was still checked in the Balkans by the resistance of Belgrade and in the Mediterranean by that of Rhodes.[7] The growth of Turkish sea-power under Selim I (1512–20) made possible the conquest of Syria and Egypt. Only under Suleiman II (1520–66) was the advance into Europe resumed, while Charles V warred with Francis I of France. Then the king of Bohemia and Hungary was killed in the decisive battle at Mohács (1526) and, with the acquisition of Hungary, the Ottoman Empire became a greater power in Europe than its Byzantine predecessor had been, even in its heyday before the First Crusade. Not only had the territorial problems set by Byzantine decline been settled for centuries, but the western European states had to reckon with a mighty neighbour whose weight was to count for much in the balance of power diplomacy of the 'early modern' period. By splitting Christian Europe, the Reformation served to make the domination of the Turks yet more secure. The crusading ideal lived on strongly in the ideas of the Counter-Reformation, but even the naval victory of Lepanto (1571) failed to check the Ottoman advance: a century after this the Turks captured Crete and besieged Vienna. The replacement of a stricken Christian empire by an aggressive Islamic autocracy was certainly the greatest change in the map of Europe between the thirteenth century and the early years of the sixteenth.

FURTHER READING

General

The themes covered here are so intertwined that the bibliography follows a more detailed scheme than the text. Chapters 4–6 of Robert Fossier, ed., *The Cambridge Illustrated History of the Middle Ages*, 3, *1250–1520* (Cambridge, 1986) together constitute a wide-ranging introduction to the themes covered here.

Byzantium

D. M. Nicol, *The End of the Byzantine Empire* (London, 1979) is an introductory textbook, complementing his extensive *The Last Centuries of Byzantium, 1261–1453* (2nd edition, Cambridge, 1993). *See also* the standard general histories, of which the most authoritative and extensive is now Warren Treadgold, *A History of the Byzantine State and Society* (Stanford, Cal., 1997) (pp. 709–853 for this period); D. Obolensky, *The Byzantine Commonwealth: Eastern Europe, 500–1453* (London, 1971), ch. 8, and G. Ostrogorsky, *History of the Byzantine State* (2nd edition, tr. Oxford, 1968), ch. 8. On religion, *see* D. M. Nicol, *Church and Society in the Last Centuries of Byzantium* (Cambridge, 1979), and J. Gill, *Byzantium and the Papacy, 1198–1400* (New Brunswick, N.J., 1979).

Two of the last emperors have found English-language biographers: John W. Barker, *Manuel II Palaeologus (1391–1425): a Study in Late Byzantine Statesmanship* (New Brunswick, N.J., 1969), and Donald Nicol, *The Immortal Emperor: the Life and Legend of Constantine Paliologos, Last Emperor of the Romans* (Cambridge, 1992). On the Ottoman capture of Constantinople, S. Runciman, *The Fall of Constantinople, 1453* (Cambridge, 1965); his *Mistra. Byzantine Capital of the Peloponnese* (London, 1980) is a sympathetic study of the final focus of Byzantine history and culture, as is his *The Last Byzantine Renaissance* (Cambridge, 1970).

Latins in the East; Late Medieval Crusading

Peter Lock, *The Franks in the Aegean, 1204–1500* (London, 1995, paperback 1998) is a wide-ranging synthesis. B. Arbel, B. Hamilton and D. Jacoby, eds, *Latins and Greeks in the Eastern Mediterranean after 1204* (London, 1989), and B. Arbel, ed., *Intercultural Contacts in the Medieval Mediterranean* (London, 1996) include a range of relevant essays, all reprinted from volumes 4 and 10 respectively of *Mediterranean Historical Review; see also* K. Setton, *Catalan Domination of Athens, 1311–1388* (2nd edition, London, 1975), and C. Frazee and K. Frazee, *The Island Princes of Greece. The Dukes of the Archipelago* (Amsterdam, 1988). On Venice and the East, D. M. Nicol, *Byzantium and Venice. A Study in Diplomatic and Cultural Relations* (Cambridge, 1988), and for both Venice and Genoa, E. Ashtor, *Levant Trade in the Later Middle Ages* (Princeton, N.J., 1984). *See also* under Chapter 2, above.

On late medieval crusading, N. Housley, *The Later Crusades. From Lyons to Alcazar 1274–1580* (Oxford, 1992) is the best introduction; *see also* his *The Avignon Papacy and the Crusades, 1305–1378* (1986); A. Luttrell, 'The crusade in the fourteenth century', in *Europe in the Late Middle Ages*, eds J. R. Hale, J. R. L. Highfield and B. Smalley (London, 1965), pp. 122–54 is a briefer introduction. Introductions to medieval crusading in general, albeit with quite different interpretations, include H. E. Mayer, *The Crusades* (2nd edition, Oxford, 1988); J. Riley-Smith, *What were the Crusades?* (London, 1977), and *The Crusades. A Short History* (London, 1987); and Christopher Tyerman, *The Invention of the Crusades* (London, 1998). K. M. Setton, gen. ed., *A History of the Crusades*, III, *The Fourteenth and Fifteenth Centuries*, ed. Harry W. Hazard (Madison, Wis., 1969), and VI, *The Impact of the Crusades in Europe*, eds Harry W. Hazard and Norman P. Zacour (Madison, Wis., 1989) have a number of chapters on westerners in the East; P. W. Edbury, *The Kingdom of Cyprus and the Crusades, 1191–1374* (Cambridge, 1991) is a useful case study. Amadeus of Savoy is the subject of Eugene L. Cox, *The Green Count of Savoy. Amadeus VI and Transalpine Savoy in the Fourteenth Century* (Princeton, N.J., 1967). The writings of Ramon Llull can be sampled in translation in Anthony Bonner, *Selected Works of Ramon Llull*, 2 vols (Princeton, N.J., 1985), and in his *Doctor Illuminatus. A Ramon Llull Reader* (Princeton, N.J., 1993).

The Balkans

John V. A. Fine, Jr., *The Late Medieval Balkans. A Critical Survey from the Late Twelfth Century to the Ottoman Conquest* (Ann Arbor, Mich., 1987, paperback 1994) is now the standard work. On specific regions or states *see*, among other works, the following: Noel Malcolm, *Bosnia. A Short History* (2nd edition, London, 1996); Noel Malcolm, *Kosovo. A Short History* (London, 1998): ch. 4 is an up-to-date assessment of the Battle of Kosovo, on which *see also* T. A. Emmert, *Serbian Golgotha: Kosovo, 1389* (New York, 1990), and W. S. Vucinich and T. A. Emmert, eds, *Kosovo: Legacy of a Medieval Battle* (Minneapolis, Minn., 1991). Susan Mosher Stuard, *A State of Deference. Ragusa/Dubrovnik in the Medieval Centuries* (Philadelphia, Pa., 1992) is a fine study of this remarkable city-state; *see also* Francis W. Carter, *Dubrovnik (Ragusa). A Classic City-State* (London and New York, 1972) (a full account with emphasis on economic history), and Bariša Krekić, *Dubrovnik, Italy and the Balkans in the Late Middle Ages* (London, 1980) (collected essays). D. M. Nicol, *The Despotate of Epiros, 1267–1479. A Contribution to the History of Greece in the Middle Ages* (Cambridge, 1984) covers a territory which underwent more changes of control than most; Nicholas Cheetham, *Medieval Greece* (New Haven, Conn., and London, 1981) gives a rounded picture. On Romania, A. Oṭetea (ed.), *The History of the Romanian People* (Bucharest, 1970) is a full official publication of its time; G. Castellan, *A History of the Romanians* (Boulder, Colo., 1989), and K. W. Treptow, ed., *A History of Romania* (Iasi, 1996); Dinu C. Giurescu and Stephen Fischer-Galati, eds, *Romania: a Historical Perspective* (Boulder, Colo.. distrib. N.Y., 1998) includes two useful articles: Stefan Andreescu, 'The making of the Romanian principalities' (pp. 77–104) and Mihai Maxim, 'The Romanian principalities and the Ottoman Empire (1400–1878)' (pp. 105–32). Finally S. Pollo and A. Puto, *The History of Albania from Its Origins to the Present Day* (tr. London, 1981) is one of the few English publications on Albania to give much weight to the late medieval period.

The Ottomans

Halil Inalcık, *The Ottoman Empire: the Classical Age, 1300–1600* (tr. London, 1973, repr. 1997) is the standard work. C. Imber, *The Ottoman Empire 1300–1481* (Istanbul, 1990) is a fuller political account; P. F. Sugar, *Southeastern Europe under Ottoman Rule, 1354–1804* (Seattle, 1977) concentrates on Ottoman government; Halil Inalcık, *An Economic and Social History of the Ottoman Empire*, 1, *1300–1600* (Cambridge, 1994) is a detailed socio-economic survey. Godfrey Goodwin, *The Janissaries* (London, 1994) is a lively investigation of a key aspect of Ottoman military history. The Mongol incursions around 1400 can be followed in B. F. Manz, *The Rise and Rule of Tamerlane* (Cambridge, 1989). Franz Babinger, *Mehmed the Conqueror and His Time* (ed. and tr. Princeton, N.J., 1978) is a classic biography. Kate Fleet, *European and Islamic Trade in the Early Ottoman State. The Merchants of Genoa and Turkey* (Cambridge, 1999) is a thorough examination of trade between western Europe and the Ottomans.

NOTES

1. Ricaut Bonomel, in V. de Bartholomaeis, *Poesie provenzali storiche relative all'Italia*, 2 vols (Rome, 1931), II, pp. 222–4.
2. R. Muntaner, *Cronica*, in Ferran Soldevila, *Les quatre grans cròniques (Jaume I, Bernat Desclot, Ramon Muntaner, Pere III)* (Barcelona, 1971), §228, pp. 869–70.
3. Ibid., §240, pp. 882–3.
4. *See* Map 5.
5. Llull, *Liber de fine*, in *Raimundi Lulli Opera Latina*, eds F. Stegmüller *et al.* (Turnhout, 1959–), 9 (1981), pp. 233–91 (this passage is on p. 283).
6. *See above*, pp. 255–6.
7. *See* Map 6.

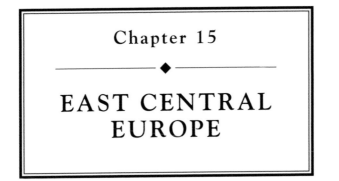

Chapter 15

◆

EAST CENTRAL
EUROPE

CHANGING CONCEPTS OF EAST AND WEST

Mention has been made of the *Drang nach Osten*, the prolonged and multi-phased eastward expansion of German people, authority and culture. Since the nineteenth century there has been a strong tendency to view the history of Germany's eastern neighbours in these terms—indeed to see the whole history of the region as one of the relationship between 'Germans' and 'Slavs'. Both German and pan-Slavic nationalists contributed to this dualistic and conflictual approach, and just as its flaws—and above all the political dangers inherent in it—were becoming evident, it was succeeded by an equally insidious variant, fostered by the ideological division of late twentieth-century Europe into two power-blocks. The notions of 'Western' and 'Eastern' Europe have a long, unhappy, mutating pedigree. Yet it would be impossible to exaggerate the inadequacy of this approach from the medieval viewpoint. To assume any sort of homogeneity in the area of what is geographically considered Europe that is populated by Slavic peoples—from the Baltic to the Adriatic and the Black Sea, from Prague to the Urals (not to mention the non-Slavic peoples, such as the Hungarians and Albanians, enclosed in that area)—would be as outrageous as to assume it for the area from Iceland to Sicily, or from Lisbon to Berlin. The historical outlook which tends to see 'Eastern Europe' as 'Slav' Europe is characteristic of an outlook in which race is emphasised as an historical factor. Moreover, historians have shown how complex the ethnic terms 'Germanic' and 'Slavic' actually are, and have sometimes come close to rejecting their use altogether as more pernicious than useful.[1]

The term 'East Central Europe', as used here, has come into common currency in the last 20 years, partly to reflect growing dissatisfaction with the old dichotomy, and partly to reflect the older truth that culturally 'Central' Europe, including the Germanic and even the north Italian lands, had a great deal in common, not only from the long hegemony of the Habsburgs but from still further back in time. 'East Central Europe' is used here to denote the westernmost band of those linguistically non-Germanic territories to the east or south-east of the German-speaking world, which from the Second World War to the collapse of communism found themselves on the east side of the famous 'Iron Curtain'.[2] Yet there are other historical reasons for studying these lands together, and particularly for examining their medieval history in comparative light. As will be seen below, they have a number of features and circumstances in common. The most important of these was that by the later Middle Ages they both shared with their western neighbours a full membership of the Roman Catholic obedience and at the same time were in the special position of being on the borders of that obedience. Which of these two features was the more significant is impossible to say; both have to be taken fully into account. Of those inclined to typologise and draw lines on maps—and this is still often an ethnocentric exercise—an increasing number now stress that in many ways the line between Western and Eastern Christianity (with, later on, Islam on the 'Eastern' side as well) has been culturally more fundamental than that between 'German' and 'Slav', or its approximate twentieth-century counterpart, the Iron Curtain. As far as the late Middle Ages are concerned, no such borders were yet fixed. 'East Central Europe' was a huge space in transition. At the beginning of our period it was still subject to eastward (Germanic) expansion; by the end it was in retreat in the face of Ottoman Turkish aggrandisation, as has been seen in Chapter 14. In between there were many opportunities for the formation of states, and for social, economic and cultural development, which the rulers of the different regions took up in often similar (though not identical) ways, and sometimes in co-operation rather than conflict. The results included, for a time, immense territorial agglomerations, dwarfing anything in the 'west', but also participating fully in 'western' cultural and economic life.

HUNGARY

Throughout its pre-twentieth century history the kingdom of Hungary was much larger than is today's modern state. By 1100 the territory under some form of Hungarian control included Slovakia to the north, Croatia and much of Dalmatia to the south (to which was soon added a claim over Bosnia), and Transylvania to the east; by the thirteenth century it extended further eastwards, across the Carpathians, to Wallachia and Moldavia.[3] Several of these territories retained effective independence under Hungarian overlordship, or were contested by local princes, but the fact remains that in the later Middle Ages this power block stretched at least notionally from the Adriatic almost to the Black Sea, covering much of the northern part of the Balkan peninsula, and at one stage extending west over much of Austria and as far north as Silesia. The late medieval history of the Hungarian monarchy itself reflects this international position. Its centrality brought Hungary into Italian, Byzantine, Ottoman, Austrian, German, Bohemian and Polish politics.

This internationalism goes back to the origins of the kingdom, and affected the internal life of the country as well as its foreign relations. The Magyars were a nomadic tribe from the steppes, whose sudden appearance at the very end of the ninth century terrified much of Europe.[4] Fifty years of almost annual marauding raids ended with their defeat at the battle of Lechfeld in 955, and they settled in the great plain circled by the Carpathian mountains, and soon converted. By that is meant that the monarch became Christian and imposed the Christian faith, to a large extent, on his subjects, though that process was for a long time far from complete. To bring this about, the kings relied heavily on foreign help; missionaries and churchmen from France, Germany, Italy and Slavic lands. Foreign input was not confined to the religious sphere; for at least three centuries the Crown strongly encouraged settlers from elsewhere, including Slavic lands but above all from the empire.[5] The early Hungarian monarchy was precocious in its comparative centralisation and international in outlook, arranging dynastic marriages with German, Croatian, French and Byzantine royalty and nobility, adopting western culture and methods of government and playing its part on the international political stage, particularly in the Adriatic. This policy had a mixed reception among the Hungarian nobility, the heirs of those who had participated in the original settlement, some of whom remained suspicious of the king's motives. But this was far from a simple, dual antagonism. Hungary also remained a Christian outpost. The Carpathians were a poor barrier to further incursions, and the twelfth-century monarchs had to defend the realm against Pechenegs, Cumans and others. Most of these were fleeing from Mongol expansion, and many were in fact absorbed, though not necessarily converted; the kings were happy to have Cumans, for example, as front-line defences against further invaders, and they remained both pagan and nomadic, occupying the eastern part of the great plain. The nobility was unhappy about these migrants as well. That the fears of fresh invasions were not idle was demonstrated cataclysmically in 1241, with the second swoop of the Mongols into Europe. The buffer of the Cumans in the event failed; four weeks before the invasion they had left, outraged that Hungarian nobles, believing them to be agents of the Mongols, had assassinated their leader.

The whirlwind incursion of the Mongols in 1241 produced, in Hungary, perhaps the worst atrocities seen in Europe before the twentieth century. It has been estimated that between three and four hundred thousand people (of a population of perhaps two million) were eliminated by the Mongol warriors themselves, some dying in battle, most massacred as settlements—perhaps 60 per cent of them—were systematically ravaged. Many more died in the famine and epidemics which followed.[6] It was also a tremendous shock, both to Christian rulers generally and to Hungarians; the precarious nature of their role as *antemurale christianitatis*, the bulwark of Christendom, could not have been more starkly demonstrated. But the invasion also brought about an assessment of what had gone wrong, and was soon followed by real recovery. Béla IV (1235–70), who had seen it coming and issued unheeded warnings, was quick to learn lessons and rebuild his kingdom. Defences were substantially improved, with the construction of stone castles (which had proved to be the only effective defence against the Mongol horsemen). No fewer than 55 such fortifications had been built by Béla's death. Land grants to nobles were confined to those loyal to him and made conditional on their building castles in the territory awarded them. The lesser nobility was integrated into the political order with the creation of a system of county courts. Towns were fortified and given royal charters with privileges to encourage extensive repopulation, and Béla renewed the invitation to foreign colonisers from all over the region. By the end of his reign some of the political problems appeared to have been resolved. But the monarchy remained essentially personal, and Béla's successors were not able to maintain the uneasy harmony. Lászlo IV (1272–90), half-Cuman, soon managed to alienate first the barons and then the pope, who excommunicated him; he repudiated his wife, broke with the Church, married a Cuman in a pagan ceremony and ended up living among these nomads in a tent. He was eventually assassinated; but his successor, Andrew III (1290–1301), was unable to end the disorders reopened by Lászlo, and with him the founding dynasty petered out.

The end of the Árpád line was a turning-point in a particular sense. While there had occasionally been foreign rulers for brief periods in the previous centuries, after 1301 it was Hungarian-born monarchs who would be the exception. In matters of succession power reverted to the nobles, whose independence, large number and extensive ownership of land made them perennially difficult to control. The succession squabbles of the later Middle Ages arose where the nobility could not agree, but it is significant that they repeatedly went for foreign rulers, and often for men who already had another royal title. The Árpád period, the ethnic mix and Hungary's border role in western Christendom had at least made the idea of a foreigner on the throne uncontroversial, and of course it can be found elsewhere as well, for example in southern Italy. The calculation of the nobility was often that they would benefit from rulers who had broader interests and less commitment to indigenous factions. There was also the hope that they would leave the nobles alone, though it was accompanied by fear that the kingdom might be exploited or neglected. The relationship of kings to the nobility has to be seen in that light. In 1301 the nobles were divided between support of king Wenceslas II of Bohemia, who gave up his claim in 1304, and Charles Robert of Anjou, member of the astonishingly versatile family whose various branches between them ruled so much of the Mediterranean. Charles Robert's road to real control was protracted. He was crowned properly in 1310, but it was some time before he felt secure enough to move his operational base from Temesvár (now Romanian Timişoara) in the south to Visegrád, near Buda, and make it his capital.

In the seven decades under Angevin rule Hungary can be said to have reached an apogee. Charles Robert (1310–42) and his son Louis the Great (1342–82) gave the country a period of prominence and political centrality. Charles Robert is credited with reuniting the country after decades of instability. He kept Czech and Austrian aspirants at bay, and established good relations with his northern and southern neighbours—to the point of becoming the arbiter between Poland and Bohemia at a meeting of the three monarchs, the 'Congress of Visegrád', that he hosted in 1335.[7] He restored Hungarian sovereignty in Bosnia and consolidated power in other regions bordering on the kingdom of Serbia. Louis' foreign policy was altogether more aggressive (and costly). His ambitions extended first of all in the direction of Naples, where his younger brother Andrew was claimant to the throne. After Andrew was killed in 1345, Louis mounted two expeditions to southern Italy, gaining the title 'king of Jerusalem and Sicily', but losing control again almost immediately on departure. His Balkan policy was more successful; he established Hungarian protectorship over the most important Dalmatian city-state, Ragusa (now Dubrovnik), and temporarily won other ports from the Venetians; he took advantage of the collapse of Štefan Dušan's Serbian empire with his death in 1355, extending control into northern Serbia; Wallachia accepted Hungarian overlordship, previously thrown off, in 1369; and he even briefly established a power-base in Bulgaria. From the point of view of status and prestige these were significant achievements, but not as much as that of his final years, namely the acquisition through marriage of the Crown of Poland in 1370,[8] which briefly made him the ruler of the largest territory in Europe.

The internal history of Angevin rule also had many positive features. The greater achievements were undoubtedly those of Charles Robert; he laid foundations, while Louis built on them. Early in Charles Robert's reign the oligarchical power of the greater nobility was checked; lands seized by nobles during the years of instability were recovered, and royal powers of taxation reasserted. Land, the determining qualification for membership of the nobility, became increasingly a matter of royal gift and favour. The administration at Visegrád became more organised, and the court expanded and flourished. Above all a clearer legal structure was evolved, confirming the status of the nobility and of serfs. The embodiment of these reforms was the legal code issued by Louis in 1351. A measure of success was that there was barely any internal opposition to Louis' expensive campaigns; they were prestigious (which suited the nobles, who also did not have to pay for them directly). But an important key to this success has not yet been mentioned. In the gold mines of northern Hungary and of Transylvania the monarchs held society's most highly prized commodity, and in the fourteenth century Europe was starved of it. It has been estimated that under Charles Robert, Hungary produced 80 per cent of Europe's gold.[9] It was this (and other mineral resources) that gave Hungary, which was not particularly urbanised or populated, and which since the rise of the Mongols no longer found itself on a significant trade route, special economic significance in the European context, and ensured the continued and indeed growing presence of foreign merchants and financiers, mainly German but also Italian. It also gave the monarchs added status and leeway in political enterprises—though the most dramatic example of this, Louis' use of over five tonnes of gold in his campaign to get Andrew crowned king of Naples in 1343, had no outcome other than the flooding of the market.[10]

The death of Louis saw a return to the cycle of succession problems, but this time in an international context. The eventual beneficiary was Sigismund of Luxembourg, husband of Louis' daughter Maria—but not before a bitter contest with Charles of Durazzo, king of Naples. Sigismund's approach to the Crown of Hungary might be described as the opposite of that of the Angevins; he was determined to use the title as a lever on the European stage, and handing power to the Hungarian barons was the first step towards this, but it did not satisfy them for long. In 1401 the king was briefly imprisoned by a group of them, and the baronial council administered the country in the name of the 'Holy Crown of Hungary', an interesting conceptual innovation. This set the pattern for his later career; in 1410 he became emperor, and thereafter devoted most of his time to non-Hungarian matters, as described elsewhere in this book.[11] Internal government was left entirely to the barons, but the frequent absences did take their toll on the extent of territory controlled, with

Venice benefiting by regaining some of Dalmatia, and many of the southern lands, together with Wallachia, accepting or falling to Ottoman rule.

Sigismund had no male heir. His Habsburg son-in-law, Albert, was elected king of Hungary but died two years later. For the first time the nobles elected not only a foreigner but one with no blood ties with Hungary, Úlászló I (Władysław) of Poland (1440–44), and then Albert's son Ladislas Posthumus (1446–57), who only came of age and was released from Viennese clutches in 1453. Out of the power vacuum of these years there emerged a Wallachian nobleman, János (John) Hunyadi, the *voyvode* or ruler of Transylvania, whose defence of the kingdom against the Turks raised him to the status of national hero. His career is discussed elsewhere in this book;[12] he became regent in 1446, and continued to dominate after Ladislas's assumption of power. Hunyadi's greatest and last moment was the lifting of the Ottoman siege of Belgrade in 1456; but perhaps his greatest legacy was his son, Matthias Corvinus (1458–90), the first nobleman to be elevated to royalty for centuries. In this ruler Hungary found its Indian summer, reaping the benefits of centuries of western influence; an international 'Renaissance' court, with a 'Renaissance prince' at its head, and once again a vigorous political programme on the international stage. Corvinus —the epithet was a typical humanist one, referring to the raven on the family crest—surrounded himself with trained non-aristocratic advisers and humanists. Under these the rhetoric of absolute and centralised monarchy developed. The Italian humanist Aurelio Brandolini attributed to Corvinus the statement that 'the king himself is no slave or tool to the law, he is above it, ruling over it'.[13] The characteristics of such ideals of government will be examined in Chapter 18. Firm, often confrontational rule was the hallmark of Corvinus. He soon ditched the baronial faction that had brought him to power. Feudal privileges were eliminated, and when a number of barons turned against him and offered the Crown to the Polish king, an invading force, and then the offending barons, were crushed. Once firmly in control he seldom called meetings of the diet, though less public alliances with lesser nobles were made, and in 1486 their privileges (as opposed to those of the greater barons) were extended.

The main preoccupations of the monarch lay northwards and westwards. Bohemia, by now in virtual European isolation, was exposed and tempting; Corvinus offered to crusade against the Hussites, and allied himself with Catholic nobles in Moravia and Silesia, who helped to get him crowned in 1469 in opposition to the official king, George of Poděbrady.[14] When the latter died in 1471 the Hussite nobles offered the Crown to the Polish prince Władisław, who in turn brought the (Habsburg) emperor Frederick III into the conflict. Eventually the country was divided, both claimants unusually recognising the other as kings of Bohemia, with Corvinus retaining Moravia and Silesia (1478). Austria, of which little mention has been made so far, was an equally attractive prospect for economic as well as political reasons. A brief period in which the Crowns of Austria, Hungary and Bohemia had been united (1438–9) had had no practical consequences but left a vision of what might be possible, while the fact that Frederick was also emperor provided an opportunity for mischief. By 1477 Corvinus had forged an alliance with the archbishop of Salzburg and occupied most of Styria. In 1485 he took Vienna itself, and made it his capital. With this the Hungarian state reached its greatest extent.

Corvinus has often been accused of doing too little to defend Hungary—and the 'west'—against the Ottomans. There is some truth in this; although the improvements in defence and the modern standing army he created—the largest in central Europe—were directed against Hungary's southern neighbours as well as the others, he doubted that more could be done against Turkish advances without help from other European powers. He was probably right. The years after Corvinus's death saw what could best be described as protracted implosion. The estates deliberately chose a weak successor, Władisław of Bohemia (in Hungarian Úlászló II, 1490–1516), who had promised to reverse those of Corvinus's reforms to which the nobles objected, and who presided ineffectually over financial decline, baronial excesses, peasant uprisings and steady Turkish advances.[15] A decade after his death the Ottomans inflicted their massive and historic defeat at the battle of Mohács (1526). Hungary ended carved up between Turkish rule in the core of the country (including the great plain and Buda/Pest), and Habsburg control on the northern fringes, with an independent Transylvanian state to the east. The two neighbours which had come to dominate Hungarian politics for so much of the fifteenth century thus swallowed it up for the next four centuries.

BOHEMIA

Less will be said here about Bohemia because it is also discussed in other chapters. The smallest of the three states that form the main subject of this chapter, it shared many of the characteristics of its two neighbours, including the interconnectedness of their history. However the effective ostracism of the nation by Roman Christendom in the fifteenth century meant that the outcome of medieval Czech history could not but be different.

A Czech 'state' had existed since the Přemyslide dynasty's ascendancy in the late tenth century, and given that it died out in 1306 this house can be described as almost exactly coterminous with that of the Árpáds of Hungary. Bohemia's evolution was if anything even more closely bound to 'western' Europe than that of Hungary. The compact region inhabited by the westernmost group of Slavs became more densely colonised, and also more quickly urbanised. There was little space for expansion, and relatively little appetite for it once Moravia, to the south-east of Bohemia, had become permanently joined to Bohemia in a subordinate capacity in the eleventh century. A critical factor was that Bohemia was part of the empire, albeit with even more autonomy than its other components; from 1158 Bohemia had its own monarch. In the thirteenth century the potential impact of a king within an empire became clear with the dynamic Ottokar II (1253–78), whose role in the double imperial election of 1257 has already been mentioned.[16] Ottokar had already been elected duke of Austria in 1251, after the extinction of the house of Babenberg, though it was almost a decade before he defeated the rival claimant, king Béla of Hungary. Expansion did not stop with Austria; Styria, Carinthia, Carniola and Friuli were added in the 1260s, giving Bohemia access to the Adriatic for the first time. Ottokar also had ambitions to the north, crusading against the Prussians, founding the Baltic port of Königsberg (named thus in his honour—now Kaliningrad, after

M. I. Kalinin) and antagonising Polish interests in the process. By the time the imperial interregnum ended in 1273 Ottokar had become the most powerful figure in east central Europe. But the election of Rudolf—whom Ottokar refused to recognise, scorning the choice of 'a poor count of Habsburg'—soon brought him a powerful new enemy. By 1276 Rudolf had enlisted the Hungarians in a pincer campaign, forcing Ottokar to renounce his claim to Austria and two years later defeating him personally in battle at Dürnkrut, in the Marchfeld, near Vienna, where Ottokar died at the hand of his own cupbearer. It was the beginning of the Habsburg's Austrian power-base, and as such had far-reaching consequences, though entirely unpredictable ones that the time—who could have foretold that this dynasty, rather than that of Přemyslide or Árpád or Piast, or their many successors, would be stamped for centuries on central European history? Ottokar's 'empire', like so many others of the period, did not last, and in his territorial ambitions he was unusual, indeed almost unique in Bohemia's history; but as the first Czech king to operate on the grand European scale he set a precedent which was followed up. After Dürnkrut Bohemian attentions turned towards the north-east, and Ottokar's successor, Wenceslas II (1278–1305), became king of Poland in 1300.

As the Přemyslide line ended in 1306, the Bohemians, like the Hungarians, took a new and decisive route. Both of the rival candidates of that year were foreigners, as was the eventual recipient of the Crown, John of Luxembourg (1310–46). The extensive presence and profound influence of 'westerners' in Bohemia, Germans in particular, has already been noted. A foreign monarch was a natural step; the international character of monarchy was widespread and increasing, and a ruler with international connections and ambitions was seen as an asset rather than a liability. Even growing 'national' sentiment proved no obstacle to the repeated choice of foreign rulers in later years. In John, the Bohemians undoubtedly acquired a typical foreign king, with both the accruing prestige and the less obvious drawbacks. Under John and his son Charles IV (1346–78) there were marriage alliances with France, Germany, Hungary and Poland, close relations with the papacy at Avignon, and extensive involvement in Italian politics. John was largely an absentee ruler, who used the coffers of state for his foreign enterprises and in the process placed great strain on them. Charles, himself half-Bohemian, took his dual lineage very seriously, and brought Bohemia more tangible results: an international profile and court, prestige and extensive development for Prague. In this respect the German accusation that he mortgaged the empire for Bohemia, whether justified or not, speaks for itself.[17] Like Hungary, Bohemia experienced its greatest glories in the mid-fourteenth century, under 'foreign' rulers.

The decline of the kingdom into full-blown crisis has been recounted above in Chapter 6. Its complexity ensures that the roots and significance of the Hussite revolution will continue to be hotly debated for a long time. Here we shall confine the discussion to the political consequences for the monarchy and the way in which Bohemia was governed, and to the regional context. The story 'at the top' is quickly told. The disastrous Wenceslas, deposed as emperor in 1400, lasted as king of Bohemia until his death in 1419, by which time the revolt was in full flood and the country ungovernable. His popularity in Bohemia had increased with the country's rapidly growing isolation, but that was of no lasting benefit. It took 17 years of campaigning before Sigismund brought the rebels to a compromise and was finally accepted as king, and he died a year later (1437). In a further parallel with Hungary there followed 20 years of power vacuum—Albert of Bavaria refused the crown as too burdensome, Albert I of Habsburg, king of Hungary and emperor, accepted the Bohemian crown two years before dying, and Ladislas V, yet another Hungarian, had only four years of rule. Eventually a Bohemian nobleman, George of Poděbrady (1457–71), came to power as heroic defender of the nation, in an echo of the career of John Hunyadi in Hungary. After his death the Crown passed again to a 'foreign' line, in the shape of the eldest son of the Polish king, Ladislas II (1471–1516), who in 1490 became king of Hungary and from then on devoted an increasing amount of attention to it. Under him and his son Louis (1516–26), royal power experienced a similar decline to that in Hungary, and with the same dynastic outcome in that the two joined the Habsburg empire in tandem.

The rise and fall of Bohemian independence in the Middle Ages has obvious parallels with Hungary, as we have seen, and also some with other smaller states that did not survive. The trajectory of that rise and fall was different in each case, and in Bohemia there were some singular conditions. At the same time as being geo-politically in an unfavourable position, surrounded by larger powers, from the early fifteenth century it also experienced isolation to a degree that was unique in medieval Christendom. Hussitism both profoundly split the country and got it ostracised. It could be argued that, while Hungary and Poland-Lithuania represented geographical frontiers of Christendom, Bohemia came to represent a kind of spiritual frontier. The difficulties of succession after the truce of 1436–7 and the death of Sigismund were not unconnected with the traumatic experience of the previous two decades; it was not easy to persuade foreigners to accept the Crown of a partly heretical country. The division was ultimately one that only the Czechs could sort out for themselves. The coronation ceremony of George of Poděbrady in 1457 was a careful compromise between the two religious obediences, the Cross and the Chalice, as they are sometimes described. Yet in its isolation—and in some respects perhaps even because of it—Bohemia evolved in an unusual political direction. For much of the period under Přemyslide rule it had been more urbanised, with a more developed bourgeoisie, than its neighbours, though at the same time the nobility, that is, the landowning class, was the key participant in government after the king. The changing fortunes and priorities of the monarchy over time had left a delicate balance between these forces; for example, whereas by the late thirteenth century the kings were regularly relying on the support of townsmen and gentry to keep the great landowners in check, king John reversed the trend in 1310 by granting the nobles extensive privileges. The balance was still in evidence during the Hussite revolution, which could not have followed the course it did without a highly educated bourgeoisie or a nobility jealous of privilege and conscious of ethnic divisions. The rest of the century saw a continuation of this duality. Despite the deep divisions among them the power of the nobles increased steadily; in electing the king, keeping the peasantry tied to the land, resisting the influence of the towns and often coming together effectively to dictate policy. These features can be found in Hungary and

Poland as well; but in Bohemia at the end of the century they had a unique result. The ineffective and eventually absentee rule of the Jagiełłonian kings initially left the country in the grip of the nobles, but the royal towns retaliated by forming a union and developing into a 'third power'. The 'monarchy of the estates' is the expression used to describe the government; a highly developed Diet or parliament, whose decisions, reached by a sophisticated procedure, became law without royal action. Such an advanced manifestation of the corporate state within a monarchy was unique not just in the region but in Europe. It would not have been possible without the high conceptual level at which Bohemians considered their politics, as they did their religion.

POLAND

Polish history is full of paradoxes, including borders that changed dramatically over time, and the emergence of a sense of national identity notwithstanding profound intermixing and influences of others. By the end of our period it was both the largest kingdom in Europe west of Muscovy and the most decentralised. The Piast dynasty that had established control of Greater Poland in the north-west, and by the tenth century annexed Little Poland in the south-east, held sway until 1305, though in a highly fragmented way; from 1138 the territory disintegrated, going to members of the same family who controlled swathes of land of varying areas and often competed with each other. This unusual dynastic continuity was one reason why some sense of Polish identity persisted throughout the period. (Another was that it was kept alive by the Polish Church.) As with the other lands we have been discussing, German colonisers played a great part in the history of Poland; but so did Bohemia, through which Poland was first christianised and brought into the 'western' ambit. The culmination of this close relationship was the brief rule of the Bohemian king Wenceslas over Poland (1300–5). This provided the final impetus for the reintegration of Polish lands, which was achieved with comparative speed by the Piast king Vladislav IV Łokietek ('the Short') (1320–33). Łokietek had aspired to the throne for years, but was only able to obtain it after the Bohemian, who had exiled him, had died, and the Přemyslide dynasty with him. He returned to Cracow in 1306 and made it the base of his campaign to revive royal fortunes (it remained the seat of the monarchy thereafter). The fuelling of anti-foreign sentiment played a large part in this revival. The Bohemians were represented as occupiers, of whose influence the country was to be purged. There was also hostility towards Germans, who dominated the towns, and who by 1311 had come together in a rebellion, which was suppressed. On the northern borders Łokietek became embroiled in a protracted and indecisive war against the Teutonic knights. Internal 'Polish' divisions also had to be tackled; Łokietek's long-standing enemy, Henry II of Głogów, controlled Greater Poland, and after Henry's death in 1309 it took another five years before his sons were driven out. By the time of his coronation, at the age of 60, in 1320, Łokietek's authority exceeded that of any of his predecessors of almost two centuries.

Łokietek's son and successor, Casimir III 'the Great' (1333–70), was able to build on his father's work. The contest with the Teutonic knights in the north was still a burning issue, and there were tensions with Bohemia (John of Luxembourg had taken Silesia in 1327). Casimir, who had already been active in government during the last year of his father's reign, recognised the political realities and wrought a fundamental shift in policy. He made peace with the Teutonic knights, and in 1335 also came to a formal settlement with the house of Luxembourg, recognising its rights over Silesia and obtaining—for a large sum—the renunciation of Luxembourg claims over the Polish Crown. This cleared the way for Casimir's real aim, the redirection of Polish territorial aspirations towards its eastern borders. Mazovia (the area around Warsaw) was established as a Polish fief in 1351. Red Ruthenia, wedged between Little Poland, Hungary and Lithuania, was taken in 1340, lost again to Lithuania in 1352 and regained, together with substantial additional territories to the north and the east of it, in 1366. Casimir made full use of a long-standing alliance with Hungary (whose king, Louis the Great, was his nephew), but also engaged in constructive diplomatic relations with many other powers. Indeed he is remembered above all as a diplomat. The culmination of his career was the Congress of Cracow, 1364, called to help the visiting king of Cyprus, Peter of Lusignan, launch a crusade.[18] Though it failed in its official purpose, this grand event brought to Poland the emperor, the kings of Hungary and Denmark, and princes and nobles from much of the region. Amid the sumptuous reception Cracow, already the stage for the emperor's fourth marriage (to Casimir's granddaughter) the previous year, showed off the fruits of Casimir's building programme and its newly founded university, only the second in central Europe.

With Casimir the Piast line ended; the throne passed, as has been seen, to Louis of Hungary (1370–82), for whom Poland was not much more than a prestigious appendage. After his death the nobility made an historic decision. In 1374 Louis had obtained their agreement that one of his daughters should succeed him, and shortly before his death he appointed his elder daughter, Maria, aged 11, as regent. Since she was betrothed to Sigismund of Luxembourg this implied that Poland would continue under Hungarian rule. After much controversy the nobles agreed instead on Louis' younger daughter, Hedwig, on condition that the union with Hungary was abandoned. She was crowned in 1384, at the age of 10, as Queen Jadwiga. The most dramatic aspect of the succession came two years later, when she was prevailed upon to marry not the duke of Austria (to whom she had been promised), nor even a member of 'western' or even 'central' European royalty or aristocracy, but a pagan ruler, Jogaila, of neighbouring Lithuania. In the space of a century Poland's eastern neighbour had grown from modest beginnings in Žemaitija or Samogitia (roughly present-day north-western Lithuania, and ethnically Lithuanian) to include vast territories, mainly populated by Slavs, stretching almost as far as Moscow in the east, and including Novgorod and Kiev further south. This Grand Duchy now became formally christianised (as much of its subject territory already was). Jogaila took the Polish name Władysław Jagiełło (the dynasty became known as Jagiełłonian), and there began a period of first personal and then constitutional union that was to last until the late sixteenth century. Jagiełło assumed power in Poland (1386–1434), leaving his cousin Vytautas (Witold) as governor and then grand duke of Lithuania, but it was the combined forces of the two territories that proved impressive, as the

Teutonic Order was soon to discover.[19] For most of the fifteenth century, under Jagiełło's sons Władysław VI (1434–44) and Casimir IV Jagiełłończyk (1444–92), this dual monster continued to grow, northwards towards the Baltic, south-east to Galicia, Moldavia and the Black Sea. Yet control over the vast territory of Lithuania was never very effective, and at moments threatened to break down altogether. By the end of the century it was also losing territory, and especially political incentive, to the rulers of Russia.

Poland continued to have close, and by and large co-operative, relations with Hungary and Bohemia. Władysław VI's election as king of Hungary (1440) was part of a plan to strengthen defences against the Turks, and as has been seen the late fifteenth century saw a Jagiełłonian line on the thrones first of Bohemia (from 1471) and then of Hungary (from 1490). These constructive relations, as well as those with the empire, ensured that Poland's western borders remained largely unchanged throughout the period, and also facilitated participation in 'western' life. Poland, like Hungary, saw various manifestations of 'Renaissance' culture, sending its share of law students to Italy, receiving and adopting the ideas of the humanists, and commissioning many works by Renaissance artists. Poland also shared in some of the political characteristics of the other states examined here. Polish monarchs, like those of other states, could only build their authority if they commanded the support or at least the neutrality of the nobles. This was particularly true of a large territory, lightly populated, less urbanised than most. Given the protracted period of weakness in the high Middle Ages, the Polish kings were highly dependent on the support of the landowning class. They needed approval of their authority in the first place—the monarchy was in practice elective—as well as co-operation in raising military forces and taxes, the maintenance of public order and, of particular importance with a comparatively underdeveloped administrative system, the meting out of justice. The monarchs' foreign adventures were designed to maintain that approval and help them rise above local power struggles, but to gain support for these policies they often had to give something in return. Examples of this are the Košice charter of 1374, under which the Louis exempted the nobility from the plough tax and agreed not to raise taxes without the approval of the nobility; the agreement in 1388 that the king would pay knights for foreign military service; guarantees of immunities for the nobility in 1422–34; and the charter of Nieszawa (1454), whereby Casimir IV reaffirmed and expanded the charter of Košice. These measures ensured that the nobility gained steadily over the late Middle Ages. By the late fifteenth century this was increasingly formalised and institutionalised. Approval for fiscal and legislative measures was sought in the two diets of Greater and Little Poland, and by the end of the century a national Diet (*Sejm*) had been established. In 1493 the king's own role in this process was reduced; the free movement of peasants was abolished in 1495, and in 1505 it was established that only nobles could introduce new laws. There are parallels with the Bohemian 'monarchy of the estates', with the difference that the *Sejm* was overwhelmingly dominated by the one group. It has been observed that the true inheritors of Poland on the international scene were the Habsburgs, and on the domestic scene the nobility.[20]

THE TEUTONIC KNIGHTS

It was said at the beginning of this chapter that the view of central European history as dominated by German colonisation and the *Drang nach Osten* was a distortion. In one specific case, however, it is accurate. The German or Teutonic Order of knights, established for crusading purposes, sought new areas of operation after the Third Crusade. King Andrew of Hungary invited them in to Transylvania in 1211, but when they attempted to have the lands they were defending transferred to papal protection they were expelled (1225). Duke Conrad of Mazovia then asked them for assistance against the Prussians, a heathen Baltic people, and in 1226 they began operations in the Baltic. To describe the Order as a political 'loose cannon' would be an understatement. Though the charges levelled against them by contemporaries, as they were against the Templars, took on fanciful dimensions (witchcraft, the murder of their own wounded), there seems little doubt that they were an exceptionally brutal group of fighting men. It was clear from the outset that their mission work was entirely subordinate to their main aim, conquest and empire building. The last of the Prussians was conquered by 1288, but the state kept growing. The extent of the territory they amassed was formidable; 400 miles of coastline, from Gdańsk (which they captured and sacked in 1308, and renamed Danzig) to Estonia, with a substantial hinterland. Moreover, they were highly organised; each new conquest was followed by a programme of colonisation, the establishment of communications and an efficient administration.

While supported by the church, the Teutonic Order also caused moral outrage. To the Polish kings, however, it was seen as a direct challenge. As well as Gdańsk, Pomerania was lost to the Order in 1308 and became its chief power-base, with neighbouring Marienburg (Malbork) the centre of operations. The seemingly unending growth of the state was one of the main motives for the union of Poland and Lithuania in 1386. Over time the new alliance contrived to diminish the Order's authority, though this was a slow process. With the conversion of the Lithuanians the excuse that the Order was there for missionising finally evaporated, but that had no effect. In 1404 the Order took Žemaitija, the ethnic cradle of Lithuania. In 1409 an alliance against it was formed, and the following year it defeated the Order, which had Luxembourg (and therefore Hungarian and Bohemian) support, at the battle of Grunwald (Tannenberg). The battle was subsequently ascribed great significance in the 'German *versus* Slavic' view of history described above, but its only practical outcome was that under the First Peace of Thorn (1411) the Order had to return Žemaitija. Poland launched further military expeditions in the 1430s, in which Czech Taborites joined, and by the 1450s, when the Order was for the first time plagued by serious internal difficulties, Casimir IV felt strong enough to declare his claim to Prussia. A Thirteen Years War followed (1454–66), in which the church continued to support the Order, placing Poland under interdict. It ended with the Peace of Torun (Thorn), and at last some significant gains for Poland in the shape of the western territories, known thereafter as Royal Prussia. The conflict was still not over. A third war, in 1519–21, was also inconclusive, but the Order was then suddenly disbanded in 1525. 'The Reformation achieved at a stroke what the combined forces of Poland and Lithuania had failed to achieve over one and a half centuries.'[21]

CONCLUSION

The story of the Teutonic knights, while untypical in its entirely conflictual history and in the kind of state established, is nonetheless in many ways typical of what east central Europe had to offer. To the end of the Middle Ages, Roman Catholic Europe's easternmost realms consisted of large swathes of territory, with relatively low population levels, enticing opportunities for aggrandisement, trade and the exploitation of resources. The strength of the westernised fourteenth-century monarchies gave the late Middle Ages a new dynamism in the region. Further to the east, 'states', 'empires' and boundaries were volatile, but the comparative stability of the three major powers we have examined gave the European polity a rich additional dimension. That all three of these powers were eventually subsumed into other empires was not of their doing. Ultimately the much larger forces of Istanbul, Moscow and Vienna prevailed. In each case, though, the profound 'European' influence of the Middle Ages remained.

FURTHER READING
General

Jean W. Sedlar, *East Central Europe in the Middle Ages, 1000–1500* (Seattle, Wash., and London, 1994) (vol. 3 of *A History of East Central Europe*, eds Peter F. Sugar and Donald W. Treadgold) is a comprehensive thematic survey; *see also* the older O. Halecki, *Borderlands of Western Civilization: a History of East Central Europe* (New York, 1952). S. C. Rowell, 'The central European kingdoms', in *NCMH*, 5, pp. 753–78, and C. Michaud, 'The kingdoms of central Europe in the fourteenth century', in *NCMH*, 6, pp. 735–63. K. Bosl, A. Gieysztor, F. Graus, M. M. Postan and F. Seibt, *Eastern and Western Europe in the Middle Ages* (1970) contains still useful introductory essays. Lonnie R. Johnson, *Central Europe. Enemies, Neighbors, Friends* (New York and Oxford, 1996), and Robert Bideleux and Ian Jeffries, *A History of Eastern Europe* (London and New York, 1998) are stimulating outlines with good medieval chapters. A. Mączak, H. Samsonowicz and P. Burke, eds, *East-Central Europe in Transition from the Fourteenth to the Seventeenth Century* (Cambridge and Paris, 1985) is a collection of essays, mainly on economic history, on which *see also* M. Małowist, 'Problems of the growth of the national economy of Central-Eastern Europe in the late middle ages', *Journal of European Economic History*, 3 (1974), pp. 319–57; and Bariša Krekić, ed., *Urban Society of Eastern Europe in Pre-Modern Times* (Berkeley and Los Angeles, Cal., 1987). A comparative study of aspects of kingship is G. Klaniczay, 'The cult of dynastic saints in Central Europe: fourteenth-century Angevins and Luxembourgs', in his *The Uses of the Supernatural Power: the Transformation of Popular Religion in Medieval and Early Modern Europe* (tr. Cambridge, 1990, ch. 7, pp. 111–28. For atlases *see* P. R. Magocsi, *Historical Atlas of East Central Europe* (Toronto, 1993) (vol. 1 of *A History of East Central Europe*, cit.), and D. P. Hupchick and H. E. Cox, *A Concise Historical Atlas of Eastern Europe* (London, 1996). *See also* suggestions under Chapter 10.

Hungary

The fullest account in English is now Pál Engel, *Realm of St Stephen. A History of Medieval Hungary*, 895–1526 (London, 2000). P. F. Sugar, P. Hanák and T. Frank, eds, *A History of Hungary* (Bloomington, In., 1990) is an up-to-date introduction; *see also* E. Pamlényi, ed., *A History of Hungary* (London, 1975), and C. A. Macartney, *Hungary. A Short History* (Edinburgh, 1962). Z. J. Kosztolnyk, *Hungary in the Thirteenth Century* (Boulder, Col., 1996) is a full account of the late Árpád period; on the Mongol incursion *see* P. Jackson, 'The Mongols and Europe', in *NCMH*, 5, pp. 703–19, J. R. S. Phillips, *The Medieval Expansion of Europe* (2nd edition, Oxford, 1998), ch. 4, and A. R. Lewis, *Nomads and Crusaders, a.d. 1000–1368* (Bloomington and Indianapolis, In., 1988); on the fifteenth century J. Bak, 'Hungary: crown and estates', in *NCMH*, 7, pp. 707–26. On specific themes *see* S. B. Vardy, G. Grosschmid and L. S. Domonkos, eds, *Louis the Great, King of Hungary and Poland* (New York, 1986); J. Held, *Hunyadi: Legend and Reality* (New York, 1985); J. M. Bak and B. K. Király, eds, *From Hunyadi to Rákóczi: War and Society in Late Medieval and Early Modern Hungary* (Budapest, 1984); E. Fügedi, *Castle and Society in Medieval Hungary* (Budapest, 1984); L. Gerevich, ed., *Towns in Medieval Hungary* (Boulder, Col., 1990); and M. C. Rady, *Medieval Buda: a Study of Municipal Government and Jurisdiction in the Kingdom of Hungary* (New York, 1985).

Bohemia

The richest overview in English is chapter 7 of Robert Bideleux and Ian Jeffries, *A History of Eastern Europe* (London and New York, 1998). M. Teich, ed., *Bohemia. A History* (Cambridge, 1998) is a useful sequence of introductory essays; W. Eberhard, 'The political system and the intellectual traditions of the Bohemian Ständestaat from the thirteenth to the sixteenth century', in *Crown, Church and Estates. Central European Politics in the Sixteenth and Seventeenth Centuries*, eds R. J. W. Evans and T. V. Thomas (London, 1991), pp. 23–47 is useful on the development of the estates. For Bohemia under the house of Luxembourg *see* under chapter 4; on the Hussite revolution *see* under chapter 6. Alfred Thomas, *Anne's Bohemia. Czech Literature and Society, 1310–1420* (Minneapolis, Minn., 1998) is the first full survey in English of the Czech literature of the period.

Poland and Lithuania

N. Davies, *God's Playground: A History of Poland*, vol. 1: *The Origins to 1795* (Oxford, 1981), and O. Halecki, *A History of Poland* (1961; revised edition with additional material by A. Polonsky and T. V. Grommada, London, 1993) are standard works. W. F. Reddaway *et al.*, eds, *The Cambridge History of Poland. I. From the Origins to Sobieski (to 1696)* (Cambridge, 1950, repr. New York, 1978) is still valuable especially for its account of political history, as is A. Gieysztor, 'Medieval Poland', in *History of Poland*, eds A. Gieysztor, S. Kieniewicz, E. Rostworowski, J. Tazbir and H. Wereszycki (Warsaw, 1968). On specific periods *see* P. W. Knoll, *The Rise of the Polish Monarchy. Piast Poland in East Central Europe, 1320–1370* (Chicago, Ill., 1972); O. Halecki, *Jadwiga of Anjou and the Rise of East Central Europe* (New York, 1991); and A. Gieysztor, 'The kingdom of Poland and the grand duchy of Lithuania, 1370–1506', in *NCMH*, 7, pp. 727–47. Collections of essays include A. Gąsiorowski, ed., *The Polish Nobility in the Middle Ages* (Warsaw, 1984) and J. Kłoczowski, ed., *The Christian Community of Medieval Poland* (Warsaw, 1981). On questions of identity Paul Knoll, 'Economic and political institutions on the Polish-German frontier in the middle ages: action, reaction, interaction', in *Medieval Frontier Societies*, eds Roger Bartlett and Angus Mackay (Oxford, revised edition 1992), pp. 151–74 is a wide-ranging and thoughtful article; Andrzej Wyczański, 'The system of power in Poland, 1370–1648', in *East-Central Europe in Transition*, cit., pp. 140–52 is a succinct overview. S. C. Rowell, *Lithuania Ascending. A Pagan Empire within East-Central Europe, 1295–1345* (Cambridge, 1994) charts the dramatic rise of Lithuania before its union with Poland. Finally R. C. Hoffman, *Land, Liberties and Lordship in a Late Medieval Countryside: Agrarian Structures and Change in the Duchy of Wrocław* (Philadelphia, Pa., 1989) is a magisterial study of agrarian history.

The Teutonic Order, the Baltic and beyond

Eric Christiansen, *The Northern Crusades. The Baltic and the Catholic Frontier 1100–1525* (London, 1980, repr. 1997) gives the broadest overview; *see also* M. Burleigh, 'The military orders in the Baltic', in *NCMH*, 5, pp. 743–53, S. C. Rowell, 'Baltic Europe', in *NCMH*, 6, pp. 699–734 and K. Górski, 'The Teutonic Order in Prussia', *Medievalia et Humanistica*, 17 (1966), pp. 20–37; and for the later period M. Burleigh, *Prussian Society and the German Order. An Aristocratic Corporation in Crisis, c.1410–1466* (Cambridge, 1984).

For some of the areas not covered in this book, *see* Birgit Sawyer and Peter Sawyer, *Medieval Scandinavia. From Conversion to Reformation, circa 800–1500* (Minneapolis, Minn., 1993). On Russia three textbooks: J. Fennell, *The Crisis of Medieval Russia, 1200–1304* (London, 1983); R. O. Crummey, *The Formation of Muscovy, 1304–1613* (London, 1987); and J. Martin, *Medieval Russia, 980–1584* (Cambridge, 1995).

NOTES

1. A forceful summary in English of this case is F. Graus, 'Slavs and Germans', in *Eastern and Western Europe in the Middle Ages*, ed. G. Barraclough (London, 1970), pp. 15–42.
2. For discussions on this terminology, *see* Robert Bideleux and Ian Jeffries, *A History of Eastern Europe* (London and New York, 1998), pp. 8–15; Lonnie R. Johnson, *Central Europe. Enemies, Neighbors, Friends* (New York and Oxford, 1996), pp. 3–12; and P. Burke, 'Introduction: a note on the historiography of East-Central Europe', in *East-Central Europe in Transition from the Fourteenth to the Seventeenth Century*, eds. A. Mączak, H. Samsonowicz and P. Burke (Cambridge and Paris, 1985), pp. 1–5.
3. For these territories and others discussed in this chapter, *see* Map 7.
4. The image of these tribes was enhanced, from the late thirteenth century, from the mis-identification of the Magyars with the Huns, at the time a convenient national myth.
5. The demographic consequences of this are particularly important. It is often pointed out that the settlement of the Magyars, as a non-Slavic tribe, drove a wedge between what then came to be thought of as western and southern Slavs. Within a few centuries, though, the intermingling of Germans, Slavs, Magyars, migrant tribes from the east (*see below*) and Jews meant that these ethnic differences were fundamentally attenuated. Hungary was subsequently held together much more by linguistic than by ethnic unity.
6. F. Glatz, *A magyarok krónikayá* (Budapest, 1996), p. 99.
7. *See below*, p. 273.
8. *See below*, p. 273.
9. P. Lendvai, *Die Ungarn. Ein Jahrtausend Sieger in Niederlagen* (Munich, 1999), pp. 78–9.
10. M. de Ferdinandy, 'Ludwig I. von Ungarn (1342–1382)', in *Louis the Great, King of Hungary and Poland*, eds S. B. Vardy, G. Grosschmid and L. S. Domonkos (New York, 1986), pp. 3–48 (pp. 9–10). *See above*, p. 234.
11. *Above*, Chapters 4 and 6.
12. *Above*, p. 258.

13. P. Pamlényi (ed.), *A History of Hungary* (London, 1975), p. 108.

14. *See below*, p. 271, and Chapter 6.

15. He was nicknamed *dobže* ('all right') because of his habit of agreeing to everything.

16. *Above*, p. 70.

17. *Above*, pp. 73–4.

18. *See above*, p. 256.

19. *See below*, pp. 275–6.

20. A. Mączak, 'Poland', in *The Renaissance in National Context*, eds Roy Porter and Mikuláš Teich (Cambridge, 1992), pp. 180–96 (p. 186).

21. N. Davies, *God's Playground: A History of Poland*, vol. 1: *The Origins to 1795* (Oxford, 1981), p. 121.

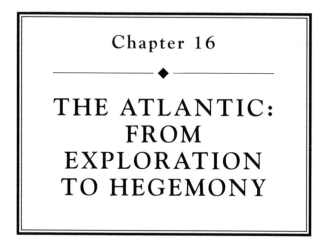

Chapter 16

◆

THE ATLANTIC: FROM EXPLORATION TO HEGEMONY

INTRODUCTION

It is a commonplace that the 'closure' of the eastern Mediterranean world in the fourteenth and fifteenth centuries in due course provided the stimulus for the opening up of other frontiers, eventually resulting in the spectacular 'discovery' of the New World in 1492. This is almost by definition an economic interpretation, yet it is clear from the history of the explorations and discoveries that political interest and will was also necessary if they were to be translated into something permanent. Long-distance travel and exploration were hardly new phenomena; Vikings had reached North America centuries before (though colonies were not sustained beyond Greenland), while the many eastward journeys of Italian and other merchants and missionaries, epitomised above all in the *Travels of Marco Polo*, are ample evidence of curiosity and appetite for trade and souls. Nor were such activities limited to particular countries; the Atlantic, indeed, was being explored, fished and colonised by Danes, Icelanders, Basques, Castilians, Portuguese, English, Flemish and French, sometimes in co-operation and often with multinational financial support. The transformation of this free-for-all into a world of imperial powers had a more than purely economic explanation. This chapter focuses on the country whose initiatives were to prepare the world for the idea of maritime empires based in the Atlantic, even if like so many pioneers it was not destined to become the greatest beneficiary of that effort.

PORTUGAL AND OVERSEAS ENTERPRISE

The fundamental divisions between Portugal and 'Spain' that are so evident from the late fifteenth century were far from obvious at the time.[1] The history of medieval Portugal demonstrates several parallels with that of the other parts of the Iberian peninsula that were discussed in Chapter 12. Like both Castile and Aragon, Portugal provides strong contrasts between north and south; like both it had had its Reconquest, with all the social consequences that entailed; and like both, it had a chequered late medieval political history. By and large the Portuguese monarchy proved more stable than either. Successions and regencies were in the main handled better, or at least with less damaging consequences. There were quarrels over the succession at the beginning of the reign of Dinis (1279–1325); actual rebellion after the death of Fernando I (1367–83), which led to the accession of João I (1385–1433) and the new dynasty of Avis; and divisions over the regency of Afonso V (1438–81), aged six at his father's death. The second of these was Portugal's biggest late medieval crisis, but in each of these cases the outcome was a long and comparatively peaceful reign. As in Aragon but in contrast to Castile, in the more compact Portugal the Crown had a stronger and from its point of view ultimately more successful relationship with its subjects. Although the revolution that established the house of Avis in 1385 has sometimes been portrayed as a triumph of bourgeois over aristocratic interests, this is a simplification. In fact the interrelationship between nobility and merchant interests was intricate, if often tense, and this relationship was to be a determinant feature of the course of Portuguese exploration and expansion.

A recurrent theme of Portuguese politics was the uneasy relationship with its sole land neighbour, Castile. This has already been mentioned in connection with the dynastic rivalries that preceded the marriage of Ferdinand and Isabella;[2] it was nothing new, and indeed had dominated the second half of the fourteenth century. War broke out between the two countries in 1335–6 (under Afonso IV, 1325–57), and three times under Fernando I, when Portugal became involved in the 'Iberian phase' of the Hundred Years War, allying itself with England and Aragon in opposition to Castile.[3] With the unrest after the death of Fernando relations with Castile reached a low point; within months of João's proclamation as king a substantial Castilian invasion force was dispatched to contest the succession. The smaller Portuguese forces successfully resisted it at Aljubarrota (14 August 1385), ensuring the independence of Portugal for two centuries, but the state of war between the two countries persisted from 1385 to 1411. The crisis of the 1380s has thus often been seen as a turning-point in the formation of Portuguese national identity, in much the same way as the Hundred Years War for France.

Notwithstanding what it had in common with other parts of Iberia, in geographical terms Portugal was quite differently situated. Like Aragon on the other side of the peninsula, it had an extensive and dominant seaboard, but, uniquely, one with no obvious European counterparts. Its access to the most obviously thriving theatre of trade of the time, the Mediterranean, was restricted by Castile. Geographical circumstance thus meant that any foreign enterprise other than direct conflict with Castile would be maritime, and would take unusual forms. Maritime trade, exploration and eventually colonisation were simply natural activities for a people in this position, though there is nothing preordained or inevitable about the energy and resilience with which they pursued them.

In fact Portugal's geographical isolation was more apparent than real. As has been seen, sea travel in this period was much more important than is often imagined; it could certainly be quicker than many land routes, and in some respects safer and cheaper as well.[4] Remote as it was from many areas, Portugal had a considerable Hanseatic trade, while its position made it a natural refuelling point for traffic between the Mediterranean and the Atlantic. Moreover, the technical problems and initial investment necessary for maritime activity, not to mention its purpose and variety of destinations, gave the world of the sea a cosmopolitan flavour that descriptive accounts of national endeavour cannot adequately convey. The Portuguese employed the technological innovations that made possible long-distance navigation and sailing. Improvements in manoeuvrability such as the central rudder and the triangular or lateen sail, and navigational tools such as the compass and later the astrolabe and the quadrant, were taken from elsewhere, while the caravel, the most typically Portuguese vessel that allowed fast coastal and shallow-water travel, may well have been a perfection of an Arabic model. An understanding of the world was equally international. The names of Spanish, Italian and German geographers and cartographers are inseparably interwoven with the history of Portuguese exploration. If the leaders of Portuguese-backed expeditions—mostly Portuguese but including a number of Italians—acquired their expertise and knowledge during their voyages, they also passed at least some of it on to an eager cosmopolitan community. The Portuguese had no monopoly of explorations, still less of the technical achievements and the financial backing that made them possible. It was a genuinely international enterprise. What they did was to develop a sustained and systematic programme of exploration that became a focus for international interest and eventually, after almost a century, culminated in the celebrated discoveries that unleashed European 'expansion' across the globe. The Portuguese role in this process has aptly been described as that of 'detonator'.[5] If in retrospect it has been eclipsed by the even more significant discovery of the Americas, it is nonetheless an indispensable preliminary to it. The foundations of colonialism and global empire building were laid by them, and the rapidity with which this was achieved was due to the solidity and extent of those foundations.

Portuguese outward enterprises fall into discrete geographical categories, each with its own rationale.[6] Chronologically the first is Morocco; the near-continuous story of Portuguese expansion is usually dated back to 1415, when the thriving Muslim city of Ceuta, on the north African coast but at the Mediterranean end of the straits of Gibraltar, was captured, after preparations which began soon after the cessation of hostilities between Portugal and Castile in 1411. The event was a landmark, of more symbolic than actual significance, and it illustrates the complex mix of Portuguese interests. The rulers of the Maghrib had been responsible for the last attempted Islamic invasion of the peninsula in 1340 (they were beaten off by a rare alliance of Portugal and Castile), and since that time the Portuguese were mindful of their claims in Africa, which they saw as a legitimate objective of reconquest; Morocco had once been Visigothic. The Maghrib also offered trading opportunities, and the strategic value of a hold on the straits of Gibraltar—together with the possibility of blocking putative Castilian interests in Morocco—were also factors according to the later fifteenth-century chronicler Azurara. Government documents of the period tell us little about the reasons for the decision to attack Ceuta, but it is clear that it caused some concern in the Mediterranean, and also that it was controversial at home. Both the capture of Ceuta and the continuation of Portuguese interests in the Maghrib throughout the fifteenth century were expensive in terms of resources—economic and human—and it is doubtful whether they were of any long-term economic or political benefit. But the symbolic value of the holding was clear, and is perhaps the main explanation for the persistence with which the Portuguese conducted their Moroccan policy.

The Moroccan enterprise was soon followed by others in different directions. A second area of activity was the Atlantic islands. Interest in these dated back to the fourteenth century if not earlier. The Canaries, known since Roman times and redis-covered probably in the late 1330s by Portuguese and other sailors, were the largest group in extent, but were already the subject of conflicting attentions; a Catalan expedition had been there in 1342, Castile had applied to the pope for the right of possession in 1344 and began to settle in the islands in 1402. In the 1420s Portugal began to colonise those islands not yet in Castilian hands, but the two countries con-tinued to dispute them until Castile's rights were confirmed and accepted in 1479. Meanwhile in 1420 the Portuguese settled on Madeira, also known since the mid-fourteenth century but uninhabited. Further north but considerably further from the mainland lay the Azores, which the Portuguese may have reached by accident in the 1340s[7] and which they began to colonise in the late 1420s. The final archipelago to become Portuguese was the much more southerly Cape Verde Islands, reached in the late 1450s or early 1460s and colonised soon after. Considered as specks on the map, none of these small clusters of islands appears very promising, even though some—notably the larger of the Canaries and Madeira—were by no means insig-nificant in size and, eventually, population. Their value was in the first instance strategic, as forward positions and provisioning stops for seafarers bound further, as trading posts and as garrisoned deterrents to other potential interlopers. Small islands could be held much more easily than mainland territory, as Venetian and Genoese sailors and entrepreneurs, already heavily involved in Portuguese enter-prises, knew well from their experiences in the Mediterranean. But beyond that, all these archipelagos very soon acquired considerable economic importance of their own, as will be seen. Taking all these possessions together Portugal already had an empire of sorts, even if it was nothing compared with what was to follow.

To posterity the most famous of the Portuguese areas of enterprise was of course west Africa. For 60 years a series of expeditions steadily advanced European knowledge of the coastline of Africa. Despite the excitement these discoveries clearly generated, we will eschew 'the cape-by-cape depiction of the building of empire' which has rightly been described as a 'heroic distortion'.[8] It must be pointed out, though, that the efforts were consistent (often with several expeditions per year), cumulative in effect (unsurprisingly, since it is a coastline that was being 'discovered') and rapidly consolidated. The most significant highlights were perhaps not so much the rounding of capes or landmarks as the discovery of river-mouths and indigenous populations—for example the discovery of the river Senegal (1444), to which the Portuguese soon returned, exploration of the Gulf of Guinea generally (1470–5), and the discovery by Diogo Cão of the Congo (1483, with a second venture soon after). The culmination of these successive expeditions came at the end of the century, first with the rounding of the Cape of Good Hope by Bartolomeu Dias in 1487, which in turn gave the green light for the key Portuguese achievement, Vasco da Gama's extension of that journey across the Indian Ocean to Calicut on the southwestern Indian coast (1497–99).

Of course it would be another false perspective to assume that, because the Portuguese reached India by sea in 1498, that was where the expansion had been directed since 1415. However there is one element of truth in this, in turn obscured by the accidental discovery of America; Asia had indeed been a key objective in much of the exploratory efforts of the fifteenth century. This in turn leads us to the question of what motivated the explorations. Of the standard possible causes of 'outthrust', two can quickly be discounted. There seems to have been no serious demographic pressure for expansion in Portugal, whose population probably did not exceed one and a half million by the end of the fifteenth century,[9] and in which there are none of the standard signs of excessive population density relative to its capacity to feed itself. Indeed, it may be significant that an estimated two-thirds of the crews of these expeditions came from the more sparsely populated part of Portugal that lay to the south of Lisbon.[10] Second, intellectual curiosity may well have existed, both among geographers influenced by humanistic culture and among the explorers themselves; but it could hardly be said to have played a key part. The figure most closely connected with this is supposed to have been prince Henry, brother of king Duarte and son of João I and Philippa of Lancaster, whose reputation and nickname, 'The Navigator', were the creation of nineteenth-century Portuguese and English historians. Although Henry's responsibility for much of the exploration has not been questioned—it is claimed that 74 per cent of recorded voyages between 1415 and 1460 are attributed to his initiative[11]—his status as intellectual inspiration, creator of the astronomical and cartographic school of Sagres and so on has been completely demolished. A third motive, religious fervour, is more complex. Undoubtedly the theme of reconquest in the first instance, and subsequently of proselytisation among pagans, accompany the Portuguese initiatives throughout, and a recurring theme is the desire to find the kingdom of Prester John, the legendary Christian ruler beyond the Muslim world whose aid in suppressing Islam had been sought variously from the thirteenth century onwards. However it is questionable whether, for example, the force which reached the Gambia in 1445–6 and captured more than 100 slaves, by going into action with cries of 'São Jorge, Santiago, Portugal' were expressing more than the standard and obligatory pieties. It would be as misleading to diagnose religious fervour from the standard imprecatory heading of late medieval account books. None of the more revealing indicators— the degree of involvement of the Church, the number and role of priests on the expeditions, the extent of conversion—point to religious motivation as the predominant factor, at least during the fifteenth century.[12]

By contrast, the economic motives of the organisers, investors and explorers are beyond question. The seas beyond Portuguese waters offered richer fishing opportunities, and seals—used for oil and for their skins—became a sought-after commodity. These represent extensions of an important existing element of the

Portuguese economy. The desire to access the luxury eastern markets—spices above all—while bypassing the tightening Muslim grip on the eastern Mediterranean and Near East undoubtedly weighed not only with the Portuguese but with other merchants, notably Italians, who offered to participate in the Portuguese ventures, though these were slow to yield the full results anticipated from the east itself. The most high-profile appetite was for gold, which several historians describe as the driving force behind the explorations. This financially high-risk quest paid off from the 1440s when gold and pepper began to be brought back from Guinea, though it is questionable whether the volume of gold imported ever matched the expectations of investors. In terms of results, two other commodities came to play a much greater role, and in tandem they transformed the nature of colonialism. Sugar, long a small-scale product of the Iberian peninsula, but more traditionally an import from the Muslim world, was ideally suited to the climate and terrain of many of the Portuguese islands which, being uninhabited, needed settlers and agriculture if they were to be held. Sugar has been described as the key to Portuguese colonisation. Sugar cane was planted in Madeira from the mid-fifteenth century, and within a decade had transformed the island, bringing spectacular prosperity and an international community. By the end of the century its population had risen from an estimated 800 to perhaps 20,000.[13] It also came to dominate the economy of the Canaries in the years after the final decision in favour of Castilian sovereignty, with large merchant proprietors and sharecroppers from many parts of Europe, among them a predominance of Portuguese, setting up and prospering.

Sugar cultivation in these islands depended on a form of organisation, the plantation, found chiefly in border and colonial territories. The sugar boom of the Atlantic islands was consolidated with the help of the other, darker economic achievement of Portuguese expansion, the dramatic revival of the slave trade. Though long abolished in much of Europe and frowned on by the Church and specially in northern Europe, slavery had been reintroduced, particularly in the Mediterranean; in some Italian cities eastern domestic slaves were almost a fashion accessory by the fifteenth century. The indigenous population of the Canaries had provided an early new source of slaves, and here Castilian, French and Italian freebooters had indulged in the trade before the Portuguese. The expeditions along the west African coast, however, opened up a new source and a new dimension of the traffic in humans. From 1441, when the first black slaves were captured, the growth in the trade was dramatic. At least a thousand slaves were imported into Portugal in the following seven years, and by the 1450s an average of seven to eight hundred entered Europe each year through the Algarve and Lisbon. The Guinea coast was a particular target. The trade soon developed its own structures on and off the coast, first with trading posts at Arguim (from the late 1450s or early 1460s) and later São Jorge de Mina (1482), and on a larger scale with the colonisation of the Cape Verdes in the 1460s. These were used both as a holding area and as an experiment in a new model of farming, the slave-based plantation, producing cotton. The success of this encouraged the further use of slaves in the sugar economies of Madeira and eventually the Canaries. Most slaves were in fact not captured but bought, either from Muslim traders or from black rulers who had criminals or prisoners of war for sale.

Throughout this discussion initiatives have been described as Portuguese, but frequent references have also been made to international interests and participation. It is worth noting how this functioned. The Portuguese Crown had a central place in all such voyages, since from pope Nicholas V's bull of 1434 it had exclusive rights over all discoveries '*usque ad Indios*' (as far as the Indies). In practice this control could be delegated, as it was to the king's brother, Henry the Navigator, and even auctioned off, as later in the century. In economic terms, this was basically franchising. The Crown licensed and controlled both expeditions and trade within current and future Portuguese territory, took a healthy cut of revenue, kept a close eye on operations through government *feitores* or factors and could make stipulations about their destinations or results (for example, blocking the export of slaves to Castile). What the Crown never did in the fifteenth century was to finance the expeditions directly; and by and large the kings also refrained from excessive intervention in the commercial decisions of the entrepreneurs themselves. This 'decentralised' model worked particularly well for the island colonies, which drew in venturers from France, Flanders, Italy and elsewhere. The capital-intensive sugar industry of Madeira was funded largely by Genoese bankers, and all the islands had an international merchant presence. 'The Iberian islands formed a sort of "enterprise zone" of new exploitation.'[14] This liberal approach meant that, rather than competing *with* Portuguese trade, the more centrally placed international merchants were competing *for* it, and bringing their experience, capital and contacts to Portugal. One further example: the intense Flemish interest in the Azores—known as the 'Flemish Isles' because of the widespread belief that the Flemish had discovered them—increased contacts with Flanders and eventually gave Portugal a more important northern European outlet. By the sixteenth century the sugar staple (market) at Antwerp was the largest dealer in Portuguese sugar.

Royal control was not always beneficial. The franchising arrangements, or the programme of expeditions itself, could be interrupted or deflected for political reasons; Portuguese 'overseas' policy was a proper issue for debate and often a matter of controversy. In the later fifteenth century a number of political factors led to the interruptions of the programme at some critical junctures. A couple of examples will suffice to illustrate the kind of factors at work. In 1469 Afonso V granted the entrepreneur Fernão Gomes a six-year monopoly of exploration. Despite Gomes's many achievements in this period, the auctioning of licences that had brought about this monopoly led to mounting opposition, and in 1474 the monopoly was rescinded and oversight was given to the Infante (heir to the throne), Dom João. Another change to policy was made in the same year; the successful expansion of Portuguese territory in Morocco was halted in favour of Afonso's grand designs on the Castilian throne. Conflict with Castile effectively held up expansion for five years, until the treaty of Alcáçovas settled that the Canaries would remain Spanish and the islands south of it and the African coast Portuguese. The early 1480s saw an energetic resumption of expeditions, but after Dias' rounding of the south of Africa there followed another pause, this time of 10 years, for reasons that have never been satisfactorily fathomed. Divisions over the policy of expansion, other domestic and foreign distractions, the news of Columbus' discovery and the death of João II in

1495 probably played their part; in any case, the pause was not so long as to threaten what had been achieved, though it did critically offer Castile the chance to seize the limelight.

THE FOUNDATIONS FOR TWO EMPIRES

The peculiarities of royal control are at least part of the explanation for what is usually presented as one of the most famous missed opportunities in history, Portugal's rejection of the proposals of Columbus. The tale is almost too well known to need recounting. The Genoese sailor arrived in Portugal in 1476 after being shipwrecked; he married there and spent years in Portuguese service, acquiring the skills of Atlantic navigation and building on the experiences of others. In 1483 or 1484 he asked João II to fund his plans to reach India by sailing westward; they were rejected by the king's experts (and also incidentally by Ferdinand and Isabella, whose efforts were focused on the conquest of Granada, in the following year). It seems likely that João's scholars recognised behind the proposal the calculations of the Florentine mathematician Paolo Toscanelli, who grossly underestimated the circumference of the globe and thus the distances and dangers of the enterprise; ironically the Portuguese may have had enough geographical sophistication to reject the very foolhardiness that would eventually take Columbus to the New World. It must also be said that the request for finance was highly unusual; as has been seen at this stage the Portuguese monarchy was not in the habit of funding expeditions, let alone outrageously expensive ones such as this. Columbus laid a second proposal before João in 1487/88, arousing more interest, but when the news of Dias' rounding of Africa arrived he was rejected again. In the fateful hiatus of the Portuguese exploration programme that followed, Columbus finally persuaded the Catholic kings to give their support—though it was a close call—and the rest is a story that the Portuguese would rather forget or, in some cases, attempt to modify.

The episode also neatly epitomises the essential differences in approach between the two future colonial powers. During the course of the fifteenth century the Portuguese approach of behind-the-scenes control of essentially independent capital venture had opened up the Atlantic for overseas exploration, yet at the critical moment what turned out to be the biggest prize in that undertaking went elsewhere. The Castilians—and Columbus—had the immense fortune of making a discovery that no one had or could have anticipated (and that the discoverer himself refuted, believing until his death that he had reached India), and the Portuguese can hardly be blamed for not discovering something that was neither on the conceptual map nor anywhere near their sphere of operations. However the point to be stressed is that Castile was also far better placed to exploit that discovery immediately and to the full. If for the Portuguese trade had come first, for the Castile the priority was conquest, and the momentum for Crown-led, religiously inspired unification extended readily into the New World. Much was made in Spain of the 'meaningful chronology'[15] of the events of 1492 (Columbus himself recalled it as the year of conquest, expulsion and discovery), but behind the instant opportunity for mythologising were also a number of solid factors that help to explain the conquests. Many historians have stressed the continuity between the political, socioeconomic and cultural mechanisms of the Reconquest—from El Cid in the eleventh century through to Granada in 1492—and the construction of the empire in the New World. The primacy of religion as underpinning territorial conquest, the subjugation and colonial rule of an indigenous population, the control and exploitation of vast underpopulated tracts of land—all these were familiar challenges. And while it would be simplistic to argue for exact parallels, in respect of at least one fresher component of the problem—long-distance control over not an infidel but a pagan population—the Castilians had effectively had the opportunity of a 'dress rehearsal' in the Canaries, thanks to which the intellectual questions about how Christians should treat pagans—with the full gamut of approaches from mystification and disgust through to the idealisation of the 'noble savage'—had already been widely aired. The code for the treatment of indigenous peoples that would become the basis for the Spanish empire in the New World was enacted by Isabella in 1504, just over a decade after the news of the discovery.

The Portuguese programme of exploration was not deflected by the discovery of the New World; on the contrary, it was accelerated and refined. The Treaty of Tordesillas (1494) resolved the decades-old conflict over the demarcation line between Spanish and Portuguese possessions, and over the following decades its implications, and the outlines of the future empires, soon became clear. Vasco da Gama's pioneering voyage was followed in the opening years of the sixteenth century by Afonso de Albuquerque's occupation and control of the Persian Gulf, from which in the first two decades of the century the Portuguese established naval supremacy in the Indian Ocean. Meanwhile in 1500 Pedro Álvares Cabral had also landed in the New World, paving the way for Brazil to become Portugal's westernmost colony. Spain financed further expeditions by Columbus, who himself became a viceroy and governor in the New World; with the establishment of a court in Haiti in 1511 Spanish colonial administration began a continuous history, on which were built the conquest of Mexico (initiated in 1519) and Peru (from 1532). The geographical division of power is only one aspect; the style and approach of the two empires also varied, though competition drew them closer, and in time the Portuguese empire too became more centralised and absolute in its stance. The relationship between Spanish and Portuguese expansion had both serendipitous and symbiotic elements, a combination of complementary features that was felicitous for both powers, though hardly for its countless victims.

FURTHER READING

Introduction

The history of Portuguese and Spanish explorations and discoveries is best studied in the context of Europe's perceptions and exploration of the outside world throughout the period. Felipe Fernández-Armesto, 'Exploration and discovery', in *NCMH*, 7, pp. 175–207 is a cogent overview; *see also* Wolfgang Reinhard, 'The seaborne empires', in *Handbook of European History 1400–1600*, eds Thomas A. Brady jr., Heiko A. Oberman and James D. Tracy (Leiden, 1994–5, paperback Grand Rapids, Mich., 1996), vol. 1, pp. 637–64. J. R. S. Phillips, *The*

Medieval Expansion of Europe (2nd edition, Oxford, 1998) is the best full introduction, and has an extensive bibliography. *See also* F. Fernández-Armesto, *Before Columbus. Exploration and Colonisation from the Mediterranean to the Atlantic, 1229–1492* (London, 1987); P. Chaunu, *European Expansion from the 13th to the 15th Centuries* (tr. Amsterdam, 1978); E. Burman, *The World before Columbus, 1100–1492* (London, 1990), an accessible read; more broadly still, G. V. Scammell, *The World Encompassed: the First European Maritime Empires, c.800–1650* (London, 1981), and M. Mollat du Jourdain, *Europe and the Sea* (Oxford, 1993). K. A. Seaver, *The Frozen Echo. Greenland and the Exploration of North America ca A.D. 1000–1500* (Stanford, Cal., 1996) has much of relevance to Iberian exploration despite its title. Lohn Larner, *Marco Polo and the Discovery of the World* (New Haven, Conn., and London, 1999) is an important work tracing the influence of this pioneer on both understanding and imagination; Janet L. Abu-Lughod, *Before European Hegemony. The World System A.D. 1250–1350* (New York and Oxford, 1989) is a stimulating assessment of European culture in the global context in the earlier half of the period. Finally two useful collections of essays are Felipe Fernández-Armesto ed., *The European Opportunity* (Aldershot, 1995) and Stuart B. Schwartz, ed., *Implicit Understandings. Observing, Reporting, and Reflecting on the Encounters Between Europeans and Other Peoples in the Early Modern Era* (Cambridge, 1994).

Portugal and overseas enterprise

Armindo de Sousa, 'Portugal', in *NCMH*, 7, pp. 627–44 is a recent general introduction to the fifteenth century. General histories in English are A. H. de Oliveira Marques, *A History of Portugal*, 2 vols (New York, 1972); H. V. Livermore, *A New History of Portugal* (Cambridge, 1966) and H. V. Livermore, *Portugal. A Short History* (Edinburgh, 1973); the latter focuses on the social history of the country. Ferrão Lopes, *The English in Portugal, 1383–1387* (Warminster, 1988) is a translation of chronicles.

Bailey W. Diffie and George D. Winius, *Foundations of the Portuguese Empire 1415–1580* (Minneapolis, Minn., 1977) gives the fullest account of the Portuguese explorations and expansion; *see also* C. R. Boxer, *The Portuguese Seaborne Empire, 1415–1825* (2nd edition, Manchester, 1991), ch. 1, and A. J. R. Russell-Wood, *A World on the Move. The Portuguese in Africa, Asia and America, 1415–1808* (Manchester, 1992), a broad, non-chronological portrait. On prince Henry and the legend that has accrued around him, P. E. Russell, *Prince Henry 'the Navigator'. A Life* (New Haven, Conn., and London, 2000); and M. Newitt, 'Prince Henry and the origins of Portuguese expansion', in M. Newitt, ed., *The First Portuguese Colonial Empire* (Exeter, 1986), pp. 9–35. On the context of Portugal's interest in Africa, *see* Robert Mantran and Charles de la Roncière, 'Africa opens up to the old worlds', in *The Cambridge Illustrated History of the Middle Ages, III, 1250–1520*, ed. Robert Fossier (Cambridge, 1986), pp. 256–95. E. Axelson, *Congo to Cape. Early Portuguese Explorers* (New York, 1973) covers the voyages of Diogo Cão and Bartolomeu Dias; Sanjay Subrahmanyam, *The Career and Legend of Vasco da Gama* (Cambridge, 1997) is a much acclaimed study from a multicultural perspective.

On the technical aspects of exploration, *see* the extensive bibliography in Phillips, *Medieval Expansion of Europe*, cit. R. W. Unger, *The Ship in the Medieval Economy, 600–1600* (London and Montreal, 1980) is an authoritative introduction to many aspects of shipping. Jerry Brotton, *Trading Territories. Mapping the Early Modern World* (London, 1997), ch. 2 is a penetrating study of cartographic aspects of the Portuguese initiatives; for a fuller overview of the subject *see* J. B. Harley and D. Woodward, eds, *The History of Cartography*, I. *Cartography in Prehistoric, Ancient and Medieval Europe and the Mediterranean* (Chicago, Ill., and London, 1987). The colonisation of the Canaries is covered thoroughly in Felipe Fernández-Armesto, *Before Columbus*, chs 6 and 8; Eduardo Aznar Vallejo, 'The conquests of the Canary Islands', in Schwartz,

Implicit Understandings, cit., pp. 134–56; John Mercer, *The Canary Islanders: Their Prehistory, Conquest, and Survival* (London, 1980); Joseph F. O'Callaghan, 'Castile, Portugal, and the Canary Islands: claims and counterclaims, 1344–1479', *Viator*, 24 (1993), pp. 287–309; and for the later period in Felipe Fernández-Armesto, *The Canary Islands after the Conquest. The Making of a Colonial Society in the Early Sixteenth Century* (Oxford, 1982). James Muldoon, *Popes, Lawyers and Infidels: The Church and the Non-Christian World, 1250–1550* (Philadelphia, Pa., and Liverpool, 1979) discusses the church's attitude to non-Christians generally. For the legend of Prester John, *see* R. Silverberg, *The Realm of Prester John* (Athens, O., 1972, paperback 1996).

On the slave trade *see* A. C. de C. M. Saunders, *A Social History of Black Slaves and Freedom in Portugal, 1441–1555* (Cambridge, 1982), and more generally Hugh Thomas, *The Slave Trade The History of the Atlantic Slave Trade 1440–1870* (London, 1997), William D. Phillips, *Slavery from Roman Times to the Early Transatlantic Trade* (Minneapolis, Minn., 1985), and C. Verlinden, 'Some aspects of slavery in medieval Italian colonies', in his *The Beginnings of Modern Colonization* (Ithaca, N.Y., 1970), ch. 4.

The foundations for two empires

On Columbus the best of many biographies is Felipe Fernández-Armesto, *Columbus* (Oxford, 1991); *see also* W. D. Phillips, Jr., and C. R. Phillips, *The Worlds of Christopher Columbus* (Cambridge, 1992). On the Spanish empire, *see* J. H. Parry, *The Spanish Seaborne Empire* (London, 1966), and his *The Age of Reconnaissance: Discovery, Exploration and Settlement, 1450–1650* (London, 1963, 3rd edition Berkeley, Cal., and London, 1981).

NOTES

1. Even the linguistic division is not clear-cut; the future Spain included Catalan and Basque speakers, while the Galician of the north-western corner of the peninsula had much in common with Portuguese.
2. *Above*, p. 222.
3. *Above*, p. 219. The alliance made in 1373 with England, and confirmed in 1386, had a long subsequent history. Its consequences included a dynasty which was partially English by descent, but it was of little significance during the fifteenth century and lay in abeyance in the sixteenth.
4. *See above*, p. 29.
5. F. Braudel, *Civilization and Capitalism, 15th–18th Century*, vol. 3, *The Perspective of the World* (tr. London, 1984), p. 138.
6. *See* Map 8.
7. For a discussion of this contentious matter *see* F. Fernández-Armesto, *Before Columbus. Exploration and Colonisation from the Mediterranean to the Atlantic, 1229–1492* (London, 1987), pp. 161–6.
8. F. Fernández-Armesto, 'Exploration and discovery', in *NCMH*, 7, pp. 175–201 (p. 191), quoting A. J. R. Russell-Wood, *The Black Man in Slavery and Freedom in Colonial Brazil* (London, 1982), p. 20.
9. H. V. Livermore, *Portugal. A Short History* (Edinburgh, 1973), p. 77.
10. J. Serrão and A. H. de Oliveira Marques, eds, *Nova Historia da Expansão Portuguesa*, II, *A Expansão Quatrocentista*, eds A. H. de Oliveira Marques and Paulo Drumond Braga (Lisbon, 1998), pp. 207–8.
11. Ibid., p. 166.

12. With papal approval the Portuguese Church contributed to the Ceuta campaign to the modest tune of 9,000 florins per annum for a period of three years, but there is little evidence of subsequent contributions.

13. Bailey W. Diffie and George D. Winius, *Foundations of the Portuguese Empire 1415–1580* (Minneapolis, Minn., 1977), p. 305.

14. Fernández-Armesto, *Before Columbus*, cit., p. 200.

15. Miguel Angel Ladero Quesada, 'Spain, circa 1492: social values and structures', in *Implicit Understandings. Observing, Reporting, and Reflecting on the Encounters Between Europeans and Other Peoples in the Early Modern Era*, ed. Stuart B. Schwartz (Cambridge, 1994), pp. 96–133 (p. 131).

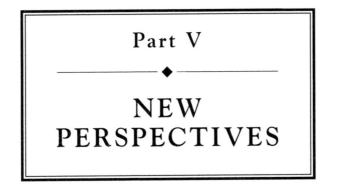

Part V

NEW
PERSPECTIVES

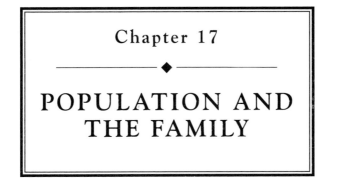

Chapter 17

◆

POPULATION AND
THE FAMILY

INTRODUCTION: MEDIEVAL DEMOGRAPHY

The rise of demographic history in recent years has brought a very technical subject to the attention of more general historians. Clearly nothing could be more crucial to an understanding of Europe's medieval past than a knowledge of how many people inhabited it and their life expectation. Here there can be room only to suggest the interest of the subject by putting forward some general considerations; to attempt a full coverage would be quite impracticable.

Many of the principal factors affecting the population structure of medieval Europe are so different from those prevailing in Europe (but not in parts of the developing world) in the late twentieth century that some preliminary discussion is necessary. It should first be noted that historical studies of population are dogged by inadequate sources and hence there is a natural tendency for writing on demographic history to be much concerned with these sources. A consequence of the patchy and controversial nature of the evidence is the need to present conclusions with the greatest caution, though in practice this had not always prevailed. The high incidence of infant mortality (birth, followed by death within one week, which was extremely common, often went unreported) is merely one of the elements which make statistical treatment unreliable. Direct information regarding the birth rate is rarely available, therefore it is usually necessary to investigate it by means of calculations concerning the distribution of the population into different age-groups. At times when the recent birth rate had been high the percentage of the population that was still in childhood could be very high indeed.

Crucial for the birth rate and for the size of the population was the normal age at marriage, particularly that of women. Much depended on whether women married early on in their fertile years; if they did not do so they were likely to give birth to a smaller number of offspring. The average age of men at marriage was also a factor of some (though less) importance. There was probably a general tendency for husbands to be considerably older than wives and this increased the chances that the wife would be widowed. Widowhood was a common experience for both women and men, but they would normally expect—perhaps with more certainty in the case of men than of women—to remarry. The widowhood of women, when experienced during their fertile years, even if it was not lengthy, served as a check on the birth rate. To have been married several times was not at all uncommon, to have never married was much more unusual than in the western world today. In particular it seems to have been rare for women to remain unmarried. The English poll tax returns of 1377 suggest that 70 per cent of women aged above 15 were married. Remarriage for widows did not, of course, necessarily imply new families of off-spring; the tendency to find a new spouse was marked among women above child-bearing age, as well as among younger ones.

For many couples the advent of another child meant an increasing burden and greater poverty. Did many medieval families seek to prevent the regular appearance of new offspring requiring to be fed? The question is a difficult one and the little evidence available is controversial and hard to interpret. When the gaps between the births of later offspring are longer than those between earlier births there is a presumption that some form of birth control was practised, but there was never any system of reporting births anywhere in medieval Europe such as to leave certain evidence of this state of affairs. Nevertheless some statistics suggest quite strongly the limitation of the number of births. Moreover passages in medieval religious manuals and sermons, emanating from various parts of Europe, imply that married couples were guilty of the sin of having 'unnatural' marital relations in order not to conceive. In *The Parson's Tale* Chaucer mentions abortion and also, as contraceptive measures, the drinking of 'herbs' and 'unnatural' intercourse. Altogether it seems highly probable that some parents took successful measures to avoid the burden of nourishing an additional child.[1]

In many parts of Europe it was normal for those possessing sufficient money to employ the services of a wet-nurse. In Florence, as we shall see, this practice was widespread. Humanists and churchmen alike condemned it, though the validity of their claim that children 'out to wetnurse' were less likely to survive infancy is debat-able. Another factor defying investigation is the 'exposure' of infants. In the late Middle Ages the foundation of the Roman hospital of S. Spirito by Pope Innocent III (1198–1216) was attributed to his having had a dream of fishermen in the Tiber bringing back nets full of the bodies of unwanted babies. The pope's dream, or the story of it, is likely to have had at least some foundation in fact.

To suggest a correlation between poverty and birth rates is perhaps to imply the Malthusian view that when standards of living were low any rise in population would necessarily be halted. However there is a good deal of evidence to suggest that the population continued to increase over much of Europe in the thirteenth and early fourteenth centuries despite the pressures of food shortage and malnutrition. Poor harvests and low real wages were not on their own direct causes of death and enough children survived to give birth to new generations. The experience of being predeceased by the majority of the children born to them was common to most mar-ried partners and in wills the wish to be buried 'next to my children' was frequently expressed.[2] Naturally the better-off married younger, had more (surviving) children and lived longer. A study of British ducal families in the fourteenth and fifteenth centuries suggests that even in this favoured milieu 36 per cent of males and 29 per cent of females died before the age of five. For those who reached 20, the further expectation of life was 21.7 years for males and 31.1 for females. If these figures seem surprisingly weighted against the men it needs to be recalled that nearly half (46 per cent) of the males in these families who attained the age of 15 met with a violent death; in the period 1730–79 the figure was a mere 4 per cent. Expectations, however, were high for those tough individuals who attained 60. The males among them had a further life expectancy of 10 years, the females of 8.2.[3]

The medieval mortality rate was always subject to great fluctuations and this applied particularly to that for children. The summer months were the worst season, at least in England and Italy, both for the gastro-intestinal deaths common among children, and for death from fever or plague among those of all ages. Child mortality from the plague was always extremely high. Young adults stood a better chance of survival but with the onset of age the chances probably diminished, though there is some evidence that those exposed to the disease may have gained immunity or at least stronger biological resistance.

Estimates that one-quarter of Europe's population perished in the Black Death of 1348–9 are probably too cautious. Figures from particular localities are always open to the well-founded objection that they may not be typical (and Europe comprises so large an area that no specimen regions can be a statistically respectable sample). The manor of Halesowen, in the English Midlands, is known from surviving court records to have had 203 male tenants at the outbreak of the Black Death. During the three months between May and July 1349, at least 68 of the 203 met their deaths. In all some 40 to 45 per cent of the adult male inhabitants of Halesowen died during this outbreak of plague.[4] Figures for manors in various other parts of England, for the parish clergy and for certain monastic houses, suggest that Halesowen escaped comparatively lightly. The lowest percentage of mortality for these, in the Black Death, is 45 per cent, the highest 65 per cent. Yet it should be clear that historians cannot hope to chart statistically the demographic consequences of the plague, partly because, whereas the most widespread outbreaks were recorded at the time, serious local and regional ones were less remarked. The converse, namely local and regional areas of immunity amid large-scale epidemics, may also apply.

Rates of demographic recovery after the great plagues of the mid- and late fourteenth century have been much debated by historians. Everywhere plague remained endemic in the fifteenth century. In Tuscany two deaths out of five were from the plague as late as 1424–30. In Provence recovery began in some areas in the 1430s, in others not till the 1470s. Demographic decline in England probably continued to the mid-fifteenth century (when the population was perhaps equal to that of William the Conqueror's time) and the level of the fourteenth century may not have been equalled again till the middle of the sixteenth. The immediate consequences of the Black Death included a greatly increased number of marriages, since many had been widowed and others who could not normally have expected to marry so soon had unexpectedly inherited land and money. Peasants would only marry when they had the wherewithal in the form of a cottage and smallholding—they did not have to be on a considerable scale—to start a family. The plague of 1348–9 brought such circumstances to many sooner than anticipated, though in their turn many of these would be prematurely swept away.

The preceding general remarks have done no more than introduce some aspects of medieval demographic history. Nothing has been said of psychological aspects— on which future historians will certainly have plenty of theories to propound— though one can hardly pass by the normal age difference of a decade or so between husband and wife without mentioning that this must have reinforced the former's commanding status. Nor is it adequate to discuss population in terms of total numbers while saying nothing of location. Many studies have shown striking changes in the whereabouts of settlement. Travellers in the Val di Spoleto in Umbria looking towards Monte Subasio and the bare hilly region above Assisi would be surprised to learn that in the thirteenth century this zone teemed with flourishing villages and farmsteads which did not go into decline until the sixteenth.[5] Elsewhere such changes have affected even larger areas. In the early Middle Ages the population of inland (upper) Provence had been greater than that of maritime Provence, but the late medieval demographic decline was far more acute in the former region, where the population decreased by perhaps 75 per cent between the mid-fourteenth and mid-fifteenth centuries. Now 90 per cent of the population of Provence lives on or close to the sea. In general the late medieval and subsequent decline was most marked on the higher land and in mountainous areas, where hilltop sites were deserted in favour of the plain or the route thereto. Montaillou, 1,300 metres up in the Pyrenees and the subject of a famous book by Emmanuel Le Roy Ladurie, had some 250 inhabitants in the early fourteenth century, although methods of transport were so primitive that no wheeled vehicle was known there. By the late fourteenth century the population was no more than a hundred, and the medieval site is no longer occupied, though the present village is not far from it.

However meagre the sources for the demography of medieval Europe may be, exceptional patches of information have survived. Among these, evidence concerning food consumption in towns may be included, but not the area occupied by the site of the towns, which in itself gives little indication of the size of the population. The overwhelming majority of medieval Europeans, however, lived not in towns but in the countryside. Figures concerning their numbers, when known, have been preserved through the activities of various institutions of government and these had in view their own fiscal requirements—not the requirements of future historians. One consequence is that the very poor, capable of yielding nothing to the tax gatherer, tend to be absent. An authority on Provence suggests that the fiscal returns there in the late Middle Ages omitted between one-sixth and one-third of the male population on the grounds that they were exempt through poverty, but such generalisations can only indicate an average, and at Tarascon in 1392 there were more exempt (421) than payers (360).[6] The privileged, or those taxed in other ways, might also be omitted, and such elements—the clergy, Jews, sometimes nobles and 'foreigners'— could be very numerous.

A CASE STUDY: FLORENTINE TUSCANY IN THE EARLY FIFTEENTH CENTURY

After all these explanations and provisos it is time to present a single source and to see what may be learnt from it. In 1427 the ruling magistrates of Florence decreed the introduction of a form of tax (technically it was a loan) known as the *catasto*. This involved the preparation of an inventory of the wealth of households in Florence and its territory, an area which extended over most of Tuscany, including the regions formerly under Pisa and Arezzo.[7] Some 11,000 square kilometres came into the survey, which included about 60,000 households, possessing between them rather over a quarter of a million members. There was no intention of listing the population as such, the *catasto*'s concern being the financial assets of households, not their numerical strength. The returns had, however to include the ages of members of households, though the ages given are approximate only. They were 'rounded off' and the proportion which are multiples of 10 (in particular), 5 and 6 is far too high. Apart from the omission of the clergy and a few territories which secured an early exemption, the *catasto*'s main imperfection from the viewpoint of the demographer is the considerable under-registration of women and children.

For all their deficiencies, there is a great deal to be gained from the *catasto* returns, and not merely about demographic matters. We learn that one Tuscan in seven (in the region covered) lived in Florence, one in four in the 10 largest towns (including Florence) of the region, one in three in 'a town' (taking a population of 800 to constitute the dividing line between town and village). Over 60 per cent of the 'populated places' recorded had fewer than 100 inhabitants and one in five lived in such a locality. The distribution of resources was very uneven indeed, in every respect. The wealth of a Florentine household was, on average, some five times greater than that for the territory as a whole and Florentines owned over half the landed wealth, as well as three-quarters of the commercial wealth and almost the entire stock of the republic's funded debt. The average household in a secondary town declared a figure for wealth which was one-quarter that of the average Florentine household, while for rural areas the figure was only one-quarter that of the secondary towns. In other words, the figure for Florence was 16 times that for the countryside. The average investment in commerce for a Florentine household was over 600 florins; Pisa, with 154, came far behind, yet it was ahead of the other cities. Within Florence itself the richest 1 per cent of the population (some 100 households) had over a quarter of the city's wealth and thus one-sixth of that of the territory as a whole. Among these a very few outstandingly wealthy families, such as the Strozzi, Bardi and Medici predominated. While the wealthiest 5 per cent of Florentine households had more than all the rest combined, nearly one household in three in the city had no taxable wealth. The concentration in the other cities was similar.

Florence differed greatly from its subject area, including the towns, in that more than half its families were engaged in trade, industry or crafts. The proportion in the other considerable urban centres was about one-quarter. In these places the share of 'agriculturalists' in the population tended to be below 10 per cent (though Volterra with 23 per cent was an exception) but it rose to one in five or even one in three in lesser towns such as Montepulciano and S. Gimignano. Outside the towns some two-thirds of households lived mainly by agriculture and about one in five of these were *mezzadri* ('sharecroppers'), dividing the proceeds of their farm with the land-lord, who was himself usually a Florentine investing in agriculture. Sharecropping was commonest in the regions close to Florence itself, particularly to the south and east; in the Appenines and the largely pastoral Maremma (in the south-west) a fixed rent or peasant ownership still tended to predominate. A sharecropping tenancy implied the provision of capital by the landlord and in the zone where *mezzadria* was most frequent half the peasants had no taxable wealth to declare.

On the question of the migration of the population the *catasto* returns provide only indirect information. The little evidence there is suggests a rather low degree of mobility except within the Florentine territories themselves. Few outsiders, even from other parts of the Italian peninsula, settled in Tuscany but there was some emigration to France and Spain, no doubt connected with trading activities. The main movement in the fifteenth century, as it had been earlier, was from the countryside into the principal cities, especially Florence and Pisa. As many as one Florentine family in four or five had settled in the city within the previous decade, which had already been the case in the later fourteenth century and probably earlier still. Though these immigrants included those 'on the way up', who brought money with them, it is likely that most of them were from the poor, driven by the weight of their indebtedness and the hope of employment, perhaps as manual workers in the textile industry.

The 'rounding off' of ages mentioned above is a hindrance to an analysis of the age structure of the Tuscan population, but not a fatal one. It is clear that a quite high proportion of the population comprised what would now be called 'senior citizens'; something like one in seven was over 60, one in 10 over 65. Despite the plagues of the preceding years there had been enough births to achieve a large ele-ment of young also: some 37 per cent of the population was aged 14 or below. This left a surprisingly small proportion of adults who were not yet elderly. Only two-fifths of the population were aged between 20 and 60. The proportion of young was highest among the well-off, no doubt because more of their children survived the perils of the earliest weeks of life. The fact that the population of the city itself was younger than that of its territory is perhaps explained by the emigration in search of work mentioned above, as well as by the poverty of the mountain regions, where people married later and had fewer children.

The Tuscans married early and often. A very high proportion of the women married; of girls who reached the age of 15, nine out of ten would marry before they were 20. At the age of 50, only about one man in 20 was unmarried, though it was a good deal less rare for a man to remain unmarried at Florence than it was in the country. The average age at marriage for women was about 19 (rather below this in Florence, rather higher in the country), but in general men did not marry so young and an age gap between spouses was the rule. For men the average age at mar-riage was about 24 in the country, about 28 in towns. Thus the age difference was less marked in the countryside, though there it was subject to quite large regional variations. In rural areas the richer peasants married younger, as one would expect, whereas in the town preoccupation with economic prospects (apprenticeship in the family firm, accumulation of capital, organisation of dowries in the case of wealthier families and so on) tended to prescribe later marriage for the richer. When men became widowers they usually remarried, commonly a wife younger than the one they had lost, hence second and third families were frequent and step relationships a normal feature of life. With widowers seeking young wives, the marriage prospects of widows were less good and the proportion of widowed women remarrying was certainly much lower than that for men, although the usual age difference made widowhood a very frequent eventuality.

In general the possession of more money went with more children, or at least more surviving children. An apparent tendency for childbearing to continue longer outside the towns may be evidence for the existence of checks on fecundity. Spare hands for the work of the fields and pastures were needed and rural households welcomed children to fill gaps that had arisen from death or emigration. The very high marriage rate among sharecroppers illustrates this need for labour.

The mortality rate, like the birth rate, was extremely high by the standards of the modern West, even if it fluctuated greatly. Discussion of an 'average' year is more or less meaningless, since a bad plague year might bring about a mortality rate of over 30 per cent, which was perhaps ten times greater than the rate in a healthy year. Fluctuations probably affected the rates for children even more than those for adults; in 1400 the death rate for children was 12 times the average, for married women five times, for widows double. Perhaps half the deaths were those of children. Naturally childbirth was a perilous event, for mother as well as infant. Among all married women, one death in five was in childbirth and the incidence for those of childbearing age must have been considerably higher. Nevertheless it is probable that more women than men survived to die of old age. Although there is no great disparity, the figures suggest that Florence itself was a less healthy place to live in than the other Tuscan towns or the countryside.

The information derivable from the *catasto* returns makes our knowledge of Tuscany at this time totally exceptional, yet the fundamental question must be: to what extent can Tuscany serve as an exemplar of fifteenth century Europe as a whole? If it was not at all a typical region, the findings derived from the *catasto* clearly lose their right to take up much space in a book devoted to 'Europe'. In fact the findings of the considerable quantity of research published on the medieval demography of other parts of Europe—in particular England and France—are sufficiently in line with the *catasto* for it to be clear that it is not necessary to write off Tuscany as totally atypical. On the other hand it certainly cannot be accepted as completely representative. The predominantly agrarian nature of medieval (and early modern) Europe is not fully reflected in Tuscany, where the development of towns had been precocious. The urban element bulked larger in Tuscany than it did in almost any other part of Europe, the main exceptions being Flanders and the western and central parts of northern Italy. Even if only one in three Tuscans lived in an urban environment,[8] the proportion would have been far lower in almost any other part of Europe—probably at any period between classical antiquity and the eighteenth century. Tuscany's peasants, with their comparatively ready access to urban markets and employment, cannot figure as typical medieval peasants, whatever the continuing seclusion of their mountainous regions.

If Tuscany was considerably too urban to be average, it may also have comprised an untypically immobile population. Italian traders[9] travelled in Europe and the Levant, often settling outside the peninsula in their younger years, but it was usual for them to return to the city on which their commercial activities were based. Pisans and Florentines overseas were temporary exiles, rarely settlers. Furthermore they were unlikely to become citizens of other Italian republics except in rare circumstances of political misfortune. The situation was quite different in the Middle Ages among German merchants of the Hanse and other towns, who appear to have been willing to marry and put down roots wherever they traded. Thus the Besserer family which originated in Ulm (in Swabia) had branches at Constance, Ravensburg, Memmingen, Überlingen and Leutkirch.[10] Also there were regions of Europe which experienced immigration on a very considerable scale in the late Middle Ages, some of it from long distances. There were, for example, settlements of Germans in Slav areas, such as Bohemia, and movements by Italians into the Languedoc and other parts of France—not to mention emigration from the Balkans, the Iberian peninsula, Ireland and elsewhere, with religious division adding its contribution to the propellant force of economic circumstances. Compared with such areas Tuscany was unchanging in its population and little affected by outside developments.

FAMILY STRUCTURES, STRATEGIES AND SOLIDARITIES

The growth of research into demographic matters has been accompanied by increasing interest in the social institution of the family. Despite indications that medieval marriage could be fragile in practice, that bigamy may have been widespread and illegitimacy not uncommon, it remains true that the family is the essential unit through which population history must be approached. Fiscal records such as the Florentine *catasto* normally involved the institution of the household and hence demographic research has necessarily been driven to concern itself with that unit and particularly the vexed question of the numerical coefficient between households and total population.

'The Medieval Household Large or Small' is the characteristic title of one learned article,[11] and the answers given to this enquiry have differed very widely indeed. It is common ground that household size must itself have varied greatly according to economic and social circumstances. Analysis of the 1427 *catasto* itself makes this sufficiently clear, since the average number of residents per household was 3.8 for the city of Florence and 4.74 for rural areas. In Florence the size of household rose regularly according to wealth, but in the countryside this was often related to tenure rather than wealth; only 20 per cent of sharecropping households numbered fewer than four members, whereas the figure for peasant households possessing no taxable property was 35.5 per cent. Moreover it is not clear that in Tuscany towns had always had smaller households than the countryside. Some figures suggest the contrary situation, as do those proposed for medieval Provence (5.5 for towns, 4.5 for rural districts). At Nuremberg in 1431 there were 5.3 inhabitants per household. A coefficient of 3.6 has been offered for medieval England as a whole, but this is certainly too low.

A commonly held view is that the predominance of the 'nuclear' (two-generation) family household is a recent phenomenon—and indeed some discern in this development the root of many contemporary ills, social and psychological. Accompanying this view is a picture of an ideal household in the past, replete with wise grandmothers, sympathetic aunts and an ideal proportion of active breadwinners to domestic passengers. The notion that 'the greater the antiquity, the more extended the family' seems, however, to be a myth. The coexistence under the same roof of three (or more) generations is a possibility dependent on life expectation and age at marriage. In fifteenth century Italy joint households including brothers and involving other relatives on the husband's side were fairly common, though not so much so as to constitute the norm. In his treatment of three Florentine families F. W. Kent suggests that 'each type of household was a stage in the life cycle of a particular group of Rucellai, Ginori or Capponi'; 'most members of the three lineages spent at least one phase of their lives in a fraternal or grand-family'.[12] Thus the composition of the household (and this seems obvious enough) would depend largely on the age of its members. Although there was an inevitable process of change and development, the principal factor governing the incidence of multi-generation households must have been the length of expectation of life. However there were significant topographical differences. The 'extended' household was uncommon among the Florentines (though less so among the wealthy), rather commoner at Arezzo, more so still in Arezzo's country districts. In the city of Arezzo itself, which may be taken as coming close to the Tuscan average, 54 per cent of households were conjugal in 1427, while 11 per cent comprised a couple plus one 'ascendant' widowed person. The latter was much more likely to be related to the husband than to the wife, family sentiment and organisation being strongly agnatic (deriving from the male line).

The number of people comprised in a 'hearth' or household is a significant social datum available (in some cases) to demographers and therefore analysed by them. However, one has learnt very little indeed about a family or lineage from knowing how many of them live under the same roof. Every sort of variety is possible in the extent to which, and manner in which, families not living under the same roof keep in touch—or fail to do so. These matters are more difficult to investigate, but the scarcity of evidence does not prevent them from being the essence of social history. Some families not living together drift apart or are forced apart by the circumstances of life, others remain neighbours and meet almost daily or eat together frequently and regularly, others succeed in maintaining touch by correspondence (which can be valuable as source material for the historian) or seek to do so and fail. Weddings and funerals, business meetings formal and informal, are all relevant to an analysis of the family. Indeed the nature of the relationships between relatives who do *not* live together, rather than the 'household', is the crucial aspect of kinship and the family as a social institution, for they define the strength of its cohesion.

Legal arrangements, particularly those governing inheritance and ownership, provide evidence concerning the relative strength of family cohesion and in turn influence its operation. Joint inheritance and co-ownership were common in medieval law. While they were not guaranteed to contribute to family harmony, such arrangements necessitated continuing collaboration between brothers and other co-heirs. In Italy it was normal for all sons to inherit equally and this often involved complicated business negotiations and recourse to arbitration. A long period of co-ownership between brothers might follow their inheritance, until eventually ownership was sorted out, by a process of division, after which individual ownership would again prevail. Such temporary (but often lengthy) arrangements had to be formalised on account of the fiscal and military obligations which continued to be borne in common by the inheriting 'consorts'. The complications of co-ownership were of considerable importance. When the Florentine Guelfs were driven into exile in the 1260s[13] and their property was subject to confiscation, no less than 36 per cent of this property was found to be jointly owned by 'consorts'.

Inheritance by more distant relatives is a good test of the nature and strength of the family's fabric. In later medieval Germany the numerous legacies made by merchants to great-nephews, great-nieces, cousins and other quite distantly linked members of their families are confirmatory evidence of a strong feeling of kinship. Katharine von Wanebach of Frankfurt left money (in 1334) to no fewer than 17 relations.[14] Wills such as hers, in which the intended beneficiaries were named, even though their survival was not certain, reveal pride in a very considerable genealogical knowledge. A Pisan will of a century later (1433) shows the same awareness. Caterina de Marco, a widow, asked to be buried next to her husband in the cloister of St Francesco at Pisa and named as her heirs not the descendants of her own brother but two orphans who were grandsons of her husband by his first marriage. In the event of the failure of this line, the succession was to pass to 'whichever of their family, as closely related as possible (*in propinquiori gradu*) shall be the poorest among the *consortes*. If this (poor) man should die without leaving children' he should be succeeded by another poor relative 'and so, in perpetuity, let one poor man succeed to another. The property is never to be sold or alienated but must always pass to whomever is the poorest among the *consortes*'. Among the executors of the will were to be 'the senior (*antiquiores*) men of the said *consortes* and house of Sancasciano'. This testatrix hoped to protect representatives of her late husband's family against the danger of falling into poverty and disgrace, by providing a financial lifeline to whichever of them was most likely to suffer such a fate. Thus her intentions went beyond the mere perpetuation of the family as a co-operative and self-aware entity.[15]

Wills are more likely to be preserved than is evidence of financial assistance given to relations in the lifetime of the donor, yet such aid must have been a commonplace event. The Velluti family chronicle (to return once more to Florence) records assistance to nephews (helping them in business), to nieces (with dowries), particularly when the recipients were orphans, to a *seventh* cousin, who was set up in business as a dyer, and to the same cousin's illegitimate brother, who was given a start as a merchant.[16]

Family memoirs and chronicles. which were a feature of several parts of Renaissance Europe, were a testimony of pride and also a conscious stimulus, intended to ensure the continuation of family self-awareness. The Overstolz in fifteenth century Cologne ambitiously traced an ancestry back to the time of the emperor Trajan. The Florentine equivalents (*ricordi*) of such chronicles were less genealogically enterprising, but they were compiled in the same way from information *da piu antichi huomini di casa nostra* ('by the oldest men of our lineage') and were intended for reading aloud, within the family circle.[17]

Pride in descent and feeling for the lineage manifested themselves in public as well as private forms. The role of family patronage in the Italian Renaissance has already been mentioned.[18] The great churches of the time were to a remarkable extent churches of great families, with family chapels. The facade of S. Maria Novella at Florence, built in the 1460s and 1470s at the expense of Giovanni Rucellai, bears his signature and the Rucellai arms. The family had already provided a handsome white marble pulpit, also displaying their arms, in the same church. Family chapels within these churches provided the setting for intercessory masses said on behalf of the souls of ancestors. Tombs are perhaps the most evident surviving testimony to the dynastic ethos of the Italian Renaissance, but the churches were in continuous receipt of visible patronage from the wealthy, in the form of paintings, tabernacles, tapestries and draperies, liturgical vestments and service books.

The chapels had their secular counterparts in the major architectural manifestations, the monumental palaces, which enjoyed a particular prestige as tangible symbols of success and had to be kept within the family at all costs. The will of the Florentine Giovanni Rucellai[19] directed that his palace should not be the residence of anyone save his descendants. Any attempt at alienation was to be punished by deprivation and allocation, on the same condition, to 'the oldest member of the Rucellai family'. Like Caterina de Marco, Giovanni was willing that the most distant of his kin should be sought out as the heir, though his criterion was seniority in age, whereas hers had been poverty. It should be recorded that the *palazzo* is still occupied by the Rucellai.

The politics and the economics of the medieval or Renaissance city are incomprehensible without an understanding of the operation of the family link. In seeking purchasers or tenants for property, or in making an exchange, relatives were to be preferred. It was relations who gave financial advice, put one in touch with the right people, assisted in negotiations as agents and arbitrators. The family, naturally, was the most usual basis of the business firm.

The political way of life and constitutions of the cities, however great or small their degree of self-government, were indeed dependent on the notion of family solidarity. The most visible and extreme product of that solidarity—and at the same time the guarantor of its continuity—was the vendetta or blood feud. The fourteenth century Perugian legist Baldus explained the obligation on all members of a family to take up offensive weapons in appropriate circumstances 'since injury done to one blemishes the entire house'.[20] At a less dramatic level, men intervened constantly to seek political and fiscal advantages for their relatives, while a man unable to take up office would have his place taken by another member of the same family.

The more extensive the family, the less was it certain that all its members would agree on political issues. Nevertheless tradition was strongly influential in such matters and it was realistic of Italian cities to assume family co-operation as the norm—hence the *divieto* legislation limiting the contemporaneous holding of office by members of the same family. The effect of such laws must have been to reinforce the solidarity to which they bore witness.

Reference has already been made to temporary co-ownership within the family, but permanent corporative ownership by groups within families, by kinship groups and by allied groups drawn from more than one family was an even more important element in the social fabric. Such groups of co-possessors, commonly called *consorzerie* in Italy, sometimes evolved institutions designed to 'tie up' property within a family, sometimes comprised a sort of superstructure transcending the family group. In the latter case they were a family by analogy, comparable with 'brothers in arms'. As a social institution their role was that of a horizontal link; though they might possess clients and retainers, the 'consorts' themselves were essentially equals. The property held in common between consorts might be a city tower designed for residence and defence, but could also comprise lordship over widespread lands and associated rights. Thus the 'nobles of Ripafratta' (in the region of Lucca) had their own officials ('consuls' and 'rectors'), possessed jurisdiction over their own men and levied tolls. Such family groups were a common feature of central and northern Italy and probably of other parts of Europe.

Two further instances will serve to illustrate the phenomenon of an organised group of families. At Metz the leading patricians were organised in *paraiges*, of which there were five by the middle of the thirteenth century and later six. In time each *paraige* (like the English 'peer' the word derives ultimately from the classical Latin *par*, meaning 'equal') came to be divided into four branches. Members of a *paraige* tended to have family connections (not necessarily in the agnatic line) and to live in adjacent quarters of the city. The formal constitutional role of the *paraiges* at Metz was to divide proportionately between them the city's various municipal offices.

At Genoa the institution of *alberghi* (inns) had a not dissimilar but even more important function. These *alberghi* numbered 64 in the later fourteenth century, though the number was later diminished. Around the mid-fifteenth century the average Genoese *albergo* comprised a membership of between 20 and 30 heads of families, though one (the Spinola) had as many as 134. An *albergo* might elect annual officials to settle disputes among its own members and recourse to external law courts in matters concerning the institution itself was forbidden. These powerful states within the city-state also had their own churches and their own investments from the proceeds of which they ran systems of poor relief. The *albergo* typifies well the great wealth and diversity of social institutions in later medieval Europe. The emphasis placed in this book on the growing strength of the nation-state must not be interpreted as implying that it gained a monopoly of authority. In that respect Luther's Europe was a very long way from Orwell's 1984, or anybody else's. Family, guild, parish, city, region were all among the many forces which exerted rival magnetisms.

FURTHER READING

Introduction: medieval demography

No single work can serve as a comprehensive introduction to medieval demography; introductions to specific aspects are listed in the sections below. Overviews of the later part of our period can be found in Jan de Vries, 'Population', and Merry E. Wiesner, 'Family, household, and community', both in *Handbook of European History 1400–1600*, cit. Surveys of historiography include Janet L. Nelson, 'Family, gender and sexuality in the Middle Ages', in *Companion to Historiography*, ed. M. Bentley (London, 1997), pp. 153–76, and L. R. Poos, 'The historical demography of Renaissance Europe: recent research and current issues', *Renaissance Quarterly*, 42 (1989), pp. 794–811. Individual works on specific communities include, famously, E. Le Roy Ladurie, *Montaillou: Cathars and Catholics in a French Village, 1294–1324* (tr. London, 1978; paperback Harmondsworth, 1980); and, more technically, Z. Razi, *Life, Marriage and Death in a Medieval Parish. Economy, Society and Demography in Halesowen, 1270–1400* (Cambridge, 1980).

English evidence is plentiful. General works include J. Hatcher, *Plague, Population and the English Economy 1348–1530* (London, 1977) and B. Hanawalt, *The Ties that Bound. Peasant Families in Medieval England* (Oxford, 1986). J. L. Bolton, 'The World Upside Down: plague as an agent of economic and social change', in *The Black Death*, eds M. Ormrod and P. Lindley (Stamford, 1996), pp. 17–78 revives the theme of the rise of the nuclear family and 'individualism' as eventual outcomes of the Black Death; T. H. Hollingsworth, 'A demographic study of the British ducal families', in *Population in History: Essays in Historical Demography*, eds D. V. Glass and D. E. C. Eversley (London, 1965), pp. 354–78 studies a smaller group.

A case study: Florentine Tuscany in the early fifteenth century

The fundamental work on which much of the discussion here is based is D. Herlihy and C. Klapisch-Zuber, *Tuscans and their Families: A Study of the Florentine* catasto *of 1427* (English edition, New Haven, Conn., and London, 1985). The database which underpins the research is now consultable on the internet: http://www.stg.brown.edu/projects/catasto/overview.html. Many other scholars have contributed to the rich picture of fifteenth century Florentine families and demography: *see especially* R. A. Goldthwaite, *Private Wealth in Renaissance Florence. A Study of Four Families* (Princeton, N.J., 1968); F. W. Kent, *Household and Lineage in Renaissance Florence. The Family Life of the Capponi, Ginori and Rucellai* (Princeton, N.J., 1977); G. Brucker, *Giovanni and Lusanna. Love and Marriage in Renaissance Florence* (London, 1986), a fascinating vignette; A. Molho, *Marriage Alliance in Late Medieval Florence* (Cambridge, Mass., 1994); Louis Haas, *The Renaissance Man and His Children. Childbirth and Early Childhood in Florence, 1300–1600* (Basingstoke and London, 1998); R. C. Trexler, *The Women of Renaissance Florence* (Binghamton, N.Y., 1993) and *The Children of Renaissance Florence* (Binghamton, N.Y., 1993). On Italy more generally (though often with a Florentine focus) *see* the excellent introductory essays in Judith C. Brown and Robert C. Davis, eds, *Gender and Society in Renaissance Italy* (London, 1998); C. Klapisch-Zuber, *Women, Family and Ritual in Renaissance Italy* (Chicago, Ill., 1985); T. Kuehn, *Law, Family and Women: Toward a Legal Anthropology in Renaissance Italy* (Chicago, Ill., 1991); S. K. Cohn, Jr., *Women in the Streets. Essays on Sex and Power in Renaissance Italy* (Baltimore, Md., 1996); and T. Dean and K. J. P. Lowe, eds, *Marriage in Italy, 1300–1650* (Cambridge, 1998). Finally Duccio Balestracci, *The Renaissance in the Fields. Family Memoirs of a Fifteenth-Century Tuscan Peasant* (University Park, Pa., 1999) sheds valuable light on the life of a sharecropper.

Family structures, strategies and solidarities

Considered introductions to the history of the family over a long period are M. Mitterauer and R. Sieder, *The European Family. From Patriarchy to Partnership, from the Middle Ages to the Present* (Oxford, 1982), and J. Goody, *The European Family. An Historico-Anthropological Essay* (Oxford, 2000); *see also* J. Goody, *The Development of the Family and Marriage in Europe* (Cambridge, 1983), and J. Goody, J. Thirsk and E. P. Thompson, eds, *Family and Inheritance: Rural Society in Western Europe 1200–1800* (Cambridge, 1976). The models that have dominated discussion of marriage patterns and household formation are set out in J. Hajnal, 'European marriage patterns in perspective', in *Population in History: Essays in Historical Demography*, eds D. V. Glass and D. E. C. Eversley (London, 1965), pp. 101–43, and J. Hajnal, 'Two kinds of pre-industrial household formation system', in *Family Forms in Historic Europe*, ed. Richard Wall (Cambridge, 1983), pp. 65–104; on inheritance a similarly fundamental work is David Gaunt, 'The property and kin relationships of retired farmers in northern and central Europe', in the same volume, pp. 249–79. The reader will soon discover that these are highly technical areas.

There are several introductions to medieval households, families and family life, all syntheses of extensive detailed local work. *See* in particular D. Herlihy, *Medieval Households* (Cambridge, Mass., and London, 1985); A. Burgière, ed., *A History of the Family* (tr. Cambridge, 1996), vol. 1, *Distant Worlds, Ancient Worlds*, Part 2; and G. Duby, ed., *A History of Private Life, II. Revelations of the Medieval World* (Cambridge, Mass., and London, 1988). There is extensive literature on medieval women, and no brief survey could hope to do it justice; introductions include E. Ennen, *The Medieval Woman* (tr. Oxford, 1989); S. Shahar, *The Fourth Estate. A History of Women in the Middle Ages* (tr. London, 1983); and C. Klapisch-Zuber, ed., *Silences of the Middle Ages*, vol. 2 of *A History of Women in the West*, eds G. Duby and M. Perrot (Cambridge, 1992). M. Sheehan, *Marriage, Family, and Law in Medieval Europe*, ed. J. K. Farge (Cardiff, 1996) is a collection of essays. Many aspects of childhood and child-rearing have been explored. P. Ariès, *Centuries of Childhood* (tr. London, 1962) effectively spawned the topic by his largely rejected—but also widely misrepresented—argument that pre-industrial societies had a limited concept of childhood. S. Shahar, *Childhood in the Middle Ages* (London, 1990) is the broadest introduction. Other topics covered here are discussed more fully in J. Boswell, *The Kindness of Strangers: the Abandonment of Children in Western Europe from Late Antiquity to the Renaissance* (London, 1988), and V. Fildes, *Wet Nursing. A History from Antiquity to the Present* (Oxford, 1988). Finally S. Shahar, *Growing Old in the Middle Ages: Winter Clothes Us in Shadow and Pain* (London, 1997), M. M. Sheehan, ed., *Aging and the Aged in Medieval Europe* (Toronto, 1990), and P. Ariès, *The Hour of Our Death* (Harmondsworth, 1983) may help the student trace this immense topic to its logical conclusion.

NOTES

1. For the evidence *see* J. T. Noonan, *Contraception. A History of its Treatment by the Catholic Theologians and Canonists* (Cambridge, 1966), pp. 200–30, and Angus McLaren, *A History of Contraception from Antiquity to the Present Day* (Oxford, 1990), ch. 4. *The Parson's Tale*: see the section 'de Ira', in *The Riverside Chaucer* (3rd edition, Oxford, 1988), pp. 304–9.
2. *See* P. Ariès, *The Hour of Our Death* (tr. Harmondsworth, 1983), pp. 75–6. Ariès, concerned with people's wishes about the location of burial, makes no comment on the demographic implications of such a request!
3. T. H. Hollingsworth, 'A demographic study of the British ducal families', in D. V. Glass and D. E. C. Eversley, eds, *Population in History* (London, 1965), pp. 354–78.

4. Z. Razi, *Life, Marriage and Death in a Medieval Parish, Economy, Society and Demography in Halesowen, 1270–1400* (Cambridge, 1980), pp. 99–113.

5. A. Grohmann, 'Per una tipologia degli insediamenti umani del contado di Assisi', in *Assisi al tempo di S. Francesco. Atti del V convegno internazionale della società internazionale di studi francescani* (Assisi, 1978), pp. 181–246.

6. For all references here to the demography of Provence we are indebted to E. Baratier, *La demographie provencale du XIIIe au XVIe siècle* (Paris, 1961).

7. The following section is based on D. Herlihy and C. Klapisch-Zuber, *Les Toscans et leurs Families. Une étude du catasto florentin de 1427* (Paris, 1978), of which there is a revised and abridged English version, *Tuscans and their Families. A Study of the Florentine Catasto of 1427* (New Haven, Conn., and London, 1985).

8. *See above*, p. 299.

9. *See above*, pp. 35–6.

10. E. Maschke. *Die Familie in der deutschen Stadt des späten Altmittelalters* (Heidelberg, 1980), p. 85.

11. J. T. Krause in *Economic History Review*, 2nd ser., 9 (1956–7), pp. 420–32.

12. F. W. Kent, *Household and Lineage in Renaissance Florence. The Family Life of die Capponi. Ginori and Rucellai* (Princeton, N.J., 1977), p. 43.

13. *See above*, pp. 32–3.

14. Maschke, *Die Familie*, cit., pp. 15–16.

15. M. Luzzati, 'Familles nobles et familles marchandes à Pise et en Toscane dans le Bas Moyen Age' in *Famille el Parenté dans l'Occident Médiéval*. Collection de l'École française de Rome, 30 (Rome, 1977), pp. 275–96.

16. C. M. De la Roncière, 'Une famille florentine au XIVe siècle: les Velluti' in *Famille el Parenté*, cit., pp. 227–48.

17. Maschke, *Die Familie*, cit., p. 24: Kent, *Household and Lineage*, cit., p. 278n. The fourteenth century Florentine Giovanni Morelli remarked sceptically that 'nowadays everyone wishes to claim a foundation in great antiquity', but he merely knew that his own ancestors had come to Florence 'three centuries ago or longer'. *Ricordi*, ed. V. Branca (Florence, 1956), pp. 81, 83.

18. *Above*, pp. 161–3 and 198–200.

19. On Rucellai *see above*, pp. 157 and 160–1.

20. Cited by N. Tamassia, *La famiglia italiana nei secoli XV e XVI* (Milan, 1910), p. 61 (from Baldus's *Consilia*, where we have not succeeded in tracing the passage).

FRANCESCO GUICCIARDINI

Organisers of curricula and authors of textbooks have usually fixed and accepted a date at the end of the fifteenth century as the arbitrary dividing line between 'medieval' and 'modern' European history, the most conventional of such dates being that of the invasion of Italy by Charles VIII of France in 1494. The very idea of such a disjunction has itself a long history, and ultimately goes back, as does the concept of 'the Renaissance', to the opinions of contemporary writers. One of the most influential works in formulating this view of 1494 as a dividing line is Francesco Guicciardini's *Storia d'Italia*, written in about 1536–9 and published in 1561. Guicciardini begins his history of Italy with the year 1494 and his principal theme is the 'calamities' inflicted on a previously tranquil and wealthy peninsula by this and subsequent invasions.

Yet the opinion that 1494 marked a radical change in the texture of Italian political life was held long before Guicciardini wrote his *Storia d'Italia*, as may be seen from his own much earlier history of Florence, most of which was probably written during the year 1508. In this work he narrates the appearance of Charles VIII's army in Italy, and then breaks off to exclaim:

And there had entered Italy a flame and a plague which not only changed states,[1] but also methods of ruling them and of conducting warfare. Previously, Italy being composed to five main states (the pope's, Naples, Venice, Milan and Florence), each one of these attempted to preserve its own possessions, and watched out lest any took another's territory and gained so much that all the rest should fear it. Thus they observed every small alteration, and there was excitement when even the most insignificant of fortresses changed hands. When it came to warfare the strength was so evenly balanced and the movements of the militia and the artillery were so slow that almost a whole summer might be spent over the capture of a single castle. Wars were long-drawn-out, and when battles were fought very few men were killed in them. Now, with the coming of the French, it was as though a sudden storm had turned everything upside-down. The union of Italy was broken and torn apart, and so was the thought and care that had previously been given to the commonweal ['*cose communi*']. When cities, duchies, and kingdoms were attacked or fell prey to tumults, each state stood aside and attended to its own interests, instead of taking action lest a nearby fire or the downfall of a neighbouring town might burn or bring down its own regime. Sudden and violent wars began, and now a kingdom was destroyed and gained in less time than had previously been taken for a village to change hands. Cities were captured rapidly and fell not in months but in days or hours, and battles became ferocious and bloody. In brief, henceforward states were preserved or ruined, given away or taken, not by schemes drawn up in the study as in the past, but in the field and by armed men.[2]

Francesco Guicciardini (b. 1483) was a member of one of Florence's great patrician families. In childhood he saw the city's Medicean regime overturned as a result of Piero de' Medici's hesitant attitude and feeble opposition to the French invasion, and for the next 18 years he lived under a republic that was too democratic (one should perhaps say insufficiently oligarchic) to suit the ideas and interests of the Florentine magnates. Thereafter he entered the service of the Medicean popes (Leo X and Clement VII) as an administrator, and in 1526–7 played a particularly important role in the attempts to withstand Charles V's domination of Italy. His practical experience as an administrator and soldier, and his concern over democratic trends in Florence after 1494, are the biggest influences in Guicciardini's political writings. These are thus—as are his historical works—essentially the products of a particular situation: even when generalising they consider and criticise *contemporary* institutions, and hence they stand in complete contrast to the writings of Aquinas and other medieval authors,[3] which approach politics deductively by the application of general and universally valid principles.

His circumstances, his temperament and the wish to give practical opinions, all made Guicciardini a realist. He saw Florence's limited capacities, and thought of the city as being 'in its old age'. He prided himself, too, on not being overawed by the writers of classical antiquity—in a way he was consciously emerging from the 'Renaissance' with its uncritical enthusiasm for antiquity—and he boasted that he was no Plato, thinking up some 'imaginary government, more likely to appear in books than in reality'.[4] With characteristically cautious phraseology, he often urged a certain course of action as 'the least bad'. In a dialogue concerning the Florentine situation in 1494, written some 30 years later, he has one of the participants declare 'when judging between one government and another I should not consider so much the form of these governments, but should rather take into account which has better consequences and where men are better governed, where justice is best administered and where there is most respect for the general good, each man being in his proper rank'.[5] The practical application of Guicciardini's pragmatic approach emerges in the same Dialogue. He regretted the fall of the Medicean regime, but concluded (with the advantage of hindsight) that its restoration would be harmful, since this could only come about through external attack or internal faction, or a combination of the two, and it would lead not only to the destruction of the Medici's opponents but also to the installation of a very different type of Medicean rule. This regard for particular circumstances and caution in generalisation were to make Guicciardini the ideal critic of his dogmatic friend Machiavelli.

NICCOLÒ MACHIAVELLI

Niccolò Machiavelli (1469–1527) lived through the same critical decades of Italian history and his writings, too, are essentially the product of the humiliation of Florence and the other Italian states by the great powers, France, Spain and the Empire of Charles V. His experiences, however, differed from Guicciardini's in a way that did much to affect his ideas, for as secretary to the Florentine committee for foreign affairs he saw events from the centre without having to bear the heavy burden of responsibility and decision making which fell to Guicciardini. Machiavelli was a brilliant writer and a generaliser by temperament, but his advice comes from the study. He delighted in writing the word 'to liquidate' (*spegnere*), yet his ruthlessness somehow fails to convince. In contrast Guicciardini, who wrote in the intervals of a career as governor and military commander, had really had men put to death.

This does not mean that Machiavelli has no claim to be considered as a 'realist'. His realism is limited and generic; but in that he was obsessed by the idea of power he, too, was dealing with realities with which his medieval predecessors had had no concern. 'Power easily wins a name, but a name wins no power',[6] he wrote, and in this determination to see beneath the surface he has much in common with Guicciardini and with many contemporary writers, among them a nephew of the latter who wrote contemptuously of 'the many men in our city who consider the names of things rather than their effects and causes'.[7] Machiavelli had learnt the hard lesson of Florence's insignificance in the eyes of the great powers in a fashion that was personally humiliating. He visited France as a Florentine emissary three times between 1500 and 1510, and his treatment by the French made him realise that a state can only count with its titular allies in so far as it has power to do them good or harm. The French consistently neglected their obligations towards their Florentine ally and, to make things worst of all, they themselves met defeat in Italy in 1512, and this defeat in turn brought about that of the republican regime in Florence, as a result of which Machiavelli lost his post and was for a time imprisoned. Savonarola had failed, and 'unarmed prophets' were bound to meet with defeat. Florence could only count for something in the world of power politics if it had a formidable army and, since each state can rely solely on its own power, this would have to be an army of Florentine citizens. Mercenaries lacked any compelling bond with the states that employed them, hence the only solution was the restoration of a civic militia, based on Roman and communal models. It was in this field alone that Machiavelli held a post of real importance and had an opportunity to put his ideas into practice: he played a leading part in the organisation of a Florentine militia in 1506–7, but must have been sadly disappointed by its subsequent ineffectiveness.

Machiavelli saw not only states but also men as powers whose limits were those of their own unaided strength. Thus a dictator who had gained his position by a *coup d'état* was warned against reliance on the supporters who had brought him to power; by definition they were the malcontents of the previous regime and were likely to remain malcontents under his. On the other hand he could hope for the backing of the populace if he attended to the 'common good', and their support was preferable to that of the aristocracy not only in the dictator's own interest but also because theirs was a more widely shared 'good' and hence 'a more honest aim'.

Since the potential strength of the state was the sum of that of its own citizens, it was essential to maximise this by ensuring their full support. Patriotism, or public spirit, was the assurance of such support, and the good citizen—of whom Machiavelli found examples among classical Romans and contemporary Germans—was the man who paid his taxes honestly or delivered up to the state the loot captured in war. Feudalised states, whose nominal citizens owed allegiance to a local potentate rather than to the ruler, were enfeebled or 'corrupt'. Machiavelli relied on religion to impart public spirit, but Christianity was not well calculated to perform this role, and he criticised it for that reason. His ideal citizen, gladly paying taxes and serving in the army, was surely then, as now, 'more likely to appear in books than in reality'.

Machiavelli is best known for *The Prince*, the brilliantly written handbook for a tyrant which set up an idealised Cesare Borgia as a model to the Medici from whom the author was seeking employment. His most important political work, however, is the *Discourses on Livy*, an attempt to elucidate and propound the lessons of early Roman history. In his Introduction to the *Discourses* Machiavelli declared his inability to understand why 'in matters of constituting republics, maintaining states, governing kingdoms, forming an army or conducting a war, judging subjects, or extending rule, one finds neither prince nor republic who goes to antiquity for examples'.[8] There is expressed here a fundamental belief that the ancients can teach in politics as they have taught in architecture and literature, that the men of the 'Renaissance' may, by copying them, hope to rival their achievements in statecraft as in the other fields of human activity. In this, as in other ways, Machiavelli was more old-fashioned than Guicciardini and many of his contemporaries; at the time when he was writing his main political works, in the second decade of the sixteenth century, blind admiration for antiquity was rather out of date.

A number of letters bear witness to a most interesting friendship between the lively, rather showy Machiavelli and Guicciardini, an aloof man who was perhaps a shade patronising to Machiavelli but was attracted and stimulated by his vivacity and brilliance. Fascinated but unconvinced by Machiavelli's generalisations, Guicciardini once reminded his older friend in a typically pessimistic phrase that 'we walk in darkness, with our hands tied behind our backs so that we cannot ward off blows'.[9] 'It is a great error', he thought, 'to speak of things absolutely and without distinguishing—by rule, as it were—for there is nearly always some difference in the circumstances which prevents their being brought under the same heading, and such distinctions have to be learnt from experience, not from books.'[10] This was really his reply to the doctrine of Machiavelli's *Discourses*: 'It is quite fallacious to judge by examples. They are useless unless they are identical, because the smallest difference between them may be the cause of a great difference between their consequences, and a very perceptive eye indeed is required to discern such small differences.'[11] Again, such generalisations presuppose absolutely correct knowledge about the past, yet this is an impossibility 'if one comes to reflect that we have no sure knowledge of the present, even of events occurring from day to day in one's own city'.[12] A last quotation from Guicciardini's aphorisms (the *Ricordi*) completes the case against

Machiavelli: 'How mistaken are those people who constantly cite the example of the Romans! One would have to have a city [state] the conditions of which were the same as theirs and then follow their example fully, but our qualities are so disproportionate to theirs that this would be like trying to make a donkey gallop like a horse.'[13] When he came to write a specific criticism of the *Discourses*, Guicciardini returned once more to his friend's exaggerated classicism: 'One should not praise antiquity so much that one disapproves every modern institution that was unknown to the Romans.'[14]

Whatever their disagreements, Machiavelli, Guicciardini and their Florentine contemporaries inaugurated a new approach to political writing. This is not the same as saying that they were the first men since classical times to think inductively about politics, or even that they were the first to write in a 'practical' way about politics, and this is perhaps as well, for this book has surely had enough to say about Florence already. To find the same practical pragmatic discussion of the state and politics, however, it is necessary only to travel to Venice, where it may be encountered in the utilitarian reports (*Relazioni*) by Venetian ambassadors which are such an important source for sixteenth century history. These accounts were used as the basis for the republic's decisions concerning political and economic policy, hence they were practical by their very nature. The institution of diplomatic reports of this nature was not solely a Venetian one, and it originated before the sixteenth century; but the Venetian *relazioni* were particularly copious and, by retaining its independence, Venice kept the need for such information longer than the other Italian states.

PHILIPPE DE COMMYNES

Realistic discussion of politics is of course to be sought in historical works as well as in writings on 'current affairs', and may also be found in abundance in the *Mémoires* of Commynes (*c.*1447–1511).[15] Commynes' *Memoirs* is a fascinating and much-read book, which ran to no fewer than 25 editions in French between its appearance in 1524 and the end of the century, and was translated into many languages. Not the least of its consequences was the stimulus it gave to the great German historian Ranke, who as a boy had noted the discrepancies between Scott's *Quentin Durward* and the 'much superior' account given by Commynes of the character of Charles the Rash.[16] Philippe Commynes came of a Flemish family (feudal in standing though bourgeois by descent) settled near Lille. He early entered the service of Charles the Rash, then heir to the duchy of Burgundy, and later duke, but in 1471 accepted a pension from Louis XI and the following year turned traitor to Charles. He then took employment under Louis XI, and for some 40 years acted as an adviser and emissary for the French Crown. He was endowed with large estates by Louis, who particularly valued his first-hand knowledge of his former master. Louis also despatched him on a mission to Florence (1478), and later Commynes accompanied Charles VIII to Italy and acted as his emissary to Venice (1494–5); he also visited Milan with Louis XII (1507). Commynes' service to the French Crown was not without vicissitudes: he had great difficulty in asserting his title to the lands granted him by Louis XI, and after Louis' death he fell from favour for some years, took part in the insurrection of 1485 ('la Guerre Folle'), and was subsequently imprisoned. After a long exile from the court he was restored in 1491 only to fall into temporary disgrace once more seven years later.

There are some curiously close parallels between Commynes' career and Machiavelli's, as well as similarities in the bearing of their experiences on the framework of their ideas. Both men conceived an admiration for the statecraft of one exemplary individual: Commynes was often the confidant of Louis XI, as Machiavelli occasionally was of Cesare Borgia, and he thought Louis wise, subtle, possessing 'perfect common sense' and, above all, skilful at extricating himself from difficulties. Each of them, too, was present at a momentous occasion in his hero's career, which profoundly affected his own ideas. In the case of Commynes the 'traumatic' episode, of which he gives a highly dramatic version in the *Memoirs*, was Louis XI's meeting with Charles of Burgundy at Péronne in 1468,[17] when the king was perhaps in his enemy's power and yet was allowed to go free. The equivalent occasion in Machiavelli's experience was the trap set by Cesare Borgia at Senigallia to capture the mercenary leaders who had been plotting against him. Machiavelli was at Cesare's court as Florentine emissary when these men were apprehended and put to death (31 December 1502), and he described the entire event three times, with increasing care and admiration, first in his report to the republic, then in the brief *Description of the method whereby duke Valentino* [Cesare Borgia] *had Vitellozzo Vitelli, Oliverotto da Fermo, the lord Paolo and the duke of Gravina Orsini murdered* and finally in *The Prince*. Both of these men travelled a good deal—as we have seen, Commynes knew Italy and Machiavelli France—and both endured spells of imprisonment, the former in 1487–9, the latter in 1513 when suspected of complicity in an anti-Medicean plot. Machiavelli suffered French insults, and even for this there is a parallel, of sorts, since Commynes had to return to Venice as France's emissary in 1495, after Charles VIII's humiliating withdrawal from Italy, and the Venetians then greeted him sarcastically as a 'much thinner' man than the triumphant Commynes of the previous year.

Machiavelli thought that *The Prince* would prove his 'fifteen years study of the art of statecraft were not wasted in sleep or play' and that it would persuade the Medici that his services were too valuable to miss.[18] Commynes felt the same conviction that his *Memoirs*, the fruit of 'eighteen years or more spent in the vicinity of princes, and certain knowledge of the most important and secret affairs of this kingdom of France and the neighbouring lordships'[19] would not provide amusing reading matter for silly, simple folk, 'but I think that rulers or men at court will find good advice in them'.[20] By a natural extension of the same principle, Commynes shared the Florentine's belief in the 'lessons of history', and his pessimism concerning his own times:

One of the best ways for a man to acquire wisdom is to read histories. From these and the example of his predecessors he can learn how to act, to be cautious, and to undertake things wisely. For one man's life is so short that it does not provide sufficient experience. Moreover, we are enfeebled by age, and men live less long than they used to and their bodies are less strong. We are also weaker in observing good faith and loyalty among ourselves. I do not know where men can trust each other now, particularly among great rulers, for these are most inclined to follow their own will without considering anything else and, what is worse, they are usually surrounded by men who are intent only on pleasing their masters, and praise all their actions, both good and evil.[21]

When Commynes writes of Venice he comes closer still to Machiavelli, so close indeed that some scholars have tried to maintain that he had heard of Machiavelli's ideas, though the *Discourses* were written after his death and it is virtually certain that he never met their author. Commynes envied the Venetians because 'they know, through Livy, the mistakes that the Romans made, for they have his *History*, as they have also his bones in their palace at Padua'.[22] He himself knew no Latin and regretted this deficiency. His belief that the lessons of history were best learnt from Livy is evidence, of course, not of any dependence on Machiavelli, but of the general acceptance ot the superiority of the Romans over their debased successors and the consequent opinion that their achievements and shortcomings constituted the lessons of the past *par excellence*. This way of thinking was no less characteristic of the twelfth century than of the sixteenth, and was to be found in France as much as in Italy: we have already encountered it in the history book specially composed for Philip VI.[23]

Commynes certainly appears more 'medieval' than Machiavelli in some ways. Whereas the latter thought Fortune 'arbiter of half our actions', Commynes would have no truck with this essentially irreligious concept. 'Fortune is nothing but a poetic fiction', he wrote, and the downfall of Burgundy was no turn of Fortune's wheel but the work of 'the hand of God', but for whose special favours France 'would have been in great danger'.[24] Yet fundamentally they have much in common, and both Commynes and his master would have understood and sympathised with Machiavelli's political writings, a point that is perhaps best established by giving some sayings of Louis XI that are quoted appreciatively in the *Mémoires*:

He once said to me . . . that men are sometimes ruined by having served too well, and great services are most often repaid by great ingratitude. He said that this may come about not only through the ingratitude of rulers but also through the defects of those who have performed these services, if they speak too arrogantly and rely too much on their good fortune in their dealings with their lord as well as with their colleagues. He also said to me that, in his opinion, it was better for a man at court to have received undeserved benefits from his ruler, and thus to be much obliged to him, than to have rendered great services, so that it was the ruler who stood under a great obligation; because it is natural for a ruler to love those who are obliged to him rather than those to whom he is obliged.[25]

To Louis XI was also attributed (though not by Commynes) that quintessentially 'Machiavellian' saying: *Qui nescit dissimulare, nescit regnare* ('He who cannot dissimulate cannot rule').[26] That such an amoral aphorism should have been on the tongue of a ruler half a century before *The Prince* was written will surprise only the most naïve, but the fact may help to disprove the ridiculous and stubborn myth that rulers and statesmen needed to read Machiavelli to learn wickedness.

More striking than Machiavelli's not very successful attempt to eliminate morality as irrelevant to political discussion is the way in which he saw statecraft as the interplay of power. Commynes had emphasised strongly the element of personal decision; the downfall of the Burgundian duchy, for instance, was for him essentially the result of a series of misjudgements by Charles the Rash. Machiavelli's view of the lessons of the last decade of the fifteenth century and the first of the sixteenth was a more penetrating one, and in this he was assisted by being an Italian and hence reflecting more on the changes wrought in the peninsula by the invasions. Like Guicciardini, Machiavelli saw the Italian states as potential victims of the 'new' powerful monarchies, particularly of the French, the Spaniards and the Ottomans. These were monarchies whose rulers could 'make the rich poor and the poor rich . . . build new cities, destroy those that already exist, and move the population about from one place to another'.[27]

CONCLUSION

Machiavelli's was indeed in many ways an utterly different world from the thirteenth century Europe sketched in Chapter 1. Men still went back to the ancients— Machiavelli to Livy and Polybius, as Aquinas to Aristotle—but ways of writing about politics and the society that was written about had both changed profoundly. The Aragonese kings whose subjects would obey them if they kept their word 'and if not, not', the barons whose feudal rights made them 'sovereigns in their own baronies', the Italian 'patricians' enjoying complete political independence through the weakness of central authority, all these would have found the political atmosphere altered beyond recognition had they revisited Europe in the sixteenth century. Communications were still primitive and regional jurisdictions and loyalties, states within the state, immensely powerful; Machiavelli and men for centuries after him knew the successors of Beaumanoir's 'sovereigns in their own baronies'. Yet the main direction of change in these three centuries had been decisively in favour of the monarchies. Spain was now well on the way to becoming one powerful kingdom, France so strong that it could take Italian states 'with chalk',[28] England, Sweden and Denmark had kings who could break the bonds of Rome and change their countries' religion. The cardinal achievement was the gradual ousting of the mighty subject by a centralising bureaucracy, and this process was taking place in the later Middle Ages wherever circumstances were favourable. In Spain the circumstances were provided by a dynastic marriage, in France by the more complicated combination of the English challenge, the stimulus given by this to patriotic sentiment, and the collapse of the Burgundian duchy.

Granted the proviso that many ordinary folk would still be aware of the strength of local potentates more than that of monarchs, some apology is perhaps needed also for the choice of a political criterion in assessing the greatest changes during this period of three centuries. Among writers who have seen things differently, some would point to the geographical discoveries in America and Africa as marking a fundamental change in expanding men's intellectual horizons, revolutionising their commercial and financial existence and bringing into being new empires. The impact of these developments, though, was extremely gradual, a matter of slow dilution. The Mediterranean continued to be the most important sphere of European maritime commerce throughout most of the sixteenth century, and awareness of exotic peoples and new worlds was slow—except perhaps in the Iberian peninsula

—to work significant changes in the outlook of even the most thoughtful of Europeans. Even less convincing is the claim that a 'modern' way of thought among the educated, a sloughing off of the 'medieval mind', dates from the cosmological discoveries of the sixteenth century. Copernicus's heliocentric system was indeed published in 1543—a second edition was not required till 1566—but its effects on men's views of life were bound to be small; indeed, they remain small today. This sort of scientific truth seems compelled, in a way, to remain incomprehensible, so evident is it to each individual that there is another sense in which the earth is the centre of the universe and he or she the centre of earthly affairs.

To depict the growing power of the monarchic state as the great tendency of the times is not to suggest that all forces were conspiring in this direction or that this was a sort of magnetism predestined to prevail and to undergo no lasting reverse. The internal cohesion of imperial Germany, not comparable at the outset of the sixteenth century with that of France, England or Spain, was further impaired by Charles V's struggle to rule a vast Habsburg empire and was destroyed in the following century by the Thirty Years War. The French monarchy too was to undergo an immensely harassing crisis throughout the second half of the sixteenth century, partly due to the newly disunificatory force of religion. Nevertheless the power of Charles V's state and that of Francis I prepared that struggle between Habsburg and Valois which was to provide the main theme in European foreign relations right up to 1648 or even 1713.

FURTHER READING
General

In addition to the works suggested under Chapter 1, *see* J. H. Burns and M. Goldie, *The Cambridge History of Political Thought, 1450–1700* (Cambridge, 1991); Q. Skinner, *The Foundations of Modern Political Thought*, 2 vols (Cambridge, 1978), vol. 1; J. Hankins, 'Humanism and the origins of modern political thought', in *The Cambridge Companion to Renaissance Humanism*, ed. J. Kraye (Cambridge, 1996), pp. 118–41; and N. Rubinstein, 'Political theories in the Renaissance', in *The Renaissance: Essays in Interpretation* (London, 1992), pp. 153–200.

Francesco Guicciardini

The standard biography of Guicciardini is R. Ridolfi, *The Life of Francesco Guicciardini* (1960: tr. London, 1967). M. Phillips, *Francesco Guicciardini: the Historian's Craft* (Manchester, 1977), and F. Gilbert, *Machiavelli and Guicciardini. Politics and History in Sixteenth-Century Florence* (Princeton, N.J., 1965, paperback 1973) are important analyses of his work. Guicciardini's two major histories have been translated; *The History of Florence* by M. Domandi (New York, 1970) and *The History of Italy* in part by S. Alexander (New York and London, 1969, repr. Princeton, N.J., 1984). Excerpts from both were also translated by C. Grayson, ed. J. R. Hale (Chalfont St Giles, 1966). The *Dialogue on the Government of Florence* has been translated by Alison Brown (Cambridge, 1994); the *Ricordi* were translated as *Maxims and Reflections of a Renaissance Statesman* by M. Domandi (New York, 1965) and by M. Grayson in *Francesco Guicciardini. Selected Writings* (London, 1965), pp. 4–56, together with his 'Considerations on the "Discourses" of Machiavelli' (pp. 61–124) and the autobiographical *Ricordanze* (pp. 129–70); the treatise 'Del modo di ordinare il governo popolare' has been translated by Russell Price as 'How the popular government should be reformed', in *Cambridge Translations of Renaissance Philosophical Texts*, vol. 2: *Political Philosophy*, ed. Jill Kraye (Cambridge, 1997), pp. 200–37

Niccolò Machiavelli

Along with Dante, Machiavelli is perhaps the most written-about individual covered in this book. The following are no more than suggestions of initial approaches to the literature. Q. Skinner, *Machiavelli* (Past Masters series, Oxford, 1981) is a brief introduction. A full biography is R. Ridolfi, *The Life of Niccolò Machiavelli* (1954: tr. London, 1963); *see also* S. de Grazia, *Machiavelli in Hell* (Princeton, N.J., 1993); M. Hulliung, *Citizen Machiavelli* (Princeton, N.J., 1983); S. Anglo, *Machiavelli: a Dissection* (London, 1969); and G. Bock, Q. Skinner and M. Viroli, eds, *Machiavelli and Republicanism* (Cambridge, 1991, paperback 1993). The essay by I. Berlin, 'The originality of Machiavelli' in *Studies on Machiavelli*, ed. M. Gilmore (Florence, 1972), pp. 147–206; repr. in his *Against the Current: Essays in the History of Ideas* (Oxford, 1981 edition), pp. 25–79, has been deeply influential. Among the many translations of *The Prince*, *see* those of R. Price, ed. Q. Skinner (Cambridge, 1988), G. Bull (Harmondsworth, 1961, many reprints) and D. Wootton (Indianapolis, In., and Cambridge, 1995); the latter has an accessible introduction including a valuable contribution to the long-running question of the relationship of *The Prince* to the *Discourses*. The *Discourses* were translated by L. J. Walker, 2 vols (London, 1950, new edition by C. H. Clough, 1975); paperback version ed. B. Crick (Harmondsworth, 1970, many reprints); the *Art of War* is translated by E. Farneworth (rev. edition, New York, 1990). A study is H. C. Mansfield, *Machiavelli's New Modes and Orders. A Study on the Discourses on Livy* (Ithaca, N.Y., and London, 1979). Anthologies include: Machiavelli, *The Prince and Other Political Writings*, tr. B. Penman (London, 1981); P. Bondanella and M. Musa, eds, *The Portable Machiavelli* (Harmondsworth, 1979); and D. Wootton, *Machiavelli: Selected Political Writings* (Indianapolis, In., 1994).

Philippe de Commynes

The first six books of Commynes' *Memoirs* have been translated by Michael Jones (Harmondsworth, 1972). For further reading *see above*, under Chapter 12.

Postscript: the growth of the monarchic state

Daniel Waley's concluding portrayal of the growth of the monarchic state as the key political development of the period is as valid as it was when first written. Recent research on 'the growth of the state' has confirmed this view and greatly enriched it in matters of detail. The following suggestions are offered as introductory guidance to the burgeoning literature on the subject.

An assessment of the significance of medieval developments can by definition only be possible by placing medieval history in the context of a longer period. The following broad studies engage with this problem: Perry Anderson, *Passages from Antiquity to Feudalism* (London, 1974) and *Lineages of the Absolute State* (London, 1974); M. Mann, *The Sources of Social Power*, vol. I, *A History of Power from the Beginning to A.D. 1760* (Cambridge, 1986); S. E. Finer, *The History of Government From the Earliest Times*, 3 vols (Oxford, 1997); H. Spruyt, *The Sovereign State and Its Competitors. An Analysis of Systems Change* (Princeton, N.J., 1994); M. van Creveld, *The Rise and Decline of the State* (Cambridge, 1999); T. Ertman, *Birth of the Leviathan, Building States in Medieval and Early Modern Europe* (Cambridge, 1997); Kenneth H. F. Dyson, *The State Tradition in Western Europe* (Oxford, 1980). A study with a specifically economic slant is Charles Tilly, *Coercion, Capital, and European States, AD 990–1992* (Oxford, 1990, rev. edition

1992). The medieval origins of the modern state is one of the most intensely studied topics of recent years. In the 1990s the European Science Foundation sponsored a project on 'The Origins of the Modern State in Europe, 13th–18th Centuries', which has resulted in the publication of seven volumes in English: Richard Bonney, ed., *Economic Systems and State Finance* (Oxford, 1995); Wolfgang Reinhard, ed., *Power Elites and State Building* (Oxford, 1996); Janet Coleman, ed., *The Individual in Political Theory and Practice* (Oxford, 1996); Peter Blickle, ed., *Resistance, Representation and Community* (Oxford, 1997); Antonio Padoa-Schioppa, ed., *Legislation and Justice* (Oxford, 1997); Allan Ellenius, ed., *Iconography, Propaganda and Legitimation* (Oxford, 1998); and Philippe Contamine, ed., *War and Competition between States* (Oxford, 2000). B. Guenée, *States and Rulers in Later Medieval Europe* (1971, tr. and revised Oxford, 1985) is a systematic synthesis with an ample thematic bibliography; Susan Reynolds, 'The historiography of the medieval state', in *Companion to Historiography*, ed. M. Bentley (Routledge, 1997), pp. 117–38 surveys the subject of states from the medieval viewpoint. Since the ESF project there has been a further survey of taxation and statecraft: R. Bonney, ed., *The Rise of the Fiscal State in Europe* c.*1200–1815* (Oxford, 1999).

The concept of the State becomes intertwined with that of nation, one of several levels of 'identity' in the Middle Ages, with a complex history. For an introduction *see* H. Schulze, *States, Nations and Nationalism: From the Middle Ages to the Present* (tr. Blackwell, 1996); also J. A. Armstrong, *Nations before Nationalism* (Chapel Hill, N.C., 1982); and, for more general approaches, Benedict Anderson, *Imagined Communities. Reflections on the Origin and Spread of Nationalism* (London, 1983, revised 1991), and Anthony D. Smith, *The Ethnic Origins of Nations* (Oxford, 1986) both provide more general background. 'National' identity was subordinate to the identity conveyed by faith, the geo-political contours of which also duly emerged, though their eventual transformation into the secular concept of 'Europe' was only just beginning in the late Middle Ages. On this *see* D. Hay, *Europe. The Emergence of an Idea* (Edinburgh, 1957, 2nd edition 1968); John Hale, *The Civilization of Europe in the Renaissance* (London, 1993), Part 1; and 'Europe's Medieval Origins', a special feature of *History Workshop*, 33 (Spring 1992). The frontiers of Christendom, and the relationship of frontier and peripheral territories to those more central, are brilliantly discussed in S. Pollard, *Marginal Europe. The Contribution of Marginal Lands Since the Middle Ages* (Oxford, 1997); *see also* the essays in R. Bartlett and A. Mackay, eds, *Medieval Frontier Societies* (Oxford, 1992).

Several of the many different aspects of current research stand out. One is the increasingly important role of the courts and the court society with which monarchs surrounded themselves. A useful collection of comparative essays is R. G. Asch and A. M. Birke, eds, *Princes, Patronage, and the Nobility: the Court at the Beginning of the Modern Age,* c.*1450–1650* (Oxford and London, 1991). The attention to display, ceremonial and ritual with which both king and court were increasingly engaged are studied in Allan Ellenius, *Iconography, Propaganda and Legitimation* (Oxford, 1998); J. M. Bak, ed., *Coronations: Medieval and Early Modern Monarchic Ritual* (Berkeley and Los Angeles, Cal., 1990); R. A. Jackson, *Vive le Roi! A History of the French Coronation from Charles V to Charles X* (Chapel Hill, N.C., 1984); G. Kipling, *Enter the King. Theatre, Liturgy, and Ritual in the Medieval Civic Triumph* (Oxford, 1998); and P. Arnade, *Realms of Ritual. Burgundian Ceremony and Civic Life in Late Medieval Ghent* (Cornell, N.Y., 1996). The nobility, on whose consensus so much royal power increasingly rested in many parts of Europe, has been widely investigated. P. Contamine, 'The European nobility', in *NCMH*, 7, pp. 89–105, and T. Reuter, 'The medieval nobility in twentieth-century historiography', in *Companion to Historiography*, ed. M. Bentley (Routledge, 1997), pp. 177–202, are good introductions, as is J. Dewald, *The European Nobility, 1400–1800* (Cambridge, 1996). *See also* M. C. E. Jones, ed., *Gentry and Lesser Nobility in Late Medieval Europe* (Gloucester and New York, 1986); H. Kaminsky, 'Estate, nobility and the exhibition of estate in the later middle ages', *Speculum*, 68 (1993), pp. 684–709; and on social hierarchies generally Jeffrey Denton, ed., *Hierarchies and Orders in Late Medieval and Renaissance Europe* (London, 1998). Finally the role of cities and townspeople, both in politics and in the economy, are evaluated in a number of studies. In addition to titles listed under Chapter 5 and elsewhere, *see* C. Tilly and W. P. Blockmans, eds, *Cities and the Rise of States in Europe, AD 1000 to 1800* (Westview, Conn., 1994); Paul M. Hohenberg and Lynn Hollen Lees, *The Making of Urban Europe, 1000–1994* (Cambridge, Mass., 1985, rev. edition 1995); and Leonardo Benevolo, *The European City* (Oxford, 1993, paperback 1995).

NOTES

1. That is, changed their regimes.
2. F. Guicciardini, *Storie Fiorentine*, ed. R. Palmarocchi (Bari, 1931), pp. 92–3; translation as *The History of Florence* by M. Domandi (New York, 1970), pp. 88–9.
3. *See above*, pp. 8–10.
4. From 'Dialogo del Reggimento di Firenze' in *Dialogo e Discorsi del Reggimento di Firenze*, ed. R. Palmarocchi (Bari, 1932), p. 99; an English translation is *Dialogue on the Government of Florence*, tr. Alison Brown (Cambridge, 1994); this passage is on p. 96.
5. 'Dialogo', cit., pp. 17–18; in Brown translation, p. 15.
6. *Discorsi sopra la prima deca di Tito Livio* (*Discourses on the First Decade of Livy*), Bk. I, ch. 34; cf. the translation by L. J. Walker, paperback edition by B. Crick (Harmondsworth, 1970), p. 194.
7. Niccolò Guicciardini, 'Discorso', printed in R. von Albertini, *Das florentinische Staatsbewusstsein im Übergang von der Republik zum Prinzipat* (Bonn, 1955), pp. 352–62 (this passage occurs on p. 357).
8. *Discorsi*, cit., Bk. I, Preface: cf. Walker's translation, Crick edition, cit., p. 98.
9. Letter of 7 August 1525, in Machiavelli, *Lettere*, ed. F. Gaeta (Milan, 1961), p. 426.
10. *Ricordi*, ed. R. Spongano (Florence, 1951), no. 6, p. 11; translated as *Maxims and Reflections of a Renaissance Statesman (Ricordi)*, tr. M. Domandi (New York, 1965), and in *Selected Writings*, tr. M. Grayson (London, 1965).
11. *Ricordi*, tr. Domandi, cit., no. 117; Spongano edition, cit., p. 128.
12. *Ricordi*, cit., no. 141; Spongano edition, cit., p. 153.
13. *Ricordi*, cit., no. 110; Spongano edition, cit., p. 121.
14. *Considerazioni su i Discorsi di Machiavelli*, on *Discorsi*, Bk. II, ch. 24, in F. Guicciardini, *Opere Inedite* (Florence, 1857), p. 67; English translation as 'Considerations on the "Discourses" of Machiavelli', in *Selected Writings*, tr. M. Grayson, cit.; this passage is on p. 117.
15. Philippe de Commynes, *Mémoires*, and trans Michael Jones (Harmondsworth, 1972). *See above*, pp. 209–11 for some quotations from this work.
16. Ranke, *Sämmtiche Werke*, 54 vols (Leipzig, 1867–90), 53/54, p. 61.
17. *See above*, p. 210.
18. Machiavelli, Letter to F. Vettori, 10 December 1513, in *Lettere*, ed. F. Gaeta, cit., p. 305; English translations in *The Prince and Other Political Writings*, ed. B. Penman (London, 1981), pp. 33–7, and *The Prince*, ed. D. Wootton (Indianapolis, In., 1995), pp. 1–4.
19. Commynes, Bk. II, ch. 6; in Jones's translation, p. 137.
20. Bk. III, ch. 8; in Jones's translation, p. 200.
21. Bk. II, ch. 6; in Jones's translation, p. 137 (for the last sentence, cf. *The Prince*, chs. 18 and 23).
22. Bk.VII, 15 (not translated by Jones).

23. *Above*, p. 133.

24. *The Prince*, ch. 25: *Mémoires*, Bk. IV, chs 1, 5, 7, 12.

25. Bk. III, ch. 12 (op. cit., p. 219). There are some similar remarks in Machiavelli's *Discorsi*, Bk. I, 30; cf. Walker's translation, Crick edition, cit., pp. 176–7).

26. Giovanni Botero, *La Ragion di Stato*, Bk. V, ch. 5; English translation: *The Reason of State*, tr. P. J. and D. P. Waley (London, 1956), p. 104.

27. *Discorsi*, Bk. I, ch. 26.

28. *See above*, p. 215.

INDEX